Human Rights Law and Practice

Human Rights Law and Practice

GENERAL EDITORS

Lord Lester of Herne Hill
QC, MA (Cantab), LLM (Harvard), President of International Centre for the Legal
 Protection of Human Rights, of Lincoln's Inn, Barrister

David Pannick
QC, MA (Oxon), BCL (Oxon), Gray's Inn, Barrister, Fellow of All Souls College,
 Oxford

CONTRIBUTORS

Monica Carss-Frisk LLB (Lond), BCL (Oxon), of Gray's Inn, Barrister

Brice Dickson BA, BCL, MPhil, Barrister

Emma Dixon BA (Cantab), of Gray's Inn, Barrister

Ben Emmerson LLB (Bristol), of Middle Temple, Barrister

Kate Gallafent BA (Cantab), of Gray's Inn, Barrister

Joanna Harrington BA (UBC), LLB (UVictoria), Barrister and Solicitor
 (British Columbia)

Javan Herberg LLB (Lond), BCL (Oxon), of Lincoln's Inn, Barrister

Thomas de la Mare BA (Oxon) LLM (European University Institute),
 of Middle Temple, Barrister

Nuala Mole BA (Oxon), Diploma of College of Europe, Bruges,
 founder director of AIRE Centre

The Hon Lord Reed LLB (Edin), D Phil (Oxon), Senator of the College of
 Justice in Scotland

Dinah Rose BA (Oxon), of Gray's Inn, Barrister

Pushpinder Saini MA (Oxon), BCL (Oxon), of Gray's Inn, Barrister

Mark Shaw BA (Dunelm), LLM (Cantab), of Inner Temple, Barrister

Butterworths
London, Edinburgh and Dublin
1999

United Kingdom
Butterworths a Division of Reed Elsevier (UK) Ltd, Halsbury House, 35 Chancery Lane, *London* WC2A 1EL, and 4 Hill Street, *Edinburgh* EH2 3JZ

Australia
Butterworths, *Sydney, Adelaide, Brisbane, Canberra, Melbourne, Perth*

Canada
Butterworths Canada Ltd, *Toronto* and *Vancouver*

Ireland
Butterworth (Ireland) Ltd, *Dublin*

Malaysia
Malayan Law Journal Sdn Bhd, *Kuala Lumpur*

New Zealand
Butterworths of New Zealand Ltd, *Wellington* and *Auckland*

Singapore
Reed Elsevier (Singapore) Pte Ltd, *Singapore*

South Africa
Butterworth Publishers (Pty) Ltd, *Durban*

United States of America
Michie, *Charlottesville*, Virginia

© Reed Elsevier (UK) Ltd 1999

Reprinted 1999

A CIP Catalogue record for this book is available from the British Library.

ISBN 0-406-90126-0

9 780406 901262

LAW

Printed and bound in Great Britain by Butler & Tanner Ltd, Frome and London

Visit us at our website: www.butterworths.co.uk

To Katya and to the memory of Denise, with love and gratitude

Preface

The Lord Chancellor, Lord Irvine of Lairg, has been heard on occasions to say that the current Government is a 'reforming Government'. He has also been heard to say that it is a 'modernising Government'. In relation to human rights, he is correct on both counts. The justification is the Act to bring the European Convention on Human Rights home.

The Act will energise the whole of the United Kingdom's legal system. Its effects will be felt across the breadth of both civil and criminal justice. It will apply to both public and private law. It will be used to challenge existing procedures as well as substantive law. All legislation, existing and future, will be scrutinised to ensure it meets the standards which the Act, by incorporating the Convention, establishes. The landscape of UK law will be transformed. For the first time our entire legal system, not having a written constitution, will be judged in our own courts against objective international standards. Unlike Community law, the effects will not be restricted to a particular field of activity.

This is a challenge for which we need to prepare, but it is a challenge which we should welcome. Fortunately, we have the precedents of Canada and New Zealand from which we can learn. We can anticipate, as a result of their experiences, the problems which are likely to arise and what we should do to meet them. Advisory bodies in the community, lawyers, the court service and judges all face a steep learning curve.

The Human Rights Act 1998 gives individuals a raft of rights across the whole spectrum of social activity. Infringement of those rights will give the individual an entitlement to compensation where our administrative law previously provided none. It is possible to view what will be happening as the creation for this country of a new code of torts: 'Human Rights Torts' which will operate both in the fields of public and private law. These torts will redefine the relationship between the individual and the State but will go beyond this by operating 'horizontally' to influence the rights of individuals as well. The interests of minorities will be protected in a way which, up to now, has not been possible.

Understanding what is involved will not be achieved by merely becoming familiar with the terms of the Act in the form in which it is enacted. A knowledge of the European Convention on Human Rights will also be essential. Familiarity with the vast corpus of case law on the European Court of Human Rights will also be important. A knowledge of some of the significant decisions in the courts of other signatory states' jurisdictions will be an advantage.

The challenge and the opportunities for the judiciary are probably going to be the most dramatic. Almost all the rights contained in the Convention are qualified by exceptions. Usually the rights have to be balanced against the interests of the public as a whole. It is the judiciary who will have responsibility for determining where the balance lies. It is a heavy responsibility because if the right balance is not struck there will be the risk of UK courts' decisions being disapproved on application to the European Court of Human Rights and of the new rights being devalued in the eyes of the public. If, on the other hand, the job is done well, the judiciary of this country will have the opportunity they have so far been denied to make a significant contribution to the international jurisprudence of human rights.

Part of the preparation will be training. The government has provided resources for the Judicial Studies Board to provide the training which will be essential for judges at all levels. It is not only the High Court which will determine human rights issues. The magistrates' courts and Crown Court will also have to do so. The appeal judges will also have to be prepared for an influx of human rights issues which will need to be determined expeditiously. Both sides of the profession will have to make similar preparations, as will those who provide advice to the public, such as the Citizens Advice Bureaux. If members of the public are unable to receive advice on their new rights, those rights will be of little practical value.

There will also be the need for textbooks to which reference can be made as problems arise. Here is to be found the significance of this book. The reputation and experience of Lord Lester QC and David Pannick QC in this field means that any book for which they are responsible will inevitably command the greatest respect and can be cited with total confidence to any tribunal. Their standing has also resulted in a team of contributors joining them who ensure that every aspect of the subject of human rights is covered with unquestionable authority. This book will be of the greatest value to all those who will be engaged in responding to the challenge of the new law. With its help they will be able to take advantage of the opportunities which undoubtedly lie ahead with confidence.

The Rt Hon Lord Woolf of Barnes
Royal Courts of Justice, London

Contents

ix

Contents

Table of Statutes

All references in this table are to paragraph numbers.

Table of Statutory Instruments

All references in this table are to paragraph numbers.

Table of European Legislation

All references in this table are to paragraph numbers.

SECONDARY LEGISLATION

Directives

Table of International Legislation

All references in this table are to paragraph numbers.

Table of Cases

B

C

D

E

G

M

N

Q

R

S

T

U

V

W

X

Y

Z

Decisions of the European Court of Justice are listed below numerically. These decisions are also included in the preceding alphabetical list.

Introduction

In Charles Dickens' *Our Mutual Friend*, Mr Podsnap proudly informed 'the foreign gentleman' that:

> 'We Englishmen are very proud of our Constitution, sir. It was bestowed upon us by Providence. No other country is so favoured as this country'.

Mr Podsnap, 'gravely shaking his head', observed with regard to other countries that 'they do—I am sorry to be obliged to say it—*as* they do'.

The Human Rights Act 1998 is the long awaited, but very welcome, acknowledgement that, in relation to the protection of fundamental freedoms, the constitution of the United Kingdom needs improvement. The Act is an important step towards a new constitutional settlement for the United Kingdom, as significant as any of the great charters of rights (such as Magna Carta and the Bill of Rights 1689) in our history. Parliament has recognised that the UK can no longer remain immune from the basic constitutional principles adopted by almost all developed countries in the world. They are principles which we exported to many countries of the Commonwealth on their independence and which are enshrined in the European Convention on Human Rights as drafted primarily by British lawyers: the principles that the law must respect and protect human rights and that the judiciary should have the responsibility of interpreting and applying the basic freedoms to which we are all entitled as an aspect of our common humanity.

The recognition of fundamental rights protected by fundamental law involves consequent responsibilities, especially for lawyers and judges: a duty to understand the Human Rights Act and its objectives and to apply the European Convention on Human Rights (to which it gives effect in domestic law) with knowledge of its jurisprudence and of comparative constitutional case law. This book seeks to explain the background, content and application of the Act and the Convention, within their wider context.

We thank our distinguished contributors for finding time in their busy practices to assist in this venture. We are grateful to The Rt Hon Lord Woolf of Barnes, Master of the Rolls, for writing the preface and to Butterworths for their exceptional contribution to the production and publication of this book. We also thank Caroline Neenan for her helpful research work.

Lord Lester of Herne Hill QC and David Pannick QC
Blackstone Chambers
Temple, London
EC4Y 9BW
April 1999

Chapter 1

History and Context

A   Introduction

1.01   Since the Second World War, the universality of human rights has been recognised by the United Nations as inherent in the very nature of human beings – a reflection of their common humanity. For religious thinkers, human rights are considered to be fundamental because they are derived from divine revelation or natural law. Secular thinkers treat basic civil and political rights as fundamental in the sense that they have a special claim to protection because they are rooted in democratic concepts of popular sovereignty, government by consent, and equal rights of citizenship protected by law against what John Stuart Mill termed the 'tyranny of the majority'.

1.02   There are important English sources of the doctrine of fundamental rights[1]. However, for the past two centuries the prevailing English constitutional ideology, influenced by Burke, Bentham, Austin, Dicey, and Sir Ivor Jennings, has treated British citizens as subjects of the Crown without benefit of positive and fundamental constitutional rights giving protection to the individual against the state and its agents. What are known as 'the liberties of the subject' are residual and negative in their nature – the individual's freedom to do what he or she likes, unless forbidden by the common law or by statute.

1   See generally, H Lauterpacht *International Law and Human Rights* (1950), Ch 2.

1.03   The idea of 'fundamental rights' and of a 'fundamental' constitutional law, taking precedence over ordinary laws, became eclipsed at the end of the seventeenth century by the concept of absolute Parliamentary sovereignty. In the earlier part of that century, the judges had struggled not only for independence from the Executive but also for the right to withhold effect from laws that they regarded as unconscionable or contrary to a higher, fundamental and immutable natural law. The judges won the struggle for independence against the Crown's claim to rule by prerogative but the price paid by the common lawyers for their alliance with Parliament against the divine right of kings was that the common law could be changed by Parliament as it pleased. The 'glorious bloodless' revolution was won by Parliament; and although the Bill of Rights of 1688–89 and the Act of Settlement of 1700 recognised some important personal rights and liberties, the terms of the constitutional settlement were mainly concerned with the rights and liberties of Parliament. The alliance of Parliament and the common lawyers ensured that the supremacy of the law would mean the supremacy of Parliament; or, more realistically, the supremacy of the central government in Parliament, Lord Hailsham of St Marylebone's 'elective dictatorship'.

1.04   According to traditional, post-seventeenth century English political and legal theory, therefore, since Parliament is sovereign (acting in place of the monarch), the subject cannot possess fundamental rights, such as are guaranteed to the citizen by the many foreign and Commonwealth written constitutions containing fundamental and paramount law[1]. There are no rights that are fundamental in the sense that they enjoy special constitutional protection against interference by Parliament. The liberties of the subject are merely implications derived from two principles. The first principle is that we may say or do as we please, provided we do not transgress the substantive law, or infringe the legal rights of others. The second principle is that public authorities (including the Crown) may do only what they are authorised to do by some rule (including the royal prerogative) or by statute.

1   See 8 (2) *Halsbury's Laws* (4th edn reissue) para 101.

1.05   Again, according to traditional English theory, the role of the independent judiciary is essential in maintaining the common law principles of the rule of law, but the courts are subordinate to the Executive in Parliament; not an equal and co-ordinate branch of government; they are Francis Bacon's 'lions under the Throne'. The task of law-making is the exclusive province of Parliament. It would be undemocratic for the non-elected Judiciary to act as lawmakers. It would also be inappropriate because judges are ill-equipped by their training and professional experience, and by the very nature of the judicial process, to make law. It would be undesirable for judges to become involved in controversial issues of policy, because their decisions would make them more vulnerable to public criticism in the political arena. The judges' constitutional task is faithfully and strictly to interpret the will of Parliament, expressed in detailed legislation, to be read according to its so-called 'plain meaning', and to declare the common law where it is incomplete or obscure. If either the textual analysis of the words of a statute or the courts' interpretation of the common law has undesirable consequences, the matter must be corrected by the legislature and not by the courts.

1.06   The surest and most effective safeguards of human rights, in the opinion of Dicey and Sir Ivor Jennings, are not the rigid legalism and paper guarantees of written constitutions and Bills of Rights but the benevolent exercise of administrative discretion by public officials, acting as platonic guardians of the public interest, accountable through their political masters to the legislature and the people. Until recently, the effective safeguards against the misuse of public powers were regarded as being not legally enforceable safeguards but malleable constitutional conventions; the sense of fair play of Ministers and the professional integrity of civil servants in exercising their broad delegated public powers; the vigilance of the Opposition and of individual Members of Parliament; the influence of a free and vigorous press and a well-informed public opinion; and the periodic opportunity of changing the government through free and secret elections. It is this state of mind in the corridors of power that has underpinned the refusal by successive British governments to introduce legislation to incorporate the European Convention on Human Rights into UK law. Its great virtue is that it reminds us that a culture of liberty is more significant than formal legal rights, and that it is the duty of the Executive and Legislature, as well as of the Judiciary, to protect human rights.

1.07   Although the rights-based ideology was rejected by successive generations of governors of the United Kingdom and the British Empire, in favour of the benevolent exercise of administrative discretion, it has proved to be a potent force across the world. American and French concepts of human rights and judicial review shaped the rise of constitutionalism in Europe and elsewhere. The conquests of Napoleon's armies spread throughout the European continent not only the Code Civil but also the public philosophy and public law of the United States and France. These legal ideas and systems were also spread to other continents. Today, the many countries whose legal systems are based upon the civil law have constitutional guarantees of fundamental human rights derived from seventeenth century England, and the eighteenth century Enlightenment. Independent India's Constitution came into force in 1950 containing, to the displeasure of Sir Ivor Jennings and other British constitutional lawyers of the time, enforceable fundamental rights. By mid-century, therefore, there were three countries—the United States, India and Ireland—with legal systems based upon the common law, each giving constitutional protection to human rights.

1.08   Australia's written constitution contained a couple of fundamental rights: to property and religious freedom[1]. Canada too was governed under a rigid constitution, the British North America Act, but without expressly guaranteed fundamental rights. New Zealand had the same flexible and unwritten system as did the British. In the Colonies, British rule continued without the inconveniences (to the rulers) of political democracy or enforceable fundamental rights.

1   The High Court of Australia has recently implied fundamental rights into the Federal Constitution, notably, the right to freedom of political expression as an essential attribute of democratic government. However, it seems unlikely that the opportunity will be taken at the centenary of the Federal Constitution, in 2000, to include a modern charter of fundamental rights in the amended instrument. With the coming into force of the Human Rights Act 1998 in the UK, Australia will be the only democratic Commonwealth country without such a charter.

1.09   Within the UK, from the mid-1960s, political events occurred that were to have a profound effect in altering conventional British attitudes towards the role of the legal process in protecting human rights. They included the creation of the Law Commissions in 1966, the enactment in 1968, 1975 and 1976 of anti-discrimination legislation containing positive civil rights, acceptance in 1966 of the right of individual petition under the European Convention, and accession in 1972 to the European Community. The Law Commission for England and Wales, under the leadership of its first chairman, Lord Scarman, paved the way for the procedural reforms to English judicial review made in 1977, at a time when a new generation of judges were fashioning a modern system of administrative law, giving greater protection to the citizen against the misuse of public powers.

B   The Universal Declaration of Human Rights

1.10   The rights-based legal philosophy was profoundly influential on the international plane, in the wake of the Second World War. On 26 June 1945, the United Nations Charter was signed in San Francisco. It included several references to human rights and created a commission to act on them. Mrs Eleanor Roosevelt was appointed to chair the Commission on Human Rights and to submit proposals for an International Bill of Rights.

1.11   Within a few months, the outbreak of the Cold War had a chilling effect upon these efforts. By October 1946, when the International Military Tribunal delivered its judgment at Nuremberg, such enthusiasm as there might have been at governmental level about the development of international human rights law under UN auspices was already waning. There was still sufficient political will to enable the adoption of the Universal Declaration of Human Rights by the General Assembly of the United Nations on 10 December 1948. But behind the scenes, work on the International Bill of Rights was hindered by Western government fears that the project would be exploited by the Soviet bloc and by the movement for decolonisation and self-determination in Asia and

Africa. Henceforth, the work was to be done with all deliberate delay. What were to become the two UN Covenants on Human Rights were not ready for signature until December 1966, and they did not come into force for a further decade.

C   The origins of the European Convention on Human Rights

1.12   Meanwhile, in Western Europe, a second terrible war in half a century and the barbarous atrocities of the Nazi Holocaust convinced European politicians, as well as international jurists (such as Hersch Lauterpacht[1], Arthur Goodhart, John Foster QC, and René Cassin) of the need to forge a new Europe based on a greater degree of unity and understanding. The need to guard against the rise of new dictatorships, to reduce the risk of relapse into another disastrous European war, and to provide a beacon of hope for the peoples of Central and Eastern Europe living under totalitarian Soviet regimes, inspired the foundation in 1949 of the Council of Europe. Members of the Council are obliged to accept the principles of the rule of law and the enjoyment by all peoples within their jurisdiction of human rights and fundamental freedoms.

1   Lauterpacht's work was brilliantly original and influential, both within the United Nations and in Europe. In 1944, he completed a masterly work that was published by Columbia University Press in 1945, entitled *An International Bill of the Rights of Man*. Drawing upon international law and constitutional law, and moral and political philosophy, Lauterpacht explained why an International Bill of the Rights of Man must be an integral part of any rational scheme of world order. His book formulated concrete proposals, including a draft instrument. In 1950, he published a second edition, entitled *International Law and Human Rights*, which took account of the events which had occurred within the United Nations and the Council of Europe.

1.13   One of the Council of Europe's first tasks was to draft a legally-binding human rights Convention for Europe, conferring enforceable rights upon individuals against sovereign states. It was a revolutionary enterprise. The master builders knew why human rights protection had to transcend national boundaries, nationality and citizenship. They saw the need to link positive law with ethical values, and to protect individuals and minorities against the misuse of power by elected governments and unelected public officials in periods of emergency and in normal times.

1.14   The inventors of the European Convention were determined never again to permit state sovereignty to shield from international liability the perpetrators of crimes against humanity; never again to allow governments to shelter behind the traditional argument that what a state does to its own citizens or to the stateless is within its exclusive jurisdiction, and beyond the reach of the international community. So they resolved to create a binding international code of human rights, with effective legal safeguards and remedies for all victims of violations by contracting states.

1.15   For the first time, individual men and women would be able to exercise personally enforceable rights under public international law, before an independent international human rights court, against the public authorities of their own states. No matter whether the violation occurred because of an administrative decision by a minister or civil servant, or because of the judgment of their supreme court interpreting and applying its national constitution, or because of legislation enacted by their democratically elected legislature; there would be no privilege or immunity enabling state authorities automatically to shield themselves against supra-national European judicial scrutiny and international liability behind the walls of national sovereignty, with arguments about the special nature of local circumstances, or the citizenship or lack of citizenship of the victims, or the need to protect national security. In the words of Pierre-Henri Teitgen[1], a founding father of the Convention, and brave member of the French resistance, who was to become one of the first judges of the European Court of Human Rights, 'I think we can now unanimously confront "reasons of State" with the only sovereignty worth dying for, worthy in all the circumstances of being defended, respected and safeguarded – the sovereignty of justice and of the law.'

1   Collected Edition of the 'Travaux Préparatoires', Vol I, Preparatory Commission of the Council of Europe, Committee of Ministers, Consultative Assembly, 11 May–8 September 1949, (1975) 1st Session of Consultative Assembly, pp 50–51.

1.16   The birth pangs of the Convention were not easy[1]. The first initiative had been taken by the unofficial European Movement before the Council of Europe was established. The 'Congress of Europe' at The Hague in May 1948 adopted a 'Message to Europeans' stating that: 'We desire a Charter of Human Rights. We desire a Court of Justice with adequate sanctions for the implementation of this Charter.' The International Council of the European Movement in February 1949 approved a 'Declaration of Principles of the European Union' which stated that 'No State should be admitted to the European Union which does not accept the fundamental principles of a Charter of Human Rights and which does not declare itself willing and bound to ensure their application.' An international juridical section of the European Movement, chaired by Teitgen, with Sir David Maxwell-Fyfe (later Home Secretary and Lord Chancellor Kilmuir) as one of the joint rapporteurs, and Goodhart and Lauterpacht as members, produced a draft Convention.

1   Collected Edition of the 'Travaux Préparatoires', at p xxii, Introduction by A H Robertson. The following account draws upon the introduction to Vol I of the 'Travaux Préparatoires' as well as the primary sources contained in Vols I and II. For the political background, see Hugo Young, *This Blessed Plot*, Chapters 1 and 2.

1.17   In spite of the European Movement's proposal, the Committee of Ministers of the Council of Europe decided not to include the subject of human rights on the draft agenda which they proposed for the first session of the Consultative Assembly. However, pressure from the Consultative Assembly induced the Committee of Ministers to agree to include the subject as part of the Assembly's work. The main British protagonists within the Assembly were Churchill, Macmillan and Foster, for the Conservatives, and Lord Layton for the Liberals. Ungoed-Thomas for Labour was briefed negatively by the government.

1.18   Churchill stated that:

'We attach great importance to this ... and are glad that the obstacles to discussion by the Assembly have been removed. A European Assembly forbidden to discuss human rights would indeed have been a ludicrous proposition to put to the world ... we hope that a European Court might be set up, before which cases of the violation of these rights in our own body of twelve nations might be brought to the judgment of the civilised world.'

1.19   Under the leadership of Maxwell-Fyfe and Teitgen, the Assembly's Legal Committee proposed that the Committee of Ministers should draw up a draft Convention providing a collective guarantee designed to ensure the effective enjoyment of ten separate rights proclaimed in the Universal Declaration, and establish for the purpose a European Court and Commission of Human Rights. In August 1950, after work had been done by government officials, the Committee of Ministers were persuaded by the United Kingdom government to adopt a text that was considerably weaker than the original proposals of the Assembly; the right of petition to the Commission was made conditional and the jurisdiction of the E Ct HR optional. The main drafter of the text of what became the Convention, was Sir Oscar Dowson, who had retired as senior legal adviser to the Home Office two years earlier. The UK draft contained fifteen articles containing for the most part definitions of specific human rights taken from the Universal Declaration.

1.20   Within the Attlee government, the project was grudgingly supported by the Foreign Secretary, Ernest Bevin, and was enthusiastically backed only by his Minister of State, Kenneth Younger. It was forcefully opposed by Lord Chancellor Jowitt, by the Colonial Secretary, James Griffiths, and by the Chancellor of the Exchequer, Sir Stafford Cripps[1]. They were as hostile to proposals for an enforceable European Human Rights Convention as they were to Jean Monnet's plans for a politically integrated European Union. Attlee's colleagues and their civil servants saw themselves as protecting the integrity of the British constitution, the common law system, and the British Empire against subversive European influences. They were keen to preserve their ministerial powers from judicial review, especially by an international body of foreign judges of unknown worth.

1   See Anthony Lester 'Fundamental Rights: the United Kingdom Isolated?' [1984] PL 46, at 49–55; see also the fuller account by Geoffrey Marston 'The United Kingdom's Part in the Preparation of the European Convention on Human Rights, 1950' [1993] 42 ICLQ 796.

1.21   The Attorney-General, Sir Hartley Shawcross observed that the government should oppose the right of individual petition which seemed to him to be 'wholly opposed to the theory of responsible Government'. Cripps regarded the Convention as inconsistent with a planned economy, and he wanted to ensure that tax inspectors could exercise their powers of search and seizure free of a vaguely worded general right to personal privacy. Griffiths was worried that the Convention would be exploited by troublemakers in the colonies. Lord Chancellor Jowitt was troubled that emergency powers of detention without trial, or a judge's peremptory power to commit someone to prison for contempt, might not pass muster under the Convention. He consulted the senior judiciary who shared his hostility to the right of petition and the jurisdiction of the European Court.

1.22   Although Bevin shared his negative colleagues' views, the European tide was now strongly flowing in favour of the Convention, and the UK was in danger of being politically isolated. So Bevin persuaded the Cabinet to agree to ratification subject to the crucial condition that the UK would not accept the right of individual petition and the European Court's jurisdiction in individual cases. The government duly signed, and, on 8 March 1951, became the first state to ratify the Convention, which came into force on 23 September 1953.

1.23   Before its ratification, the Convention had been laid on the table of the House of Commons in the usual way under the so-called 'Ponsonby rule'. No objections to ratification had been made by Members of Parliament, and no reservations by the government were made upon ratification. There was, of course, no acceptance of the optional right of individual petition or of the E Ct HR's jurisdiction in individual cases; nor was there any legislation to alter existing domestic law, still less to incorporate Convention rights into UK law.

1.24 The Attlee government persuaded the Committee of Ministers to omit from the Convention the rights to property, to education and to political freedom. This was because of the Labour government's concerns about the potential impact of these rights upon compensation for the nationalisation of property, the abolition of independent fee-paying schools, and undemocratic systems of colonial government. However, each of these rights was subsequently included in the First Protocol to the Convention, ratified by the Conservative government on 3 November 1952.

D The European Convention in the Commonwealth

1.25 On 23 October 1953, the government gave notice, under art 63 of the Convention, extending it to 42 overseas territories for whose international relations they were responsible. Six years later, fundamental rights modelled on the European Convention, were included in Nigeria's pre-independence Constitution. This in turn became the model for the codes of fundamental rights which were inserted into the constitutions of the great majority of independent Commonwealth countries and British dependent territories[1].

1   Anthony Lester 'Fundamental Rights: the United Kingdom Isolated?' [1984] PL 46, pp 55–56. In 1982, the Westminster Parliament enacted the Canada Act, containing a comprehensive Charter of Rights. In 1990, the New Zealand Parliament enacted an interpretative Bill of Rights Act. In 1991, the Hong Kong Bill of Rights Ordinance incorporated the rights guaranteed by the International Covenant on Civil and Political Rights into the domestic law of Hong Kong, including a power for the courts to over-rule inconsistent legislation.

E Acceptance of the right of individual petition

1.26 From time to time throughout the 1950s, MPs pressed the Conservative government to accept the right of petition and the E Ct HR's jurisdiction. The stock response was negative on the ground that this would mean that British codes of common and statute law would become subject to review by an international court. In December 1964, a Conservative MP, Terence Higgins, urged the new Wilson Government to reverse this negative position, as privately did the eminent British judge on the European Court, Lord McNair. On 7 December 1965, after a year of official and ministerial discussion, in which Lord Chancellor Gardiner and the Foreign Secretary, Michael Stewart, pressed for an early, favourable decision, Prime Minister Harold Wilson informed the Commons that the Government had decided to accept the right of petition and the E Ct HR's jurisdiction for an initial period of three years. In spite of its importance and controversial nature in making Acts of Parliament subject to judicial review by the E Ct HR, the matter was not discussed in Cabinet or a Cabinet Committee[1].

1   Anthony Lester 'Fundamental Rights: the United Kingdom Isolated?' [1984] PL 46, at pp 58–61.

1.27　The official papers, made public under the 30-year rule, show that the reason it took so long to announce the decision and formally to accept the right of petition was not only the need to consult the Governors of the dependent territories about whether the right of petition should be extended to their inhabitants; the delay was regarded as essential by HM Treasury to prevent the Burmah Oil company from being able to challenge the compatibility of the War Damage Act 1965 with its rights under the Convention and its first protocol[1]. That Act had deprived Burmah Oil of the fruits of their legal victory[2] establishing the right to compensation for the wartime destruction of their property. It came into force on 2 June 1965. The government waited until the six month period of limitation, within which a challenge to the operation of the Act could have been mounted by Burmah Oil under art 25 of the Convention, had expired before announcing the decision to accept the right of petition. It formally accepted the right of petition on 14 January 1966.

1　Lord Lester of Herne Hill QC, 'UK Acceptance of the Statutory Jurisdiction: What Went on in Whitehall in 1965', [1998] PL 237.
2　*Burmah Oil Co (Burma Trading) Ltd v Lord Advocate* [1965] AC 75, [1964] 2 All ER 348, HL.

1.28　In 1966, the Convention was a sleeping beauty. The Commission's staff were diplomatically building confidence in the system among the governments, overcoming objections based upon their concern to preserve their national sovereignty so as to encourage them to accept the right of individual petition. Only two cases had by then been decided by the E Ct HR. No one foresaw how the E Ct HR's jurisprudence would develop, or what a powerful impact its case law would have upon the UK's constitutional and legal system.

F　British cases under the Convention

1.29　Acceptance of the right of petition gave British lawyers an important opportunity to obtain effective redress for their clients under the Convention for want of effective remedies within the UK. The first British case was brought within only a few months, and the Commission was able to achieve a friendly settlement which met the needs of the individual applicants while paving the way for a statutory system for immigration appeals in the general interest[1]. In *East African Asians v United Kingdom*[2], the Commission decided that Parliament itself had breached the Convention in enacting the Commonwealth Immigrants Act 1968, which subjected British Asian passport-holders to inherently degrading treatment by excluding them on racial grounds from their country of citizenship. The first case in which the E Ct HR found a breach by the UK was *Golder v United Kingdom*[3], which held that the Home Secretary had infringed a prisoner's right of access to the English courts and his right to respect for his correspondence. The first case in which the E Ct HR held that the Law Lords had breached the Convention was in relation to an injunction restraining *The Sunday Times* from publishing an article about the 'thalidomide' tragedy because it was prejudicial to the fair trial of pending civil proceedings. By a narrow majority the E Ct HR held the Lords' decision to have unnecessarily interfered with the right to free expression[4].

1　Application 2991/66, *Alam and Khan v United Kingdom* 24 CD 116 (1967).
2　Commission decision on admissibility of 14 December 1973; (1981) 3 EHRR 76.
3　(1975) 1 EHRR 524, E Ct HR.
4　*Sunday Times v United Kingdom* (1979) 2 EHRR 245, E Ct HR.

1.30 In all, there have been some fifty judgments in UK cases finding breaches of Convention rights, many of them controversial and far-reaching. They include: the inhuman treatment of suspected terrorists in Northern Ireland; inadequate safeguards against telephone tapping by the police; unfair discrimination against British wives of foreign husbands under the immigration rules; unjust restrictions upon prisoners' correspondence and visits; corporal punishment in schools; criminal sanctions against private homosexual conduct; ineffective judicial protection for detained mental patients, or would-be immigrants, or individuals facing extradition to countries where they risk being exposed to torture or inhuman treatment; the dismissal of workers because of the oppressive operation of the closed shop; interference with free speech by maintaining injunctions restraining breaches of confidence where information had become widely available; the right to have a detention order under the Mental Health Act reviewed; parental access to children; access to child care records; review of the continued detention of those serving discretionary life sentences; access to legal advice for fine and debt defaulters; courts-martial procedure; availability of legal aid in criminal cases; access to civil justice. 'There is hardly an area of state regulation untouched by standards which have emerged from the application of Convention provisions to situations presented by individual applicants.'[1].

1   Francis G Jacobs and Robin C A White *The European Convention on Human Rights* (2nd edn, 1996), at p 406.

G   Use of the Convention in British courts

1.31 The reasons why the UK has been found to have breached Convention rights in so many significant and far-reaching cases include the absence of effective domestic remedies, the readiness and ability of British lawyers to use the Convention system imaginatively on their clients' behalf, and the publicity given to Convention cases by the British media. The Convention has been frequently invoked in proceedings before English courts, even though it has not been incorporated by statute into domestic law[1]; and the courts have become willing to have regard to the unincorporated Convention and its case law as sources of principles or standards of public policy[2]. They have done so where a statute is ambiguous; or where the common law is developing or uncertain; or where the common law is certain but incomplete; or as a source of public policy; or when determining the manner in which judicial powers are to be exercised. Common law rights, reflected in the Convention, have been recognised in relation to free expression and to access to the courts and lawyers[3].

1   Murray Hunt *Using International Human Rights Law in English Court* (1997), Appendix I contains a chronological table of English cases in which judicial reference has been made to unincorporated international human rights law. The Universal Declaration and the International Covenant on Civil and Political Rights have been referred to much more rarely.
2   Murray Hunt *Using International Human Rights Law in English Court* (1997), at pp 207–251. See also Rabinder Singh *The Future of Human Rights in the United Kingdom* (1997) at pp 5–16.
3   See para **2.03** below.

1.32 However, Convention rights cannot be directly invoked to determine whether administrative discretion, exercised under broad statutory powers, has unnecessarily interfered with those rights, or has been disproportionate to the decision-maker's aims.

This is because a statute conferring broad discretionary powers is regarded as unambiguous, and the Convention as irrelevant, in construing the purpose of the statute. For the courts to require ministers to comply with the Convention in performing their public functions would involve a violation of the constitutional separation of powers, by incorporating the Convention through the back door when Parliament has refused to do so through the front door. However, where human rights are at stake, the courts require a stricter objective justification of the exercise of public powers than would satisfy the looser test of irrationality. Absent a clear legislative or executive statement to the contrary, they also recognise a legitimate expectation that ministers and civil servants will comply with Convention obligations[1].

1   See para **2.03** below.

1.33   English courts, influenced by the development of a modern system of public law and by the requirement to give effect to the supremacy of European Community law have done their best to give effect to Convention rights, without statutory incorporation. However, the continuing gap between Convention law and domestic law has meant that the European Court of Human Rights has become in effect a supreme constitutional court of the UK. British judges have been denied the power and responsibility of safeguarding Convention rights. Victims of violations of human rights have been unable to obtain speedy and effective domestic redress. British judges been unable to make a distinct contribution to the development of the European Court's case law by interpreting and applying the Convention directly. These considerations, together with the fact that the UK and Ireland are the only two contracting states in the Council of Europe that have not directly incorporated Convention rights, have created a compelling and widely-supported case for incorporation.

H   The campaign for incorporation

1.34   The first public call for the incorporation of Convention rights by statute was made in 1968[1]. In 1974, Lord Scarman gave his great authority to the campaign to make the Convention directly enforceable[2], in his Hamlyn lectures. In 1976, the Home Secretary, Roy Jenkins, published a little-noticed discussion paper on the subject[3], and revealed his personal support for incorporation. In 1977, the Northern Ireland Standing Advisory Commission on Human Rights published a report unanimously recommending incorporation[4]. In 1978, a Lords Select Committee also recommended incorporation[5].

1   Anthony Lester, 'Democracy and Individual Rights' Fabian Tract No 390, November 1968. See generally, Michael Zander *A Bill of Rights?* (4th edn, 1997).
2   Lord Scarman *English Law—The New Dimension* (1976).
3   'Legislation on Human Rights with particular reference to the European Convention on Human Rights' (June 1976) Home Office.
4   *The Protection of Human Rights by Law in Northern Ireland* (1977); Cmnd 7009.
5   *Report of the Select Committee on a Bill of Rights* (HL 176 (1978)). There was a bare majority in favour caused by Baroness Gaitskell's refusal to adopt the negative line of her Labour colleagues.

1.35   Later in 1978, the Select Committee's Report was debated in the Lords. The Liberal, Lord Wade, whose original Bill had led to the setting up of the Select Committee, successfully moved an amendment urging the Government to introduce incorporating legislation. In 1981, Lord Wade again succeeded in obtaining the Lords' approval of his Bill, but it was blocked in the Commons after a poorly attended debate on Alan Beith MP's unsuccessful attempt to secure a second reading. In 1986, the Conservative, Lord Broxbourne QC, obtained Lords' approval for his Bill, but, after receiving a second reading in the Commons on the initiative of the Conservative MP, Sir Edward Gardiner QC, the Bill progressed no further.

1.36 Charter 88, created in November 1988, quickly became an influential political movement supporting constitutional reforms, including the Convention's incorporation. In December 1990, the Liberal Democrat, Lord Holme of Cheltenham, whose Constitutional Reform Centre had paved the way for Charter 88, initiated a Lords' debate to urge incorporation. In 1991, two organisations, Liberty and the Institute of Public Policy Research, published separate proposals for Bills of Rights, modelled in part upon the Convention.

1.37 By now, the declared supporters of incorporation included two former Lord Chancellors, Lord Gardiner and Lord Hailsham, the Lord Chief Justice, Lord Taylor of Gosforth, the Master of the Rolls, Sir Thomas Bingham, several Law Lords, the Bar Council and the Law Society, Justice, and two former Home Secretaries, Lord Jenkins of Hillhead and Sir Leon Brittan QC. However, the two main political parties remained opposed to incorporation.

I Bringing rights home

1.38 On 1 March 1993, the Leader of the Labour Party, John Smith QC, gave a lecture entitled 'A Citizen's Democracy', under the auspices of Charter 88, calling for 'a new constitutional settlement, a new deal between the people and the state that puts the citizen centre stage'. The lecture marked a political watershed. One measure of reform which he proposed was statutory incorporation, with a Human Rights Commission to advise and support those wishing to assert their Convention rights, and, where necessary, itself to institute cases. In September 1993, John Smith's statement of policy was expressed in the Labour Party's *A new agenda for democracy: Labour's proposals for constitutional reform*. The 1993 Labour Party conference adopted a policy supporting a two-stage process: the first stage included the incorporation of the Convention; the second stage was for a Labour Government to set up an all-party commission to consider and draft a home-grown Bill of Rights.

1.39 In 1994, the Liberal Democrat, Lord Lester of Herne Hill QC, introduced the first of two Bills to incorporate the Convention[1]. It was designed to give the Convention a similar status in UK law to that of directly effective Community law. It would have empowered the courts to disapply inconsistent existing and future Acts of Parliament, imposing a duty on public authorities to comply with the Convention, and creating effective remedies (including damages) for breaches. The Bill had a turbulent passage through the Lords. It was mutilated by wrecking amendments supported by Conservative ministers.

---

1   Lord Lester of Herne Hill QC, 'First Steps towards a Constitutional Bill of Rights', [1997] EHRLR 124–31. This special issue of EHRLR was devoted to the incorporation debate.

1.40   Senior judges, including the Lord Chief Justice, Lord Taylor of Gosforth, Lord Browne-Wilkinson and Lord Woolf of Barnes supported the Bill, but, given a political climate of concern about threats to Parliamentary sovereignty perceived to come from the supremacy of European Community law, they suggested that it would be prudent to devise a measure, modelled upon New Zealand's Bill of Rights Act 1990, that did not give the courts an express power to disapply or strike down inconsistent legislation. Their advice was heeded.

1.41   Lord Lester's second Bill, given a Second Reading on 5 February 1997, was a strengthened version of the New Zealand model. It applied to any person discharging public functions, ensured that Convention rights would override inconsistent common law, and provided that, whenever an enactment can be given a meaning that is consistent with Convention rights, that meaning shall be preferred to any other meaning. It also provided that when a Government Bill is introduced, the Minister must certify whether it is or appears to be inconsistent with Convention rights. The Bill gave flexible powers to the courts to grant appropriate remedies, but no power to override inconsistent primary legislation. The Bill's success depended upon the willingness of the judiciary to treat it as a unique constitutional measure to be interpreted and applied purposively. Lord Lester also made it clear that he regarded the creation of a Human Rights Commission as indispensable in ensuring effective access to justice, providing advice and assistance and bringing proceedings in its own name.

1.42   Meanwhile, on 18 December 1996, the shadow Home Secretary, Jack Straw MP, published Labour's consultation paper, *Bringing Rights Home*, setting out the case for incorporation and proposals for the way this should be done[1]. On 5 March 1997, the Labour and Liberal Democrat Joint Consultative Committee on Constitutional Reform, co-chaired by Robin Cook MP and Robert Maclennan MP, published its report[2]. The section of the report on incorporation closely followed the scheme of the second Lester Bill. It envisaged that there would be a Human Rights Commissioner or Commission, or similar public body, to advise and assist those seeking protection of their Convention rights, and to be able to bring proceedings in its own name.

1   The text was published in [1997] EHRLR 71.
2   See the editorial by Ben Emmerson in [1997] EHRLR 115–16.

1.43   On 1 May 1997, Tony Blair's New Labour Party was returned to office, committed by its manifesto to incorporate the Convention. In October 1997, it published a White Paper, *Rights Brought Home: The Human Rights Bill*[1], together with the Bill itself for which Home Secretary Straw was the responsible minister. On 3 November 1997, the Lord Chancellor, Lord Irvine of Lairg, who had played a crucial role in persuading John Smith MP to favour incorporation, and who had significantly influenced the shaping of the Bill, introduced the second reading debate[2]. The Bill was given strong support by the Liberal Democrats, by the eminent Conservative backbenchers, Lord Renton and Lord Windlesham, and by a formidable body of jurists on the Cross-Benches, including the Lord Chief Justice, Lord Bingham of Cornhill, Lord Scarman, Lord Wilberforce, Lord Ackner, Lord Cooke of Thorndon, and (as a recent convert) Lord Donaldson of Lymington. However, the Bill was opposed by the Conservative Front Bench.

1   Cm 3782.
2   582 HL Official Report (5th series) cols 1227–34.

1.44   A half century after the publication of the Universal Declaration, and almost thirty years after incorporation had first been proposed, fundamental human rights were at last to be secured in UK law. The first historic step had been taken towards a constitutional Bill of Rights.

Chapter 2
The Human Rights Act 1998

A   The purposes of the HRA 1998

2.01   The Long Title states that the Human Rights Act 1998 (HRA 1998) is designed 'to give further[1] effect to rights and freedoms guaranteed under the European Convention on Human Rights' (and to make provision with respect to holders of certain judicial offices who become judges of the E Ct HR, and for connected purposes).

1   The Lord Chancellor, Lord Irvine of Lairg, explained during the committee stage of the Bill in the House of Lords (see 583 HL Official Report (5th series) col 478 (18 November 1997)), that 'The reason the Long Title uses the word "further" is that our courts already apply the Convention in many different circumstances.' See para **2.03**. He added during the third reading (see 585 HL Official Report (5th series) col 755 (5 February 1998)), that the HRA 1998 'does not create new human rights or take any existing human rights away. It provides better and easier access to rights which already exist'. The HRA 1998, s 11 emphasises that the Act does not remove rights previously or otherwise enjoyed: see para **2.11**.

2.02   As explained by the Prime Minister, Tony Blair, in the Preface to the White Paper *Bringing Rights Home*, the HRA 1998 is intended to 'give people in the United Kingdom opportunities to enforce their rights under the European Convention in British courts rather than having to incur the cost and delay of taking a case to the European Human Rights ... Court in Strasbourg'[1]. The White Paper added that the aim of the legislation 'is a straightforward one. It is to make more directly accessible the rights which the British people already enjoy under the Convention. In other words, to bring those rights home'[2].

1   *Rights Brought Home* (Cm 3782, 1997), p 1.
2   *Rights Brought Home* (Cm 3782, 1997), para 1.19. See also the speech by the Lord Chancellor, Lord Irvine of Lairg, on the second reading of the Bill in the House of Lords, 582 HL Official Report (5th series), col 1228 (3 November 1997): 'The Bill will bring human rights home. People will be able to argue for their rights and claim their remedies under the Convention in any court or tribunal in the United Kingdom. Our courts will develop human rights throughout society. A culture of awareness of human rights will develop ... The protection of human rights at home gives credibility to our foreign policy to advance the cause of human rights around the world ... We are not ceding new powers to Europe. The United Kingdom already accepts that Strasbourg rulings bind.' Lord Bingham of Cornhill, the Lord Chief Justice, explained at cols 1245–1246: 'It makes no sense, and, I suggest, does not make for justice that those seeking to enforce their rights have to exhaust all their domestic remedies here before embarking on the long and costly trail to Strasbourg ... British judges have a significant contribution to make in the development of the law of human rights. It is a contribution which so far we have not been permitted to make ... At present disappointed litigants leave our courts believing that there exists elsewhere a superior form of justice which our courts are not allowed to administer.' See also Lord Wilberforce at col 1279: '"Bringing home the rights" is a lovely phrase. It makes us think of the "Ashes", or perhaps the bacon.'

2.03   The general principle of United Kingdom law is that 'a treaty is not part of [domestic] law unless and until it has been incorporated into the law by legislation'[1]. Prior to the coming into force of the HRA 1998, the European Convention on Human

Rights, although an international treaty which binds the United Kingdom (and obliges the United Kingdom as a matter of international obligation to amend our laws and procedures where they are found to have breached the Convention), therefore has a limited, albeit important, effect in domestic law in creating rights and duties[2]. In particular:

(1)   courts seek to interpret ambiguous legislation consistently with the Convention[3];

(2)   courts seek to apply the common law (where it is uncertain, unclear or incomplete), and exercise judicial discretions, consistently with the Convention[4];

(3)   although public authorities, such as Ministers of the Crown, exercising discretionary powers have no duty to exercise such powers consistently with the Convention[5], the human rights context is relevant to whether the Minister or other public authority acted reasonably and had regard to all relevant considerations[6];

(4)   where a dispute concerns directly effective European Union law, the courts take account of the Convention because European Union law includes the principles recognised by the Convention[7].

1   *J H Rayner (Mincing Lane) Ltd v Department of Trade and Industry* [1990] 2 AC 418 at 500C per Lord Oliver of Aylmerton.

2   See, generally, para **8.02** for the (maiden) speech in the House of Lords by Lord Bingham, the Lord Chief Justice 575 HL Official Report, cols 1465–1467; Murray Hunt *Using Human Rights Law in English Courts* (1997); and Michael J Beloff, QC and Helen Mountfield 'Unconventional Behaviour? Judicial Uses of the European Convention in England and Wales' [1996] European Human Rights Law Review 467.

3   *R v Secretary of State for the Home Department, ex p Brind* [1991] 1 AC 696 at 747H–748A (per Lord Bridge of Harwich, with whom Lord Roskill agreed) and at 760D–G (per Lord Ackner, with whom Lord Lowry agreed).

4   See, for example, *Derbyshire County Council v Times Newspapers Ltd* [1992] QB 770 at 812D–E (Balcombe LJ), at 822D–E (Ralph Gibson LJ) and at 830A–B (Butler-Sloss LJ) in the Court of Appeal (the House of Lords dismissed an appeal, but on other grounds: [1993] AC 534); and *Rantzen v Mirror Group Newspapers (1986) Ltd* [1994] QB 670 at 691B–C (Neill LJ for the Court of Appeal).

5   *R v Secretary of State for the Home Department, ex p Brind* [1991] 1 AC 696 at 748A–F (per Lord Bridge of Harwich, with whom Lord Roskill agreed) and at 761F–762B (Lord Ackner, with whom Lord Lowry agreed).

6   'The more substantial the interference with human rights, the more the court will require by way of justification before it is satisfied that the decision is reasonable' in the sense that it was within the range of responses of a reasonable decision-maker: *R v Ministry of Defence, ex p Smith* [1996] QB 517 at 554E–G (Sir Thomas Bingham MR for the Court of Appeal) approved by Lord Woolf MR for the Court of Appeal in *R v Secretary of State for the Home Department, ex p Canbolat* [1997] 1 WLR 1569, 1579E-H. In *R v Secretary of State for the Home Department, ex p Ahmed and Patel* (1998) Times, 15 October, Lord Woolf MR for the Court of Appeal held, approving the judgment of the High Court of Australia in *Minister for Immigration and Ethnic Affairs v Teoh* (1995) 183 CLR 273, that where the state has ratified an international human rights treaty, there is a legitimate expectation that the state will take account of those international obligations in domestic decision-making where a discretion exists. However, any such expectation does not entitle the domestic court to decide whether the state has correctly interpreted the international obligation. Moreover, where the state has adopted an express policy, the only legitimate expectation is that this policy will be applied.

7   Article F(2) of the Maastricht Treaty states:

'The [European] Union shall respect fundamental rights, as guaranteed by the European Convention for the Protection of Human Rights and Fundamental Freedoms signed in Rome on 4 November 1950 and as they result from the constitutional traditions common to the Member States, as general principles of Community law.'

This confirms the prior case-law of the European Court of Justice. See, for example, Cases 46/87, 227/88: *Hoechst AG v EC Commission* [1989] ECR 2859 at 2923 (para 13 of the judgment):

'The Court has consistently held that fundamental rights are an integral part of the general principles of law the observance of which the court ensures, in accordance with constitutional traditions common to the Member States, and the international treaties on which the Member States have collaborated or of which they are signatories ... . The European Convention for the Protection of Human Rights and Fundamental Freedoms ... is of particular significance in that regard ... .'

2.04   The HRA 1998 imposes the following principal duties of constitutional significance so as to 'bring rights home'.

(1)   So far as it is possible to do so, primary legislation and subordinate legislation must be read and given effect in a way which is compatible with rights guaranteed under the Convention[1].

(2)   Where it is not possible to read other legislation compatibly with Convention rights, the HRA 1998 confers no power on the court to strike down such legislation. However, the court may make a declaration of incompatibility[2], which will encourage the government and Parliament to consider urgent amendments to the relevant legislative provision by remedial action[3]. The incompatible legislative provision remains valid and effective, unless and until legislative amendments are made[4]. And Parliament has a discretion whether to remove the incompatibility. So Parliamentary sovereignty is maintained. But a failure to make such amendment to remedy the domestic court's declaration of incompatibility will lead to a complaint to the E Ct HR and so will be a powerful incentive to the Executive to introduce, and for Parliament to enact, amending legislation.

(3)   Public authorities, which include courts and tribunals, must not act in a way which is incompatible with Convention rights[5]. Therefore, the HRA 1998 will affect the legal relationship between private parties because the courts will owe a duty to protect individuals against breaches of their rights[6]. If a public authority breaches that obligation, a victim may obtain judicial remedies[7]. Courts and tribunals therefore have a duty to comply with the Convention in applying the common law and in granting remedies.

(4)   A Minister of the Crown in charge of a Bill in either House of Parliament must, before the second reading, make a statement about the compatibility of the Bill with Convention rights. If the Minister cannot confirm that the Bill is compatible with the Convention, then he must explain that the Government nevertheless wishes the House to proceed with the Bill[8]. In the absence of a statement of incompatibility, the courts will be entitled to proceed on the assumption that the Bill was not intended to abridge or limit Convention rights.

1   HRA 1998, s 3: see para **2.3**. The HRA 1998 has replaced the insularity expressed by Lord Denning MR for the Court of Appeal in *R v Chief Immigration Officer, Heathrow Airport, ex p Bibi* [1976] 1 WLR 979 at 985B: 'The Convention is drafted in a style very different from the way which we are used to in legislation. It contains wide general statements of principle. They are apt to lead to much difficulty in application: because they give rise to much uncertainty. They are not the sort of thing which we can easily digest. Article 8 is an example. It is so wide as to be incapable of practical application. So it is much better for us to stick to our own statutes and principles, and only look to the Convention for guidance in case of doubt.' It will also be important for judges in domestic courts to avoid the more subtle insularity of Lord Donaldson MR in the Court of Appeal in *R v Secretary of State for the Home Department, ex p Brind* [1991] 1 AC 696 at 717E–F: 'you have to look long and hard before you can detect any difference between the English common law and the principles set out in the Convention, at least if the Convention is viewed through English judicial eyes'.
2   HRA 1998, s 4: see para **2.4**.

3   HRA 1998, s 10: para **2.10**.
4   HRA 1998, s 4(6). See para **2.4.5**.
5   HRA 1998, s 6: see para **2.6**.
6   See para **2.6.3**, n 3.
7   HRA 1998, ss 7–9: paras **2.7–2.9**.
8   HRA 1998, s 19: see para **2.19**. The HRA 1998, s 19 came into force on 24 November 1998: see para **2.22.2**, n 1.

2.05   The HRA 1998 thereby gives considerable further effect to the Convention in domestic law, while maintaining ultimate Parliamentary sovereignty. The HRA 1998 is no ordinary law[1]. It is a legally enforceable charter of human rights and fundamental freedoms. It secures to everyone within the jurisdiction of the United Kingdom the fundamental values and rights that are entrenched in binding international law by the United Kingdom's ratification of the European Convention and membership of the Council of Europe.

1   See para **3.01** n 1.

2.06   The scheme of the HRA 1998 recognises the responsibility of each branch of government (legislature, executive and judicial) to give effect to Convention rights in exercising public powers.

2.07   Under the scheme of the HRA 1998, Convention rights become the law's compass where human rights are involved. The HRA 1998 will create a strong magnetic field across the entire body of United Kingdom law, whether relating to statute or the common law, the duties of public bodies, and the scope of private obligations.

B The provisions of the HRA 1998[1]

SECTION 1

2.1   The HRA 1998, s 1 specifies which rights ('the Convention rights') are to be given further[2] effect in domestic law through the provisions of the HRA 1998. It also provides that the Convention rights may be amended by order to reflect the effect of a protocol to the Convention which the United Kingdom has ratified, or signed with a view to ratification.

1   The following analysis of each section of the HRA 1998 draws on the very helpful 'Notes on Clauses' produced by the Government for the House of Lords (when the Bill was introduced) and then (in an amended form) for the House of Commons.
2   See paras **2.01** and **2.03**.

2.1.1   The 'Convention rights' which are given further effect in domestic law are[1] the rights guaranteed under arts 2 to 12 and 14 of the Convention, arts 1 to 3 of the first protocol, and arts 1 and 2 of the sixth protocol[2], in each case as read with arts 16 to 18 of the Convention[3].

1   HRA 1998, s 1(1). For the content and application of each of the Convention rights, see Ch 4 below.
2   Articles 1 and 2 of the sixth protocol abolish the death penalty in peacetime. See para **4.2.16– 4.2.19**. The Bill was amended in the House of Commons Committee (on an amendment moved by Mr Kevin McNamara MP) to include arts 1 and 2 of the sixth protocol within the scope of Convention rights, against the wishes of the government: see 312 HC Official Report (6th series)

cols 987–1013 (20 May 1998). The government's position had been set out in the White Paper *Rights Brought Home* (Cm 3782, 1997), at para 4.13: the sixth protocol should not be ratified because the government regarded the issue raised by the death penalty as being 'not one of basic constitutional principle but is a matter of judgment and conscience to be decided by Members of Parliament as they see fit', that is without being constrained by the international obligations of the United Kingdom. Parliament took a different view: that the United Kingdom should ratify the sixth protocol because the death penalty is incompatible with fundamental human rights. The death penalty for murder was abolished by the Murder (Abolition of Death Penalty) Act 1965 (originally for a trial period, but then permanently). Section 36 of the Crime and Disorder Act 1998 abolished the death penalty for treason and piracy. Although art 2 of the sixth protocol allows states to make legal provision for the death penalty in respect of acts committed in time of war, or imminent threat of war, the government decided that it was also appropriate to abolish the death penalty for military offences, in all circumstances, whether in peace or in wartime. See the comments of Mr Mike O'Brien MP, Parliamentary Under-Secretary of State for the Home Department, at the report stage in the House of Commons, 317 HC Official Report (6th series) cols 1353–1356 (21 October 1998). See also para **2.21**. The decision to include the sixth protocol within the scope of Convention rights under the HRA 1998 supplements the general purposes of the Act to this extent: the HRA 1998 is primarily designed to implement in the United Kingdom the international obligations of this country, but the inclusion of the sixth protocol has encouraged the United Kingdom to adopt a new international obligation. The United Kingdom ratified the sixth protocol on 27 January 1999. The consequence of the ratification of the sixth protocol was explained by the Minister of State for the Home Office, Lord Williams of Mostyn, when the House of Lords considered the Commons' amendments to the Bill: it makes it 'impossible for Parliament to reintroduce the death penalty in future, except for acts committed in time of war or imminent threat of war, without denouncing the Convention itself': see 593 HL Official Report (5th series) col 2084 (29 October 1998).

3   On arts 17–18, see paras **3.14** and **3.17**. On art 16, see para **4.16**.

2.1.2   The 'Convention rights' therefore do not include art 1, which provides that the contracting states 'shall secure to everyone within their jurisdiction' the rights and freedoms guaranteed under the Convention. This is because the HRA 1998 itself 'gives effect to art 1 by securing to people in the United Kingdom the rights and freedoms of the Convention'[1]. Nor does the concept of 'Convention rights' include art 13, which provides that everyone whose rights and freedoms are violated shall have 'an effective remedy before a national authority'[2]. That is because the HRA 1998 'gives effect to art 13 by establishing a scheme under which Convention rights can be raised before our domestic courts'[3].

1   Lord Chancellor, Lord Irvine of Lairg, at the committee stage of the Bill in the House of Lords, 583 HL Official Reports (5th series) col 475 (18 November 1997). On art 1 see para **4.1**.

2   On art 13 see para **4.13**.

3   The Lord Chancellor, Lord Irvine of Lairg, at the committee stage of the Bill in the House of Lords, 583 HL Official Reports (5th series) col 475 (18 November 1997). However, he added, at col 477, that 'the courts may have regard to art 13'. See also the Lord Chancellor's comments on the report stage in the House of Lords, 584 HL Official Report (5th series) cols 1265–1267 (19 January 1998). The obligation imposed by art 13 'is met by the passage of the [Act]': Lord Williams of Mostyn, Under-Secretary of State at the Home Office, on the second reading of the Bill in the House of Lords, 582 HL Official Report (5th series) col 1308 (3 November 1997). During the committee stage in the House of Commons, 312 HC Official Report (6th series) cols 978–981 (20 May 1998), the Home Secretary, Mr Jack Straw MP, explained that there were two main reasons why, in the Government's view, art 13 should not be included in the Convention rights protected under the HRA 1998. 'First and foremost, it is the Bill that gives effect to art 13, so there was an issue of duplication'. The second reason is that if article 13 were to be included, 'the question would inevitably arise what the courts would make of the amendment, which, on the face of it, contains nothing new'. Mr Straw accepted (at col 981) that 'the courts must take account of the large body of Convention jurisprudence when considering remedies' (as s 2 requires: see para **2.2**). 'Obviously, in doing so, they are bound to take judicial notice of article 13, without specifically being bound by it'. Therefore, when courts and tribunals consider the scope and effect of remedies under the HRA 1998, they should proceed by reference to the principle that the Act is intended to implement the art 13 guarantee

of an 'effective' national remedy. In deciding the criteria of an 'effective' national remedy, courts and tribunals should have regard to the Strasbourg jurisprudence, on which see para **4.13**. Prior to the enactment of the HRA 1998, domestic courts were already having regard to art 13 for the purposes indicated in para **2.03**: see, for example, *R v Secretary of State for the Home Department, ex p Brind* [1991] 1 AC 696, HL: *Rantzen v Mirror Group Newspapers* [1994] QB 670, CA; *R v Khan* [1997] AC 558, HL.

2.1.3   The articles setting out Convention rights[1] are[2] to have effect for the purposes of the HRA 1998 subject to any designated derogation or reservation, as provided by HRA 1998, ss 14 and 15[3]. Because the Act gives the Convention rights effect in domestic law for the purposes of this Act, it does not remove the effect which the Convention already has in domestic law[4].

1   HRA 1998, s 1(3) adds that the articles are set out in Sch 1 to the HRA 1998 which reproduces the text of the relevant articles of the Convention and protocols.
2   HRA 1998, s 1(2).
3   For HRA 1998, ss 14 and 15, see paras **2.14** and **2.15**.
4   For the effect of the Convention in domestic law prior to the coming into force of the HRA 1998, see paras **2.0.1** and **2.0.3**. HRA 1998, s 11 emphasises that the HRA 1998 does not remove rights previously or otherwise enjoyed: see para **2.11**.

2.1.4   The Secretary of State has power[1] by order[2] to make such amendments to the HRA 1998 as he considers appropriate to reflect the effect, in relation to the United Kingdom, of a protocol.

1   HRA 1998, s 1(4). This order-making power enables the Convention rights to be updated as appropriate to keep them in line with any further obligations which the United Kingdom may assume under further protocols to the Convention from time to time.
2   HRA 1998, s 20(1) provides that the power to make an order is exercisable by statutory instrument. HRA 1998, s 20(4) provides that no order may be made under s 1(4) unless a draft has been laid before, and approved by, each House of Parliament. The use of the draft affirmative resolution procedure reflects the importance of the subject matter with which the relevant provisions are concerned.

2.1.5   'Protocol' is defined[1] to mean a protocol to the Convention which the United Kingdom has ratified, or which the United Kingdom has signed with a view to ratification. Various categories of protocol are covered by this definition: those which the United Kingdom has already signed or ratified when the HRA 1998 came into force but which are not included in the term 'Convention rights' (in particular, the United Kingdom has signed, but not ratified, the fourth protocol to the Convention)[2]; existing protocols to the Convention which the United Kingdom has neither signed nor ratified (in particular, the seventh protocol[3]); and protocols which are added to the Convention at some future date.

1   HRA 1998, s 1(5).
2   Covering the right not to be deprived of liberty on the ground of inability to fulfil a contractual obligation; the right to liberty of movement for those lawfully in a country, and the right of a person to leave any country, including his own; the right to enter the territory of a country of which one is a national and the right not to be expelled from such territory; and the prohibition on the collective expulsion of aliens. As explained in the White Paper *Rights Brought Home* (Cm 3782, 1997), para 4.10, the fourth protocol was signed by the United Kingdom in 1963 but not subsequently ratified because of concerns about the exact extent of the obligation regarding a right of entry. Paragraph 4.11 of the White Paper added that the Government had no present intention to ratify the fourth protocol. This was confirmed by Lord Williams of Mostyn, the Parliamentary Under-Secretary of State at the Home Office, during the committee stage in the House of Lords, 583 HL Official Report (5th series) col 504 (18 November 1997). On the forth protocol, see also paras **4.16.3–4.16.10**.

3   The seventh protocol concerns the right of an alien lawfully resident in the territory of a state not to be expelled therefrom except in pursuance of a decision reached in accordance with the law, with defined procedural safeguards; the right of a person convicted of a criminal offence by a tribunal to have the conviction or sentence reviewed by a higher tribunal; the right to compensation for a person whose criminal conviction leading to punishment has been reversed, or who has received a pardon, on the ground that a new or newly discovered fact shows conclusively that there has been a miscarriage of justice; the right to protection from double jeopardy in criminal proceedings; and equality of rights and responsibilities for spouses. As explained in the White Paper *Bringing Rights Home* (Cm 3782, 1997), para 4.15, in substance these principles are already contained in domestic law, and the United Kingdom intends to sign and ratify the seventh protocol once some necessary legislative changes have been made. On the content and application of the seventh protocol in the context of a fair trial, see paras **4.6.73–4.6.82**. On the seventh protocol, see also paras **4.16.11–4.16.14**.

2.1.6   No amendment to Convention rights may be made by an order[1] so as to come into force before the protocol concerned is in force in relation to the United Kingdom[2].

1   Under the powers described in para **2.1.4**.
2   HRA 1998, s 1(6). The purpose of this provision is to ensure that the Convention rights under the HRA 1998 remain consistent with the United Kingdom's international obligations under the Convention. But for s 1 (6), it would be possible for rights in a protocol to have domestic effect before the United Kingdom has an international obligation to secure those rights.

SECTION 2

2.2   The HRA 1998, s 2 requires United Kingdom courts and tribunals to take account of the judgments, decisions, declarations or opinions of the institutions established by the Convention when determining a question which has arisen in connection with a Convention right[1]. It also makes provision for how evidence of such judgments etc is to be given in relevant proceedings[2].

1   'Convention rights' are defined in s 1(1) of the HRA 1998: see para **2.1.1**.
2   See the speech by the Lord Chancellor, Lord Irvine of Lairg, on the second reading of the Bill in the House of Lords, 582 HL Official Report (5th series) col 1230 (3 November 1997): 'It is entirely appropriate that our courts should draw on the wealth of existing jurisprudence on the Convention.' Commonwealth constitutional case-law is also likely to provide a rich source of jurisprudence.

2.2.1   When determining a question which has arisen in connection with a Convention right, a court or tribunal must take into account any:

(a)   judgment, decision, declaration or advisory opinion of the E Ct HR;

(b)   opinion of the Commission given in a report adopted under art 31 of the Convention;

(c)   decision of the Commission in connection with arts 26 or 27(2) of the Convention (decisions on the admissibility of complaints); or

(d)   decision of the Committee of Ministers taken under art 46 of the Convention,

whenever made or given[1], so far as it is relevant to the proceedings[2].

1   During the House of Commons Committee Stage, the Parliamentary Secretary to the Lord Chancellor's Department, Mr Geoffrey Hoon MP, explained that the phrase 'whenever made or given' was intended to make 'clear that the domestic courts are to take into account not only existing jurisprudence of the Convention institutions, but their future jurisprudence ...': see 313 HC Official Report (6th series) col 405 (3 June 1998).
2   HRA 1998, s 2(1). Under the revised structure introduced by the eleventh protocol to the Convention (with effect from 1 November 1998), the European Commission of Human Rights

ceased to exist and the Committee of Ministers ceased to have the function of considering cases not referred by the Commission to the E Ct HR (although the Committee of Ministers still has the function of considering the execution of judgments of the E Ct HR). The eleventh protocol therefore amended the Convention in particular in articles 26, 27 and 31. Parliament has ensured that after the coming into force of the eleventh protocol amending the Convention, domestic courts and tribunals can have regard to decisions taken under the Convention prior to its amendment. HRA 1998, s 21(2) provides that, for the purposes of s 2(1)(b) and (c), references to the articles of the Convention are to those articles as they had effect immediately prior to the coming into force of the eleventh protocol (on 1 November 1998). HRA 1998, s 21(3) provides that for the purposes of s 2(1)(d), the reference to art 46 includes a reference to arts 32 and 54 of the Convention as they had effect immediately before the coming into force of the eleventh protocol. Article 46 of the Convention (as amended) and art 54 of the Convention before its amendment concern the Committee's function of supervising the implementation of judgments of the E Ct HR. Article 32 of the Convention before its amendment concerned the Committee's function of deciding, in cases which were not referred to the court, whether there had been a violation of the Convention. HRA 1998, s 21(4) states that the references in s 2(1) to a report or decision of the Commission or a decision of the Committee of Ministers include references to a report or decision made as provided by art 5 of the eleventh protocol, paras 3, 4 and 6 (transitional provisions). This is to allow for the period immediately following the coming into force of the eleventh protocol when some cases pending in Strasbourg will be addressed in accordance with transitional arrangements.

2.2.2   Courts and tribunals are required to take these judgments, decisions, declarations and opinions[1] into account because they are all potentially relevant to the correct interpretation of the Convention rights. However, our courts and tribunals are not bound to follow the Strasbourg judgments and other decisions[2].

1   Whether or not delivered in cases concerning the United Kingdom: see the Lord Chancellor, Lord Irvine, during the report stage in the House of Lords, 584 HL Official Report (5th series) col 1271 (19 January 1998).
2   The Lord Chancellor, Lord Irvine of Lairg, explained at the committee stage of the Bill in the House of Lords, 583 HL Official Report (5th series) cols 514–515 (18 November 1997) that s 2(1) does not make the Strasbourg judgments 'binding'. So United Kingdom courts may 'depart from existing Strasbourg decisions and upon occasion it might well be appropriate to do so, and it is possible they might give a successful lead to Strasbourg'. However, 'where it is relevant, we would of course expect our courts to apply Convention jurisprudence and its principles to the cases before them'. The Lord Chancellor added during the report stage in the House of Lords, 584 HL Official Report (5th series) cols 1270–1271 (19 January 1998) that 'the interpretation of the Convention rights develops over the years. Circumstances may therefore arise in which a judgment given by the European Court of Human Rights decades ago contains pronouncements which it would not be appropriate to apply to the letter in the circumstances of today in a particular set of circumstances affecting this country'. It is not only the age of the Strasbourg determination which will affect its persuasive force: judgments of the E Ct HR carry greater weight than decisions of the Commission, especially admissibility decisions; and a judgment based on the doctrine of the margin of appreciation may provide limited assistance to a national court (see paras **3.20–3.27**). During the House of Commons committee stage, the Parliamentary Secretary to the Lord Chancellor's Department, Mr Geoffrey Hoon MP, explained that the phrase 'must take into account' did not mean that the domestic courts were obliged to follow Strasbourg jurisprudence. He therefore resisted an amendment which would have substituted 'may take into account'. The amendment was withdrawn: see 313 HC Official Report (6th series) cols 388, 402 and 413 (3 June 1998). As well as taking into account the judgments of the E Ct HR, domestic courts should also have regard to judgments made by other national courts on the provisions of the Convention, and on analogous instruments. But because domestic courts are not bound even by the judgments of the E Ct HR, this is not a context in which one can apply the observations of Lord Browne-Wilkinson for the House of Lords in *Re H (Minors) (Abduction: Acquiescence)* [1998] AC 72 at 87: 'An international Convention [there the Hague Convention on the Civil Aspects of International Child Abduction], expressed in different languages and intended to apply to a wide range of differing legal systems, cannot be construed differently in different jurisdictions. The Convention must have the same meaning and effect under the laws of all contracting states.' Cf *Iyadurai v Secretary of State for the Home Department* [1998] Imm AR 470 where the Court of Appeal said that the observations in *Re H* did not apply to the Geneva Convention on Refugees. Lord Woolf MR concluded (at 481) that the Secretary of State may return an asylum-seeker to a third country even though it does not adopt the same interpretation of the Convention as the United

Kingdom, so long as the third country's interpretation is not 'outside the range of responses of a contracting state acting in good faith to implement its obligations under the Convention'.

2.2.3 Rules may provide for how evidence of the Strasbourg judgments, decisions, declarations and opinions is to be given in relevant proceedings[1].

1 HRA 1998, s 2(2). HRA 1998, s 2(3) adds that 'rules' means rules of court or, in the case of proceedings before a tribunal, rules made for the purposes of this section by appropriate Ministers. HRA 1998, s 20(2) states that the power to make rules (other than rules of court) under s 2(3) is exercisable by statutory instrument.

SECTION 3

2.3 The HRA 1998, s 3 deals with the relationship between the Convention rights[1] and United Kingdom legislation. It requires primary and subordinate legislation to be interpreted and applied consistently with Convention rights, so far as possible.

1 'Convention rights' are defined in HRA 1998, s 1(1): see para **2.1.1**.

2.3.1 So far as it is possible to do so, primary legislation and subordinate legislation[1] must be read and given effect in a way which is compatible with the Convention rights[2]. All courts and tribunals are required to interpret and apply legislation in this way where it is relevant to any case before them (whether or not a public authority is a party to the proceedings[3]). Indeed, the obligation imposed by s 3 applies to all concerned in interpreting a legislative provision, including the executive and administrators.

1 'Primary legislation' and 'subordinate legislation' are defined in HRA 1998, s 21(1).
2 HRA 1998, s 3(1). On the interpretative obligation imposed by s 3(1), see also paras **3.18–3.19** and Lord Lester of Herne Hill QC 'The Art of the Possible: Interpreting Statutes under the Human Rights Act' [1998] Human Rights Law Review 665.
3 See para **2.6.3**, n 3 on the obligations imposed by the Convention in relation to proceedings between private parties.

2.3.2 The crucial words in relation to this interpretative obligation are 'possible' and 'must'. As the White Paper explained:

'This goes far beyond the present rule which enables the courts to take the Convention into account in resolving any ambiguity in a legislative provision. The courts will be required to interpret legislation so as to uphold the Convention rights unless the legislation itself is so clearly incompatible with the Convention that it is impossible to do so.'[1].

So courts and tribunals must strive for compatibility between legislation and Convention rights, so far as possible, if necessary reading down (that is limiting in scope and effect) provisions which would otherwise breach Convention rights, and reading in necessary safeguards to protect such rights. In this context, the role of the court is not (as in traditional statutory interpretation) to find the true meaning of the provision, but to find (if possible) the meaning which best accords with Convention rights[2].

1 *Rights Brought Home* (Cm 3782, 1997), para 2.7. See also the speech by the Lord Chancellor, Lord Irvine of Lairg, on the second reading of the Bill in the House of Lords, 582 HL Official Report (5th series) cols 1230–1231 (3 November 1997): s 3 'will ensure that, if it is possible to interpret a statute in two ways—one compatible with the Convention and one not—the courts will always choose the interpretation which is compatible. In practice, this will prove a strong form of incorporation ... [H]owever, the [Act] does not allow the courts to set aside or ignore Acts of Parliament. [Section] 3 preserves the effect of primary legislation which is incompatible with the Convention. It does the same for secondary legislation where it is

inevitably incompatible because of the terms of the parent statute'. During the committee stage in the House of Lords, 583 HL Official Report (5th series) col 535 (18 November 1997) the Lord Chancellor said: 'We want the courts to strive to find an interpretation of legislation which is consistent with Convention rights so far as the language of the legislation allows, and only in the last resort to conclude that the legislation is simply incompatible with them.' On the third reading in the House of Lords, the Lord Chancellor added that 'in 99% of the cases that will arise, there will be no need for judicial declarations of incompatibility' (under HRA 1998, s 4: see para **2.4**): 585 HL Official Report (5th series) col 840 (5 February 1998). See similarly the Home Secretary, Jack Straw MP, during the second reading debate in the House of Commons, 306 HC Official Report (6th series) col 780 (16 February 1998): 'We expect that, in almost all cases, the courts will be able to interpret legislation compatibly with the Convention.' During the committee stage in the House of Commons, when refusing to accept proposed amendments to replace 'possible' with 'reasonable' or with the phrase 'where ambiguous', the Home Secretary said (see 313 HC Official Report (6th series) cols 415 and 421–422 (3 June 1998):

> 'we want the courts to strive to find an interpretation of legislation that is consistent with Convention rights, so far as the plain words of the legislation allow, and only in the last resort to conclude that the legislation is simply incompatible with them. The Opposition want the courts to arrive somewhat earlier at the conclusion that the legislation is simply incompatible with the Convention. I cannot see what would be gained by that, bearing in mind our responsibilities under the Convention, apart from the prospect of more cases ending up in Strasbourg because fewer people would be satisfied with the interpretation of the United Kingdom courts.'

Mr Straw also stated (at col 422): 'for the avoidance of doubt, I will say that it is not our intention that the courts, in applying [section] 3, should contort the meaning of words to produce implausible or incredible meanings'. But he added (at col 423) that the clause 'moves us on from the way in which the courts currently interpret Convention legislation'. The proposed amendments were withdrawn: col 426.

2   Lord Steyn has pointed out that 'Traditionally the search has been for the one true meaning of a statute. Now the search will be for a possible meaning that would prevent the need for a declaration of incompatibility [see para **2.4**]. The questions will be: (1) What meanings are the words capable of yielding? (2) And, critically, can the words be made to yield a sense consistent with Convention rights? In practical effect there will be a rebuttable presumption in favour of an interpretation consistent with Convention rights. Given the inherent ambiguity of language the presumption is likely to be a strong one': 'Incorporation and Devolution—A Few Reflections on the Changing Scene' [1998] European Human Rights Law Review 153 at 155. See also Lord Cooke of Thorndon during the second reading debate in the House of Lords, 582 HL Official Report (5th series) col 1272 (3 November 1997): s 3(1) 'will require a very different approach to interpretation from that to which the United Kingdom courts are accustomed. Traditionally, the search has been for the true meaning; now it will be for a possible meaning that would prevent the making of a declaration of incompatibility' (on which see s 4 and para **2.4**).

2.3.3   Although it is expected that it will normally be possible for legislation to be construed consistently with Convention rights[1], there may, in extreme circumstances, come a point where the legislation is plainly incompatible with Convention rights, and so the latter must give way to the former. In such circumstances, the court or tribunal has no power to strike down or ignore such legislation, whether enacted before or after the coming into force of the HRA 1998[2].

1   See para **2.3.2**.
2   HRA 1998, s 3(2). During the committee stage in the House of Commons, the Home Secretary, Mr Jack Straw MP, said that 'no group of senior judges looking at the clause will come to any other view but that the intention of Parliament is that there may be legislation that is incompatible with the Convention—either in future or previously—and, that even if it is found to be incompatible, it will remain in force unless and until the House, by accelerated or normal procedure, decides otherwise' see 313 HC Offical Report (6th series) col 421 (3 June 1998).

2.3.4   The interpretative obligation imposed by the HRA 1998, s 3 applies to primary and subordinate legislation 'whenever enacted'[1], that is both to existing legislation and to future legislation[2].

1   HRA 1998, s 3(2)(a).
2   Because of the fundamental nature of the rights protected by the HRA 1998, the international
    obligations of the United Kingdom, and the requirement imposed by HRA 1998, s 3(1) (see paras
    2.3.1 and **2.3.2**) to interpret legislation in a manner compatible with the Convention 'so far
    as it is possible to do so', the courts will be very reluctant to conclude that *future* legislation
    is inconsistent with Convention rights without an unequivocal statement of legislative intent
    to depart from Convention rights. Such an unequivocal statement will plainly not exist where
    there is a Ministerial statement of compatibility pursuant to s 19(1)(a) (see para **2.19**).

2.3.5   If primary legislation cannot be interpreted consistently with Convention
rights, this does not affect the validity, continuing operation or enforcement of that
legislation[1].

1   HRA 1998, s 3(2)(b). The Lord Chancellor, Lord Irvine of Lairg, explained during the
    committee stage of the Bill in the House of Lords, 583 HL Official Report (5th series) col 522
    (18 November 1997) that 'this scheme is consistent with the sovereignty of Parliament as
    traditionally understood ... [I]f statutes are held incompatible on Convention grounds, then it
    is for Parliament to remedy that' after a declaration of incompatibility under s 4 (see para **2.4**)
    by use of the procedure in s 10 (see para **2.10**). See similarly the statement made by the Home
    Secretary, Jack Straw MP, during the second reading debate in the House of Commons, 306 HC
    Official Report (6th series) col 772 (16 February 1998): 'The sovereignty of Parliament must
    be paramount. By that, I mean that Parliament must be competent to make any law on any
    matter of its choosing ... To allow the courts to set aside Acts of Parliament would confer on
    the judiciary a power that it does not possess, and which could draw it into serious conflict with
    Parliament ... [T]he courts and the senior judiciary do not want such a power, and we believe
    that the people do not wish the judiciary to have it.'

2.3.6   Similarly, the HRA 1998 does not affect the validity, continuing operation or
enforcement of any subordinate legislation which is incompatible with Convention
rights if (disregarding the possibility of revocation) primary legislation prevents
removal of the incompatibility[1]. However, if subordinate legislation is incompatible
with Convention rights, and the incompatibility is not required by primary legislation,
then the HRA 1998 will affect the validity, continuing operation or enforcement of that
subordinate legislation[2].

1   HRA 1998, s 3(2)(c). During the committee stage debates in the House of Commons, the
    Parliamentary Secretary at the Lord Chancellor's Department, Mr Geoffrey Hoon MP,
    explained the theory of s 3(2)(c) (see 313 HC Official Report (6th series) col 433 (3 June 1998)):

    'it is perfectly reasonable to require that subordinate legislation be consistent both with
    the terms of its parent statute and with the Human Rights Act. That is what the Bill provides.
    It is inherent in the public authority provisions in [section] 6 that Ministers will be acting
    unlawfully if they make subordinate legislation that is incompatible with a Convention
    right, unless the parent statute requires the subordinate legislation to take that form ... If
    it is the will of Parliament that something should be done that is incompatible with a
    Convention right, Parliament must be prepared to say so in primary legislation ... The
    nature of the primary legislation under which an order is made may be such that any
    subordinate legislation will necessarily be in conflict with Convention rights. If the courts
    were to have the power to strike down such subordinate legislation, it would, at least
    indirectly, amount to a challenge to the primary legislation itself. That would place the
    courts at odds with Parliament.'

2   Either the court would interpret the subordinate legislation compatibly with Convention rights
    under s 3(1), or the court would set aside the subordinate legislation under s 6(1), on which see
    paras **2.6.1** and **2.6.2**. It will be rare for the courts to have to declare subordinate legislation
    to be incompatible with Convention rights. Indeed, in relation to *future* subordinate legislation
    the Minister will, by reason of his duty under HRA 1998, s 6(1) (see para **2.6**), be acting ultra
    vires by introducing subordinate legislation incompatible with Convention rights unless primary
    legislation unequivocally so requires.

2.3.7   The continuing validity and enforcement of incompatible legislation (primary or subordinate) applies whether or not that incompatible legislation has been the subject of a formal declaration of incompatibility.[1]

1   See HRA 1998, s 4(6): para **2.4.5**.

SECTION 4

2.4   The HRA 1998, s 4 provides a judicial mechanism for bringing to the attention of Government and Parliament any provision of primary legislation which cannot be read and given effect in a manner compatible with Convention rights[1], and any provision of subordinate legislation where such an incompatibility cannot be removed because of the terms of the relevant primary legislation. Section 4 sets out the circumstances in which courts may make a 'declaration of incompatibility'; it specifies which courts have such power; and it makes provision for the effect of such a declaration on the legislation in respect of which it is given. The HRA 1998, s 4 is 'central to the careful compromise' adopted by the Act 'between parliamentary sovereignty and the need to give proper effect to the European Convention'[2].

1   'Convention rights' are defined in s 1(1): see para **2.1.1**.
2   Mr Geoffrey Hoon MP, Parliamentary Secretary at the Lord Chancellor's Department, House of Commons committee stage, 313 HC Official Report (6th series) col 458 (3 June 1998).

2.4.1   Specified courts[1] have power to make declarations of incompatibility when determining that a provision of primary legislation, or a provision of subordinate legislation[2] (made in the exercise of a power conferred by primary legislation), is incompatible with a Convention right[3].

1   See para **2.4.4**.
2   'Primary legislation' and 'subordinate legislation' are defined in HRA 1998, s 21(1).
3   HRA 1998, s 4(1) and (3). On the limited circumstances in which subordinate legislation will be incompatible with Convention rights, see para **2.3.6**. The Lord Chancellor, Lord Irvine of Lairg, explained during the House of Lords committee stage, that there is no power to make a declaration of incompatibility 'in cases where the problem is an absence of legislation, because there is nothing to stop the courts providing a remedy in those cases' (see 583 HL Official Report (5th series) col 815 (24 November 1997)).

2.4.2   Where the court is satisfied that a provision of primary legislation is incompatible with a Convention right, then the court may make a declaration to that effect.[1] This is a discretionary power[2], but one which the court would almost inevitably exercise[3].

1   HRA 1998, s 4(2).
2   During the committee stage in the House of Lords, the Lord Chancellor, Lord Irvine of Lairg, explained that the reason why s 4 'only confers a discretion is in part that in our domestic law a declaration is generally a discretionary remedy' (see 583 HL Official Report (5th series) col 546 (18 November 1997)). See Zamir and Woolf *The Declaratory Judgment* (2nd edn, 1993), p 106. The Lord Chancellor added: 'I certainly would expect courts generally to make declarations of incompatibility when they find an Act to be incompatible with the Convention. However, we do not wish to deny them a discretion not to do so because of the particular circumstances of any case.'.
3   During the committee stage in the House of Lords, the Lord Chancellor, Lord Irvine of Lairg, gave examples of cases where it might possibly be appropriate not to make a declaration of incompatibility: '[T]here might be an alternative statutory appeal route which the court might think it preferable to follow, or there might be any other procedure which the court in its discretion thought the applicant should exhaust before seeking a declaration which would then put Parliament under pressure to follow a remedial route' (see 583 HL Official Report (5th series)

col 546 (18 November 1997)). But unless the declaration of incompatibility is made, the expedited Parliamentary procedure under s 10 (see para **2.10**) for amendment to the relevant legislation would not apply, and so the effective domestic remedy intended by Parliament for a breach of Convention rights would not be available. Moreover, it is difficult to see any good reason for the court not normally to make a declaration of incompatibility where an incompatibility exists (on the finding of the court) since such a declaration merely empowers (rather than obliges) the Government and Parliament to remedy the incompatibility found by the court. Parliament would not be 'under pressure' to take remedial action: it would have the opportunity to do so if it thought fit.

2.4.3   Where a court is satisfied that a provision of subordinate legislation (made in the exercise of a power conferred by primary legislation) is incompatible with a Convention right, and that (disregarding any possibility of revocation) the primary legislation under which it is made prevents removal of that incompatibility[1], then the court may make a declaration to that effect[2].

1   See para **2.3.6**.
2   HRA 1998, s 4(4). Again, this is a discretionary power: see para **2.4.2** n 3.

2.4.4   Only specified, higher courts may make a declaration of incompatibility: the House of Lords; the Judicial Committee of the Privy Council; the Courts-Martial Appeal Court; in Scotland, the High Court of Justiciary sitting otherwise than as a trial court, or the Court of Session; and in England and Wales or Northern Ireland, the High Court or the Court of Appeal[1]. The power is so confined because of the constitutional importance of such a declaration, and also because the government did 'not believe that [criminal] trials should be upset, or potentially upset, by declarations of incompatibility'[2].

1   HRA 1998, s 4(5).
2   The Lord Chancellor, Lord Irvine of Lairg, during the committee stage in the House of Lords, 583 HL Official Report (5th series) col 551 (18 November 1997).

2.4.5   A declaration of incompatibility does not affect the validity, continuing operation or enforcement of the provision in respect of which it is given[1]. Nor is it binding on the parties to the proceedings in which it is made[2]. So the relevant legislative provision will continue to have force and effect, notwithstanding its incompatibility with Convention rights, until such time as it may be amended[3].

1   HRA 1998, s 4(6)(a). Geoffrey Hoon MP, Parliamentary Secretary at the Lord Chancellor's Department, explained during the House of Commons committee stage that 'this is because we think that any decision to change primary legislation should be reserved for the consideration of Parliament' (see 313 HC Official Report (6th series) col 460 (3 June 1998)). The Lord Chancellor, Lord Irvine of Lairg, explained on the second reading of the Bill in the House of Lords that: 'A declaration of incompatibility will not itself change the law. The statute will continue to apply despite its incompatibility. But the declaration is very likely to prompt the Government and Parliament to respond' (see 582 HL Official Report (5th series) col 1231 (3 November 1997)). See also the comments of the Home Secretary, Mr Jack Straw MP, during the committee stage of the Bill in the House of Commons at 313 HC Official Report (6th series) cols 419–420 (3 June 1998). See similarly para **2.3.5** on HRA 1998, s 3(2)(b). If Parliament does not respond to a declaration of incompatibility by amending domestic law, then the complainant would be able to pursue the matter by making an application to the E Ct HR in Strasbourg. See the comments of the Home Secretary, Mr Jack Straw MP, during the report stage in the House of Commons, 317 HC Official Report (6th series) cols 1299–1307 (21 October 1998). If the E Ct HR finds a violation of the Convention, then Parliament would be obliged (as a matter of international law) to amend domestic law, unless the United Kingdom were to derogate from the Convention under art 15 and s 14 (see para **2.14**). See also para **2.10**, n 3. That a declaration of incompatibility does not affect the validity of legislation poses

particular difficulties if someone is being detained contrary to Convention rights. The domestic court will have no power to order release, whether by habeas corpus or otherwise. The unfortunate victim will have to wait for parliament, or the government, to secure release and then rely on art 13 (see para **4.13**) in Strasbourg to complain about the lack of an effective remedy. Note also that the court is not given power to adjourn an application while the government and Parliament give consideration to amending relevant legislation.

2   HRA 1998, s 4(6)(b). This enables the government to continue to argue, for example in Parliament or in Strasbourg, that the legislative provision is not incompatible with Convention rights.

3   HRA 1998, s 10 provides for remedial action to amend the relevant provision: see para **2.10**. If a declaration of incompatibility is made by a court, an applicant should recover the costs of the legal proceedings. The applicant will have secured the only remedy allowed by domestic law for the breach of his Convention rights, and will have triggered the application of the fast-track procedure for possible amendment of domestic law under s 10. If the applicant does not receive a satisfactory ex gratia remedy from the government, and successfully pursues the matter to the E Ct HR in Strasbourg, the government would be required there to pay the costs of the domestic proceedings.

SECTION 5

2.5   The HRA 1998, s 5 gives the Crown the right to intervene in any proceedings where the court is considering making a declaration of incompatibility under the provisions of s 4[1]. This is because of the constitutional importance of such a declaration, because the government answers for the United Kingdom in proceedings in Strasbourg, and because the government has the responsibility for considering whether to propose to Parliament the amendment of any legislation in respect of which such a declaration is made[2].

1   See para **2.4**.
2   At common law, 'the Attorney-General has a right of intervention in a private suit whenever it may affect the prerogatives of the Crown, including its relations with foreign states ...; and he certainly has in such circumstances a locus standi at the invitation of the court ... I think that the Attorney-General also has the right of intervention at the invitation or with the permission of the court where the suit raises any question of public policy on which the executive may have a view which it may desire to bring to the notice of the court': *Adams v Adams* [1971] P 188 at 197H–198B, per Sir Jocelyn Simon P.

2.5.1   Where a court is considering whether to make a declaration of incompatibility, the Crown is entitled to notice in accordance with rules of court[1]. The Crown may already be a party to the proceedings, in which case it may agree to waive the requirement for such notice. But there may be occasions where the Crown is not a party to the proceedings[2], or where the Crown is involved but its representative (for example the Crown Prosecution Service) may not be the appropriate person to present relevant arguments in relation to possible declarations of incompatibility.

1   HRA 1998, s 5(1).
2   HRA 1998, s 4 does not limit the power to make a declaration to cases involving the Crown.

2.5.2   Where a court is considering whether to make a declaration of incompatibility, a Minister of the Crown[1], or a person nominated by him[2], or a member of the Scottish Executive, or a Northern Ireland Minister (or Department), is entitled, on giving notice in accordance with rules of court, to be joined as a party to the proceedings[3]. Such notice may be given at any time during the proceedings[4].

1   Defined by s 21(1) to have the same meaning as in the Ministers of the Crown Act 1975. The Ministers of the Crown Act 1975, s 8(1) defines 'Minister of the Crown' to mean 'the holder

of an office in her Majesty's Government in the United Kingdom, and includes the Treasury, the Board of Trade and the Defence Council'.

2   For example, the Director General of Fair Trading: see the comments of the Lord Chancellor, Lord Irvine of Lairg, during the committee stage in the House of Lords at 583 HL Official Report (5th series) col 555 (18 November 1997).

3   HRA 1998, s 5(2).

4   HRA 1998, s 5(3).

2.5.3   While there is a right for the Crown to be notified, the government has no duty to intervene, although it would be surprising were it not to do so by an appropriate representative at some stage of the proceedings where the court is seriously considering making a declaration of incompatibility.

2.5.4   A person who has been made a party to criminal proceedings[1] (other than in Scotland[2]) as a result of a notice under s 5(2) for the purpose of an application for a declaration of incompatibility may (with leave[3]) appeal to the House of Lords against any declaration of incompatibility made in those proceedings[4]. Only criminal proceedings are mentioned because in civil proceedings any person joined as a party is able to exercise the rights of appeal open to any other party. The special right of appeal created by this provision is confined to issues relating to the declaration of incompatibility; it confers no right of appeal on other grounds. The right of appeal created by this provision does not affect the existing rights of appeal of the defendant and the prosecutor.

1   HRA 1998, s 5(5) defines 'criminal proceedings' to include all proceedings before the Courts-Martial Appeal Court.

2   This provision does not apply to Scotland because there is no right of appeal to the House of Lords in relation to criminal matters in Scotland.

3   'Leave' is defined by s 5(5) to mean leave granted by the court making the declaration of incompatibility or by the House of Lords. Only specified courts may make a declaration of incompatibility: see para **2.4.4**.

4   HRA 1998, s 5(4).

SECTION 6

2.6   The HRA 1998, s 6 imposes a duty on public authorities to act in a manner compatible with Convention rights[1], save in specified circumstances (designed to preserve Parliamentary sovereignty). It also makes provision for identifying a 'public authority' for the purposes of the Act[2].

1   'Convention rights' are defined in s 1(1): see para **2.1.1**.

2   The Home Secretary, Mr Jack Straw MP, told the House of Commons during the committee stage that 'the matter is extremely complicated' and the Cabinet Committee 'devoted a great deal of time and energy to this issue' (314 HC Official Report (6th series) cols 408–409 (17 June 1998). He explained (at cols 409–410), that the effect of s 6 'is to create three categories, the first of which contains organisations which might be termed "obvious" public authorities, all of whose functions are public. The clearest examples are government departments, local authorities and the police ... The second category contains organisations with a mix of public and private functions ... The effect of [s 6(5)] [on which see para **2.6.4**] is that those organisations, unlike the "obvious" public authorities, will not be liable in respect of their private acts. The third category is organisations with no public functions—accordingly, they fall outside the scope of [section] 6'. During the House of Lords committee stage, the Lord Chancellor, Lord Irvine of Lairg, explained that s 6 applies to two types of body: 'in the first place to bodies which are quite plainly public authorities such as government departments; and, secondly, to other bodies whose functions include functions of a public nature, and therefore the focus should be on their functions and not on their nature as an authority. In the latter case

the provisions of the [Act] would not apply to the private acts of the bodies in question' (583 HL Official Report (5th series) col 797 (24 November 1997)) (see para **2.6.4**). See also the speech by the Lord Chancellor on the second reading of the Bill in the House of Lords: 'We decided, first of all, that a provision of this kind should apply only to public authorities, however defined, and not to private individuals. That reflects the arrangements for taking cases to the Convention institutions in Strasbourg. The Convention has its origins in a desire to protect people from the misuse of power by the state, rather than from the actions of private individuals. Someone who takes a case to Strasbourg is proceeding against the United Kingdom government, rather than against a private individual. We also decided that we should apply the Bill to a wide rather than a narrow range of public authorities, so as to provide as much protection as possible to those who claim that their rights have been infringed' (see 582 HL Official Report (5th series) cols 1231–1232 (3 November 1997)).

2.6.1   It is unlawful for a public authority to act in a way which is incompatible with a Convention right[1].

1   HRA 1998, s 6(1). 'An act' is defined by s 6(6) to include a failure to act, but it does not include a failure to introduce in, or lay before, Parliament a proposal for legislation, or a failure to make any primary legislation or remedial order. This is because the Act preserves Parliamentary sovereignty, and the prerogatives of the Executive concerning the introduction of legislation. For the consequences of an unlawful act contrary to s 6(1), see ss 7–9, discussed at paras **2.7–2.9**.

2.6.2   An exception[1] is that it is not unlawful for a public authority to act in a way which is incompatible with a Convention right if:

(a)   as the result of one or more provisions of primary legislation, the authority could not have acted differently[2]; or

(b)   in the case of one or more provisions of, or made under, primary legislation which cannot be read or given effect in a way which is compatible with the Convention rights, the authority was acting so as to give effect to or enforce those provisions[3].

This exception will not apply if it possible to construe the relevant primary legislation[4] consistently with Convention rights, but the public authority has exercised a discretion in a manner incompatible with a Convention right.

1   HRA 1998, s 6(2). This subsection is designed to preserve Parliamentary sovereignty.
2   HRA 1998, s 6(2)(a). This covers a case where the public authority is required by primary legislation to take the action in question, even though it conflicts with Convention rights.
3   HRA 1998, s 6(2)(b). This covers the case where primary legislation confers a choice on the public authority, but the choice is restricted to options each of which would involve a breach of Convention rights.
4   By reason of HRA 1998, s 3(1): see para **2.3.1**.

2.6.3   The HRA 1998, s 6(3) states that 'public authority'[1] includes[2]:

(a)   a court[3] or tribunal[4]; and

(b)   any person certain of whose functions[5] are functions of a public nature[6],

but does not include[7] either House of Parliament[8] or a person exercising functions in connection with proceedings in Parliament[9].

1   HRA 1998, s 6 is 'designed to invite the civil courts of the United Kingdom, as far as possible, to treat as a "public authority" those bodies which the Strasbourg institutions would treat as bodies whose acts engage the responsibility of the state' (per Lord Hardie, the Lord Advocate, third reading of the Bill in the House of Lords, 585 HL Official Report (5th series) col 794 (5 February 1998)). See similarly the observations of the Home Secretary, Jack Straw MP, during the committee stage in the House of Commons, 314 HC Official Report (6th series) cols 406, 432–433 (17 June 1998): 'The principle of bringing rights home suggested that liability

in domestic proceedings should lie with bodies in respect of whose actions the United Kingdom Government were answerable in Strasbourg ... [W]e could not directly replicate in the Bill the definition of public authorities used by Strasbourg because, of course, the respondent to any application in the Strasbourg court is the United Kingdom, as the state. We have therefore tried to do the best we can in terms of replication by taking into account whether a body is sufficiently public to engage the responsibility of the state.' See also the comments of the Home Secretary during the second reading debate in the House of Commons at 306 HC Offical Report (6th series) col 775 (16 February 1998). On the responsibility of the state, including a responsibility for the determination of actions between private persons, see n 3 below.

2   The Act does not define 'public authority'. The Lord Chancellor, Lord Irvine of Lairg, stated that 'We think that it is far better to have a principle rather than a list which would be regarded as exhaustive' (583 HL Official Report (5th series) col 796 (24 November 1997)). He commented (at col 808) that the principle is deliberately broad 'because we want to provide as much protection as possible for the rights of individuals against the misuse of power by the state ...'. The White Paper *Rights Brought Home* (Cm 3782, 1997), para 2.2, stated that the concept of a 'public authority' is intended to be broad. It includes 'central government (including executive agencies); local government; the police; immigration officers; prisons; courts and tribunals themselves; and, to the extent that they are exercising public functions, companies responsible for areas of activity which were previously within the public sector, such as the privatised utilities'. See also the speech by the Parliamentary Under-Secretary of State, Home Office, Lord Williams of Mostyn, on the second reading of the Bill in the House of Lords: 'we would anticipate the BBC being a public authority and that Channel 4 might well be a public authority, but that other commercial organisations, such as private television stations, might well not be public authorities. I stress that that is a matter for the courts to decide as the jurisprudence develops ... [A] newspaper is not a public authority' (see 583 HL Official Report (5th series) cols 1309–1310 (3 November 1997)). See similarly the Home Secretary, Jack Straw MP, during the second reading debate in the House of Commons, 306 HC Official Report (6th series) col 778 (16 February 1998). During the committee stage, on 20 May 1998, the Home Secretary, Mr Jack Straw MP, stated that the Jockey Club carries out public functions and so would fall within s 6 in relation to those functions (see 312 HC Official Report (6th series) col 1018). See n 6 below at (3) on the Jockey Club and judicial review. In an analogous context, the December 1997 White Paper *Your Right to Know: The Government's Proposals for a Freedom of Information Act* (Cm. 3818, 1997) listed 'public authorities' which will have a duty to provide access to records and information relating to 'public functions', and stated that legislation 'will contain a list, showing which public authorities and other organisations are covered, so that there will be no ambiguity about which bodies are included and which are not' (paras **2.2** and **2.4**). The government has yet to place a Bill before Parliament. See also the Northern Ireland Act 1998, s 75(3) which defines 'public authority' by reference to departments, corporations or bodies listed in Schedule 2 to the Parliamentary Commissioner Act 1967 (and similar legislation) and 'any other person designated for the purposes of this section by order made by the Secretary of State'.

3   Therefore, the courts 'have the duty of acting compatibly with the Convention not only in cases involving other public authorities but also in developing the common law in deciding cases between individuals' (per the Lord Chancellor, Lord Irvine of Lairg, House of Lords Committee Stage, 583 HL Official Report (5th series) col 783 (24 November 1997)). Because the courts are public authorities, they have a duty to ensure that Convention rights are protected even in litigation between private parties. The obligation of the court under s 6 will apply where the Convention has effect on the legal relationship between private parties because the state (acting through its courts) is obliged, under the Convention, to protect individuals against breaches of their rights. See, for example, *Costello-Roberts v United Kingdom* (1993) 19 EHRR 112 at 132, E Ct HR, paras 26–27 (concerning corporal punishment of children) where the ECt HR emphasised that it:

'has consistently held that the responsibility of a state is engaged if a violation of one of the rights and freedoms defined in the Convention is the result of non-observance by that state of its obligation under article 1 to secure those rights and freedoms in its domestic law to everyone within its jurisdiction. ... [T]he state cannot absolve itself from responsibility by delegating its obligations to private bodies or individuals.'

See, similarly, *A v United Kingdom* [1998] 3 FCR 597, [1998] 5 BHRC 137, 141–142, E Ct HR, para 22 (also on corporal punishment of children) and *Young, James and Webster v United Kingdom* (1981) 4 EHRR 38, 52, E Ct HR, para 49 (legislation which breached the Convention by allowing a closed shop in employment). In relation to the right to private and family life (on which see para **4.8**), the E Ct HR explained in *X and Y v Netherlands* (1985) 8 EHRR 235 at 239–240, E Ct HR, para 23, that:

'although the object of article 8 is essentially that of protecting the individual against arbitrary interference by the public authorities, it does not merely compel the state to abstain from such interference: in addition to this primarily negative undertaking, there may be positive obligations inherent in an effective respect for private or family life. These obligations may involve the adoption of measures designed to secure respect for private life even in the sphere of the relations of individuals between themselves.'

Another example of the impact on the Convention on private law rights is in relation to damages for libel: see *Tolstoy v United Kingdom* (1995) 20 EHRR 442, E Ct HR. Therefore, the HRA 1998 will have an indirect but powerful influence upon private law rights and obligations in tort, contract and other contexts in which the Convention imposes minimum standards which the United Kingdom must guarantee. The Parliamentary Under-Secretary of State for the Home Department, Mr Mike O'Brien MP, correctly stated during the committee stage in the House of Commons that 'newspapers will not be public authorities and could not be proceeded against directly under the [Act], but an article 8 point could be raised in proceedings for harassment or a libel action, for example' (see 315 HC Official Report (6th series) col 561 (2 July 1998)). On the application of the Act to the press, see s 12: para **2.12**. Similar issues have been addressed in other jurisdictions. See Cory J for the Supreme Court of Canada in *Vriend v Alberta* [1998] 4 BHRC 140 at 159 (para 66) concerning the application of the Canadian Charter of Rights: 'The respondents' submission has failed to distinguish between "private activity" and "laws that regulate private activity". The former is not subject to the Charter, while the latter obviously is.' The Canadian Supreme Court has recognised that where the common law is concerned, the Charter of Rights may also have a strong indirect effect. In *Hill v Church of Scientology of Toronto* [1995] 2 SCR 1130 at 1170–1171, Cory J said (on behalf of the Can SC): 'Private parties owe each other no constitutional duties and cannot found their cause of action upon a Charter right. The party challenging the common law cannot allege that the common law violates a Charter *right* because, quite simply, Charter rights do not exist in the absence of state action. The most that the private litigant can do is argue that the common law is inconsistent with Charter *values* ... Therefore in the context of civil litigation, involving only private parties, the Charter will "apply" to the common law only to the extent that the common law is found to be inconsistent with Charter values.' A similar approach was adopted in South Africa by the Constitutional Court in relation to the Interim Constitution. In *Du Plessis v De Klerk* [1996] 5 BCLR 658, Kentridge AJ (for the court) explained (in particular at 684– 685 and 691–692) that constitutional rights may be invoked against an organ of government but not by one private litigant against another. He emphasised (at 682H–683H) that the relevant article of the Interim Constitution applied to the legislature and the executive, but not to the judiciary (by contrast with the Human Rights Act 1998, s 6(1)). Nevertheless, Kentridge AJ concluded that in private litigation, any litigant may contend that a statute or executive act relied on by the other party is invalid as being inconsistent with the limitations placed on the legislature and executive; and, approving the principle stated by the Canadian Supreme Court in *Hill* (see above), he held that the court should have regard to the values contained in the constitution when developing the common law. Prior to the coming into force of the HRA 1998, English courts were already having regard to the Convention when considering the content of the common law: see para **2.03**. For a different approach, see *Tam Hing-yee v Wu Tai-wai* [1992] 1 HKLR 185, where the Hong Kong Court of Appeal held that the Bill of Rights Ordinance 1991 had no application to disputes between private individuals. That was because s 7 states that the Ordinance 'binds only (a) the Government and all public authorities; and (b) any person acting on behalf of the Government or a public authority'. Therefore, the Court of Appeal concluded (at 189), 'private individuals should not be adversely affected by the Ordinance'. Note, however, *Hong Kong Polytechnic University v Next Magazine Publishing Ltd* [1996] 2 HKLR 260 at 264, where Mr Justice Keith, in the Hong Kong High Court, concluded that 'the Government' for the purpose of s 7 of the Ordinance means 'the legislative, executive and judicial organs of the state'. (He held that the University was a 'public authority' given the nature of its functions and the use of public funds, even though it was not subject to government control.) On the impact of the HRA 1998 on litigation between private parties, see Murray Hunt 'The "Horizontal Effect" of the Human Rights Act' (1998) PL 423.

4   HRA 1998, s 6(3)(a). 'Tribunal' means any tribunal in which legal proceedings may be brought, see s 21(1). On the application of s 6(3)(a) to religious courts and tribunals, Lord Hardie, the Lord Advocate, explained during the third reading of the Bill in the House of Lords, that the government did not regard courts of the Church of Scotland as within the scope of the sub-section because they 'do not, as a matter either of their constitution or practice, carry out any judicial functions on behalf of the state. Nor do they adjudicate upon a citizen's legal rights or obligations, either common law or statutory. They operate in relation to matters which are essentially of a private nature. Unlike the courts of the Church of England—this is one of the differences—they do not have the right to compel the attendance of witnesses or the production

of documents' (see 585 HL Official Report (5th series) col 794 (5 February 1998)). See, similarly, the comments of the Secretary of State for Scotland, Mr Donald Dewar MP, during the committee stage in the House of Commons, 312 HC Official Report (6th series) cols 1064–1067 (20 May 1998). Other religious courts or tribunals would not be within the scope of s 6(3)(a) for the same reason. It is well established that they are not public bodies for the purposes of judicial review: see *R v Chief Rabbi of the United Hebrew Congregations of Great Britain and the Commonwealth, ex p Wachmann* [1992] 1 WLR 1036 (per Simon Brown J), approved by Hoffmann LJ in *R v Disciplinary Committee of the Jockey Club, ex p Aga Khan* [1993] 1 WLR 909, 932H, CA (Parliament regards religion as 'something to be encouraged but not the business of government'); *Ali v Imam of Bury Park Jame Masjid, Luton* (12 May 1993, unreported), CA, and *R v London Beth Din (Court of the Chief Rabbi), ex p Michael Bloom* (18 November 1997, unreported), per Lightman J. On the application of the HRA 1998 to religious bodies, see also s 13, discussed at para **2.13**, n 2.

5   It is therefore not necessary for all of the person's functions to be 'of a public nature' before that person is a public authority. But note the exception in s 6(5) where the nature of the particular act is private: see para **2.6.4**.

6   HRA 1998, s 6(3)(b). Assistance in applying the concept of 'functions of a public nature' may be obtained from five main sources:

(1) The principle stated by the E Ct HR in *Costello-Roberts v United Kingdom* (1993) 19 EHRR 112 at 132, E Ct HR, paras 26–27: see n 3 above.

(2) In EC law, a Directive only has direct effect against the state. In *Foster v British Gas plc* [1991] 1 QB 405 at 427G–H, the ECJ stated that this covers 'a body, whatever its legal form, which has been made responsible, pursuant to a measure adopted by the state, for providing a public service under the control of the state and has for that purpose special powers beyond those which result from the normal rules applicable in relations between individuals ...'.

(3) The Home Secretary, Mr Jack Straw MP, observed during the committee stage in the House of Commons, 17 June 1998, that '[t]he most valuable asset that we had to hand was jurisprudence relating to judicial review' (see 314 HC Official Report (6th series) col 409). A body is performing public functions for the purpose of the law of judicial review of administrative action 'when it seeks to achieve some collective benefit for the public or a section of the public and is accepted by the public or that section of the public as having authority to do so' see de Smith, Woolf and Jowell *Judicial Review of Administrative Action* (5th edn, 1995), p 167 at para 3-024. See generally their analysis at pp 167–191, paras 3-024 to 3-066. The essential criteria for liability to judicial review are 'a public element, which can take many different forms, and the exclusion from the jurisdiction of bodies whose sole source of power is a consensual submission to its jurisdiction': *R v Panel on Take-Overs and Mergers, ex p Datafin plc* [1987] QB 815 at 838E–F (per Sir John Donaldson MR for the CA). The body must be exercising powers which are 'governmental' in nature: see *R v Disciplinary Committee of the Jockey Club, ex p Aga Khan* [1993] 1 WLR 909 at 923G–924C (per Sir Thomas Bingham MR), at 929H–930E (per Farquharson LJ), and at 932E–F, 932H–933A, 933E–F (per Hoffmann LJ) (but see n 2 above on the *Jockey Club* and the concept of a 'public authority'). In *R v Press Complaints Commission, ex p Stewart-Brady* (1996) 9 Admin LR 274, the CA proceeded on the assumption that the PCC is a public body. The Home Secretary, Mr Jack Straw MP, stated during the Committee Stage in the House of Commons that the government considered that the PCC 'undertakes public functions but the press does not ...' (see 314 HC Official Report (6th series) col 414 (17 June 1998)). On the application of the HRA 1998 to the press, see s 12 and para **2.12**.

(4) Under the Public Authorities Protection Act 1893 (now repealed), special limitation periods applied to actions against a 'public authority'. In *Griffiths v Smith* [1941] AC 170 at 205–206, Lord Porter said, approving the observations of Sir Gorell Barnes P in *The Johannesburg* [1907] P 65 at 78–79, that a body is a 'public authority' if it performs statutory duties and exercises public functions, and is not 'carrying out transactions for private profit ... Profit they may undoubtedly make for the public benefit ... but they must not be a trading corporation making profits for their corporators ...'. (See similarly Viscount Simon LC at 178–179, and Viscount Maugham at 186.) That principle is similar to the conclusion stated by Mr Justice Patteson in *R v Woods and Forests Comrs, ex p Budge* (1850) 15 QB (Adolphus & Ellis) 761 at 774 (rejecting an application for mandamus to compel the Commissioners to proceed after they had given notice that they intended to take lands for the purpose of forming Battersea Park): 'a private company to whom an Act is granted for their profit differs materially from commissioners appointed under a public Act to do on behalf of the executive government certain things for the benefit of the public'.

(5) The Prevention of Corruption Act 1916, s 2 creates a presumption, in proceedings for an offence under the Prevention of Corruption Act 1906, that any money, gift or other

consideration paid or given to, or received by, a person in the employment of 'a public body' was paid or given and received corruptly unless the contrary is proved. In *DPP v Manners* [1978] AC 43, the HL approved the reasoning and conclusion of the CA (at 49G–50D) that the North Thames Gas Board was 'a public body' in this context because it had public or statutory duties to perform, and performed those duties and carried out its transactions for the benefit of the public and not for private profit.

7   This is to preserve Parliamentary sovereignty which would be infringed were the actions of Parliament to be subject to challenge in the courts.

8   HRA 1998, s 6(4) explains that 'Parliament' does not include the House of Lords in its judicial capacity. In that capacity, the HL is a public authority, and so has a duty to act in a way which is compatible with Convention rights.

9   HRA 1998, s 6(3). Judicial review does not apply to a person exercising functions in connection with proceedings in Parliament, see *R v Parliamentary Comr for Standards, ex p Al Fayed* [1998] 1 WLR 669, CA. So s 6 would not apply in relation to a Parliamentary Committee considering whether to impose disciplinary sanctions. However, the United Kingdom would be liable in proceedings before the E Ct HR were such a Committee to act in breach of Convention rights (see *Demicoli v Malta* (1991) 14 EHRR 47, E Ct HR). See para **4.21.6**.

2.6.4   In relation to a particular act, a person is not a public authority by virtue only of being a person certain of whose functions are functions of a public nature[1] if the nature of the act is private[2].

1   So this provision does not apply to persons who are, in any event, public authorities. Such obvious public authorities, such as central government, owe the duty imposed by s 6(1) in relation to all their functions. See para **2.6**, n 2 for an analysis of the different categories of body. See also para **2.6.3**, n 2 for Ministerial comments on the identity of public bodies in this context. This provision applies to bodies who are on the borderline of being public authorities in that some of their functions are public in nature: for example, privatised utilities, which have a mixture of public and private functions. In relation to such bodies, each act must be considered separately, and whether s 6(1) applies will depend upon the nature of the act in question. Examples of such borderline bodies were given by the Lord Chancellor, Lord Irvine of Lairg, during the committee stage in the House of Lords: 'Railtrack would fall into that category because it exercises public functions in its role as a safety regulator, but it is acting privately in its role as a property developer. A private security company would be exercising public functions in relation to the management of a contracted-out prison but would be acting privately when, for example, guarding commercial premises. Doctors in general practice would be public authorities in relation to their National Health Service functions, but not in relation to their private patients' (see 583 HL Official Report (5th series) col 811 (24 November 1997)). See similarly Lord Williams of Mostyn (Parliamentary Under-Secretary of State, Home Office), House of Lords committee stage, 583 HL Official Report (5th series) col 758 (24 November 1997); and the Home Secretary, Mr Jack Straw MP, during the committee stage in the House of Commons, 314 HC Official Report (6th series) cols 409–410 and 433 (17 June 1998), where he pointed out that it was necessary, for example, to 'provide a level playing field between BT and other, wholly private, operators ... As we are dealing with public functions and with an evolving situation, we believe that the test must relate to the substance and nature of the act, not to the form and legal personality'.

2   HRA 1998, s 6(5). It is well established in public law that there are some acts of public bodies which are not subject to judicial review. See, for example, the employment disputes in *R v BBC, ex p Lavelle* [1983] ICR 99 at 107H (per Woolf J) and *R v Derbyshire County Council, ex p Noble* [1990] ICR 808, CA where Woolf LJ concluded (at 820G) that the case did not have 'the public law element which is required to make it an appropriate subject of an application for judicial review'. Similarly, contractual functions of public bodies may be private, and not public, for the purposes of judicial review: see de Smith, Woolf and Jowell *Judicial Review of Administrative Action* (5th edn, 1995), pp 177–179 at paras 3-040 to 3-043. See also *Mass Energy Ltd v Birmingham City Council* [1994] Env LR 298, CA.

SECTION 7

2.7   The purpose of the HRA 1998, s 7 is to identify how a person may pursue a claim before the appropriate domestic court or tribunal[1] against a public authority alleged to be in breach of s 6 in relation to Convention rights[2].

1   During the second reading debate in the House of Commons, the Home Secretary, Mr Jack Straw
    MP, explained that s 7 'enables individuals who believe that they have been a victim of an
    unlawful act of a public authority to rely on the Convention rights in legal proceedings. They
    may do so in a number of ways : by bringing proceedings under the [Act] in an appropriate court
    or tribunal; in seeking judicial review; as part of a defence against a criminal or civil action
    brought against them by a public authority; or in the course of an appeal. [Section] 7 ensures
    that an individual will always have a means by which to raise his or her Convention rights. It
    is intended that existing court procedures will, wherever possible, be used for that purpose' (see
    306 HC Official Report (6th series) col 780 (16 February 1998)).
2   'Convention rights' are defined in HRA 1998, s 1(1): see para **2.1.1**.

2.7.1   A person who claims that a public authority[1] has acted (or proposes to act) in
a manner made unlawful by the HRA 1998, s 6(1)[2] may[3]:

(a)   bring proceedings against the public authority under the Act in the appropriate
      court or tribunal[4]; or

(b)   rely on the relevant Convention right(s) in any legal proceedings[5],

but only if he is (or would be), a victim of that unlawful act[6].

1   For the meaning of 'public authority', see HRA 1998, s 6(3) at para **2.6.3**.
2   See para **2.6**.
3   HRA 1998, s 7(1).
4   HRA 1998, s 7(2) defines 'appropriate court or tribunal' to mean 'such court or tribunal as may
    be determined in accordance with rules'. It adds that 'proceedings against an authority' includes
    a counterclaim or similar proceedings. HRA 1998, s 7(9) defines the meaning of 'rules' for the
    purposes of s 7. The power to make rules (other than rules of court) under s 7(9) is exercisable
    by statutory instrument, see s 20(2). HRA 1998, s 7(10) states that in making rules, regard must
    be had to s 9, on which see para **2.9**. HRA 1998, s 7(11) states that the Minister who has power
    to make rules in relation to a particular tribunal may, to the extent he considers it necessary
    to ensure that the tribunal can provide an appropriate remedy in relation to an act (or a proposed
    act) of a public authority which is (or would be) unlawful as a result of s 6(1), by order add to
    the relief or remedies which the tribunal may grant, or the grounds on which it may grant any
    of them. This power is needed because although it is the intention of the Act that tribunals should
    consider and apply Convention rights insofar as they are relevant to the subject-matter of the
    cases before them (see ss 3(1), 6(3)(a) and 7(1)(b)), there may be tribunals (special adjudicators
    hearing cases under the Asylum and Immigration Appeals Act 1993 are the only example
    identified by the government) which have a limited jurisdiction which would otherwise prevent
    them from considering Convention rights. The use of the order-making power is intended to
    be a short-term solution until a suitable opportunity arises to amend the primary legislation
    in question. See the explanation by Lord Williams of Mostyn, the Under-Secretary of State,
    Home Office, during the report stage in the House of Lords on 19 January 1998 (584 HL Official
    Report (5th series) cols 1360–1362) and the explanation during the committee stage in the
    House of Commons by the Parliamentary Under-Secretary of State for the Home Department,
    Mr Mike O'Brien MP on 24 June 1998 (314 HC Official Report (6th series) cols 1109–1111).
    Under s 20(1), a power to make an order is exercisable by statutory instrument. Under s 20(4),
    no order may be made under s 7(11) unless a draft has been laid before, and approved by, each
    House of Parliament. The use of the draft affirmative resolution procedure reflects the
    importance of the subject matter with which the relevant provisions are concerned. HRA 1998,
    s 7(12) adds that an order made under s 7(11) may contain such incidental, supplemental,
    consequential or transitional provision as the Minister (which includes the Northern Ireland
    Department concerned, see s 7(13)) making it considers appropriate. The Supreme Court of
    Canada has held that the Canadian Charter of Rights and Freedoms implicitly confers power
    on statutory tribunals (charged with the duty to uphold the 'law') to hear and determine
    challenges based on the Charter: *Cuddy Chicks Ltd v Ontario Labour Relations Board* [1991]
    2 SCR 5 and *Tétreault-Gadoury v Canada Employment and Immigration Commission* [1991]
    2 SCR 22.
5   HRA 1998, s 7(6) defines 'legal proceedings' to include proceedings brought by or at the instigation
    of a public authority, and an appeal against the decision of a court or tribunal. The latter part
    of the definition is intended to ensure that Convention points can be raised for the first time
    on an appeal against a decision of a court or tribunal which is said itself to be incompatible with
    Convention rights. During the committee stage of the Bill in the House of Commons, the

Parliamentary Under-Secretary of State for the Home Department, Mr Mike O'Brien MP, said that criminal proceedings were covered, either because they are brought by a public authority or because (in the case of a private prosecution) s 7(6) is not an exhaustive definition (see 314 HC Official Report (6th series) col 1057 (24 June 1998)). HRA 1998, s 22(4) states that s 7(1)(b) applies to proceedings brought by or at the instigation of a public authority whenever the act in question took place, but otherwise that sub-section does not apply to an act committed before the coming into force of that section. This means that it will be possible for an individual to rely on Convention arguments after commencement in any civil or criminal action brought by a public authority, irrespective of when the events took place. Otherwise, however, acts of public authorities committed before s 7 came into force will not be capable of challenge. For commencement, see the HRA 1998, s 22, para **2.22**.

6   In *Motsepe v IRC* (1997) (6) BCLR 692 at 705, para 30, Ackermann J for the Constitutional Court of South Africa made some observations about claims for costs against applicants who have failed in constitutional claims: 'one should be cautious in awarding costs against litigants who seek to enforce their constitutional rights against the state, particularly where the constitutionality of a statutory provision is attacked, lest such orders have an unduly inhibiting or "chilling" effect on other potential litigants in this category. This cautious approach cannot, however, be allowed to develop into an inflexible rule so that litigants are induced into believing that they are free to challenge the constitutionality of statutory provisions in this court, no matter how spurious the grounds for doing so may be or how remote the possibility that this court will grant them access. This can neither be in the interests of the administration of justice nor fair to those who are forced to oppose such attacks.' If the court applying the HRA 1998 were to apply a less generous approach to the award of costs, this could well amount to a breach of art 6 and the right to a fair hearing (see para **4.6**) because it may impede access to justice.

2.7.2   For the purposes of the HRA 1998, s 7, a person is a victim of an unlawful act only if he would be a victim for the purposes of art 34[1] of the Convention if proceedings were brought in the E Ct HR in respect of that act[2]. Under the Convention jurisprudence[3], the following principles have been established:

(1)   The court must 'confine itself, as far as possible, to an examination of the concrete case before it. It is accordingly not called upon to review the system of the [domestic law] *in abstracto*, but to determine whether the manner in which this system was applied to or affected the applicants gave rise to any violations of the Convention'[4]. So there is no '*actio popularis*' permitting individuals 'to complain against a law *in abstracto* simply because they feel that it contravenes the Convention'[5].

(2)   However, the procedural provisions are part of a Convention designed 'to protect the individual', and so they must 'be applied in a manner which serves to make the system of individual applications efficacious'[6].

(3)   To establish that they are 'victims', individual complainants do not need to show that their rights have been violated by 'an individual measure of implementation'. It suffices that they 'run the risk of being directly affected by' the measure of which complaint is made[7].

(4)   An applicant may claim to be an indirect victim, for example when he or she is a close relative (such as a spouse or parent) of the affected person[8].

(5)   A trade union, or other organisation, cannot itself claim to be a victim on the ground that it represents the interests of its members[9]. But a trade union may, however, be the victim of a breach of its own rights under the Convention[10], or it may provide assistance to individual applicants who are complaining about breaches of their rights.

(6)   A company may be the victim of a breach of its rights[11] but shareholders cannot claim to be a victim because of alleged infringements of the rights of a company (other than in exceptional circumstances, for example where it is impossible for the company itself to make complaint)[12]. A 'governmental organisation', such as a local authority, cannot claim to be a victim[13].

(7)   A person does not cease to be a victim because the impugned measure has caused no prejudice, except possibly where 'the national authorities have acknowledged either expressly or in substance, and then accorded redress for, the breach of the Convention'[14].

(8)   A person may not claim to be a victim where he has not previously asserted the right on which he now relies[15].

(9)   An applicant who is faced with an imminent act (such as deportation) which might expose him or her to a breach of the Convention can claim to be a victim[16], but not until there has been a final decision which is not open to further domestic challenge[17].

1   As amended by the eleventh protocol. It was formerly art 25. It provides that an application may only be received from 'any person, non-governmental organisation or group of individuals claiming to be the victim of a violation by one of the High Contracting Parties of the rights set forth in the Convention or the protocols thereto'.

2   HRA 1998, s 7(7).

3   See Harris, O'Boyle and Warbrick *Law of the European Convention on Human Rights* (1995), pp 630–638.

4   *Hakansson and Sturesson v Sweden* (1990) 13 EHRR 1 at 11–12, E Ct HR, para 46. See similarly *Young, James and Webster v United Kingdom* (1981) 4 EHRR 38 at 53–54, E Ct HR, para 53, and *Buckley v United Kingdom* (1996) 23 EHRR 101 at 125–126, E Ct HR, para 59. See also *Salabiaku v France* (1988) 13 EHRR 379 at 390, E Ct HR, para 30.

5   *Klass v Federal Republic of Germany* (1978) 2 EHRR 214 at 227, E Ct HR, para 33. See also *Norris v Ireland* (1988) 13 EHRR 186 at 195, E Ct HR, para 30, and *Leigh, Guardian Newspapers Ltd and The Observer Ltd v United Kingdom* 38 DR 74 (1984) at 78 (admissibility decision of the European Commission of Human Rights).

6   *Klass v Federal Republic of Germany* (1978) 2 EHRR 214 at 227–228, E Ct HR, para 34.

7   See, for example, *Marckx v Belgium* (1979) 2 EHRR 330 at 340, E Ct HR, para 27. In *Norris v Ireland* (1988) 13 EHRR 186 at 195–196, E Ct HR, paras 32–34, a man complaining about the Irish criminal law prohibiting homosexual relations between consenting male adults was held to be a 'victim' even though he had not been prosecuted and even though (as the E Ct HR accepted at 196, para 33) 'the risk of prosecution in the applicant's case was minimal' because the policy was, and had been for some time, not to enforce the prohibition. The applicant, as an active homosexual, was held to 'run the risk of being directly affected by the legislation in question' because a change of policy was possible at any time, and the existence of the legal prohibition reinforced popular prejudice and increased the anxiety of homosexuals. The decision on whether the applicant was a 'victim' was reached by eight votes to six. In *Open Door Counselling and Dublin Well Woman v Ireland* (1992) 15 EHRR 244 at 258, E Ct HR, para 44, the E Ct HR accepted that all women of child-bearing age were victims of an injunction granted by the domestic court concerning the provision of information about abortion facilities abroad. See also *Campbell and Cosans v United Kingdom* (1980) 3 EHRR 531 at 547, EComHR, para 116 (attendance at a school at which corporal punishment was practised was sufficient to entitle a child to complain that such punishment breached the Convention even though that child had not personally been subjected to such punishment). But cf Application 22170/93: *V, W, X, Y and Z v United Kingdom* (EComHR, admissibility decision, 18 January 1995) dismissing a complaint by various Applicants that the decision by the House of Lords in *R v Brown* [1994] 1 AC 212 upholding criminal convictions against sadomasochists had a direct effect on their own private lives, even though they had not been prosecuted or threatened with prosecution.

8   For example, in *McCann v United Kingdom* (1995) 21 EHRR 97, E Ct HR. See also *Campbell and Cosans v United Kingdom* (1980) 3 EHRR 531 at 545, EComHR, para 112. See the discussion in Harris, O'Boyle and Warbrick *Law of the European Convention on Human Rights* (1995), p 637.

9   Application 15404/89: *Purcell v Ireland* 70 DR 262 (1991) at 272–273 (admissibility decision of the European Commission of Human Rights).

10   See, for example, Application 11603/85: *Council of Civil Services Unions v United Kingdom* 50 DR 228 (1987), EComHR.

11   And not just in relation to rights of property under art 1 of protocol 1, on which see para **4.19**. A company may, for example, be the victim of a breach of its rights to freedom of expression under art 10: see Application 6538/74: *Times Newspapers Ltd v United Kingdom* 2 DR 90 (1975) at 95, EComHR, and *Observer Ltd and Guardian Newspapers Ltd v United Kingdom* (1991) 14 EHRR 153, E Ct HR. But there are some rights which, by their nature, cannot be enjoyed

by a company. For example, the right to private life, which is, at root, a right to *personal* privacy: see William L Prosser 'Privacy' (1960) 48 CalifLR 383 at 408–409.

12   *Agrotexim v Greece* (1995) 21 EHRR 250 at 284, E Ct HR, para 66.

13   This is because it is not 'any person, non-governmental organisation or group of individuals' (see n 1 above). See the admissibility decisions of the Commission in *Rothenthurm Commune v Switzerland* 59 DR 251 (1988) and *Ayuntamiento de M v Spain* 68 DR 209 (1991).

14   *Eckle v Federal Republic of Germany* (1982) 5 EHRR 1 at 24, E Ct HR, para 66, and *Ludi v Switzerland* (1992) 15 EHRR 173 at 197, E Ct HR, para 34. The existence, or absence, of prejudice is relevant to the award of a remedy under art 50: see para **2.8.4**.

15   Application 13562/88: *Guenoun v France* 66 DR 181 (1990) (admissibility decision of the European Commission of Human Rights: the applicant claimed to be the victim of a breach of the right to a public hearing before a medical disciplinary tribunal, but he had not previously asserted such a claim).

16   *Soering v United Kingdom* (1989) 11 EHRR 439 at 489 (para 106 of the Report of the European Commission of Human Rights).

17   *Vijayanathan and Pusparajah v France* (1992) 15 EHRR 62 at 75–76, E Ct HR, paras 43–46.

2.7.3   Because (in other contexts) an applicant may be able to bring proceedings for judicial review even though not a victim of the unlawful act[1], it is provided that where proceedings against the public authority alleging a breach of a Convention right are brought by way of judicial review, the applicant must show that he is, or would be, a victim of the unlawful act[2]. A sufficient interest (for example, that of a representative body or a pressure group) does not suffice[3].

1   A sufficient interest suffices to establish standing for judicial review: see de Smith, Woolf and Jowell *Judicial Review of Administrative Action* (5th edn, 1995), paras 2-019–2-050.

2   HRA 1998, s 7(3) and (4).

3   During the committee stage of the Bill in the House of Commons, the Parliamentary Under-Secretary of State for the Home Department, Mr Mike O'Brien MP, said that a 'victim' test was adopted because '[t]he purpose of the [Act] is to give effect in our domestic law to the Convention rights. It is in keeping with that approach that people should be able to rely on those rights before our courts in the same circumstances as they can rely on them before the Strasbourg institutions' (see 314 HC Official Report (6th series) col 1083 (24 June 1998)). Mr O'Brien added (at col 1086) that 'our aim is to grant access to victims. It is not to create opportunities to allow interest groups ... to venture into frolics of their own in the courts. The aim is to confer access to rights, not to licence interest groups to clog up the courts with test cases ...'. It is understandable that the 'victim' test should be applied under the Act where Convention rights are relevant to private law proceedings where a plaintiff needs to have a direct personal interest. But the test is unsuitable for public law proceedings raising issues of general importance where reliance on Convention rights may form only part of the case being presented by an applicant who is not a victim but has a sufficient interest to bring judicial review proceedings on other grounds. Unless flexibly applied, the 'victim' test will have the unfortunate consequence that an applicant will be able to raise some grounds of challenge, but not others, and the court will be prevented from considering whether Convention rights are being denied. The dangers were explained by Lord Lester of Herne Hill, QC during the committee stage of the Bill in the House of Lords on 24 November 1997 (see 583 HL Official Reports (5th series) cols 823–837), and by Lord Slynn of Hadley and Lord Lester of Herne Hill, QC during the third reading debate in the House of Lords on 5 February 1998 (see 585 HL Official Report (5th series) cols 805 –812, where the House of Lords rejected a proposed amendment to substitute a 'sufficient interest' test for raising Convention issues in judicial review proceedings. In a letter to the Lord Chancellor, dated 17 February 1998, Lord Woolf MR expressed his concern, and that of other members of the judiciary, about the adoption of a 'victim' test.

2.7.4   Nothing in the HRA 1998 creates a criminal offence[1].

1   HRA 1998, s 7(8). Some acts which are incompatible with the Convention may constitute criminal offences under existing law. The HRA 1998 does not affect this. During the committee stage in the House of Commons, the Parliamentary Under-Secretary of State for the Home Department, Mr Mike O'Brien MP, gave examples: 'ill-treatment that is contrary to article 3 of

the Convention on the prohibition of torture may amount to an offence under the Offences Against the Person Act 1861. In such circumstances, criminal proceedings could be brought, but they would be for an alleged breach of the 1861 Act, not for an alleged failure to comply with article 3' (see 314 HC Official Report (6th series) col 1107 (24 June 1998)). In relation to the impact of a breach of the Convention on criminal proceedings, Mr O'Brien observed (at col 1107) that it would depend on the circumstances, but if 'a fair trial is impossible, an acquittal would be the appropriate outcome'. He added (at col 1108) that the Convention 'would be used in the same way as the rules in the Police and Criminal Evidence Act 1984 and as any of the other provisions of natural justice'.

2.7.5 Proceedings brought against a public authority under the HRA 1998[1] must be brought[2] before the end of the period of one year beginning with the date on which the act complained of took place, or such longer period as the court or tribunal considers equitable[3] having regard to all the circumstances. However, this is subject to any rule imposing a stricter time limit in relation to the procedure in question[4].

1   That is, proceedings under s 7(1)(a), see para **2.7.1**. For proceedings under s 7(1)(b) (that is relying on Convention rights in other legal proceedings: see para **2.7.1**), the limitation provision will be that imposed in relation to such other proceedings. See also para **2.22.3** on proceedings under s 7(1)(b).
2   HRA 1998, s 7(5). This limitation provision is concerned only with proceedings brought on Convention grounds. It does not concern proceedings under an existing cause of action (which will have its own limitation periods), with Convention rights being relied on for supplementary purposes, for example in relation to the interpretation of legislation (see s 3(1) and para **2.3**). During the committee stage in the House of Commons, the Parliamentary Under-Secretary of State for the Home Department, Mr Mike O'Brien MP, explained that the 12 month limitation period was being introduced because '[w]e want to ensure that public authorities are made subject to the legislation, but we want to do that in a fair and balanced way, remembering that public authorities are often acting in the interests of the taxpayer and the citizen ...' (see 314 HC Official Report (6th series) col 1095 (24 June 1998)).
3   See the similar discretion enjoyed by an employment tribunal under the Sex Discrimination Act 1975, s 76(5) and the Race Relations Act 1976, s 68(6). On the width of the power to extend time under the 1975 Act, see *Mills and Crown Prosecution Service v Marshall* [1998] IRLR 494, EAT. The discretion to extend time under the HRA 1998 is likely to receive a similarly generous construction.
4   For example, in relation to judicial review, where the time-limit is normally three months, unless this is extended by the court. See the Rules of the Supreme Court 1965 (as amended), Ord 53, r 4(1), and the Supreme Court Act 1981, s 31(6).

SECTION 8

2.8   The purpose of the HRA 1998, s 8 is to enable a court or tribunal[1] to grant appropriate remedies when it finds that a public authority has acted (or proposes to act) in a way which is incompatible with Convention rights[2] and has therefore acted unlawfully.

1   HRA 1998, s 8(6) provides that in s 8, 'court' includes a tribunal.
2   'Convention rights' are defined in s 1(1), see para **2.1.1**.

2.8.1   Where a court or tribunal finds that any act (or proposed act) of a public authority is (or would be) unlawful[1], it may grant such relief or remedy, or make such order, within its powers, as it considers just and appropriate[2].

1   HRA 1998, s 8(6) defines 'unlawful' to mean 'unlawful under HRA 1998, s 6(1)', that is unlawful because the act is incompatible with a Convention right. HRA 1998, s 8 is not concerned with remedies for acts which are unlawful for other reasons. See also para **2.8.5**. On s 6(1), see para **2.6.1**.
2   HRA 1998, s 8(1). So the HRA 1998 does not create new types of remedy not previously within the powers of the court or tribunal.

2.8.2   Damages[1] may be awarded only by a court or tribunal which has power to award damages, or to order the payment of compensation, in civil proceedings[2]. This means that a criminal court will not be able to award damages or compensation for a breach of Convention rights[3]. Nor are tribunals which otherwise lack the power to award compensation given any such power under the HRA 1998.

1   'Damages' are defined by s 8(6) to mean 'damages for an unlawful act of a public authority'. HRA 1998, s 8(5) provides that where damages are awarded against a public authority, the principles of contribution apply in relation to persons who are jointly and severally liable. See the Civil Liability (Contribution) Act 1978.
2   HRA 1998, s 8(2).
3   As the Lord Chancellor, Lord Irvine of Lairg, explained in the House of Lords during the committee stage of the Bill on 24 November 1997, 'it is not the Bill's aim that, for example, the Crown Court should be able to make an award of damages where it finds, during the course of a trial, that a violation of a person's Convention rights has occurred. We believe that it is appropriate for an individual who considers that his rights have been infringed in such a case to pursue any matter of damages through the civil courts where this type of issue is normally dealt with ...' (see 583 HL Official Report (5th series) col 855). More difficult is a case where the Criminal Division of the Court of Appeal, allows an appeal against conviction because of a breach of Convention rights. That court probably then does have power to award damages under s 8(2) because the Court of Appeal, generally, does have 'power to award damages ... in civil proceedings'.

2.8.3   No award of damages is to be made[1] unless, taking account of all the circumstances of the case, including any other relief or remedy granted, or order made, in relation to the act in question (by that or by any other court or tribunal), and also taking into account the consequences of any decision in respect of that act, the court or tribunal is satisfied that the award is necessary to afford just satisfaction to the person in whose favour it is made[2].

1   HRA 1998, s 8(3).
2   So a court will ask itself whether other remedies (for example, certiorari and a declaration) suffice. A court asked to award damages for a breach of Convention rights will take account of an existing cause of action for damages (for example, for wrongful arrest). The award of damages is therefore a discretionary matter, not an entitlement. This is different from the normal position for private law torts. There may be cases where a court takes the view that damages are a more appropriate remedy than certiorari or other relief, for example, where the court thinks it inappropriate to annul an administrative scheme because of the adverse consequences for the rights of third parties (eg under settled transactions) but where the grievance of the individual claimant can be remedied by compensation.

2.8.4   When deciding whether to award damages, or the amount of an award, the court or tribunal must take into account[1] the 'principles' applied by the E Ct HR in relation to the award of compensation under art 41 of the Convention[2]. Those 'principles' in truth amount to little more than equitable assessments of the facts of the individual case[3]. They are as follows[4].

(1)   There is no right to compensation[5]. Compensation is awarded only if 'necessary' to 'afford just satisfaction' to the injured party. The E Ct HR adopts an equitable assessment and decides whether compensation is appropriate in the circumstances[6].

(2)   In relation to pecuniary loss, the E Ct HR sometimes states that it 'cannot speculate' as to whether the adverse consequences of which complaint is made would have occurred but for the breach of the Convention, or that it 'does not find it established that there existed a causal link between the matter found to constitute a violation and any loss or damage', and so it awards no compensation under this head[7]. But the court is prepared to award compensation for pecuniary loss when satisfied that it is necessary to do so[8].

(3)   Similarly, in relation to non-pecuniary loss, the E Ct HR sometimes states that it 'cannot speculate' as to whether the adverse consequences of which complaint is made would have occurred but for the breach of the Convention, or that, in any event, 'in the circumstances, the finding of a violation constitutes sufficient just satisfaction'[9]. On other occasions, the court is persuaded to award 'a just and equitable amount of compensation' for distress, disruption, lost opportunities of being released from detention, and other types of damage[10].

(4)   The E Ct HR has awarded interest on compensation where this is necessary to avoid unfair diminution in its value[11], but it has not awarded exemplary damages[12].

1   HRA 1998, s 8(4). The court or tribunal is obliged only to take into account the European principles. It is not obliged to apply those principles (but see the speech by the Lord Chancellor, Lord Irvine of Lairg, on the second reading of the Bill in the House of Lords on 3 November 1997: 'Our aim is that people should receive damages equivalent to what they would have obtained had they taken their case to Strasbourg' (582 HL Official Report (5th series) col 1232).

2   Formerly art 50, prior to amendment by the eleventh protocol. Article 41 states: 'If the court finds that there has been a violation of the Convention or the protocols thereto, and if the internal law of the High Contracting Party concerned allows only partial reparation to be made, the court shall, if necessary, afford just satisfaction to the injured party.'

3   The case-law of the E Ct HR lacks coherence, and advocates and judges are in danger of spending time attempting to identify principles that do not exist.

4   See Harris, O'Boyle and Warbrick *Law of the European Convention on Human Rights* (1995), pp 682–688.

5   In *Fose v Minister of Safety and Security* (1997) 2 BHRC 434, the Constitutional Court of South Africa held that 'appropriate relief' in s 7(4)(a) of the interim Constitution could include damages where this was necessary to protect and enforce constitutional rights. The court analysed the jurisprudence in various jurisdictions relating to damages for breaches of constitutional rights. See similarly the judgments of the New Zealand Court of Appeal in *Simpson v A-G* [1994] 3 NZLR 667 that damages could be claimed for a breach of the New Zealand Bill of Rights even though the Bill made no specific reference to remedies. Hardie Boys J, at 698–703, discussed the relevant international case-law.

6   See, for example, *McCann v United Kingdom* (1995) 21 EHRR 97 at 177–178, E Ct HR, para 219: the E Ct HR found a breach of art 2 of the Convention (the right to life) but 'having regard to the fact that the three terrorist suspects who were killed had been intending to plant a bomb in Gibraltar, the court does not consider it appropriate to make an award' of compensation.

7   See, for example, *Tolstoy v United Kingdom* (1995) 20 EHRR 442 at 479, E Ct HR, para 74; *Saunders v United Kingdom* (1996) 23 EHRR 313 at 342, E Ct HR, para 86; *Findlay v United Kingdom* (1997) 24 EHRR 221 at 247, E Ct HR, paras 84–85.

8   See, for example, *Pine Valley Developments Ltd v Ireland* (1993) 16 EHRR 379, E Ct HR (diminution in value of property) and *Young, James and Webster v United Kingdom* (1982) 5 EHRR 201, E Ct HR (loss of earnings and loss of employment-related benefits).

9   See, for example, *Thynne, Wilson and Gunnell v United Kingdom* (1990) 13 EHRR 666, at 696, E Ct HR, para 85; *Hussain v United Kingdom* (1996) 22 EHRR 1 at 27–28, E Ct HR, paras 65–66; *Goodwin v United Kingdom* (1996) 22 EHRR 123 at 146–147, E Ct HR, para 50; *Benham v United Kingdom* (1996) 22 EHRR 293 at 325, E Ct HR, para 68; *Saunders v United Kingdom* (1996) 23 EHRR 313 at 342, E Ct HR, paragraph 89; *Findlay v United Kingdom* (1997) 24 EHRR 221 at 247, E Ct HR, para 88; *Bowman v United Kingdom* (1998) 26 EHRR 1 at 20, E Ct HR, para 51.

10 See, for example, *Young, James and Webster v United Kingdom* (1982) 5 EHRR 201, E Ct HR; *Gillow v United Kingdom* (1987) 13 EHRR 593, E Ct HR; *Darnell v United Kingdom* (1993) 18 EHRR 205 at 212, E Ct HR, para 24; *McMichael v United Kingdom* (1995) 20 EHRR 205 at 243, E Ct HR, para 103; *Halford v United Kingdom* (1997) 24 EHRR 523 at 550, ECt HR, para 76.

11 See, for example, *Stran Greek Refineries v Greece* (1994) 19 EHRR 293 at 331, ECt HR, paras 82–83.

12 At common law, exemplary damages are available, inter alia, for 'oppressive, arbitrary or unconstitutional action by the servants of the government': *Rookes v Barnard* [1964] AC 1129 at 1226 (per Lord Devlin for the House of Lords). However, such damages are not awarded by the E Ct HR. And in *Fose v Minister of Safety and Security* (1997) 2 BHRC 434 at 466–468,

the Constitutional Court of South Africa held that 'appropriate relief' in s 7(4)(a) of the interim Constitution should not include exemplary damages because they were an anomaly, being the imposition of a penalty in civil law proceedings, which would be paid by taxpayers and provide a windfall to the victim. Exemplary damages are not awarded under art 5(5) of the Convention, see para **4.5.59**. It is very doubtful that the concept of damages under s 8(3) of the Act as 'just satisfaction to the person in whose favour it is made' (see para **2.8.3**) allows for the award of exemplary damages.

2.8.5   Because the HRA 1998, s 8 only concerns the grant of remedies for breaching Convention rights, other remedies available to an individual in relation to an act or omission by a public authority are unaffected by the HRA 1998, s 8[1].

1   See HRA 1998, s 11 at para **2.11**.

SECTION 9

2.9   The purpose of the HRA 1998, s 9 is to allow decisions of courts and tribunals to be challenged only by way of an appeal or a judicial review application or in another prescribed forum, and to prevent claims for damages in respect of judicial acts save where this is required to ensure compliance with the Convention.

2.9.1   Proceedings under the HRA 1998, s 7(1)(a)[1] in respect of a judicial act[2] may be brought only[3] by exercising a right of appeal, or on an application (in Scotland, a petition) for judicial review, or in such other forum as may be prescribed by rules[4]. Save and to the extent that another forum is so prescribed, the Act does not create new methods by which judicial decisions may be challenged.

1   See para **2.7.1**.
2   HRA 1998, s 9(5) defines 'judicial act' to mean 'a judicial act of a court and includes an act done on the instructions, or on behalf, of a judge'. HRA 1998, s 9(5) also defines 'court' to include a tribunal, and defines 'judge' to include a member of a tribunal, a justice of the peace and a clerk or other officer entitled to exercise the jurisdiction of a court.
3   HRA 1998, s 9(1).
4   HRA 1998, s 9(5) defines 'rules' as having the same meaning as is s 7(9), on which see para **2.7.1**, n 4.

2.9.2   The HRA 1998 does not affect any rule of law which prevents a court from being the subject of judicial review[1]. In such cases, the complainant would need to proceed by way of any right of appeal (unless another forum is prescribed by rules).

1   HRA 1998, s 9(2). For example, by reason of the Supreme Court Act 1981, s 29(3), the Crown Court may not be the subject of judicial review in matters relating to trial on indictment. In relation to its other jurisdictions, the Crown Court is subject to judicial review by reason of s 29(3) of the 1981 Act. In general, however, only inferior courts are subject to judicial review: see *Re Racal Communications Ltd* [1981] AC 374, HL.

2.9.3   Damages cannot[1] be awarded in proceedings under the HRA 1998[2] in respect of a judicial act done in good faith, other than damages to compensate a person to the extent required by Article 5(5) of the Convention[3]. Any such award of damages is to be made against the Crown (but no such award may be made unless the appropriate person[4], if not a party to the proceedings, is joined)[5].

1   HRA 1998, s 9(3).
2   Because s 9(3) is concerned only with new rights of action conferred by the HRA 1998, a person's right to bring other proceedings, and to rely on the Convention in those proceedings, is unaffected, see s 11, as discussed in para **2.11**.

3   On art 5.5 of the Convention, see para **4.5.58**.
4   HRA 1998, s 9(5) defines 'appropriate person' to mean the Minister responsible for the court concerned, or a person or government department nominated by him.
5   HRA 1998, s 9(4). As to the personal liability of magistrates, see the Justices of the Peace Act 1997, ss 51–52: s 51 gives immunity to a justice of the peace for acts done in the execution of his duty, provided that they are done within his jurisdiction; s 52 provides that an action may be brought against a justice for an act which is done in the purported execution of his duty but which is beyond his jurisdiction, but only if he has acted in bad faith. The HRA 1998, s 9 does not affect the personal liability of the magistrate. It imposes a liability on the Crown to pay damages for breaches of art 5 of the Convention by courts and tribunals. By reason of s 9(3), awards of damages against the Crown are limited to cases where the judicial act was done in good faith. In respect of acts done in bad faith, proceedings cannot be brought against the Crown. But proceedings for damages can be brought against magistrates acting outside their jurisdiction, and the Crown would be liable for any unlawful detention which followed.

SECTION 10

2.10   The purpose of the HRA 1998, s 10 is to enable provisions of legislation declared[1] to be incompatible with a Convention right[2] to be amended speedily. The Government has no duty to propose such an amendment to Parliament, but it would normally wish to do so following a declaration of incompatibility (and the absence of any further appeal)[3]. The power is also available following adverse findings in United Kingdom cases by the E Ct HR.

1   See HRA 1998, s 4 and para **2.4**.
2   'Convention rights' are defined in s 1(1), see para **2.1.1**.
3   There may be cases where the government does not agree with the findings of the domestic courts and waits for the applicant to take the matter to Strasbourg so that the government can seek to persuade the E Ct HR to find that there has been no breach of the Convention. As explained by the Parliamentary Under-Secretary of State for the Home Department, Mr Mike O'Brien MP, at the report stage in the House of Commons on 21 October 1998 (see 317 HC Official Report (6th series) col 1351) there may be exceptional cases where the government believes that domestic law, or a Bill bring placed before Parliament, breaches the Convention but the government intends, if necessary, to invite Parliament to derogate from the Convention (ie under art 15 and s 14: see para **2.14**). See also para **2.4.5**, n 1.

2.10.1   The power to take remedial action arises[1] in two circumstances:

(a)   where a provision of legislation[2] has been declared under s 4[3] to be incompatible with a Convention right and if there is no further appeal (that is if all persons who may appeal have stated in writing that they do not intend to do so, if the time for bringing an appeal has expired and no appeal has been brought within that time, or if an appeal brought within that time has been determined or abandoned); or

(b)   where it appears to a Minister of the Crown[4] or Her Majesty in Council that, having regard to a finding of the E Ct HR made after the coming into force of this section[5] in proceedings against the United Kingdom[6], a provision of legislation is incompatible with an obligation of the United Kingdom arising from the Convention.

1   HRA 1998, s 10(1).
2   HRA 1998, s 10(6) states that in this Act, 'legislation' does not include a Measure of the Church Assembly or of the General Synod of the Church of England. This is to respect the separate law-making powers vested in the Church of England as a legislative body.
3   See para **2.4**.
4   For the meaning of 'Minister of the Crown' see para **2.5.2**, n 1.
5   The power does not apply in relation to E Ct HR findings which pre-date the coming into force of s 10.

6   The power does not apply in relation to E Ct HR findings in cases against other contracting states, however similar the terms of United Kingdom legislation may be to the legislation found by the court to breach Convention rights. In such case, Parliament would, no doubt, wish to consider amending domestic legislation by normal means.

2.10.2   In such circumstances, if a Minister of the Crown[1] considers that there are compelling reasons for so proceeding[2], he may[3] by order[4] make such amendments to the legislation as he considers necessary to remove the incompatibility[5].

1   HRA 1998, s 10(5) states that if the legislation is an Order in Council, the relevant powers under s 10 are exercised not by a Minister of the Crown, but by Her Majesty in Council.
2   During the committee stage in the House of Commons, the Home Secretary, Mr Jack Straw MP, explained that '[t]he power to make a remedial order exists for cases—we do not think that there will be very many—when there is a very good reason to amend the law following a declaration of incompatibility or a finding by the Strasbourg court, but no suitable legislative vehicle is available' (see 314 HC Official Report (6th series) col 1137 (24 June 1998)). In response to those members of Parliament who were concerned about the power to amend primary legislation by order, he added (at col 1138) that the terms 'compelling' and 'necessary' set 'a very high test'. During the report stage, the Home Secretary successfully resisted an amendment to confine 'compelling reasons' to cases involving threats to national security, public health or the liberty of the individual. He explained that 'compelling reasons' may also apply to 'a decision of the higher courts in relation to basic provisions of criminal procedure affecting the way in which, perhaps, all criminal cases must be handled'. The government 'might need to respond very quickly simply to avoid the criminal justice system in such cases either collapsing or not being able to deliver justice and proper convictions' (see 317 HC Official Report (6th series) col 1330 (21 October 1998)).
3   During the committee stage in the House of Lords (27 November 1997), the Lord Chancellor, Lord Irvine of Lairg, explained that 'we expect that the government and Parliament will in all cases almost certainly be prompted to change the law following a declaration. However we think that it is preferable, in order to underpin Parliamentary sovereignty, to leave this on a discretionary basis. The decision whether to seek a remedial order is a matter for government to decide on a case-by-case basis. It would be wrong for a declaration automatically to lead to a remedial order' (see 583 HL Official Report (5th series) col 1139). But '[i]f a Minister's prior assessment of compatibility [under s 19, see para **2.19**] is subsequently found, by a declaration of incompatibility by the courts, to have been mistaken, it is hard to see how the Minister could withhold remedial action' (the Lord Chancellor, Lord Irvine of Lairg, 'Keynote Address' to the January 1998 Conference at the University of Cambridge Centre for Public Law, *Constitutional Reform in the United Kingdom: Practice and Principles* (1998), p 4). During the committee stage in the House of Commons (24 June 1998), the Home Secretary, Mr Jack Straw MP, explained that the Act did not contain any provision enabling the government to appeal to the E Ct HR against a declaration of incompatibility both because the Convention made no such provision and because it was unnecessary, in that Parliament has no duty to comply with such a declaration (which does not affect the validity of the provision in respect of which it is given: s 4(6), on which see para **2.4.5**) and, if Parliament chose not to do so, the complainant could take the matter to the E Ct HR (314 HC Official Report (6th series) cols 1121–1123).
4   Under HRA 1998, s 20(1), the power to make such an order is exercisable by statutory instrument.
5   HRA 1998, s 10(2).

2.10.3   The Minister has a similar power in relation to incompatible subordinate legislation. If a Minister of the Crown considers that it is necessary to amend the primary legislation under which the subordinate legislation in question was made, in order to enable the incompatibility to be removed, and that there are compelling reasons for exercising the power, then he may by order make such amendments to the primary legislation as he considers necessary[1].

1   HRA 1998, s 10(3). See para **2.4.3** on declarations of incompatibility in relation to subordinate legislation.

2.10.4 HRA 1998, s 10 also applies[1] where the relevant provision is in subordinate legislation, and has been quashed, or declared invalid, by reason of incompatibility with a Convention right[2], and the Minister proposes to proceed under the powers conferred in relation to remedial action in urgent cases[3].

1   HRA 1998, s 10(4).
2   On quashing a provision of subordinate legislation, or declaring it invalid, see para **2.3.6**, n 2.
3   See Sch 2, para 2(b) and para **2.24.3**.

2.10.5   Schedule 2 makes detailed provision as to remedial orders under the HRA 1998, s 10[1].

1   HRA 1998, s 10(7). On Sch 2, see para **2.24**.

SECTION 11

2.11   The purpose of the HRA 1998, s 11 is to safeguard more generous legal rights[1] which may be enjoyed by persons apart from the HRA 1998[2].

1   The purpose of s 11 is similar to that of art 53 of the Convention which provides: 'Nothing in this Convention shall be construed as limiting or derogating from any of the human rights and fundamental freedoms which may be ensured under the laws of any High Contracting Party or under any other agreement to which it is a Party.'
2   During the committee stage in the House of Lords (27 November 1997), the Lord Chancellor, Lord Irvine of Lairg, explained in relation to s 11 that 'it is for the court in question, and for individual judicial decision in any particular case, to decide when the point, based on Convention law, is to be adjudicated upon. It is a matter to decide in its discretion whether the argument that is put before it, based on the Convention, is one upon which it should decide as, for example, a preliminary issue at the outset' (see 583 HL Official Report (5th series) cols 1157–1158).

2.11.1   A person's reliance on a Convention right[1] does not restrict any other right or freedom conferred on him by or under any law having effect in any part of the United Kingdom[2].

1   'Convention rights' are defined in s 1(1): see para **2.1.1**.
2   HRA 1998, s 11(a). This is a saving for existing more generous provisions which a person enjoys. However, where (as is often the case, for example in relation to the potential conflict between freedom of expression under art 10 and the right to private life under art 8) the Convention requires a balance to be struck between competing rights and freedoms, the courts will need to act in conformity with the Convention when interpreting legislation (see s 3) and public authorities will have to do likewise when exercising their powers (see s 6).

2.11.2   A person's reliance on a Convention right does not restrict his right to make any claim or bring any proceedings which he could make or bring apart from the HRA 1998, ss 7 to 9[1].

1   HRA 1998, s 11(b). So the rights conferred by the HRA 1998 to bring cases on Convention grounds, or to rely on Convention grounds in legal proceedings, are additional to existing rights and remedies, not a substitute for them.

SECTION 12

2.12   The purpose of the HRA 1998, s 12 is to ensure that courts pay particular regard to the Convention right to freedom of expression[1].

1   See art 10 of the Convention: para **4.10**. Like s 13 of the HRA 1998, and the duty to pay particular regard to freedom of thought, conscience and religion (on which see para **2.13**, n 2), s 12 serves no sensible purpose. It was introduced by the government during the committee stage in the House of Commons by reason of a campaign led by Lord Wakeham, Chairman of the Press Complaints Commission, and supported by a number of newspapers, for special protection for the media under the Act because of concern that the Act might otherwise impede freedom of expression by protecting privacy. During the second reading debate in the House of Lords, the Lord Chancellor, Lord Irvine of Lairg, stated that 'the Government are not introducing a privacy statute ... They believe that strong and effective self-regulation is the best way forward in the interests of both the press and the public' (582 HL Official Report (5th series) col 1229 (3 November 1997)). During the committee stage in the House of Lords, Lord Wakeham referred to an article in (1997) Times, 18 November, by David Pannick, QC suggesting that the PCC would be a public authority for the purposes of s 6 of the Act (see para **2.6**), and expressed concern about the consequences. The Lord Chancellor said that he had reconsidered the matter in the light of an opinion by David Pannick, QC, and he agreed that the PCC would indeed be a public authority under s 6 (see 583 HL Official Report (5th series) cols 771–774 and 783–787 (24 November 1997)), and a Press Release from the Lord Chancellor's Department dated 1 December 1997)). During the second reading debate in the House of Commons, the Home Secretary, Mr Jack Straw MP, announced that an amendment would be introduced to protect press freedom, consistently with the Convention (306 HC Official Report (6th series) cols 775–777 (16 February 1998)). On introducing the amendment, now s 12, during the committee stage in the House of Commons, Mr Straw stated that the government considered that the PCC 'undertakes public functions but the press does not ...' (see 314 HC Official Report (6th series) col 414 (17 June 1998)). Journalists are right to be concerned about Her Majesty's judiciary taking greater powers to decide, in the interests of protecting privacy, what should be included in tomorrow's *Times* or *Sun*. But their alarm about the application of the Act, and any satisfaction they may have with s 12, are misguided. This is for four main reasons:

(1) Irrespective of the HRA 1998, judges were developing the common law of breach of confidence to protect privacy. See, for example, *Hellewell v Chief Constable of Derbyshire* [1995] 1 WLR 804 at 807H (per Mr Justice Laws). In *Spencer v United Kingdom* (admissibility decision of the Commission, 16 January 1998, Applications 28851/95 and 28852/95), [1998] EHRLR 348, the argument for the United Kingdom government was that the content of domestic law (including remedies for breach of confidence, trespass, nuisance, harassment and malicious falsehood, as well as remedies before the Press Complaints Commission) gave adequate protection to individuals and an appropriate balance between the competing rights guaranteed by art 8 (privacy) and art 10 (freedom of expression) of the Convention. The application was rejected by the Commission because the applicants had not brought proceedings in the domestic courts to try to use the law of breach of confidence to protect their privacy. During the committee stage in the House of Commons, the Parliamentary Under-Secretary of State for the Home Department, Mr Mike O'Brien MP, explained that 'newspapers will not be public authorities and could not be proceeded against directly under the [Act], but an article 8 point could be raised in proceedings for harassment or a libel action, for example' (see 315 HC Official Report (6th series) col 561 (2 July 1998)).

(2) The HRA 1998 will assist press freedom because judges will have a duty to recognise the fundamental right to freedom of expression. Article 8 of the Convention (see para **4.8**) guarantees the right to private life. It recognises that on occasions we all, like Greta Garbo, want to be alone. We are entitled to have our personal thoughts and private actions protected from the telephoto lens and the microphone. But art 8 is not absolute. It allows for intrusions into private life when this is necessary in a democratic society. When the intrusion is by the media, art 10 of the Convention (see para **4.10**) is also relevant, since it guarantees freedom of expression. Again, this is not an absolute right, but one which is subject to those exceptions necessary in a democratic society. However, the E Ct HR has repeatedly emphasised the primary importance of freedom of expression. It is 'one of the essential foundations of a democratic society and one of the basic conditions for its progress and for each individual's self-fulfilment', with 'freedom of political debate' being 'at the very core of the concept of a democratic society', see *Lingens v Austria* (1986) 8 EHRR 407 at 418–419, E Ct HR, paras 41–42. In Application 30552/96 *Winer v United Kingdom* 48 DR 154 (1986) at 170, the European Commission of Human Rights concluded that because of the competing right to freedom of expression, in the circumstances of that complaint it did 'not consider that the absence of an actionable right to privacy under English law shows a lack of respect for the applicant's private life'.

(3) The government did not intend, by s 12, to include in the HRA 1998 any provision which requires courts to do other than apply the principles set out in the Convention. The Home

Secretary, Mr Jack Straw MP, explained during the committee stage in the House of Commons (see 315 HC Official Report (6th series) col 543 (2 July 1998)): 'So far as we are able in a manner consistent with the Convention and its jurisprudence, we are saying to the courts that whenever there is a clash between article 8 [privacy] rights and article 10 [freedom of expression] rights, they must pay particular attention to the article 10 rights'. Indeed, were the HRA 1998 to require domestic courts to apply special principles not contained in the Convention, the Act would fail in its primary purpose to give effect to the Convention in domestic courts.

(4) It would be pointless for the HRA 1998 to create special principles not found in the Convention. The United Kingdom's international obligations under the Convention mean that persons who take the view that domestic law inadequately protects their right to privacy may bring a claim against the United Kingdom in Strasbourg.

All that can be said for s 12 is that it does no positive harm to the principles of the HRA 1998, and removed possible objections to the Act from those concerned about the Convention's impact on press freedom.

2.12.1   The HRA 1998, s 12 applies if a court[1] is considering whether to grant any relief[2] which, if granted, might affect the exercise of the Convention right to freedom of expression[3].

1   HRA 1998, s 12(5) states that in this section, 'court' includes a tribunal.
2   'Relief' includes any remedy or order, other than in criminal proceedings: s 12(5). During the committee stage debate in the House of Commons (see 315 HC Official Report (6th series) col 540 (2 July 1998)), the Home Secretary, Mr Jack Straw MP, explained that criminal proceedings were excluded because otherwise 'judges wanting to impose reporting restrictions in a criminal trial would, for example, have to consider any relevant privacy code, though plainly it would not be appropriate in that context. Nevertheless, as public authorities, the criminal courts will of course, in the same way as other courts, be required not to act in a way that is incompatible with articles 8 and 10 and other Convention rights. The special provision that we are making in new [s 12] does not therefore exempt criminal courts from the general obligations imposed by other provisions of the [Act]. However, had we included criminal proceedings under new [s 12], we would have made the running of criminal trials very complicated'. This is very difficult to understand. Mr Straw correctly confirmed that, under the Act, criminal courts are required to respect Convention rights. There is no especial difficulty about them doing so in relation to reporting restrictions. If such restrictions are necessary to protect a fair trial, that will not breach Convention rights. The confusion is the result of s 12 adding nothing of substance, but being designed to suggest that some special protection is being afforded to freedom of expression, and Mr Straw then being concerned to emphasise (correctly) that s 12 does not derogate from the Convention, under which freedom of expression is important but not absolute.
3   HRA 1998, s 12 (1). During the committee stage in the House of Commons, the Home Secretary, Mr Jack Straw MP, explained that this 'applies to the press, broadcasters or anyone whose right to freedom of expression might be affected. It is not limited to cases to which a public authority is a party. We have taken the opportunity to enhance press freedom in a wider way than would arise simply from the incorporation of the Convention into our domestic law' (see 315 HC Official Report (6th series) col 536 (2 July 1998)).

2.12.2   Where freedom of expression might be affected, the HRA 1998 makes special provision[1] for cases where the person against whom the application for relief is made ('the respondent') is neither present nor represented. In such circumstances, no such relief may be granted unless the court is satisfied that the applicant has taken all practicable steps to notify the respondent[2] or there are compelling reasons[3] why the respondent should not be notified[4].

1   HRA 1998, s 12(2).
2   During the committee stage in the House of Commons, the Home Secretary, Mr Jack Straw MP, suggested (correctly) that 'in the case of broadcasting authorities and the press, rarely would an applicant not be able to serve notice of the proceedings on the respondent' (see 315 HC Official Report (6th series) col 536 (2 July 1998)).
3   During the committee stage in the House of Commons, the Home Secretary, Mr Jack Straw MP, suggested that 'compelling reasons' might exist 'in a case raising issues of national security

where the mere knowledge that an injunction was being sought might cause the respondent to publish the material immediately. We do not anticipate that that limb would be used often' (see 315 HC Official Report (6th series) col 536 (2 July 1998).

4   This adds nothing to the common law. No judge would grant a remedy where the respondent was neither present nor represented unless either the applicant had taken all practicable steps to notify the respondent, or there were compelling reasons not to notify the respondent. During the committee stage in the House of Commons (see 315 HC Official Report (6th series) col 536, (2 July 1998)) the Home Secretary, Mr Jack Straw MP, said that 'the provision is intended overall to ensure that ex parte injunctions are granted only in exceptional circumstances. Even where both parties are represented, we expect that injunctions will continue to be rare, as they are at present'.

2.12.3   Where freedom of expression might be affected, the HRA 1998 also makes special provision by stating[1] that no relief is to be granted so as to restrain publication before trial unless the court is satisfied that the applicant is likely to establish that publication should not be allowed[2].

1   HRA 1998, s 12(3).
2   During the committee stage debate in the House of Commons, (see 315 HC Official Report (6th series) col 536 (2 July 1998)) the Home Secretary, Mr Jack Straw MP, correctly explained that this recognises a principle stated by the E Ct HR in *Observer and Guardian v United Kingdom* (1991) 14 EHRR 153 at 191, E Ct HR, para 60: 'the dangers inherent in prior restraints are such that they call for the most careful scrutiny on the part of the court. This is especially so as far as the press is concerned, for news is a perishable commodity and to delay its publication, even for a short period, may well deprive it of all its value and interest'. Mr Straw stated that because of this principle, the government believed that 'the courts should consider the merits of an application when it is made and should not grant an interim injunction simply to preserve the status quo ante between the parties'. The HRA 1998 here applies to freedom of expression generally a principle similar to that applied by libel law that a plaintiff cannot obtain an interlocutory injunction simply by establishing a seriously arguable case and relying on the balance of convenience. See *Holley v Smyth* [1998] QB 726, CA.

2.12.4   The court must have particular regard[1] to the importance of the Convention right to freedom of expression[2]. In particular, where the proceedings relate to material which the respondent claims, or which appears to the court, to be journalistic, literary or artistic material (or to conduct connected with such material[3]), the court must also have particular regard to the extent to which:

(a)   the material has, or is about to, become available to the public[4], or it is, or would be, in the public interest[5] for the material to be published; and

(b)   any relevant privacy code[6].

1   HRA 1998, s 12(4).
2   See para **2.12**, n 1 at (2) referring to *Lingens v Austria* and see n 5 to this para. During the committee stage in the House of Commons, Ross Cranston MP referred to the analysis by Professor Basil Markesinis, QC of how German law has sought to balance freedom of expression and the right to privacy (see 315 HC Official Report (6th series) cols 558–559 (2 July 1998)). In his 1998 Wilberforce Lecture, 'Privacy, Freedom of expression, and the Horizontal Effect of the Human Rights Bill: Lessons from Germany' (1999) 115 LQR 47, 62–63, Professor Markesinis observed that where free speech clashes with privacy, German courts have regard (amongst other matters) to the motives of the publisher (is he simply seeking to make a profit?), the importance of the speech (does it advance knowledge and public debate?), the way in which the information was obtained (was it by an illegal means or through the use of a telephoto lens, so suggesting that the intruder knew the plaintiff wanted to be left alone?), the extent of dissemination of the information, the accuracy of the statement, and the breadth of the restriction which the plaintiff wishes to place on the defendant's rights to free speech.
3   During the committee stage debate in the House of Commons (see 315 HC Official Report (6th series) col 540 (2 July 1998)) the Home Secretary, Mr Jack Straw MP, said that the reference to 'conduct connected with such material' was 'intended for cases where journalistic inquiries suggest the presence of a story, but no actual material yet exists—perhaps because the

story has not yet been written'. The right to freedom of expression under art 10 protects, for example, conduct concerned with the gathering of material: see *Goodwin v United Kingdom* (1996) 22 EHRR 123 at 143, E Ct HR, para 39, where the E Ct HR recognised that the ability of the press to obtain information is of vital importance to its 'public watchdog role'.

4   Where the material is (or is about to become) available to the public, and raises matters of legitimate public interest and concern, a restraint on freedom of expression is very unlikely to be justified under the Convention: see *Sunday Times Ltd v United Kingdom (No 2)* (1991) 14 EHRR 229 at 243–244, E Ct HR, para 55 and *Weber v Switzerland* (1990) 12 EHRR 508 and 524–525, E Ct HR, paras 49–51. During the committee stage debate in the House of Commons (see 315 HC Official Report (6th series) col 538 (2 July 1998)) the Home Secretary, Mr Jack Straw MP, explained that '[i]f the court and the parties to the proceedings know that a story will shortly be published anyway, for example in another country or on the internet, that must affect the decision whether it is appropriate to restrain publication by the print or broadcast media in this country'. Mr Straw added (at col 540) that the HRA 1998 did not define 'public'. It would be 'a matter for the courts to decide, based on common sense and proportionality. The fact that the information was available across the globe in very narrow circumstances would not be weighed in the balance'.

5   As the E Ct HR explained in *Sunday Times Ltd v United Kingdom (No 2)* (1991) 14 EHRR 229 at 241–242, E Ct HR, para 50, there must be a 'pressing social need' for any restriction on free speech, because it is incumbent on the press 'to impart information and ideas on matters of public interest. Not only does the press have the task of imparting such information and ideas, the public also has a right to receive them. Were it otherwise, the press would be unable to play its vital role of "public watchdog"'. The E Ct HR's case law emphasises that, as stated in *Wingrove v United Kingdom* (1996) 24 EHRR 1 at 30, E Ct HR, para 58 (concerning the law of blasphemy), 'there is little scope under art 10(2) of the Convention for restrictions on political speech or on debate of questions of public interest', but restrictions on freedom of expression are more defensible in relation to issues of morals or taste where the court is more willing to protect the 'rights of others'. See also *Muller v Switzerland* (1988) 13 EHRR 212, E Ct HR (obscenity) and *Casado Coca v Spain* (1994) 18 EHRR 1, E Ct HR (advertising by lawyers). The E Ct HR said in *Lingens v Austria* (1986) 8 EHRR 407 at 419, E Ct HR, para 42, that public figures can expect less protection under art 10(2) than private persons: '... freedom of political debate is at the very core of the concept of a democratic society which prevails throughout the Convention. The limits of acceptable criticism are accordingly wider as regards a politician as such than as regards a private individual. Unlike the latter, the former inevitably and knowingly lays himself open to close scrutiny of his every word and deed by both journalists and the public at large, and he must consequently display a greater degree of tolerance. No doubt art 10(2) enables the reputation of others—that is to say, of all individuals—to be protected, and this protection extends to politicians too, even when they are not acting in their private capacity; but in such cases the requirements of such protection have to be weighed in relation to the interests of open discussion of political issues'.

6   During the committee stage debate in the House of Commons (see 315 HC Official Report (6th series) cols 538–539 (2 July 1998)) the Home Secretary, Mr Jack Straw MP, explained that this 'could be the newspaper industry code of practice operated by the Press Complaints Commission, the Broadcasting Standards Commission code, the Independent Television Commission code, or a broadcaster's internal code such as that operated by the BBC. The fact that a newspaper has complied with the terms of the code operated by the PCC—or conversely, that it has breached the code—is one of the factors that we believe the courts should take into account in considering whether to grant relief'. Mr Straw added, at col 541, that the government's intention was to emphasise the importance of self-regulation of the newspaper and broadcasting media. What, then, will the domestic courts say if a television soap opera star, a relative of the Queen, or a backbench Member of Parliament seeks an injunction to stop a Sunday newspaper from publishing the secrets of their private life in circumstances where the article is said to involve no public interest considerations? Judges will be less likely to intervene to find that a newspaper article would unjustifiably invade privacy the more confident they are that there is an expert body which will fairly consider complaints and give effective remedies to victims of abuses of the right to freedom of expression. The Press Complaints Commission Code of Practice, for example, maintains a fair balance by protecting privacy save where there are competing public interest considerations. Applying the principles to specific cases is often a difficult question of subjective judgment. Since the PCC is a public authority under s 6 of the Act (see para **2.12**, n 1 and para **2.6.3**, n 6 at (3)), judges should be willing to leave to the PCC, other than in extreme cases, the difficult and sensitive decision on whether an article is an unjustifiable invasion of privacy, having regard to the importance of freedom of expression. The courts should recognise that other than in the most extreme circumstances, it is consistent with the Convention to leave these difficult questions of judgment to the relevant specialist

body. For the PCC to be a 'public authority' for the purposes of s 6 of the Act requires it to take account of the often conflicting demands of the right to freedom of expression and the right to privacy. That was already the task performed by the PCC. The leading textbook on public law (de Smith, Woolf and Jowell *Judicial Review of Administrative Action* (5th edn, 1995) p 182; and First Cumulative Supplement, 1998, pp 32–33) suggests that the PCC is, in any event, probably a public body subject to judicial review which gives a legal remedy for unfair or unreasonable action. In dismissing in 1996 an application for judicial review against the PCC brought by the Moors Murderer Ian Brady, who was aggrieved by a picture of him published in *The Sun*, Lord Woolf MR emphasised for the Court of Appeal that it would recognise a very broad discretion for the PCC: *R v Press Complaints Commission, ex p Stewart-Brady* (1996) 9 Admin LR 274 at 279B–C. Such an approach is entirely consistent with the Convention. When dismissing claims against the United Kingdom in planning cases, the E Ct HR has stated that questions of judgment may properly be left to qualified independent experts, so long as judicial review exists to correct perversity, or errors of law: *Bryan v United Kingdom* (1995) 21 EHRR 342 at 360–361, E Ct HR, paras 45–47. (See, similarly, the decisions by the European Commission of Human Rights in *X v United Kingdom* (1998) 25 EHRR CD 88 at 97–98; *Stefan v United Kingdom* (1997) 25 EHRR CD 130, 135; and *APB Ltd v United Kingdom* (1998) 25 EHRR CD 141 at 149–150.) It is true that the PCC cannot grant complainants an injunction to stop publication. But then the courts themselves will not grant injunctions to stop libels which the publisher intends to justify: see para **2.12.3**, n 2 above. Indeed, the E Ct HR has emphasised that prior restraints on publication require 'the most careful scrutiny': see para **2.12.3**, n 2. If the PCC were to have power, in exceptional cases, to award compensation, judges would be even more ready to leave complainants to that remedy. But the absence of compensation does not make a remedy ineffective: in judicial review proceedings, a successful applicant is not entitled to damages for ultra vires conduct, even if it has foreseeably caused loss, unless a tort has been committed. See, for example, *R v Secretary of State for Transport, ex p Factortame Ltd (No 2)* [1991] 1 AC 603 at 672H–673A (Lord Goff of Chieveley for the House of Lords). As Thomas Jefferson wrote in 1803: 'It is so difficult to draw a clear line of separation between the abuse and the wholesome use of the press, that as yet we have found it better to trust the public judgment, rather than the magistrate ...': see *Oxford Dictionary of American Legal Quotations* (1993 edn, p 173). The Act neither qualifies nor requires our judges generally to substitute their judgment for that of the PCC on where freedom of expression ends and privacy begins.

SECTION 13

2.13   The purpose of the HRA 1998, s 13 is to ensure that courts pay particular regard to the right to freedom of thought, conscience and religion[1] as exercised by religious organisations (itself or its members collectively)[2].

1   See art 9 of the Convention: para **4.9**.
2   Like the HRA 1998, s 12, on freedom of expression (on which see para **2.12**, n 1), s 13 serves no sensible purpose. During the third reading debate in the House of Lords, various amendments to the Bill were approved, contrary to the wishes of the government, to give specific protection to religious beliefs because of concern that the Bill might otherwise force churches and their members to engage in acts contrary to their religious principles, for example in relation to who they would marry in church, or who they would employ (see 585 HL Official Report (5th series) cols 747–760, 770–790, 805 and 812–813 (5 February 1998)). In particular, the House of Lords adopted an amendment which would have made it 'a defence for a person to show that he has acted in pursuance of a manifestation of religious belief in accordance with the historic teaching and practices of a christian or other principal religious tradition represented in Great Britain'. The amendments made by the House of Lords were neither necessary nor appropriate, for four reasons.
   (1) First, because the Act will operate to the considerable benefit of religious organisations, since art 9 (see para **4.9**) is one of the Convention rights and so, for the first time, English law will specifically protect religious freedom.
   (2) Second, because, as the Home Secretary, Mr Jack Straw MP, explained during the committee stage of the Bill on 20 May 1998, (see 312 HC Official Report (6th series) col 1015), the Act has a very limited inhibiting effect on the actions of churches:
      'Much of what the churches do is, in the legal context and in the context of the European Convention on Human Rights, essentially private in nature, and would not be affected by the Bill even as originally drafted. For example, the regulation of divine worship, the

administration of the sacrament, admission to church membership or to the priesthood and decisions of parochial church councils about the running of the parish church are, in our judgment, all private matters. In such matters, churches will not be public authorities; the requirement to comply with Convention rights will not bite on them.'

During the report stage in the House of Commons, (see 317 HC Official Report (6th series) col 1368 (21 October 1998)), the Home Secretary, Mr Jack Straw MP, gave an assurance that the Plymouth Brethren was not acting as a public authority when excluding people from membership. On the meaning of a 'public authority', see para **2.6**, in particular para **2.6.3**, n 4 on religious bodies. If a religious body were to act in breach of the rights established by the Convention, in a context where it was acting as a public authority, on behalf of the state, then it is right and proper that the victim should have a remedy. As the Home Secretary stated, during the committee stage of the Bill on 20 May 1998 (see HC Official Report (6th series) col 1015):

'On the occasions when churches stand in place of the state, Convention rights are relevant to what they do. The two most obvious examples relate to marriages and to the provision of education in church schools. In both areas, the churches are engaged, through the actions of the Minister or of the governing body of a school, in an activity which is also carried out by the state, and which, if the churches were not engaged in it, would be carried out directly by the state. We think it right in principle—there was no real argument about it on second reading—that people should be able to raise Convention points in respect of the actions of the churches in those areas on the same basis as they will be able to in respect of the actions of other public authorities, however rarely such occasions may arise.'

One cannot have a Human Rights Act that excludes churches from its application, even where churches act as public authorities, and whatever the extent to which their conduct infringes basic human rights.

(3) Thirdly, because in those contexts where churches do act on behalf of the state, the Convention has not hitherto been applied by the E Ct HR (or the European Commission of Human Rights) to damage the interests of religious organisations, or to force them to carry out acts contrary to religious principle, and there is no good reason for fearing that English courts will apply the Convention in any different manner in the future. As the Home Secretary, Jack Straw MP, stated during the committee stage of the Bill on 20 May 1998, (see HC 312 Official Report (6th series) col 1016), in response to specific concerns expressed by churches, Strasbourg case-law does not confer on persons of the same sex the right to marry each other (see para **4.12.10**), and, in any event, the availability of civil marriage means that there is no right to marry in a service conducted by a particular church or under the doctrine of a particular religion. The Secretary of State for Scotland, Mr Donald Dewar MP, added (at col 1036) that:

'The Convention on human rights has been relevant to the churches in this country since it was ratified here in 1953. The only change is the forum in which a case can be taken— that is, it can be taken directly in the domestic courts rather than in Strasbourg ... It seems to me that the threat—if there is one—has existed since 1953 and that it will not essentially change as a result of this legislation.'

He added, at col 1066:

'the Convention has been in being for more than 45 years. The fabric of our religious freedoms has not crumbled. The fact that we are now allowing the British courts ... to deal with the issues that come up under the Convention of human rights represents no alteration of substance to the relationship between the church and the courts'.

(4) Fourthly, because the amendments made by the House of Lords were inconsistent with the purpose of the Bill to give domestic effect to the Convention. To the extent that the Act (by making special provision for religious freedom) alters (for the purpose of domestic law) the content of the rights under the Convention, it fails to achieve its purpose and is (in any event) pointless because the problem remains in that any victim may (after exhausting domestic remedies) bring a claim against the United Kingdom before the E Ct HR.

At the committee stage in the House of Commons, the government secured the removal of the amendments approved by the House of Lords and substituted s 13 (see 312 HC Official Report (6th series) cols 1013–1974 (20 May 1998)). The Home Secretary, Jack Straw MP, explained (at col 1019) that the aim of the provision was to meet church concerns 'without violating the Convention or compromising the integrity of the Bill'. The aim is *not* to confer on churches any immunity from the Convention. As the Home Secretary stated at col 1020, the purpose of s 13 is to 'make it clear in the Bill that the churches were to have protection consistent with the Convention' and so it 'deals with the anxieties raised by the churches, without getting us into the impossible situation of risking having parts of what will become the

Act that are outwith the Convention'. See also col 1021. The Home Secretary added, at col 1022, that s 13 'will send a clear signal to the courts that they must pay due regard to the rights guaranteed by art 9, including, where relevant, the right of a Church to act in accordance with religious belief'. (See similarly the comments of the Home Secretary at the report stage on 21 October 1998, 317 HC Official Report (6th series) cols 1339–1343.)

HRA 1998, s 13 is, in truth, a provision that has no logical or legal justification. It is simply a sop to those who supported the amendments in the House of Lords because of misguided concern about the impact of the Convention. To tell courts to have 'particular regard' to art 9 rights is superfluous (no judge would be doing his duty if he failed to have due regard to art 9 rights where these are relevant) and potentially misleading (in that it may wrongly lead people to believe that churches and their members are being given a special defence when they would otherwise be in breach of Convention rights). The only positive things to be said in favour of s 13 are that it avoids excluding certain acts by religious organisations from the scope of the HRA 1998, as the House of Lords' amendments would have done, and it defused objections to the Act by those wrongly concerned about its impact on religious bodies.

2.13.1   If a court's[1] determination of any question arising under the HRA 1998 might affect the exercise by a religious[2] organisation (itself or its members collectively)[3] of the Convention right of thought, conscience and religion[4], it must have particular regard[5] to the importance of that right[6].

1   HRA 1998, s 13(2) states that 'court' here includes a tribunal. Note that a religious court or tribunal is not a 'court or tribunal' for the purposes of s 6 of the Act: see para **2.6.3**, n 4.

2   The HRA 1998 does not define a religion. The Home Secretary, Mr Jack Straw MP, explained during the committee stage of the Bill on 20 May 1998 (see 312 HC Official Report (6th series) col 1021) that this is because 'no definition is readily available, at home or in Strasbourg'. In other contexts, courts have suggested that there are two primary criteria of a religion:
(1) it addresses ultimate questions by reference to spiritual or supernatural existence or experience;
(2) it results in external manifestations of such beliefs by adherents in religious practices: for example, symbols, creeds, services, ceremonies, rituals, ministers, prayerbooks and other means of formalising and expressing spiritual or supernatural beliefs.
See *Malnak v Yogi* 592 F 2d 197 (1979) (US Court of Appeals, Third Circuit) and *Church of the New Faith v Comr for Payroll Tax* (1983) 154 CLR 120 (High Court of Australia).

3   The Home Secretary, Mr Jack Straw MP, explained during the committee stage of the Bill on 20 May 1998 (see 312 HC Official Report (6th series) col 1021) that:

'The intention is to focus the courts' attention in any proceedings on the view generally held by the church in question, and on its interest in protecting the integrity of the common faith of its members against attack, whether by outsiders or by individual dissidents'.

4   The Secretary of State for Scotland, Mr Donald Dewar MP, explained during the committee stage in the House of Commons on 20 May 1998 (see 312 HC Official Report (6th series) col 1063) that this is 'a sort of shorthand, because it is certainly intended to include the right to manifest religion or belief in worship, teaching practice and observance' under art 9 of the Convention (on which see para **4.9**).

5   This does not confer any immunity on churches and their members from the scope and effect of the Convention rights. See para **2.13**, n 2.

6   HRA 1998, s 13(1).

SECTION 14

2.14   By reason of the HRA 1998, s 1(2)[1], Convention rights[2] have effect for the purposes of the HRA 1998 subject to any designated derogation or reservation. The purpose of s 14 is to define designated derogations[3] and make further provision in relation to them.

1   See para **2.1.3**.
2   'Convention rights' are defined in HRA 1998, s 1(1): see para **2.1.1**.
3   Reservations are addressed in HRA 1998, s 15: see para **2.15**.

2.14.1   Article 15 of the Convention allows for a contracting state exceptionally to derogate from the Convention in specified circumstances[1].

1   Article 15 provides:

'1.   In time of war or other public emergency threatening the life of the nation any High Contracting Party may take measures derogating from its obligations under this Convention to the extent strictly required by the exigencies of the situation, provided that such measures are not inconsistent with its other obligations under international law.

2.   No derogation from article 2, except in respect of deaths resulting from lawful acts of war, or from articles 3, 4 (paragraph 1) and 7 shall be made under this provision.

3.   Any High Contracting Party availing itself of this right of derogation shall keep the Secretary General of the Council of Europe fully informed of the measures which it has taken and the reasons therefor. It shall also inform the Secretary General of the Council of Europe when such measures have ceased to operate and the provisions of the Convention are again being fully executed.'

In art 15(1), the words 'threatening the life of the nation' refer to 'an exceptional situation of crisis or emergency which affects the whole population and constitutes a threat to the organised life of the community of which the state is composed': *Lawless v Ireland* (1961) 1 EHRR 15 at 31, E Ct HR, para 28. Despite the language of art 15(1) ('strictly required'), the E Ct HR has recognised a margin of appreciation for the contracting state in assessing whether such an emergency exists and, if so, what steps are necessary to overcome it: *Ireland v United Kingdom* (1978) 2 EHRR 25 at 91–92, E Ct HR, para 207 and *Brannigan and McBride v United Kingdom* (1993) 17 EHRR 539 at 569–570, E Ct HR, para 43. See generally Harris, O'Boyle and Warbrick *Law of the European Convention on Human Rights* (1995), pp 489–507.

2.14.2   The term 'designated derogation'[1] is defined to mean[2]:

(a)   the United Kingdom's existing derogation from art 5(3)[3] of the Convention[4]; and

(b)   any derogation by the United Kingdom from an article of the Convention, or of any protocol to the Convention, which is designated for the purposes of the Act in an order[5] made by the Secretary of State[6].

1   The period for which designated derogations have effect is regulated by s 16: see para **2.16**.
2   HRA 1998, s 14(1).
3   For art 5(3), see paras **4.5.37–4.5.47**.
4   HRA 1998, s 14(1)(a). As s 14(2) explains, the derogation from art 5(3) is set out in the HRA 1998, Sch 3, Pt I. It includes the 1988 notification and the 1989 updating notification. It is the only derogation which the United Kingdom currently has in place in respect of the Convention and its protocols. It was entered into in 1988 following the judgment of the E Ct HR in *Brogan v United Kingdom* (1988) 11 EHRR 117, E Ct HR, that the detention of the applicants under the Prevention of Terrorism (Temporary Provisions) Act 1984 for more than four days constituted a breach of art 5(3) (and consequently also of art 5(5)) of the Convention because they had not been brought promptly before a judicial authority. The derogation preserves the Secretary of State's power under what is now the Prevention of Terrorism (Temporary Provisions) Act 1989 to extend the period of detention of persons suspected of terrorism connected with the affairs of Northern Ireland for a total of up to seven days. The validity of the derogation was upheld by the E Ct HR in *Brannigan and McBride v United Kingdom* (1993) 17 EHRR 539, E Ct HR.
5   HRA 1998, s 20(1) states that the power to make an order is exercisable by statutory instrument, and s 20(3) requires a statutory instrument made under s 14 to be laid before Parliament.
6   HRA 1998, s 14(1)(b). This is to cover any future derogations. In practice, the Secretary of State for Foreign and Commonwealth Affairs would exercise the power since he is responsible for giving notice of any derogation by the United Kingdom from an article of the Convention or a protocol to the Convention.

2.14.3   The HRA 1998 seeks to ensure that any designated derogation reflects the exact terms of any derogation which the United Kingdom currently has in place in respect of an article of the Convention or protocol, and hence that the effect in United Kingdom law of the particular Convention right is consistent with the United Kingdom's obligations in international law with respect to that article. Therefore:

(a)   if a designated derogation is amended or replaced, it ceases to be a designated derogation[1];

(b)   but this does not prevent the Secretary of State from exercising his power to make a fresh designation order in respect of the Article concerned[2];

(c)   the Secretary of State must by order make such amendments to Sch 3 of the Act (in Pt I of which derogations are set out) as he considers appropriate to reflect any designation order and the effect of the amendment or replacement of such an order[3].

1   HRA 1998, s 14(3). On the consequences of a withdrawal of a designated derogation, see para **2.16.4**.
2   HRA 1998, s 14(4). A fresh designation order would need to be made under s 14(1)(b).
3   HRA 1998, s 14(5).

2.14.4   A designation order may be made in anticipation of the making by the United Kingdom of a proposed derogation[1].

1   The HRA 1998, s 14(6). This helps to ensure that any derogation applies for the purposes of the HRA 1998 at the same time as it takes effect to modify the United Kingdom's international obligations under the Convention and protocols.

SECTION 15

2.15   By reason of the HRA 1998, s 1(2)[1], Convention rights[2] have effect for the purposes of the HRA 1998 subject to any designated derogation or reservation. The purpose of the HRA 1998, s 15 is to define designated reservations[3] and make further provision in relation to them.

1   See para **2.1.3**.
2   'Convention rights' are defined in HRA 1998, s 1(1): see para **2.1.1**.
3   Derogations are addressed in HRA 1998, s 14: see para **2.14**.

2.15.1   Article 57 of the Convention allows for a contracting state to make a reservation in relation to a provision of the Convention in specified circumstances[1].

1   Article 57 (which was art 64 before amendment by the eleventh protocol) provides:

'1. Any state may, when signing this Convention or when depositing its instrument of ratification, make a reservation in respect of any particular provision of the Convention to the extent that any law then in force in its territory is not in conformity with the provision. Reservations of a general character shall not be permitted under this article.

2. Any reservation made under this article shall contain a brief statement of the law concerned'.

The E Ct HR has held that the requirement imposed by art 57(2) 'both constitutes an evidential factor and contributes to legal certainty'. Its purpose is to 'provide a guarantee—in particular for the other contracting parties and the Convention institutions—that a reservation does not go beyond the provisions expressly excluded by the state concerned'. See *Weber v Switzerland* (1990) 12 EHRR 508 at 521, E Ct HR, para 38, and *Chorherr v Austria* (1993) 17 EHRR 358 at 374, E Ct HR, para 21.

2.15.2   'Designated reservation'[1] is defined to mean[2]:

(a)   the United Kingdom's existing reservation to art 2 of the first protocol to the Convention[3]; and

(b)   any other reservation by the United Kingdom to an article of the Convention, or of any protocol to the Convention, which is designated for the purposes of the Act in an order[4] made by the Secretary of State[5].

1   The periodic review of designated reservations is required by s 17: see para **2.17**.
2   HRA 1998, s 15(1).
3   HRA 1998, s 15(1)(a). For art 2 of the first protocol, see para **4.20**. As s 15(2) notes, the reservation to art 2 of the first protocol is set out in HRA 1998, Sch 3, Pt 2. The second sentence of art 2 of the first protocol states that in exercising any functions in relation to education and teaching, the state shall respect the right of parents to ensure that such education and teaching is in conformity with their own religious and philosophical convictions. The reservation states that the United Kingdom accepts this principle 'only so far as it is compatible with the provision of efficient instruction and training, and the avoidance of unreasonable public expenditure'. The reservation is designed to reflect the principle now contained in the Education Act 1996, s 9 that 'pupils are to be educated in accordance with the wishes of their parents, so far as that is compatible with the provision of efficient instruction and training and the avoidance of unreasonable public expenditure'.
4   HRA 1998, s 20(1) states that the power to make an order is exercisable by statutory instrument, and s 20(3) requires a statutory instrument made under s 15 to be laid before Parliament.
5   HRA 1998, s 15(1)(b). This is to cover any future reservations. A state cannot add a reservation after ratification. So this concerns any future reservation which may be made when the United Kingdom ratifies a further protocol to the Convention, or if the current reservation to art 2 of the first protocol were to be partially withdrawn. In practice, the Secretary of State for Foreign and Commonwealth Affairs would exercise the power since he is responsible for giving notice of any reservations by the United Kingdom.

2.15.3   The HRA 1998 seeks to ensure that any designated reservation reflects the exact terms of any reservation which the United Kingdom currently has in place in respect of an article of the Convention or protocol, and hence that the effect in United Kingdom law of the particular Convention right is consistent with the United Kingdom's international obligations with respect to that article. Therefore:

(a)   if a designated reservation is withdrawn wholly or in part it ceases to be a designated reservation[1];

(b)   but this does not prevent the Secretary of State from exercising his power to make a fresh designation order in respect of the Article concerned[2];

(c)   the Secretary of State must by order make such amendments to the Act as he considers appropriate to reflect any designation order or the effect of the withdrawal (in whole or in part) of a designated reservation[3].

1   HRA 1998, s 15(3). By contrast with s 14(3) in relation to derogations (see para **2.14.3**), the Act does not refer to a reservation being amended or replaced since the Convention does not so allow. It is, however, possible to withdraw part of a reservation leaving another part intact.
2   HRA 1998, s 15(4). A fresh designation order would then need to be made under s 15(1)(b).
3   HRA 1998, s 15(5).

SECTION 16

2.16   The HRA 1998, s 16 provides that, because of the essentially temporary and exceptional nature of any derogation[1], the effect of a derogation for the purposes of the Act is limited in time, unless extended by Parliament. For the purposes of the Act[2], derogations are therefore subject to regular Parliamentary oversight and approval[3].

1   Under s 14: see para **2.14**.
2   HRA 1998, s 16 only affects the status and effect of a derogation under the Act. It does not affect the continuing effect of a derogation (whether designated or otherwise) on the United Kingdom's international obligations under the Convention.
3   There was, prior to the HRA 1998, no such legal obligation.

2.16.1   If a designated derogation has not already been withdrawn by the United Kingdom, it will cease to have effect for the purposes of the HRA 1998[1]:

(a)   in the case of the derogation which is currently in place in relation to art 5(3) of the Convention[2], at the end of the period of five years beginning with the date when the HRA 1998, s 1(2)[3] came into force[4];

(b)   in the case of any other (future) derogation, at the end of the period of five years beginning with the date on which the order designating it was made.

1   HRA 1998, s 16(1).
2   HRA 1998, s 14(1)(a): see para **2.14.2**.
3   See para **2.1.3**.
4   For commencement provisions, see HRA 1998, s 22: para **2.22**.

2.16.2   The Secretary of State has power by order[1] (made at any time before the period of five years expires) to extend the continuing effect of a derogation for a further period of five years. This period may be extended on more than one occasion[2].

1   The power to make such an order is exercisable by statutory instrument: HRA 1998, s 20(1). A draft of the order must be laid before, and approved by, each House of Parliament: s 20(4). The use of the draft affirmative resolution procedure reflects the importance of the subject matter with which the relevant provisions are concerned.
2   HRA 1998, s 16(2).

2.16.3   An order designating a new derogation[1] ceases to have effect at the end of the 40 day period for consideration[2] unless a resolution has been passed by each House approving the order[3].

1   Under HRA 1998, s 14(1)(b): see para **2.14.2(b)**.
2   That is the period beginning with the day on which the order was made: s 16(5). In calculating the period for consideration, no account is to be taken of any time during which Parliament is dissolved or prorogued, or both Houses are adjourned for more than four days: s 16(6).
3   HRA 1998, s 16(3). This ensures that the order is subject to Parliamentary scrutiny whilst enabling designation orders to take effect immediately so that United Kingdom law is kept in line with our international obligations. The concern is that it might become necessary to make a derogation urgently and before it would be possible to obtain Parliament's approval to the making of a designation order for the derogation. HRA 1998, s 16(4) states that, should the designation order cease to have effect by reason of s 16(3), this does not affect anything done in reliance on the order, and does not affect the power to make a fresh order under s 14(1)(b) (para **2.14.2(b)**).

2.16.4   If a designated derogation is withdrawn by the United Kingdom, the Secretary of State must by order[1] make such amendments to the HRA 1998 as he considers are required to reflect that withdrawal[2].

1   The power to make an order is exercisable by statutory instrument: HRA 1998, s 20(1). Such a statutory instrument must be laid before Parliament: HRA 1998, s 20(3).

2   HRA 1998, s 16(7). This is designed to ensure that the content of the Act is consistent with
the international obligations of the United Kingdom from time to time. On the consequences
of the amendment or replacement of a designated derogation, see para **2.14.3**.

SECTION 17

2.17   The HRA 1998, s 17 provides that, because of the essentially temporary and
exceptional nature of any reservation[1], the effect of a reservation for the purposes of
the Act is limited in time, unless extended by Parliament. For the purposes of the Act[2],
reservations are therefore subject to regular Parliamentary oversight and approval[3].

1   Under HRA 1998, s 15: see para **2.15**.
2   HRA 1998, s 17 only affects the status and effect of a reservation under the Act. It does not
affect the continuing effect of a reservation (whether designated or otherwise) on the United
Kingdom's international obligations under the Convention.
3   There was, prior to the HRA 1998, no such legal obligation.

2.17.1   The appropriate Minister[1] is required[2] to review the United Kingdom's current
designated reservation to art 2 of the first protocol[3] before the end of the period of five
years beginning with the date on which s 1(2)[4] came into force, and (if that designation
is still in force) before the end of the period of five years beginning with the date on
which the last report relating to it was laid before Parliament[5].

1   Defined by HRA 1998, s 21(1) to mean the Minister of the Crown having charge of the
appropriate authorised government department (within the meaning of the Crown Proceedings
Act 1947).
2   HRA 1998, s 17(1).
3   See HRA 1998, s 15(1)(a): para **2.15.2**.
4   See para **2.1.3**. For commencement provisions, see HRA 1998, s 22: para **2.22**.
5   Under HRA 1998, s 17(3): see para **2.17.3**.

2.17.2   The appropriate Minister is also required[1] to review any further (future)
designated reservation before the end of the period of five years beginning with the
date on which the order designating the reservation first came into force and (if that
designation is still in force) before the end of the period of five years beginning with
the date on which the last report relating to it was laid before Parliament[2].

1   HRA 1998, s 17(2).
2   Under HRA 1998, s 17(3): see para **2.17.3**.

2.17.3   The Minister conducting a review of designated reservations must prepare
a report on the result of such a review and lay a copy of it before each House of
Parliament[1].

1   HRA 1998, s 17(3).

SECTION 18

2.18   The purpose of the HRA 1998, s 18 is to enable a serving United Kingdom judge
to accept appointment to the E Ct HR without resigning from United Kingdom judicial
office. This is designed to remove unnecessary legal obstacles to the best candidates
coming forward when the position of United Kingdom judge on the E Ct HR is being
filled[1]. The HRA 1998, s 18 also makes provision for judicial pensions.

1   See the speech by the Lord Chancellor, Lord Irvine of Lairg, on the Second Reading of the Bill
     in the House of Lords on 3 November 1997 (582 HL Official Report (5th series) col 1233):
     a disincentive under the previous law was that 'a judge would have to resign his office here in
     order to take up the appointment at Strasbourg, with no guarantee of reinstatement at the end
     of the term of office'. See also the Lord Chancellor's comments during the committee stage
     in the House of Lords, 27 November 1997, 583 HL Official Report (5th series) col 1160. The
     first appointee to the E Ct HR under these provisions was Nicolas Bratza, QC (who became
     Mr Justice Bratza), formerly the British member of the European Commission of Human Rights.
     On the appointment process see the debate initiated by Lord Lester of Herne Hill, QC in the
     House of Lords on 13 July 1998 (592 HL Official Report (5th series) cols 75–100), and David
     Pannick, QC, 'Political meddling in rights is wrong' (1998) Times, 19 May.

2.18.1   The holder of a judicial office[1] in the United Kingdom may become a judge of
the E Ct HR without being required to relinquish his office[2]. He is not required to perform
the duties of his judicial office while he is a judge of the E Ct HR[3].

1   'Judicial office' is defined by HRA 1998, s 18(1) to mean the office of:
     (a) Lord Justice of Appeal, Justice of the High Court or Circuit judge, in England and Wales;
     (b) judge of the Court of Session or sheriff, in Scotland;
     (c) Lord Justice of Appeal, judge of the High Court or county court judge, in Northern Ireland.
2   HRA 1998, s 18(2).
3   HRA 1998, s 18(3). This provision is necessary because judges are otherwise appointed and paid
     to fulfil the judicial office which they hold in the United Kingdom.

2.18.2   Statutory provisions relating to the maximum number of judges in the United
Kingdom do not apply to a serving judge who is appointed to the E Ct HR[1].

1   HRA 1998, s 18(4). HRA 1998, s 18(5) adds that if a sheriff principal is appointed as a judge
     of the E Ct HR, it will be possible to appoint a temporary sheriff principal as if the office were
     vacant. These provisions allow the domestic judicial strength to be kept up to complement
     notwithstanding the absence of a judge serving in Strasbourg. Under s 18(7), the Lord Chancellor
     or the Secretary of State may by order make such transitional provision (including provision
     for a temporary increase in the maximum number of judges) as he considers appropriate in
     relation to any holder of a judicial office who has completed his service as a judge of the E Ct
     HR. This would include a temporary increase in the maximum number of judges allowed in the
     judicial office holder's United Kingdom office. Power to make such an order is exercisable by
     statutory instrument: s 20(1). Such a statutory instrument is subject to annulment in pursuance
     of a resolution of either House of Parliament: s 20(5).

2.18.3   Nor do statutory provisions relating to the payment of judicial salaries
apply in such circumstances[1]. Special provision is made for judicial pensions in relation
to the holder of a judicial office who serves as a judge of the E Ct HR[2].

1   HRA 1998, s 18(4). Domestic salary provisions do not apply because, during the period of his
     appointment to the E Ct HR, the judge will be paid by the Council of Europe.
2   HRA 1998, s 18(6) and Sch 4.

SECTION 19

2.19   The purpose of the HRA 1998, s 19 is to ensure that in the preparation of a Bill and
its consideration by Parliament, consideration is given to any implications the Bill may have
in relation to Convention rights[1], and to ensure that any relevant issues are identified at an
early stage so that they can be the subject of informed debate in Parliament[2].

1   'Convention rights' are defined in HRA 1998, s 1(1): see para **2.1.1**.
2   The Lord Chancellor, Lord Irvine of Lairg, said on the second reading of the Bill in the House
     of Lords, 3 November 1997, (see 582 HL Official Report (5th series) col 1233) that the
     requirements imposed by s 19 will have 'a significant impact on the scrutiny of draft legislation

within government. Where such a statement cannot be made, Parliamentary scrutiny of the Bill would be intense'. The Lord Chancellor added during the committee stage, 27 November 1997 (see 583 HL Official Report (5th series) col 1163), that 'if there had been no such provision in the Bill, that might have given a quieter life for Ministers'. See also Lord Lester of Herne Hill, QC during the second reading debate (House of Lords, 3 November 1997, 582 HL Official Report (5th series) col 1240): 'In the absence of a formally expressed intention to enact inconsistent legislation, the courts will be able to act on the basis that the legislation was intended by Parliament to be compatible with Convention rights.' Note that s 19 is already in force: para **2.22.2**, n 1. In answer to a question posed by Lord Lester of Herne Hill QC, the government promised on 17 December 1998 that 'we will of course explain the thinking behind a section 19 statement if the issue is raised in debate': Lord Williams of Mostyn, Under-Secretary of State, Home Office, 595 HL Official Report (5th series) col 186.

2.19.1   A Minister of the Crown[1] in charge of a Bill in either House of Parliament must, before the second reading of the Bill[2]:

(a)   make a statement to the effect that in his view the provisions of the Bill are compatible with Convention rights; or

(b)   make a statement to the effect that although he is unable to make such a statement of compatibility, the government nevertheless wishes the House to proceed with the Bill[3].

1   HRA 1998, s 21(1) provides that this has the same meaning as in the Ministers of the Crown Act 1975. Ministers of the Crown Act 1975, s 8(1) defines 'Minister of the Crown' to mean 'the holder of an office in her Majesty's Government in the United Kingdom, and includes the Treasury, the Board of Trade and the Defence Council'.
2   The timing of the statement is designed to be sufficiently early to enable Parliamentary proceedings to take it into account.
3   HRA 1998, s 19(1). Paragraph (b) is included so as not to prejudice the right of Parliament (exercising Parliamentary sovereignty) to make provision which appears in some respects to be contrary to Convention rights. There may also be occasions when a positive statement cannot be made because of uncertainty about the exact implications of a Bill for Convention rights. 'Where a Minister states that he is unable to make a positive statement, that will be a very early signal to Parliament that the human rights implications of the Bill will need to receive the closest consideration': the Lord Chancellor, Lord Irvine of Lairg, 'Keynote Address' to the January 1998 Conference at the University of Cambridge Centre for Public Law, *Constitutional Reform in the United Kingdom: Practice and Principles* (1998), p 4.

2.19.2   The statement must be in writing and be published in such manner as the Minister making it considers appropriate[1].

1   HRA 1998, s 19(2). The adequacy or otherwise of such a statement is not a justiciable issue. See *Mangawaro Enterprises Ltd v A-G* [1994] 2 NZLR 451 where Gallen J in the High Court of New Zealand held that the obligation imposed on the Attorney-General by the New Zealand Bill of Rights Act 1990, s 7 to bring to the attention of the House of Representatives any provision in a Bill that appears to be inconsistent with any of the rights and freedoms contained in the Bill did not create individual rights for citizens. The obligation concerned an aspect of Parliamentary proceedings, and so was covered by the immunity conferred by the Bill of Rights 1688, art 9. See similarly para **2.6.3**, n 9 on a person exercising functions in connection with proceedings in Parliament not being a public authority for the purposes of s 6 of the Act.

SECTION 20

2.20   The HRA 1998, s 20 makes provision in respect of order-making powers contained in the Act.

2.20.1   Any power of a Minister of the Crown to make an order under the HRA 1998 is exercisable by statutory instrument[1].

1   HRA 1998, s 20(1).

2.20.2   The power of the Lord Chancellor or the Secretary of State to make rules (other than rules of court) under the HRA 1998, s 2(3)[1] or the HRA 1998, s 7(9)[2] is exercisable by statutory instrument[3].

1   See para **2.2.3**.
2   See para **2.7.1**, n 4.
3   HRA 1998, s 20(2).

2.20.3   Any statutory instrument made under the HRA 1998, s 14[1], s 15[2] or s 16(7)[3] must be laid before Parliament[4].

1   See para **2.14**.
2   See para **2.15**.
3   See para **2.16.4**.
4   HRA 1998, s 20(3).

2.20.4   No order may be made by the Lord Chancellor or the Secretary of State under the HRA 1998, s 1(4)[1], s 7(11)[2] or s 16(2)[3] unless a draft of the order has been laid before, and approved by, each House of Parliament[4].

1   See para **2.1.4**.
2   See para **2.7.1**, n 4.
3   See para **2.16.2**.
4   HRA 1998, s 20(4). The use of the draft affirmative resolution procedure reflects the importance of the subject matter with which the relevant provisions are concerned.

2.20.5   Any statutory instrument made under the HRA 1998, s 18(7)[1], or Sch 4[2], or to which s 20(2)[3] applies, shall be subject to annulment in pursuance of a resolution of either House of Parliament[4].

1   See para **2.18.2**, n 1.
2   See paras **2.18.3** and **2.26**.
3   See para **2.20.2**.
4   HRA 1998, s 20(5). Special provision is made by s 20(6) to (8) in relation to the making of rules and orders in Northern Ireland.

SECTION 21

2.21   The HRA 1998, s 21 defines various terms used in the Act[1]. It also implements the abolition of the death penalty for military offences[2]. Any liability to the death penalty under the Armed Forces Acts is replaced by a liability to imprisonment for life or some lesser penalty instead[3].

1   HRA 1998, s 21 also explains how references in the Act to Articles of the Convention are to be read before and after the coming into force of the eleventh protocol (see para **2.2.1**, n 2).
2   See para **2.1.1**, n 2.
3   HRA 1998, s 21(5). During the report stage in the House of Commons (see 317 HC Official Report (6th series) cols 1353–1354 (21 October 1998)), Mr Mike O'Brien MP, Parliamentary Under-Secretary of State for the Home Department, explained that more detailed amendments would be made to the Armed Forces Acts when the next legislation to consolidate them was introduced. By reason of HRA 1998, s 22(7), s 21(5) has effect in any place where the Armed Forces Acts apply, unlike the HRA 1998 generally, which is confined in territorial effect to the United Kingdom. See para **2.22.4**.

SECTION 22

2.22   The HRA 1998, s 22 makes provision about the commencement, application and extent of the Act, and confers the short title, the Human Rights Act 1998[1].

1   HRA 1998, s 22(1) confers the short title, the Human Rights Act. During the Committee Stage in the House of Lords, Lord Monson suggested an amendment to add the word 'additional' before 'Human Rights' to avoid a 'propagandistic title'. He was concerned that 'the sort of voter who reads only the tabloids and watches only commercial television could be forgiven for being persuaded that prior to 1 May 1997 [the date of the general election won by the Labour Party led by Tony Blair MP] the United Kingdom was in a state of semi-tyranny compared with the liberal paradise to be found on the Continent of Europe'. Lord Williams of Mostyn, Under-Secretary of State, Home Office, responded that 'if it is an additional human rights Bill, that would be additionally propagandist'. The amendment was withdrawn (see 583 HL Official Report (5th series) cols 1167–1169 (27 November 1997)).

2.22.1   The HRA 1998, s 18[1], s 20[2], and s 21(5)[3] (as well as s 22 itself) come into force on the passing of the Act[4].

1   See para **2.18**.
2   See para **2.20**.
3   See para **2.21**, n 3.
4   HRA 1998, s 22(2). The date on which the Act received Royal Assent was 9 November 1998.

2.22.2   The other provisions of the HRA 1998 come into force on such day as the Secretary of State may by order appoint, and different days may be appointed for different purposes[1].

1   HRA 1998, s 22(3). By reason of the Human Rights Act 1998 (Commencement) Order 1998 SI 1998/2882, HRA 1998, s 19 (see para **2.19**) came into force on 24 November 1998.

2.22.3   A person may rely on Convention rights in any proceedings brought by or at the instigation of a public authority whenever the act in question took place, but otherwise a person may not rely on Convention rights under the HRA 1998, s 7(1)(b)[1] in relation to an act taking place before the coming into force of that sub-section[2].

1   See para **2.7.1**.
2   HRA 1998, s 22(4). This provision, as part of the HRA 1998, s 22, is already in force. See para **2.22.1**.

2.22.4   The HRA 1998 binds the Crown[1] and extends to Northern Ireland[2].

1   HRA 1998, s 22(5).
2   HRA 1998, s 22(6). The Act is generally confined in territorial effect to the United Kingdom, but by reason of s 22(7), s 21(5) on the abolition of the death penalty for military offences has effect in any place where the Armed Forces Acts apply: see para **2.21**, n 3. However, the Act does not apply to the Isle of Man or the Channel Islands. The House of Lords rejected an amendment proposed by Lord Lester of Herne Hill, QC to extend the geographical scope of the Act so as to ensure compliance by the United Kingdom with the obligation under art 13 of the Convention (see para **4.13**) to secure effective remedies in respect of the Isle of Man and the Channel Islands for which the United Kingdom is responsible under the Convention: see the report stage, 19 January 1998, 584 HL Official Report (5th series) cols 1303–1311. During the committee stage in the House of Commons, an amendment was proposed, but withdrawn, to extend the Bill to cover the Channel Islands and the Isle of Man: 313 HC Official

Report (6th series) cols 464–475 (3 June 1998). The proposed amendment was withdrawn because the Home Secretary, Mr Jack Straw MP, explained that the authorities in the islands had stated their intention to incorporate the Convention into their domestic law: see cols 471–474.

SCHEDULE 1

2.23   Schedule 1 sets out the text of the Convention rights[1] which are to be given further effect by the HRA 1998.

1   'Convention rights' are defined in s 1(1): see para **2.1.1**. They are arts 2–12, 14, and 16–18 of the Convention, arts 1–3 of the first protocol, and arts 1 and 2 of the sixth protocol.

SCHEDULE 2

2.24   Schedule 2 makes further provision in relation to remedial orders under s 10[1]. It ensures proper Parliamentary supervision of such orders[2].

1   See para **2.10**.
2   See the speech by the Lord Chancellor, Lord Irvine of Lairg, on the Second Reading of the Bill in the House of Lords, 3 November 1997 (see 582 HL Official Report (5th series) col 1231): 'We recognise that a power to amend primary legislation by means of a statutory instrument is not a power to be conferred or exercised lightly. [The provisions of the Act] therefore place a number of procedural and other restrictions on its use ... [W]e have built in as much parliamentary scrutiny as possible. In addition, the power to make a remedial order may be used only to remove an incompatibility or a possible incompatibility between legislation and the Convention. It may therefore be used only to protect human rights, not to infringe them.' In the House of Commons, during the committee stage, a government amendment introduced Sch 2, containing additional controls on the use of the remedial order procedure to those originally contained in the Bill (see 314 HC Official Report (6th series) cols 1130–1143 (24 June 1998)).

2.24.1   A remedial order may contain such incidental, supplemental, consequential or transitional provision as the person making it considers appropriate[1]; may have retrospective effect; may make provision for the delegation of specific functions; and may make different provision for different cases[2]. It may be made so as to have the same extent as the legislation which it affects[3].

1   Under HRA 1998, Sch 2, para 1(2), this includes power to amend primary legislation (including primary legislation other than that which contains the incompatible provision), and power to amend or revoke subordinate legislation (including subordinate legislation other than that which contains the incompatible provision).
2   HRA 1998, Sch 2, para 1(1). A remedial order could make provision for compensation for victims. Indeed, it would be desirable for it to do so to ensure that victims do not need to bring proceedings against the United Kingdom in the E Ct HR for an effective remedy. During the committee stage in the House of Lords (27 November 1997), the Lord Chancellor, Lord Irvine of Lairg (responding to concern about compensation for the complainant where a declaration of incompatibility has been made under s4 of the Act), explained that in addition to the powers under the Act, 'there are prerogative powers which can be exercised and other ex gratia actions that could be taken to grant remedies in appropriate circumstances' (see 583 HL Official Report (5th series) col 1108).
3   HRA 1998, Sch 2, para 1(3).

2.24.2   No person is to be guilty of an offence solely as a result of the retrospective effect of a remedial order[1].

1   HRA 1998, Sch 2, para 1(4). This is to ensure compliance with art 7 of the Convention: see para **4.7**.

2.24.3   No remedial order may be made unless[1]:

(a)   a draft of the order[2] has been approved by a resolution of each House of Parliament made after the end of the period of 60 days beginning with the day on which the draft was laid; or

(b)   it is declared in the order that it appears to the person making it that, because of the urgency of the matter, it is necessary to make the order without a draft being so approved[3].

1   HRA 1998, Sch 2, para 2.
2   HRA 1998, Sch 2, para 3(1) states that no such draft may be laid unless
    (a) the person proposing to make the order has laid before Parliament a document which contains a draft of the proposed order and the required information; and
    (b) the period of 60 days, beginning with the day on which the document was laid, had ended. If representations are made during that period, the draft laid must be accompanied by a statement containing a summary of the representations and (if as a result of the representations, the proposed order has been changed), details of the changes: HRA 1998, Sch 2, para 3(2).
3   There may be occasions where there is an urgent need to remove an incompatibility, a need which would be frustrated if the draft affirmative resolution procedure were invariably to apply. A precedent for the procedure is to be found in the Northern Ireland (Emergency Provisions) Act 1996, s 60(2).

2.24.4   If a remedial order is made without being approved in draft[1], the person making it must lay it before Parliament, accompanied by the required information[2], after it is made. If representations[3] have been made during the period of 60 days beginning with the day on which the original order was made, the person making it must (after the end of that period) lay before Parliament a statement containing a summary of the representations and, if as a result of the representations he considers it appropriate to make changes to the original order, details of the changes[4]. In a case where the person has, as a result of representations, considered it appropriate to make changes, that person must make a further remedial order replacing the original order and lay the replacement order before Parliament[5]. If at the end of the period of 120 days beginning with the day on which the original order was made, a resolution has not been passed by each House approving the original or replacement order, then the order ceases to have effect (but without that affecting anything previously done under either order or the power to make a fresh remedial order)[6].

1   HRA 1998, Sch 2, para 4(1).
2   Defined by HRA 1998, Sch 2, para 5 to mean an explanation of the incompatibility which the order (or proposed order) seeks to remove, including particulars of the relevant declaration, finding or order, and a statement of the reasons for proceeding under s 10 and for making an order in those terms.
3   HRA 1998, Sch 2, para 5 defines 'representations' to mean representations about a remedial order (or proposed remedial order) made to the person making (or proposing to make) it and includes any relevant Parliamentary report or resolution.
4   HRA 1998, Sch 2, para 4(2).
5   HRA 1998, Sch 2, para 4(3).
6   HRA 1998, Sch 2, para 4(4).

2.24.5   In calculating any period for the purposes of the HRA 1998, Sch 2, no account is to be taken of any time during which Parliament is dissolved or prorogued, or both Houses are adjourned for more than four days[1].

1   HRA 1998, Sch 2, para 6.

SCHEDULE 3

2.25   The HRA 1998, Sch 3 sets out the text of the derogation made by the United Kingdom in respect of art 5(3) of the Convention[1] and the text of the reservation entered by the United Kingdom in respect of art 2 of the first protocol[2].

1   See HRA 1998, s 14(1)(a): para **2.14.2**.
2   See HRA 1998, s 15(1)(a): para **2.15.2**.

SCHEDULE 4

2.26   The HRA 1998, Sch 4 makes provision in relation to judicial pensions[1].

1   See HRA 1998, s 18(6): para **2.18.3**. During the committee stage in the House of Commons, 2 July 1998, (see 315 HC Official Report (6th series) col 572) the Parliamentary Under-Secretary of State for the Home Department, Mr Mike O'Brien MP, explained that Sch 4 makes provision for the pension of a holder of judicial office in the United Kingdom who serves as a judge of the E Ct HR: 'It places a duty on the relevant Minister—the Lord Chancellor for a judge serving in England and Wales or Northern Ireland and the Secretary of State for a Scottish judge—to make an order ensuring that a UK serving judge's pension position will not be prejudiced as a result of his or her appointment to the court.'

Chapter 3
Principles of Interpretation

A The general approach to interpretation

3.01 Special principles of interpretation apply to the Human Rights Act 1998. Such a constitutional instrument, giving effect to fundamental rights, is:

'sui generis, calling for principles of interpretation of its own, suitable to its character ... without necessary acceptance of all the presumptions that are relevant to legislation of private law.'[1].

This is because:

'The context and purpose of a commercial contract is very different from that of a constitution. The background of a constitution is an attempt, at a particular moment in history, to lay down an enduring scheme of government in accordance with certain moral and political values. Interpretation must take these purposes into account. Furthermore, the concepts used in a constitution are often very different from those used in commercial documents. They may expressly state moral and political principles to which the judges are required to give effect in accordance with their own conscientiously held views of what such principles entail'[2].

---

1 *Ministry of Home Affairs v Fisher* [1980] AC 319, PC per Lord Wilberforce at 329C–E. cf Chief Justice Marshall in *M'Culloch v Maryland* 17 US 316 (1819) at 407: 'we must never forget that it is a *constitution* we are expounding'. In the Preface to the White Paper, *Rights Brought Home: The Human Rights Bill 1997* (Cm 3782), p 1, the Prime Minister, Tony Blair, explained that the Bill was part of 'a comprehensive programme of constitutional reform'. On the second reading in the House of Lords, on 3 November 1997 (582 HL Official Reports (5th series) col 1227), the Lord Chancellor, Lord Irvine of Lairg, said that the Bill 'occupies a central position in our integrated programme for constitutional change'.
2 *Matadeen v Pointu* [1998] 3 WLR 18, PC per Lord Hoffmann at 25G–H. Similar views were expressed in *James v Commonwealth of Australia* [1936] AC 578, PC at 614, per Lord Wright MR. See also 44 (1) *Halsbury's Laws* (4th edn) para 1221, which notes that although the British constitution is said to be unwritten, there are, nevethleless, 'a number of historic statutes regarded as embodying and setting forth the state's constitutional principles. Any modern Act which amends or adds to these may also be regarded as a constitutional Act. The main significance of classing an Act as a constitutional Act lies in the nature of the interpretative criteria which then apply to it. In particular, the rights the Act confers, having the quality of constitutional rights, will be regarded by the courts as fundamental and not to be displaced except by clear words'.

3.02 In particular, the provisions of an enactment giving effect to basic freedoms 'call for a generous interpretation avoiding what has been called the "austerity of tabulated legalism", suitable to give to individuals the full measure of the fundamental rights and freedoms referred to'[1]. This 'require[s] the courts to adopt a non-rigid and generous approach' in which the court 'looks at the substance and reality of what was involved and should not be over-concerned with what are no more than technicalities'[2]. The issues 'should be approached with realism and good sense, and kept in proportion'[3].

1   *Ministry of Home Affairs v Fisher* [1980] AC 319, PC per Lord Wilberforce at 328G–H. Similarly
     A-G of the Gambia v Jobe [1984] AC 689, PC per Lord Diplock at 700H, approved in
     A-G of Hong Kong v Lee Kwong-kut [1993] AC 951, PC per Lord Woolf at 966B–E. See also
     Ministry of Transport v Noort [1992] 3 NZLR 260, NZ CA per Cooke P at 271: the New Zealand
     Bill of Rights Act should be given 'such fair, large and liberal construction and interpretation
     as will best ensure the attainment of its object according to its true intent, meaning and spirit'.
     Similarly Richardson J at 276–278. And see, similarly, Dickson J for the Supreme Court of
     Canada in *R v Big M Drug Mart Ltd* (1985) 18 DLR (4th) 321 at 360: the method of
     interpretation of the Canadian Charter of Rights and Freedoms should be 'a generous rather
     than a legalistic one, aimed at fulfilling the purpose of the guarantee and securing for individuals
     the full benefit of the Charter's protection'.
2   *Huntley v A-G for Jamaica* [1995] 2 AC 1, PC per Lord Woolf at 12G–H.
3   *A-G of Hong Kong v Lee Kwong-kut* [1993] AC 951, PC, per Lord Woolf at 975B–C.
     See similarly *R v Grayson and Taylor* [1997] 1 NZLR 399, NZ CA at 409: 'The [New
     Zealand] Bill of Rights is not a technical document. It has to be applied in our society
     in a realistic way'.

3.03   However,

> 'This is in no way to say that there are no rules of law which should apply to the
> interpretation of a Constitution. A Constitution is a legal instrument giving rise, amongst
> other things, to individual rights capable of enforcement in a court of law. Respect must be
> paid to the language which has been used and to the traditions and usages which have given
> meaning to that language.'[1].

It is therefore 'a mistake' to consider that the special features of constitutional
provisions 'release judges from the task of interpreting the statutory language and
enable them to give free rein to whatever they consider should have been the moral and
political views of the framers of the constitution. What the interpretation of commercial
documents and constitutions have in common is that in each case the court is
concerned with the meaning of the language which has been used'[2].

1   *Ministry of Home Affairs v Fisher* [1980] AC 319, PC, per Lord Wilberforce at 329E–F. See
     also the observations of Judge Kentridge for the Constitutional Court of South Africa in *State
     v Zuma* [1995] (4) BCLR 401 at 412H, approved by Lord Woolf for the PC in *La Compagnie
     Sucriere de Bel Ombre Ltee v Government of Mauritius* (13 December 1995, unreported) at
     p 5 and approved by Lord Hoffmann in *Matadeen v Pointu* [1998] 3 WLR 18, PC at 26A–
     B: 'If the language used by the lawgiver is ignored in favour of a general resort to "values", the
     result is not interpretation but divination.'
2   *Matadeen v Pointu* [1998] 3 WLR 18, PC, per Lord Hoffmann at 25H–26A.

B   The basic principles derived from the European Convention on Human Rights

1   THE PURPOSE OF THE HUMAN RIGHTS ACT

3.04   Because the purpose of the Human Rights Act is to give effect in our domestic
law to the rights guaranteed by the European Convention on Human Rights[1], the
principles recognised by the European Commission of Human Rights and the European
Court of Human Rights for the interpretation of the Convention will have considerable
value for the interpretation of the Act[2].

1   See paras **2.01–2.08** above.
2   The Human Rights Act 1998, s 2(1) requires courts and tribunals to take into account the
     judgments of the European Court of Human Rights (and the decisions and opinions of the
     European Commission of Human Rights): see para **2.2** above.

2 INTERPRETING AN INTERNATIONAL TREATY

3.05 The Convention is an international treaty, the general principles for the interpretation of which are set out in arts 31–33 of the Vienna Convention on the Law of Treaties, which incorporate generally accepted principles of international law[1]. A treaty must be interpreted in good faith, by reference both to its wording and to its object and purpose, and having regard to subsequent practice[2]. The existence, or absence, of a 'generally shared approach' in contracting states is relevant to the application of the Convention[3]. But this 'does not mean that absolute uniformity is required'[4].

1   *Golder v United Kingdom* (1975) 1 EHRR 524 at 532, E Ct HR, paras 29–30.
2   See also *A v Minister for Immigration and Ethnic Affairs* (1997) 142 ALR 331 at 349–352 (McHugh J, with whom Brennan CJ agreed at 333, in the High Court of Australia).
3   *X, Y and Z v United Kingdom* (1997) 24 EHRR 143 at 171–172, E Ct HR, para 52. See similarly *Dudgeon v United Kingdom* (1981) 4 EHRR 149 at 167, E Ct HR, para 60 and *Petrovic v Austria* (1998) 4 BHRC 232, 238, E Ct HR, para 38. See also *Sheffield and Horsham v United Kingdom* (1998) 27 EHRR 163.
4   *Sunday Times v United Kingdom* (1979) 2 EHRR 245 at 277, E Ct HR, para 61. The European Court has repeatedly recognised that 'it is not possible to find in the legal and social orders of the contracting states a uniform European conception of morals' and that each contracting state has a margin of appreciation in deciding its own approach to such matters: see, for example, *Muller v Switzerland* (1988) 13 EHRR 212 at 228–229, E Ct HR, para 35, and *Wingrove v United Kingdom* (1996) 24 EHRR 1 at 30–31, E Ct HR, para 58. In *F v Switzerland* (1987) 10 EHRR 411 at 420, E Ct HR, para 33, the court noted that 'the fact that, at the end of a gradual evolution, a country finds itself in an isolated position as regards one aspect of its legislation does not necessarily imply that that aspect offends the Convention, particularly in a field – matrimony – which is so closely bound up with the cultural and historical traditions of each society and its deep-rooted ideas about the family unit'. On the margin of appreciation, see para **3.20** below.

3   A DYNAMIC INTERPRETATION

3.06 The Human Rights Act requires a dynamic, evolving interpretation, as it is seeking to give effect to a Convention which 'is a living instrument which ... must be interpreted in the light of present-day conditions'[1].

1   *Tyrer v United Kingdom* (1978) 2 EHRR 1 at 10, E Ct HR, para 31. See also *Marckx v Belgium* (1979) 2 EHRR 330 at 346, E Ct HR, para 41. But note that in *Johnston v Ireland* (1986) 9 EHRR 203, E Ct HR, where the E Ct HR held that the right to marry (under art 12) does not confer a right to divorce (see para **4.12.12** below), the E Ct HR said, at 219, para 53, that it could not 'by means of an evolutive interpretation, derive ... a right that was not included therein at the outset. This is particularly so here, where the omission was deliberate'.

4   THE OBJECTS AND PURPOSES OF THE CONVENTION

3.07 When interpreting the Act, courts should have regard to the general objects and purposes of the Convention, which is 'an instrument designed to maintain and promote the ideals and values of a democratic society'[1]. Particularly important features of a 'democratic society' are 'pluralism, tolerance and broadmindedness'[2]; 'the rule of law' with 'access to the courts'[3]; and freedom of expression, which is 'one of the essential foundations of a democratic society and one of the basic conditions for its progress and for each individual's self-fulfilment'[4], with 'freedom of political debate' being 'at the very core of the concept of a democratic society'[5].

1   *Kjeldsen, Busk, Madsen and Pedersen v Denmark* (1976) 1 EHRR 711 at 731, E Ct HR, para 53; and *Soering v United Kingdom* (1989) 11 EHRR 439 at 467, E Ct HR, para 87. See also *Ministry of Transport v Noort* [1992] 3 NZLR 260, NZ CA at 271 per Cooke P:

'[the] courts will be expected to try to approach the Bill of Rights Act with a sense of the democratic values for which the Bill of Rights Act stands. This may seem to be asking much, but it is asking no more than that we in New Zealand try to live up to international standards or targets and to keep pace with civilization.'.

2   *Handyside v United Kingdom* (1976) 1 EHRR 737 at 754, E Ct HR, para 49. See similarly *Dudgeon v United Kingdom* (1981) 4 EHRR 149 at 165, E Ct HR, para 53. See para **3.16, n 1** below for the particular protection accorded to 'intimate aspect[s] of private life'. See also the judgment of Chief Justice Dickson for the Supreme Court of Canada in *R v Oakes* (1986) 26 DLR (4th) 200 at 225 concerning the Canadian Charter of Rights and Freedoms, s 1, which states that rights and freedoms are guaranteed 'subject only to such reasonable limits prescribed by law as can be demonstrably justified in a free and democratic society'. Chief Justice Dickson explained that:

> 'the values and principles essential to a free and democratic society ... embody, to name but a few, respect for the inherent dignity of the human person, commitment to social justice and equality, accommodation of a wide variety of beliefs, respect for cultural and group identity, and faith in social and political institutions which enhance the participation of individuals and groups in society.'.

3   *Golder v United Kingdom* (1975) 1 EHRR 524, 535, E Ct HR, para 34. In *Engel v Netherlands* (1976) 1 EHRR 647 at 672, E Ct HR, para 69, the E Ct HR referred to 'the notion of the rule of law from which the whole Convention draws its inspiration'. In *Klass v Germany* (1978) 2 EHRR 214 at 235, E Ct HR, para 55, the E Ct HR noted that: 'One of the fundamental principles of a democratic society is the rule of law, which is expressly referred to in the preamble to the Convention. The rule of law implies, inter alia, that an interference by the executive authorities with an individual's rights should be subject to an effective control which should normally be assured by the judiciary, at least in the last resort, judicial control offering the best guarantees of independence, impartiality and a proper procedure.' See also *Raymond v Honey* [1983] 1 AC 1, HL, per Lord Wilberforce at 12H–13A, and *R v Secretary of State for the Home Department, ex p Leech* [1994] QB 198, CA, per Steyn LJ at 210A. See also para **4.14** on the right to equality of treatment without arbitrary discrimination, in particular para **4.14.19** concerning discrimination on invidious grounds.
4   *Lingens v Austria* (1986) 8 EHRR 407 at 418–419, E Ct HR, paras 41–42.
5   *Lingens v Austria* (1986) 8 EHRR 407 at 419, E Ct HR, para 42.

5   PRACTICAL AND EFFECTIVE RIGHTS

3.08   Courts should bear in mind that 'the Convention is intended to guarantee not rights that are theoretical or illusory but rights that are practical and effective'[1]. The conditions imposed for the exercise of a right must not 'impair their very essence and deprive them of their effectiveness'[2]. Because the interpretation of the Convention is concerned with substance, not form, courts may need to 'look behind the appearances and investigate the realities of the procedure in question'[3].

1   *Airey v Ireland* (1979) 2 EHRR 305 at 314, E Ct HR, para 24; and *Artico v Italy* (1980) 3 EHRR 1, 13, ECt HR, para 33.
2   *Mathieu-Mohin v Belgium* (1987) 10 EHRR 1 at 16, E Ct HR, para 52.
3   *Deweer v Belgium* (1980) 2 EHRR 439 at 458, E Ct HR, para 44. Note also that the Convention does not involve consideration of statutes (or other laws) in the abstract, but whether their application in the circumstances of the individual case involved a breach: see para **2.7.2**, n 4.

6   A FAIR BALANCE

3.09   Interpretation of the Human Rights Act should strive to give effect to the general principle, 'inherent in the whole of the Convention', that it is seeking to strike a 'fair balance ... between the demands of the general interest of the community and the requirements of the protection of the individual's fundamental rights'[1].

1   *Sporrong and Lönnroth v Sweden* (1982) 5 EHRR 35 at 52, E Ct HR, para 69. See similarly *Soering v United Kingdom* (1989) 11 EHRR 439 at 468, E Ct HR, para 89. On the extent to

which the Convention requires states to protect this fair balance in disputes arising as between private individuals, see para **2.6.3, n 3**.

7 THE PRINCIPLE OF PROPORTIONALITY

3.10 Central to the principle of a 'fair balance' is the doctrine of proportionality. A restriction on a freedom guaranteed by the Convention must be 'proportionate to the legitimate aim pursued'[1]. There must be 'a reasonable relationship of proportionality between the means employed and the legitimate objectives pursued by the contested limitation'[2]. A measure will satisfy the proportionality test only if three criteria are satisfied:

(1)   the legislative objective must be sufficiently important to justify limiting a fundamental right;

(2)   the measures designed to meet the legislative objective must be rationally connected to that objective – they must not be arbitrary, unfair or based on irrational considerations;

(3)   the means used to impair the right or freedom must be no more than is necessary to accomplish the legitimate objective – the more severe the deleterious effects of a measure, the more important the objective must be if the measure is to be justified in a democratic society[3].

1   *Handyside v United Kingdom* (1976) 1 EHRR 737 at 754, ECt HR, para 49. On the principle of proportionality, see generally de Smith, Woolf and Jowell *Judicial Review of Administrative Action* (5th edn, 1995), pp 593–606. As they explain, in the application of the principle of proportionality, courts recognise a discretionary area of judgment for the decision-maker, the width of which varies according to the context. In the context of EC law, see the discussions in *R v Ministry of Agriculture, Fisheries and Food, ex p First City Trading Ltd* [1997] 1 CMLR 250 at 278–279 (paragraphs 67–69) (Mr Justice Laws), and Lord Hoffmann 'A Sense of Proportion' in *European Community Law in the English Courts* (eds Mads Andenas and Francis Jacobs, 1998), p 149.
2   *Fayed v United Kingdom* (1994) 18 EHRR 393, 432, E Ct HR, para 71. See also para **3.15** below.
3   See *De Freitas v Permanent Secretary of Ministry of Agriculture, Fisheries, Lands and Housing* [1998] 3 WLR 675, PC per Lord Clyde at 684A–F; *Germany v Council of the European Union* [1995] ECR I–3723 at 3755–3756 (paragraph 42 of the Judgment of the ECJ); 51 *Halsbury's Laws* (4th edn) para 2.296 on proportionality in EU law; Jurgen Schwarze *European Administrative Law* (1992), ch 5, on the principle of proportionality; and *R v Oakes* (1986) 26 DLR (4th) 200, Can SC, per Chief Justice Dickson at 227–228, considering the Canadian Charter of Rights and Freedoms, s 1 (on which see para **3.07, n 2** above). The Supreme Court of Canada has emphasised that the principles of proportionality 'should be applied flexibly, so as to achieve a proper balance between individual rights and community needs': *Ross v New Brunswick School District No 15* [1996] 1 SCR 825 at 872 (La Forest J for the court). See also para **3.24** below.

C   Burden of proof

3.11   It is for the complainant to show that there has been an infringement of his or her rights[1] under the Convention. Where the right is not absolute but is subject to exceptions, it is for the respondent to show that there is a justification for the prima facie breach[2].

1   In a claim under the HRA 1998, s 7(1) alleging that a public authority has acted unlawfully contrary to s 6(1), the applicant must show that he or she is a 'victim' for the purposes of art 25 of the Convention. See para **2.7** above.
2   See the approach of the Supreme Court in Canada in relation to the Canadian Charter of Rights and Freedoms in *Andrews v Law Society of British Columbia* (1989) 56 DLR (4th) 1 at 21 (per

McIntyre J dissenting on the merits, but speaking for the court on this issue of principle) and *R v Cobham* (1994) 118 DLR (4th) 301 at 309 (per Chief Justice Lamer for the court). See similarly *R v Butcher* [1992] 2 NZLR 257 at 266 (Cooke P for the NZ CA on the New Zealand Bill of Rights Act 1990).

D   Limitations on rights

1   INTRODUCTION

3.12   Articles 8–11 of the Convention contain limitations in similar terms. Where there is a prima facie breach of the right to respect for private and family life, home and correspondence, or the right to freedom of thought, conscience and religion, or the right to freedom of expression, or the right to freedom of peaceful assembly and freedom of association with others, the state must show that any restriction on the exercise of such rights is prescribed by law (or in accordance with law), and is necessary in a democratic society for the advancement of one or more specified objectives (such as the protection of public order, health or morals, or the interests of others). Because the state may 'interfere' with the exercise of rights where these conditions are satisfied, the rights themselves should be broadly interpreted[1]. Exceptions to the rights recognised under the Convention 'must be narrowly interpreted'[2].

1   *Niemietz v Germany* (1992) 16 EHRR 97 at 112, E Ct HR, para 31.
2   *Sunday Times v United Kingdom* (1979) 2 EHRR 245 at 281, E Ct HR, para 65.

2   'IN ACCORDANCE WITH THE LAW/PRESCRIBED BY LAW'

3.13   Where the Convention requires that the state has acted 'in accordance with the law' or in a manner 'prescribed by law'[1], the state must be able to show that its conduct 'must have some basis in domestic law', whether statute or common law[2]. But the Convention 'does not merely refer back to domestic law but also relates to the quality of the law, requiring it to be compatible with the rule of law', so that there is 'a measure of legal protection in domestic law against arbitrary interference by public authorities with the rights safeguarded'[3]. This is 'especially so where ... the law bestows on the executive wide discretionary powers'[4]. To avoid arbitrary laws, there are two fundamental requirements:

'First, the law must be adequately accessible: the citizen must be able to have an indication that is adequate in the circumstances of the legal rules applicable to a given case. Secondly, a norm cannot be regarded as a "law" unless it is formulated with sufficient precision to enable the citizen to regulate his conduct: he must be able – if need be with appropriate advice – to foresee, to a degree that is reasonable in the circumstances, the consequences which a given action may entail. Those consequences need not be foreseeable with absolute certainty: experience shows this to be unattainable. Again, whilst certainty is highly desirable, it may bring in its train excessive rigidity and the law must be able to keep pace with changing circumstances. Accordingly, many laws are inevitably couched in terms which, to a greater or lesser extent, are vague and whose interpretation and application are questions of practice.'[5]

1   There is no difference in substance between these requirements: *Silver v United Kingdom* (1983) 5 EHRR 347 at 371, E Ct HR, para 85.
2   *Silver v United Kingdom* (1983) 5 EHRR 347 at 372, E Ct HR, para 86, and *Sunday Times v United Kingdom* (1979) 2 EHRR 245 at 270, E Ct HR, para 47.
3   *Malone v United Kingdom* (1984) 7 EHRR 14 at 40, E Ct HR, para 67.
4   *Silver v United Kingdom* (1983) 5 EHRR 347 at 373, E Ct HR, para 90. See similarly *De Freitas v Permanent Secretary of Ministry of Agriculture, Fisheries, Lands and Housing* [1998] 3 WLR 675, PC per Lord Clyde at 682C–H.

5   *Sunday Times v United Kingdom* (1979) 2 EHRR 245 at 271, E Ct HR, para 49. In *Muller v Switzerland* (1988) 13 EHRR 212 at 226, E Ct HR, para 29, the court recognised that: 'The need to avoid excessive rigidity and to keep pace with changing circumstances means that many laws are inevitably couched in terms which, to a greater or lesser extent, are vague.'

3   PERMITTED AIMS

3.14   Where the Convention identifies the legitimate objectives of an interference with a right, the respondent must establish that it was, in good faith, seeking to advance one or more of those objectives. To similar effect, art 18 of the Convention provides that: 'The restrictions permitted under this Convention to the said rights and freedoms shall not be applied for any purpose other than those for which they have been prescribed.'[1].

1   Human Rights Act 1998, s 1(1) states that Convention rights are defined 'as read with', inter alia, art 18 of the Convention.

4   'NECESSARY IN A DEMOCRATIC SOCIETY'

3.15   The European Court of Human Rights has explained that the adjective 'necessary':

'is not synonymous with "indispensable", neither has it the flexibility of such expressions as "admissible", "ordinary", "useful", "reasonable" or "desirable" and that it implies the existence of a "pressing social need".'[1].

The court must assess 'whether the interference complained of corresponded to a pressing social need, whether it was proportionate to the legitimate aim pursued, whether the reasons given by the national authorities to justify it are relevant and sufficient ...'[2].

1   *Sunday Times v United Kingdom* (1979) 2 EHRR 245 at 275, E Ct HR, para 59, and *Handyside v United Kingdom* (1976) 1 EHRR 737 at 753–754, E Ct HR, para 48.
2   *Sunday Times v United Kingdom* (1979) 2 EHRR 245 at 277–278, E Ct HR, para 62. On the principle of proportionality, see para **3.10** above.

3.16   In applying these principles, regard should be had, in particular, to the importance of the relevant right[1].

1   The European Court of Human Rights has recognised certain rights as being of especial importance. For example, in *Dudgeon v United Kingdom* (1981) 4 EHRR 149, E Ct HR (concerned with criminal sanctions for homosexual acts between adult males), the court said (at p 165, para 52) that the case concerned 'a most intimate aspect of private life' in respect of which 'there must exist particularly serious reasons before interferences on the part of the public authorities can be legitimate ...'. See also para **3.07** above for other rights of especial importance.

E   Abuse of rights

3.17   Article 17 of the Convention provides:

'Nothing in this Convention may be interpreted as implying for any State, group or person any right to engage in any activity or perform any act aimed at the destruction of any of the rights and freedoms set forth herein or at their limitation to a greater extent than is provided for in the Convention.'[1].

Although this means that 'no person may be able to take advantage of the provisions of the Convention to perform acts aimed at destroying the ... rights and freedoms' of others set out in the Convention, art 17 does not deprive persons such as terrorists of the benefit of the rights and freedoms set out in the Convention[2]. An example of the application of art 17 to prevent persons from claiming to use the Convention to further acts aimed at destroying the rights of others was the decision of the European Commission of Human Rights to dismiss the complaint by people who had been convicted of distributing racist pamphlets and who had been prevented from standing as candidates in municipal elections on a racist platform[3].

1   Human Rights Act 1998, s 1(1) states that Convention rights are defined 'as read with', inter alia, art 17 of the Convention.
2   *Lawless v Ireland* (1961) 1 EHRR 15 at 22, E Ct HR, para 7.
3   *Glimmerveen and Hagenbeek v Netherlands* (1979) 18 DR 187, EComHR.

F   Interpretation of other legislation to ensure conformity with the Human Rights Act 1998

1   THE INTERPRETATIVE OBLIGATION IMPOSED BY THE HUMAN RIGHTS ACT 1998

3.18   The Human Rights Act 1998, s 3(1) states that: 'so far as it is possible to do so, primary legislation and subordinate legislation must be read and given effect in a way which is compatible with the Convention rights'[1]. The crucial words are 'possible' and 'must'. As the White Paper explained:

'This goes far beyond the present rule which enables the courts to take the Convention into account in resolving any ambiguity in a legislative provision. The courts will be required to interpret legislation so as to uphold the Convention rights unless the legislation itself is so clearly incompatible with the Convention that it is impossible to do so.'[2].

So courts and tribunals must strive for compatibility, applying 'a presumption of constitutionality' by implying words necessary to give effect to Convention rights (so long as this does not contradict the express words of the relevant legislation) and where necessary reading down (that is limiting in scope and effect) provisions which would otherwise breach the Act[3].

1   For a detailed discussion of the meaning and effect of the Human Rights Act 1998, s 3(1), see para **2.3** above.
2   *Rights Brought Home: The Human Rights Bill* (1997) (Cm 3782), para 2.7.
3   See *A-G of the Gambia v Jobe* [1984] AC 689, PC, per Lord Diplock at 702B–F. But although courts will adopt a strained interpretation, they will not be willing to rewrite a statute in order to avoid unconstitutionality: *De Freitas v Permanent Secretary of Ministry of Agriculture, Fisheries, Lands and Housing* [1998] 3 WLR 675, PC per Lord Clyde at 681F–682A. See, generally, Lord Lester of Herne Hill QC 'The Art of the Posssible: Interpreting Statutes under the Human Rights Act' [1998] EHRLR 665.

2   THE SIMILAR OBLIGATION IN OTHER AREAS OF) LAW

3.19   In performing the duty imposed by the Human Rights Act 1998, s 3(1), courts and tribunals should note the extent to which they perform a similar function in relation to statutes which are affected by EC rights, where they give statutory provisions a meaning which they would not normally bear, in order to ensure compatibility with EC law[1]. On one occasion, in order to give effect to legislation designed to further fundamental rights guaranteed by EC law, Lord Russell of Killowen (on behalf of the House of Lords) concluded his analysis of the provisions of the Equal Pay Act 1970 with the words 'This beats me', and announced that he would 'jettison the words in dispute as making no contribution to the manifest intention of Parliament'[2]. Courts should also have regard to the general doctrine of statutory interpretation that judges may be: 'driven to disregard particular words or phrases [in a statute] when, by giving effect to them, the operation of the statute would be rendered insensible, absurd or ineffective to achieve its evident purpose.'[3].

1   See, for example, *Litster v Forth Dry Dock and Engineering Co Ltd* [1990] 1 AC 546, HL, per Lord Keith of Kinkel at 554A–B and G–H, explaining and following *Pickstone v Freemans plc* [1989] AC 66, HL: in order to achieve the manifest purpose of the regs to implement EC law, 'words must be read in by necessary implication'. See also *Webb v EMO Air Cargo (UK) Ltd (No 2)* [1995] ICR 1021, HL.
2   *O'Brien v Sim-Chem Ltd* [1980] ICR 573, HL, per Lord Russell of Killowen at 580F.
3   *McMonagle v Westminster City Council* [1990] 2 AC 716, HL, per Lord Bridge of Harwich at 726E.

G   Margin of appreciation and the discretionary area of judgment

1   THE DOCTRINE OF THE MARGIN OF APPRECIATION

3.20   The doctrine of the 'margin of appreciation'[1] concerns the reluctance of an international court to substitute its judgment for that of the domestic authorities. As the European Court has explained, 'the machinery of protection established by the Convention is subsidiary to the national systems safeguarding human rights'[2].

The European Court has recognised that: 'By reason of their direct and continuous contact with the vital forces of their countries, the national authorities are in principle better placed than an international court to evaluate local needs and conditions.'[3].

Although national authorities therefore enjoy a 'margin of appreciation', this 'goes hand in hand with a European supervision'[4]. The attitude adopted by the European Court of Human Rights 'will vary according to the context. Relevant factors include the nature of the Convention right in issue, its importance for the individual and the nature of the activities concerned'[5].

1   See Paul Mahoney 'Marvellous Richness of Diversity or Invidious Cultural Relativism' (1998) 19 Human Rights LJ 1, and the other contributions at pp 6–36 discussing 'The Doctrine of the Margin of Appreciation under the European Convention on Human Rights: Its legitimacy in Theory and Application in Practice'.
2   *Handyside v United Kingdom* (1976) 1 EHRR 737 at 753, E Ct HR, para 48.
3   *Buckley v United Kingdom* (1996) 23 EHRR 101 at 129, E Ct HR, para 75. See also para **3.28** below on how this margin of appreciation varies according to the context. The margin of appreciation is particularly broad in relation to moral issues: see, para **3.05, n 4** above.
4   *Handyside v United Kingdom* (1976) 1 EHRR 737 at 754, E Ct HR, para 49.
5   *Buckley v United Kingdom* (1996) 23 EHRR 101 at 129, E Ct HR, para 74. The intensity of the European supervision depends, in particular, on the importance of the rights (see paras **3.07** and **3.16, n 1** above) and the extent to which the justification for the state conduct raises matters of social or moral judgment on which there is no consensus (see para **3.05, nn 3–4**).

2   WHY THE DOCTRINE OF MARGIN OF APPRECIATION HAS NO APPLICATION IN THE PRESENT CONTEXT

3.21   This doctrine of margin of appreciation does not apply when a national court is considering the Human Rights Act[1]. However, an analogous doctrine should be recognised by national courts. Just as there are circumstances in which an international court will recognise that national institutions are better placed to assess the needs of society, and to make difficult choices between competing considerations, so national courts will accept that there are some circumstances in which the legislature and the executive are better placed to perform those functions.

1   As Lord Woolf explained (for the Privy Council) in *A-G of Hong Kong v Lee Kwong-kut* [1993] AC 951 at 966H–967A, the European Court of Human Rights 'is not concerned directly with the validity of domestic legislation but whether, in relation to a particular complaint, a state has in its domestic jurisdiction infringed the rights of a complainant under the European Convention'.

3   THE APPROACH TO BE ADOPTED BY THE NATIONAL COURT

3.22   The manner in which the domestic court exercises its responsibilities will depend on the nature of the dispute.

3.23   The dispute may concern whether facts have occurred which (if found) will amount to a breach of the Convention. In such circumstances, the task of the court is to find the facts, unless that task has already been carried out (in a satisfactory manner) by a lower court or tribunal, or other quasi-judicial body. The European Court of Human Rights has recognised that it is 'frequently a feature in the systems of judicial control of administrative decisions found throughout the Council of Europe Member States' that a court or appeal tribunal interferes with findings of fact by a lower body only on limited grounds (such as perversity) where that lower body has established the facts 'in the course of a quasi-judicial procedure governed by many of the safeguards required by art 6(1)'[1].

1   *Bryan v United Kingdom* (1995) 21 EHRR 342 at 361, E Ct HR, para 47. On art 6(1) of the Convention, see para **4.6** below.

3.24   The dispute may concern matters of judgment: do the facts (as found) establish a breach of the Convention? It would be wrong for the national court or tribunal to apply the Wednesbury principle of domestic judicial review[1], and simply ask itself whether an impugned decision is 'so unreasonable that no reasonable authority could ever have come to it' in the light of the contents of the Convention. The task of the court is to decide the issue of judgment for itself, applying the principle of proportionality[2].

1   *Associated Provincial Picture Houses Limited v Wednesbury Corporation* [1948] 1 KB 223, at 230, CA.
2   See para **3.10** above. Although the principle of proportionality is different from the principle of Wednesbury unreasonableness (see *R v Secretary of State for the Home Department, ex p Brind* [1991] 1 AC 696, per Lord Ackner at 762E–763B and Lord Lowry at 763C and 766C–767G), in many cases they will provide the same result: *R v Chief Constable of Sussex, ex p International Trader's Ferry Ltd* [1998] 3 WLR 1260, per Lord Slynn of Hadley at 1277B–C and Lord Cooke of Thorndon at 1288G–1289C.

4 DEFERENCE BY THE COURT

3.25 Some questions in relation to the application of the Convention raise issues of judgment on which the body under review (the legislature, the executive or another relevant person or body authorised to take the decision under English law) has already adopted a view. It is, nevertheless, for the court to reach its own judgment on whether there is a breach of the Human Rights Act. But there are some circumstances in which the court will defer to the opinion of the legislature, executive or other relevant person or body[1].

1 As Lord Hoffmann explained for the Privy Council in *Matadeen v Pointu* [1998] 3 WLR 18, at 27A, in many areas of constitutional law 'sonorous judicial statements of uncontroversial principle often conceal the real problem, which is to mark out the boundary between the powers of the judiciary, the legislature and the executive in deciding how that principle is to be applied'.

3.26 Particular factors to which a court will have regard in deciding to what extent (if at all) to defer to the opinion of the legislature, executive or other relevant person or body are as follows.

(1) The nature of the Convention right. Many of the rights protected by the Convention (for example arts 8–11 and art 1 of Protocol no 1) require a balance to be struck between competing considerations. Other rights (such as art 3) are absolute;

(2) The extent to which the issues require consideration of social, economic or political factors. As the Supreme Court of Canada has explained, when applying the Canadian Charter of Rights and Freedoms, there are cases in 'the social, economic and political spheres where the legislature [or other authorised person] must reconcile competing interests in choosing one policy among several that might be acceptable'.

In such circumstances, 'the courts must accord great deference to the legislature's choice because it is in the best position to make such a choice'.

The legislature (or the person or body to whom it has delegated this type of decision) will normally receive deference in such contexts because:

'courts are not specialists in the realm of policy-making, nor should they be. This is a role properly assigned to the elected representatives of the people, who have at their disposal the necessary institutional resources to enable them to compile and assess social science evidence, to mediate between competing social interests and to reach out and protect vulnerable groups.'[1].

(3) The extent to which the court has special expertise, for example in relation to criminal matters[2].

(4) Where the rights claimed are of especial importance, 'a high degree of constitutional protection' will be appropriate[3]. The European Court of Human Rights has recognised as being of especial importance rights to freedom of expression (especially in relation to political speech), access to the courts, and protection of intimate aspects of private life[4]. In such contexts, judicial deference is far less appropriate, and the courts will carry out particularly strict scrutiny of state conduct.

1 *Libman v A-G of Quebec* (1998) 3 BHRC 269 at 289 (Can SC, para 59). See similarly Lord Woolf for the Judicial Commitee of the Privy Council in *A-G of Hong Kong v Lee Kwong-kut* [1993]

AC 951 at 975C–D on the Hong Hong Bill of Rights: 'In order to maintain the balance between the individual and the society as a whole, rigid and inflexible standards should not be imposed on the legislature's attempts to resolve the difficult and intransigent problems with which society is faced when seeking to deal with serious crime. It must be remembered that questions of policy remain primarily the responsibility of the legislature.' See also the approach of the European Court of Justice in relation to the concept of objective justification in indirect sex discrimination in EC social security law, that 'social policy is a matter for the member states ... . Consequently, it is for the member states to choose the measures capable of achieving the aim of their social and employment policy. In exercising that competence, the member states have a broad margin of discretion': *Nolte* [1995] ECR I-4625 at 4660 (para 33). See also Sir John Laws 'Wednesbury' *in The Golden Metwand and the Crooked Cord: Essays on Public Law in Honour of Sir William Wade QC* (1998), p 201: it is necessary 'to distinguish the idea of a margin of appreciation, which is apt for an international court reviewing a national decision, from the different idea of a discretion left to elected authorities on democratic grounds'.

2   *Libman v A-G of Quebec* (1998) 3 BHRC 269 at 289 (Can SC, para 59).
3   *Libman v A-G of Quebec* (1998) 3 BHRC 269 at 289–290 (Can SC, para 60).
4   See paras **3.07** and **3.16, n 1** above.

3.27   Even where the court thinks it appropriate to accord some degree of deference to the decisions of the legislature or other bodies, the court must comply with its responsibility to give a judgment consistent with the Convention, having regard to the principles set out above, in particular whether the principle of proportionality has been satisfied[1].

1   See para **3.10** above.

Chapter 4

The European Convention on Human Rights

4.1

Article 1 Obligation to respect human rights

The High Contracting Parties shall secure to everyone within their jurisdiction the rights and freedoms defined in Section 1 of this Convention
---

4.1.1 Article 1 obliges the contracting states to secure to everyone within their jurisdiction, without limitation to citizens or permanent residents, the rights and freedoms protected by the Convention. State responsibility is therefore invoked under the Convention if the violation of a Convention right or freedom arises as the result of the state's failure to secure that right or freedom in its domestic law[1].

1   See eg *Costello-Roberts v United Kingdom* (1993) 19 EHRR 112, E Ct HR, para 26.

4.1.2 The concept of 'jurisdiction' under art 1 is not restricted to the national territory of the contracting states. A state's responsibility can be invoked as a result of acts or omissions by its public authorities which produce effects outside its own territory. For example, responsibility can arise when as a result of military action, whether lawful or unlawful, a state exercises effective control of an area outside its national territory[1]. The obligation to secure Convention rights and freedoms in such an area derives from the fact of such control, whether it be exercised directly through its armed forces, or through a subordinate local administration[2].

1   See eg *Loizidou v Turkey* (1996) 23 EHRR 513, E Ct HR, para 52.
2   *Loizidou v Turkey (Preliminary Objections)* (1995) 20 EHRR 99, E Ct HR, para 62.

4.1.3 Article 1 requires contracting states to secure directly the Convention rights and freedoms but, even though incorporation is a particularly faithful reflection of the object and purpose of art 1, that provision does not require states to incorporate the Convention rights and freedoms into their domestic law. In practice, however, every contracting state has now incorporated the convention rights into their domestic law, except Ireland some of whose constitutional provisions on fundamental rights mirror the rights and freedoms protected by the Convention.

4.1.4 A state may satisfy art 1 by ensuring, in whatever manner it chooses, that its law and practice secure the rights and freedoms[1]. A violation of art 1 follows automatically from, but adds nothing to, a breach of any of the Convention rights and freedoms. Article 1 does not therefore confer enforceable rights upon individuals (as distinct from other contracting states) to complain of a breach of the obligation to secure Convention rights and freedoms. Such claims may, however, arise because of a breach of the right of access to a court (under art 6[2]) or of a failure to provide an effective national remedy (under art 13[3]).

1   *Ireland v United Kingdom* (1978) 2 EHRR 25, E Ct HR, paras 238–240.
2   See para **4.6**.
3   See para **4.13**.

Article 2 Right to life

1. Everyone's right to life shall be protected by law. No one shall be deprived of his life intentionally save in the execution of a sentence of a court following his conviction of a crime for which this penalty is provided by law.

2. Deprivation of life shall not be regarded as inflicted in contravention of this article when it results from the use of force, which is no more than absolutely necessary:

(a) in defence of any person from unlawful violence;

(b) in order to effect a lawful arrest or to prevent the escape of a person lawfully detained;

(c) in action lawfully taken for the purpose of quelling a riot or insurrection.

The Sixth Protocol Abolition of the death penalty

1. The death penalty shall be abolished. No one shall be condemned to such penalty or executed.

2. A State may make provision in its law for the death penalty in respect of acts committed in time of war or of imminent threat of war; such penalty shall be applied only in the instances laid down in the law and in accordance with its provisions. The State shall communicate to the Secretary-General of the Council of Europe the relevant provision of that law.

A General considerations

4.2.1 Article 2 is recognised as one of the most important rights in the Convention. According to the E Ct HR, it is a 'fundamental' right which, together with art 3, 'enshrines one of the basic values of the democratic societies making up the Council of Europe'[1]. The Inter-American Commission on Human Rights has also described the right to life as 'fundamental'[2] while the UN Human Rights Committee, in its General Comment on the equivalent provision in the ICCPR[3], describes the right as a 'supreme right' and a right 'basic to all human rights'[4].

---

1   *McCann v United Kingdom* (1996) 21 EHRR 97, E Ct HR, para 147 and *Andronicou and Constantinou v Cyprus* (1997) 25 EHRR 491, E Ct HR, para 171.

2   (1986-87) IA Comm HR Annual Report 271. On the right to life generally in the Inter-American system, see Davidson *The Civil and Political Rights Protected in the Inter-American Human Rights System* in Harris and Livingstone (eds) *The Inter-American System of Human Rights* (1998) at 214–225.

3   See ICCPR, art 6. On art 6 generally, see McGoldrick *The Human Rights Committee: Its Role in the Development of the International Covenant on Civil and Political Rights* (1994) at pages 328–361.

4   See General Comment 14, reproduced in (1994) 1 IHRR 15–16, confirming earlier General Comment 6, reproduced in (1994) 1 IHRR 4–5.

4.2.2 The interpretation of the right to life must be guided by the fact that the object and purpose of the Convention as an instrument for the protection of individual human beings requires its provisions to be interpreted and applied so as to make its safeguards practical and effective[1]. Article 2 however not only safeguards the right to life but also sets out the circumstances when the deprivation of life may be justified. These circumstances must be strictly construed in light of the fundamental nature of the right at stake[2] and the fact that no derogation from art 2 is permitted in peacetime[3].

1   *McCann v United Kingdom* (1995) 21 EHRR 97, E Ct HR, para 146; *Soering v United Kingdom* (1989) 11 EHRR 439, E Ct HR, para 89 and *Loizidou v Turkey* (1995) 20 EHRR 99, E Ct HR, para 72. See para **3.08**.
2   *McCann v United Kingdom* (1995) 21 EHRR 97, E Ct HR, para 147 and *Soering v United Kingdom* (1989) 11 EHRR 439, E Ct HR, para 88.
3   Art 15(2) permits derogation in respect of deaths resulting from lawful acts of war. See para **2.14.1**.

4.2.3   Article 2(1) places on the state both a positive duty to safeguard the lives of those within its jurisdiction and a negative duty to refrain from the intentional and unlawful taking of life[1]. The second sentence of art 2(1) facilitates the retention of the death penalty[2].

1   *LCB v United Kingdom* (1998) 27 EHRR 212, E Ct HR, para 36 and Application 7154/75 *Association X v United Kingdom* 14 DR 32 (1987), EComHR.
2   On the death penalty, see paras **4.2.24–4.2.26**.

4.2.4   Article 2(2) provides an exhaustive list of the three situations where the use of force resulting in the deprivation of life is permitted. According to the E Ct HR, this paragraph does not primarily define instances where it is permitted intentionally to kill an individual, but describes the situations where it is permitted to 'use force' which may result, as an unintended outcome, in the deprivation of life[1]. The use of force, however, must be no more than 'absolutely necessary' for the achievement of one of the purposes set out in sub-paras (a), (b) or (c)[2]. The use of the adverb 'absolutely' indicates that a stricter and more compelling test of necessity must be applied under art 2 than the proportionality test used in relation to other Convention articles[3].

1   *McCann v United Kingdom* (1995) 21 EHRR 97, E Ct HR, para 148. See also Application 10044/82 *Stewart v United Kingdom* 39 DR 162 (1984), EComHR.
2   *McCann v United Kingdom* (1995) 21 EHRR 97, E Ct HR, para 148 and Application 10044/82 *Stewart v United Kingdom* 39 DR 162 (1984), EComHR at 169–171.
3   *McCann v United Kingdom* (1995) 21 EHRR 97, E Ct HR, para 149 and *Andronicou and Constantinou v Cyprus* (1997) 25 EHRR 491, E Ct HR, para 171.

4.2.5   Complaints under art 2 are most often bought by a deceased's spouse or child[1]. Other close relatives may also be granted standing to bring a claim under art 2 both in their own right (as persons affected by the death) and in the name of the deceased. In *Yasa v Turkey*[2] the E Ct HR held that a deceased's nephew had the necessary standing, even though he was not joined in his complaint by other closer relatives. The court agreed with the Commission's Delegate that 'if a relative wished to complain about a question as serious as the murder of one of his close relations, that ought to suffice to show that he felt personally concerned by the incident'[3] and, on the facts, concluded that the nephew could legitimately claim to be a victim of an act as tragic as the murder of his uncle. Potential relatives may also, in certain circumstances, be considered a victim provided they are closely affected[4].

1   See, for example, *Osman v United Kingdom* [1999] 1 FLR 193, E Ct HR, where a son brought a claim under art 2 in his own right, having been wounded in the attack, and on behalf of his deceased father.
2   Case No 63/1997/847/1054 (2 September 1998, unreported), E Ct HR.

3   *Yasa v Turkey*, Case No 63/1997/847/1054 (2 September 1998, unreported), E Ct HR, para 66, read with para 63.
4   See *Paton v United Kingdom* (1981) 3 EHRR 408, EComHR, where a potential father was so closely affected by the termination of his wife's pregnancy that he was able to claim to be a victim.

B   Scope of article 2

4.2.6   Article 2 may give rise to positive, as well as negative, obligations on the part of the state[1]. However, as with all positive duties to ensure rights, a court will be likely to accord a broad discretion to a national legislature in fulfilling its positive duty to protect life given the political and operational choices that must be made in terms of priorities and resources.

1   *McCann v United Kingdom* (1995) 21 EHRR 97, E Ct HR, para 184 and Application 9438/81 *W v United Kingdom* 32 DR 190 (1983) at 200, EComHR.

4.2.7   A variety of complaints have been raised under art 2, including a possible but not indefinite requirement for police protection for terrorist targets[1]. The Commission has also considered, without deciding, whether art 2 obliges a state to impose a legal duty on members of the public to assist in an emergency[2] and whether art 2 may be applicable to the eviction of a vulnerable person from her home[3]. In most cases however the Commission has found that the steps taken by the state were, in all the circumstances, adequate, thereby avoiding any liability under art 2.

1   See Application 9438/81 *W v United Kingdom* 32 DR 190 (1983), EComHR.
2   Application 11590/85 *Hughes v United Kingdom* 48 DR 258 (1986), EComHR.
3   Application 5207/71 *X v Federal Republic of Germany* 14 YB 698 (1971), EComHR.

4.2.8   A state's obligation to secure the right to life also requires it to put in place effective criminal law provisions to deter the commission of offences against the person, backed by the law-enforcement machinery necessary for the prevention, suppression and sanctioning of any breaches of these provisions[1]. However, in *Dujardin v France*[2] the Commission found that an amnesty law adopted in New Caledonia which resulted in the discontinuance of prosecutions for murder did not infringe art 2 when the protection of the individual's right to life was weighed against the state's legitimate interests. The Commission found that an amnesty for the crime of murder does not in itself contravene the Convention unless it can be seen to form part of a general practice aimed at the systematic prevention of prosecution of the perpetrators of such crimes[3].

1   *Osman v United Kingdom* [1999] 1 FLR 193, E Ct HR, para 115.
2   Application 16734/90 72 DR 236 (1992), EComHR.
3   Application No 16734/90 *Dujardin v France* 72 DR 236 (1992) at 240, EComHR.

4.2.9   It is not always necessary that death should have actually occurred in order for art 2 to be engaged. A threat or attempt may be sufficient[1]. In *Osman v United Kingdom*[2] the E Ct HR was concerned with the alleged failure of the police to take the necessary steps to protect a family who had been repeatedly threatened and intimidated by the mentally disturbed teacher of one of their children. The teacher shot the father dead and seriously wounded the child. The court had no difficulty in recognising the potential application of art 2 to the surviving family members but, on the facts of the case, it found no violation. In the view of the court, the applicants had failed to point to any decisive stage in the sequence of events leading to the shooting when it could be said that the police knew or ought to have known that the lives of the Osman family were at real and immediate risk from the criminal acts of a third party[3].

1   But see Application 26985/95 *Poku v United Kingdom* (15 May 1996, unreported), discussed at para **4.2.18**.
2   [1999] 1 FLR 193, E Ct HR.
3   *Osman v United Kingdom* [1999] 1 FLR 193, E Ct HR, paras 116 and 121.

4.2.10   Although the scope for art 2 is theoretically very broad, both the E Ct HR and Commission have been reluctant to find a state in violation of its positive obligations under art 2. There is a tendency for the E Ct HR and Commission to consider the application of other articles of the Convention, thereby making it unnecessary to adjudicate on the art 2 claim[1].

1   See for example *Brüggeman and Scheuten v Federal Republic of Germany* (1981) 3 EHRR 244, EComHR where an abortion case was decided under the rubric of art 8 and *D v United Kingdom* (1997) 24 EHRR 423, E Ct HR where the withdrawal of life-sustaining treatment as a consequence of expulsion was decided under art 3.

C   Medical care and attention

4.2.11   The positive nature of the obligation in art 2 raises the question of a state's duty to provide the health care necessary to save life. This issue was raised in *X v Ireland*[1] but it was held unnecessary to determine the appropriate level of health care since the applicant had in fact received treatment and her life had not been endangered. A similar complaint was raised in *Association X v United Kingdom*[2] in relation to the steps taken by a state to reduce the risks to life by introducing a vaccination programme for children. The Commission accepted that a state was under an obligation to take adequate measures to protect life and suggested that this might raise issues with respect to the adequacy of medical care[3]. However, on the facts of the case before it, the Commission found no evidence to suggest that the vaccinations had been administered poorly or that proper steps had not been taken to minimise any risks[4].

1   Application 6839/74 7 DR 78 (1974), EComHR concerning the denial of a medical card for a severely disabled woman which would have provided free medical care.
2   Application 7154/75 14 DR 31 (1978), EComHR.
3   Application 7154/75 *Association X v United Kingdom* 14 DR 31 (1978) at 32, EComHR.
4   Negligence will be a relevant factor: see Application 28323/95 *Buckley v United Kingdom* 26 February 1997, summarised in (1997) 23 EHRR CD 129, where the administration of drugs in circumstances leading to a patient's death did not disclose grounds for negligence in domestic law, thereby prompting the Commission to find the art 2 complaint to be manifestly ill-founded. However, there is likely to be no need to establish gross negligence or wilful disregard for life given the E Ct HR's comments, albeit in a policing context, in *Osman v United Kingdom* [1999] 1 FLR 193, E Ct HR, para 116.

4.2.12   The UN Human Rights Committee has also recognised a connection between the right to life and a state's obligation to provide medical care. In its General Comment on the right to life, the Committee urged all state parties to take all possible measures to reduce infant mortality and to increase life expectancy, especially in adopting measures to eliminate malnutrition and epidemics[1].

1   UN Human Rights Committee, General Comment 6, reprinted in (1994) 1 IHRR 4–5, para 5.

4.2.13   A successful complaint under art 2 is however highly unlikely in relation to the general standard of health care available, the financial arrangements for such care, and the policies governing its organisation and delivery within the state. Under the doctrine of the margin of appreciation, it is the place of national courts to determine compliance with the Convention given their direct and continuous contact with the vital forces of the responsible state[1]. Domestically, the courts have taken the view that they cannot make judgments about how health authorities decide to allocate a limited budget, even when a child's brief life expectancy is in issue[2]. Only an exceptional case will dislodge the deference accorded to a state's decision on how best to allocate scarce resources.

1   *Handyside v United Kingdom* (1976) 1 EHRR 737, E Ct HR, paras 48–49. See para **3.20**.
2   *R v Cambridge Health Authority, ex p B* [1995] 1 WLR 898, CA. See also James and Longley 'Judicial Review and Tragic Choices' [1995] PL 367 and O'Sullivan 'The allocation of scarce resources and the right to life under the ECHR' [1998] PL 389. For comparative jurisprudence, see the decision of the South African Constitutional Court in *Soobramoney v Minister of Health (KwaZulu-Natal)* (1998) 4 BHRC 308, concerning the refusal of dialysis treatment due to insufficient hospital resources.

4.2.14   In *D v United Kingdom*[1] the E Ct HR considered a case of exceptional circumstances arising within a deportation context. The case concerned the proposed expulsion of a convicted drug trafficker in the terminal stages of AIDS to a country where it was accepted that the absence of vital medical treatment would rapidly accelerate his death. Both the E Ct HR and the Commission however found it unnecessary to decide whether the risk to the applicant's life expectancy created by his expulsion disclosed a breach of art 2, preferring instead to address this allegation as it related to the applicant's complaint of inhuman treatment under art 3[2]. A violation of art 3 was found but the E Ct HR laid much emphasis on the exceptional circumstances of the particular case and the compelling humanitarian considerations at stake[3].

1   (1997) 24 EHRR 423, E Ct HR.
2   *D v United Kingdom* (1997) 24 EHRR 423, E Ct HR, paras 58 and 59. In a similar case involving the return of an AIDS sufferer to a country where no medical treatment would be available, the respondent state undertook not to deport the individual thereby avoiding a violation of the Convention: Application 30930/96 *BB v France* (7 September 1998, unreported), E Ct HR.
3   *D v United Kingdom* (1997) 24 EHRR 423, E Ct HR, paras 50–54.

4.2.15   The medical care given in prison may also attract a complaint under art 2[1] although a claim under art 3 is more common.

1   Application 4340/69 *Simon-Herold v Austria* 14 YB 698 (1971), EComHR.

D   Unborn children

4.2.16   Under UK law, an unborn child has no existence separate from its mother[1] nor is it a person for the purposes of the law of murder and manslaughter[2]. An unborn child may also be aborted in the United Kingdom under the terms of the Abortion Act 1967.

1   *Re F (in utero)* [1988] Fam 122, CA. See *St George's Healthcare National Health Service Trust* [1998] 3 WLR 936 at 957A, CA.
2   *A-G's Reference (No 3 of 1994)* [1998] AC 245, HL.

4.2.17   No consensus exists across Europe on the issue of abortion, and given the difficult moral and ethical issues involved, the Strasbourg organs have been understandably reluctant to pronounce substantively on whether the protection in art 2 for 'everyone' extends to an unborn child[1]. In light of the differing national laws, a state will have a broad margin of appreciation with regard to the Convention on the issue of abortion[2].

1   Contrast with article 4 of the American Convention on Human Rights 1969 which expressly protects the right, 'in general, from the moment of conception'. See also the *Baby Boy* case, (1980-81) IA Com HR Annual Report 25, reprinted in (1981) 2 HRLJ 110, and Shelton, 'Abortion and the Right to Life in the Inter-American System' (1980) 1 HRLJ 316. Contrast with the position of the Supreme Court of Canada that the common law does not recognise the unborn child as a legal or juridical person possessing rights: *Winnipeg Child and Family Services (Northwest Area) v G* [1997] 3 SCR 925.
2   Application 17004/90 *H v Norway* 73 DR 155 (1992), EComHR.

4.2.18   An illustration of the Commission's view can be found in *Paton v United Kingdom*[1] where it was held that the termination of a 10-week foetus to protect the health of the mother did not breach art 2[2]. The Commission however left open the question of whether this was because the foetus was not included in the word 'everyone' or because, if included, its rights were not absolute and on the facts were subject to permissible limitations[3]. More recently, in *Poku v United Kingdom*[4], an application was made under art 2 on behalf of a third trimester unborn child whose life was threatened by the mother's imminent deportation from the UK because of a risk to the pregnancy from severe complications. The Commission found the art 2 claim to be inadmissible because the mother had not been deported, following an initial request by the Commission to the government, and so the child had in fact been born alive. The Commission therefore found it unnecessary to rule expressly as to the admissibility of a complaint initiated by a child whilst still unborn.

1   (1981) 3 EHRR 408, EComHR.
2   See Application 17004/90 *H v Norway* 73 DR 155 (1992), EComHR. Compare *Roe v Wade* 410 US 113 (1973) and *R v Morgentaler* [1988] 1 SCR 30, Supreme Court of Canada.
3   See also *Brüggeman and Scheuten v Federal Republic of Germany* (1981) 3 EHRR 244, EComHR, where the issue was avoided by deciding the case under art 8 and Application 17004/90 *H v Norway* 73 DR 155 (1992), EComHR, where the Commission noted that the laws on abortion differed considerably and accorded the state a degree of discretion in determining its obligation to protect life in the context of abortion.
4   Application 26985/95 (15 May 1996, unreported).

4.2.19   The E Ct HR has yet to decide whether the term 'everyone' includes an unborn child. In *Open Door Counselling and Dublin Well Woman v Ireland*[1] the Commission had recognised the possibility that art 2 might in certain circumstances offer protection to an unborn child, but took the point no further, and the E Ct HR offered no guidance.

1   (1992) 15 EHRR 244, E Ct HR.

4.2.20   These cases do not necessarily exclude the application of art 2 to an unborn child in a non-abortion context. In *Mentes v Turkey*[1] an art 2 claim was made by a woman who had given birth prematurely to twins, who later died, following her forced eviction from her village by the state security forces. The E Ct HR however could not decide the issue since the claim lacked substantiation because the claimant had failed to give evidence before the Commission.

1   (1997) 26 EHRR 595, E Ct HR.

E Euthanasia

4.2.21 A lack of consensus among the member states of the Council of Europe also exists on the issue of euthanasia. Neither the European Commission nor the E Ct HR has so far given a substantive ruling on this issue and a wide margin of appreciation is likely in light of the variance in state practice.

4.2.22 It is clear from the wording of art 2(1) that there is little room to reject in principle a case brought by the relatives of a deceased complaining that a life had been deliberately terminated. What is less clear is what the content of the relevant law must be, taking into account the state's margin of appreciation[1]. Nor is it clear how the deceased's rights under art 2 are to be balanced against the prohibition on inhuman and degrading treatment under art 3 or the right to 'moral and physical integrity' in art 8. In *D v United Kingdom*[2] the E Ct HR emphasised, albeit within the context of art 3, the importance of dying in dignity, but although the art 2 complaint was declared admissible both the Commission and the E Ct HR declined to rule on it substantively. Nothing can at present be extrapolated from the Strasbourg case law to suggest that the life of a person in a persistent vegetative state is outside the protection of the first sentence of art 2(1)[3] or that the termination of life falls within the exceptions set out in either art 2(1) or art 2(2). However, this article does not stipulate that everyone has the right to life, only the right to have that right protected by law[4].

1   The Commission has held that art 2 does not require passive euthanasia to be a crime. Passive euthanasia is when a person is allowed to die by not being given treatment: see Application 20527/92 *Widmer v Switzerland* unreported, but cited in Harris, O'Boyle and Warbrick *Law of the European Convention on Human Rights* (1995) at p 38, note 7.
2   (1997) 24 EHRR 423, E Ct HR.
3   See *Airedale National Health Service Trust v Bland* [1993] AC 789, HL. See also *In the matter of a ward of court* [1995] 2 ILRM 401, Irish Supreme Court, which permitted the withdrawal of tube feeding from a patient who was not in a persistent vegetative state and retained some cognitive function, and *Re G* [1997] 4 LRC 146, New Zealand High Court.
4   Contrast with ICCPR, art 6 which provides that 'Every human being has the inherent right to life. This right shall be protected by law. No-one shall be arbitrarily deprived of his life'. Nowak *CCPR Commentary* (1993) at pp 124–125: 'If a national legislature limits criminal responsibility here after carefully weighing all affected rights and takes adequate precautions against potential abuse, this is within the scope of the legislature's discretion in carrying out its duty to ensure the right.'

4.2.23 The question arises whether the right can be violated if death is the express wish of the individual concerned[1]. In the vagrancy cases[2], the E Ct HR noted that the fact that a person gave himself up to the police for detention did not mean that he was not entitled to the guarantees in art 5: 'The right to liberty is too important in a democratic society ... for a person to lose the benefit of the Convention for the single reason that he gives himself up to be taken into detention. Detention might violate article 5 even though the person concerned might have agreed to it.'[3]. It could however be argued that a person's consent to the termination of their own life takes the matter outside art 2.

1   For comparative jurisprudence, see the Supreme Court of Canada's decision in *Rodriguez v A-G of British Columbia* [1993] 3 SCR 519, the US Supreme Court's decision in *Washington v Glucksberg* (1997) 2 BHRC 539 and the Indian Supreme Court's decision in *Gian Kaur v State of Punjab* [1996] 2 LRC 264.
2   *De Wilde, Ooms and Versyp v Belgium* (1971) 1 EHRR 373, E Ct HR.
3   *De Wilde, Ooms and Versyp v Belgium* (1971) 1 EHRR 373, E Ct HR, para 65.

F   The death penalty

4.2.24   Article 2(1) expressly provides for the continued use of the death penalty[1]. However a state which ratifies the sixth protocol must abolish the death penalty in peacetime. The United Kingdom ratified the sixth protocol on 27 January 1999 and 'Convention rights' under the HRA 1998 expressly include the substantive rights in the sixth protocol[2].

1   For a complete study of the institution of the death penalty under international, European and Inter-American law, see Schabas *The Abolition of the Death Penalty in International Law* (2nd edn, 1997).
2   See paras **2.1.1** and **2.21**.

4.2.25   The sixth protocol prohibits both the passing of death sentences and actual executions. It permits no derogation and can only be ratified without reservation. Its application is, however, limited to times of peace. Under the terms of the sixth protocol, a state party may still make provision in its laws for the death penalty in time of war or imminent threat of war, provided that the law lays down the instances in which the death penalty may be applied and that the relevant provisions are communicated to the Secretary General of the Council of Europe[1]. Such provisions may be adopted post-ratification provided notification occurs in the proper way. Unlike art 15(1), which refers to 'war or other public emergency threatening the life of the nation', the sixth protocol refers to 'war or imminent threat of war' presumably to indicate a narrower scope of application.

1   Contrast with the *Second Optional Protocol* to the ICCPR and the *Second Protocol* to the American Convention on Human Rights 1969 which abolish the death penalty in times of peace and war, but allow reservations for serious crimes of a military nature in wartime. A new additional protocol to abolish the death penalty in wartime was proposed by the Council of Europe's Parliamentary Assembly in Recommendation 1246 (1994). No action has as yet been taken. On art 15, see para **2.14.1**.

4.2.26   Reference to the sixth protocol in peacetime is most likely to be made in extradition or deportation cases where the receiving state still applies the death penalty. The leading E Ct HR decision is *Soering v United Kingdom*[1] where the proposed extradition of a German national to face capital charges in the US had to be considered under art 3 in the light of the inhuman and degrading treatment which prisoners are likely to suffer on death row since the UK was not yet a party to the sixth protocol. Future extradition and deportation cases involving the UK will, however, have to give effect to the sixth protocol's ratification. This will be likely to prevent the expulsion or extradition from the UK of any individual where there is an actual risk of the death penalty being applied to the individual concerned[2]. Death penalty states may, however, provide an assurance that the penalty will not be carried out in order to secure the extradition.

1   (1989) 11 EHRR 439, E Ct HR. In a deportation context, see *Cruz Varas v Sweden* (1991) 14 EHRR 1, E Ct HR.
2   The Commission declined to resolve this issue in Application 25342/94 *Raidl v Austria* 82-A DR 134 (1995) at 146, EComHR. But see the decision of the French Conseil d'Etat in *Aylor v France*, 15 October 1993, reprinted in (1994) 100 ILR 665 and the decision of the Netherlands Supreme Court in *Short v Netherlands* (1990) Rechtspraak van de Week 358, reprinted in (1990) 29 ILM 1378. See also the view of the UN Human Rights Committee on extradition from an abolitionist to a non-abolitionist state in *Kindler v Canada*, Communication No 470/1991, reported in (1994) 1 IHRR 98 and *Ng v Canada*, Communication No 469/1991, reported in (1992) 1 IHRR 161.

G   Extra-judicial killings

4.2.27   One of the primary aims of art 2 is to prohibit the execution of persons by the state outside the judicial process. However, where individuals have claimed that they would be at risk of extra-judicial killings on expulsion to a jurisdiction outside the Convention, the Commission and E Ct HR have normally examined the issue under art 3[1]. Nevertheless, the Commission has recognised since 1976[2] the possibility of liability under art 2 for a decision to expel someone in circumstances where there was a real risk of that person being killed in the recipient state. More recently, the Commission has declared admissible a complaint under arts 2 and 3 based on an applicant's fears that he would be at risk of an extra-judicial killing, among other forms of ill treatment, if he were returned to his home country[3].

1   See, for example, *Chahal v United Kingdom* (1997) 23 EHRR 413, E Ct HR; *Ahmed v Austria* (1997) 24 EHRR 278, E Ct HR; and *HLR v France* (1998) 26 EHRR 29, E Ct HR.
2   Application 7317/75 *Lynas v Switzerland* 6 DR 141 (1976), EComHR.
3   Application 28038/95 *MAR v United Kingdom* 16 January 1996, summarised in (1996) 23 EHRR CD 120, EComHR. A friendly settlement was later reached between the parties and accepted by the Commission on 19 September 1997. A possible art 2 claim was also raised in *Bahddar v Netherlands* (1998) 26 EHRR 278, E Ct HR, but failed for non-exhaustion of domestic remedies.

4.2.28   In the leading case under art 2, the E Ct HR was required to determine a state's liability following three extra-judicial killings which took place on the state's own territory. In *McCann v United Kingdom*[1] the E Ct HR was concerned with the killing by SAS soldiers of three suspected IRA terrorists who were believed to be planning to set off an explosion in Gibraltar. As this was a case where deliberate lethal force was used, the court subjected the deprivations of life to the most careful scrutiny, taking into consideration not only the actions of the agents of the state who actually administered the force but also all the surrounding circumstances, including such matters as the planning and control of the SAS operation[2]. The court accepted that the soldiers honestly believed, in light of the information given them by their superiors, that it was necessary to shoot the suspects in order to prevent them from detonating a bomb and causing serious loss of life[3]. Nevertheless, the court, by ten votes to nine, found the state in violation of art 2. Several factors influenced the court's ruling, including the fact that the authorities had decided to allow the suspects to enter Gibraltar when they could have arrested them at the border on suspicion of carrying a bomb. The court also noted that the soldiers had failed to consider that their intelligence assessment could be wrong with respect to the suspects' capacity to detonate a bomb from a distance and also observed that the soldiers had immediately used lethal force when they opened fire on the suspects. This reflex action, according to the court, lacked the 'degree of caution in the use of firearms to be expected from law enforcement personnel in a democratic society, even when dealing with dangerous terrorist suspects ... '[4] and so the E Ct HR was not persuaded that the use of force had been no more than absolutely necessary.

1   (1995) 21 EHRR 97, E Ct HR.
2   *McCann v United Kingdom* (1995) 21 EHRR 97, E Ct HR, para 151.
3   *McCann v United Kingdom* (1995) 21 EHRR 97, E Ct HR, para 200.
4   *McCann v United Kingdom* (1995) 21 EHRR 97, E Ct HR, para 212.

4.2.29   *McCann*[1] has since been applied by the E Ct HR to the killing of two people by a special police force following a failed attempt to rescue by negotiation one of the individuals who was being held hostage by the other[2]. The E Ct HR took note of the planning and control of the rescue operation but could find no evidence to show that the authorities had not taken appropriate care to ensure that any risk to the lives of the couple had been minimised[3]. The court also found that the authorities were not negligent in their choice of action, taking into account the circumstances, and concluded that the killing of the two people had resulted from a use of force which was no more than absolutely necessary to defend persons from unlawful violence[4].

1   *McCann v United Kingdom* (1995) 21 EHRR 97, E Ct HR.
2   *Andronicou and Constantinou v Cyprus* (1997) 25 EHRR 491, E Ct HR.
3   *Andronicou and Constantinou v Cyprus* (1997) 25 EHRR 491, E Ct HR, para 186.
4   *Andronicou and Constantinou v Cyprus* (1997) 25 EHRR 491, E Ct HR, para 194.

4.2.30   Several cases against Turkey have also applied the principles established in *McCann*[1] with respect to the application of art 2[2]. Proportionality has been a key factor. In *Güleç v Turkey*[3], the E Ct HR found that shots fired from armoured vehicles into a crowd of violent demonstrators constituted a disproportionate use of force, and accordingly a violation of art 2 was found. The E Ct HR was particularly influenced by the fact that the security forces had not been provided with any conventional equipment for dealing with disorder such as truncheons, riot shields, water cannons, rubber bullets[4] or tear gas, a fact made 'all the more incomprehensible and unacceptable' in light of the declared state of emergency[5]. In *Ogur v Turkey*[6] a violation of art 2 was found when security forces fired on a night watchman they suspected of being a terrorist. The security forces were not in danger at the time and the Commission was particularly concerned by the absence of a verbal warning or a warning shot before the fatal blow.

1   *McCann v United Kingdom* (1995) 21 EHRR 97, E Ct HR.
2   See *Kaya v Turkey*, 1998-I No 65, 19 February 1998, E Ct HR; *Kurt v Turkey*, Case No 15/1997/
     799/1002, 25 May 1998, E Ct HR; *Mentes v Turkey* (1997) 26 EHRR 595, E Ct HR; *Ergi v
     Turkey*, Case No 66/1997/850/1057, 28 July 1998, E Ct HR; *Güleç v Turkey*, Case No 54/1997/
     838/1044, 27 July 1998, E Ct HR; and *Yasa v Turkey*, Case No 63/1997/847/1054, 2 September
     1998, E Ct HR.
3   Case No 54/1997/838/1044, 27 July 1998, E Ct HR.
4   On the use of plastic bullets or 'baton rounds', see Jason-Lloyd 'Plastic Bullets on the Mainland'
     (1990) 140 NLJ 1492 and Robertson 'Baton Rounds in 39 DR 162 (1984) concerning the death
     of the applicant's son after being hit on the head by a plastic bullet fired into a crowd of rioters.
5   *Güleç v Turkey*, Case No 54/1997/838/1044, 27 July 1998, E Ct HR, para 71.
6   Application 21594/93 (30 October 1997, unreported), EComHR.

H   Procedural safeguards

4.2.31   The E Ct HR has attached particular weight to the procedural safeguards implicit in art 2. The absence of these procedural safeguards may constitute a violation of art 2 even where there is insufficient evidence, or it would be otherwise inappropriate, to hold the state responsible for the actual death or risk to life that has occurred.

4.2.32   Whenever there is a deprivation of the right to life through the use of lethal force, a state has a duty to carry out an adequate and effective investigation. As the E Ct HR held in *McCann v United Kingdom*[1], the obligation to protect the right to life under art 2, read in conjunction with a state's general obligation under art 1 to secure to everyone within its jurisdiction the rights and freedoms defined in the Convention, requires by implication that there should be some form of effective official investigation when individuals have been killed as a result of the use of force[2]. This obligation is not confined to killings caused by agents of the state. Nor is it decisive whether members of the deceased's family or others have lodged a formal complaint about the killing with the competent investigatory authority. As the E Ct HR held in *Ergi v Turkey*[3], the mere knowledge of the killing on the part of the authorities can give rise to an obligation under art 2 to carry out an effective investigation into the circumstances surrounding the death[4].

1 (1995) 21 EHRR 97, E Ct HR.
2 *McCann v United Kingdom* (1995) 21 EHRR 97, E Ct HR, para 161. See also *Kaya v Turkey*, 1998-I No 65, 19 February 1998, E Ct HR, paras 78 and 86.
3 Case No 66/1997/850/1057, 28 July 1998, E Ct HR.
4 *Ergi v Turkey*, Case No 66/1997/850/1057, 28 July 1998, E Ct HR, para 82.

4.2.33 In some of the recent cases against Turkey, the absence of procedural safeguards has led to a violation of art 2 even when the applicants have failed to provide the E Ct HR with sufficient factual and evidentiary material to conclude that the deceased was intentionally killed by the state. Often these cases have involved deaths as a result of clashes with the security forces. In *Kaya v Turkey*[1] the E Ct HR could not conclude on the evidence presented that the deceased had been intentionally killed by the security forces, but held that the investigation into the death was so inadequate that it amounted to a failure to protect the right to life thereby violating article 2[2]. The E Ct HR was particularly critical of the public prosecutor's role:

'As an independent investigating official he should have been alert to the need to collect evidence at the scene, to make his own independent reconstruction of the events and to satisfy himself that the deceased, despite being dressed as a typical farmer, was in fact a terrorist as alleged ... It cannot be maintained that the perfunctory nature of the autopsy performed or the findings recorded in the report could lay the basis for any effective follow-up investigation or indeed satisfy even the minimum requirements of an investigation into a clear-cut case of lawful killing since it left too many critical questions unanswered'[3].

1 *Kaya v Turkey*, 1998-I No 65, 19 February 1998, E Ct HR.
2 See also *Yasa v Turkey*, Case No 63/1997/847/1054, 2 September 1998, E Ct HR. But see *Aytekin v Turkey*, Case No 102/1997/886/1098, 23 September 1998, E Ct HR where the E Ct HR rejected a complaint about the adequacy of an investigation because of the non-exhaustion of domestic remedies.
3 *Kaya v Turkey*, 1998-I No 65, 19 February 1998, E Ct HR, para 89.

4.2.34 The requirements for an adequate investigation will however vary with the circumstances of each particular case. In a case concerning a series of murders by a hospital nurse, the Commission found that the prosecution of the nurse, the possibility of civil proceedings against the health authority, and the publication of the findings of a private enquiry into the procedures at fault were sufficient to meet the procedural requirements inherent in art 2[1].

1 See Application 23412/94 *Taylor v United Kingdom* 79-A DR 127 (1994), EComHR.

I Deaths in custody

4.2.35 Article 2 issues may also arise in connection with the investigation of deaths in custody. In relation to art 3, the E Ct HR has found that where someone has been injured whilst in custody, it is incumbent on the state to provide a plausible explanation as to the cause of that injury[1]. The burden is placed not on the victim or his representatives to identify the cause or author of the injury, but on the state to explain how the injuries occurred. This principle should apply a fortiori to art 2 when a death in custody occurs. As yet, the E Ct HR has not been required to decide this issue, but the Commission has declared admissible a claim under art 2 concerning the death in prison of a young man suffering from a chronic mental illness who was a known suicide risk[2]. The prisoner had been placed in a segregation unit in the punishment block rather than a hospital wing and the relatives allege that there were no effective procedural safeguards available in respect of the measures taken against the deceased.

1   See *Ribbitsch v Austria* (1995) 21 EHRR 573, E Ct HR and *Aksoy v Turkey* (1997) 23 EHRR 553, E Ct HR.
2   Application 27229/95 *Keenan v United Kingdom* 93-A DR 45 (1998), summarised in (1998) 26 EHRR CD 64, EComHR.

4.2.36   The E Ct HR has recently considered the issue of 'disappearances' following the taking of individuals into custody[1]. Disappearances constitute a serious violation of the right to life given the secrecy of the killing, followed by the concealment or elimination of any material evidence to ensure the impunity of those responsible. However, in *Kurt v Turkey*[2], the E Ct HR required the production of 'concrete evidence' which would lead it to conclude that the individual concerned was, beyond a reasonable doubt, killed by the authorities in order to ground a violation under art 2[3]. This differs from the approach taken by the Inter-American Court of Human Rights in disappearance cases. In the *Velásquez Rodríguez* case[4], the Inter-American Court would not allow the state to rely on the defence that the complainant had failed to present evidence when such evidence could not be obtained without the state's co-operation[5].

1   *Kurt v Turkey*, Case No 15/1997/799/1002, 25 May 1998, E Ct HR. Similar claims have arisen before the Commission in relation to Turkey's invasion of Cyprus in 1974: see for example *Cyprus v Turkey* (1983) 4 EHRR 482, EComHR. See also *Vernave, Loizides v Turkey* (1998) 25 EHRR CD 9, EComHR, concerning a state's continuing obligation to account for the fate of 'missing persons'. The Inter-American Commission takes a similar view: see for example Cases 2488 and 3482 in 1980-81 IA Comm HR Annual Report 19-25 concerning the continuing obligation for disappeared persons in Argentina.
2   Case No 15/1997/799/1002, 25 May 1998, E Ct HR.
3   *Kurt v Turkey*, Case No 15/1997/799/1002, 25 May 1998, E Ct HR, para 107.
4   Series C No 4, reprinted in (1988) 9 HRLJ 212, IA Ct HR.
5   *Velásquez Rodríguez*, Series C No 4, reprinted in (1988) 9 HRLJ 212, IA Ct HR, paras 134–135.

4.2.37   Disappearances can also raise procedural issues if the investigative authorities have been unable or unwilling, possibly because of political intimidation, to carry out their functions in the proper manner. In both *Mojica v Dominican Republic*[1] and *Laureano Atachahua v Peru*[2] the UN Human Rights Committee held that states should take 'specific and effective measures to prevent the disappearance of individuals and establish effective facilities and procedures to investigate thoroughly, by an appropriate and impartial body, cases of missing and disappeared persons in circumstances which may involve a violation of the right to life'[3]. In *Ogur v Turkey*[4] the European Commission found a violation of the procedural safeguards required by art 2 when the investigation of a death was carried out by a member of the police who belonged to the same 'administrative hierarchy' as the security forces whose conduct was being investigated.

1   Communication No 449/1991, reprinted in [1995] 2 IHRR 86, UNHRC, para 5.5.
2   Communication No 540/1993, reprinted in (1997) 1 BHRC 338, UNHRC, para 8.3.

3   See also General Comment 6, reprinted in (1994) 1 IHRR 4, UNHRC, para 4.
4   Application 21594/93 (30 October 1997, unreported), EComHR.

J   Environmental hazards

4.2.38   A state's obligation under art 2 may also include a duty to protect the general public from life-threatening hazards present in the environment, insofar as such hazards can be attributed to the state[1]. Other than in excpetional circumstances, causation will be very difficult to establish, and a high degree of discretion is likely to be accorded to the steps that were taken by the state to regulate the hazard in light of the known risks. The test to be applied is whether, given the circumstances of the case, the state did all that could have been required of it to prevent a life from being avoidably put at risk[2].

1   Consider, for example, the right to life issues raised by the Bhopal gas leak disaster in India and the subsequent litigation: *Charan Lal Sahu v Union of India* [1990] LRC (Const) 638, Indian Supreme Court and *Indian Council for Enviro-Legal Action v Union of India* [1996] 2 LRC 226, Indian Supreme Court.
2   *LCB v United Kingdom* (1998) 27 EHRR 212, E Ct HR, para 36.

4.2.39   In *LCB v United Kingdom*[1] the E Ct HR considered a claim under art 2 brought by a woman diagnosed with leukaemia, allegedly caused by her father's exposure to radiation while serving with the Royal Air Force during the nuclear tests that were conducted on Christmas Island in the late 1950s. Since these tests were conducted before the UK's acceptance of the right of individual petition under the Convention, the daughter could not successfully attack the exposure to radiation itself[2]. However, she also alleged that the state had failed in its duty to warn and advise her parents or monitor her health prior to the diagnosis of leukaemia. The E Ct HR dismissed the claim on the ground that no causal link had been established between the father's exposure to radiation and the daughter's illness, but its judgment confirms that the state could have been required to take steps to warn and advise if it had appeared likely at the time that the irradiation of the father would endanger the health of a daughter not yet conceived[3].

1   (1998) 27 EHRR 212, E Ct HR.
2   See also *McGinley and Egan v United Kingdom* (1998) 27 EHRR 1, E Ct HR.
3   *LCB v United Kingdom* (1998) 27 EHRR 212, E Ct HR, paras 38 and 40.

4.2.40   Such claims may also be decided under another article of the Convention instead of art 2. In *Guerra v Italy*[1] a claim was made concerning the Convention liability for illegal toxic emissions from a factory which resulted in 150 people being admitted to hospital with acute arsenic poisoning. Since some of the workers from the factory had died of cancer, the applicants argued that the state's failure to provide information about the risks was a violation of art 2. The E Ct HR, however, found it unnecessary to consider the case under art 2 since it had found that the absence of information about living near the factory breached the applicants' rights to respect for their private and family life under art 8 of the Convention[2].

1   (1998) 26 EHRR 357, E Ct HR.
2   *Guerra v Italy* (1998) 26 ECHR 357, E Ct HR, para 62. On art 8 and the environment, see para **4.8.39**.

4.2.41   As modern medicine and science evolve to bring to the attention of both the public and government the dangers present in our environment, it is likely that new and possibly more creative grounds for complaint may arise under art 2. The dangers of passive smoking, for example, may in future form the basis for a complaint, although again success would be unlikely, in light of the margin of appreciation to be given to the state, particularly if the state has taken some steps towards the regulation of the harm[1].

1   See Application 32165/96 *Wockel v Germany* 93-A DR 82 (1998), summarised in (1997) 25 EHRR CD 156 where the Commission found a passive smoking complaint in relation to a public bus service to be manifestly unfounded. See also *Barratt v United Kingdom* (1997) 23 EHRR CD 185 where the Commission recognised that the absence of measures designed to discourage drinking alcohol to excess in state-provided facilities could raise issues under art 2.

> ### Article 3 Prohibition of torture, and of inhuman or degrading treatment or punishment
>
> No one shall be subjected to torture or to inhuman or degrading treatment or punishment

A Introduction

4.3.1 The basic right to physical integrity contained in art 3 ranks among the most important guaranteed by the Convention. The article reflects abhorrence at the systematic abuse of prisoners and use of torture in Europe during the Third Reich and the Second World War, and enshrines one of the fundamental values of the democratic societies making up the Council of Europe.

4.3.2 The prohibition on torture and other forms of inhuman or degrading treatment is absolute, and is generally enforced by the Commission and the court with rigour. As the court has repeatedly stressed, unlike most provisions of the Convention, art 3 is not limited by exceptions, regardless of the reprehensible conduct of the victim, the aims of the state, or the difficulties faced by states in relation to the investigation of organised crime or terrorism[1]. No derogation from its provisions is permitted in times of war or public emergency[2]. On the other hand, in some cases, particularly those concerning conditions of detention, or other treatment falling short of deliberate assault, the court has tended to have regard to considerations which might be thought of as justifications for the treatment in question as being criteria relevant to the classification of the treatment as inhuman or degrading. For example, in *Herczegfalvy v Austria*[3], the court found that forcible medical treatment and forced feeding could not be categorised as inhuman or degrading where therapeutically necessary. Similarly, prison conditions which might otherwise be considered degrading may be lawful if they are necessary to prevent suicide or escape[4].

1 See, for example, *Chahal v United Kingdom* (1996) 23 EHRR 413, E Ct HR, at paras 79–80; *Aksoy v Turkey* (1997) 23 EHRR 553, E Ct HR at para 62; and *Selçuk and Asker v Turkey* (1998) 26 EHRR 477, at para 75.
2 European Convention on Human Rights, art 15. See also the *Report of the Committee of Privy Councillors Appointed to Consider Authorised Procedures for Interrogation of Persons Suspected of Terrorism* (Cmnd 4901), which considered (without finding any justification for treatment contrary to art 3) various hypothetical situations such as where, for example, information is sought from a terrorist suspect about an impending explosion. See also the Inter-American Convention to Prevent and Punish Torture 1985, art 5.
3 (1992) 15 EHRR 437, E Ct HR, para 82.
4 *Kröcher and Möller v Switzerland* 34 DR 25 (1982), EComHR.

4.3.3 The prohibition contained in art 3 is closely modelled on the Universal Declaration of Human Rights, art 5[1]. A number of international instruments contain similar prohibitions, including: the International Covenant on Civil and Political Rights, art 7[2]; the American Convention on Human Rights 1969, art 5, para 2[3]; and the African Charter on Human and Peoples' Rights 1981, art 5[4]. More detailed measures adopted by the international community to combat torture are contained in the United Nations' Declaration against Torture in 1975 (the 'Declaration on the Protection of All Persons from Being Subjected to Torture or Other Cruel, Inhuman or Degrading Treatment or Punishment')[5], the UN Convention against Torture and other Cruel, Inhuman or Degrading Treatment or Punishment 1984[6] (ratified by the United Kingdom in December 1988), and the European Convention for the Prevention of Torture and Inhuman or Degrading Treatment or Punishment 1987[7] (ratified by the United Kingdom in June 1988).

1   'No one shall be subjected to torture or to cruel, inhuman or degrading treatment or punishment'.
2   Which adopts the wording of art 5 of the Universal Declaration, adding the words, 'In particular, no one shall be subjected without his free consent to medical or scientific experimentation'. See also art 10 ('Right of detained persons to humane and dignified treatment'), and see below, paras **5.19–5.22**.
3   Signed at the Inter-American Specialized Conference on Human Rights, San Jose, Costa Rica, 22 November 1969. See also Inter-American Convention to Prevent and Punish Torture, adopted in December 1985 by the General Assembly of the Organization of American States (OAS, Treaty Series, No 67).
4   Organisation of African Unity, adopted by the 18th Assembly of Heads of State and Government, Nairobi, Kenya, June 1981.
5   General Assembly Resolution 3452, 9 December 1975.
6   General Assembly Resolution 3946, 10 December 1984. See paras **5.56–5.69**, and see generally Martinus Nijhoff *The United Nations Convention Against Torture: A Handbook on the Convention Against Torture and Other Cruel, Inhuman or Degrading Treatment or Punishment* (1988) and N Rodley *The Treatment of Prisoners under International Law* (1987). The definition of torture, and positive obligations imposed on states to investigate allegations of torture contained in the 1984 UN Convention were considered as a guide to the interpretation of art 3 by the Commission and the court in *Aydin v Turkey* (1997) 25 EHRR, 251, E Ct HR.
7   Council of Europe, 26 November 1987 (TS 5 (1991), Cmd 1634; ETS 126). See below, paras **5.70–5.74**.

B   The meaning of torture, and inhuman or degrading treatment or punishment[1]

4.3.4   Mistreatment must attain a minimum level of severity in order to fall within the scope of art 3. The assessment of this minimum is relative, and depends on factors including the duration of the treatment, its physical or mental effects, and the age, sex, vulnerability and state of health of the victim[2]. In *Costello-Roberts v United Kingdom*[3], the court held, albeit with some misgivings, that three blows inflicted by a headmaster with a slipper on the clothed buttocks of a seven year old boy did not attain the minimum level of severity necessary to engage the provisions of art 3. Other conduct which has been held to fall below the necessary minimum includes the interference with human dignity resulting from the surveillance of an applicant's home[4], and the embarrassment caused to transsexuals under the French legal system arising from the fact that identity documents, including passports, could not be altered to show their new sex[5]. The court has adopted a low threshold for the necessary minimum in the case of individuals who are assaulted while in detention. In *Ribitsch v Austria*[6], the court stated that any recourse to physical force which has not been made strictly necessary by the applicant's own conduct diminishes his human dignity and is in principle a breach of art 3. Nevertheless, in *Raninen v Finland*[4] the E Ct HR held that the handcuffing of a detainee did not violate art 3, even though the detention was unlawful and the handcuffing unnecessary.

1   See generally, Klayman 'The Definition of Torture in International Law' (1978) 51 *Temp Lq* 449; Rodley *The Treatment of Prisoners under International Law* (1987), ch 3.
2   *Ireland v United Kingdom* (1978), 2 EHRR 25, E Ct HR, para 162.

3 (1993) 19 EHRR 112, at para 32.
4 *D'Haese, Le Compte v Belgium* (1983) 6 EHRR 114, EComHR. It is strongly arguable that a far reaching or very long exclusion order from the home or home area may constitute inhuman treatment: *Abuki v A-G of Uganda* (1997) 3 BHRC 199, Constitutional Court of Uganda (sentence of banishment for 10 years from home area, and restraining defendant from having contact with anybody from that area, was a cruel and inhuman punishment since its effect would be to render the petitioner homeless, without shelter, food or any means of livelihood).
5 *B v France* (1992) 16 EHRR 1, E Ct HR.
6 (1995) 21 EHRR 573, at para 38.
7 (1997) 26 EHRR 563.

4.3.5 Treatment causing mental suffering is sufficient to fall within art 3, provided a sufficient degree of intensity is reached[1]. In *Kurt v Turkey*[2], the E Ct HR held that a mother who suffered anguish as the result of the disappearance of her son following his detention by the authoriaties was herself to be regarded as the victim of a violation of art 3. Provided it is sufficiently real and immediate, a mere threat of inhuman or degrading treatment may itself violate art 3[3].

1 See, for example, *Ireland v United Kingdom* (1978), 2 EHRR 25, E Ct HR, para 162.
2 E Ct HR, 25 May 1998. See also the decision of the United Nations Human Rights Committee in *Quinteros v Uruguay*, 21 July 1983.
3 Although the mere threat of corporal punishment in Scottish schools caused insufficient suffering or humiliation to surmount the minimum threshold for the applicability of art 3: *Campbell and Cosans v United Kingdom* (1982) 4 EHRR 293, E Ct HR, para 26.

4.3.6 The court has drawn a distinction between inhuman treatment generally, and torture. Although any form of inhuman treatment will violate art 3, the special stigma of torture attaches only to deliberate inhuman treatment causing very serious and cruel suffering[1]. Perhaps surprisingly, in *Ireland v United Kingdom*[2], the court held that techniques used to interrogate Nationalist detainees in Northern Ireland, while they constituted inhuman treatment, were not sufficiently severe or cruel to amount to torture, notwithstanding the fact that the treatment was deliberately inflicted for the purpose of extracting information, and caused intense physical and mental suffering and acute psychiatric disturbance to the victims. The techniques included forcing the detainee to stand spread-eagled against a wall for lengthy periods, with the majority of his weight on his fingertips; covering a detainee's head with a hood; subjection of the detainee to a loud hissing noise; deprivation of sleep; and deprivation of food and drink. By contrast, in the case of *Aydin v Turkey*[3] the court held that rape constituted torture[4], as did the accumulation of a series of acts of physical and mental violence over a period of time, deliberately inflicted by security forces to elicit information from a 17-year-old girl.

1 *Ireland v United Kingdom* (1978) 2 EHRR 25, E Ct HR, para 167, in which the court referred to Resolution 3452 of the General Assembly of the United Nations, 9 December 1975, which declared that 'torture constitutes an aggravated and deliberate form of cruel, inhuman or degrading treatment or punishment'; *Denmark v Greece ('the Greek case')* (1972) 12 YB 186. See also Application 25803/94 *Selmonni v France*, in which the Commission found that the beating of a suspect in custody constituted torture.
2 (1978) 2 EHRR 25, E Ct HR. Compare *Bazzano and Massera (Hernandez) v Uruguay* (5/1977), report of the Human Rights Committee, GAOR, 35th Session, Supp No 40 (1979) (treatment including requirement to stand hooded for long period, leading to a fall and a broken leg which went untreated causing permanent deformity, constituted torture).
3 (1998) 25 EHRR 251.
4 See also, *Mejia Egocheaga v Peru* (1996) 1 BHRC 229, Inter-American Commission on Human Rights (rape of applicant by soldiers constituted torture within arts 2 and 3 of Inter-American Convention to Prevent and Punish Torture 1985, being intentional acts of violence causing physical and mental pain and suffering, which were carried out with the purpose of punishing and intimidating applicant by members of the security forces).

4.3.7   Treatment is 'degrading' if it arouses in the victim feelings of fear, anguish and inferiority capable of humiliating and debasing him and possibly breaking his physical or moral resistance[1]. An action which lowers a person in rank, position, reputation or character may be degrading, provided the treatment reaches a certain level of severity, as may be an action which grossly humiliates a victim before others, or drives him to act against his will or conscience[2]. Racial discrimination may in some circumstances be considered degrading treatment. In the *East African Asians Cases*[3], the Commission stressed the special importance to be attached to discrimination based on race as an affront to human dignity, and indicated that racial discrimination might therefore be capable of constituting degrading treatment when differential treatment on some other ground would raise no such question. In particular circumstances, legislation discriminating against women or illegitimate children has not been held to be degrading[4].

1   *Ireland v United Kingdom* (1978) 2 EHRR 25, E Ct HR, at para 167.
2   *East African Asians Cases* (1973) 3 EHRR 76 at 80, EComHR. See also *Denmark v Greece* (1972) 12 YB 186, where the European Commission defined 'degrading treatment' as treatment of an individual that grossly humiliates him before others or drives him to act against his will or conscience.
3   (1973) 3 EHRR 76, EComHR.
4   *Abdulaziz, Cabales and Balkandali v United Kingdom* (1985), 7 EHRR 471, E Ct HR, para 91; *Marckx v Belgium* (1979) 2 EHRR 330, E Ct HR. As to the prohibition of discrimination under art 14 of the Convention, see para **4.14** below.

4.3.8   A punishment will be degrading if it entails a degree of humiliation and debasement which attains a particular level, and which is other than that usual element of humilation almost inevitably involved in punishment. The assessment is relative, and depends on all the circumstances of the case and in particular on the nature and context of the punishment itself and the manner and method of its execution. Publicity may be relevant but its absence does not prevent a punishment from being degrading: it may suffice if the victim is humiliated in his own eyes. The birching of a teenage boy by a stranger in humiliating circumstances was held to constitute a degrading punishment in the case of *Tyrer v United Kingdom*[1]. On the other hand, the court held in *Albert and Le Compte v Belgium*[2] that striking a doctor off a medical register did not constitute a degrading punishment. The Commission has held that a disciplinary penalty pronounced on a prisoner by a court, consisting of seven days sleeping without a bed, with a diet restricted to bread and water, was not inhuman or degrading, although it did not correspond to modern standards[3]. In some jurisdictions there has been consideration of the question whether imprisonment for debt or other civil imprisonment is degrading; despite some suggestions to the contrary[4], the balance of authority is that in appropriately limited circumstances, civil imprisonment is permitted[5].

1   (1978) 2 EHRR 1, E Ct HR, para 30. Contrast *Costello-Roberts v United Kingdom* (1993) 19 EHRR 112, E Ct HR.
2   (1983), 5 EHRR 533.
3   *X v Federal Republic of Germany* 10 DR 221, EComHR.
4   See eg Sieghart *The International Law of Human Rights* (1983), p 83. See further, art 11 of the International Covenant on Civil and Political Rights: 'No one shall be imprisoned merely on the ground of inability to fulfil a contractual obligation'. See similarly art 1 of protocol 4 to the Convention: para **2.1.5** above, at n 2.
5   See *Hicks v Fejock* 485 US 624 (1988) ('purgable' imprisonment for remedial purposes to compel performance of an obligation is permissible); *Bux v Officer Commanding Pietermaritzburg Prison* 1994 (4) SA 562 at 564; *Chinamora v Angwa Furnishers (Private) Ltd* (1997) 1 BHRC 460 at 475–477 (Sup Ct of Zimbabwe), where Gubbay CJ reviewed authorities from a number of jurisdictions and concluded that imprisonment of 'debt-dodger' for maximum permissible period of three months did not offend the Declaration of Rights, s 15(1) (protection against 'degrading treatment').

C   The state's responsibility

4.3.9   States are unlikely to be able to escape liability for torture and other ill treatment committed by their public officials. In *Cyprus v Turkey*[1], Turkey was liable for acts, including rape, committed by Turkish soldiers during the invasion of Northern Cyprus in 1974, because it was not shown that adequate measures had been taken to prevent them occurring, or that the perpetrators had been disciplined. In *Ireland v United Kingdom*[2], the court declared that states were 'strictly liable for the conduct of their subordinates; they are under a duty to impose their will on subordinates and cannot shelter behind their inability to ensure that it is respected'. 'Strict' liability should probably be understood as indicating not automatic liability, but that liability will attach unless it can be clearly shown that all reasonable measures have been taken to prevent such acts occurring, and to investigate and punish where appropriate.

1   (1976) 4 EHRR 282, E Ct HR.
2   (1978) 2 EHRR 25, E Ct HR, para 159.

4.3.10   In addition, the court has imposed a positive obligation on contracting states, under arts 3 and 13 of the Convention, to carry out a prompt, impartial and effective investigation into allegations of torture, which is capable of leading to the identification and punishment of those responsible[1]. Failure to carry out such an investigation will result in a finding of a violation of art 3.

1   *Aksoy v Turkey* (1997) 23 EHRR 553, E Ct HR, paras 98–99; *Assenov v Bulgaria* E Ct HR, 28 October 1998, para 102; *Aydin v Turkey* (1998) 25 EHRR 251. In imposing this positive obligation, the court referred to art 12 of the 1984 UN Convention Against Torture, which expressly provides: 'Each State Party shall ensure that its competent authorities proceed to a prompt and impartial investigation, wherever there is reasonable ground to believe that an act of torture has been committed in any territory under its jurisdiction'. See also the Inter-American Convention to Prevent and Punish Torture, art 7.

4.3.11   States may be responsible for acts contrary to art 3 committed by 'unofficial' groups[1] or even private individuals. In *Costello-Roberts v United Kingdom*[2], the court held that a contracting state may be held responsible for degrading corporal punishment in private schools, because the state has an obligation under art 2 of the First Protocol to secure to children their right to education, of which a school's disciplinary system forms a part. The state cannot absolve itself of responsibility by delegating that obligation to private bodies or individuals. In *A v United Kingdom*[3], the Court held that, pursuant to their obligations under art 1, states are required to take measures designed to ensure that individuals are not subjected to torture of inhuman or degrading treatment or punishment, including such treatment administered by private individuals. Children and other vulnerable individuals in particular are entitled to state protection, in the form of effective deterrence, against such serious breaches of personal integrity. In this case the United Kingdom was found to have violated art 3 on the grounds that national law failed adequately to protect a child who was caned by his step-father, because of the availability of the defence of 'reasonable chastisement' to a criminal charge of assault.

1   The UN Convention Against Torture provides in terms in art 1 that torture must be 'inflicted by or at the instigation of or with the consent or acquiescence of a public official or person acting in an official capacity'; but 'acquiescence' may extend to failures by government officials to prevent or stop torture by private persons or unofficial groups, such as 'death squads'; see eg *Laureano Atachahua v Peru* (1997) 1 BHRC 338, UN HRC (abduction and disappearance of L by kidnappers appearing to belong to the military or special police forces

constituted a breach by Peru of art 7 of the International Covenant on Civil and Political Rights).
2   (1993) 19 EHRR 112, paras 26–28.
3   E Ct HR, 23 September 1998.

D   Arrest and detention

4.3.12   Individuals who have been arrested, detained by police or held in custody in prison or mental hospital are particularly vulnerable to assault in violation of their rights under art 3. Since they are often isolated from medical or legal help, or contact with the outside world, they may have difficulty in proving that they have suffered the mistreatment they allege. Thus, the court has repeatedly held that where a person is taken into custody in good health, found to be injured at the time of release, and alleges that he has been ill-treated, it is incumbent on the state to provide a plausible explanation as to the cause of his injuries, in order to avoid a finding of a violation of art 3[1]. In *Ribitsch v Austria*[2], for example, the court found that the Austrian Government had failed to establish that the bruises suffered by the applicant were not the result of inhuman treatment inflicted on him by the police. The state had committed a breach of art 3 even though the national criminal court had acquitted the police officer concerned.

1   *Tomasi v France* (1992) 15 EHRR 1, E Ct HR; *Aksoy v Turkey* (1997) 23 EHRR 553, E Ct HR, at para 61.
2   (1995) 21 EHRR 573.

4.3.13   The conditions in which a person is detained may violate art 3[1]. For example, solitary confinement may in some circumstances violate art 3, depending on its stringency and duration, and the effect on the prisoner[2]. Excessive and physically intrusive security measures may be unlawful[3]. Where degrading or inhuman conditions are self-imposed (as during a 'dirty protest'), the state is not responsible for those conditions, but has an obligation to exercise custodial authority to safeguard the health and well-being of the prisoners who have imposed such conditions upon themselves[4].

1   Although the Convention does not contain an equivalent of art 10 of the International Covenant on Civil and Political Rights, which provides that: 'All persons deprived of their liberty shall be treated with humanity and with respect for the inherent dignity of the human person'. The American Convention on Human Rights contains the same provision, although it is there located within the article prohibiting torture (art 5(2)).
2   Applications 7572/76, 7586/76 and 7587/76: *Ensslin, Baader and Raspe v Federal Republic of Germany* 14 DR 64 (1978)(on the facts the conditions of detention not inhuman, and justified by security requirements). See also *Kröcher and Möller v Switzerland* 34 DR 25 (1982), EComHR. The Human Rights Committee has in a number of cases placed weight on the fact of solitary confinement in finding breaches of arts 7 and/or 10(1) of the International Covenant on Civil and Political Rights; see eg *Marais v Madagascar* (49/1979), Report of the Human Rights Committee, GAOR, 38th Session, Supp No 40, Annex XI; *Larrosa v Uruguay* (88/1981), Report of the Human Rights Committee, GAOR, 38th Session, Supp No 40, Annex XVI. See also the Human Rights Committee's General Comment 20 on art 7 (1992).
3   As in *Weems v US* 217 US 349 (1910)(US Supreme Court)(penal code imposing imprisonment with hard and painful labour involving the carrying of a chain at the ankle and hanging from the wrist contravened the Eighth Amendment prohibiting cruel and unusual punishment).
4   *McFeeley v United Kingdom* 20 DR 44 (1980), EComHR.

4.3.14   Some guidance as to prison conditions which may violate art 3 can be obtained from the Standard Minimum Rules for the Treatment of Prisoners adopted in 1955 by the First UN Congress on the Prevention of Crime and the Treatment of Offenders, and endorsed in 1957 by the Economic and Social Council[1]. Although the rules do not set out enforceable minimum standards, let alone standards below which conditions are or are presumed to be inhuman or degrading, certain rules do refer expressly to inhuman or degrading punishments[2]. Reference has been made to the rules by the European Commission in considering whether conditions of detention constitute inhuman or degrading treatment[3].

1 Ecosoc resolution 663 C (XXIV), 31 July 1957, as amended by Ecosoc resolution 2076 (LXII), 13 May 1977.
2 For example, rule 31, relating to inter alia corporal punishment.
3 *Denmark v Greece ('the Greek case')* (1972) 12 YB 186.

4.3.15 The continued detention of a prisoner whose state of health has deteriorated is not inhuman provided that the necessary medical care is provided[1]. On the other hand, the inadequate provision of medical care for detainees may constitute inhuman treatment[2].

1 Application 7994/77: *Kotälla v Netherlands* 14 DR 238 (1978), EComHR
2 *Hurtado v Switzerland* A 280-A (1994)(friendly settlement); Application 23636/94 *PM v Hungary* (the inadequate hygienic care of an incontinent, partially-paralysed prisoner violated art 3). Cf *Estelle v Gamble* 429 US 97 (1976), where the majority of the US Supreme Court held that 'deliberate indifference to serious medical needs of prisoners' would violate the eighth amendment prohibition on cruel and unusual punishment, whilst expressing no view in relation to inattention that could not be characterised as 'deliberate'. But see the dissent of Justice Stevens, arguing that the prison conditions in question, whether 'the product of design, negligence, or mere poverty, ... were cruel and inhuman' (at 116–117).

4.3.16 Although art 3 does not prohibit the death penalty per se[1], the treatment of prisoners on death row awaiting execution may in some circumstances be considered to be inhuman or degrading. In *Soering v United Kingdom*[2], the court held that the applicant faced a real risk of treatment contrary to art 3 if he was extradited to Virginia on a charge of capital murder, because of the risk of exposure to the suffering experienced by condemned prisoners who spent, on average, six to eight years on death row. It was immaterial that delay was likely to be due in part to appeals pursued by the applicant.

1 As to which, see art 2 and the Sixth Protocol at para **4.2**. See also para **2.1.1** above, at n 2.
2 (1989) 11 EHRR 439, E Ct HR.

4.3.17 The Privy Council has followed *Soering* in holding, in a number of decisions, that an excessively long period of time spent on death row will, per se, amount to inhuman or degrading treatment, and has laid down guideline periods of delay after which execution will be unlawful[1]. The Board has expressly adopted the approach that 'a state that wishes to retain capital punishment must accept the responsibility of ensuring that execution follows as swiftly as practicable after sentence, allowing a reasonable time for appeal ...'[2]. This rejection of the American death row phenomenon is in marked contrast to the approach of the UN Human Rights Committee, which has held that the length of the period spent on death row does not in itself, and in the absence of further compelling circumstances, amount to cruel and degrading treatment or punishment under arts 7 or 10(1) of the International Covenant on Civil and Political Rights, precisely because if the mere length of detention were determinative, the effect would be to expedite executions, which would be inconsistent with the objective of the International Covenant on Civil and Political Rights of reducing the use of the death penalty[3].

1   *Pratt v A-G for Jamaica* [1994] 2 AC 1, PC (which adopted as a guideline an overall five-year limit from sentence to execution), departing from the decision of the Privy Council in *Riley v A-G of Jamaica* [1983] 1 AC 719; *Guerra v Baptiste* [1996] AC 397, PC (Trinidad) (where the Board took into account a serious delay in providing the notes of the petitioner's trial as well as the overall period); *Reckley v Minister of Public Safety and Immigration (No 2)* [1996] AC 527, PC (Bahamas); *Henfield v A-G of the Bahamas; Farrington v Minister of Public Safety and Immigration* [1997] AC 413, PC (Bahamas) (overall guidline limit for The Bahamas should be three and a half years, taking into account (together with the 'agony of mind' of the petitioner) the absence of any right of appeal to the UN Human Rights Commission, and the accordingly shorter period required for exhaustion of rights of appeal); *Fisher v Minister of Public Safety and Immigration* [1998] AC 673, PC (Bahamas)(guideline period in the Bahamas extended to five years where appeals to UN Human Rights Commission allowed; pre-trial period of detention usually irrelevant); cf *Fisher v Minister of Public Safety and Immigration (No 2)* [1999] 2 WLR 349, PC.
2   *Pratt v A-G for Jamaica* [1994] 2 AC 1, PC at 33.
3   *Johnson v Jamaica* (1996) 1 BHRC 37. The Committee made reference to General Comment 6(16) of 27 July 1982 and the Preamble to the Second Optional Protocol to the Covenant Aiming at the Abolition of the Death Penalty (15 December 1989; Annex to GA Resolution 44/128) as establishing that reducing recourse to the death penalty was 'one of the objects and purposes of the covenant' (at 43).

E   Immigration control, asylum seekers and extradition

4.3.18   The responsibility of contracting states under art 3 is engaged not only where individuals are mistreated, or degrading or inhuman punishments inflicted, in the contracting state itself, but also where states have sought to deport or extradite individuals to third countries where they face a real risk of torture or other treatment or punishment contrary to art 3.

4.3.19   Although there is no right under the Convention to political asylum as such, nor any right not to be expelled or extradited from a state, the expulsion or extradition of a person to another state where there are substantial grounds for believing that there is a real risk that he may be subjected to torture, or to inhuman or degrading treatment or punishment in the receiving state, constitutes a breach of the Convention by the state which takes the decision to deport or extradite[1]. The same position holds under the International Covenant on Civil and Political Rights, art 7 and under the Convention against Torture and other Cruel, Inhuman or Degrading Treatment or Punishment 1984, art 3[2].

1   *Soering v United Kingdom* (1989) 11 EHRR 439, E Ct HR, para 88.
2   See eg *Alan v Switzerland* (1996) 1 BHRC 598, UN Committee Against Torture (the applicant's ethnic background, political affiliation and history of detention and internal exile, combined with systemic torture in Turkey and activities of security forces, constituted substantial grounds for believing that he would be in danger of being subjected to torture if deported).

4.3.20   Account may be taken of the risk of ill-treatment by private groups or individuals, as well as the state, provided that it is shown that the risk is real and that the authorities of the receiving state are not able to obviate the risk by providing appropriate protection. However, a general situation of violence in the receiving state is not sufficient to entail a violation of art 3 in the event of deportation[1].

1   *HLR v France* (1997) 26 EHRR 29, E Ct HR, at paras 40–41; *Altun v Federal Republic of Germany* 36 DR 209 (1983), EComHR; *Kirkwood v United Kingdom* 37 DR 158 (1984), EComHR. But see Application 7216/75 *X v Federal Republic of Germany* 5 DR 137 (1976), EComHR; *X v United Kingdom* 29 DR 48 (1980), EComHR; and *YH v Federal Republic of Germany* 51 DR 258 (1986), EComHR.

4.3.21 Deportation may violate art 3 not only where the risk to the individual emanates from the intentionally-inflicted acts of public bodies in the receiving state, or of non-state bodies when the authorities are unable or unwilling to provide appropriate protection, but also where the risk stems from factors which in themselves do not infringe the standards of art 3. Thus, in the case of *D v United Kingdom*[1], the court held that art 3 would be violated if a man was deported to his native St Kitts, having served a sentence for importing drugs. He was in the last stages of AIDS, and, if deported, would be deprived of vital medical treatment, and exposed to a real risk of dying in destitution under most distressing circumstances. The E Ct HR held that it would be inhuman for the United Kingdom to deport him, even though the conditions he would face in St Kitts did not themselves amount to a breach of art 3 standards on the part of the St Kitts Government.

1 (1997) 24 EHRR 423. See also Application 30930/96 *BB v France* (7 September 1998, unreported).

4.3.22 The expulsion of a person who faces a real risk of treatment contrary to art 3 in the receiving state will breach art 3 even if the individual has committed serious crimes, or if the decision is taken in the interests of national security, or to combat terrorism. The absolute protection provided by art 3 does not permit the risk to the applicant to be balanced against the interests of the state in expelling him[1]. In this respect, art 3 gives greater protection than the UN Convention on the Status of Refugees 1951, art 33[2], by which a refugee may be returned to a country in which he fears persecution, if he is a danger to the state or community.

1 *Chahal v United Kingdom* (1996) 23 EHRR 413, E Ct HR, paras 73 and 74; *Ahmed v Austria* (1997) 24 EHRR 278, E Ct HR, paras 40 and 41; Application 32448/96 *Hatami v Sweden* (9 October 1998, unreported), paras 93–96.
2 UN TS Vol 189, p 137. Furthermore, the Refugee Convention does not apply to a person with respect to whom there are serious reasons for considering that he committed a serious non-political crime outside the country of refuge prior to his admission there: art 1 of the Convention and *T v Immigration Officer* [1996] AC 742, HL.

4.3.23 Where a state is threatening to deport or extradite a person, the extent of the risk to him of treatment contrary to art 3 if he is expelled is to be assessed as at the date of the court's consideration of the case. To that end, the court will assess all material before it, and may obtain further material by its own motion[1].

1 *Chahal v United Kingdom* (1997) 23 EHRR 413, E Ct HR, at para 86; *Ahmed v Austria* (1997) 24 EHRR 278, E Ct HR, at para 43.

F Corporal punishment

4.3.24 Corporal punishment, whether inflicted as a criminal penalty, by a parent, or in schools, may constitute a violation of art 3, provided it exceeds the minimum threshold for inhuman or degrading treatment[1]. Corporal punishment is not addressed in most international human rights instruments[2], but the UN Human Rights Committee has, in General Comment 7 (1982) on the International Covenant on Civil and Political Rights, art 7, expressed the view that the prohibition on torture and cruel, inhuman or degrading treatment or punishment 'must extend to corporal punishment'[3].

1 As to which, compare *Tyrer v United Kingdom* (1978), 2 EHRR 1, E Ct HR; *A v United Kingdom*

E Ct HR, 23 September 1998; and *Costello-Roberts v United Kingdom* (1993) 19 EHRR 112, E Ct HR, considered at paras **4.3.8** and **4.3.10** above. The Commission has held that the caning of school pupils constituted degrading punishment contrary to art 3 in two cases, *Y v United Kingdom* A 247-A (1992), 17 EHRR 238, and *Warwick v United Kingdom* 60 DR 5 (1986), EComHR. Cf *Ingraham v Wright* 430 US 651 (1977), where the majority of the US Supreme Court held that the ban on cruel and unusual punishments was inapplicable to school discipline (at 671).

2   An exception being the Third and Fourth Geneva Conventions of 12 August 1949 (Treatment of Prisoners of War, art 87 and Protection of Civilian Persons in Time of War, art 32, respectively), which expressly prohibit corporal punishment.

3   See further, N Rodley *The Treatment of Prisoners under International Law* (1987), ch 10.

Article 4   Prohibition of slavery and forced labour

1. No one shall be held in slavery or servitude.
2. No one shall be required to perform forced or compulsory labour.
3. For the purpose of this Article the term 'forced or compulsory labour' shall not include:
   (a) any work required to be done in the ordinary course of detention imposed according to the provisions of Article 5 of this Convention or during conditional release from such detention;
   (b) any service of a military character or, in case of conscientious objectors in countries where they are recognised, service exacted instead of compulsory military service;
   (c) any service exacted in case of an emergency or calamity threatening the life or well-being of the community;
   (d) any work or service which forms part of normal civic obligations.

A   Introduction

4.4.1   The right not to be enslaved is one of the oldest internationally-recognised basic human rights[1]. Article 4 combines an absolute prohibition on slavery and servitude, from which no derogation is permitted, with a limited prohibition on forced or compulsory labour, which is restricted by provisions excluding from its scope various forms of labour which individuals may be compelled to perform by the state.

1   For a review of international instruments aimed at the abolition of slavery and the slave trade, see Nina Lassen *The Universal Declaration of Human Rights: A Commentary* (1992) art 4, pp 87–99.

4.4.2   The wording of the article reflects the Universal Declaration of Human Rights 1948, art 4[1], and has been closely followed by the International Covenant on Civil and Political Rights 1966, art 8, although it differs from both instruments in omitting an express prohibition on the slave-trade.

1   Universal Declaration of Human Rights 1948, art 4 provides: 'No one shall be held in slavery or servitude; slavery and the slave trade shall be prohibited in all their forms.'

B   Article 4(1): slavery and servitude

4.4.3   The terms 'slavery' and 'servitude' are not defined in art 4 itself.

4.4.4   The Commission and the court have not yet had occasion to consider the meaning of 'slavery'. However, it is likely that they would adopt the definition of slavery contained in the Slavery Convention 1926, art 1 of which defines slavery as 'the status or condition of a person over whom any or all of the powers attaching to the right of ownership are exercised'[1].

1   Slavery Convention 1926 (Cmd 2910), art 1. The Supplementary Convention on the Abolition
    of Slavery, the Slave Trade, and Institutions and Practices Similar to Slavery (Cmnd 257)
    provides for the abolition of practices such as debt bondage, serfdom, servile forms of marriage,
    and the exploitation of children, while leaving open the question whether these conditions are
    themselves covered by the definition of slavery in the 1926 Convention. Compare the
    Constitution of India, art 23, which prohibits inter alia 'traffic in human beings'.

4.4.5   'Servitude' has been distinguished by the Commission from forced labour on
the basis that a 'serf', in addition to being compelled to work, is obliged to live on
another's property, and that it is impossible for him to change his condition[1].

1   *Van Droogenbroeck v Belgium* B 44 (1980) Comm Rep, para 79; see also the judgment of the
    court (1982) 4 EHRR 443, E Ct HR. On the facts of the case, the court found that an applicant
    who was placed at the 'disposal of the state' for ten years following the completion of a prison
    sentence was not held in servitude contrary to this provision; his situation did not violate art
    5(1) of the Convention (see para **4.5.9** below), and accordingly could have been regarded as
    servitude only if it involved a particularly serious form of denial of freedom.

4.4.6   No derogation from art 4(1) is permitted, even in time of war or other public
emergency[1].

1   ECHR, art 15(2).

C   Articles 4(2) and 4(3): forced or compulsory labour

4.4.7   Forced and compulsory labour refers to work exacted from a person under the
threat of a penalty, for which he has not voluntarily offered himself. 'Forced' labour
suggests physical or mental constraint[1]. Under a similar provision in the Indian
Constitution[2], it has been held that where a person provides labour or service for
remuneration which is less than the minimum wage prescribed by statute, he renders
forced service such that the constitutional provision is engaged[3].

1   *Van der Mussele v Belgium* (1983), 6 EHRR 163, E Ct HR. The definition adopted is derived
    from ILO Convention 29 on Forced or Compulsory Labour 1930. See also the Abolition of
    Forced Labour Convention 1957, ILO Convention 105.
2   Article 23(1) provides, 'Traffic in human beings and *begar* and other similar forms of forced
    labour are prohibited ...'. 'Begar' has been described as 'labour or service exacted by a
    Government or a person in power without giving remuneration for it' (H M Seervai
    Constitutional Law of India, Vol 2 (1993), para 11.487, quoting Molesworth).
3   *People's Union for Democratic Rights v Union* (1983) 1 SCR 456; see H M Seervai
    Constitutional Law of India, Vol 2 (1993) at para 11.488. See also, in relation to the question
    of the extent to which the system of bonded labour infringes the article, *Bandhua Mukti Morcha
    v Union* (1984) 2 SCR 67.

4.4.8   An obligation to work will not violate art 4(2), provided it is not excessive or
disproportionate in the circumstances. In *Iversen v Norway*[1], a Norwegian dentist was
compelled to work in northern Norway for two years, later reduced to one. The
assignment was for a short period, was well-remunerated, and fell within the applicant's
profession. The fact that the work was compulsory and was enforced under threat of
punishment was not conclusive as to whether it violated art 4(2). In *Van der Mussele
v Belgium*[2], a Belgian pupil advocate was obliged under the rules of the *Ordre des
avocats* to represent a client without remuneration or reimbursement of his expenses.
The court held that the requirement was not disproportionate or excessive in the
circumstances, considering various factors, including the fact that he was required to

undertake the normal activities of a lawyer; that there was a professional benefit to him in undertaking the work; and that his services secured to the client the benefit of a fair hearing as guaranteed by art 6 of the Convention. The fact that he had consented to the application of professional rules to him, by becoming a pupil advocate, was not conclusive of the question of whether he had offered himself voluntarily for the work in question. However, in a case of prior consent, there would have to be a considerable and unreasonable imbalance between the aim pursued and the obligation upon the individual for the requirement to work to constitute forced labour.

1   Application 1468/62 6 YB 278 (1963), EComHR.
2   A 70 (1983) 6 EHRR 163, E Ct HR.

D   Forms of labour excluded from Article 4(2)

4.4.9   A number of forms of labour are wholly excluded from the definition of forced or compulsory labour by virtue of art 4(3). Article 4(3) is not intended to limit the protection of the right guaranteed by art 4(2). Rather, it delimits the content of that right, in that it indicates what the term 'forced or compulsory labour' does not include, and so aids the interpretation of art 4(2)[1].

1   See *Schmidt v Germany* (1994) 18 EHRR 513, E Ct HR, para 22. Compare the Abolition of Forced Labour Convention 1957, ILO Convention 105, which as well as identifying (by art 2) various forms of labour as falling outside the definition of 'forced or compulsory labour', also lays down criteria which any authority competent to exact forced or compulsory labour shall in advance satisfy itself exists, namely: '(a) that the work to be done or the service to be rendered is of important direct interest for the community called upon to do the work or render the service; (b) that the work or service is of present or imminent necessity; (c) that it has been impossible to obtain voluntary labour for carrying out the work or rendering the service by the offer of rates of wages and conditions of labour not less favourable than those prevailing in the area concerned for similar work or service; and (d) that the work or service will not lay too heavy a burden on the present population, having regard to the labour available and its capacity to undertake the work'.

1   WORK DONE DURING DETENTION

4.4.10   Any work required to be done in the ordinary course of detention imposed according to the provisions of art 5 of the Convention or during conditional release from such detention does not constitute forced or compulsory labour. It is immaterial that the conviction of the detained person is later quashed[1], or that the terms of the detention violate art 5(4)[2]. There is no breach of art 4(2) if a prisoner is obliged to work in prison in return for insufficient pay and without social security benefits[3]. Compulsory work demanded of convicts in a forced labour institution is not forced or compulsory labour within the meaning of the Convention[4], nor is the practice of hiring out prisoners for work to private enterprises[5].

1   Application 3245/67 *X v Austria* 12 YB 206 (1969), EComHR; Application 3485/68 *X v United Kingdom* 12 YB 288 (1969), EComHR.
2   *De Wilde, Ooms and Versyp v Belgium (Vagrancy Cases)* A 12 (1971) 1 EHRR 373, E Ct HR.
3   Application 833/60 *X v Austria* 3 YB 428 (1960), EComHR; Application 2742/66 *X v Germany* 23 CD 1 (1965), EComHR.
4   Application 770/60 *X v Germany* 6 CD 1 (1960), EComHR; Application 2742/66 *X v Austria* 9 YB 550 (1966), EComHR.
5   Although it is contrary to art 2(c) of ILO Convention No 29 for detainees or convicts to be hired to or placed at the disposal of private individuals, companies or associations, this

prohibition was deliberately omitted from the Convention for the Protection of Human Rights and Fundamental Freedoms, art 4: Applications 3134/67, 3172/67 *Twenty-one Detained Persons v Germany* 11 YB 528 (1968), EComHR.

2   MILITARY SERVICE

4.4.11   Forced and compulsory labour does not include any service of a military character or, in case of conscientious objectors in countries where they are recognised, service exacted instead of compulsory military service[1].

1   Application 2299/64 *Grandrath v Germany* 8 YB 324, 10 YB 626 (1965), EComHR, see para **4.9.5**.

4.4.12   'Military service' includes voluntary as well as compulsory military service. Thus, the Commission rejected complaints from boys who had committed themselves at the ages of 15 or 16 to service in the armed forces of the Crown until they were 18, and for a further nine years thereafter[1].

1   Applications 3435-3438/67 *W, X, Y and Z v United Kingdom* 11 YB 562 (1968), EComHR.

4.4.13   States have the freedom to recognise or not to recognise conscientious objections as exempting persons from military service[1].

1   Application 5591/72 *X v Austria* 43 CD 161 (1973), EComHR.

3   EMERGENCY SERVICE

4.4.14   Forced or compulsory labour does not include any service exacted in case of an emergency or calamity threatening the life or well-being of the community. Two members of the Commission relied on this ground in concluding that the requirement on the applicant in *Iversen*[1] to practise for a limited period of time as a dentist in northern Norway, where there was a shortage of dentists, did not constitute forced or compulsory labour.

1   Application 1468/62 *Iversen v Norway* 6 YB 278 (1963), EComHR. See para **4.4.8** above.

4   NORMAL CIVIC OBLIGATIONS

4.4.15   Any work or labour forming part of normal civic obligations is not within the scope of art 4(2). Normal civic obligations include: a lessor's obligation to maintain his building[1]; the obligation on a holder of a shooting licence to participate in gassing fox holes to help eradicate rabies[2]; an employer's obligation to deduct tax from his employees' income[3]; and both compulsory fire service, and a financial contribution payable in lieu of such service[4].

1   Application 5593/72 *X v Austria* 45 CD 113 (1973), EComHR.
2   Application 9686/82 *X v Federal Republic of Germany* 39 DR 90 (1984), EComHR.
3   Application 7427/76 *Four Companies v Austria* 7 DR 148 (1976), EComHR.
4   *Schmidt v Germany* (1994) 18 EHRR 513, E Ct HR, para 22.

Article 5   Right to liberty and security of person

(1) Everyone has the right to liberty and security of person. No one shall be deprived of his liberty save in the following cases and in accordance with a procedure prescribed by law:

(a) the lawful detention of a person after conviction by a competent court;

(b) the lawful arrest or detention of a person for non-compliance with the lawful order of a court or in order to secure the fulfilment of any obligation prescribed by law;

(c) the lawful arrest or detention of a person effected for the purpose of bringing him before the competent legal authority on reasonable suspicion of having committed an offence or when it is reasonably considered necessary to prevent his committing an offence or fleeing after having done so;

(d) the detention of a minor by lawful order for the purpose of educational supervision or his lawful detention for the purpose of bringing him before the competent legal authority;

(e) the lawful detention of persons for the prevention of the spreading of infectious diseases, of persons of unsound mind, alcoholics or drug addicts or vagrants;

(f) the lawful arrest or detention of a person to prevent his effecting an unauthorised entry into the country or of a person against whom action is being taken with a view to deportation or extradition.

(2) Everyone who is arrested shall be informed promptly, in a language which he understands, of the reasons for his arrest and of any charge against him.

(3) Everyone arrested or detained in accordance with the provisions of paragraph (1)(c) of this Article shall be brought promptly before a judge or other officer authorised by law to exercise judicial power and shall be entitled to trial within a reasonable time, or to release pending trial. Release may be conditioned by guarantees to appear for trial.

(4) Everyone who is deprived of his liberty by arrest or detention shall be entitled to take proceedings by which the lawfulness of his detention shall be decided speedily by a court and his release ordered if his detention is not lawful.

(5) Everyone who has been the victim of arrest or detention in contravention of the provisions of this Article shall have an enforceable right to compensation.

A   Introduction

4.5.1 Article 5 protects the liberty and security of the person and occupies an important position in the Convention system[1]. It contemplates individual liberty 'in its classic sense, that is to say the physical liberty of the person'[2]. The underlying aim of art 5 is 'to ensure that no one should be dispossessed of this liberty in an arbitrary fashion'[3]. The E Ct HR has consistently emphasised that it is one of the fundamental principles of a democratic society that the state must strictly adhere to the rule of law when interfering with the right to personal liberty[4].

1   *Brogan v United Kingdom* (1988) 11 EHRR 117, para 58; *De Wilde, Ooms and Versyp v Belgium* (1971) 1 EHRR 373, para 65.
2   *Engel v Netherlands* (1976) 1 EHRR 647, para 58. The phrase 'security of the person' must also be understood in the context of physical liberty rather than physical safety: *East African Asians v United Kingdom* (1973) 3 EHRR 76, EComHR, para 220. The inclusion of the word 'security' simply serves to emphasise the requirement that the detention may not be arbitrary: *Bozano v France* (1986) 9 EHRR 297, paras 54 and 60. 'Liberty of the person' in art 5(1) means freedom from arrest and detention, and 'security of the person' means protection against arbitrary interference with this liberty: *Adler and Biras v Germany* 20 YB 102 (1977) at 146. Article 5 does not therefore afford a right to *social* security: Application 5287/71 *X v Federal Republic of Germany* (1972) 1 Digest 288. Nor does it impose positive obligations on the state to provide physical protection against threats to personal safety by private individuals: Application 6040/73 *X v Ireland* 16 YB 388 (1973). On the positive obligations of the state and the application of the Human Rights Act 1998 to disputes between individuals, see para **2.6.3** at n 3.
3   *Engel v Netherlands* (1976) 1 EHRR 647, para 58; *Winterwerp v Netherlands* (1979) 2 EHRR 387, para 37; *Guzzardi v Italy* (1980) 3 EHRR 333, para 92; *Bozano v France* (1986) 9 EHRR 297, para 54; *Van Droogenbroeck v Belgium* (1982) 4 EHRR 443, para 40; *Weeks v United Kingdom* (1987) 10 EHRR 293, para 49.
4   *Brogan v United Kingdom* (1988) 11 EHRR 117, para 58; *Engel v Netherlands* (1976) 1 EHRR 647, para 69.

B   Scope

1   DEPRIVATION OF LIBERTY

4.5.2   Article 5 is concerned with the *deprivation* of liberty and not with mere *restrictions* on freedom of movement[1]. The distinction is not always easy to identify since the difference is 'merely one of degree or intensity, and not one of nature or substance'[2]. In determining whether the level of restraint involved amounts to a detention regard should be had to 'a whole range of criteria such as the type, duration, effects and manner of implementation of the measure in question'[3].

1   *Engel v Netherlands* (1976) 1 EHRR 647, para 58; *Guzzardi v Italy* (1980) 3 EHRR 333, para 92; *Raimondo v Italy* (1994) 18 EHRR 237, para 39. Lesser restrictions on freedom of movement are governed by art 2 of the fourth protocol, to which the United Kingdom is not a party. See paras **4.16.3–4.16.7**.
2   *Guzzardi v Italy* (1980) 3 EHRR 333, para 93; *Ashingdane v United Kingdom* (1985) 7 EHRR 528, para 41.
3   *Guzzardi v Italy* (1980) 3 EHRR 333, para 92; *Ashingdane v United Kingdom* (1985) 7 EHRR 528, para 41; *Engel v Netherlands* (1976) 1 EHRR 647, paras 58–59. As to the position in domestic law see *Clerk and Lindsell on Torts* (17th edn) paras 12–17 to 12–18.

4.5.3   Applying these criteria, the E Ct HR has held that 'strict arrest' imposed on soldiers for disciplinary offences amounted to a deprivation of liberty despite the different standards which apply to military personnel[1]. A person detained under house arrest was deprived of his liberty as was a person who was confined in a hospital, school or church which was used in a similar fashion to a detention centre[2]. But a curfew or an order preventing an individual from leaving a particular area is not a deprivation of liberty[3]. A person held in a mental hospital under a compulsory detention order could rely on art 5 even though he was kept in an open ward for part of the time and could leave the hospital unaccompanied on occasions[4]. On the other hand, a patient who, whilst remaining subject to a detention order, was provisionally released, was no longer deprived of her liberty[5]. In *Guzzardi v Italy*[6], the E Ct HR held that a suspected mafia member was deprived of her liberty during one phase of his detention, when he was made the subject of a compulsory residence order requiring him to live on a small island subject to strict police supervision. In its admissibility decision in the *Guzzardi* case, the Commission distinguished this regime from the circumstances prevailing during another phase of the applicant's detention when he was held on the Italian mainland, subject to a less strict regime[7]. Whether a person is deprived of his liberty may also depend on the degree of freedom otherwise enjoyed. In *X v Switzerland*[8] the Commission held that a disciplinary order confining a prisoner to his cell did not lead to an additional deprivation of liberty[9], whereas in *Campbell and Fell v United Kingdom*[10] an order for the forfeiture of remission was held to have imposed an additional period of detention.

1   *Engel v Netherlands* (1976) 1 EHRR 647, para 63. In *Engel* the E Ct HR distinguished 'strict arrest' from so-called 'light arrest' and 'aggravated arrest', neither of which were found to amount to a deprivation of liberty because the soldiers concerned were not confined and were able to perform their normal service.
2   *Greek Case* 12 YB (1969) at 134–135.
3   *Cyprus v Turkey* (1976) 4 EHRR 482, para 235; *Raimondo v Italy* (1994) 18 EHRR 237, para 39.
4   *Ashingdane v United Kingdom* (1985) 7 EHRR 528, para 42.
5   *W v Sweden* 59 DR 158 (1988).
6   (1980) 3 EHRR 333.
7   *Guzzardi v Italy* (1980) 3 EHRR 333, EComHR, para 56
8   Application 7754/77 11 DR 216 (1978), para 2.
9   Cf *R v Deputy Governor of Parkhurst Prison, ex p Hague* [1992] 1 AC 58 where the House of Lords came to the same conclusion in relation to the tort of false imprisonment.
10   (1984) 7 EHRR 165, para 72.

4.5.4   The duration of the detention is not necessarily decisive[1]: art 5 has been held to apply to detention for the purposes of carrying out a compulsory blood test[2], or during the course of a journey in a moving vehicle[3], or an aircraft[4]. Detention does however depend upon the intention of the authorities. Where the police intend merely to question a suspect without detaining him[5], art 5 will not apply. In *X v Federal Republic of Germany*[6] the Commission held that a ten year old girl who was questioned at a police station for two hours without being arrested, locked into a cell or formally detained was not deprived of her liberty for the purposes of art 5. Similarly, art 5 will not apply where the individual consents to the restriction, providing the consent is clearly established and unequivocal. But the fact that a person initially agreed to enter into an institution does not prevent him from relying on art 5 if he subsequently wishes to leave[7]. Neither is an asylum seeker who is housed in an airport transit area prevented from relying on art 5 simply because it is possible for him voluntarily to leave the country in which he seeks refuge[8]. In 1989, in the case of *Nielsen v Denmark*[9], the E Ct HR held that where the detention of a child was in issue, consent of the parent or guardian might be sufficient, even if the detention was contrary to the child's wishes. The E Ct HR, however, noted that parental rights were not absolute and that it was incumbent on the State to provide safeguards against abuse[10].

1   *X and Y v Sweden* 7 DR 123 (1976); Application 8278/78 *X v Austria* 18 DR 154 (1979).
2   Application 8278/78 *X v Austria* 18 DR 154 (1979).
3   *Bozano v France* (1986) 9 EHRR 297.
4   *X and Y v Sweden* 7 DR 123 (1976).
5   The powers of the police in England and Wales to question a suspect without arrest are governed by the Police and Criminal Evidence Act 1984, s 29 ff and para 3.15 of the Code of Practice on Detention, Treatment and Questioning (Code C).
6   Application 8819/79 24 DR 158 (1981) at 161.
7   *De Wilde, Ooms and Versyp v Belgium* (1971) 1 EHRR 373, para 65.

8   *Amuur v France* (1996) 22 EHRR 533, para 48.
9   (1988) 11 EHRR 175.
10   But note that the UN Convention on the Rights of the Child (1989) affords the child the right to be consulted over decisions affecting its future and provides express protection against arbitrary deprivation of liberty.

2   TERRITORIAL APPLICATION

4.5.5   Article 5 applies to an arrest or detention by agents of the contracting state, even if it is effected outside the jurisdiction[1]. However, where a contracting party receives custody of a person detained by a non-Convention country, that person cannot claim a violation of art 5 by the receiving state, even though the return may amount to a breach of the returning state's laws or the Convention[2]. Where the detention is based on a criminal conviction under art 5(1)(a), a conviction of a foreign court is sufficient[3], even if the state concerned is not party to the Convention, unless the conviction resulted from a 'flagrant denial of justice'[4].

1   Contracting States are bound to secure the Convention rights 'to all persons under their actual authority and responsibility, whether that authority is exercised within their own territory or abroad': *Cyprus v Turkey* 2 DR 125 (1975) at 136. See also *Freda v Italy* 21 DR 250 (1980).
2   *Altmann v France* 37 DR 225 (1984); *Reinette v France* 63 DR 189 (1989) at 193; *Freda v Italy* 21 DR 250 (1980).
3   Application 1322/62 *X v Federal Republic of Germany* 6 YB 494 (1963) at 516.
4   *Drozd and Janousek v France and Spain* (1992) 14 EHRR 745, para 110.

3   DEROGATION

4.5.6   Article 15 of the Convention permits a state to derogate from art 5 in times of war or other public emergency threatening the life of the nation. The United Kingdom's only derogation applies to art 5(3). It was entered in response to the judgment in *Brogan v United Kingdom*[1] where the E Ct HR held that detention for four days and six hours under the Prevention of Terrorism (Temporary Provisions) Act 1984 was incompatible with the requirement that a detained person should be brought promptly before a judge or judicial officer. The derogation preserves the power of the Secretary of State to extend the period of detention of persons suspected of terrorism in connection with Northern Ireland for a total of up to seven days[2]. The Human Rights Act 1998 expressly retains the derogation to art 5(3)[3] but places a time limit of five years on its operation[4] subject to renewal by order of the Secretary of State.

1   (1988) 11 EHRR 117.
2   The derogation was subsequently held to be compatible with art 15: *Brannigan and McBride v United Kingdom* (1993) 17 EHRR 539. See para **2.14.2**.
3   HRA 1998, s 14. See para **2.14**. The text of the derogation is set out in the Human Rights Act 1998, Sch 3.
4   HRA 1998, s 16. See para **2.16**.

D   Permissible grounds for deprivation of liberty

1   GENERAL

4.5.7   Article 5(1) provides an exhaustive[1] definition of the circumstances in which a person may be lawfully deprived of his liberty and is to be given a narrow construction[2]. In addition to falling within sub-paras (a)–(f)[3], any detention must be:

(i) 'lawful' and (ii) carried out 'in accordance with a procedure prescribed by law'[4]. These terms refer to conformity with national law and procedure and it is therefore 'in the first place for the national authorities, notably the courts, to interpret and apply domestic law'[5]. Nevertheless, it remains the function of the E Ct HR to determine whether art 5 has been violated, and the court therefore has the ultimate power to interpret and apply national law[6]. The scope of the court's task in this connection 'is subject to limits inherent in the logic of the European system of protection'[7], so that on the international level[8] a certain margin of appreciation will be afforded to the decisions of the domestic courts[9].

1   *Ireland v United Kingdom* (1978) 2 EHRR 25, para 194.
2   *Guzzardi v Italy* (1980) 3 EHRR 333, paras 98 and 100; *Winterwerp v Netherlands* (1979) 2 EHRR 387, para 37; *Quinn v France* (1995) 21 EHRR 529, para 42.
3   The grounds enumerated in sub-paras (a)–(f) are not mutually exclusive: *McVeigh, O'Neill and Evans v United Kingdom* 25 DR 15 (1981).
4   *Winterwerp v Netherlands* (1979) 2 EHRR 387, para 39.
5   *Bozano v France* (1986) 9 EHRR 297, para 58; *Winterwerp v Netherlands* (1979) 2 EHRR 387; *Wassink v Netherlands* (1990) Series A/185-A, para 24; *Benham v United Kingdom* (1996) 22 EHRR 293, para 41.
6   *Bozano v France* (1986) 9 EHRR 297, para 58; *Benham v United Kingdom* (1996) 22 EHRR 293, para 41.
7   *Bozano v France* (1986) 9 EHRR 297, para 58.
8   As to the relevance of the 'margin of appreciation' doctrine before the national courts see paras**3.20– 3.27**.
9   *Weeks v United Kingdom* (1987) 10 EHRR 293, para 50; *Winterwerp v Netherlands* (1979) 2 EHRR 387, para 40.

4.5.8   For a detention to comply with art 5, the procedure followed must be in conformity with the applicable municipal law[1] and with the Convention[2], including the general principles contained in the Convention[3]. Moreover, the term 'lawful' implies that the domestic law on which the detention is based must itself be 'accessible and precise'[4]. Thus the E Ct HR has held that an 'arrested or detained person is entitled to a review of the "lawfulness" of his detention in the light not only of the requirements of domestic law, but also of the text of the Convention, the general principles embodied therein, and the aim of the restrictions permitted by article 5(1)'[5].

1   This includes directly applicable EC law: *Caprino v United Kingdom* 12 DR 14 (1978).
2   *Winterwerp v Netherlands* (1979) 2 EHRR 387, para 37; *Herczegfalvy v Austria* (1992) 15 EHRR 437, para 63; *Bozano v France* (1986) 9 EHRR 297, para 54; *Weeks v United Kingdom* (1987) 10 EHRR 293, para 42.
3   The 'general principles' contained in the Convention include the 'rule of law':*Engel v Netherlands* (1988) 11 EHRR 117, para 69; *Brogan v United Kingdom* (1988) 11 EHRR 117, para 58.
4   Application 9174/80 *Zamir v United Kingdom* 40 DR 42 (1983); *Sunday Times v United Kingdom* (1979) 2 EHRR 245, para 49; *Amuur v France* (1992) 22 EHRR 533, para 50.
5   *E v Norway* (1990) 17 EHRR 30, para 49.

4.5.9   Article 5 has been held to prohibit deprivation of liberty which is 'arbitrary' in its motivation or effect[1]. A detention will be arbitrary if it is not in keeping with the purpose of the restrictions permissible under art 5(1) or with art 5 generally[2]. Detention which is ostensibly for the purpose of deportation but which is in reality a disguised illegal extradition is arbitrary[3]. Even if properly motivated, a detention may be arbitrary if it is disproportionate to the attainment of its purpose[4]. Thus in *Bouamar v Belgium*[5] detention of a minor for the purposes of educational supervision was held to be arbitrary where it involved 'fruitless repetition' of placements in institutions with inadequate educational facilities. Detention imposed on grounds of dangerousness by reference to characteristics which are susceptible to change with the passage of time will become arbitrary if those characteristics are no longer present[6]. On the other hand, the fact that time spent in custody abroad is not taken into account in computing the length of a prison sentence does not render the additional period of detention arbitrary[7]. Nor does the fact that detention results from a 'loss of time' order by the Court of Appeal Criminal Division under the Criminal Appeal Act 1968, s 29(1)[8].

1   *Winterwerp v Netherlands* (1979) 2 EHRR 387, paras 37–39; *Van Droogenbroeck v Belgium* (1982) 4 EHRR 443, para 48; *Weeks v United Kingdom* (1987) 10 EHRR 293, para 49; *Bozano v France* (1986) 9 EHRR 297, para 54; *Ashingdane v United Kingdom* (1985) 7 EHRR 528, para 44. Cf *Ong Ah Chuan v Public Prosecutor* [1981] AC 648, PC.
2   *Winterwerp v Netherlands* (1979) 2 EHRR 387, para 39; *Bouamar v Belgium* (1988) 11 EHRR 1, para 50; *Weeks* (1987) 10 EHRR 293, para 42; *Ashingdane* (1985) 7 EHRR 528, para 44.
3   *Bozano v France* (1986) 9 EHRR 297.
4   *Winterwerp v Netherlands* (1979) 2 EHRR 387 para 39; *Van Droogenbroeck v Belgium* (1982) 4 EHRR 443.
5   (1988) 11 EHRR 1, para 53.
6   *Van Droogenbroeck v Belgium* (1982) 4 EHRR 443; *Weeks v United Kingdom* (1987) 10 EHRR 293; *Thynne, Wilson and Gunnell v United Kingdom* (1990) 13 EHRR 666; *Abed Hussain v United Kingdom* (1996) 22 EHRR 1.
7   *C v United Kingdom* 43 DR 177 (1985).
8   *Monnell and Morris v United Kingdom* (1987) 10 EHRR 205. Under the Criminal Appeals Act 1968, s 29(1) the Court of Appeal may, if it considers that an appeal is without merit, direct that time served between the imposition of the sentence and the disposal of the appeal should not count towards the accused person's sentence. As to the circumstances in which such an order may be made see *Practice Direction (Crime: Sentence: Loss of Time)* [1980] 1 WLR 270.

2   DETENTION FOLLOWING CONVICTION

4.5.10   The first exception to the rule that no one may be deprived of his liberty is the lawful[1] detention[2] of a person after conviction by a competent court[3]. The word 'after' does not simply mean that the detention must follow the conviction in point of time[4]. There must also be a sufficient causal connection between the conviction and the deprivation of liberty at issue[5]. In *Monnell and Morris v United Kingdom*[6] the E Ct HR found a sufficient causal connection between a criminal conviction and an additional period of detention which resulted from a 'loss of time' order[7] by the Court of Appeal (Criminal Division) since the intention of the provision was to prevent abuse of the right of appeal.

1   As to the meaning of 'lawful' see paras **4.5.7–4.5.9**.
2   As to the meaning of 'detention' see paras **4.5.2–4.5.4**.
3   Article 5(1)(a).
4   *Van Droogenbroeck v Belgium* (1982) 4 EHRR 443, para 35; *Bozano v France* (1986) 9 EHRR 297, para 53.
5   *Weeks v United Kingdom* (1987) 10 EHRR 293, para 42. In the words of the E Ct HR, 'the detention must result from, follow and depend upon, or occur by virtue of the conviction': *B v Austria* (1990) Series A/175, para 38.
6   (1987) 10 EHRR 205.
7   See further para **4.5.9**, n 8.

4.5.11   A detention is not rendered retroactively unlawful under art 5(1)(a) because the conviction or sentence on which it was based is overturned on appeal[1]. But the position is different where the court of first instance had no power to order detention[2]. If an error made by the trial court was such as to deprive it of its jurisdiction to commit a person to custody[3], the detention will be unlawful for the purposes of art 5[4].

1   *Krzycki v Fegeral Republic of Germany* (1978) 13 DR 57 at 61; *Benham v United Kingdom* (1996) 22 EHRR 293, para 42.
2   *Van der Leer v Netherlands* (1990) 12 EHRR 567; *Artico v Italy* 8 DR 73 (1977) at 88–89. Cf *Benham v United Kingdom* (1996) 22 EHRR 293.

3   As to the circumstances in which an error by a Magistrates Court will deprive the court of jurisdiction to imprison see *Re McC* [1985] AC 528, HL; *R v Manchester City Justices, ex p Davies* [1989] QB 631, CA.
4   In *Benham v United Kingdom* (1996) 22 EHRR 293, paras 42–46 the E Ct HR examined whether the Magistrates' Court had made a jurisdictional error in the decision which led to the applicant's detention. Cf the decision of the Commission in the same case, paras 45–52.

(a)   Conviction

4.5.12   A conviction means a 'finding of guilt' in respect of an offence and the imposition of a penalty[1]. Thus, an order for detention in a mental institution which follows conviction will fall within art 5(1)(a)[2] whereas such an order imposed following an acquittal must be examined under art 5(1)(e)[3]. A conviction justifying detention under art 5(1)(a) may be for a disciplinary offence as well as a criminal offence[4] or a finding of guilt in proceedings defined as civil by domestic law[5]. The conviction may be that of a foreign court[6], even if the state is not party to the Convention, unless the conviction resulted from a 'flagrant denial of justice'[7]. The conviction referred to in art 5(1)(a) is a decision of a court of first instance so that detention pending appeal falls within art 5(1)(a) of the Convention rather than art 5(1)(c)[8].

1   *X v United Kingdom* (1981) 4 EHRR 188, para 39; *B v Austria* (1990) 13 EHRR 20, para 38. See also *Guzzardi v Italy* (1980) 3 EHRR 333, para 100, where the E Ct HR held that art 5(1)(a) did not permit detention as a preventative or security measure since such detention did not involve a finding of guilt.
2   *X v United Kingdom* (1981) 4 EHRR 188, para 39.
3   *Luberti v Italy* (1984) 6 EHRR 440, para 25; *Herczegfalvy v Austria* (1992) 15 EHRR 437.
4   *Engel v Netherlands* (1976) 1 EHRR 647, para 68.
5   As to the Convention's autonomous approach to the interpretation of the term 'criminal' in art 6 see para **4.6.13**.
6   Application 1322/62 *X v Federal Republic of Germany* 6 YB 494 (1963) at 516.
7   *Drozd and Janousek v France and Spain* (1992) 14 EHRR 745, para 110.
8   *Wemhoff v Federal Republic of Germany* (1968) 1 EHRR 55, para 9.

(b)   Competent court

4.5.13   The judicial guarantees required by art 5(1)(a) are not necessarily the same as those required by art 6[1]. In order to qualify as a 'court' for the purposes of art 5 the body in question must be one which 'gives to the individuals concerned guarantees appropriate to the kind of deprivation of liberty in question'[2]. It does not therefore need to be a 'court of law of the classic kind integrated within the standard judicial machinery of the country'[3], but it must be independent both of the executive and of the parties[4], and it must have power to give a legally binding judgment concerning a person's release[5]. A court will be 'competent' for the purposes of art 5(1)(a) providing it has jurisdiction under national law to hear the case and to determine whether an individual should be detained[6].

1   *Engel v Netherlands* (1976) 1 EHRR 647, para 68 (public hearing required in a criminal case not obligatory in military disciplinary proceedings). On art 6, see para **4.6**.
2   *De Wilde, Ooms and Versyp v Belgium* (1971) 1 EHRR 373, para 76.
3   *Weeks v United Kingdom* (1987) 10 EHRR 293, para 61.
4   *De Wilde, Ooms and Versyp v Belgium* (1971) 1 EHRR 373, para 77; *Weeks v United Kingdom* (1987) 10 EHRR 293, para 61; *Engel v Netherlands* (1976) 1 EHRR 647, para 68. The following have been held not to satisfy this requirement: the medical officer of a person of unsound mind, and a government minister (*X v United Kingdom* (1981) 4 EHRR 188, para 61); and a public prosecutor (*Winterwerp v Netherlands* (1979) 2 EHRR 387, para 64).
5   *X v United Kingdom* (1981) 4 EHRR 188, para 61 (Mental Health Review Tribunal); *Weeks v United Kingdom* (1987) 10 EHRR 293 (Parole Board).
6   Application 2645/65 *X v Austria* 11 YB 322 (1968) at 348; *Weeks v United Kingdom* (1987) 10 EHRR 293, paras 64–68.

3   DETENTION FOR NON-COMPLIANCE WITH COURT ORDERS/ TO SECURE COMPLIANCE WITH A LEGAL OBLIGATION

4.5.14   The second exception to the general rule in art 5(1) is the lawful arrest or detention of a person for non-compliance with the lawful order of a court or in order to secure the fulfilment of an obligation prescribed by law.

(a)   Non-compliance with a court order

4.5.15   The first limb of art 5(1)(b) provides for detention in civil matters where the applicant has failed to comply with an injunction or other court order. The order must have been made by a court of competent jurisdiction[1] and it must be capable of enforcement. Article 5(1)(b) has been held to permit detention for failure to pay a fine[2], for refusal to undergo a blood test[3] or medical examination[4] ordered by a court; and for failure to observe a residence restriction[5]. Imprisonment for a failure to fulfil a contractual obligation is not a violation of art 5(1) since it is separately protected under art 1 of protocol 4 to which the United Kingdom is not a party[6].

1   A warning by the Chief of Police does not constitute an order of a court for the purposes of art 5(1)(b): *Guzzardi v Italy* (1980) 3 EHRR 333, para 101.
2   Application 6289/73 *Airey v Ireland* 8 DR 42 (1977).
3   Application 8275/78 *X v Austria* 18 DR 154 (1979).
4   Application 6659/74 *X v Federal Republic of Germany* 3 DR 92 (1975).
5   Application 8916/80 *Freda v Italy* 21 DR 250 (1980).
6   See para **2.1.5**, n 2.

(b)   Compliance with legal obligations

4.5.16   The second limb of art 5(1)(b) has been narrowly construed so as to refer only to the situation where a person is detained 'to compel him to fulfil a specific and concrete obligation which he has until then failed to satisfy'[1]. Thus, art 5(1)(b) cannot be relied upon to justify detention of a person in order to compel him to discharge his general duty of obedience to the law[2], and cannot justify internment or preventative detention of the kind that may be introduced during a state of emergency[3]. Similarly, an obligation imposed on a suspect to 'change his behaviour' has been held insufficiently specific to fall within this definition[4], as has a power of detention for the 'preservation of peace and the maintenance of order'[5]. On the other hand, an obligation to carry an identity card and to submit to an identity check has been held to be sufficiently specific[6], as has an obligation to do military service[7], an obligation to live in a designated locality[8]; and an obligation to provide information and documentation when passing through border controls[9].

1   *Engel v Netherlands* (1976) 1 EHRR 647, para 69; *Guzzardi v Italy* (1980) 3 EHRR 333, para 101.
2   *Engel v Netherlands* (1976) 1 EHRR 647, para 69; *Guzzardi v Italy* (1980) 3 EHRR 333, para 101.
3   *Lawless v Ireland* (1961) 1 EHRR 15, paras 9 and 12.
4   *Ciulla v Italy* (1989) Series A/148, EComHR.
5   *Ireland v United Kingdom* (1978) 2 EHRR 25, para 195 concerning the Civil Authorities (Special Powers) Act (NI) 1922.
6   Application 10179/82 *B v France* 52 DR 111 (1987); *Reyntjens v Belgium* 73 DR 136 (1992).
7   Application 10600/83 *Johansen v Norway* 44 DR 155 (1985).
8   *Ciulla v Italy* (1989) 13 EHRR 346.
9   Applications 8022, 8025, 8027/77 *McVeigh, O'Neill and Evans v United Kingdom* 25 DR 15 (1981).

4.5.17   Detention may only be imposed under the second limb of art 5(1)(b) if its purpose is to *secure fulfilment* of the obligation, rather than merely to punish the person concerned for its breach[1]. In general, the obligation must be one which is 'already incumbent on the person concerned'[2]. However, in *McVeigh, O'Neill and*

Evans v United Kingdom[3] the Commission held that in certain 'limited circumstances of a pressing nature' a coercive power of detention may be permissible where it is necessary to secure fulfilment of a specific obligation at the time when it arises[4]. This principle may only be invoked where there is an immediate necessity for the fulfilment of the obligation, and where there is no reasonably practicable alternative means available for securing compliance[5]. Assuming these criteria are satisfied, the importance and urgency of the obligation must nevertheless be balanced against the individual's right to liberty and the length of the period of the detention. Thus, in *McVeigh* the Commission held that there was no breach of art 5(1) where persons entering the United Kingdom were required to submit to 'further examination' at the point of entry pursuant to the Prevention of Terrorism (Supplemental Temporary Provisions) Order 1976[6]. The applicants were detained for that purpose and released after 45 hours, having been questioned, searched, photographed and fingerprinted but not charged with any offence. In finding no violation the Commission attached importance to the fact that the obligation applied only on entering and leaving the United Kingdom and in order to verify the particular matters referred to in the legislation[7]. The same principle would also apply to other powers of temporary detention exercisable by the police without reasonable suspicion, such as the power to detain for the purpose of verifying ownership of a vehicle or the power to establish a roadblock.

1 Application 10600/83 *Johansen v Norway* 44 DR 155 (1985). In *Benham v United Kingdom* (1996) 22 EHRR 293, the E Ct HR held that it was sufficient that the legislative scheme was aimed at securing the fulfilment of an obligation to pay the Community Charge even though the applicant was unable to meet the obligation since he did not have the means to pay.
2 *Ciulla v Italy* (1989) 13 EHRR 346, para 36; *Guzzardi v Italy* (1980) 3 EHRR 333, para 101.
3 (1981) 5 EHRR 71.
4 (1981) 5 EHRR 71, paras 175 and 190–191.
5 (1981) 5 EHRR 71, para 191.
6 SI 1976/465.
7 Cf *Ireland v United Kingdom* (1978) 2 EHRR 25.

4   ARREST ON REASONABLE SUSPICION

4.5.18   Article 5(1)(c) authorises lawful arrest or detention for the purpose of bringing a person before the competent legal authority on reasonable suspicion of having committed a criminal offence, or when it is reasonably considered necessary to prevent him committing an offence or fleeing having done so. It has to be read in conjunction with art 5(3) which provides additional protection for persons detained under art 5(1)(c)[1].

1 *Ciulla v Italy* (1989) 13 EHRR 346, para 38; *Lawless v Ireland* (1961) 1 EHRR 15, para 14. On art 5(3), see paras **4.5.37–4.5.47**.

(a)   Competent legal authority

4.5.19   The requirement that detention must have been effected for the purpose of bringing a person before the competent legal authority is not confined to arrest on reasonable suspicion. It applies to all three grounds of detention in art 5(1)(c)[1]. Thus, in *Lawless v Ireland*[2] the E Ct HR held that the internment of a suspected terrorist could not be justified under art 5(1)(c) on the ground that it was necessary to prevent him committing an offence, since the detention was not effected for the purpose of initiating a criminal prosecution. The term 'competent legal authority' has the same meaning as the term 'judge or other officer authorised by law to exercise judicial power' in art 5(3)[3]. The competent legal authority in England and Wales is a magistrates' court.

1   *Lawless v Ireland* (1961) 1 EHRR 15, para 14; *De Jong, Baljet and Van Den Brink v Netherlands* (1984) 8 EHRR 20, paras 43 and 44.
2   (1961) 1 EHRR 15, paras 14 and 15.
3   *Schiesser v Switzerland* (1979) 2 EHRR 417, para 29.

(b)   Reasonable suspicion

4.5.20   In order for an arrest on reasonable suspicion to be justified under art 5(1)(c) it is not necessary to establish either that an offence has been committed or that the person detained has committed it[1]. Neither is it necessary that the person detained should ultimately have been charged or taken before a court. As the E Ct HR observed in *Murray v United Kingdom*[2], the object of detention for questioning is to further a criminal investigation by confirming or discounting suspicions which provide the grounds for detention.

1   *X v Austria* (1989) 11 EHRR 112.
2   (1994) 19 EHRR 193, para 55.

4.5.21   However the requirement that the suspicion must be based on reasonable grounds 'forms an essential part of the safeguard against arbitrary arrest and detention'[1]. The fact that a suspicion is honestly held is insufficient[2]. The words 'reasonable suspicion' mean the existence of facts or information which would satisfy an objective observer that the person concerned may have committed the offence[3]. What may be regarded as reasonable will depend on all the circumstances. Even in relation to offences with national security implications however, the state must be in a position to provide evidence which is capable of satisfying a court that the arrested person was reasonably suspected of having committed the offence[4].

1   *Fox, Campbell and Hartley v United Kingdom* (1990) 13 EHRR 157, para 32.
2   *Fox, Campbell and Hartley v United Kingdom* (1990) 13 EHRR 157, para 32.
3   *Fox, Campbell and Hartley* (1990) 13 EHRR 157, para 32. Cf *Hussein v Kam* [1970] AC 942 at 946.
4   *Fox, Campbell and Hartley* (1990) 13 EHRR 157, para 34. Cf *Murray v United Kingdom* (1994) 19 EHRR 193, paras 56, 61–63.

(c)   Criminal offence

4.5.22   Article 5(1)(c) is confined to criminal proceedings[1]. The term 'offence' means a criminal or military[2] offence which is 'concrete and specified'[3]. Article 5(1)(c) is not therefore capable of authorising a general power of preventative detention since this would lead to 'conclusions repugnant to the fundamental principles of the Convention'[4]. In *Brogan v United Kingdom*[5] the applicants were detained for questioning in connection with alleged involvement in 'acts of terrorism'. The E Ct HR held that although an 'act of terrorism' (which was defined as 'the use of violence for political ends'[6]) was not a criminal offence in itself under domestic law, it was 'well in keeping with the idea of an offence' for the purposes of art 5(1)(c), particularly since the applicants had been questioned about specific offences immediately after their arrests.

1   *Ciulla v Italy* (1989) 13 EHRR 346, para 38, where the E Ct HR held that detention of the applicant in order to bring him before a competent legal authority in connection with a compulsory residence order did not fall within art 5(1)(c).
2   *De Jong, Baljet and Van Den Brink v Netherlands* (1984) 8 EHRR 20.
3   *Guzzardi v Italy* (1980) 3 EHRR 333, para 102.
4   *Lawless v Ireland* (1961) 1 EHRR 15, para 14.
5   (1988) 11 EHRR 117, para 51. Cf *Ireland v United Kingdom* (1978) 2 EHRR 25, para 196.
6   See the Prevention of Terrorism (Temporary Provisions) Act 1984, s 14.

5   DETENTION OF MINORS

4.5.23   Article 5(1)(d) authorises the detention of a minor by lawful[1] order for the purposes of educational supervision or in order to bring him before the competent legal authority[2]. The term 'minor' has an autonomous definition within the Convention, although no contracting state has an age of majority less than 18, so that a person younger than 18 may be taken to be a minor. Above that age, national law will continue to be relevant[3].

1   As to the meaning of 'lawful' see para **4.5.7–4.5.9**.
2   As to the meaning of 'competent legal authority' see para **4.5.19**.
3   See Application 8500/79 *X v Switzerland* (1979) 18 DR 238. The Council of Europe has by resolution recommended that member states should reduce the age of majority from 21 to 18 (Resolution CM(72)29 of the Committee of Ministers of the Council of Europe). See also the UN Human Rights Committee General Comment 21 (44th Session, 1992), para 13, which suggests that all persons under the age of at least 18 should be treated as juveniles for the purposes of the ICCPR, art 10. See further the United Nations Standard Minimum Rules for the Administration of Juvenile Justice (the Beijing Rules (1987)).

(a)   Educational supervision

4.5.24   Detention of a minor under art 5(1)(d) may only be for one of two identified purposes. First, detention is permitted for the purposes of educational supervision. This will clearly include detention in a reformatory for the purpose of educational supervision, but will also cover an order requiring attendance at an ordinary school (which will itself involve a deprivation of liberty). Such an order may be made by an administrative authority rather than a court, provided that there is an opportunity to challenge the order by way of court proceedings under art 5(4)[1]. Detention in a remand prison or other institution without educational facilities may be permitted as an interim custody measure whilst arrangements are made for transfer to an institution with such facilities, but such custody must be strictly limited. In *Bouamar v Belgium*[2] the E Ct HR held that detention of a 16 year old boy in a remand prison with no educational facilities for a total period of 119 days (spread over nine periods within a year) was a violation of art 5(1)(d).

1   See para **4.5.48** ff.
2   (1987) 11 EHRR 1. The E Ct HR rejected the argument that the detention in the remand prison was itself for the purposes of educational supervision, since there were no educational facilities in the prison. See also *Nielsen v Denmark* (1988) 11 EHRR 175.

(b)   Detention of juveniles on remand

4.5.25   The second limb of art 5(1)(d) permits the lawful detention of a minor for the purpose of bringing him before the competent legal authority. This must be done within a reasonable time, although the Commission has held that an eight month period of detention of a minor accused of a criminal offence, pending preparation of the necessary psychiatric reports, was not a violation of art 5[1]. A stricter standard would appear to apply under the ICCPR, art 10(2)(b), which requires juveniles to be 'brought as speedily as possible for adjudication'[2].

1   Application 8500/79 *X v Switzerland* 18 DR 238 (1979).
2   The UN Human Rights Committee has commented on the importance of this requirement: General Comment 21 (44th Session, 1992) para 13.

6   DETENTION FOR THE PREVENTION OF THE SPREADING OF INFECTIOUS DISEASES AND OTHER PURPOSES

4.5.26   Article 5(1)(e) authorises the detention by lawful order of persons for the prevention of the spreading of infectious diseases, of persons of unsound mind, alcoholics, drug addicts or vagrants. In general, persons falling into any of these categories may be detained not only for reasons of public safety, but also because their own interests may necessitate their detention: the clause contemplates inter alia the social protection of vulnerable groups[1]. There have been no cases before the E Ct HR or Commission dealing with the prevention of the spread of infectious diseases, or of the detention of alcoholics or drug addicts. However, the cases relating to persons of unsound mind, and vagrants, provided some general guidance as to the operation of the clause.

1   *Guzzardi v Italy* (1980) 3 EHRR 333, para 98.

(a)   Persons of unsound mind

4.5.27   In relation to persons of unsound mind, the stipulation of lawfulness[1] in art 5(1)(e) has been held to require first, that the individual concerned must be reliably shown by objective medical expertise to be of unsound mind (although this condition does not apply in emergencies)[2]; second, that the individual's mental disorder is of a kind or degree which warrants compulsory confinement[3]; and third, that the disorder persists throughout the period of detention (ie that detention continues to be justified)[4]. The state has a certain discretion in making its own initial assessment[5].

1   See generally paras **4.5.7–4.5.9**. See, relating to mental illness cases, *Van der Leer v Netherlands* (1990) 12 EHRR 567; *Wassink v Netherlands* (1990) Series A/185–A.
2   *Winterwerp v Netherlands* (1979) 2 EHRR 387, para 42; *X v United Kingdom* (1981) 4 EHRR 188.
3   Cf the decision of the Supreme Court of Canada in *R v Swain* [1991] 1 SCR 933 that an automatic detention order for persons acquitted by reason of insanity under s 542(2) of the Criminal Code was contrary to the Canadian Charter of Rights, s 9 ('everyone has the right not to be arbitrarily detained or imprisoned'); in the absence of any standards for detention, 'this court cannot imagine a detention being ordered on a more arbitrary basis'.
4   *Winterwerp v Netherlands* (1979) 2 EHRR 387, para 39. There is no express or implied limitation on the length of detention; indefinite detention (providing it is accompanied with periodic review required by art 5(4)) is permitted: *X v Denmark* 8 YB 370 (1965): *X v Belgium* 40 CD 21 (1972).
5   *Winterwerp v Netherlands* (1979) 2 EHRR 387, para 40. Indeed, there have been no cases in which any of the three tests laid down in *Winterwerp* have been held to be violated. See also *Luberti v Italy* (1984) 6 EHRR 440; *X v United Kingdom* (1982) 4 EHRR 188 (criteria apply to recall of patient).

4.5.28   Article 5(1)(e) does not govern conditions of confinement or govern the provision of suitable treatment, which are matters for art 3[1]. However in *Ashingdane v United Kingdom*[2], the E Ct HR held that the detention of persons of unsound mind is required to be in a hospital, clinic, or other appropriate institution authorised for the detention of such persons. No definition of 'unsound mind' has been attempted by the E Ct HR or Commission, but it has been emphasised that the deprivation of a person's liberty cannot be justified simply because his views or behaviour deviate from the norms prevailing in a particular society[3].

1   Cf Application 11703/85 *D v Federal Republic of Germany* 54 DR 116 (1987) at 121. On art 3 see para **4.3**.
2   (1985) 7 EHRR 528, para 44.
3   *Winterwerp v Netherlands* (1979) 2 EHRR 387, para 37.

(b) Vagrants

4.5.29 The definition of 'vagrants' in the Belgian Criminal Code, namely 'persons who have no fixed abode, no means of subsistence, and no regular trade or profession' has been held to be within the meaning of the term 'vagrants' in art 5(1)(e)[1]. In *De Wilde, Ooms and Versyp v Netherlands*[2] the E Ct HR held that the detention in 'vagrancy centres' of three applicants by order of a Belgian Magistrate was not a violation of art 5(1)(e) because, on the facts of the case, the applicants satisfied the criteria for vagrancy. The E Ct HR rejected however the submission of the Belgian Government that the applicants had not in any event been deprived of their liberty because they had initially reported voluntarily to the police[3]. In view of the fundamental importance of the right to liberty under the Convention, which concerns the *ordre public* of the Council of Europe, the E Ct HR held that detention may violate art 5 even if the person concerned has initially agreed to it[4].

1 *De Wilde, Ooms and Versyp v Netherlands* (1971) 1 EHRR 373, para 68. See also *Guzzardi v Italy* (1980) 3 EHRR 333, para 98 (suspected Mafia members who lacked identifiable sources of income could not be classed as 'vagrants').
2 Above, paras 68 and 69.
3 See para **4.5.4**.
4 (1971) 1 EHRR 373, para 65.

7 DEPRIVATION OF LIBERTY IN CONNECTION WITH IMMIGRATION, DEPORTATION OR EXTRADITION

4.5.30 Article 5(1)(f) authorises the lawful arrest or detention of a person to prevent his effecting unauthorised entry into the country, or of a person against whom action is being taken with a view to deportation or extradition. National law authorising the detention must be accessible and foreseeable[1]. Although the term 'lawful' means, as elsewhere in art 5(1), that the arrest or detention must be lawful under domestic law and must not be arbitrary[2], it is not clear when a ruling by a national court that a measure such as a deportation notice is invalid will be held to have retrospective effect so as to render the detention contrary to art 5(1). In *Bozano v France*[3] the E Ct HR appeared to draw a distinction between agents of the state acting in good faith but subsequently found to have acted illegally, and the abuse of power ab initio. In the latter case it would be much more likely for a finding of retrospective effect to be made[4]. On the facts of the case, where an Italian national who had been convicted in absentia of murder by an Italian court was forcibly taken by French police officers by car to the Swiss border and handed to Swiss police custody, pursuant to what subsequently turned out to be an invalid deportation order, the E Ct HR held that the detention violated art 5(1), taking into account: (a) the fact that French law may have been infringed when the applicant was handed into Swiss custody; and (b) the element of 'arbitrariness' in the circumstances in which the applicant was forcibly taken to the Swiss border. The applicant's detention was not lawful, but was designed to achieve a 'disguised extradition' to Italy which could not be justified under art 5(1)(f).

1 Application 9174/80 *Zamir v United Kingdom* 40 DR 42 (1983), paras 90–91.
2 See para **4.5.9** and see *De Jong, Baljet and Van Den Brink v Netherlands* (1984) 8 EHRR 20, para 44; *Kemmache v France (No 3)* (1994) 19 EHRR 349, para 42; and *Chahal v United Kingdom* (1996) 23 EHRR 413, para 118.
3 (1986) 9 EHRR 297, para 55.
4 Cf Application 6871/75 *Caprino v United Kingdom* 22 DR 5 (1980) (invalidity of deportation order did not affect the lawfulness of detention based upon it, because it was still action being taken 'with a view' to deportation); *Zamir v United Kingdom* (1983) 40 DR 42 (requirement of non-arbitrariness in art 5(1)(f) does not permit the E Ct HR a challenge to a decision to deport on its facts).

4.5.31   The requirement that a person detained under art 5(1)(f) be detained 'with a view to deportation' does not import a requirement that the detention must be necessary to prevent him from committing an offence or absconding[1]. The reasons for detention may, however, be of relevance in relation to the question of whether the detention is arbitrary. In *Chahal v United Kingdom*[2] the E Ct HR noted the Secretary of State's assertion that national security considerations required the applicant's detention pending deportation, and noted that this decision was open to a limited form of review by the immigration advisory panel procedure, in holding that there were on the facts sufficient guarantees against arbitrary detention[3].

1   *Bozano v France* (1986) 9 EHRR 297, para 60.
2   (1997) 23 EHRR 413, paras 120–123.
3   Note however that the E Ct HR found a violation of art 5(4): see paras **4.5.50** and **4.5.52**.

4.5.32   Deprivation of liberty under art 5(1)(f) will be justified only for so long as the deportation or extradition proceedings remain in progress, and will cease to be justified if such proceedings are not prosecuted with 'due' or 'requisite' diligence[1]. In *Chahal v United Kingdom*[2] the E Ct HR held that the applicant's detention, which lasted for just over four years and six months[3] was not excessive in the light of the complexity of the proceedings and the need for detailed and careful consideration of the applicant's request for asylum[4].

1   See Application 7317/75 *Lynas v Switzerland* 6 DR 141 (1976) (requirement that deportation or extradition proceedings be conducted with 'requisite diligence' was an aspect of the requirement that the detention be 'lawful'); *X v United Kingdom* 12 DR 207 (1978) at 209; *Farmakopoulos v Belgium* 64 DR 52 (1990); *Kolompar v Belgium* (1992) 16 EHRR 197 (no violation although delay of over two years and eight months, since not attributable to authorities). See also *Tan Te Lam v Superintendant of Tai A Chau Detention Centre and A-G of Hong Kong* [1997] AC 97, where the Privy Council held that detention under the Hong Kong Immigration Ordinance pending deportation would only be lawful: (a) during the period necessary to effect removal; (b) so long as it was not evident that removal would not be possible within a reasonable period; and (c) so long as all reasonable steps were taken to ensure the removal within such a period (at 107).
2   (1997) 23 EHRR 413.
3   The end of the period under consideration by the E Ct HR being the date upon which leave to appeal to the House of Lords was refused.
4   (1997) 23 EHRR 413, paras 113–117.

E   Procedural Rights under art 5

1   THE RIGHT TO BE INFORMED OF THE GROUND FOR DETENTION

4.5.33   Article 5(2) requires that anyone arrested or detained should be 'informed promptly, in a language which he understands, of the reasons for his arrest and of any charge against him'. This requirement is not confined to arrest for a criminal offence. It applies to detention on any ground including the compulsory detention of a mental patient[1]. The requirement to give reasons arises not only where a person is initially detained but also where a person is recalled after conditional release, even if the legal basis for the detention remains unchanged[2].

1   *Van der Leer v Netherlands* (1990) 12 EHRR 567, paras 27 to 29.
2   *X v United Kingdom* (1981) 4 EHRR 188, para 66.

4.5.34 The detained person must be told 'in simple, non-technical language that he can understand, the essential legal and factual grounds for his arrest so as to be able, if he sees fit, to apply to a court to challenge its lawfulness' in accordance with art 5(4) of the Convention[1]. Where a person has been arrested in connection with a criminal offence, art 5(2) is also intended to enable the detained person to deny the offence at the earliest opportunity[2].

1   *Fox, Campbell and Hartley v United Kingdom* (1990) 13 EHRR 157, para 40. Cf *Christie v Leachinsky* [1947] AC 573; the Police and Criminal Evidence Act 1984, s 28. On art 5.4, see paras 4.5.48–4.5.57.
2   *X v Germany* 16 DR 111 (1978) at 114.

4.5.35 It is not always necessary for the relevant information to be given at the very moment of the arrest, provided it is given within a sufficient period following the arrest[1]. In a number of cases the E Ct HR and Commission have held that the obligation in art 5(2) will be met if the information is provided during the course of questioning following an arrest[2]. In *Delcourt v Belgium*[3] an arrest warrant was issued in Dutch in respect of a French speaking detainee. The Commission found no violation because the subsequent questioning, in which the reasons for the arrest became apparent, was conducted in French.

1   *Fox, Campbell and Hartley v United Kingdom* (1990) 13 EHRR 157, para 40. Cf *Van der Leer v Netherlands* (1990) 12 EHRR 567 where a delay of ten days was held to violate art 5(2) in the context of detention of a mental patient.
2   *Fox, Campbell and Hartley v United Kingdom* (1990) 13 EHRR 157, para 41; *Murray v United Kingdom* (1994) 19 EHRR 193, para 77.
3   10 YB 238 (1967) at 270–272.

4.5.36 The extent of the information required will depend on the circumstances[1]. Mere reference to the applicable statutory provision is generally insufficient[2]. Where the reason for the arrest is suspicion of involvement in a particular offence, the detainee must be informed of the facts which are the foundation of the decision to detain, and in particular he should be asked whether he admits or denies the allegation[3]. It will not always be necessary to inform a detained person of every charge which may later be brought, providing the information supplied is sufficient to justify the arrest[4]. Once a person has been charged, however, there is an additional entitlement under art 6(3)(a) to be informed in detail of the nature and cause of the accusation against him[5].

1   *Fox, Campbell and Hartley v United Kingdom* (1990) 13 EHRR 157, para 40.
2   *Ireland v United Kingdom* (1978) 2 EHRR 25, para 198; *Fox, Campbell and Hartley v United Kingdom* (1990) 13 EHRR 157, para 41; *Murray v United Kingdom* (1994) 19 EHRR 193, para 76.
3   *X v Germany* 16 DR 111 (1978), para 114.
4   Application 4220/69 *X v United Kingdom* 14 YB 250 (1971) at 278; *McVeigh, O'Neill and Evans v United Kingdom* (1981) 5 EHRR 71, para 210.
5   See para **4.6.63**.

2   RIGHT TO RELEASE PENDING TRIAL

4.5.37 Article 5(3) provides that every person who has been arrested or detained in accordance with art 5(1)(c) must be brought promptly before a judge or other judicial officer and is entitled to trial within a reasonable time or to release pending trial. It applies only to criminal offences[1]. The twin aims of this provision are: (a) to limit the period of detention by the police before a detainee's first court appearance; and (b) to establish a prima facie right to bail pending trial.

1   *De Wilde, Ooms and Versyp v Netherlands* (1971) 1 EHRR 373, para 71.

(a)   Limits on police detention

4.5.38   The first court appearance must be 'prompt'[1]. This requirement is to be construed in the light of the object and purpose of art 5 which is 'the protection of the individual against arbitrary interferences by the state with his right to liberty'[2] and in the context of the importance attached to art 5 within the Convention legal order[3]. In the context of art 5(3) the E Ct HR has observed that 'the degree of flexibility attached to the notion of "promptness" is limited'[4]. Whilst allowance will be made for the special features of each case, the E Ct HR has held that the significance attached to those features can never be taken to the point 'of effectively negativing the state's obligation to ensure a prompt release or a prompt appearance before a judicial authority5.

1   Note that the French text uses the word 'aussitôt' which connotes a greater degree of immediacy: *Brogan v United Kingdom* (1988) 11 EHRR 117 paras 59.
2   *Brogan v United Kingdom* (1988) 11 EHRR 117, para 58.
3   *Brogan v United Kingdom* (1988) 11 EHRR 117, para 58.
4   *Brogan v United Kingdom* (1988) 11 EHRR 117, para 59; *Koster v Netherlands* (1991) 14 EHRR 396, para 24.
5   *Brogan v United Kingdom* (1988) 11 EHRR 117, para 59; *Koster v Netherlands* (1991) 14 EHRR 396, para 24.

4.5.39   Although the E Ct HR and Commission have refrained from setting abstract time limits, it seems certain that the general regime established by the Police and Criminal Evidence Act 1984, ss 41–46 would be found to comply with art 5(3). By contrast, detention for four days and six hours under the Prevention of Terrorism (Temporary Provisions) Act 1984 was found to breach art 5(3) in *Brogan v United Kingdom*[1].

1   (1988) 11 EHRR 117; see para **4.5.6** on the United Kingdom's subsequent derogation. See also *Koster v Netherlands* (1991) 14 EHRR 396 (five days in the context of military criminal law: violation of art 5(3)); *McGoff v Sweden* (1984) 8 EHRR 246 (15 days; violation of art 5(3)); *De Jong, Baljet and Van Den Brink v Netherlands* (1984) 8 EHRR 20 (six days; violation of art 5(3)); *Duinhoff and Duif v Netherlands* (1984) 13 EHRR 478 (eight days 'far in excess' of time limits laid down in art 5(3)).

4.5.40   The term 'judge or other officer authorised by law' has the same meaning as the term 'competent legal authority' in art 5(1)(c)[1]. The tribunal must be independent of the investigating and prosecuting authorities[2], and it must be impartial in the sense of being free from actual bias and from the appearance of bias[3]. It must also be empowered to make a legally binding decision ordering release[4]. In addition:

'under art 5(3) there is both a procedural and a substantive requirement. The procedural requirement places the "officer" under the obligation of himself hearing the individual brought before him; the substantive requirement imposes on him the obligations of reviewing the circumstances militating for or against detention, of deciding, by reference to legal criteria, whether there are reasons to justify detention and of ordering release if there are no such reasons'[5].

The state is obliged to take the initiative for a detained person to be brought before an appropriate tribunal[6].

1   *Lawless v Ireland (No 3)* (1961) 1 EHRR 15, paras 13–14; *Ireland v United Kingdom* (1978) 2 EHRR 25, para 199; *Schiesser v Switzerland* (1979) 2 EHRR 417, para 29. On art 5(1)(c), see para **4.5.19**.
2   *De Jong, Baljet and Van Den Brink v Netherlands* (1984) 8 EHRR 20, para 49; *Schiesser v Switzerland* (1979) 2 EHRR 417, paras 29 and 30.
3   *Huber v Switzerland* (1990) Series A/188, para 43. Cf the E Ct HR's interpretation of the impartiality requirement in art 6(1) (see paras **4.6.55–4.6.57**).
4   *Ireland v United Kingdom* (1978) 2 EHRR 25, para 199.

5   *Schiesser v Switzerland* (1979) 2 EHRR 417, para 31.
6   Application 9017/80 *McGoff v Sweden* 31 DR 72 (1982)(art 5(3) imposes an 'unconditional obligation' on the State to bring the accused 'automatically and promptly' before a court). This decision does not appear to have been cited in *Olotu v Home Office* [1997] 1 WLR 328 where Lord Bingham CJ held that detention following the expiry of custody time limits did not involve a breach of art 5(3) because the relevant legislation placed the onus on the defendant to make an application for bail.

(b)   The right to bail pending trial

4.5.41   The second limb of art 5(3) entitles an accused person 'to trial within a reasonable time or to release pending trial'. The use of the word 'or' does not indicate that prompt trial is an alternative to release on bail[1]. A person charged with an offence must always be released pending trial unless the state can show that there are 'relevant and sufficient' reasons to justify his continued detention[2]. This obligation applies throughout the period from the arrest of an accused to his conviction or acquittal by the trial court, but not to detention pending appeal[3]. The procedural requirements imposed by art 5(4) where a court is considering bail in criminal proceedings are discussed at para **4.5.51** below. The defence must be afforded adequate access to the evidence in the possession of the prosecution, and the procedure must ensure equality of arms and be 'truly adversarial'[4]. The court is obliged to pay due regard to the presumption of innocence[5] and must record the arguments for and against release in a reasoned ruling[6]. Acceptable reasons for refusing bail fall into the following four categories.

1   *Neumeister v Austria* (1968) 1 EHRR 91, para 4; *Wemhoff v Germany* (1968) 1 EHRR 55, paras 4–5.
2   *Wemhoff v Germany* (1968) 1 EHRR 55, para 12; *Yagi and Sargin v Turkey* (1995) 20 EHRR 505, para 52.
3   *Wemhoff v Germany* (1968) 1 EHRR 55, paras 7–9; *B v Austria* (1990) 13 EHRR 20, paras 36–40.
4   *Lamy v Belgium* (1989) 11 EHRR 529, para 29.
5   *Letellier v France* (1991) 14 EHRR 83, para 35.
6   *Letellier v France* (1991) 14 EHRR 83, para 35; *Yagi and Sargin v Turkey* (1995) 20 EHRR 505, para 52.

(i)   Risk that the accused will fail to appear for trial

4.5.42   Refusal of bail on this ground requires 'a whole set of circumstances ... which give reason to suppose that the consequences and hazards of flight will seem to him to be a lesser evil than continued imprisonment'[1]. Relevant considerations are those 'relating to the character of the person involved, his morals, his home, his occupation, his assets, his family ties, and all kinds of links with the country in which he is being prosecuted'[2]. The severity of the potential sentence, though important, is not an independent ground and cannot itself justify the refusal of bail[3]. If the risk of absconding is the only justification for the detention, release of the accused pending trial should be ordered if it is possible to obtain guarantees that will ensure his appearance at trial[4]. In *Neumeister v Austria*[5] the E Ct HR pointed out that:

'The danger of flight necessarily decreases as the time spent in detention passes by, for the probability that the length of detention on remand will be deducted from the period of imprisonment which the person concerned may expect, if convicted, is likely to make the prospect seem less awesome to him and reduce his temptation to flee'.

1   *Stögmüller v Austria* (1969) 1 EHRR 155, para 15.
2   *Neumeister v Austria* (1968) 1 EHRR 91, para 10.
3   *Neumeister v Austria* (1968) 1 EHRR 91, para 10; *Letellier v France* (1991) 14 EHRR 83, para 43.
4   *Wemhoff v Germany* (1968) 1 EHRR 55, para 15.
5   *Neumeister v Austria* (1968) 1 EHRR 91, para 10.

(ii)   Interference with the course of justice

4.5.43   Bail may be refused where there is a well-founded risk that the accused, if released, would take action to prejudice the administration of justice[1]. The risk may involve interference with witnesses, warning other suspects, or the destruction of relevant evidence[2]. A generalised risk is insufficient. The risk must be identifiable and there must be evidence in support[3]. Further the court should bear in mind that this risk will often diminish with time once the investigation has concluded[4].

1   *Wemhoff v Germany* (1968) 1 EHRR 55, para 14.
2   *Letellier v France* (1991) 14 EHRR 83, para 39; *Wemhoff v Germany* (1968) 1 EHRR 55.
3   *Clooth v Belgium* (1991) 14 EHRR 717, para 44; *Tomasi v France* (1992) 15 EHRR 1, paras 84 and 91.
4   *Clooth v Belgium* (1991) 14 EHRR 717, para 43; *W v Switzerland* (1993) 17 EHRR 60, para 35; *Letellier v France* (1991) 14 EHRR 83, para 39.

(iii)   Prevention of further offences

4.5.44   The public interest in the prevention of crime may justify detention on remand where there are good reasons to believe that the accused, if released, would be likely to commit further offences[1]. However, the danger must be 'a plausible one' and the appropiateness of a remand in custody on this ground must be considered 'in the light of the circumstances of the case and, in particular, the past history and the personality of the person concerned'[2]. The E Ct HR should consider whether any previous convictions are 'comparable, either in nature or in the degree of seriousness to the charges preferred against [the accused]'[3]. Where the mental condition of a person charged with murder is cited as a ground for refusal of bail, steps should be taken to provide him with the necessary psychiatric care whilst on remand[4].

1   *Matznetter v Austria* (1969) 1 EHRR 198, para 9; *Toth v Austria* (1991) 14 EHRR 551, para 70; *Clooth v Belgium* (1991) 14 EHRR 717, para 40.
2   *Clooth v Belgium* (1991) 14 EHRR 717, para 40.
3   *Clooth v Belgium* (1991) 14 EHRR 717, para 40.
4   *Clooth v Belgium* (1991) 14 EHRR 717, para 40.

(iv)   The preservation of public order

4.5.45   Where the nature of the crime alleged and the likely public reaction are such that the release of the accused may give rise to public disorder, then temporary detention on remand may be justified[1]. The offence must however be one of particular gravity. The E Ct HR has held that a premeditated act of terrorism by an organisation which has caused death or serious injury may qualify as such a risk[2], but detention on this ground may only continue for as long as the threat to public order remains[3].

1   *Letellier v France* (1991) 14 EHRR 83, para 51.
2   *Tomasi v France* (1992) 15 EHRR 1, para 91.
3   *Letellier v France* (1991) 14 EHRR 83, para 51; *Tomasi v France* (1992) 15 EHRR 1, para 91.

4.5.46   Article 5(3) expressly provides that 'release may be conditioned by guarantees to appear for trial'. Permissible conditions of bail under art 5(3) include a requirement to surrender travel documents and driving documents[1], the imposition of a residence requirement[2], and the provision of a sum of money as a surety or security[3]. Where a financial condition is imposed the figure must be assessed by reference not to the financial loss occasioned by the alleged offence but by reference to the means of the accused, if it is a security, or of the person standing surety, and of the relationship between the two[4]. If the accused refuses to furnish the necessary information to enable an assessment to be made of his assets, it is permissible to establish a bail figure based on hypothetical assets[5].

1 *Stögmüller v Austria* (1969) 1 EHRR 155, para 15; Application 10670/83 *Schmid v Austria* 44 DR 195 (1985).
2 Application 10670/83 *Schmid v Austria* 44 DR 195 (1985).
3 *Wemhoff v Germany* (1968) 1 EHRR 55.
4 *Neumeister v Austria* (1968) 1 EHRR 91, para 14; *Schertenleib v Switzerland* 23 DR 137 (1980) at 196.
5 *Bonnechaux v Switzerland* 18 DR 100 (1979) at 144.

4.5.47 Where the court orders that a person should remain in custody pending trial there will nevertheless be a breach of art 5(3) if the proceedings are not conducted with appropriate expedition[1]. The fact that an accused has been refused bail requires special diligence in the conduct of the proceedings[2] and entitles him to have his case treated as a priority by the prosecution and the court[3]. There is however no absolute limit to the permissible period of pre-trial detention; the reasonableness of the length of the proceedings depends on the facts of the case[4]. The requirement for expedition has to be balanced against the duty of the court to ascertain the facts and to allow both parties to present their case[5].

1 The standard of diligence required is the same as under art 6(1) see para **4.6.51**: *Abdoella v Netherlands* (1992) 20 EHRR 585, para 24.
2 *Clooth v Belgium* (1991) 14 EHRR 717, para 36; *Tomasi v France* (1992) 15 EHRR 1, para 84; *Herczegfalvy v Austria* (1992) 15 EHRR 437, para 71.
3 *Wemhoff v Germany* (1968) 1 EHRR 55, para 17.
4 *W v Switzerland* (1993) 17 EHRR 60 (four years: no breach of art 5(3)); *Toth v Austria* (1991) 14 EHRR 551 (two years and one month: violation of art 5(3); *Tomasi v France* (1992) 15 EHRR 1 (five years and seven months: violation of art 5(3)).
5 *Wemhoff v Germany* (1968) 1 EHRR 55, para 17.

3 HABEAS CORPUS

4.5.48 Article 5(4) provides that everyone who is deprived of his liberty is entitled to take proceedings by which the lawfulness of his detention can be decided speedily by a court and his release ordered if his detention is not lawful[1]. This guarantees the right to *habeas corpus* in order to challenge the legality of executive detention. It also applies to other proceedings in which a court is called upon to determine whether a person should be detained, including a Mental Health Review tribunal or a bail application in criminal proceedings. The right to make such an application applies to all grounds for detention, and does not depend upon the detention being unlawful under art 5(1)[2]. Since the purpose of art 5(4) is to secure release from detention, it cannot be invoked by a person who is lawfully free in order to mount a retrospective challenge to the legality of detention[3], although complaint may nevertheless be made about the speediness of any review which has taken place[4].

1 The term 'lawfulness' in art 5(4) has the same meaning as the term 'lawful' in art 5(1): *Brogan v United Kingdom* (1988) 1 EHRR 117, para 65.
2 *De Wilde, Ooms and Versyp v Belgium* (1971) 1 EHRR 373, para 73; *Kolompar v Belgium* (1992) 16 EHRR 197, para 45.
3 Application 10230/82 *X v Sweden* 32 DR 303 (1983) at 305. Where a person absconds, art 5(4) continues to apply since he is still liable to be detained: *Van der Leer v Netherlands* (1990) 12 EHRR 567.
4 Application 9403/81 *X v United Kingdom* 28 DR 235 (1982) at 239.

(a)   The scope of the review

4.5.49   On any art 5(4) review, the burden of proving the lawfulness of the detention rests with the state[1]. The extent of the remedy required will vary according to the nature of the detention in issue[2]. As the E Ct HR observed in *E v Norway*[3]:

> 'Article 5(4) does not guarantee a right to judicial review of such a scope as to empower the court, on all aspects of the case including questions of pure expediency, to substitute its own discretion for that of the decision-making authority. The review should however be wide enough to bear on those conditions which are essential for the "lawful" detention of a person according to article 5(1).'

1   Application 9174/80 *Zamir v United Kingdom* 40 DR 42 (1983), para 58.
2   *Bouamar v Belgium* (1988) 11 EHRR 1, para 60.
3   (1990) 17 EHRR 30, para 50.

4.5.50   In *X v United Kingdom*[1] the English remedy of habeas corpus was found insufficient in a case involving the detention of a mentally disordered person because it did not enable a challenge to be made to the medical grounds for the detention. Similarly, in *Weeks v United Kingdom*[2] judicial review was found to be insufficient as a means of challenging the recall of a post-tariff discretionary life sentence prisoner because of the limited grounds of challenge available. In *Chahal v United Kingdom*[3] the E Ct HR found that neither habeas corpus nor judicial review was sufficient since the domestic courts were not in a position to review the merits of the decision to detain the applicant with a view to deportation on national security grounds. By contrast in *Brogan v United Kingdom*[4] the E Ct HR found that habeas corpus was an adequate procedure for challenging detention under art 5(1)(c); and in *Zamir v United Kingdom*[5] judicial review was found sufficient as a means of establishing the lawfulness of detention under art 5(1)(f) where the applicant was detained as an illegal immigrant with a view to deportation and there was no national security element involved.

1   (1981) 4 EHRR 188, paras 58 to 61.
2   (1987) 10 EHRR 293, para 69.
3   (1996) 23 EHRR 413, para 130.
4   (1988) 11 EHRR 117, para 65.
5   40 DR 42 (1983).

(b)   Procedural requirements

4.5.51   The minimum requirements for a 'court' are the same under art 5(4) and art 5(1)(a)[1], namely independence of the executive and the parties, impartiality[2], and a power to give a legally binding judgment concerning a person's release. The E Ct HR has held that art 5(4) requires procedural guarantees appropriate to the kind of deprivation of liberty in question[3]. The 'equality of arms' principle[4] which has been inferred by the E Ct HR into art 6, also applies to art 5(4) review[5]: the procedure adopted must 'ensure equal treatment' and be 'truly adversarial'[6]. The detained person must be told the reasons for his detention[7] and be given disclosure of all relevant evidence in the possession of the authorities[8]. He must also have adequate time to prepare an application for release[9]. Where the detention may be for long periods the procedural guarantees should not be 'markedly inferior' to procedures in the criminal courts[10]. Article 5(4) requires the provision of legal assistance, whenever this is necessary to enable the detained person to make an effective application for release[11]. In *Woukam Moudefo v France*[12] the Commission considered that legal assistance should be available prior to the hearing as well as during it. The onus is on the state to take the initiative to provide legal representation[13] and to provide legal aid where representation is necessary and the detained person has insufficient means to pay for it[14]. Furthermore, art 5(4) generally requires that a detained person or his legal representative be permitted to participate in an oral hearing[15]. There are inconsistent statements in the E Ct HR's case law as to whether the proceedings must take place in public[16]. If a state provides a right of appeal against a refusal to order release, the appeal body must itself comply with the requirements of art 5(4)[17].

1 See para **4.5.13**.
2 In *K v Austria* (1993) Series A/255-B the Commission ruled that the requirement for impartiality was not satisfied where a judge who imposed a fine later ruled upon a person's detention for failure to pay the fine.
3 *Wassink v Netherlands* (1990) Series A/185-A, para 30. See also *Winterwerp v Netherlands* (1979) 2 EHRR 387, para 60 (the procedural guarantees required by art 5(4) are 'not always' the same as those required by art 6(1) for criminal or civil litigation). Cf *Lamy v Belgium* (1989) 11 EHRR 529, para 29 (the appraisal of the need for a remand in custody in a criminal case and the subsequent assessment of guilt are 'too closely linked' to permit different rules on the extent of prosecution disclosure); *De Wilde Ooms and Versyp v Belgium* (1971) 1 EHRR 373, paras 78–79 (procedural guarantees appropriate to a criminal prosecution required in proceedings leading to the detention of vagrants).
4 See paras **4.6.31–4.6.33**.
5 See eg *Toth v Austria* (1991) 14 EHRR 551, para 84 (prosecutor present at an appeal on the question of detention while the applicant was not: violation of art 5(4)). there are suggestions in some of the early cases that the 'equality of arms' guarantee does not apply in art 5(4) proceedings: *Neumeister v Austria* (1968) 1 EHRR 91 at 132, paras 22–25; approved in *Matznetter v Austria* (1969) 1 EHRR 198 at 228, para 13. these decisions havenot, however, been followed: see *Toth v Austria* (1991) 14 EHRR 551, para 84; *Lamy v Belgium* (1989) 11 EHRR 529, para 29; *Sanchez-Reisse v Switzerland* (1986) 9 EHRR 71, paras 52–52.
6 *Toth v Austria* (1991) 14 EHRR 551, para 84; *Lamy v Belgium* (1989) 11 EHRR 529, para 29.
7 *X v United Kingdom* (1981) 4 EHRR 188, para 66.
8 *Lamy v Belgium* (1989) 11 EHRR 529, para 29; *Weeks v United Kingdom* (1987) 10 EHRR 293, para 66. Cf *Wassink v Netherlands* (1990) Series A/185-A, para 28. In Application 28901/95 *Rowe and Davies v United Kingdom* (1998) , para 71 the Commission observed that the disclosure requirements imposed by art 6 are 'more extensive' than those imposed by art 5(4).
9 *Farmakopoulos v Belgium* (1992) 16 EHRR 187, EComHR.
10 *De Wilde Ooms and Versyp v Belgium* (1971) 1 EHRR 373, paras 78–79. Cf *Wassink v Netherlands* (1990) Series A/185-A (less strict procedural standards may apply where a person is detained for a short time in an emergency). See also *Lamy v Belgium* (1989) 11 EHRR 529, para 29.
11 *Winterwerp v Netherlands* (1979) 2 EHRR 387, para 60; *Bouamar v Belgium* (1987) 11 EHRR 1, para 60; *Megyeri v Germany* (1992) 15 EHRR 584, paras 23–25; *Woukam Moudefo v France* (1988) 13 EHRR 549, EComHR.
12 (1988) 13 EHRR 549.
13 *Megyeri v Germany* (1992) 15 EHRR 584, para 27; *Winterwerp v Netherlands* (1979) 2 EHRR 387, para 66.
14 Application 9174/80 *Zamir v United Kingdom* 40 DR 42 (1983) at 60.
15 *Keus v Netherlands* (1991) 13 EHRR 700, para 27; *Farmakopoulos v Belgium* (1992) 16 EHRR 187, EComHR, para 46; *Winterwerp v Netherlands* (1979) 2 EHRR 387, para 60; *Bouamar v Belgium* (1987) 11 EHRR 1, para 60; Cf *Sanchez-Reisse v Switzerland* (1986) 9 EHRR 71, para 51 (written proceedings held sufficient in a case under art 5(1)(f)).
16 In *Neumeister v Austria* (1968) 1 EHRR 91 at 132, para 23, in the context of a remand in custody in criminal proceedings, the E Ct HR observed that 'publicity in such matters is not … in the interest of accused persons as it is generally understood'. However, in *De Wilde Ooms and Versyp v Belgium* (1971) 1 EHRR 373 at 409, para 79, the E Ct HR suggested that a requirement for a public hearing and public pronouncement of judgment were 'judicial features' required by art 5(4).
17 See *Toth v Austria* (1991) 14 EHRR 551, para 84, where the E Ct HR held that although art 5(4) does not require states to establish a second level of jurisdiction for applications for release from detention, where a system of appeal is established it 'must in principle accord to the detainees the same guarantees on appeal as at first instance'; *Navarra v France* (1993) 17 EHRR 594, para 28.

4.5.52 In *Weeks v United Kingdom*[1] the E Ct HR held that although the Parole Board satisfied the requirements of independence and impartiality, and had the power to make a binding recommendation, it lacked the procedural safeguards necessary to ensure the effective participation of the detained person. In *Chahal v United Kingdom*[2] the Home Office advisory panel on deportation in national security cases (the so-called 'three wise men') was found to be incapable of satisfying the requirements of a 'court' for a combination of reasons: the applicant had no right to legal representation before the panel; he was given only an outline of the grounds for the notice of intention to deport; the panel had no power to make a binding decision; and its advice to the Home Secretary was not disclosed to the applicant.

1   (1987) 10 EHRR 293, paras 65–68.
2   (1996) 23 EHRR 413, para 130. Parliament responded by enacting the Special Immigration Appeals Commission Act 1997.

(c)   Speedy determination

4.5.53   The application for release must be determined 'speedily'[1]. Article 5(4) will therefore be violated of a person has to wait for an unreasonably long period before being able to make an application to challenge the legality of his detention. In*Sanchez-Reisse v Switzerland*[2] the E Ct HR emphasised that the term 'speedily' cannot be defined in the abstract. As with the 'reasonable time' stipulations in art 5(3) and art 6(1) it must be determined in the light of the circumstances of the individual case. Relevant considerations include the diligence shown by the authorities, any delay caused by the detained person, and any other factors causing delay that do not engage the state's responsibility[3]. Time begins to run from the moment the proceedings are instituted[4] and ends with the final determination of the legality of the applicant's detention (including any appeal)[5]. Periods of four days[6] and sixteen days[7] have been held compatible with the notion of speediness, but delays of 31 and 46 days have been held to violate art 5(4)[8]. Detention on remand in criminal cases calls for short intervals between reviews[9]. If the length of time before a decision is taken is prima facie incompatible with the notion of speediness, the court will look to the state to explain the reason for the delay[10]. The workload of the domestic courts does not excuse excessive delays when a person is in custody, because it is incumbent on contracting states to organise their legal system so as to be able to discharge their obligations under the Convention[11].

1   The requirement of 'promptness' in art 5(3) connotes a greater degree of urgency than the term 'speedily' in art 5(4): *E v Norway* (1990) 17 EHRR 30, para 64.
2   (1986) 9 EHRR 71, para 55.
3   *Sanchez-Reisse v Switzerland* (1986) 9 EHRR 71, para 56.
4   *Van der Leer v Netherlands* (1990) 12 EHRR 567, para 35. If an administrative remedy has to be exhausted before recourse can be had to a court, time begins to run when the administrative authority is seized of the matter: *Sanchez-Reisse v Switzerland* (1986) 9 EHRR 71, para 54.
5   *Luberti v Italy* (1984) 6 EHRR 440.
6   Application 11256/84 *Egue v France* 57 DR 47 (1988) at 71. The circumstances of this case were unusual; the applicant had been detained for many years and the court was considering an extension for five years.
7   Application 7648/76 *Christinet v Switzerland* 17 DR 35 (1979) at 57.
8   *Sanchez-Reisse v Switzerland* (1986) 9 EHRR 71, paras 54–60. See also *Bezicheri v Italy* (1989) 12 EHRR 210, paras 22–25 (five and a half months delay: violation of art 5(4)).
9   *Bezicheri v Italy* (1989) 12 EHRR 210, para 21.
10   *Koendjbiharie v Netherlands* (1990) 13 EHRR 820, para 29.
11   *Bezicheri v Italy* (1989) 12 EHRR 210, para 25; *Cf. Zimmermann and Steiner v Switzerland* (1983) 6 EHRR 17.

(d)   Preventative detention

4.5.54   Article 5(4) does not generally apply to detention following conviction, since the requisite element of supervision is usually incorporated in the original decision to detain[1]. However, it has a special application in cases of preventative detention[2], since 'the very nature of the deprivation of liberty under consideration would appear to require a review of lawfulness to be available at reasonable intervals'[3]. Thus, where the justification for detention relates to characteristics of the individual which are susceptible to change with the passage of time, such as mental instability and dangerousness, art 5(4) requires regular periodic access to a judicial tribunal in order to determine whether detention continues to be justified[4]. This principle was applied in *X v United Kingdom* where the E Ct HR held that a person detained in a mental institution for a lengthy or indefinite period is entitled to automatic periodic review or to take proceedings at reasonable intervals so that new issues affecting the lawfulness of the detention can be considered by an independent judicial body. This was so 'whether the detention was ordered by a civil or criminal court or by some other authority'[5].

1   *De Wilde, Ooms and Versyp v Belgium* (1971) 1 EHRR 373, para 76; *Winterwerp v Netherlands* (1979) 2 EHRR 387, para 55.
2   *Van Droogenbroeck v Belgium* (1982) 4 EHRR 443.
3   *Winterwerp v Netherlands* (1979) 2 EHRR 387, para 55.
4   *Weeks v United Kingdom* (1987) 10 EHRR 293 (recall of a discretionary life sentence prisoner following release on licence).
5   (1981) 4 EHRR 188, paras 51 and 52.

4.5.55   In *Thynne Wilson and Gunnell v United Kingdom*[1] the E Ct HR held that periodic review was required in the post-tariff phase of a discretionary life sentence. The E Ct HR noted that the discretionary life sentence had developed in English law as a measure to deal with mentally unstable and dangerous offenders. Such sentences were composed of two phases: a 'punitive phase' in which detention was justified solely by reference to the requirements of retribution and deterrence (the tariff period), and a 'security phase' during which continued detention was justified by considerations of public safety:

> '[T]he factors of mental instability and dangerousness are susceptible to change over the passage of time and new issues of lawfulness may thus arise in the course of detention. It follows that at this phase in the execution of their sentences the applicants are entitled under article 5(4) to take proceedings to have the lawfulness of their continued detention decided by a court at reasonable intervals.'[2].

1   (1990) 13 EHRR 666.
2   *Thynne Wilson and Gunnell v United Kingdom* (1990) 13 EHRR 666, para 76. The Criminal Justice Act 1991, s 34 was enacted in order to give effect to the decision in *Thynne*. It introduced a procedure for art 5(4) review of the post-tariff phase of a discretionary life sentence by a system of oral hearings before a Discretionary Lifer Panel of the Parole Board. It also formalised the sentencing procedure so that a judge imposing a discretionary life sentence must now specify in open court the 'relevant part' or tariff which is to be served to meet the requirements of retribution and deterrence: see now the Crime (Sentences) Act 1997, s 28 and the *Practice Direction (Crime: Life Sentences)* [1993] 1 WLR 223. As to the frequency of reviews see Application 20448/92 *AT v United Kingdom* in which the Committee of Ministers held that the statutory interval of two years was insufficiently frequent on the facts of that case.

4.5.56   In *A Hussain v United Kingdom*[1] the E Ct HR held that juveniles convicted of murder and detained during Her Majesty's Pleasure under the Children and Young Persons Act 1933, s 53(1) are entitled to the same regular periodic review by the Parole Board as discretionary life sentence prisoners. The sentence was preventative in origin, having been modelled on the sentence of detention for criminal lunatics at the turn of the century. The E Ct HR held that indeterminate detention of a child or young person for a period which could be as long as that person's life could only be justified by considerations based on the need to protect the public. These factors centred on the child's character, mental state and resulting dangerousness and were susceptible to change as the child grew older. Accordingly new issues of lawfulness might arise in the course of detention and the applicant was entitled therefore to art 5(4) review at periodic intervals, once the tariff period had expired[2].

1   (1996) 22 EHRR 1.
2   Parliament has given effect to this ruling in the Crime (Sentences) Act 1997, s 28. This extends to juveniles the same rights in the post-tariff phase of detention as those which apply to a discretionary life sentence prisoner. It does not however permit the trial judge to fix the tariff, which remains a matter for the Secretary of State. At the time of writing this aspect of the procedure is under challenge in Strasbourg: Application 24888/94 *Venables and Thompson v United Kingdom* (ref?).

4.5.57   In *Wynne v United Kingdom*[1] the applicant argued that the distinctions between the discretionary life sentence and the mandatory life sentence for murder had narrowed to such an extent that it was no longer possible to distinguish between them for the purposes of art 5(4)[2]. The E Ct HR however considered that the essential rationale of the mandatory life sentence – that the crime of murder was so serious that the offender must be considered to have forfeited his liberty to the state for life – meant that early release in this context was a privilege rather than a right. Accordingly, there was no right under art 5(4) to periodic review in the post-tariff phase of detention. In *Mansell v United Kingdom*[3] the Commission rejected an argument that art 5(4) required periodic review in the extended period of a 'longer than normal sentence' imposed under the Criminal Justice Act 1991, s 2(2)(b).

1   (1994) 19 EHRR 333. See also *Ryan v United Kingdom* [1998] EHRLR 763, where the EComHR found, in an admissibility decision, that the sentence of custody for life for those convicted of murder aged 18–21 was comparable to a mandatory life sentence for adults and so there was no right to periodic review.
2   Relying on the dicta of Lord Mustill in *R v Secretary of State for the Home Department, ex p Doody* [1994] 1 AC 531, HL.
3   [1997] EHRLR 666.

4   COMPENSATION FOR UNLAWFUL DETENTION

4.5.58   Article 5(5) provides that everyone who has been the victim of arrest or detention in contravention of the provisions of Article 5 shall have an enforceable right to compensation. This is the only provision of the Convention which expressly requires monetary compensation for its breach, and is without prejudice to the E Ct HR's power to award just satisfaction under art 50[1]. The remedy required is one before a *national* court which leads to a legally binding award[2]. The detainee must have suffered damage in order to claim compensation[3]. Damage can include both pecuniary and non-pecuniary loss including pain, suffering and emotional distress. Compensation may be broader than mere financial recompense[4], but the obligation cannot be discharged merely by an order for release since this is separately protected under art 5(4). Where the applicant relies on a breach of one of the other provisions of art 5 the E Ct HR will examine whether the breach is established and, if so, whether the requirements of art 5(5) have been satisfied[5]. Where art 5(5) alone is alleged to have been breached, the application will only succeed if there has been a declaration by the domestic courts, either expressly or in substance, that art 5 has been violated[6].

1   *Neumeister v Austria (No 2)* (1974) 1 EHRR 136, para 30; *Ciulla v Italy* (1989) 13 EHRR 346, para 45. Where there has been a breach of art 5(5) the E Ct HR may award just satisfaction under art 50 in order to remedy the violation: *Brogan v United Kingdom* (1988) 11 EHRR 117, para 67. On art

50 and the award of damages under the Human Rights Act 1998, see para **2.8.4**.

2   *Brogan v United Kingdom* (1988) 11 EHRR 117, para 67; *Fox, Campbell and Hartley v United Kingdom* (1990) 13 EHRR 157, para 46.

3   *Wassink v Netherlands* (1990) Series A/185–A, para 38. Cf *Eggs v Switzerland* 39 DR 225 at 235 (1984).

4   Application 9990/82 *Bozano v France* 39 DR 119 (1984) at 144.

5   *Benham v United Kingdom* (1996) 22 EHRR 293; *Ciulla v Italy* (1989) 13 EHRR 346, paras 43–45.

6   *Eggs v Switzerland* 39 DR 225 at 235 (1984); *X, Y and Z v Austria* 19 DR 213 (1980).

4.5.59   Article 5(5) does not give rise to any entitlement to exemplary damages since it is concerned exclusively with compensation. In *Cumber v United Kingdom*[1] the Commission held that if the level of compensation awarded was so low as no longer to be 'enforceable' this would not discharge the obligation under art 5(5). The applicant had been awarded £350 for five hours' false imprisonment. The Commission considered that the award was low but that it was not negligible, and declared the application manifestly ill-founded. Since *Cumber* was decided the Court of Appeal has issued guidelines for the assessment of damages in cases of false imprisonment. In *Thompson and HSU v Metropolitan Police Comr*[2] the Court of Appeal expressly disapproved the award in *Cumber* and held that in a straightforward case, awards of basic damages should start at £500 per hour, on a decreasing hourly rate, up to a maximum of about £3,000 for the first twenty-four hours. The court also gave guidance for the assessment of aggravated damages.

1   [1997] EHRLR 191.

2   [1998] QB 498. On exemplary damages, see also para **2.8.4**, n 12.

4.5.60   The right to compensation does not arise merely because a decision authorising detention has been overturned on appeal. Such a right will however arise if the decision has been overturned on the ground that the court of first instance had no jurisdiction to order the detention[1]. Moreover, a right to compensation for a miscarriage of justice is expressly provided by art 3 of protocol 7, which the United Kingdom intends to ratify and incorporate[2]. A procedure already exists under the Criminal Justice Act 1988, s 133[3] to provide compensation in accordance with this requirement.

1   *Van der Leer v Netherlands* (1990) 12 EHRR 567; *Wassink v Netherlands* (1990) Series A/185–A; *Benham v United Kingdom* (1996) 22 EHRR 293; *Krzycki v Federal Republic of Germany* 13 DR 57 (1987).

2   See para **2.1.5**, n 3 and paras **4.6.76–4.6.78**.

3   Where the criteria established under the Criminal Justice Act 1988 are not satisfied, an applicant may apply for an ex gratia payment: see HC Official Report (6th series) cols 691–692 (29 November 1985).

Article 6   Right to a fair trial

(1) In the determination of his civil rights and obligations or of any criminal charge against him, everyone is entitled to a fair and public hearing within a reasonable time by an independent and impartial tribunal established by law. Judgment shall be pronounced publicly but the press and public may be excluded from all or part of the trial in the interest of morals, public order or national security in a democratic society, where the interests of juveniles or the protection of the private life of the parties so require, or to the extent strictly necessary in the opinion of the court in special circumstances where publicity would prejudice the interests of justice.

(2) Everyone charged with a criminal offence shall be presumed innocent until proved guilty according to law.

(3) Everyone charged with a criminal offence has the following minimum rights:

(a) to be informed promptly, in a language which he understands and in detail, of the nature and cause of the accusation against him;

(b) to have adequate time and facilities for the preparation of his defence;

(c) to defend himself in person or through legal assistance of his own choosing or, if he has not sufficient means to pay for legal assistance, to be given it free when the interests of justice so require;

(d) to examine or have examined witnesses against him and to obtain the attendance and examination of witnesses on his behalf under the same conditions as witnesses against him;

(e) to have the free assistance of an interpreter if he cannot understand or speak the language used in court.

A   Introduction

4.6.1 Article 6 is predominantly concerned with procedural fairness in the determination of both criminal charges and civil rights and obligations. The object and purpose of art 6 is 'to enshrine the fundamental principle of the rule of law'[1]. In a democratic society, the right to the fair administration of justice holds such a prominent place that a restrictive interpretation of the article would not correspond to the aim and purpose of the Convention. Accordingly, the article is to be given a broad and purposive interpretation[2].

1   *Salabiaku v France* (1988) 13 EHRR 379, E Ct HR, para 28; *Golder v United Kingdom* (1975) 1 EHRR 524, E Ct HR, para 35. The rule of law is, moreover, expressly referred to in the Preamble to the Convention: see *Klass v Federal Republic of Germany* (1978) 2 EHRR 214, E Ct HR, para 55.
2   See, in relation to art 6(1), *Delcourt v Belgium* (1970) 1 EHRR 355, E Ct HR, para 25; *Moreira de Azevedo v Portugal* (1990) 13 EHRR 721, E Ct HR, para 66. This principle of interpretation applies to art 6 as a whole, not merely to art 6(1).

4.6.2 The fundamental importance of procedural fairness has long been recognised in the law of the United Kingdom[1] and in international human rights instruments[2], as well as in the constitutions of other common law jurisdictions. The United States Constitution (by its Fifth and Fourteenth Amendments) prohibits depriving 'any person of life, liberty or property without due process of law'[3]. The Canadian Charter of Rights and Freedoms (s 7) secures the 'right to life, liberty and security of the person and the right not to be deprived thereof except in accordance with the principles of fundamental justice[4]'. The New Zealand Bill of Rights Act 1990 provides that every person has the right to 'the observance of the principles of natural justice by any tribunal or other public authority which has the power to make a determination in respect of that person's rights, obligations or interests protected or recognised by law'[5]. All three instruments, moreover, make specific, detailed provision for the procedural rights of criminal defendants[6].

1   Magna Carta, 1215, compelled the King to pledge that '[t]o no one we will sell, to no one will we deny or delay right or justice'.
2   See the Universal Declaration of Human Rights, 1948, arts 10–11, and the International Covenant on Civil and Political Rights, art 14 (a draft version of which appears to have influenced the drafting of art 6 of the Convention: see *Feldbrugge v The Netherlands* (1986) 8 EHRR 425, E Ct HR, joint dissenting opinion of Judges Ryssdal, Bindschedler-Robert, Lagergren, Matscher, Sir Vincent Evans, Berhardt and Gersing, para 20). Article 14 has been the subject of a General Comment by the Human Rights Committee, number 13/21, Doc A/39/40, adopted 12 April 1984 and 23 July 1984: for a recent decision of the Committee on the right to be tried without undue delay, see *Johnson v Jamaica* (1996) 1 BHRC 37.
3   See Nowak and Rotunda *Constitutional Law* (5th edn, 1995), Ch 13.
4   See Mullan *Administrative Law* (3rd edn, 1996), paras 78–87.
5   Section 27: for the concept of procedural fairness in Australian administrative law see 10*Halsbury's Laws of Australia*, especially at paras 10–1775 ff.
6   See the United States Constitution, Fourth, Fifth, Sixth and Eighth Amendments; Canadian Charter of Rights and Freedoms, ss 8–14; New Zealand Bill of Rights Act 1990, ss 21–26.

B   Article 6(1)

1   SCOPE

(a)   In the determination of civil rights and obligations

(i)   The need for a 'contestation' or dispute

4.6.3   For art 6 to apply in the context of civil rights and obligations, there must be a 'contestation' or dispute at the national level over civil rights and obligations which can be said, at least on arguable grounds, to be recognised under domestic law[1]. The word 'contestation' in the French text of the Convention has no counterpart in the English text. The E Ct HR has held that conformity with the spirit of the Convention requires that the word 'contestation' should not be construed too technically[2], and in one case went so far as to doubt whether the requirement existed at all[3].

1   *H v Belgium* (1987) 10 EHRR 339, E Ct HR, para 40, recently applied in *Hamer v France* (1996) 23 EHRR 1, E Ct HR, para 73 and *Georgiadis v Greece* (1997) 24 EHRR 606, E Ct HR, para 30.
2   *Le Compte, Van Leuven and De Meyere v Belgium* (1981) 4 EHRR 1, E Ct HR, para 45.
3   *Moreira de Azevedo v Portugal* (1990) 13 EHRR 721, E Ct HR, para 66.

4.6.4   A 'contestation' may relate not only to the actual existence of a right, but also to its scope or the manner in which the right may be exercised, and may concern matters of both fact and law, provided that the dispute is 'genuine and of a serious nature'[1].

1   *Benthem v Netherlands* (1985) 8 EHRR 1, E Ct HR, para 32; *Le Compte, Van Leuven and De Meyere v Belgium* (1981) 4 EHRR 1, E Ct HR, para 49.

4.6.5   Article 6 does not control the content of a state's substantive domestic law. If there is no actionable domestic claim as a matter of substantive national law, then the article will not apply. Thus, in the case of *Powell and Rayner v United Kingdom*[1], the E Ct HR held that art 6 did not apply when the applicants complained that because of the substantive national law (which consisted of a statutory exclusion of liability), they could not bring an action in relation to noise nuisance caused by aircraft overflight[2]. By contrast, however, art 6(1) may apply where there are procedural, rather than substantive, bars preventing or limiting the possibility of bringing a domestic claim to court. This is because:

> 'it would not be consistent with the rule of law in a democratic society or with the basic principle underlying article 6 para.1 — namely that civil claims must be capable of being submitted to a judge for adjudication — if ... a State could, without restraint or control by the Convention enforcement bodies, remove from the jurisdiction of the courts a whole range of civil claims or confer immunities from civil liability on large groups or categories of persons ...'[3].

It is, however, not always an easy matter to trace the dividing line between substantive limitations (to which art 6 will not normally apply) and procedural limitations (to which it may well apply)[4].

1   (1990) 12 EHRR 355, E Ct HR, para 36; see similarly Application 10475/83 *Dyer v United Kingdom* 39 DR 246 (1984) at 251, EComHR.
2   Similarly, in *Masson and van Zon v Netherlands* (1995) 22 EHRR 491, E Ct HR, paras 50–52, the E Ct HR held that there was no 'right' for the purposes of the article where a public authority merely had an equitable discretion (but no obligation) to award compensation.
3   *Fayed v United Kingdom* (1994) 18 EHRR 393, E Ct HR, para 65; *Tinnelly and McElduff v United Kingdom* (1998) Times, 16 July, E Ct HR, para 62 (operation of national security certificates barring further proceedings in Fair Employment Tribunal fell to be examined under art 6(1)).
4   See *Fayed v United Kingdom* (1994) 18 EHRR 393, E Ct HR, at para 67, and *Osman v United Kingdom*, judgment of 28 October 1998, E Ct HR, paras 133–140 (police immunity from common law negligence claims: E Ct HR rejected respondent Government's argument that applicants had no substantive right for purposes of applicability of art 6(1)). See also Application 28945/95 *TP and KM v United Kingdom*, EComHR Report of 26 May 1998 (local authority's immunity from suit in negligence in child care cases: complaints under art 6(1) declared inadmissible); *Waite and Kennedy v Germany*, judgment of 18 February 1999, E Ct HR, paras 63–74 (international organisation's immunity from suit in employment litigation: no violation of art 6(1) because immunity pursued a legitimate aim and did not, in the circumstances, breach principle of proportionality.

(ii)   'In the determination of' civil rights and obligations

4.6.6   Article 6 covers all proceedings, whether between two private individuals or between an individual and the state, and including constitutional court proceedings[1], the result of which is 'decisive' for civil rights and obligations[2]. However, a tenuous connection or remote consequences do not suffice: the civil rights and obligations must be the object, or one of the objects, of the 'contestation'; and the result of the proceedings must be directly decisive of such a right. Thus, in the *Le Compte v Belgium* case[3], the E Ct HR held that art 6 did apply to proceedings before a medical disciplinary tribunal which had suspended the applicant Belgian doctors, because those proceedings were directly decisive of the applicants' private law right to practise medicine. By contrast, in *Fayed v United Kingdom*[4] the mere fact that an official investigation had made findings detrimental to the applicants did not bring that investigation within the scope of art 6, because the report was not dispositive of any legal right or obligation[5].

1   *Süßmann v Germany* (1996) 25 EHRR 64, E Ct HR, paras 39, 41; *Pauger v Austria* (1997) 25 EHRR 105, E Ct HR, para 46; *Pammell v Germany* (1997) 26 EHRR 100, E Ct HR, para 53: but cf *Pierre-Bloch v France* (1997) 26 EHRR 202, E Ct HR, paras 49–52 (proceedings before constitutional court

about right to stand for election involved political, rather than civil, right – therefore art 6(1) inapplicable).
2　*Ringeisen v Austria* (1971) 1 EHRR 455, E Ct HR, para 94 (proceedings before administrative tribunal for the statutory approval of a contract between private individuals for the sale of land held to fall within art 6(1)).
3　*Le Compte, Van Leuven and De Meyere v Belgium* (1981) 4 EHRR 1, E Ct HR.
4　*Fayed v United Kingdom* (1994) 18 EHRR 393, E Ct HR.
5　See, similarly, *Saunders v United Kingdom* (1996) 23 EHRR 313, E Ct HR, para 67; and see *Hamer v France* (1996) 23 EHRR 1, E Ct HR, paras 73–78 (civil party in criminal proceedings had not claimed damages; outcome of proceedings not, therefore, decisive of her right to compensation and art 6(1) thus inapplicable).

4.6.7　Proceedings determining a preliminary point on liability, liability itself, costs, or the quantum of damages are 'decisive' of civil rights for the purposes of art 6[1].

1　*Obermeier v Austria* (1990) 13 EHRR 290, E Ct HR, paras 66–67; *Robins v United Kingdom* (1997) 26 EHRR 527, E Ct HR, paras 28–29; *Silva Pontes v Portugal* (1994) 18 EHRR 156, paras 30–36, E Ct HR.

(iii)　'Civil rights and obligations'

4.6.8　The early jurisprudence of the E Ct HR[1] established that the use of the word 'civil' in art 6(1) incorporated the distinction between private and public law, with civil rights and obligations being rights and obligations in private law. 'Civil' has an autonomous Convention meaning[2], taking into account any 'uniform European notion' (in the law of the contracting parties) as to the nature of the right[3], so that the classification of a right in domestic law is not decisive. (In *Feldbrugge v Netherlands*[4], for example, the right to health insurance benefits under social security schemes was treated as a public law right in the law of The Netherlands, but was held by the Court to amount to a civil right within the meaning of art 6(1)). It is, nonetheless, relevant to have regard to domestic law in that such law necessarily determines the substantive content and effect of the right at issue[5]. For art 6 purposes, it is the character of the right at issue, rather than that of the parties (whether private or public bodies), the governing legislation or the authority invested with jurisdiction in the matter, which is relevant[6].

1　See eg *Ringeisen v Austria* (1971) 1 EHRR 455, E Ct HR, para 94.
2　*König v Federal Republic of Germany* (1978) 2 EHRR 170, E Ct HR, para 88.
3　See *Feldbrugge v Netherlands* (1986) 8 EHRR 425, E Ct HR, para 29.
4　*Feldbrugge v Netherlands* (1986) 8 EHRR 425, E Ct HR.
5　See *König v Federal Republic of Germany* (1978) 2 EHRR 170, E Ct HR, para 89: in that case, the E Ct HR decided that the right to practise medicine in West Germany was a 'civil' right. It was relevant to the court's decision that as a matter of West German law, the medical profession did not provide a public service.
6　See eg *Stran Greek Refineries and Stratis Andreadis v Greece* (1994) 19 EHRR 293, E Ct HR, para 39.

4.6.9　The rights and obligations of private persons in their relations inter se are always civil rights and obligations. Areas include where civil rights or obligations have been found; the law of tort; family law; employment law; and the law of real property[1].

1　See, respectively *Axen v Federal Republic of Germany* (1983) 6 EHRR 195, E Ct HR; *Airey v Ireland* (1979) 2 EHRR 305, E Ct HR; *Buchholz v Federal Republic of Germany* (1980) 3 EHRR 597, E Ct HR; *Langborger v Sweden* (1989) 12 EHRR 416, E Ct HR.

4.6.10　In cases concerning relations between the individual and the state, the E Ct HR initially employed an inductive approach, identifying certain 'rights and obligations' of individuals, of a very general kind, as 'civil rights' attracting the protection of art

6 where state action is directly decisive of them. The most significant of the rights so identified are the right to real property (for example, claims concerning the expropriation of property and the application of the planning laws[1] have been held subject to the right to a fair hearing) and to personal property (including decisions in relation to bankruptcy and patent rights[2]); the right to engage in a commercial activity (so that state action by way of the withdrawal of an alcohol licence from a restaurant, or refusal to issue a licence to operate a liquid petroleum gas installation[3], is within the scope of art 6) or to practise a liberal profession[4]; the right to compensation for financial loss resulting from illegal state acts (which is broad enough to include a claim for compensation for damage caused by an illegal decision by a public authority on a tax matter: *Editions Périscope v France*[5]) including claims in respect of personal injury or ill-treatment by the state[6]. In the E Ct HR's recent case-law, however, a principle appears to be emerging to the effect that, in general, all rights of a 'pecuniary' nature are 'civil' rights within the meaning of the article[7].

1   See, respectively, *Holy Monasteries v Greece* (1994) 20 EHRR 1, E Ct HR, para 85; and *Bryan v United Kingdom* (1995) 21 EHRR 342, E Ct HR, para 31.
2   Respectively Application 10259/83, *Anca v Belgium*, 40 DR 170 (1984) and Application 7830/77, *X v Austria,* 14 DR 200 (1978).
3   Respectively, *Tre Traktörer Aktiebolag v Sweden* (1989) 13 EHRR 309, E Ct HR; *Benthem v Netherlands* (1985) 8 EHRR 1, E Ct HR: see also *Fischer v Austria* (1995) 20 EHRR 349, E Ct HR, para 40 (tipping licence).
4   See eg *König v Federal Republic of Germany* (1978) 2 EHRR 170, E Ct HR; *Diennet v France* (1995) 21 EHRR 554, E Ct HR.
5   (1992) 14 EHRR 597, E Ct HR, paras 35–40, applied in *National and Provincial Building Society v United Kingdom* (1997) 25 EHRR 127, E Ct HR, paras 97–98 (judicial review proceedings relating to claims for restitution of monies paid as tax fell within art 6(1)).
6   See eg *X v France* (1991) 14 EHRR 483, E Ct HR (claim for damages for negligence for contracting AIDS from blood transfusion); *Aksoy v Turkey* (1996) 23 EHRR 553, E Ct HR, para 92 (compensation in respect of ill-treatment committed by the state); *Georgiadis v Greece* (1997) 24 EHRR 606, E Ct HR and *Werner v Austria* (1997) 26 EHRR 310, E Ct HR, para 39 (compensation for wrongful detention).
7   See *Editions Périscope v France* (1992) 14 EHRR 597, E Ct HR, followed in *Stran Greek Refineries and Stratis Andreadis v Greece* (1994) 19 EHRR 293, E Ct HR, para 40; *Ortenberg v Austria* (1994) 19 EHRR 524, E Ct HR, para 28; and *Procola v Luxembourg* (1995) 22 EHRR 193, E Ct HR, paras 38–39. The E Ct HR has also held, however, that the fact that a dispute is 'pecuniary' in nature is not always sufficient to bring it within the scope of art 6(1): see *Schouten and Meldrum v Netherlands* (1994) 19 EHRR 432, E Ct HR, paras 50, 57 and *Pierre-Bloch v France* (1997) 26 EHRR 202, E Ct HR, para 51.

4.6.11   In the particular area of the rights of individuals to social security and social assistance, the E Ct HR initially approached the issue of whether there was a 'civil right' by examining the nature of the benefit at issue and weighing the private law features of the particular insurance scheme against its public law features[1]. More recently, however, the court has held that the 'principle of equality of treatment' now warrants taking the view that the general rule is that art 6(1) does apply in the field of social insurance[2], even where the benefit was a non-contributory form of public assistance granted unilaterally by the state, with the full cost borne by the public purse, and with no link to a private contract of employment[3]. The court has not yet, however, adopted this broad approach to 'civil' rights uniformly in other areas involving state intervention[4].

1   See eg *Feldbrugge v Netherlands* (1986) 8 EHRR 425, E Ct HR.
2   *Salesi v Italy* (1993) 26 EHRR 187, E Ct HR.
3   Where the pension is linked to employment, including civil service employment, there will certainly be an art 6(1) right: see *Lombardo v Italy* (1992) 21 EHRR 188, E Ct HR, paras 14–17; *Süßmann v Germany* (1998) 25 EHRR 64, E Ct HR, para 42; *McGinley and Egan v United Kingdom* (1998) 27 EHRR 1, E Ct HR, para 84.

4   Note in particular the jurisprudence of the E Ct HR (for example recently in *Huber v France* (1998) 26 EHRR 457, E Ct HR, by a majority of 5:4) rejecting claims by public employees concerning appointment, dismissal, conditions of service and discipline as being outside the scope of the Convention. Cf *Vogt v Germany* (1995) 21 EHRR 205, E Ct HR, para 43 applied in *Ahmed v United Kingdom* (1998) Times, 2 October, E Ct HR (no principle that civil servants fall outside the scope of the Convention), the dissenting opinion of Judges Casadevall and Lohmus in *Huber* (criticising the 'thin reasoning' of the majority), and the concurring opinion of Judge Jambrek in *Maillard v France* (1998) 27 EHRR 232 (extension of art 6(1) to careers of civil servants, so as to end current inequality of treatment, was 'a problem to be solved by the new court'). See also *Schouten and Meldrum v Netherlands* (1994) 19 EHRR 432, E Ct HR, para 50 (more restrictive approach to benefit contributions than to benefit entitlements).

4.6.12   Certain rights involving an individual and the state have consistently been categorised by the E Ct HR as public law rights falling outside the scope of art 6(1). The most important examples are cases involving criminal fines and obligations deriving from tax legislation[1].

1   *Schouten and Meldrum v Netherlands* (1994) 19 EHRR 432, E Ct HR, para 50; but cf *Editions Périscope v France* (1992) 14 EHRR 597, E Ct HR (tax) and *Procola v Luxembourg* (1995) 22 EHRR 193, E Ct HR (fines).

(b)   In the determination of a criminal charge

(i)   'Criminal'

4.6.13   The application of art 6(1) to criminal proceedings is confined to proceedings which determine a criminal charge. In considering whether the proceedings are 'criminal' for the purposes of art 6, the Convention organs adopt an autonomous approach to interpretation. Three criteria are to be applied, namely: (a) the classification of the proceedings in domestic law; (b) the nature of the offence itself; and (c) the severity of the penalty which may be imposed[1]. If the applicable domestic law defines the offence as criminal, this will be decisive. But where domestic law classifies the proceedings as civil, the domestic classification will be 'no more than a starting point'[2]. The E Ct HR will conduct an independent assessment of the true nature of the proceedings, taking into account in particular the severity of the penalty which may be imposed[3]. If a domestic court has the power to impose imprisonment, this will generally be sufficient to define the proceedings as 'criminal', unless the 'nature, duration or manner of execution of the imprisonment' is not 'appreciably detrimental'[4]. Thus, prison disciplinary proceedings[5], proceedings for tax evasion leading to large financial penalties[6], commitment to prison for non-payment of the community charge[7] and contempt proceedings[8] have all been held to be criminal proceedings for the purposes of art 6.

1   *Engel v Netherlands* (1976) 1 EHRR 647, para 82.
2   *Engel v Netherlands* (1976) 1 EHRR 647, para 82.
3   See *Öztürk v Germany* (1984) 6 EHRR 409; *Lutz v Germany* (1987) 10 EHRR 182; *Demicoli v Malta* (1992) 14 EHRR 47; *Garryfallow AFBE v Greece*, 1997-V, 29 September 1997.
4   *Engel v Netherlands* (1976) 1 EHRR 647, para 82.
5   *Campbell and Fell v United Kingdom* (1984) 7 EHRR 165.
6   *Bendenoun v France* (1994) 18 EHRR 54.
7   *Benham v United Kingdom* (1996) 22 EHRR 293.
8   Application 10038/82 *Harman v United Kingdom* 38 DR 53 (1984) (admissibility decision resulting in a friendly settlement).

(ii)   'Charge'

4.6.14   A person is subject to a charge within the meaning of art 6(1) when he is 'substantially affected' by the proceedings taken against him[1]. This will usually be the date of charge by the police[2] but in a case where the charge is delayed or subsequent charges are added it may be the date of a person's initial arrest or the date upon which he becomes aware that 'immediate consideration' is being given to the possibility of a prosecution[3]. Article 6 will continue to apply until the conclusion of any appeal[4]. Where an accused is not finally brought to trial, art 6 ceases to apply as at the date of discontinuance[5].

1 *Deweer v Belgium* (1980) 2 EHRR 439 at para 46; *Eckle v Federal Republic of Germany* (1982) 5 EHRR 1.
2 *Ewing v United Kingdom* (1986) 10 EHRR 141; Application 8233/78 *X v United Kingdom* 17 DR 122 (1979).
3 *X v United Kingdom* 14 DR 26 (1978).
4 *Eckle v Federal Republic of Germany* (1982) 5 EHRR 1, paras 76–77; *Neumeister v Austria* (1968) 1 EHRR 91 at para 19.
5 *Orchin v United Kingdom* (1983) 6 EHRR 391 (nolle prosequi). If charges have been left to lie on the file, art 6 ceases to apply if the prosecution undertake not to proceed with them (Application 8233/78 *X v United Kingdom* 17 DR 122 (1979)) or if it is established practice not to do so (*X v United Kingdom* (1983) 5 EHRR 508).

4.6.15 Article 6 extends only to proceedings by which a charge is finally determined. It does not therefore apply to preliminary hearings concerning trial arrangements and matters of procedure[1], nor to civil proceedings brought by a third party to recover goods declared forfeit in earlier criminal proceedings[2], nor to an application for clemency[3], nor to the classification of a prisoner[4], nor, generally, to extradition proceedings[5].

1 *X v United Kingdom* (1982) 5 EHRR 273.
2 *Allgemeine Gold-und Silverscheideanstalt v United Kingdom* (1986) 9 EHRR 1.
3 *X v Federal Republic of Germany* 25 CD 1 (1967).
4 *X v United Kingdom* 20 DR 202 (1979).
5 *Soering v United Kingdom* (1989) 11 EHRR 439; note however para 113 and *Drozd and Janousek v France and Spain* (1992) 14 EHRR 745 at para 110.

2 THE RIGHTS GUARANTEED BY ARTICLE 6(1)

(a) The right of access to a court

(i) Generally

4.6.16 There is no express guarantee of the right of access to a court in the text of art 6, but in *Golder v United Kingdom*[1], a case involving a refusal to permit a convicted prisoner to write to his solicitor with a view to instituting civil proceedings for libel against a prison officer, the E Ct HR (holding in the applicant's favour) decided that such a right of access was inherent in the right stated by art 6(1). A procedure whereby civil rights are determined without ever hearing the parties' submissions is, moreover, plainly incompatible with the article[2]. The right applies also to criminal proceedings (ie an accused is entitled to be tried on the charge against him in court)[3].

1 (1975) 1 EHRR 524, E Ct HR. The English courts, influenced in part by art 6 and by the decision in *Golder*, have established that there is a constitutional right of access to the courts at common law: see *Raymond v Honey* [1983] 1 AC 1, HL; *R v Secretary of State for the Home Department, ex p Anderson* [1984] QB 778, Div Ct; *R v Secretary of State for the Home Department, ex p Leech* [1994] QB 198, CA; *R v Lord Chancellor, ex p Witham* [1998] QB 575, Div Ct.
2 *Georgiadis v Greece* (1997) 24 EHRR 606, E Ct HR, para 40 (tribunal ruling on compensation of its own motion without hearing argument).
3 *Deweer v Belgium* (1980) 2 EHRR 439, E Ct HR, paras 48–49.

4.6.17 The right is a right of effective access to court. It may, therefore, require the provision of civil legal aid to an indigent person in a particular case, even though there is no specific provision for such assistance in the Convention[1]. For example, in

Airey v Ireland[2], the applicant was an indigent Irish woman seeking an order for judicial separation from her husband. The E Ct HR held that Ireland had infringed art 6 by not providing legal aid to her in circumstances where it was 'not realistic' to suppose that she could effectively conduct her own case (which potentially involved complicated points of law and the tendering of factual and expert evidence). This was so even though Ireland had ratified the Convention subject to a reservation[3] in respect of the legal aid obligation in *criminal* cases expressly included in art 6(3)(c). The right also requires that a person be given personal and reasonable notice of an administrative decision which interferes with his civil rights and obligations, so that he has an adequate opportunity to challenge it in court[4].

1   See eg *Airey v Ireland* (1979) 2 EHRR 305, E Ct HR, para 26 (family proceedings) (and, to similar effect, the US case of *MLB v SLJ* (1997) 3 BHRC 47, US SC (parental rights)); and cf the explicit requirement that criminal legal aid be provided in certain circumstances: art 6(3)(c), para **4.6.69**.
2   (1979) 2 EHRR 305, E Ct HR.
3   See para **2.15** on reservations.
4   *De La Pradelle v France* (1992) A 253–B, E Ct HR, para 34.

4.6.18   The right of access is not absolute but may be subject to limitations, since the right 'by its very nature calls for regulation by the state, regulation which may vary in time and place according to the needs and resources of the community and of individuals'[1]. States enjoy a certain margin of appreciation in laying down such regulation. Nonetheless, the limitations applied to the right of access to court must not be such that the very essence of the right is impaired; they must, moreover, pursue a legitimate aim and comply with the principle of proportionality[2]; and should be legally certain[3]. Thus, in *Ashingdane v United Kingdom*[4], the E Ct HR held that a provision in a statute under which mental patients were detained excluding liability for acts done under the statute unless there was negligence or bad faith did not violate the applicant's right of effective access to a court, because the limitation of liability pursued a legitimate aim (namely preventing those caring for mental patients from being unfairly harassed by litigation); the essence of the right was not impaired; and the restrictions were consistent with the principle of proportionality in that it was possible for the applicant to claim bad faith or absence of reasonable care. The same principles will apply in determining whether art 6 is violated by a procedural bar (such as an immunity or defence pleaded by the defendant) to the bringing of a claim[5].

1   *Golder v United Kingdom* (1975) 1 EHRR 524, E Ct HR, at para 38 (civil); *Deweer v Belgium* (1980) 2 EHRR 439, E Ct HR, para 49 (criminal).
2   *Ashingdane v United Kingdom* (1985) 7 EHRR 528, E Ct HR, para 57. See, recently, *Stubbings v United Kingdom* (1996) 23 EHRR 213, E Ct HR, para 48 and *National and Provincial Building Society v United Kingdom* (1997) 25 EHRR 127, E Ct HR, para 105. On proportionality, see para **3.10**.
3   See *Société Levage Prestations v France* (1996) 24 EHRR 351, E Ct HR, paras 40–50 (procedural requirements should be based on 'sufficiently clear and coherent' case-law). On certainty, see para **3.13**.
4   (1985) 7 EHRR 528, E Ct HR, para 57.
5   Application 10475/83 *Dyer v United Kingdom* 39 DR 246 (1984), EComHR; *Fayed v United Kingdom* (1994) 18 EHRR 393, E Ct HR. See para **4.6.5**.

4.6.19   Restrictions on the right of access to a court have also been allowed in relation to: vexatious litigants[1]; minors[2]; bankrupts[3]; prisoners[4]; a requirement for the payment of fines for abuse of process[5]; reasonable time limits in respect of proceedings[6]; a requirement for payment of security for costs[7]; in a criminal case, a practice whereby there is no hearing as to guilt or innocence (only as to sentence) where an accused pleads guilty at the beginning of his trial[8]; and privilege available in defamation proceedings concerning allegations of fraud in a government inspector's report[9]. Restrictions have been held to be in breach of the Convention where, for example, certain bodies were prevented by statute from bringing proceedings in respect of their property[10]; and where a professional person was compelled to bring a claim for fees for work done through a professional organisation[11].

1   Application 11559/85 *H v United Kingdom* 45 DR 281 (1985), EComHR.
2   See *Golder v United Kingdom* (1975) 1 EHRR 524, E Ct HR, para 39.
3   Application 12040/86 *M v United Kingdom* 52 DR 269 (1987), EComHR.
4   *Campbell and Fell v United Kingdom* (1984) 7 EHRR 165, E Ct HR.
5   Application 10412/83 *P v France* 52 DR 128 (1987), EComHR.
6   *Stubbings v United Kingdom* (1996) 23 EHRR 213, E Ct HR, paras 54–55 (limitation period for claims of childhood sexual abuse did not violate art 6(1)).
7   *Tolstoy Miloslavsky v United Kingdom* (1995) 20 EHRR 442, E Ct HR, paras 61–67.
8   Application 5076/71 *X v United Kingdom* 40 CD 64 (1972), EComHR.
9   *Fayed v United Kingdom* (1994) 18 EHRR 393, E Ct HR.
10 *Holy Monasteries v Greece* (1994) 20 EHRR 1, E Ct HR, para 83.
11 *Philis v Greece* (1991) 13 EHRR 741, E Ct HR.

4.6.20   The right of access to a court in both criminal and non-criminal cases may be waived, for example by means of an arbitration agreement, but such waiver should be subjected to 'particularly careful review' to ensure that the applicant was not subject to constraint[1].

1   *Deweer v Belgium* (1980), 2 EHRR 439, E Ct HR, para 49.

4.6.21   The right of access to a court overlaps with the right (under art 13 of the Convention[1]) to an effective national remedy in respect of a breach of a Convention right, insofar as the Convention right is also a civil right[2].

1   See para **4.13**.
2   See *De La Pradelle v France* A 253-B (1992), E Ct HR, para 37; *Aksoy v Turkey* (1996) 23 EHRR 553, E Ct HR, paras 93–94; *Matos e Silva, Lda v Portugal* (1996) 24 EHRR 573, E Ct HR, para 64.

4.6.22   Article 6(1) does not guarantee a right of appeal from a decision of a court, whether in a criminal[1] or non-criminal case, which complies with the requirements of that article. If, however, a contracting state provides a right of appeal, art 6 will apply to the appeal proceedings[2].

1   As to the right of appeal in criminal cases provided for by the seventh protocol, art 2, see paras **4.6.74– 4.6.75**.
2   *Delcourt v Belgium* (1970) 1 EHRR 355, E Ct HR, para 25, applied to the United Kingdom Court of Appeal in *Tolstoy Miloslavsky v United Kingdom* (1995) 20 EHRR 442, E Ct HR, para 59.

(ii)   Application to administrative decision-making

4.6.23   Where a decision determinative of an individual's 'civil rights and obligations' is taken by the executive, or by an adjudicatory body not complying with art 6(1), the article requires (in accordance with the right of access to a court) that the state provide a right to challenge the decision before a judicial body with full jurisdiction providing the guarantees of art 6(1)[1]. If such an appeal is provided, there will be no violation of the article. In contrast, where 'courts of the classic kind' (rather than administrative tribunals) are concerned, art 6 must be fully complied with at the trial stage[2] (although an appeal court may sometimes 'make reparation' for a breach of the article at trial[3]).

1   *Albert and Le Compte v Belgium* (1983) 5 EHRR 533, ECt HR, para 29; see also *Kaplan v United Kingdom* (1980) 4 EHRR 64, EComHR, para 161 (an interpretation of art 6 (1) under which it was held that to provide a right to a full appeal on the merits of every administrative decision affecting private rights would lead to a result which was inconsistent with the long-standing legal position in most of the Contracting States).
2   *De Cubber v Belgium* (1984) 7 EHRR 236, ECt HR, para 32 (applied to a court-martial in *Findlay v United Kingdom* (1997) 24 EHRR 221, ECt HR, para 79).
3   *Adolf v Austria* (1982) 4 EHRR 313, ECt HR, paras 38–41; *De Cubber v Belgium* (1984) 7 EHRR 236, ECt HR, para 33; *Edwards v United Kingdom* (1992) 15 EHRR 417, ECt HR, paras 34 and 39.

4.6.24   The E Ct HR has recognised that in specialised areas of law such as (for example) planning law, it may be expedient for an administrative body to make findings of fact and to exercise discretionary judgment in relation to policy matters; and that in such cases art 6(1) may be satisfied by an appeal on a point of law to a judicial body with limited jurisdiction as to matters of fact, rather than requiring a full judicial rehearing of all matters of fact and discretion[1]. This is particularly so where the facts have already been established by a quasi-judicial procedure governed by many of the safeguards required by the article. The recognition of this principle stems in part from the fact that such an approach by an appeal tribunal to questions of fact is 'frequently a feature in the systems of judicial control of administrative decisions found throughout the Council of Europe Member States'[2]. In cases involving applications for judicial review under Enlgish law, the sufficiency of the review exercised by the High Court must be assessed having regard to matters such as the subject-matter of the decision appealed against, the manner in which the decision was arrived at, and the content of the dispute, including the desired and actual grounds of appeal[3].

1   *Bryan v United Kingdom* (1995) 21 EHRR 342, E Ct HR, paras 44–47 (appeal on judicial review principles from decision of a planning inspector satisfied the requirements of art 6(1)): see also *Zumtobel v Austria* (1993) 17 EHRR 116, E Ct HR, paras 31–32; *Ortenberg v Austria* (1995) 19 EHRR 524, E Ct HR, para 34; and *Kaplan v United Kingdom* (1980) 4 EHRR 64, EComHR, para 161, n which see para **4.6.23**, n 1.
2   *Bryan v United Kingdom* (1995) 21 EHRR 342, E Ct HR, at para 47.
3   *Bryan v United Kingdom* (1995) 21 EHRR 342, E Ct HR, at para 45, applied by the EComHR (in each case rejecting the applicant's complaints) in Application 28530/95 *X v United Kingdom*, decision of 19 January 1998; Application 29419/95 *Stefan v United Kingdom*, decision of 9 December 1997, see further *Stefan v General Medical Council* (8 March 1999, unreported), PC; Application 30552/96 *APB and others v United Kingdom*, decision of 15 January 1998; and Application 31503/96 *Wickramsinghe v United Kingdom*, decision of 9 December 1997.

4.6.25   By contrast, in several cases not involving specialised decisions of this kind, the E Ct HR has found violations of art 6(1) on the basis of the lack of an appeal on the merits (rather than merely on a point of law) from an administrative decision determinative of civil rights which did not itself comply with art 6(1). Such violations were found, for example, in *Albert and Le Compte v Belgium*[1] (disciplinary decisions relating to doctors taken by professional associations not complying with art 6(1); appeal to the Belgian Court of Cassation only on a point of law); *W v United Kingdom*[2] (local authority decision restricting access to a child in care; held that the availability of judicial review in a case concerning access to children was insufficient where the parents wished to challenge the merits of the decision); *Obermeier v Austria*[3] (decision by a government body as to the justifiability of the applicant's dismissal; no appeal on the merits available); and *Schmautzer v Austria*[4] (administrative body convicting applicant of road traffic offence; appeal to the Constitutional Court only as to conformity of conviction with the Constitution). Even in this type of case, however, a violation will not be found if in fact the appeal court has been able to consider on their merits all points raised by the applicant (for example, because the applicant only wishes to appeal on a point of law, not a question of fact)[5].

1   (1983) 5 EHRR 533, ECt HR, para 36.
2   (1987) 10 EHRR 29, E Ct HR, para 82.
3   (1990) 13 EHRR 290, E Ct HR, para 70.
4   (1995) 21 EHRR 511, E Ct HR, para 36; see, similarly, *Umlauft v Austria* (1996) 22 EHRR 76, E Ct HR, para 39.
5   See eg *Fischer v Austria* (1995) 20 EHRR 349, E Ct HR, paras 33–34.

(b)   The right to a fair hearing

(i)   Introduction

4.6.26   The right to a fair hearing guaranteed by art 6 applies to both civil and criminal cases, although 'the Contracting States have a greater latitude when dealing with civil cases concerning civil rights and obligations than they have when dealing with criminal cases'[1]. In determining whether there has been a breach of the right to a fair hearing, the E Ct HR may consider the trial 'as a whole' as well as individual deficiencies in the trial process[2].

1   *Dombo Beheer v Netherlands* (1993) 18 EHRR 213, E Ct HR, para 32.
2   See *Barberà, Messegué and Jabardo v Spain* (1988) 11 EHRR 360, E Ct HR, paras 68, 89 (cumulative effect of a number of features of trial was unfair).

4.6.27   The guarantee of a fair hearing relates to the implementation of judicial decisions as well as the trial itself[1].

1   *Hornsby v Greece* (1997) 24 EHRR 250, E Ct HR, paras 40–41 (Greek authorities refraining for more than five years from taking necessary measures to comply with a judicial decision; held, art 6(1) violated).

(ii)   A hearing in one's presence

4.6.28   There is, in both criminal and civil cases, a general right to an oral hearing, which derives from the guarantee in art 6 of a 'public' hearing[1]. Moreover, in a criminal case, a right to a hearing in the presence of the accused flows from the notion of a fair trial[2]. In civil cases, however, the right of a party to be present at the hearing has been held to extend only to certain kinds of cases, such as cases which involve an assessment of a party's personal conduct[3].

1   See paras **4.6.40–4.6.43**.
2   *Ekbatani v Sweden* (1988) 13 EHRR 504, E Ct HR, para 25.
3   See, respectively, *Muyldermans v Belgium* (1991) 15 EHRR 204, E Ct HR, para 64.

4.6.29   It seems that a party may waive his right to be present at an oral hearing, provided that such a waiver is unequivocal and is 'attended by minimum safeguards commensurate to its importance'[1]. Trial in absentia may be permitted where the state has acted diligently, but unsuccessfully, to give an accused effective notice of the hearing[2]; and may be permitted in the interests of the administration of justice in some cases of illness[3].

1   *Poitrimol v France* (1993) 18 EHRR 130, E Ct HR, para 31. Where this occurs, however, a defendant in criminal proceedings must be permitted legal representation: *Lala v Netherlands* (1994) 18 EHRR 586; *Pelladoah v Netherlands* (1994) 19 EHRR 81; *Van Geyseghem v Belgium* (21 January 1999, unreported).
2   *Colozza and Rubinat v Italy* (1985) 7 EHRR 516, E Ct HR, paras 28–29.
3   Applications 7572/76, 7586/76 and 7587/76, *Ensslin, Baader and Raspe v Federal Republic of Germany* 14 DR 64 (1979), para 22 (hunger strike).

4.6.30   As to the right of a party to be present in person on any appeal, this may not be guaranteed by art 6 in cases where there has been an oral hearing at first instance at which he was entitled to be present. In such cases, the right to be present at an appeal depends upon the nature of the appeal hearing (whether the court hears questions of fact as well as law), the need for the applicant's presence in order to determine any questions of fact and the importance of what is at stake for him. In *Monnell and Morris v United Kingdom*[1], the E Ct HR held that there was no violation of art 6(1) in circumstances where the applicants were not entitled to be present in the Court of Appeal on their applications for leave to appeal against conviction and sentence, it being sufficient that they had the right to make written submissions or representations through a lawyer.

1   (1987) 10 EHRR 205, E Ct HR, paras 68–70.

(iii)   'Equality of arms'

4.6.31   The right to a fair hearing requires that everyone who is a party to proceedings must have a reasonable opportunity of presenting his case to the court under conditions which do not place him at a substantial disadvantage vis-à-vis his opponent. This is the principle of 'equality of arms' and involves striking a 'fair balance' between the parties[1].

1   See eg *Neumeister v Austria* (1968) 1 EHRR 91, E Ct HR, para 22; *Delcourt v Belgium* (1970) 1 EHRR 355, E Ct HR, para 28; *Dombo Beheer v Netherlands* (1993) 18 EHRR 213, E Ct HR, para 33; *De Haes and Gijsels v Belgium* (1997) 25 EHRR 1, E Ct HR, para 53.

4.6.32   In criminal cases, the principle of equality of arms overlaps with the specific guarantees of art 6(3), though it is not confined to those aspects of the proceedings[1]. Thus, for example, it will be a breach of the principle where an expert witness appointed by the defence is not accorded the same facilities as one appointed by the prosecution or the court[2]. In *Jespers v Belgium*[3], the Commission held that the 'equality of arms' principle imposes on prosecuting and investigating authorities an obligation to disclose any material in their possession, or to which they could gain access, which may assist the accused in exonerating himself or in obtaining a reduction in sentence. This principle extends to material which might undermine the credibility of a prosecution witness[4].

1   *Jespers v Belgium* 27 DR 61 (1981), para 54; see also *Edwards v United Kingdom* (1992) 15 EHRR 417; *Foucher v France* (1997) 25 EHRR 234.
2   *Bonisch v Austria* (1985) 9 EHRR 191.
3   27 DR 61 (1981).
4   27 DR 61 (1981) at para 58; non-disclosure of evidence relevant to credibility may also raise an issue under art 6(3)(b): *Edwards v United Kingdom* (1992) 15 EHRR 417, EComHR opinion para 50.

4.6.33   The principle also applies in 'civil rights and obligations' cases, whether between two private parties or between an individual and the state[1]. The principle will, in certain circumstances, require in particular that the parties to civil proceedings should be entitled to cross-examine witnesses[2]. More generally, a principle underlying art 6 as a whole is that judicial proceedings should be adversarial[3]. In proceedings involving the state, the principle may be breached if the legislature interferes with the administration of justice in a way designed to influence judicial determination of the dispute[4].

1   See (respectively) *Dombo Beheer v Netherlands* (1993) 18 EHRR 213, E Ct HR, para 33 and *Ruiz-Mateos v Spain* (1993) 16 EHRR 505, E Ct HR.
2   Application 5362/72 *X v Austria* 42 CD 145 (1972), EComHR.

3   For examples of violations of this principle, see *McMichael v United Kingdom* (1995) 20 EHRR 205, E Ct HR, paras 80, 83 (non-disclosure of 'vital documents' in family proceedings: as to documents, see also *McGinley and Egan v United Kingdom* (1998) 27 EHRR 1, E Ct HR, para 86); and *Mantovanelli v France* (1997) 24 EHRR 370, E Ct HR, paras 33–36 (applicants unable to comment effectively on court expert's report); *Van Orshoven v Belgium* (1997) 26 EHRR 55, E Ct HR, paras 41–42.
4   *Stran Greek Refineries and Stratis Andreadis v Greece* (1994) 19 EHRR 293, E Ct HR, para 49; but cf *National and Provincial Building Society v United Kingdom* (1998) 25 EHRR 127, E Ct HR, para 112 (retrospective legislation of a 'much less drastic nature' than in the former case, with a public interest motive, and in a sector – taxation – where retrospective legislation was not confined to the United Kingdom: held, no violation).

(iv)   The rules of evidence

4.6.34   The rules of evidence are in principle a matter for each contracting state. It is not for the E Ct HR to substitute its own view as to the admissibility of evidence for that of the national courts, although the court will nevertheless examine whether the proceedings as a whole were fair[1].

1   *Miailhe v France (No 2)* (1996) 23 EHRR 491, E Ct HR, para 43.

4.6.35   In criminal cases, the E Ct HR has held[1] that art 6 does not necessarily require the exclusion of illegally obtained evidence, but that the admission of such evidence can give rise to unfairness on the facts of a particular case[2]. The use of evidence obtained as a result of ill-treatment with the aim of extracting a confession will inevitably violate art 6[3]. The admission of hearsay evidence without an opportunity to cross-examine may render the trial unfair if the conviction is based wholly or mainly on such evidence[4]. The evidence of an accomplice who has been offered immunity from prosecution may be admitted without violating art 6, provided the defence and the jury are made fully aware of the circumstances[5]. Nor is it a breach of art 6 to admit the evidence of an undercover agent placed in a prison to eavesdrop on conversations involving the accused[6].

1   Cf the position in New Zealand, where the criminal courts have adopted a rule of prima facie exclusion of evidence obtained in consequence of a breach of the Bill of Rights Act 1990: *Simpson v A-G (Baigent's Case)* [1994] 3 NZLR 667, NZCA. As to the resolution of this conflict by the Privy Council, see *Allie Mohammed v State* [1999] 2 WLR 552, PC.
2   *Schenck v Switzerland* (1988) 13 EHRR 242 at paras 46–48; *X v Federal Republic of Germany* (1989) 11 EHRR 84.
3   *Austria v Italy* 6 YB 740 (1963).
4   *Unterpetinger v Austria* (1986) 13 EHRR 175: see art 6(3)(d) at paras **4.6.70–4.6.71**.
5   *X v United Kingdom* 7 DR 115 (1976).
6   *X v Federal Republic of Germany* (1989) 11 EHRR 84.

(v)   Freedom from self-incrimination

4.6.36   The right to a fair trial in a criminal case includes 'the right of anyone charged with a criminal offence ... to remain silent and not to contribute to incriminating himself'[1]. In *Saunders v United Kingdom*[2], the E Ct HR considered that the admission in evidence at the applicant's trial of transcripts of interviews with DTI inspectors violated art 6(1) since at the time of the interrogation the applicant was under a duty to answer the questions which was enforceable by criminal proceedings for contempt. The court considered that the right to silence and the right not to incriminate oneself were generally recognised international standards which lay at the heart of the notion of a fair procedure under art 6. This presupposed that the prosecution in a criminal case must prove its case without resort to evidence obtained through methods of coercion and oppression in defiance of the will of the accused.

1   *Funke v France* (1993) 16 EHRR 297.
2   (1996) 23 EHRR 313.

4.6.37   Different considerations apply to rules permitting the drawing of adverse inferences from the silence of an accused under interrogation or at trial. In *Murray v United Kingdom*[1], the E Ct HR found that the Criminal Evidence (Northern Ireland) Order 1988[2], as applied to the facts of that case, did not constitute a violation of art 6(1). The court emphasised that the independent evidence of guilt was strong, and that the Northern Ireland legislation incorporated a number of safeguards: in particular, the adverse inferences had been drawn by a judge sitting without a jury, and his decision was recorded in a reasoned judgment which was susceptible to scrutiny on appeal[3].

1   (1996) 22 EHRR 29.
2   SI 1988/1987.
3   Cf *Dermott Quinn v United Kingdom* [1997] EHRLR 167.

(vi)   Prejudicial publicity

4.6.38   In criminal cases, 'a virulent press campaign against the accused' is capable of violating the right to a fair trial[1], particularly if the case is to be tried by a jury. Account must be taken of the fact that some press comment on a trial involving a matter of public interest is inevitable[2]; and of any steps which the judge has taken to counter the effect of the prejudice in his directions to the jury[3].

1   *X v Austria* 11 CD 31 (1963) at 43. As to prejudicial statements by public officials see art 6(2) (paras **4.6.59–4.6.61**), and *Allenet de Ribemont v France* (1995) 20 EHRR 557.
2   *X v Norway* 35 CD 37 (1970).
3   Application 7542/76 *X v United Kingdom* 2 Digest 688 (1978).

(vii)   A reasoned judgment

4.6.39   It is a requirement of a fair trial in both civil and criminal matters that a court should give reasons for its judgment[1]. The extent of the duty to give reasons may vary according to the nature of the decision[2]. A failure by a court specifically to address a limitation argument raised by a party may amount to a breach of the duty[3].

1   For recent consideration of the duty to give reasons both at common law and under the Convention see *Stefan v General Medical Council* (8 March 1999, unreported), PC, where the Privy Council referred to the 'possible reappraisal of the whole position [in relation to the duty to give reasons] which the passing of the Human Rights Act 1988 may bring about', and commented that the provisions of art 6 'will require closer attention to be paid to the duty to give reasons, at least in relation to those cases where a person's civil rights and obligations are being determined'.
2   *Ruiz Torija v Spain* (1994) 19 EHRR 553, E Ct HR, para 29; *Georgiadis v Greece* (1997) 24 EHRR 606, paras 42–43 (violation where court found applicant guilty of 'gross negligence' without particularising matters said to constitute such negligence); *Helle v Finland* (1997) 26 EHRR 159, E Ct HR, paras 55–60 (where national court gives 'sparse' reasons for a decision, a fair procedure requires that it did in fact address the essential issues submitted to its jurisdiction); Stefan v General Medical Council (8 March 1999, unreported), PC.

3   *Ruiz Torija v Spain* (1994) 19 EHRR 553, E Ct HR, para 30.

(c)   The right to a public hearing and the public pronouncement of judgment

(i)   The right to a public hearing

4.6.40   Article 6(1) provides a right to a public hearing[1], which implies a right to an oral hearing at the trial court level[2], unless there are exceptional circumstances which justify dispensing with such a hearing[3]. The purpose of this fundamental[4] guarantee is to protect litigants from 'the administration of justice in secret with no public scrutiny'[5], and to maintain public confidence in the courts and the administration of justice[6], and for this reason the presence of the press is of particular importance[7].

1 For the position in relation to hearings in chambers in the High Court, see *Hodgson v Imperial Tobacco Ltd* [1998] 2 All ER 673, [1998] 1 WLR 1056, CA.
2 *Fredin v Sweden (No 2)* A 283–A (1994), E Ct HR, para 21; *Fischer v Austria* (1995) 20 EHRR 349, E Ct HR, para 44.
3 *Allan Jacobsson v Sweden (No 2)*, Judgment of 19 February 1998, E Ct HR, para 46 (no violation even though first and only judicial body considering applicant's case did not afford an oral hearing, because no issue of fact or law requiring such a hearing arose); cf eg *Stallinger and Kuso v Austria* (1997) 26 EHRR 81, E Ct HR, paras 50–51. See also *Werner v Austria* (1997) 26 EHRR 310, E Ct HR, para 50 (protection of private life of applicant did not override art 6(1) principle that proceedings must be in public).
4 See eg *Schuler-Zgraggen v Switzerland* (1993) 16 EHRR 405, E Ct HR, para 58.
5 *Pretto v Italy* (1983) 6 EHRR 182, E Ct HR, para 21.
6 *Diennet v France* (1995) 21 EHRR 554, E Ct HR, para 33.
7 See para **4.10** on art 10 and the duty of the press to impart information and ideas to the public.

4.6.41 The right to a public hearing is subject to the express restrictions set out in the text of the article. In contrast to the position under arts 8 to 10 of the Convention, there is no express requirement that interference with the right to a public hearing should be 'necessary in a democratic society' (which has been interpreted as requiring a proportionate response to a pressing social need)[1]. However, in a leading case, *Campbell and Fell v United Kingdom*, the E Ct HR did have regard to broad considerations of proportionality, deciding that prison disciplinary proceedings could be conducted in camera for 'reasons of public order and security' because a requirement that such proceedings would be in public would 'impose a disproportionate burden on the authorities of the state'[2]. The court has, moreover, required that derogations from the right to a public hearing should be 'strictly required by the circumstances'[3].

1 See paras **3.15–3.16**.
2 (1984) 7 EHRR 165, E Ct HR, para 37.
3 *Diennet v France* (1995) 21 EHRR 554, E Ct HR, para 34.

4.6.42 Hearings in camera have been held justified in, for example, cases involving sexual offences against children, divorce proceedings and medical disciplinary proceedings[1]. A hearing in private of a case at first instance will not, however, be justified simply to help reduce the court's workload[2].

1 See, respectively, Application 1913/63 *X v Austria* 2 Digest 438 (1965), EComHR; Application 7366/76 *X v United Kingdom* 2 Digest 452 (1977), EComHR; Application 15561/89 *Imberechts v Belgium* 69 DR 312 (1991), EComHR.
2 Cf the position on appeal, where the absence of a public hearing may be justified on this ground: *Helmers v Sweden* (1991) 15 EHRR 285, E Ct HR, para 36. See further para **4.6.30**.

4.6.43 The Convention does not require a public hearing if an accused or a party has waived his right to such a hearing, provided that the waiver is unequivocal and there is no important public interest consideration that calls for the public to have the opportunity to be present[1]. It is permissible for a body determining civil rights and obligations to have a practice that it will not hold oral hearings unless one of the parties expressly requests it to do so. If no such request is made, then the parties may be deemed unequivocally to have waived the right to an oral hearing[2]. The failure to provide a public hearing before an administrative or other tribunal determining 'civil rights and obligations' may not constitute a violation of art 6 if the case is dealt with on appeal by a court sitting in public[3].

1 *Håkansson v Sweden* (1990) 13 EHRR 1, E Ct HR, para 66, applied in *Pauger v Austria* (1997) 25 EHRR 105, E Ct HR, para 58.

2   *Zumtobel v Austria* (1993) 17 EHRR 116, E Ct HR, para 34.
3   *Schuler-Zgraggen v Switzerland* (1993) 16 EHRR 405, E Ct HR, para 58, where the E Ct HR recognised that there were technical areas of decision-making where there are good reasons for avoiding oral hearings. See paras **4.6.22** and **4.6.30** on appeal proceedings.

(ii)   The right to public pronouncement of judgment

4.6.44   The right to public pronouncement of judgment, like the right to a public hearing, is intended to contribute to a fair trial through public scrutiny. The right is not subject to any of the express limitations in the text of art 6(1), which apply only to the right to a public hearing[1]. However, the right may be satisfied by judgment being made available to the public in the court registry, or otherwise published in writing, without being pronounced orally in open court[2].

1   *Campbell and Fell v United Kingdom* (1984) 7 EHRR 165, E Ct HR, para 90.
2   See *Preto v Italy* (1983) 6 EHRR 182, E Ct HR, para 26 and *Axen v Federal Republic of Germany* (1983) 6 EHRR 195, E Ct HR, paras 29–32 (civil) and Application 11826/85, *Helmers v Sweden* 61 DR 138 (1989), EComHR (criminal). Cf *Werner v Austria* (1997) 26 EHRR 310, E Ct HR, paras 56–59 (violation where judgment merely served on parties and not available to public at large).

(d)   The right to a hearing within a reasonable time

(i)   Introduction

4.6.45   Article 6(1) guarantees a right to a hearing within a reasonable time in both civil and criminal cases. Its purpose is to protect all parties to court proceedings against excessive procedural delays, and, in criminal cases, to prevent a person charged remaining too long in a state of uncertainty about his fate[1].

1   *Stögmüller v Austria* (1969) 1 EHRR 155, E Ct HR, para 5.

4.6.46   Most of the cases involving breaches of the 'reasonable time' guarantee come from civil law jurisdictions[1]. Examples of United Kingdom cases in which a breach has been found by the E Ct HR are *H v United Kingdom*[2] (period of two years and seven months taken to decide on the applicant's access to her child in public care was unreasonable), *Darnell v United Kingdom*[3] (claim for unfair dismissal from the NHS took nearly nine years) and *Robins v United Kingdom*[4] (over four years to resolve dispute over legal aid costs).

1   As is noted by Harris, O'Boyle and Warbrick *Law of the European Convention on Human Rights* (1995), p 229.
2   (1987) 10 EHRR 95, E Ct HR, para 86.
3   (1993) 18 EHRR 205, E Ct HR, para 21.
4   (1997) 26 EHRR 527, E Ct HR, para 35.

(ii)   The period of time to be considered

4.6.47   In civil cases, time usually begins to run for the purposes of the reasonable time guarantee from the initiation of court proceedings[1], although it may start to run even before the issue of proceedings in certain situations, as for example where an applicant is required to exhaust a preliminary administrative remedy under national law before having recourse to a court or tribunal[2]. In criminal cases, the reasonable time guarantee runs from the time of charge[3]. In either case, the guarantee continues to apply until the case is finally determined (which may include appeal and judicial review proceedings[4], and proceedings determining the quantum of damages[5]).

1   See eg *Guincho v Portugal* (1984) 7 EHRR 223, E Ct HR, para 29; *Ausiello v Italy* (1996) 24 EHRR 568, E Ct HR, para 18.
2   *König v Federal Republic of Germany* (1978) 2 EHRR 170, E Ct HR, para 98.

3   See para **4.6.14** on when a person is subject to a 'charge'.
4   *Eckle v Federal Republic of Germany* (1982) 5 EHRR 1, E Ct HR, para 76 (criminal); *König v Federal Republic of Germany* (1978) 2 EHRR 170, E Ct HR, at para 98 (civil).
5   *Silva Pontes v Portugal* (1994) 18 EHRR 156, E Ct HR, paras 30, 33.

(iii) 'Reasonable time'

4.6.48   In determining what constitutes a 'reasonable time' for the purposes of the article, regard is to be had to the particular circumstances of each case including, in particular, the complexity of the factual or legal[1] issues raised by the case; the conduct of the applicant and of the competent administrative and judicial authorities; and what is 'at stake' for the applicant[2]. In some cases, the E Ct HR makes an overall assessment rather than specifically referring to these criteria[3]. There is no absolute time limit.

1   If a particular case will have important repercussions on the national case-law in a particular area, this may be a relevant consideration: *Katte Klitsche de la Grange v Italy* (1994) 19 EHRR 368, E Ct HR, para 62.
2   *Zimmerman and Steiner v Switzerland* (1983) 6 EHRR 17, E Ct HR, para 24.
3   Eg *Ferrantelli and Santangelo v Italy* (1996) 23 EHRR 288, E Ct HR, paras 39, 42–43 (16 years from offences occurring while applicants still minors to conviction: held, art 6(1) violated).

(iv)   Conduct of the state and of the applicant

4.6.49   The state is not responsible for delay that is attributable to the applicant: only delays attributable to the state may justify a finding of failure to comply with the 'reasonable time' requirement. The state is, however, responsible for delays by its administrative or judicial authorities. In a civil case, these might include the adjournment of proceedings pending the outcome of another case, delay in the conduct of the hearing by the court or in the presentation or production of evidence by the state, or delays by the court registry or other administrative authorities[1]. In a criminal case, unjustified delays by the state have been found in relation to the entering of a *nolle prosequi*; the transfer of cases between courts; the hearing of cases against two or more accused together; the communication of judgment to the accused; and the making and hearing of appeals[2].

1   See *König v Federal Republic of Germany* (1978) 2 EHRR 170, E Ct HR, paras 104–105; *H v United Kingdom* (1987) 10 EHRR 95, E Ct HR, paras 83–86; *Allenet de Ribemont v France* (1995) 20 EHRR 557, E Ct HR, para 56; *Weisinger v Austria* (1991) 16 EHRR 258, E Ct HR, paras 61–64.
2   See Application 8435/78 *Orchin v United Kingdom* 34 DR 5 (1982), EComHR; *Foti v Italy* (1982) 5 EHRR 313, E Ct HR, para 72; *Hentrich v France* (1994) 18 EHRR 440, E Ct HR, para 61; *Eckle v Federal Republic of Germany* (1982) 5 EHRR 1, E Ct HR, para 84; *Ferraro v Italy* A 197–A (1991).

4.6.50   In addition to their duty to ensure the reasonably expeditious conduct of individual cases, states are also obliged to organise their legal systems so as to allow the courts to comply with the requirements of art 6(1). Thus, breaches of the Convention have been found in cases where the reason for the delay was a long-term backlog of work in the defendant state's court system, if the state has not taken adequate measures (eg the appointment of additional judges or administrative staff) to cope with the situation[1]. No violation will, however, normally be found where the backlog is a temporary or exceptional one in relation to which the state has reasonably promptly taken any necessary remedial action[2]. Moreover, the E Ct HR has recognised that special considerations (including the political and social importance of particular cases) apply in relation to the organisation of constitutional courts[3].

1   *Zimmerman and Steiner v Switzerland* (1983) 6 EHRR 17, E Ct HR, at paras 27–32; *Guincho v Portugal* (1984) 7 EHRR 223, E Ct HR, paras 40–41.
2   *Buchholz v Federal Republic of Germany* (1981) 3 EHRR 597, E Ct HR, para 51.
3   *Süßmann v Germany* (1996) 25 EHRR 64, E Ct HR, paras 55–60 (Federal Constitutional Court entitled to give priority to cases concerning reunification).

(v)   Urgent cases

4.6.51   Certain types of case may require greater urgency than others: in particular, criminal cases generally require more urgency than civil ones and a particularly strict standard applies where the applicant is in detention pending the outcome of the case[1]. In civil cases, there is particular urgency where what is at stake is the applicant's mental health, parental rights, employment, or his title to land, or where delay might render the proceedings pointless[2].

1   *Abdoella v Netherlands* (1992) 20 EHRR 585, E Ct HR, para 24.
2   See, respectively, *Bock v Germany* (1989) 12 EHRR 247, E Ct HR, paras 47–48; *Johansen v Norway* (1996) 23 EHRR 33, E Ct HR, para 88; *Buckholz v Federal Republic of Germany* (1981) 3 EHRR 597, E Ct HR, para 52; *Hentrich v France* (1994) 18 EHRR 440, E Ct HR, at para 61; *A v Denmark* (1996) 22 EHRR 458, E Ct HR, para 78 (compensation for HIV infection).

(e)   The right to an independent and impartial tribunal established by law

(i)   A 'tribunal'

4.6.52   For the purposes of art 6(1) a 'tribunal' is characterised by its judicial function. The tribunal must have jurisdiction to examine all questions of fact and law relevant to the dispute before it[1]. It must determine matters within its competence on the basis of rules of law; and its decisions must be legally binding rather than merely advisory[2]. A tribunal may be composed of persons (for example, civil servants) who are not professional judges; and the fact that a body has other, non-judicial, functions (such as administrative functions) does not prevent it being a tribunal[3].

1   See eg *Terra Woningen v Netherlands* (1996) 24 EHRR 456, para 52; and cf *Bryan v United Kingdom* (1995) 21 EHRR 342 (see para **4.6.24**).
2   See *Belilos v Switzerland* (1988) 10 EHRR 466, E Ct HR, para 64; *Benthem v Netherlands* (1985) 8 EHRR 1, E Ct HR, para 40; *Van de Hurk v Netherlands* (1994) 18 EHRR 481, para 52, E Ct HR (government empowered by law not to implement court decision, although the power was never used; held, art 6 infringed).
3   See, respectively, *Ettl v Austria* (1987) 10 EHRR 255, E Ct HR, para 38 and *Campbell and Fell v United Kingdom* (1984) 7 EHRR 165, E Ct HR, para 81.

(ii)   'Independent'

4.6.53   The E Ct HR has consistently held that in order to establish whether a tribunal can be considered 'independent', 'regard must be had, *inter alia,* to the manner of appointment of its members and to their term of office, to the existence of guarantees against outside pressures and to the question whether the body presents an appearance of independence'[1]. 'Independent' means independent of the executive, of the parties, and of Parliament.

1   *Bryan v United Kingdom* (1995) 21 EHRR 342, E Ct HR, para 37.

4.6.54   As to the manner of appointment of a tribunal's members, appointment by the executive is permissible, as is appointment by Parliament[1]. In order for a challenge under this heading to succeed, it would need to be shown that the practice of appointment as a whole was unsatisfactory or that the establishment of the particular court deciding a case was influenced by motives suggesting an attempt at influencing its outcome[2]. As to the members' term of office, relatively short terms (eg a term of three years for prison visitors in *Campbell and Fell v United Kingdom*[3]) have been accepted in relation to administrative or disciplinary tribunals. Members must be protected from removal during their term of office, although the E Ct HR has held that this need not be recognised in law if it is recognised in practice[4]. In relation to 'guarantees against outside pressure', tribunal members should not be subject to instructions from the executive: breaches of art 6 have been found where a tribunal sought and accepted as binding Foreign Office advice on the meaning of a treaty which it had to apply; where a member of a tribunal was a civil servant whose immediate superior was representing the government as a party to the case; and where all members of a court-martial were subordinate in rank to its convening officer and fell within his chain of command[5]. As to the final requirement, the 'appearance of independence', this entails an objective test, bearing in mind the importance of justice not only being done, but being seen to be done[6]. In *Bryan v United Kingdom*[7], the requirement was held to have been infringed in relation to a planning Inspector because of the existence of a power in the Secretary of State to 'call in' and determine planning appeals.

1 *Campbell and Fell v United Kingdom* (1984) 7 EHRR 165, E Ct HR, para 79; Application 8603/79 *Crociani v Italy* 22 DR 147 (1980), EComHR.
2 Application 7360/76, *Zand v Austria* 15 DR 70 at 81 (1978), EComHR.
3 (1984) 7 EHRR 165, E Ct HR, para 80.
4 *Campbell and Fell v United Kingdom* (1984) 7 EHRR 165, E Ct HR, para 80.
5 Respectively, *Beaumartin v France* (1994) 19 EHRR 485, E Ct HR, para 38; *Sramek v Austria* (1984) 7 EHRR 351, E Ct HR, paras 41–42; *Findlay v United Kingdom* (1997) 24 EHRR 221, E Ct HR, paras 73–77.
6 *Campbell and Fell v United Kingdom* (1984) 7 EHRR 165, E Ct HR, at para 81 (requirement of independence not infringed by Board of Visitors, because prisoners were not 'reasonably entitled' to believe the Board to be dependent upon the executive). In Application 28488/95 *McGonnell v United Kingdom*, EComHR Report of 20 October 1998, the EComHR held that the position of the Bailiff in Guernsey, who was 'not only a senior member of the judiciary of the island, but was also a senior member of the legislature ... and, in addition, a senior member of the executive' was incompatible with the requirement of an appearance of independence. See also *Incal v Turkey*, judgment of 9 June 1998, E Ct HR, paras 65–73.
7 *Bryan v United Kingdom* (1995) 21 EHRR 342, E Ct HR at para 38.

(iii) 'Impartial'

4.6.55 Impartiality for the purposes of art 6 denotes an absence of prejudice or bias. Impartiality is to be examined on the basis of both a subjective test of the personal conviction of a particular judge in a given case, and an objective test of whether the judge offered guarantees sufficient to exclude legitimate doubt[1].

> 'What is at stake is the confidence which the courts in a democratic society must inspire in the public and, above all, as far as criminal proceedings are concerned, in the accused.'[2]

If a party believes that the court or tribunal is not impartial, his standpoint is important but not decisive: the question is whether that doubt as to impartiality can be objectively justified[3]. A judge will be presumed impartial until there is proof to the contrary.[4] If there is legitimate doubt as to impartiality, the judge must withdraw from the case[5].

1 *Piersack v Belgium* (1982) 5 EHRR 169, E Ct HR, para 30, recently applied in *Ferrantelli and Santangelo v Italy* (1996) 23 EHRR 288, E Ct HR, para 56; *Bulut v Austria* (1996) 24 EHRR 84, E Ct HR, para 31; *Thomann v Switzerland* (1996) 24 EHRR 553, E Ct HR, para 30.
2 *Fey v Austria* (1993) 16 EHRR 387, E Ct HR, para 30.
3 *Ferrantelli and Santangelo v Italy* (1996) 23 EHRR 288, E Ct HR, para 58; *Incal v Turkey*, judgment of 9 June 1998, E Ct HR, para 71.
4 *Piersack v Belgium* (1982) 5 EHRR 169, E Ct HR, at para 30(a); *Thomann v Switzerland* (1997) 24 EHRR 553, E Ct HR, para 31.
5 *Hauschildt v Denmark* (1989) 12 EHRR 266, E Ct HR, paras 46, 48.

4.6.56 Violations of the requirement of impartiality have been found in cases where the trial judge had previously been the head of the section of the public prosecutor's department which had investigated the applicant's case and commenced proceedings against him[1]; where a judge trying a criminal case had previously decided a bail application against the defendant on the ground that there was a 'particularly confirmed suspicion of guilt'[2]; where the judge had a financial or personal interest in the case[3]; and where members of the court carried out both advisory and judicial functions[4]. There is, however, no breach of impartiality where (without more) a court which convicted an accused in absentia presides over a retrial of his case; where a case is remitted for retrial to the same tribunal; where the trial judge has dealt with the case at the pre-trial stage; or where that judge has previously presided over the trial of a defendant's co-accused[5].

1　*Piersack v Belgium* (1982) 5 EHRR 169, E Ct HR, paras 30–32.
2　*Hauschildt v Denmark* (1989) 12 EHRR 266, E Ct HR, at para 50: see, similarly, *Ferrantelli and Santangelo v Italy* (1996) 23 EHRR 288, E Ct HR, paras 59–60 (judge had presided over trial of co-accused and made statements suggesting he had formed a conviction as to the applicants' guilt).
3　See *Demicoli v Malta* (1991) 14 EHRR 47, E Ct HR, paras 36–42 (members of the House of Representatives who were the subject of alleged offence of breach of parliamentary privilege were among those who sat in judgment); *Langborger v Sweden* (1989) 12 EHRR 416, E Ct HR, para 35 (lay members of tribunal adjudicating on deletion of clause in tenancy agreement were nominated by organisations having an interest in the clause's continued existence).
4　*Procola v Luxembourg* (1995) 22 EHRR 193, E Ct HR, paras 44–45.
5　See, respectively, *Thomann v Switzerland* (1996) 24 EHRR 553, E Ct HR, paras 33–36; *Ringeisen v Austria* (1971) 1 EHRR 455, para 97; *Bulut v Austria* (1996) 24 EHRR 84, E Ct HR, para 33; *Ferrantelli and Santangelo v Italy* (1996) 23 EHRR 288, EComHR, para 57.

4.6.57　The requirement of impartiality also applies to jury trials[1]. It is unclear whether the requirement of impartiality may be waived by an accused or a party[2].

1　*Remli v France* (1996) 22 EHRR 253, E Ct HR, paras 46–48 (violation where trial court took no steps to investigate racist remark by juror); but cf *Gregory v United Kingdom* (1997) 25 EHRR 577, E Ct HR, paras 43–50 (no violation where judge directed jury to put prejudice out of their minds in response to jury note alleging 'racial overtones' to deliberations); and see *Pullar v United Kingdom* (1996) 22 EHRR 391, E Ct HR, paras 36–41 (defendant's misgivings about impartiality of one juror not objectively justified).
2　*Oberschlick v Austria* (1994) 19 EHRR 389, E Ct HR, para 51 (waiver 'in so far as it is permissible' must be established in unequivocal manner); *Bulut v Austria* (1996) 24 EHRR 84, E Ct HR, para 30 ('regardless of whether a waiver was made or not' E Ct HR had to determine question of impartiality).

(iv)　'Established by law'

4.6.58　The requirement that a tribunal be 'established by law' is intended to ensure that the judicial organisation in a democratic society should not depend upon the discretion of the executive, but should be regulated by law emanating from Parliament setting out the basic framework concerning the courts' organisation[1]. Particular matters of detail may, however, be left to the executive acting by way of delegated legislation and subject to judicial review[2]. The requirement will be infringed if a tribunal does not function in accordance with the particular rules governing it.

1　Application 7360/76, *Zand v Austria* 15 DR 70 at 80 (1978), EComHR.
2　For example, in *Campbell and Fell v United Kingdom* (1984) 7 EHRR 165, E Ct HR, the rules concerning prison visitors were mostly contained in delegated legislation.

C　Article 6(2): The Presumption of Innocence in Criminal Cases

4.6.59　Article 6(2) guarantees the presumption of innocence in criminal proceedings. Article 6(2) does not prohibit rules which transfer the burden of proof to the accused to establish a defence, provided the overall burden of establishing guilt remains with the prosecution[1]. Neither does it necessarily prohibit presumptions of law or fact. However, any rule which shifts the burden of proof or which applies a presumption operating against the accused must be confined within reasonable limits[2]. In *X v United Kingdom*[3] the Commission upheld a rebuttable presumption that a man proved to be living with or controlling a prostitute was living off immoral earnings. Offences of strict liability do not violate art 6(2) providing the prosecution retains the burden of proving the commission of the offence[4].

1   *Lingens and Leitgens v Austria* (1981) 4 EHRR 373 at 390–391.
2   *Salabiaku v France* (1988) 13 EHRR 379, para 28; *Hoang v France* (1992) 16 EHRR 53. As to the approach of the Privy Council, see *A-G of Hong Kong v Lee Kwong Kut* [1993] AC 951. see also the decisions of the South African Constitutional Court in *State v Mbatha* [1996] 2 LRC 208; *State v Bhulwana* [1996] 1 LRC 194; *State v Coetzee* [1997] 2 LRC 593.
3   42 CD 135 (1972).
4   *Salabiaku v France* (1988) 13 EHRR 379; *Bates v United Kingdom* [1996] EHRLR 312, EComHR (Dangerous Dogs Act 1991).

4.6.60   Adverse comment by public officials runs the risk of violating the presumption of innocence. In *Allenet de Ribemont v France*[1] the French Interior Minister and a number of senior police officers held a press conference shortly after the applicant's arrest in which they named him as the one of the instigators of the murder of a French MP. The E Ct HR held that the presumption of innocence could be violated not only by a judge or a court but also by other public officials. Although art 6(2) could not prevent the authorities from informing the public about investigations in progress, it required that they did so with all discretion and circumspection necessary if the presumption of innocence was to be respected. The statements carried a clear implication that the applicant was guilty and therefore violated art 6(2).

1   (1995) 20 EHRR 557.

4.6.61   Similarly, a refusal to order the payment of costs to an acquitted defendant will violate the presumption of innocence if the ground for the refusal reflects a suspicion that the accused is guilty. In *Minelli v Switzerland*[1] the E Ct HR found a violation of art 6(2) where an acquitted defendant had been ordered to pay costs on the basis that he would 'very probably' have been convicted had he he not been saved by the operation of a limitation period for the offence.

1   (1983) 5 EHRR 554.

D   Article 6(3): Specific guarantees in criminal cases

1   GENERALLY

4.6.62   The minimum guarantees set out in art 6(3)(a)–(e) are specific aspects of the general right to a fair trial, and are not therefore exhaustive[1]. The relationship between art 6(1) and art 6(3) 'is that of the general to the particular': accordingly, a criminal trial could fail to fulfil the general conditions of art 6(1), even though the minimum rights guaranteed by art 6(3) are respected[2].

1   *Artico v Italy* (1980) 3 EHRR 1, para 32; *T v Italy* (1992) Series A/245–C, para 25; *Edwards v United Kingdom* (1992) 15 EHRR 417, para 33.
2   *Jespers v Belgium* 27 DR 61 (1981), para 54.

2   THE SPECIFIC GUARANTEES

(a)   Right to be informed of the charge

4.6.63   Article 6(3)(a) provides that a criminal defendant has the right to be informed promptly, in a language which he understands and in detail, of the nature and cause of the accusation against him. This is aimed at the information required to be given at the time of charge or the commencement of proceedings, rather than the disclosure of evidence necessary to enable the accused to prepare for trial, which is governed by the general right to equality of arms in art 6(1) coupled with the right to adequate time and facilities in art 6(3)(b). Thus, art 6(3)(a) has been restrictively interpreted so as to require that the accused be informed of the nature of the charge against him and the material facts upon which it is based, but not necessarily the evidence in support[1].

1   *Brozicek v Italy* (1989) 12 EHRR 371 at paras 38–42.

(b)   Adequate time and facilities for the preparation of the defence

4.6.64   Article 6(3)(b) guarantees the right to adequate time and facilities for the preparation of the defence. The adequacy of the time allowed will depend on the complexity of the case[1]. It is fundamental to art 6(3)(b) that the defence lawyer must be appointed in sufficient time to allow proper preparation to take place[2]. Although it was formerly the practice of the Commission to examine a case to determine whether the late appointment of the defence lawyer had actually prejudiced the accused[3], the more recent emphasis by the E Ct HR is on the appearance of fairness and upon 'the increased sensitivity of the public to the fair administration of justice'[4].

1   *Albert and LeCompte v Belgium* (1983) 5 EHRR 533, para 41.
2   *X and Y v Austria* 15 DR 160 (1978); *Goddi v Italy* (1984) 6 EHRR 457.
3   *X v United Kingdom* 13 YB 690 (1970).
4   See, in another context, *Borgers v Belgium* (1991) 15 EHRR 92, para 24.

4.6.65   The requirement to afford adequate facilities for the preparation of the defence case creates more than a negative obligation on the state to refrain from interference. There is, in addition, a positive obligation to adopt appropriate measures to place the defence in a position of parity with the prosecution[1].

1   *Jespers v Belgium* 27 DR 61 (1981); *Pataki and Dunshirn v Austria* 6 YB 714 (1963).

(c)   Right to legal representation and legal aid

4.6.66   Article 6(3)(c) provides a defendant with the right to represent himself in person, or through legal assistance of his own choosing, or be provided with free legal aid if the interests of justice require it and he does not have sufficient means to pay for a lawyer.

(i)   Legal representation

4.6.67   The use of the word 'or' in the English text of art 6 indicates that the rights set out in paragraph 3(c) are alternative means of securing equality of arms for the defence. Subject to the requirement to provide legal aid in appropriate cases it is, in the first place, for the national authorities to determine whether the accused should have the right to defend himself in person, or through a lawyer. In *Croissant v Germany*[1] the E Ct HR held that the state may place reasonable restrictions on the right of the accused to counsel of his choice. In general, an accused's choice of lawyer should be respected[2], and an appointment made against the wishes of the accused will be 'incompatible with the notion of a fair trial ... if it lacks relevant and sufficient justification'[3]. Factors to be taken into account include the basis of the accused's objection to the appointment and the existence or absence of prejudice. Article 6(3)(c) does not however guarantee the accused the right to choose a court-appointed lawyer, nor to be consulted with regard to the choice of an official defence counsel[4]. This principle has been held to apply to legally aided defendants in the United Kingdom[5]. A lawyer may be excluded by the court for good reason[6]. Thus, in *X v United Kingdom*[7] the Commission found no violation of art 6(3)(c) where the Professional Conduct Committee of the Bar Council had ruled that it would be improper for defence counsel to represent his father in a criminal trial.

1 (1992) 16 EHRR 135; see also *Philis v Greece* 66 DR 260 (1990).
2 *Goddi v Italy* (1984) 6 EHRR 457.
3 *Croissant v Germany* (1992) 16 EHRR 135, para 27.
4 *X v Germany* 6 DR 114 (1976).
5 *X v United Kingdom* (1982) 5 EHRR 273.
6 Application 6298/73 *X v United Kingdom* 2 Digest 831 (1975)(disrespect to the court); *Ensslin, Baader and Raspe v Federal Republic of Germany* (1978) 14 DR 64 (breach of professional ethics).
7 15 DR 242, paras 243–244.

4.6.68   In order to meet the requirements of art 6(3)(c), representation provided by the state must be effective. The state will not generally be responsible for shortcomings in the way a legal aid lawyer performs his duties[1], but the relevant authorities may be required to intervene where the failure to provide effective representation is manifest and has been brought to their attention[2]. Denial of access to a solicitor during police detention may violate art 6(3)(c) in conjunction with art 6(1), particularly if adverse inferences are subsequently drawn from a defendant's failure to answer questions in an interview[3]. Article 6(3)(c) has also been interpreted as requiring confidentiality of communications between a detained person and his lawyer. Eavesdropping or interception by the police violates 'one of the basic requirements of a fair trial in a democratic society'[4].

1 *Artico v Italy* (1980) 3 EHRR 1, para 36.
2 *Artico v Italy* (supra); *Kamasinki v Austria* (1989) 13 EHRR 36, para 65.
3 *Murray v United Kingdom* (1996) 22 EHRR 29.
4 *S v Switzerland* (1991) 14 EHRR 670, para 48.

(ii)   Legal aid in criminal cases

4.6.69   The second limb of art 6(3)(c) imposes a requirement to provide legal aid in criminal cases. This is not however confined to proceedings designated as criminal in domestic law since the term 'criminal charge' has an autonomous Convention meaning. In *Benham v United Kingdom*[1] the E Ct HR held that proceedings which resulted in imprisonment for non-payment of the community charge were criminal for the purposes of art 6, so that the absence of a general right to legal aid violated art 6(3)(c). The obligation to provide legal aid is subject to the means of the defendant and is confined to cases where the interests of justice require it. The 'interests of justice' criterion will take account of the complexity of the proceedings, the capacity of the individual to represent himself, and the severity of the potential sentence[2]. Where the accused faces imprisonment, this will usually be sufficient in itself to require the grant of legal aid[3].

1 (1996) 22 EHRR 293. On the meaning of 'criminal charges', see paras **4.6.13–4.6.14**.
2 *Quaranta v Switzerland* (1991) Series A/205; *Granger v United Kingdom* (1990) 12 EHRR 469.
3 *Benham v United Kingdom* (1996) 22 EHRR 293; *Quaranta v Switzerland* (1991) Series A/205.

(d)   Right to confront prosecution witnesses

4.6.70   Article 6(3)(d) guarantees the right of the accused to examine or have examined witnesses against him and to obtain the attendance and examination of witnesses on his behalf under the same conditions as witnesses against him. The term 'witness' has been held to include a person whose statements are produced as evidence before a court, but who is not called to give oral evidence[1]. Article 6(3)(d) gives the accused the right to have such a 'witness' called to give oral evidence and subjected to cross-examination. It thus amounts to a prima facie prohibition on the admission of hearsay evidence adduced by the prosecution[2]. However, the E Ct HR has not applied the rule inflexibly. In keeping with the general approach to art 6, the court will examine the importance of the prohibited hearsay evidence in the context of the proceedings as a whole[3]. Thus, the admission of hearsay evidence pursuant to the Criminal Justice Act 1988, ss 23 and 24 will not necessarily violate art 6(3)(d)[4]. In *Trivedi v United Kingdom*[5] an application based on s 23 was declared inadmissible by the Commission. The Commission attached particular importance to the fact that the disputed evidence was confirmed by independent admissible evidence and to the fact that evidence relevant to the credibility of the absent witness had also been admitted.

1   *Kostovski v Netherlands* (1989) 12 EHRR 434 at paras 40–41.
2   The right to cross-examine need not be available at the trial itself, provided the accused has had the right to confront the witness at an earlier stage: *Kostovski v Netherlands* (1989) 12 EHRR 434, para 41.
3   See *Unterpertinger v Austria* (1986) 13 EHRR 175; *Kostovski v Netherlands* (1989) 12 EHRR 434; *Windisch v Austria* (1990) 13 EHRR 281; *Lüdi v Switzerland* (1992) 15 EHRR 173; *Barberà, Messegué and Jabardo v Spain* (1988) 11 EHRR 360; *Bricmont v Belgium* (1989) 12 EHRR 217; *Delta v France* (1990) 16 EHRR 574; *Saidi v France* (1993) 17 EHRR 251; *Asch v Austria* (1992) 15 EHRR 597; *Artner v Austria* (1992) Series A/242-A; *Isgro v Italy* (1990) Series A/194.
4   For an analysis by the Court of Appeal of the effect of art 6(3)(d) on the Criminal Justice Act 1988, ss 23 to 26 see *R v Abbas Gokal* [1997] 2 Cr App Rep 266, CA.
5   [1997] EHRLR 520.

4.6.71   The E Ct HR has held that if the defence are deprived of information necessary to challenge a witness's credibility, then this will constitute an insurmountable obstacle to a fair trial. Ignorance of the identity of a witness may deprive the defence of the particulars which would enable it to demonstrate that he is prejudiced, hostile or unreliable[1]. In *Doorsen v Netherlands*[2], however, the E Ct HR held that arrangements to preserve the anonymity of a witness could in principle be justified where there was an identifiable threat to the life or physical safety of the witness. If such arrangements are put in place the judge should be made aware of the witness's identity; the defence should have an opportunity to question the witness; the evidence should be treated with 'extreme care'; and a conviction should not be based 'solely or to a decisive extent' on evidence given anonymously[3].

1   *Kostovski v Netherlands* (1989) 12 EHRR 434, para 42; *Windisch v Austria* (1990) 13 EHRR 281.
2   (1996) 22 EHRR 330.
3   See also *Van Mechelen v Netherlands* (1997) 25 EHRR 647 (the court should adopt the least intrusive method available); *Lüdi v Switzerland* (1992) 15 EHRR 173 (use of undercover officers).

(e)   Right to free interpretation

4.6.72   Article 6(3)(e) provides that the accused has the right to the free assistance of an interpreter if he cannot understand or speak the language used in court. This right is part of the state's duty to run its judicial system fairly and is unqualified. In *Luedicke, Belkacem and Koç v Federal Republic of Germany*[1] the E Ct HR held that art 6(3)(e) absolutely prohibits a defendant being ordered to pay the costs of an interpreter since it provides 'neither a conditional remission, nor a temporary exemption, nor a suspension, but a once and for all exemption or exoneration'.

1   (1978) 2 EHRR 149, para 40.

E   The Seventh Protocol: Additional Fair Trial Guarantees in Criminal Cases

1   INTRODUCTION

4.6.73   The government has indicated its intention to sign, ratify and incorporate protocol 7 to the Convention which provides inter alia certain additional fair trial guarantees in criminal cases. As the White Paper *Rights Brought Home* makes clear, 'In general the provisions of protocol 7 reflect principles already inherent in our law.'

1   Cm 3782, 1997, p 18. See para **2.1.5**, n 3.

2   THE RIGHTS GUARANTEED

(a)   Right to review of a criminal conviction or sentence

4.6.74   Article 2 of the seventh protocol reads:

'1   Everyone convicted of a criminal offence by a tribunal shall have the right to have his conviction or sentence reviewed by a higher tribunal. The exercise of this right, including the grounds on which it may be exercised, shall be governed by law.

2   This right may be subject to exceptions in regard to offences of a minor character[1], as prescribed by law, or in cases in which the person concerned was tried in the first instance by the highest tribunal, or was convicted following an appeal against acquittal.'

1   In determining whether an offence is minor for this purpose, the explanatory memorandum to the seventh protocol, CE Doc H (83) 3, para 21, states that 'an important criterion is whether the offence is punishable by imprisonment or not'.

4.6.75   The ratification and incorporation of art 2 of protocol 7 will not substantially alter the operation of the Human Rights Act 1998. Although art 6 itself does not guarantee a right of appeal, the E Ct HR has held that where domestic law *does* provide a right of appeal, the appeal proceedings are to be treated as 'an extension of the trial process' and accordingly will be subject to the requirements of art 6[1]. Whether a right of appeal exists by virtue of domestic law, or by virtue of art 2 of the seventh protocol, the requirements of fairness will not necessarily be the same as at first instance, since:

'[t]he manner of application of Article 6 to proceedings before courts of appeal ...depend[s] on the special features of the proceedings involved; account must be taken of the entirety of the proceedings in the domestic legal order and of the role of the appellate court therein.'[2]

The use of the term 'tribunal' in art 2 is intended to limit the right of appeal to proceedings which have been tried at first instance by a court or similar body[3]. The explanatory memorandum to the seventh protocol[4] confirms that a refusal of leave to appeal is sufficient to satisfy the requirements of art 2, and suggests that where a person has pleaded guilty to an offence, the right of appeal may be confined to questions of sentence only.

1　*Delcourt v Belgium* (1970) 1 EHRR 355 at para 25; *Edwards v United Kingdom* (1992) 15 EHRR 417, para 34. This will include the hearing of a renewed application for leave to appeal: *Monnell and Morris v United Kingdom* (1987) 10 EHRR 205; and a reference to the Court of Appeal by the Criminal Cases Review Commission: cf *Callaghan v United Kingdom* 60 DR 296 (1986) (reference by the Secretary of State under the Criminal Appeal Act 1968, s 17). On art 6 and appeals, see paras **4.6.22** and **4.6.30**.

2　*Ekbatani v Sweden* (1988) 13 EHRR 504, para 27. See also *Andersson v Sweden* (1991) 15 EHRR 218, para 22; *Helmers v Sweden* (1991) 15 EHRR 285, para 31; *Edwards v United Kingdom* (1992) 15 EHRR 417.

3　See explanatory memorandum to the seventh protocol, CE Doc H (83) 3, para 7. The right of appeal does not therefore apply *directly* to disciplinary proceedings before an administrative body. But this restriction is of little relevance in practice. If the proceedings qualify as 'criminal' within the autonomous definition which is given to that term under art 6 (see para**4.6.13**), there is a right to have the charge determined (or reviewed) by a court.

4　CE Doc H (83) 3.

(b)　Right to compensation following a miscarriage of justice

4.6.76　Article 3 of the seventh protocol provides:

'When a person has by a final decision been convicted of a criminal offence and when subsequently his conviction has been reversed, or he has been pardoned, on the ground that a new or newly discovered fact shows conclusively that there has been a miscarriage of justice, the person who has suffered punishment as a result of such conviction shall be compensated according to the law or the practice of the state concerned, unless it is proved that the non-disclosure of the unknown fact in time is wholly or partly attributable to him.'

4.6.77　Article 3 follows the wording of the International Covenant on Civil and Political Rights, art 14(6)[1] which the United Kingdom ratified in 1976. The right to compensation does not apply either to acquittals or to convictions which have been quashed through the ordinary appeals process. It only arises where the conviction was final and irrevocable, 'that is to say when no further ordinary remedies are available or when the parties have exhausted such remedies or have permitted the time limit to expire without availing themselves of them'[2]. Compensation will only be payable where new or newly discovered evidence establishes conclusively that there has been a miscarriage of justice. A miscarriage of justice is defined as a 'serious failure in the judicial process involving grave prejudice to the convicted person'[3].

1　Cmnd 6702 (1977).
2　Explanatory memorandum to the seventh protocol, CE Doc H (83) 3, para 22.
3　Explanatory memorandum to the seventh protocol, CE Doc H (83) 3, para 23.

4.6.78　The Criminal Justice Act 1988, s 133 was enacted in order to give effect to the United Kingdom's obligations under the ICCPR. Prior to that time, there was no legally enforceable right to compensation for miscarriages of justice, although the Home Office operated an ex gratia payments scheme[1]. Section 133 applies only to cases where a conviction has been quashed on an appeal brought out of time or in consequence of a reference to the Court of Appeal by the Criminal Cases Review Commission[2]. Under s 133 it is for the Secretary of State to determine whether the fresh evidence 'shows beyond reasonable doubt' that there has been a miscarriage of justice[3]. If so, then compensation is mandatory. The amount of the compensation is determined by an assessor[4], who must have regard inter alia to the seriousness of the offence, the severity of the penalty imposed, the conduct of the investigation and prosecution, and any previous convictions of the claimant[5]. There is no entitlement to exemplary damages since these are intended not to compensate a victim but to punish the wrongdoer.

1   See HC Official Report (6th series) 87, cols 691–692 (29 November 1985). This scheme still applies
    where the statutory criteria are unfulfilled.
2   CJA 1988, s 133(5).
3   CJA 1988, s 133(1) and (3).
4   CJA 1988, s 133(4). The current assessor is Sir David Calcutt, QC.
5   CJA 1988, s 133(4A) as inserted by the Criminal Appeal Act 1995, s 28.

(c)   Prohibition on double jeopardy in criminal cases

4.6.79   Article 4 of protocol 7 provides:

'1   No one shall be liable to be tried or punished again in criminal proceedings
       under the jurisdiction of the same State for an offence for which he has already
       been finally acquitted or convicted in accordance with the law and penal
       procedure of that State.

2   The provisions of the preceding paragraph shall not prevent the reopening of
       the case in accordance with the law and penal procedure of the State concerned,
       if there is evidence of new or newly discovered facts, or if there has been a
       fundamental defect in the previous proceedings, which could affect the
       outcome of the case.

3   No derogation from the Article shall be made under Article 15 of the Convention.'

4.6.80   This provision embodies the prohibition on double jeopardy in criminal cases
which is reflected in the English pleas in bar of *autrefois convict* and *autrefois acquit*.
The Commission has in the past left open the question whether the right to a fair hearing
in art 6 already incorporates this protection[1], but in *S v Federal Republic of Germany*[2]
the Commission held that art 6 guarantees 'neither expressly nor by way of implication
the principle of *ne bis in idem*'. The extent of the protection provided by art 4 of the
seventh protocol is qualified. It is confined to prosecutions in the same jurisdiction,
and so does not prevent successive prosecutions for the same offence in different
countries[3]. Nor does it prevent separate disciplinary and criminal proceedings in
respect of the same allegation. In *Gradinger v Austria*[4] the E Ct HR held that there had
been a violation of art 4 where the applicant had been convicted and sentenced for a
criminal offence of causing death by negligent driving and the administrative authorities
subsequently fined him for driving under the influence of alcohol[5]. Although the
elements of the two offences were different, they were 'based on the same conduct'.

1   *X v Austria* 35 CD 151 (1970). The Commission held that the fact that express protection against
    double jeopardy was provided by protocol 7 did not necessarily mean that such protection was not
    inherent in art 6 for those states which were not parties to the protocol.
2   Cf *S v Federal Republic of Germany* 39 DR 43 (1983).
3   Cf *S v Federal Republic of Germany* 39 DR 43 (1983).
4   (1995) Series A/328-C.
5   The E Ct HR assumed that the administrative proceedings were 'criminal' for the purpose of art 4
    of the seventh protocol, having found that they were 'criminal' for the purpose of art 6.

4.6.81   As to the position in English law, Lord Morris set out the governing principles
in *Connelly v DPP*[1]. A defendant may not be tried for a crime in respect of which he
has been previously acquitted or convicted[2] or in respect of which he could, on a
previous indictment, have been convicted as an alternative verdict to the offence with
which he was charged. This rule applies to all proceedings:

'on the well established common law principle that where a person has been convicted and
punished for an offence by a court of competent jurisdiction ... the conviction shall be a
bar to all further proceedings for the same offence, and he shall not be punished again for
the same matter'[3].

This principle applies to courts martial so as to prevent subsequent trial in the civilian courts[4]. It has also been assumed to apply to decisions of foreign courts[5].

1   [1964] AC 1254, HL.
2   As to what constitutes a conviction for this purpose see *Richards v R* [1993] AC 217.
3   Per Blackburn J in *Wemyss v Hopkins* (1875) LR 10 QB 378 at 381.
4   Army Act 1955, s 133(1) as amended by the Armed Forces Act 1966, s 25 and the Armed Forces Act 1991, s 26 and Sch 2, para 5(1).
5   *R v Roche* (1775) 1 Leach 134; *R v Aughet* (1918) 13 Cr App Rep 101; *R v Lavercombe* [1988] Crim LR 435; Cf *R v Thomas* [1985] QB 604. To that extent English law provides a greater degree of protection than the seventh protocol demands.

4.6.82   Article 4(2) of the seventh protocol provides an exception to the general prohibition on double jeopardy where fresh evidence has come to light or where there was a fundamental defect in the earlier proceedings which could have affected the outcome. The 'fresh evidence' exception is capable of seriously undermining the value of art 4 and has no parallel in English law. The 'fundamental defect' exception on the other hand is now reflected in the Criminal Procedure and Investigations Act 1996, ss 54 to 56, which provide a means of reopening an acquittal where it appears to be tainted by intimidation. If a person has been convicted of an administration of justice offence which involved interference with or intimidation of a juror or witness in the proceedings which led to the acquittal, and there is a 'real possibility' that the result was affected, the prosecution may apply to the High Court for an order quashing the acquittal. This will pave the way for a second prosecution.

Article 7 Freedom from retroactive criminal legislation

(1) No one shall be held guilty of any criminal offence on account of any act or omission which did not constitute a criminal offence under national or international law at the time when it was committed. Nor shall a heavier penalty be imposed than the one that was applicable at the time the criminal offence was committed.

(2) This article shall not prejudice the trial and punishment of any person for any act or omission which, at the time when it was committed, was criminal according to the general principles of law recognised by civilised nations.

A   Introduction

4.7.1   Article 7 creates a non-derogable[1] prohibition on the retrospective application of the criminal law. However, the E Ct HR has held that it also;

'embodies, more generally, the principle that only the law can define a crime and prescribe a penalty (*nullum crimen, nulla poena sine lege*) and the principle that the criminal law must not be extensively construed to an accused's detriment, for instance by analogy'[2].

1   See art 15(2) of the Convention, discussed in para **2.14**.
2   *Kokkinakis v Greece* (1993) 17 EHRR 397 at para 52. The Commission has held that art 7 incorporates the principle that penal provisions are to be restrictively interpreted:*X v Belgium* (1962) 5 YB 168 at 190.

4.7.2   Article 7 applies only to criminal proceedings resulting in a conviction[1] or the imposition of a criminal penalty. It does not therefore apply to extradition[2], or deportation[3], to alterations in the rules governing parole[4], to changes in the law of evidence[5], or to rules governing the entry of a conviction on a person's criminal record[6]. Nor does it apply to internment[7] or other forms of preventative detention which do not depend upon a criminal conviction or sentence[8]. Article 7 does not generally apply to civil proceedings[9]. But proceedings which are defined as civil in domestic law may nevertheless qualify as criminal proceedings for this purpose. The E Ct HR and Commission have adopted an autonomous approach to the term 'criminal' in arts 5 and 6[10] which also extends to art 7[11].

1   A prosecution which does not result in a conviction cannot raise an issue under art 7:*X v United Kingdom* 3 Digest 211 (1973). Note however that in the inter-state case of*Ireland v United Kingdom* 15 YB 76 (1972) the Irish Government argued that the Northern Ireland Act 1972 created a retroactive offence of failing to comply with an order issued by the security forces. The application was withdrawn when the Attorney General gave an undertaking that the Act would not be applied retrospectively.
2   *X v Netherlands* 6 DR 184 (1976). Where however a decision to extradite would result in a real risk that the person concerned would face a prosecution for a retrospectively applied offence in the receiving state it is arguable that art 7 would apply to the decision to return, by analogy with*Soering v United Kingdom* (1989) 11 EHRR 439.
3   *Moustaquin v Belgium* (1991) 13 EHRR 802.
4   *Hogben v United Kingdom* 46 DR 231 (1986) (retrospective change in parole policy concerned the execution of a sentence, not the imposition of a penalty).
5   *X v United Kingdom* 3 DR 95 (1975). It has however been suggested that where a change in the law of evidence is inextricably linked to the accused person's guilt or innocence, art 7 would apply: see Harris O'Boyle and Warbrick *Law of the European Convention on Human Rights* (1995), p 275.

6   *X v Federal Republic of Germany* 3 YB 254.
7   *Lawless v Ireland (No 3)* (1961) 1 EHRR 15 at para 19.
8   *De Wilde Ooms and Versyp v Belgium* (1971) 1 EHRR 373 para. 87 (preventative detention of vagrants); *X v Austria* 26 DR 248 (1981) (preventative detention in institution for recidivists).
9   See eg *X v Belgium* 24 DR 198 (1981) (bankruptcy order by a commercial court); *X v Sweden* (1985) 9 EHRR 244 (penalties for non-compliance with building regulations).
10   See generally, para **4.6.13**.
11   In *Harman v United Kingdom* 38 DR 53 (1984) the Commission declared admissible a complaint under art 7 which arose out of the applicant's conviction for civil contempt of court. The case resulted in a friendly settlement involving an amendment to the Rules of the Supreme Court.

B   Retroactive offences

4.7.3   The first limb of art 7(1) prohibits the retroactive application of criminal offences so as to penalise conduct which was not criminal at the time when the relevant act or omission occurred. This corresponds to the general prohibition on retroactivity in English criminal law[1]. Article 7 prohibits not only the creation of retroactive offences by legislation, but also the retroactive application of criminal offences through the development of the common law, so as to encompass conduct which would not previously have been regarded as a crime[2]. Thus it requires that the criminal law should be sufficiently accessible and precise to enable an individual to know in advance whether his conduct is criminal[3]. The E Ct HR and the Commission have adopted a rather loose approach to this requirement of legal certainty. In *Handyside v United Kingdom*[4] (a case concerning the definition of obscenity in the Obscene Publications Acts 1959 and 1964) the Commission held that art 7 'includes the requirement that the offence should be clearly described by law', but held that it was sufficient if the legislation provided a general description which was then interpreted and applied by the courts. The same principle was applied to a common law offence in *X Ltd and Y v United Kingdom*[5] (the 'Gay News' case). In that case the House of Lords held that the mens rea for the offence of blasphemous libel required only an intention to publish and not an intention to blaspheme. The Commission considered that this ruling was not a change in the law but an 'acceptable clarification' since there was no prior authority which decided the point clearly one way or the other. More recently, in *SW and CR v United Kingdom*[6] the E Ct HR held that the removal of the marital rape exemption by the House of Lords[7] did not amount to a retrospective change in the elements of the offence. Article 7 allowed for the 'gradual clarification' of the rules of criminal liability through judicial interpretation from case to case, provided the resultant development was consistent with the essence of the offence and could reasonably be foreseen. The E Ct HR held that the domestic law in this area had evolved progressively, and that the decision of the House of Lords was reasonably foreseeable with appropriate legal advice. Moreover, the abandonment of the immunity was itself in conformity with the fundamental objectives of the Convention. The principle *nullum crimen sine lege* also prohibits the prosecution of an accused person under a law which had been abrogated or had fallen into desuetude when the offence was committed[8]. But art 7 does not entitle an accused person to the benefit of an alteration in the law which has occurred between the commission of the offence and the trial[9].

1   See for example *Waddington v Miah* [1974] 1 WLR 683, HL where Lord Reid observed (at p 694) that 'it is hardly credible that any government department would promote, or that Parliament would pass, retrospective criminal legislation'.
2   *X Ltd and Y v United Kingdom* 28 DR 77 (1982).
3   *Handyside v United Kingdom* 17 YB 228 (1974) at 290; see also *Kokkinakis v Greece* (1993) 17 EHRR 397 at para 52, where the E Ct HR observed that the condition that an offence must be clearly

defined by law 'is satisfied where the individual can know from the wording of the relevant provision and, if need be, with the assistance of the courts' interpretation of it, what acts and omissions will make him liable.

4   17 YB 228 (1974).
5   28 DR 77 (1982).
6   (1995) 21 EHRR 363.
7   See *R v R* [1992] 1 AC 599.
8   *X v Federal Republic of Germany* 6 YB 520 (1963); *X v Netherlands* (1978) 11 DR 209 at 211.
9   *X v United Kingdom* 31 CD 120 (1969); *X v Federal Republic of Germany* 13 DR 70 (1978). In this respect art 7 differs from the ICCPR, art 15(1) which expressly requires the accused to be given the benefit of any subsequent change in his favour in relation to the applicable penalty. Article 7 does not, however, prohibit rules of national law which require the retrospective application of a change in the criminal law which benefits the accused: *G v France* (1995) 21 EHRR 288.

4.7.4   A conviction which results from the retrospective application of domestic law will not breach art 7(1) if the conduct of the accused was a crime under international law at the time that it occurred. Certain offences, such as war crimes, piracy, torture and genocide are treated as crimes of universal jurisdiction under public international law. A state may prosecute individuals for such offences, wherever committed, solely on the basis that it has custody of the alleged offender. The United Kingdom has given effect to this principle in a number of statutes[1], which can therefore be retrospectively applied[2] without violating art 7.

1   The War Crimes Act 1991, s 1 (offences of murder, manslaughter, or culpable homicide committed in German occupied territory during the Second World War to be triable in United Kingdom courts); the Criminal Justice Act 1988, s 134 (torture, wherever committed, to be triable in the United Kingdom); the Genocide Act 1969, s 1 (genocide, wherever committed, to be triable in the United Kingdom); the Geneva Conventions Act 1957, s 1 (grave breaches of the Geneva Conventions, wherever committed, to be triable in the United Kingdom).
2   Providing the relevant rule of international law was in existence at the time of the offence. As to the War Crimes Act 1991 see further art 7(2), para **4.7.6** n 2.

C   Retroactive penalties

4.7.5   The second limb of art 7(1) prohibits a retroactive increase in the penalty applicable to an offence. The term 'penalty' has an autonomous meaning, defined by reference to criteria analogous to those which apply to the term 'criminal charge' in art 6[1]. Providing the measure was imposed following conviction for a criminal offence, the E Ct HR will examine its substance and severity in determining whether or not it amounts to a penalty. Thus, in *Welch v United Kingdom*[2] a confiscation order was made under the Drug Trafficking Offences Act 1986 in respect of an offence committed before the Act entered into force. In deciding that the confiscation order was an additional penalty, and therefore a violation of art 7(1), the E Ct HR noted that the measure had punitive as well as preventative and reparative aims; that the order was calculated by reference to 'proceeds' rather than profits; that the amount of the order could take account of culpability; and that the order was enforceable by a term of imprisonment in default. Similarly, in *Jamil v France*[3] an order for imprisonment in default of the payment of a customs fine was held to be a penalty for the purposes of art 7. It had been ordered by a criminal court; was intended to act as a deterrent; and could lead to a punitive deprivation of liberty.

1   *Welch v United Kingdom* (1995) 20 EHRR 247 at paras 27–35. As to the approach taken in relation to art 6 see para **4.6.13**.
2   *Welch v United Kingdom* (1995) 20 EHRR 247.
3   (1995) 21 EHRR 65, para 31.

D   Article 7(2): war crimes

4.7.6   The exception created by art 7(2) was intended to allow the application of national and international legislation enacted during and after the Second World War to punish war crimes, treason and collaboration with the enemy[1]. The practical effect of art 7(2) is simply to make it clear that the international law exception in art 7(1) is not confined to treaty-based or customary international law, but extends to conduct regarded as criminal under 'the general principles of law recognised by civilised nations'. This expression is drawn directly from the Statute of the International Court of Justice, art 38, which recognises such general principles as a third formal source of public international law[2].

1   *X v Belgium* 1 YB 239 (1957).
2   This is of particular significance for prosecutions under the War Crimes Act 1991 since the existence of a rule of universal jurisdiction for war crimes was uncertain prior to and during the Second World War.

> ## Article 8 Right to respect for private and family life, home and correspondence
>
> 1. Everyone has the right to respect for his private and family life, his home and his correspondence.
> 2. There shall be no interference by a public authority with the exercise of this right except such as is in accordance with the law and is necessary in a democratic society in the interests of national security, public safety or the economic well-being of the country, for the prevention of disorder or crime, for the protection of health or morals, or for the protection of the rights and freedoms of others.

A Introduction

4.8.1 It is often said that there is no general right to privacy as such in English statute and common law[1]. Instead, there is a system of specific civil and (although more rarely) criminal remedies for specific wrongs: for example, breach of confidence, copyright, trespass (to the person and to property), nuisance, defamation, malicious falsehood and harassment[2]. Recently, however, the judiciary has indicated a willingness to create a 'law of privacy', by developing the common law of breach of confidence in particular[3]. Thus, in *A-G v Guardian Newspapers (No 2)*[4] Lord Keith observed that 'the right to personal privacy is clearly one which the law should in this field seek to protect'. Similarly, in *Hellewell v Chief Constable of Derbyshire*[5], Laws J stated:

> 'If someone with a telephoto lens were to take from a distance and with no authority a picture of another engaged in some private act, the subsequent disclosure of the photograph would, in my judgment, as surely amount to a breach of confidence as if he had found or stolen a letter or diary in which the act was recounted and proceeded to publish it. In such a case, the law should protect what might reasonably be called a right of privacy, although the name accorded to the cause of action would be a breach of confidence.'

The influence of art 8, through the HRA 1998, on English law could well be greater than the influence of any other article.

---

1 *Malone v Metropolitan Police Comr* [1979] Ch 344 and *Kaye v Robertson* [1991] FSR 62 at 66 ('... it is well-known that in English law there is no right to privacy, and accordingly there is no right of action for breach of a person's privacy ...' per Glidewell LJ), at 70 (per Bingham LJ) and at 71 (per Leggatt LJ) and, the *Report of the Younger Committee*, Cmnd 5012, 1972, especially paras 74–97. See, however, *Morris v Beardmore* [1981] AC 446 and *R v Khan* [1997] AC 558, 582–583A (Lord Nicholls of Birkenhead). For a general analysis of privacy in English law see Feldman 'Secrecy, Dignity or Autonomy? Views of Privacy as a Civil Liberty' [1995] CLP 41 and Lester and Oliver, *Constitutional Law and Human Rights* (Butterworths, 1997) para 110.
2 In recent years English courts have recognised and developed the tort of harassment to give relief to those who are harassed, molested and pestered: see *Patel v Patel* [1988] 2 FLR 179 at 182, *Khorasandjian v Bush* [1993] QB 727, CA and *Burris v Azadassi* [1995] 1 WLR 1372. However, in *Hunter v Canary Wharf Ltd* [1997] AC 655, the House of Lords stated that only a person with an interest in land can sue for private nuisance.
3 Ironically, the US courts long ago developed a 'right to be left alone' relying on English common law authorities: see *Barber v Time Inc* 159 SW 2d 291 (1942)(where the publication of a photograph of the plaintiff in her hospital bed taken without her consent was held to be an invasion of a private right); *Union Pacific Rly Co v Botsford* 141 US 250 (1891); and *Cruzan v Director, Missouri Department of Health* 497 US 261 (1990). See also *Case v Minister of Safety and Security* 1996 (5) BCLR 609 (where the South African Constitutional Court held that a statute making it an offence

to possess 'any indecent or obscene pornographic matter' was inconsistent with the constitutional right to privacy).

4   [1990] 1 AC 109 at 255H (the 'Spycatcher' case concerning the former secret service agent, Peter Wright. The subject matter of the case was, in contrast to the early confidence cases, confidences owed to public bodies).

5   [1995] 1 WLR 804 at 807. See also *R v Khan* [1997] AC 558 (where a majority in the House of Lords stated, relying on *Schenk v Switzerland* (1988) 13 EHRR 242, that art 8 was relevant to deciding whether a illegally-obtained police tape recording of a conversation which took place in a private home was admissible evidence in a criminal trial). The willingness and ability of the judges to develop a law of privacy has also been emphasised in extra-judicial statements by members of the senior judiciary: see, for example, Sir Thomas Bingham 'Should there be a Law to Protect Rights of Personal Privacy?' (1996) EHRLR 450. See also Lester 'English Judges as Lawmakers' (1993) PL 269.

4.8.2   The willingness of English judges to develop the law of confidence has already been noted with approval by the Commission. In 1986 in *Winer v United Kingdom*[1] the Commission rejected a complaint about the inadequate range of civil remedies available under English law to protect the applicant's reputation from true and false statements about his sexual relations with his wife published in a book. The Commission found that, in general, the remedies offered in English law, including libel proceedings, were adequate. But it said that the failure to take proceedings for breach of confidence did not constitute a failure to exhaust domestic remedies in view of the uncertainty as to the precise scope and extent of that remedy[2]. In 1998 in *Earl and Countess Spencer v United Kingdom*[3] the Commission considered a complaint about a number of newspaper articles and photographs concerning events in the applicants' marriage and, in particular, the second applicant's health problems. The Commission referred[4] to the detailed submissions it had received about the jurisprudential developments since *Winer* and concluded:

' ... that there has been significant clarification of the scope and extent of a breach of confidence action ... the domestic courts having extended and developed certain relevant principles though their case-law by interpretation.'

The complaint was declared inadmissible because of the applicants' failure to demonstrate the insufficiency or ineffectiveness of the domestic remedies which they had failed to exhaust.

1   Application 10871/84, 48 DR 154 (1986) EComHR.
2   At page 170.
3   Application 28851/95, (1998) 25 EHRR CD 105, EComHR.
4   Pages 18–19 of the Commission's Report.

4.8.3   However, art 8 protects more than privacy *simpliciter*. It covers a broad range of personal interests: family life, home and correspondence[1]. It imposes primarily negative[2] but also positive obligations on the state[3]. Negatively, for example, public authorities must not disclose or pry into matters confidential to an individual in violation of art 8 and the state must refrain from making laws which oblige or permit unwarranted interferences with the interests protected by art 8. Positively, the state must adopt measures to secure respect for an individual's art 8 rights by others (for example, the media)[4]. Sometimes, negative and positive duties overlap[5]. The state will enjoy a particularly broad margin of appreciation when deciding how to implement a positive obligation[6]. It must have regard:

' ... to the fair balance that has to be struck between the general interest of the community and the interests of the individual, the search for which balance is inherent in the whole Convention.'[7]

1　See, similarly, International Convention on Civil and Political Rights, art 17. The rights sometimes overlap and the jurisprudence avoids delineating the precise boundaries of each: see, for example, *Klass v Federal Republic of Germany* (1978) 2 EHRR 214, E Ct HR, para 41 (telephone conversations are part of private life, family life and correspondence).

2　*Belgian Linguistics Case (No 2)* (1968) 1 EHRR 252, E Ct HR, and *Lingens v Austria* (1986) 8 EHRR 407, E Ct HR.

3　See *Kroon v Netherlands* (1994) 19 EHRR 263, E Ct HR, para 31 where the E Ct HR described the 'essential object' of art 8 as being ' ... to protect the individual against arbitrary action by the public authorities. There may in addition be positive obligations inherent in "effective" respect for family life [and the other rights guaranteed by art 8]'. Unfortunately, the case law often fails properly to distinguish between the two types of obligation.

4　*X and Y v Netherlands* (1985) 8 EHRR 235, E Ct HR, para 23; *Johnston v Ireland* (1986) 9 EHRR 203, E Ct HR, para 55.

5　*Lopez Ostra v Spain* (1994) 20 EHRR 277, E Ct HR, paras 52 and 55–56 (no state protection against environmental damage caused by a private waste disposal plant built on public land). See also *Guerra v Italy* (1998) 26 EHRR 357, 4 BHRC 63, E Ct HR

6　*Abdulaziz, Cabales and Balkandali v United Kingdom* (1985) 7 EHRR 471, para 67, E Ct HR; Application 10871/84 *Winer v United Kingdom* 48 DR 154 (1986) at 169–171, EComHR (limited range of civil remedies available to the applicant to protect his reputation from both true and false statements about his sexual relations with his wife did not amount to a failure to protect his family life); *Buckley v United Kingdom* (1996) 23 EHRR 101, E Ct HR (legitimate balance struck between the right of a gypsy to live where she choses and the interests of the general community as reflected in planning controls); and *Handyside v United Kingdom* (1976) 1 EHRR 737, E Ct HR. This is especially true when there is a tension between art 8 and some other Article of the Convention: for example, art 10 on freedom of expression is relevant when a newspaper wishes to publish long-lens photographs of a public figure in a private context: see Applications 28851/95 and 28852/95 *Earl Spencer and Countess Spencer v United Kingdom* (1998) 25 EHRR CD 105.

7　*Cossey v United Kingdom* (1990) 13 EHRR 622, E Ct HR, para 37.

4.8.4　The reference to *respect* for these rights makes it clear that not all acts or omissions of a public authority which have an impact on the exercise of the protected interest will constitute an interference with art 8 rights. The following failures by a state have all been held to violate art 8: to make legal aid provision for a woman seeking judicial separation from violent husband[1]; to provide for full legal status of the child of an unmarried couple[2]; to allow a second-generation immigrant to remain in the country where his family lived[3]; to provide for independent adjudication on the question of confidentiality of documents relating to foster care[4]; to consult the natural father of a child before placing the child for adoption[5]; and to protect a person from pollution[6].

1　*Airey v Ireland* (1979) 2 EHRR 305, E Ct HR.

2　*Johnston v Ireland* (1986) 9 EHRR 203, E Ct HR.

3　*Moustaquim v Belgium* (1991) 13 EHRR 802, E Ct HR; *Beljoudi v France* (1992) 14 EHRR 801, E Ct HR; and *Nasri v France* (1995) 21 EHRR 458, E Ct HR.

4　*Gaskin v United Kingdom* (1989) 12 EHRR 36, E Ct HR.

5　*Keegan v Ireland* (1994) 18 EHRR 342, E Ct HR.

6　Application 7889/77 *Arrondelle v United Kingdom* 26 DR 5 (1982) EComHR; *Lopez Ostra v Spain* (1994) 20 EHRR 277, E Ct HR; Application 9310/81 *Rayner v United Kingdom* 47 DR 5 (1986), EComHR; and *Guerra v Italy* (1998) 26 EHRR 357, 4 BHRC 63, E Ct HR.

4.8.5　Even if the state has failed to secure respect for a right which is protected by art 8(1), an applicant still needs to establish that he is a 'victim' in that there has been an interference with his right. The burden is upon the applicant to establish a sufficient degree of likelihood that an interference has occurred[1]. But this requirement is not always rigorously applied. It is not always necessary for an applicant to show that legislation which affects his private life has been, or will be, actually applied to him by way of a prosecution. The mere existence of such legislation may amount to a sufficient interference because of the threat or risk of prosecution[2]. Medical treatment administered to an individual without consent does not amount to an interference if that individual cannot give informed consent[3]. There is no interference if the matters complained of result directly from an applicant's own decisions and conduct[4].

1   *Campbell v United Kingdom* (1992) 15 EHRR 137, E Ct HR, paras 32–33 (applicant prisoner unable to show that any particular letter had been opened or read but he was held to be a victim of an interference because the prison régime allowed for this).

2   *Dudgeon v United Kingdom* (1981) 4 EHRR 149, E Ct HR; *Norris v Ireland* (1988) 13 EHRR 186, E Ct HR; and *Modinos v Cyprus* (1993) 16 EHRR 485, E Ct HR. All these cases concerned legislation prohibiting homosexual activities in private but consenting adults had not been prosecuted for some time. The existence of such laws were held to interfere with the applicants' rights under art 8 because the threat of their use was not illusory or theoretical and had, therefore, had a continuous and direct impact on the applicants' lives. See also *Klass v Federal Republic of Germany* (1978) 2 EHRR 214, E Ct HR, and *Leander v Sweden* (1987) 9 EHRR 433, E Ct HR. Both of these cases concerned the existence of legislation authorising the state to tap telephones covertly. By definition, surveillance of the applicants could not be established. But the E Ct HR noted that the mere existence of the legislation involved the threat of surveillance. In these circumstances, it would be enough that the applicant could show some reason why he might be a target.

3   *Herczegfalvy v Austria* (1992) 15 EHRR 437, E Ct HR: nor, similarly, did the appointment of a guardian ad litem on the application of legal advisers of a person of full age: see Application 7940/77 *X v United Kingdom* 14 DR 224 (1978), EComHR.

4   Application No 8317/78 *McFeely v United Kingdom* 20 DR 44 (1980), EComHR ('dirty protest' by terrorist prisoners in Northern Ireland who refused to wear prison clothes or use prison toilets: held, inadmissible).

4.8.6   The rest of this chapter will take the following structure. First, the broad categories of right or interest protected by art 8(1) will be considered, namely: (a) respect for private life; (b) respect for family life; (c) respect for the home; (d) respect for correspondence and confidential information. Interferences will be considered in the context of each right. Finally, justification under art 8(2) will be dealt with separately, but with specific reference to each interest protected by art 8(1).

B   Private life

1   THE CONCEPT OF PRIVATE LIFE

4.8.7   The categories of private life under the Convention are not closed; nor are they clearly defined. It is already well-established, however, that they range wider than the notion of personal privacy at common law, which focuses on the 'right to be left alone', the secrecy of information and the seclusion of individuals. Article 8 encompasses, more broadly, the right to *be* oneself, to *live* as oneself and to *keep* to oneself. In the leading case of *Niemietz*[1], the E Ct HR pronounced that:

'... it would be too restrictive to limit the notion [of private life] to an "inner circle" in which the individual may live his own personal life as he chooses and to exclude therefrom entirely the outside world not encompassed within that circle. Respect for private life must also comprise to a certain degree the right to establish and develop relationships with other human beings.'

An individual's right to inter-relate socially with others is part of the right to develop and fulfil one's own personality[2].

1   *Niemietz v Germany* (1992) 16 EHRR 97, E Ct HR, para 29.

2   Application 6825/74 *X v Iceland* 5 DR 86 (1976), EComHR; Application 8317/78 *McFeeley v United Kingdom* 20 DR 44 (1980), EComHR (respect for private life requiring prisoners to be permitted a degree of association with others). In *Niemietz v Germany* (1992) 16 EHRR 97, E Ct HR, para 29, the E Ct HR contemplated that art 8 might even extend to some business relationships. In

Beldjoudi v France (1992) 14 EHRR 801, E Ct HR, Judge Martens (echoing Mr Schermers in the Commission) emphasised the importance of opportunities to develop personal relationships beyond the 'inner circle'. The right to form and maintain various types of relationship may also fall within other articles of the Convention: for example, the right to freedom of association (art 11) and the right to marry and found a family (art 12) – see, respectively, paras **4.11** and **4.12**.

4.8.8   Within such a broad definition various aspects of private life can be distinguished. It is useful to consider each aspect of private life alongside the equivalent notion of 'respect' for that right as the demands of that requirement are highly contextual. As the E Ct HR pointed out in the recent case of *Sheffield & Horsham*[1]:

> '[T]he notion of "respect" is not clear-cut, especially as far as the positive obligations inherent in that concept are concerned: having regard to the diversity of practices followed and the situations obtaining in the Contracting States, the notion's requirements will vary considerably from case to case. In determining whether or not a positive obligation exists, regard must be had to the fair balance that has to be struck between the general interests of the community and the interests of the individual, the search for which balance is inherent in the whole of the Convention.'

In attempting to find such a 'fair balance' the state in question can consider matters ranging well beyond the narrower art 8(2) legitimate interests[2].

1   *Sheffield and Horsham v United Kingdom* (1998) 27 EHRR 163, E Ct HR, para 52.
2   *Rees v United Kingdom* (1986) 9 EHRR 56 E Ct HR, para 37.

(a)   Respect for physical and moral integrity

4.8.9   A person's physical and moral integrity, and his right to protect them, are important aspects of private life. Thus, the failure of domestic law to provide the right for a mentally handicapped person to bring a prosecution for sexual assault amounted to a failure to secure respect for her private life[1]. Individuals have the right not to be subjected to compulsory physical interventions and treatments, such as blood[2] and urine tests[3] or corporal punishment. However, not every measure adversely affecting a person's physical and moral integrity necessarily involves an interference with respect for his private life. Thus, in *Costello-Roberts v United Kingdom*[4] the relatively slight nature of the corporal punishment combined with its infliction in the non-personal context of discipline in a (private) school was not sufficiently adverse to amount to a violation of art 8. Contrast, however, *A v United Kingdom*[5] in which the Commission indicated a violation where excessive force had been used in the home by a step-father. In *Raninen*[6] the applicant had been unlawfully detained and unnecessarily handcuffed by the military authorities following his repeated refusal to undergo military service. The E Ct HR emphasised that the right to physical and moral integrity guaranteed by art 8 may come into operation where the minimum level of severity required in art 3 cases was not attained. Physical well-being may also be impaired by non-physical assaults such as pollution[7], including noise pollution[8], but not by the compulsory wearing of seat belts[9].

1   *X and Y v Netherlands* (1985) 8 EHRR 235, E Ct HR, paras 22–27. Although civil remedies were available, they had certain procedural disadvantages. The E Ct HR held that because fundamental values and essential aspects of private life were at stake effective deterrence was indispensable and could be achieved only by criminal sanctions.
2   Application 8278/78 *X v Austria* 18 DR 154 (1979), EComHR (compulsory blood tests in paternity proceedings).
3   Application 21132/93 *Peters v Netherlands* 77-A DR 75 (1994), EComHR (compulsory random drug testing by urine sample in prisons: held inadmissible because within art 8(2)).
4   (1995) 19 EHRR 112, E Ct HR, especially para 36. In *Stubbings v United Kingdom* (1996) 23 EHRR 213 complaints about failures to provide sufficient remedies for or against child sex abuse were found to concern 'family life' in the sense of the right to physical and moral integrity. This right could

impose positive obligations on the state, though its margin of appreciation was wide. Applying the 'fair balance' test, no infringement of art 8(1) was found as ample and stringent remedies and sanctions were applied.
5   Application 25599/94 *A v United Kingdom* (1998) 5 BHRC 137, E Ct HR. The facts were that the stepfather who had beaten the child in question with a garden cane on several occasions with considerable force had been acquitted at trial of assault occasioning actual bodily harm. The Commission also criticised the uncertainty of the level of punishment permitted by the defence of reasonable chastisement in English law. As to corporal punishment and art 3, see further paras **4.3.24** and **4.3.4–4.3.8**. The E Ct HR decided the case on the basis of art 3 alone: (1998) 5 BHRC 137, E Ct HR, paras 25–28.
6   *Raninen v Finland* (1997) 26 EHRR 563, E Ct HR.
7   *Lopez Ostra v Spain* (1995) 20 EHRR 277, E Ct HR (failure of the state to prevent, or protect against, serious pollution caused by fumes from a plant disposing of waste from a tannery). See also *Guerra v Italy* (1998) 25 EHRR 357, 4 BHRC 63, E Ct HR.
8   Application 9310/81 *Rayner v United Kingdom* 47 DR 5 (1986), EComHR (art 8 held to cover intense and persistent aircraft noise although it was not directed against specific private individuals). See also Application 7889/77 *Arrondelle v United Kingdom* 26 DR 5 (1982), EComHR, F Sett and Application 9310/81 *Baggs v United Kingdom* 52 DR 29 (1987), EComHR, F Sett. As to environmental claims under art 8, see further paras **4.8.33–4.8.39**.
9   Application 8707/79 *X v Belgium* 18 DR 255 (1979), EComHR (regulations justified in the interests of public safety).

(b)   Right to a personal identity

4.8.10   The right to determine one's identity is also a fundamental part of private life: to choose or discover who one is and then to live in public (that is, outside merely one's 'inner circle') accordingly. This covers such personal characteristics as name and sexual orientation. In *Gaskin v United Kingdom*[1] Mr Gaskin had spent most of his childhood in the care of either a local authority or foster parents. On reaching majority, he sought to secure access to the confidential records of his care placements, claiming that he had been ill-treated while in care. The local authority refused access because the information had been given under express or implied duties of confidence and consent had not been forthcoming from the contributors and sources of the records. The E Ct HR found that the application raised an issue about Mr Gaskin's private and family life within art 8, rather than about a general right of access to information (which would not be protected), and declined to specify a general right of access. Instead, it recognised the need to balance the rights of the subject of the information with the need to protect contributors and sources so as to ensure their safety and candour in the general interest. In Mr Gaskin's case, however, there had been a violation of art 8 because, in the absence of any independent appeal mechanism to determine access, the local authority's refusal was disproportionate. Thus, it is not enough to establish that the applicant's interest falls within art 8: there may be some countervailing considerations of public interest. Similarly, the right to use a name is an aspect of private life[2], as is the right to choose one's mode of dress and appearance[3].

1   (1989) 12 EHRR 36, E Ct HR. See also *Rasmussen v Denmark* (1984) 7 EHRR 371, E Ct HR (determination of parentage held to be relevant to establishing personal identity).
2   *Burghartz and Burghartz v Switzerland* (1994) 18 EHRR 101, E Ct HR (refusal to allow a change of surname to be registered in official records); E Ct HR; *Stjerna v Finland* (1994) 24 EHRR 195.
3   Application 8317/78 *McFeeley v United Kingdom* 20 DR 44 at 91 (1980), EComHR (prison clothing) and Application 8209/78 *Sutter v Switzerland* 16 DR 166 (1979) (haircut).

(c)   Respect for personal or private space

4.8.11   The geographical limits of art 8 are not confined to those places where an individual has exclusive rights of occupation (his own land) but may extend to places and situations where it can be said that an individual has the right to quiet enjoyment of a private space. Hotel rooms and prison cells can be protected, as can private events in semi-public places such as vehicles and restaurants. An individual's 'inner circle' mentioned by the E Ct HR in *Niemietz*[1] refers not just to people but also to places. However, the more public the context the more difficult it is for an applicant to establish the right to private life or to acceptance of any action in that personal space. Thus, in *Friedl v Austria*[2] the Commission decided that art 8 had not been infringed when the applicant had been photographed by the police during a political demonstration. It appears that the same approach would apply to photographs taken by paparazzi, especially of public figures[3]. On the other hand, it is not an interference with private life to prevent someone from keeping a dog[4] or to institute a purely voluntary vaccination system without proper information as to the risks involved[5].

1 Para **4.8.7**.
2 *Friedl v Austria* (1995) 21 EHRR 83, EcomHR, para 48 to 51.
3 In *Costello-Roberts v United Kingdom* (1995) 19 EHRR 112, E Ct HR, the E Ct HR assumed that art 8 could apply in a private school but recognised that the protection it afforded was diminished by the slight nature of the interference and the semi-public nature of the environment.
4 Application 6825/74 *X v Iceland* 5 DR 86 (1976), EComHR.
5 Application 7154/75 *X v United Kingdom* 14 DR 31 (1978), EComHR.

(d)   Respect for sexual orientation, identity and relations

4.8.12   Sexual relations[1], orientation and identity are all intimate aspects of an individual's private life[2]. A series of cases has considered the extent of the rights of homosexuals and transsexuals under art 8.

1 The boundary of those sexual activities falling within art 8(1) was called into question in *Laskey, Jaggard and Brown v United Kingdom* (1997) 24 EHRR 39, para 36. Whilst sexual orientation and activity in general form part of private life, the E Ct HR indicated that it did not necessarily follow that all forms of sexual proclivity (such as the sado-masochistic activities in question) did as well. Since it was not disputed between the parties that there had been an art 8(1) interference the E Ct HR did not feel it necessary to determine the issue finally.
2 See also on the topic of sexual freedom and integrity: *SW v United Kingdom* [1996] 1 FLR 434, E Ct HR and *CR v United Kingdom* (1996) 21 EHRR 363, E Ct HR (common law removal of the marital exemption from criminal liability for rape, in *R v R* [1992] 1 AC 599, HL, held to conform with the Convention).

4.8.13   The E Ct HR's approach to state regulation of homosexual relations from the perspective of art 8 is best illustrated by the case of *Dudgeon v United Kingdom*[1]. Mr Dudgeon was a homosexual living in Northern Ireland who complained of the legislation that applied there. In Northern Ireland, quite distinctly from the rest of country, homosexual conduct, was an offence whether conducted in private or not, whether conducted between mature and consenting adults or not. The applicant's prime complaint, based on the general reasoning in the earlier E Ct HR decision in *Brüggemann*[2], was that the criminal offences as defined in Northern Ireland amounted to an unjustified interference with his right to respect for his private life and he had personally suffered fear and distress both generally and in questioning by the police. The E Ct HR upheld this complaint, finding that the prohibition of homosexual conduct carried out between consenting adults in private is an interference with 'a most intimate aspect' of private life[3] which was not necessary in a democratic society[4].

1 *Dudgeon v United Kingdom* (1981) 4 EHRR 149, E Ct HR.
2 In Application 6959/75 *Brüggemann and Scheuten v Federal Republic of Germany* 10 DR 100 (1977), the EComHR considered the right to an abortion. The Commission stated:

> 'The right to respect for private life is of such a scope as to secure to the individual a sphere within which he can freely pursue the development and fulfilment of his personality. To this effect, he must also have the possibility of establishing relationships of various kinds, including sexual, with other persons. In principle, therefore, whenever the State sets up rules

for the behaviour of the individual within this sphere, it interferes with the respect for private life and such interference must be justified in the light of paragraph (2) of Article 8.',

(see para 55 of the Commission's report).

3   *Dudgeon v United Kingdom* (1981) 4 EHRR 149, E Ct HR, paras 40–41 and 52. This followed the Commission's reasoning in Application 5935/72, *X v Federal Republic of Germany* 3 DR 46 (1975), an earlier case concerning homosexuality where it found, as in *Brüggeman*, that a person's sexual life is an important aspect of private life. The reasoning in *Dudgeon* has been consistently followed in *Norris v Ireland* (1988) 13 EHRR 186, E Ct HR and in *Modinos v Cyprus* (1993) 16 EHRR 485, E Ct HR 186 (where the applicant succeeded in his challenge to legislation prohibiting private, consensual homosexual relations between adults that remained in force but was unenforced. The E Ct HR held that a policy of non-prosecution was no sufficient guarantee of Convention freedoms).

4   *Dudgeon v United Kingdom* (1981) 4 EHRR 149, E Ct HR, paras 42–61.

4.8.14   The position of transsexuals has been considered in a number of cases raising issues under art 8. Typically the cases involve the refusal on the part of the state to recognise in some official form the applicant's change of identity and thus question what positive duties are required from the state in order to show respect for transsexuals' identity and private life. In the first case of *Van Oosterwijk*[1] the Commission was persuaded that art 8 was breached by the Belgian state's refusal to amend the applicant's birth certificate which constituted a refusal 'to recognise an essential element of his personality'. When the issue was considered by the E Ct HR in *Rees*[2] and then later in *Cossey*[3] no violation was found on similar facts. Great emphasis was put on the notion of the 'fair balance required'. The majority found that in the absence of any consensus between contracting states the UK authorities' refusal to amend the applicants' birth certificates struck a fair balance as the positive obligations imposed on the state did not extend so far as to require the introduction of detailed legislation that would change the very nature of the register which was viewed as a strictly historical record[4]. The E Ct HR was strongly influenced by the limited use of birth certificates in the United Kingdom and by the fact that transsexuals were free to change their name, and to use this on official documents such as passports[5]. These factors explain the different result reached by the E Ct HR (by 16 votes to 5) in *B v France*[6] where a failure to amend the French register along with a consequential refusal to amend official identity documents used on an everyday basis was held to constitute a violation of the positive duties imposed by art 8. The E Ct HR relied upon three factual differences from the *Rees* case, namely the fact that the French register was not an historical record, the refusal to allow a change of forename, and the greater impact upon social and professional life stemming from these refusals[7].

1   *Van Oosterwijk v Belgium* (1981) 3 EHRR 557, EComHR. The E Ct HR took no view on the merits, finding there to be no exhaustion of domestic remedies.

2   *Rees v United Kingdom* (1986) 9 EHRR 56, E Ct HR.

3   *Cossey v United Kingdom* (1990) 13 EHRR 622, E Ct HR.

4   In *Rees* a minority of three judges out of 15 agreed with the Commission that art 8 had been violated, essentially for the same reasons as in *Van Oosterwijk*: see (1981) 3 EHRR 557, E Ct HR, pp 68–70. In *Cossey* the dissenting minority had increased to eight votes out of eighteen.

5   *Rees v United Kingdom* (1986) 9 EHRR 56 E Ct HR, para 40.

6   *B v France* (1993) 16 EHRR 1, E Ct HR.

7   *B v France* (1993) 16 EHRR 1, E Ct HR, paras 55–62 for the material factual differences from the *Rees* and *Cossey* cases.

4.8.15   The E Ct HR revisited the issue in *Sheffield and Horsham*[1]. The court reiterated its case law and stated that notwithstanding changes in attitudes and some legal and scientific developments, the UK was still entitled in the absence of any clear consensus amongst contracting states to rely upon its margin of appreciation in order to defend its refusal to recognise post-operative transsexual identity in its births register. The E Ct HR re-emphasised that the detriments suffered by transsexuals in the United Kingdom in certain contexts were not of sufficient seriousness to displace this conclusion.

1 *Sheffield and Horsham v United Kingdom* (1998) 27 EHRR 163, E Ct HR. See also *X, Y and Z v United Kingdom* (1997) 24 EHRR 143, E Ct HR concerning the failure to recognise a transsexual as the father of a child born after artificial insemination by a donor.

(e) Privacy and instrusive publications

4.8.16 Another difficult issue is the extent to which the art 8(1) notion of 'private life' can be invoked in order to establish a duty on the state to take positive steps or provide remedies to prevent certain publications of or revelations about an individual's private life: ie to create a broad right to privacy. In *Winer*[1] the applicant complained of the publication of true and false statements about his sex life. He had obtained a settlement in respect of the false allegations in domestic libel proceedings but complained of the inadequacy of the range of civil remedies available under English law to protect his private life; in particular, he had not brought breach of confidence proceedings in respect of the true allegations. The Commission found that the range of remedies then open to Mr Winer provided sufficient protection[2]. The refusal to provide a remedy going beyond breach of confidence to prevent the publication of true but embarrassing factual material may be justified by countervailing free press and freedom of expression considerations. A fair balance was therefore struck by the United Kingdom's position.

1 Application 10871/84 *Winer v United Kingdom* 48 DR 154 (1986), EComHR.
2 In the later case of Application 28851/95 *Earl Spencer and Countess Spencer v United Kingdom* (1998) 25 EHRR CD 105, the applicants complained of intrusive revelations about their private life. The EComHR found this case to be inadmissible; developments in the law of confidence made that a potentially useful domestic remedy that should have been exhausted before an application was made.

C Family life

1 GENERAL

4.8.17 The notion of 'family' is an entirely social and contextual one. It is therefore unsurprising that its Convention meaning has evolved in step with the social developments that have occurred over the last forty years. The structure of this section is as follows. First, the range of relationships covered by the term 'family life' is considered along with the positive duties that it imposes upon the state. Next, the various discrete types of interference that commonly occur are considered[1]. The final step, namely the examination of any justification for the interference under the provisions of art 8(2) are considered in the final section[2].

1 This clear and logical approach has unfortunately become obfuscated by a jurisprudence which was described by Judge Martens in his dissenting opinion in the case of *Boughanemi v Belgium* (1996) 22 EHRR 228, E Ct HR as 'incoherent', 'arbitrary' and 'resulting in a lack of legal certainty'. This lack of coherence is attributable in part to a reluctance on the part of the Commission to accord relationships the same status when they consider immigration cases as they do when considering divorce or the taking of children into public care. A further complication has arisen in recent years by the increasing incidence of atypical households composed of same sex partners or transsexuals and their partners and children and the need to adopt an appropriate response to their demands. It is to be hoped that the British courts may be able to restore some logic in their application of this confused case-law following the coming into force of the Human Rights Act 1998.

2   In some cases this logical structure may break down or be elided. For instance, in *Nsona v Netherlands* RJD 1996-V 1979, E Ct HR a child had been falsely entered on an adult's passport as her daughter. When the forgery was discovered it was claimed that she was in fact her niece, a claim maintained throughout the proceedings. The Dutch government alleged that there could be no family life of the kind protected by the Convention because of the uncertainty surrounding the relationship. The Commission and E Ct HR leapfrogged the first two steps of the process, making no separate decision about either the relationship or the family life and went directly to decide that there had been no interference with 'their family life' because they had resorted to deceit and '[t]he Netherlands authorities cannot be blamed ... for refusing to accept allegations unsupported by evidence': para 113.

2   THE CONCEPT OF FAMILY LIFE

4.8.18   The existence of family life is ultimately a question of fact, the test being one of substance not form. As the Commission stated in *K v UK* the existence of family life depends upon 'the real existence in practice of close personal ties'[1]. The object of family life is living together (not necessarily physically) in order that family relationships can 'develop normally' and family members can enjoy one another's company[2].

1   Application 11468/85 *K v United Kingdom* (1986) 50 DR 199 at 207.
2   *Marckx v Belgium* (1979) 2 EHRR 330, E Ct HR, para 31; *Olsson v Sweden* (1988) 11 EHRR 259, E Ct HR, para 59.

4.8.19   The first key relationship is that between husband and wife[1]. The existence of a formal union accompanied by some evidence of cohabitation or consummation should be sufficient to give rise to the existence of family life. Indeed, engagements to marry, when accompanied by sufficient evidence of the strength of intention or establishment of relations, may give rise to family life[2]. But the notion of family life goes beyond the merely formal and covers other 'de facto family ties'[3]. It covers the relationship between unmarried adults even if not formally or legally endorsed or recognised provided such relationships constitute a sufficient commitment. Key factors are the stability of the relationship, the intention of the parties and (though by no means determinative) cohabitation[4]. Even polygamous unions (especially if celebrated and recognised in other jurisdictions) may give rise to family life notwithstanding the absence of any obligation to recognise such marriages as formal unions[5].

1   Sham marriages entered into, eg for immigration purposes, might fall outside art 8(1) on this test though in Application 18643/91 *Benes v Austria* 72 DR 271 (1992) the EComHR treated annulment of such marriages as a matter for justification under art 8(2).
2   Application 15817/89 *Wakefield v United Kingdom* 66 DR 251 (1990), para 255.
3   *Kroon v Netherlands* (1995) 19 EHRR 263, E Ct HR, para 30
4   *Kroon v Netherlands* (1995) 19 EHRR 263, E Ct HR, para 30.
5   Application 2991/66 *Alam and Khan v United Kingdom* 10 YB 478 (1967); Application 14501/89 *A and A v Netherlands* 72 DR 118 (1992).

4.8.20   The other focal relationship is that between parent and child[1]. Family life clearly exists between biological parents and their dependent children[2] unless fairly exceptional circumstances militate otherwise. The E Ct HR has held in *Berrehab* that:

'the concept of family life embraces, even where there is no cohabitation, the tie between a parent and his or her child regardless of whether or not the latter is legitimate ... Although that may be broken by subsequent events, this can only happen in exceptional circumstances'[3].

The tie includes that between parents to an existing, informal union and their illegitimate child[4]; equally, family life may exist between an unmarried father and his biological child[5] provided that sufficient nexus or connection between the two is maintained[6], or between a parent and child even after divorce and considerable periods of separation[7] or the break-up of a settled union[8]. Where blood ties exist 'there is a strong presumption that family life will exist'[9]. For instance, in *Moustaquim v Belgium*[10] family life was still held to exist between a young man, his parents and his siblings even though he had spent considerable periods of time separated from them after running away, being in prison and being deported. The key facets of all of these parent/child relationships is continued contact, emotional linkage and dependency. As the child matures, the burden in showing ongoing family life by reference to substantive links or factors grows[11], though of course emotional or social dependency may in fact be reversed as parents age.

1   See, for example, *Johansen v Norway* (1997) 23 EHRR 33, E Ct HR, para 52; *Ahmut v Netherlands* (1997) 24 EHRR 62, E Ct HR, para 60.
2   In *S and S v United Kingdom* 40 DR 196 (1984), EComHR (an immigration case concerning a widowed mother) the Commission held that for family life to exist between a mother and her adult son there must be elements of dependency going beyond the normal emotional ties.
3   *Berrehab v Netherlands* (1988) 11 EHRR 322, E Ct HR, para 21; *Gul v Switzerland* (1996) 22 EHRR 93, E Ct HR at para 32.
4   *Johnston v Ireland* (1986) 9 EHRR 203, E Ct HR.
5   *Kroon v Netherlands* (1994) 19 EHRR 263, E Ct HR.
6   No sufficient nexus existed between the father of an unborn foetus and that foetus: see Application 8416/78 *X v United Kingdom* 19 DR 244 (1980), at 253 to 254. As a result he had no basis upon which to be consulted on or object to an abortion.
7   *Berrehab v Netherlands* (1988) 11 EHRR 322, E Ct HR, where family life still existed between a divorced father and his child whom he visited four days a week; and *Gul v Switzerland* (1996) 22 EHRR 93, E Ct HR. Where both the parental relationship no longer subsists and normal cohabitation between parent and child has ceased it may be necessary to adduce evidence of a genuine and close family tie. Certainly, the strength of the ties that do exist will affect the assessment of the state's positive duties, the assessment of the interference and justification therefor.
8   *Keegan v Ireland* (1994) 18 EHRR 342, E Ct HR.
9   *X, Y and Z v United Kingdom* (1997) 24 EHRR 143, E Ct HR, para 52 citing *Keegan v Ireland* (1994) 18 EHRR 342, E Ct HR.
10   *Moustaquim v Belgium* (1991) 13 EHRR 802, E Ct HR.
11   See, for example, Application No 2992/66 *Singh v United Kingdom* (1967) 10 YB 478.

4.8.21   Generally, the protection of family life under art 8 involves cohabiting adults such as parents and/or step-parents and their dependent minor children. Beyond the central parent/parent and parent/child units the notion of 'family life' also extends to grandparents and grandchildren, and may extend to other relatives such as aunts, uncles[1] and so on provided that sufficiently close links (in the form of demonstrable interest, commitment and dependency between them) are shown[2]. A formal adoption creates family life between the adoptive parents and the child in question[3]. In appropriate contexts the same may also be true in a foster family relationship, though the range in the quality and duration of such relationships calls for careful analysis[4].

1   See for example Application 16580/90 *Boyle v United Kingdom* (1994) 19 EHRR 179 where it was held that an uncle had family life with a nephew because of their especially close relations. The uncle lived nearby and was a father figure to the child.
2   *Marckx v Belgium* (1980) 2 EHRR 330, E Ct HR.
3   Application 9993/82 *X v France* 31 DR 241 (1992), EComHR.
4   See *Gaskin v United Kingdom* (1989) 12 EHRR 36, E Ct HR; and Application 8257/78 *X v Switzerland* 13 DR 248 (1978), where the existence of family life between a foster parent and a foster child was raised but not decided by the Commission.

4.8.22   As to less conventional family structures, the E Ct HR and Commission have taken a fairly broad, purposive stance. The Commission was not prepared to extend the concept of 'family life' to include a homosexual relationship, though it has confirmed that respect for such a relationship nevertheless comes within the ambit of 'private life'[1]. In *Kerkhoven*[2] the Commission held that family life did not exist between a non-biological parent and a child born to a long-term lesbian relationship with the use of artificial insemination. As such, there was no positive duty on the state to grant parental rights to the partner who was not the child's biological parent. However, in the case of *X, Y and Z v United Kingdom*[3] the E Ct HR found a family relationship to exist between a woman, her female to male transsexual partner and the child she had conceived by artificial insemination by an anonymous donor[4]. In *G v Netherlands*[5] the Commission found that a man who had donated his sperm to enable a lesbian woman to become pregnant did not have family life with the resulting child, notwithstanding the fact that he had been involved in looking after the baby for seven months[6].

1   Application 11716/85 *S v United Kingdom* (1986) 47 DR 274; *B v United Kingdom* 64 DR 278 (1990). Ongoing social changes necessitate constant reappraisal of this jurisprudence.
2   Application 15666/89, *Kerkhoven v Netherlands* (19 May 1992, unreported), EComHR.
3   *X, Y and Z v United Kingdom* (1997) 24 EHRR 143, E Ct HR.
4   The E Ct HR in *X, Y and Z* distinguished *Kerkoven* on account of the fact that the child's social (but not biological) father although biologically female, suffered from gender dysphoria and as a post-operative transsexual lived in society as a man: see paras 55–56. Judge de Mayer dissented, holding that the relationship belonged properly to the sphere of private life. The E Ct HR held that there was no breach of art 8, however, by refusing to register the transsexual as the father of the child.
5   *G v Netherlands* (1993) 16 EHRR CD 38.
6   The man was refused access to the child as a result. It is unclear whether the absence of family life was as a result of the relationship between them being inherently non-familial in nature or because the facts of the case were insufficient to establish family life.

4.8.23   Certain formal or other events may terminate or severely curtail family life or aspects of it, most commonly divorce (though the parent-child relationship will probably be unaffected as in *Berrehab*[1]), legal separation, adoption. The potential for family life between adopted or fostered child and natural parents, and between a child born from donated gametes or embryos in modern fertility treatment and the donor parent or parents is an area of considerable uncertainty.

1   *Berrehab v Netherlands* (1989) 11 EHRR 322, E Ct HR.

3   RESPECT FOR FAMILY LIFE

(a)   General

4.8.24   As with all art 8 interests, the notion of respect does not imply that any state action impacting upon the interest will constitute an interference. Merely incidental matters do not raise questions of interference. Equally, it is apparent that the positive aspects of the notion 'respect' are of especial importance in the context of family life. The extent to which art 8 imposes on states not only a general duty to refrain from interfering in an individual's private life, but also a duty to act positively to protect private and family life was explained in *Marckx v Belgium*[1] where the E Ct HR held that art 8(1):

'does not merely compel the state to abstain from ... interference: in addition to this primarily negative undertaking, there may be positive obligations inherent in an effective "respect" for family life'.

On the facts of *Marckx* the E Ct HR required the state to provide sufficient domestic legal safeguards to ensure an illegitimate child's integration into its family. By requiring further steps beyond registration at birth to establish maternal affiliation,

Belgium failed to accord sufficient respect to the mother and child's family life[2]. In other contexts this positive duty has required the state to: provide a natural father (who had had family life with the mother) with an opportunity for consultation before placing the child in adoptive care[3]; provide an effective remedy to protect a family against a violent father[4]; take sufficient steps to ensure that the orders of a national court relating to a father's right of access to his child (who lived with maternal grandparents) were complied with[5]; provide a procedure by which contested paternity could be resolved[6]; and to assist serving prisoners or those on remand to maintain contact with their families[7]. It does not require the state to tax unmarried de facto couples in the same way as married couples, or to provide married couples with the option of divorce[8].

1 *Marckx v Belgium* (1979) 2 EHRR 330, E Ct HR.
2 See, similarly, *Kroon v Netherlands* (1995) 19 EHRR 263, E Ct HR where positive obligations on the state required it allow a father to establish relations and complete legal family ties with his illegitimate son as quickly as possible without necessary recourse to marriage of the mother.
3 *Keegan v Ireland* (1994) 18 EHRR 342, E Ct HR. It should be noted that there is no automatic or automatic but defeasible paternal right to care where the mother was unwilling to keep the child: see para 52; see also Application 13557/88 *N v Denmark* 63 DR 167 (1989).
4 *Airey v Ireland* (1979) 2 EHRR 305, E Ct HR.
5 *Hokkanen v Finland* (1994) 19 EHRR 139, E Ct HR. At para 61 the E Ct HR noted that 'the inaction of the authorities placed the burden on the applicant to have constant recourse to a succession of time-consuming and ultimately ineffectual remedies to enforce his rights'. See also Application 32842/96 *Nuutinen v Finland* (1996, unreported).
6 *Rasmussen v Denmark* (1984) 7 EHRR 371, E Ct HR.
7 Application 9054/80 *X v United Kingdom* 30 DR 113 (1982), EComHR; Application 18632/91 *McCotter v United Kingdom* (1993) 15 EHRR CD 98. Only exceptionally will this positive duty require prisoners to be moved; the mobility of children might be an especially relevant factor. See also the Commission admissibility decision in Application 28555/95 *Togher v United Kingdom* (1998) 25 EWHRR CD 99, EComHR which partly concerned the separation of a mother from her new-born, breast-fed baby when she was arrested and detained on remand. Because the mother was a Category A remand prisoner it was argued by the government that there was no possibility for her to keep the baby with her as convicted prisoners were able to do. But the Commission held this part of the complaint to be inadmissible.
8 *Johnston v Ireland* (1986) 9 EHRR 203, E Ct HR.

(b)   Children: care proceedings, adoption, custody

4.8.25 The Commission and E Ct HR have been particularly vigilant to ensure respect for family life in cases where the state intervenes by removing children into care or puts them under compulsory supervision or sanctions adoption or fostering (the existence of an 'interference' rarely being in dispute[1]). In adoption cases art 8 requires that the natural parents be properly involved in the decision-making process and that full account is taken of their views and wishes[2]. The E Ct HR has emphasised the importance of decisions being taken speedily in situations where the procedural delay leads to a de facto determination of the matter at issue[3]. The central consideration in such cases, as the court emphasised in *W v UK*, is that art 8(1) requires the state to put procedures in place that are sufficient to ensure that the interests of all affected family members are sufficiently protected[4].

1 See, for example, *Johansen v Norway* (1996) 23 EHRR 33, E Ct HR at para 52; *Rieme v Sweden* (1993) 16 EHRR 155, E Ct HR, para 55.
2 In *McMichael v United Kingdom* (1995) 20 EHRR 205, E Ct HR it was held that whilst art 8 contains no express procedural requirements, the decision making process leading to measures of interference must be fair and such as to afford due respect for the interests safeguarded by art 8. Save in genuine and grave emergencies, affected family members should be involved at all stages in any decision making process which might result in the state interfering with family life and should have the opportunity to be properly informed and to have their views taken into account. This approach supplements rights conferred by art 6(1) of the Convention, on which see para **4.6**. The E Ct HR made

it clear *Johansen v Norway* (1996) 23 EHRR 33, E Ct HR that this protection applies to administrative procedures as well as to any subsequent judicial proceedings.

3   In Application 9580/81 *H v United Kingdom* (1987); similarly in Application 23715/94 *SP,D P and AT v United Kingdom* (1997) the Commission found admissible a complaint made on behalf of three children involved in protracted (15 months) wardship/care proceedings, as a result of which the boys spent too long with a temporary foster parent and bonded to her, jeopardising the eventual planned permanent placement; see also *Bronda v Italy* RJD 1998-IV 1476.

4   *W v United Kingdom* (1987) 10 EHRR 29, E Ct HR.

(c)   Private law family proceedings

4.8.26   Article 8 applies to private family law proceedings, just as much as to proceedings in which the state (in whatever form) is a party. For instance, the notion of respect requires that non-custodial parents have the right of contact with their children unless particularly serious grounds exist to the contrary[1]. The custodial parent's objections to contact, which might put the child under stress, are not in themselves a ground of sufficient seriousness to prevent contact[2]. Further, the Commission has held that whilst compulsory paternity blood tests constitute an interference under art 8(1), they are justified under art 8(2) as necessary for the protection of the rights of others[3].

1   Application 9427/78 *Hendricks v Netherlands* 29 DR 5 (1982), EComHR. See also the recent admissibility decision in Application 28422/95 *Hoppe v Germany* and *Elsholz v Germany*, both unreported.

2   18 DR 225.

3   18 DR 154.

(d)   Respect, aliens and residence

4.8.27   Given the centrality of 'living together, in one another's company' to the enjoyment of family life, the notion of respect has in recent times had increasing prominence in immigration cases where one or more family members do not have a right of residence in the Convention state in question or where a right to reside is revoked or not renewed. Whether a proposed exclusion, deportation or expulsion of one or more family members constitutes an interference is a question of some sophistication.

4.8.28   Where a fresh right of residence is being sought, the starting point of the modern case law is *Abdulaziz, Cabalas and Balkandali v United Kingdom*[1]. The E Ct HR acknowledged that art 8 did not create a general right (and correlating obligation on the part of the state) to respect for a married couple's choice of matrimonial residence and thus to acceptance of the non-national spouse for settlement in that country[2]. Article 8(1) only protects the rights of existing, established families not the right of a person to enter a country in order to found a new family[3]. Deportation, or a refusal of entry, can violate art 8 if it separates an existing family.

1   *Abdulaziz, Cabales and Balkandali v United Kingdom* (1985) 7 EHRR 471, E Ct HR; the earlier cases, such as *Agee v United Kingdom* 7 DR 164 (1976) focused exclusively (and, arguably, discriminatorily) on the husband's ability to relocate.

2   *Abdulaziz, Cabales and Balkandali v United Kingdom* (1985) 7 EHRR 471, E Ct HR, para 67.

3   In *Abdulaziz, Cabales and Balkandali v United Kingdom* (1985) 7 EHRR 471, E Ct HR the E Ct HR was prepared to accept that an 'existing family' could include an engaged couple.

4.8.29   In assessing whether respect for family life gives rise to a right to residence key factors will be the length of time the other family members have resided in the contracting state, the duration of any separations, the ease of establishment of other family members in the non-national family member's state of origin (particularly whether the contracting state nationals have a right to residence there), the availability of adequate educational resources, whether children affected are of an 'adaptable age', medical imperatives, the possibility of persecution or repressive treatment, as well as other bars upon return (eg refugee or asylum based reasons). Strong grounds for suggesting legal or practical impossibility of return or substantial detrimental consequences upon such return need to be adduced in order to even give rise to a potential interference (let alone an unjustified or disproportionate one)[1]. The case of *Gul* shows how hard this test can be to satisfy[2].

1   In *Beldjoudi v France* (1992) 14 EHRR 801, E Ct HR the E Ct HR found that making the wife follow the husband back to his country of origin 'might imperil the unity or even the very existence of the marriage'. However, economic or general cultural disadvantages might be suffered is generally insufficient.

2   *Gul v Switzerland* (1996) 22 EHRR 93. However in a powerful dissenting opinion Judges Martens and Russo considered that a fair balance dad not been struck between the interests of the family and the Swiss authorities. See also *Ahmut v Netherlands* (1996) 24 EHRR 62 (again failing at the fair balance, rather than proportionality stage).

4.8.30   Probably the key factor in this equation is the extent to which family life for which protection is sought is already established in the contracting state. This then determines extent to which exclusion, deportation or expulsion would lead to separation from or destruction of that established family life[1]. Indeed, *Beldjoudi* goes so far as to change emphasis in cases where there is a substantial and (temporally) well-established family life in the contracting state. Then the focus of the E Ct HR's analysis shifts from the possibility of (re)-establishment of family life elsewhere to the proportionality of the decision in question[2].

1   See *Berrehab v Netherlands* (1989) 11 EHRR 322, E Ct HR; *Moustaquim v Belgium* (1991) 13 EHRR 802; *Beldjoudi v France* (1992) 14 EHRR 801, E Ct HR; *Boughanemi v France* (1996) 22 EHRR 228; *Bouchelkia v France* (1997) 25 EHRR 686; and *Nasri v France* (1995) 21 EHRR 458, E Ct HR. These cases all involve deportations of family members where the family had a long-standing connection with the contracting state in question. The degree of family establishment in a contracting state is likely to be a great deal lesser in the case of marriage cases such as *Abdulaziz, Cabales and Balkandali v United Kingdom* (1985) 7 EHRR 471, E Ct HR with the result that satisfying the E Ct HR that an interference exists is intrinsically harder: see generally N Mole 'Constructive Deportation' EHRLR Launch Issue; and Storey 'Implications of incorporation of the ECHR in the Immigration and asylum context' (1998) EHRLR Issue 4, p 452. In such cases, in contrast to the expulsions for criminal convictions the indigenous members of the family are expected to leave with the deportee.

2   *Beldjoudi v France* (1992) 14 EHRR 801, E Ct HR. Thus, provided a non-national demonstrates a sufficiently established family life in a state, he or she has the right to the positive benefit of being conferred with the right to remain as a manifestation of the state's respect for family life, subject to any proportionate art 8(2) public policy justification for his or her removal.

(e)   Family names

4.8.31   Article 8 does not contain any specific reference to individual names. However the E Ct HR has held that it constitutes a means of identification and a link to a family concerns his private and family life[1]. On the whole the Convention organs have preferred to consider the issue from the standpoint of private life[2]. In *Rogl v Germany*[3] the Commission found an interference with family life when the German courts overruled a father objections to his daughter's surname being changed to that of the stepfather with whom she cohabited, but that the interference was justified on the particular facts for the well being of the child and her integration into her new family[4]. The E Ct HR has not found a violation following the refusal to allow an applicant to change his surname to that of an ancestor living two hundred years earlier[5]. The court noted that states enjoy a wide margin of appreciation, as there was little common ground among the legal systems of the Convention countries regarding the circumstances in which changes of name are allowed[6].

1   *Burghhartz v Switzerland* (1994) 18 EHRR 101, E Ct HR.
2   *Guillot v France* (1996) Reports of Judgments and Decisions 1996-V 1593, E Ct HR.
3   *Rogl v Germany* 85A DR 153 85-A DR 153 (1996), EComHR.
4   Compare *W v A (Child: Surname)* [1981] Fam 14; *Re F (Child Surname)* [1994] 1 FCR 110; *Re B (Change of Surname)* [1996] 1 FLR 791.
5   *Stjerna v Finland* (1994) 24 EHRR 195.
6   *Stjerna v Finland* (1994) 24 EHRR 195, para 39.

D   Home and environment

1   GENERAL

4.8.32   This aspect of the art 8 case law is in comparative terms underdeveloped. Often the respect for the 'home' is or is treated as synonymous or coextensive with respect for family life[1]. At other times the notion of a 'home' overlaps heavily with the property rights protected by art 1 of the first protocol[2]. Alternatively, more specific matters such as a search of correspondence, which affects private life, may make it unnecessary to consider whether the action in question took place 'at home'[3]. However, whilst these overlaps do exist, respect for the home does give rise in some cases to independent considerations. The text below considers the content of the right, interferences and justification.

1   See eg *Murray v United Kingdom* (1994) 19 EHRR 193, E Ct HR; *Lopez Ostra v Spain* (1995) 20 EHRR 277, E Ct HR, para 51; and *Akdivar v Turkey* (1996) 23 EHRR 143, E Ct HR, para 88.
2   See eg *Howard v United Kingdom* 52 DR 198 (1987)(concerning the compulsory purchase of the applicants home). The Commission examined the case under art 8 as well as art 1 of the first protocol. On art 1 of the first protocol see para **4.19**.
3   Eg *Miaihle v France* (1993) 16 EHRR 332, para 28.

2   THE NOTION OF A 'HOME'

4.8.33   The term home would seem to cover a range of dwellings provided that a sufficient degree of connection and permanence is established by the applicant. The best illustration of the purposive approach to be taken towards the definition of the notion of a 'home' is the *Gillow* case[1]. Mr and Mrs Gillow had lived at the house in Guernsey for five years and then travelled extensively for eighteen years for Mr Gillow's work. They were then refused a residence licence by the Guernsey authorities so as to enable them to return to live in Guernsey for their retirement. The Commission and the E Ct HR were persuaded (especially in view of a concession that another UK property could not be viewed as the Gillows' 'home') that the Guernsey house was their home because of their 'sufficient links' with it in the form of their long-standing intention to return.

1   *Gillow v United Kingdom* (1986) 11 EHRR 335.

4.8.34   The notion of a home would thus appear to embrace, for example, a place of settled residence[1], a residence one owns where one intends to live in future (despite a long absence or period of residence elsewhere as in *Gillow*[2]) and a businessman's or professional's office[3], and more transitory abodes such as holiday homes or camper vans[4], or temporary hostels where there is a sufficiently strong linkage to the applicant. In *Buckley v United Kingdom*[5]. Mrs Buckley was a gypsy who lived continuously but without the requisite planning permission with her three children on land that she owned. In 1990 retrospective planning permission for her caravans was refused by the District Council and she was required by enforcement notice to remove the caravans. The E Ct HR had little difficulty in concluding on those facts that, whether legally established or not, the case concerned a 'home' within the meaning of art 8[6].

1   *Murray v United Kingdom* (1994) 19 EHRR 193, E Ct HR, paras 84 to 96.
2   *Gillow v United Kingdom* (1986) 11 EHRR 335, E Ct HR.
3   *Niemietz v Germany* (1992) 16 EHRR 97, E Ct HR, para 30.
4   See, eg, *Kanthak v Federal Republic of Germany* 58 DR 94 (1988).
5   *Buckley v United Kingdom* (1996) 23 EHRR 101, E Ct HR.
6   *Buckley v United Kingdom* (1996) 23 EHRR 101, E Ct HR, paras 52–55.

4.8.35   However, in the case of *Loizidou*[1] the E Ct HR held that it would overly strain the meaning of the word 'home' to extend it to cover property on which it was intended to build a home in the future. Nor could it be so widely defined as to mean 'homeland', ie an area where one has grown up or where a family has roots. That is not to say, however, that the idea of a home is restricted in any way to the physical confines of the property. The notion of 'home' also connotes the ability (facilitated by the state) to live freely in it and enjoy it, not merely as a property right[3].

1   *Loizidou v Turkey* (1996) 23 EHRR 513, E Ct HR, para 66.
2   The idea of 'enjoyment of a home' is becoming increasing important in the E Ct HR's environmental cases: see *Lopez Ostra v Spain* (1994) 20 EHRR 277, E Ct HR; *Guerra v Italy* (1998) 26 EHRR 357, E Ct HR.
3   *Howard v United Kingdom* 52 DR 198 (1987).

4.8.36   The extension of the notion of a 'home' or (in the French) 'domicile' to business premises, whilst consistent with the object and purpose of art 8, is of considerable significance. However, in practice it is likely to be accorded less intense protection under art 8(2) than a purely private residence[1].

1   *Niemietz v Germany* (1992) 16 EHRR 97, E Ct HR, para 30.

3   INTERFERENCE

4.8.37   The interference with respect for the home complained of may be in the nature of a personal invasion that takes place *at* home, such as a forcible entry or arrest at home[1]; alternatively the interference might be directed at the home *itself*, such as a denial of a right of access to the home[2], requisition or compulsory occupation, compulsory purchase[3], destruction[4] or removal of the property[5], eviction or expulsion. The potential for overlap with property rights (and particularly a claim for constructive deprivation or interference) obtained under art 1 of the first protocol is therefore apparent[6].

1   *Chappell v United Kingdom* (1990) 12 EHRR 1, E Ct HR (concerning the legality of *Anton Piller* orders); *Murray v United Kingdom* (1994) 19 EHRR 193, E Ct HR, para 86 (anti-terrorism powers of arrest); *Niemietz v Germany* (1992) 16 EHRR 97, E Ct HR (search of a lawyer's offices).
2   *Cyprus v Turkey* (1983) 15 EHRR 509, E Ct HR.
3   *Howard v United Kingdom* 52 DR 198 (1985).
4   See eg *Akdivar v Turkey* (1996) 23 EHRR 143, E Ct HR, para 88.
5   As in *Buckley v United Kingdom* (1996) 23 EHRR 101, E Ct HR, para 60.
6   On art 1 of the first protocol, see para **4.19**.

4.8.38   More recently, the interferences considered by the E Ct HR has widened out further to include environmental blighting or pollution. Thus in*Lopez Ostra*[1] the court found that the applicants' homes had not been respected where a waste treatment plant had been built close to her homes in a town with a heavy concentration of leather manufacturing and industry. The treatment plant began to operate without a licence releasing fumes and vapours that caused health problems to residents. The court held that severe environmental pollution may affect individuals' well-being and prevent them from enjoying their homes in such a way as to affect their private and family life[2]. The state had failed in its duty of respect by failing to exercise the powers that it had to prevent the nuisance and by failing to take the measures necessary to protect the applicant's home[3]. However, the court was careful, notwithstanding the fairly extreme facts, to emphasise the need to strike a fair balance between individual and collective or community interests.

1   *Lopez Ostra v Spain* (1994) 20 EHRR 277, E Ct HR, paras 51–58. See also Application 9310/81 *Baggs v United Kingdom*, (1987) 9 EHRR 235, 241 and 375, EComHR (aircraft noise); and *Guerra v Italy* (1998) 26 EHRR 357, E Ct HR (a case very similar to *Lopez Ostra* concerning a failure on the part of the state to act to protect the home environment from pollution).
2   *Lopez Ostra v Spain* (1994) 20 EHRR 277, E Ct HR, para 51
3   *Lopez Ostra v Spain* (1994) 20 EHRR 277, E Ct HR, para 55–56.

E   Correspondence, communications and confidential data

4.8.39   What constitutes an interference on the part of the state with correspondence or communications is largely self-evident. Equally, where the state uses its powers to gather personal or private details about an individual without his or her consent there may be a lack of respect for private life. Ready examples of the above infringements (often uncontested) are: the collection of private details in a security check[1]; or enforced fingerprinting or photographing as part of a criminal investigation[2]. An individual's privacy may also be infringed if the authorities keep him under surveillance[3], tap his telephone[4], check, intercept or stop mail[5] or collect and maintain data about him[6] by, for example, a record of his financial affairs or security vetting[7], information collected by way of census[8], police fingerprinting[9], or maintaining medical records[10].

1   *Hilton v United Kingdom* 57 DR 108 (1988) at 117 (the Commission emphasised that a security check would not per se consist of an interference).
2   *Murray v United Kingdom* (1994) 19 EHRR 193, E Ct HR.
3   *Klass v Federal Republic of Germany* (1978) 2 EHRR 214, E Ct HR.
4   *Malone v United Kingdom* (1984) 7 EHRR 14, E Ct HR; *Klass v Federal Republic of Germany* (1978) 2 EHRR 214, E Ct HR, para 49 (holding that tapping in fact constituted interference with the right to respect for private and family life and correspondence).
5   *Hewitt and Harman v United Kingdom* (1992) 14 EHRR 657, E Ct HR; *Herczegfalvy v Austria* (1992) 15 EHRR 437, E Ct HR; *Silver v United Kingdom* (1983) 5 EHRR 347; *McCallum v United Kingdom* (1990) 13 EHRR 596; *Campbell v United Kingdom* (1992) 15 EHRR 137, E Ct HR. There is no right to respect for correspondence once it is in the hands of the intended recipient: Application 21962/93 *AD v Netherlands* 76A DR 157 (1994).
6   *Hewitt and Harman v United Kingdom* (1992) 14 EHRR 657, E Ct HR.
7   Application 10439/83 *Mersch v Luxembourg* 43 DR 34 (1985), EComHR; and *Leander v Sweden* (1987) 9 EHRR 433, E Ct HR.
8   Application 9702/82 *X v United Kingdom* 30 DR 239 (1982), EComHR.
9   *Murray v United Kingdom* (1994) 19 EHRR 193, E Ct HR.
10   Application 14461/88 *Chare (née Jullien) v France* 71 DR 141 (1991), EComHR.

4.8.40   The case of *Halford*[1] emphasised that the basic approach of the E Ct HR to be a broad one. Respect for correspondence was held to include respect for private telephone calls albeit ones that took place at work in a private office on a personal line[2]. Equally, in correspondence cases the protection conferred is on the means of correspondence and not the content, though of course the latter is relevant to the question of justification[3], as is the identity of the correspondents[4].

1   *Halford v United Kingdom* (1997) 24 EHRR 523, E Ct HR.
2   *Halford v United Kingdom* (1997) 24 EHRR 523, E Ct HR, paras 53–58, relying in part upon *Huvig v France* (1990) 12 EHRR 538, E Ct HR paras 8 and 25 (an earlier case holding that even calls of a business nature are covered by the term 'correspondence'); and *Niemietz v Germany* (1992) 16 EHRR 97, E Ct HR.
3   *A v France* (1993) 17 EHRR 462, E Ct HR, paras 34–37 (telephone calls did not fall outside art 8(1) simply because they concerned criminal activities).
4   Most obviously, legal correspondence receives particularly anxious protection. See para **4.8.56**.

4.8.41   The extent to which the respect for correspondence imposes positive duties on the state actively to facilitate such correspondence is one area of controversy. Plainly such duties are not so general as to amount require the state to guarantee full and perfect functioning of the national postal services[1]. But in other contexts, notably imprisonment or mental health detention, the state also controls the individual's access to the postal system which may itself provide the sole means of communication. In such cases the failure to provide an internal means of access to an external facility may amount to censorship or a barrier to correspondence. In such circumstances, it is the substantive effect of the arrangements rather than their formal analysis in terms of positive or negative duties that is of interest[2].

1   Application 8383/78 *X v Federal Republic of Germany* 17 DR 227 (1979).
2   Application 11523/85 *Grace v United Kingdom* 62 DR 22 (1988), EComHR (where it was held that there are positive obligations on prison authorities to ensure letters were posted and delivered); Application 9659/82 *Boyle v United Kingdom* 41 DR 90 (1985), EComHR (where it was held that exceptionally an obligation to pay for a prisoner's post might arise given the absence of financial means. This must be particularly so where the correspondence is with legal advisers and the refusal to pay amounts to a constructive denial of access to the courts: see by analogy *R v Lord Chancellor, ex p Witham* [1998] QB 575, [1997] 2 All ER 779. On legal correspondence, see para **4.8.56**.

F   Article 8(2) justification

1   GENERAL

4.8.42   Such is the width of the rights protected by art 8(1) that the state often does not dispute that its measures have interfered with the respect for one or other of those rights: for example by photographing and fingerprinting suspects[1], covertly tapping a telephone or intercepting correspondence, by taking children into state or local authority care, or by demolishing an individual's home. The real question is whether the interference can be justified under art 8(2). If it is to be, the state must first demonstrate that the interference is 'in accordance with the law' (that is, the applicable domestic law). Applicants cannot usually rely on a complete absence, or a direct breach, of domestic law[2]. If they could, they would normally have a national remedy to be exhausted. Rather, they claim that domestic law is too uncertain or gives unduly wide discretion to public officials[3].

1   *Murray v United Kingdom* (1994) 19 EHRR 193, E Ct HR.

2   For some cases where they could, see *Eriksson v Sweden* (1989) 12 EHRR 183, E Ct HR, para 67, and *Olsson v Sweden (No 2)* (1992) 17 EHRR 134, E Ct HR, para 76 (gap in Swedish child-care law gave no legal basis for social workers to restrict the access of parents to children in care); and*Halford v United Kingdom* (1997) 24 EHRR 523,E Ct HR, para 61–63.

3   *Olsson v Sweden* (1988) 11 EHRR 259, E Ct HR (the E Ct HR's concerns about the general terms of Swedish law authorising children to be taken into care were assuaged by domestic procedural safeguards). See also *Leander v Sweden* (1987) 9 EHRR 433, E Ct HR; and *Hewitt and Harman v United Kingdom* (1992) 14 EHRR 657, E Ct HR. On the meaning of 'in accordance with the law' see para **3.13**.

4.8.43   Any interference by a public authority with the exercise of the rights guaranteed by art 8(1) must be in accordance with the law[1], for a legitimate aim and necessary in a democratic society[2] in the interests of national security[3], public safety or the economic well-being of the country[4], for the prevention of disorder or crime[5], for the protection of health or morals[6], or for the protection of the rights[7] and freedoms of others. The test of necessity involves deciding whether there is a 'pressing social need' for the interference and whether the means employed are proportionate to the legitimate aim(s) pursued by the state. In conducting such an examination, it is the nature, context and importance of the right asserted and the extent of interference that must be balanced against the nature, context and importance of the public interest asserted as justification[8].

1   See *Klass v Federal Republic of Germany* (1978) 2 EHRR 214, E Ct HR (German statute governing surveillance was sufficiently precise, and the procedures for ensuring compliance strict enough to meet the legality requirement of art 8(2) of the Convention); see also Application 10628/83 *M S v Switzerland* 44 DR 175 (1985), EComHR. See however, in *Malone v United Kingdom* (1984) 7 EHRR 14, E Ct HR (unpublished administrative practice regulating wiretapping in the absence of legislative regime too vague to be 'in accordance with the law'). A challenge to the United Kingdom statutory regime implemented by the Interception of Communications Act 1985 was declared inadmissible in Application 21482/93 *Christie v United Kingdom* 78-A DR 119 (1994), EComHR. European Union law regulating telephone tapping satisfied the legality requirement: see Application 10439/83 *Mersch v Luxembourg* 43 DR 34 (1985), EComHR. See also *Huvig v France* (1990) 12 EHRR 528, E Ct HR; and *Kruslin v France* (1990) 12 EHRR 547, E Ct HR (French statutory provisions and case-law on telephone surveillance failed to meet legality requirement); *Eriksson v Sweden* (1989) 12 EHRR 183, E Ct HR; *Olsson v Sweden (No 2)* A 250 (1992) 17 EHRR 134, E Ct HR (conditions imposed by social workers restricting access of parents to children in care had no legal basis and were therefore not in accordance with the law); *Silver v United Kingdom* (1983) 5 EHRR 347, E Ct HR (stopping prisoner's correspondence on the basis of Standing Orders and Circular Instructions issued to governors but not accessible to the prisoners was not in accordance with the law). See also *Campbell v United Kingdom* (1992) 15 EHRR 137, E Ct HR; and *Herceze-gfalvy v Austria* (1992) 15 EHRR 437, E Ct HR.

2   See *Dudgeon v United Kingdom* (1981) 4 EHRR 149, E Ct HR; and *Norris v Ireland* (1988) 13 EHRR 186, E Ct HR. In both cases, the E Ct HR was not satisfied that the criminalisation of homosexual acts in private was necessary in a democratic society; the E Ct HR required particularly serious reasons to justify interference with private enjoyment of sexual relations. However, in *Laskey, Jaggard and Brown v United Kingdom* (1997) 24 EHRR 39, convictions for consensual sado-masochistic sexual assaults were considered necessary in a democratic society to protect the health of the participants. The E Ct HR has accorded high importance to privilege between lawyer and client, and the right to communicate with legal advisers in rejecting state arguments seeking to justify interference: see *Golder v United Kingdom* (1975) 1 EHRR 524, E Ct HR (not necessary to refuse to transmit letter from prisoner to his solicitor about the possibility of bringing civil proceedings against a police officer); *Campbell v United Kingdom* (1992) 15 EHRR 137 (reasonable cause must be shown for suspecting that letter from prisoner contains illicit material before intercepting and opening it); *Niemietz v Germany* (1992) 16 EHRR 97, E Ct HR (search of premises of lawyer in quest for documents to be used in criminal proceedings was disproportionate to purpose of preventing crime and protecting the 'rights of others'). Execution of an Anton Piller Order in civil proceedings can be justified as being necessary for the protection of rights of others: *Chappell v United Kingdom* (1989) 12 EHRR 1, E Ct HR. See also *Klass v Federal Republic of Germany* (1978) 2 EHRR 214, E Ct HR, where a government's claim that secret surveillance was justified in the interests of national security and public safety was accepted, with the independent judicial

supervision of exercise of powers of surveillance as a check against abuse; see also *Leander v Sweden* (1987) 9 EHRR 433, E Ct HR (need to collect and maintain information in secret dossiers on applicants for public employment in security sensitive areas is not an interference provided that there are adequate and effective safeguards against abuse). In Application 21780/93 *T V v Finland* 76-A DR 140 (1994), EComHR, disclosure that a prisoner was HIV-positive to the prison staff involved in his custody, and who were themselves the subject of a duty of confidentiality, was justified as being necessary for the 'protection of the rights of others'. The state will be required to provide procedural safeguards against arbitrary treatment as a condition of justifying interference: *W v United Kingdom* (1987) 10 EHRR 29, E Ct HR (exclusion of parents from decisions as to placing children in foster-care or for adoption not necessary for the protection of the rights of the child); *Olsson v Sweden* (1988) 11 EHRR 259, E Ct HR (positive duty on social workers to involve parents in decisions as to care of children). States do, however, enjoy a wide margin of appreciation in deciding what steps are necessary in ensuring re-union of parents and children and protection of children, and the E Ct HR has emphasised that national courts are better placed to assess the evidence upon which such decisions are made: *Olsson v Sweden (No 2)* (1992) 17 EHRR 134, E Ct HR; *Andersson (M and R) v Sweden* (1992) 14 EHRR 615, E Ct HR; *Hokkanen v Finland* (1994) 19 EHRR 139, E Ct HR. See also *Funke v France* (1993) 16 EHRR 297, E Ct HR (absence of prior judicial authorisation required for search and seizure).

3   For example, *Leander v Sweden* (1987) 9 EHRR 433, E Ct HR.

4   *Funke v France* (1993) 16 EHRR 297, E Ct HR (search by French customs officials of individual's home was held to be in the interests of the economic well-being of the country, but the scope of the powers of search and seizure was too wide to be proportionate to this legitimate aim); similarly *Miailhe v France* (1993) 16 EHRR 332, E Ct HR; and *Berrehab v Netherlands* (1988) 11 EHRR 322, E Ct HR (explusion of Moroccan citizen following divorce from Dutch wife pursued legitimate aim of protecting the Dutch labour market, but was a disproportionate interference with his family relationship with the child of the marriage). See also Application 14501/89 *A and A v Netherlands* 72 DR 118 (1992), 89 LS Gaz, EComHR; and *Gül v Switzerland* (1996) 22 EHRR 93, E Ct HR.

5   *Campbell and Fell v United Kingdom* (1984) 7 EHRR 165, E Ct HR; *Moustaquim v Belgium* (1991) 13 EHRR 802, E Ct HR; and *Nasri v France* (1995) 21 EHRR 458, E Ct HR; *Beldjoudi v France* (1992) 14 EHRR 801, E Ct HR. In Application 11278/84 *Family K and W v Netherlands* 43 DR 216 (1985), EComHR, the interference with the family life of a convicted drug trafficker resulting from his expulsion from the Netherlands to Hong Kong was justified on grounds of prevention of crime or disorder; see also Application 16009/90 *X v United Kingdom* [1992] 89 LS Gaz R 35, EComHR. The E Ct HR and Commission have on several occasions rejected as justifiable on grounds of prevention of crime or preservation of public order the deportation of aliens with strong family ties in the host country: see *Moustaquim v Belgium* (1991) 13 EHRR 802, E Ct HR; *Beldjoudi v France* (1992) 14 EHRR 801, E Ct HR; *Bouchelkia v France*, (1997) 25 EHRR 696, E Ct HR; and *Nasri v France* (1995) 21 EHRR 458, E Ct HR.

6   Taking a child into public care may be justified as being necessary to protect the health and morals of the child, but failing to allow contact between mother and child for a substantial period is disproportionate to such legitimate aims and not necessary in a democratic society: see *Andersson v Sweden* (1992) 14 EHRR 615, E Ct HR. See also Application 11526/86 *W v Federal Republic of Germany* 50 DR 219 (1986), EComHR; Application 12523/86 *Gribler v United Kingdom* (1987) 10 EHRR 546, EComHR; Application 11588/85 *U and G F v Federal Republic of Germany* 47 DR 259 (1986), EComHR; and *Eriksson v Sweden* (1990) 12 EHRR 183, E Ct HR.

7   *Olsson v Sweden* (1989) 11 EHRR 259, E Ct HR. The compulsory psychiatric examination of a bankrupt is a justifiable interference with the right to respect for private life when ordered for the protection of the rights of creditors: see *Meeder v Netherlands* 9 EHRR 546 (1986), EComHR.

8   On the meaning of 'necessary in a democratic society' see paras **3.15–3.16**.

4.8.44   With that general test in mind certain further observations can be made, both on the requirement for legal certainty and the process of justification.

2   PRIVATE LIFE

4.8.45   The E Ct HR's reasoning in the homosexuality cases provides an illustration of these techniques, in particular the controlling influence of the doctrine of proportionality over the state's margin of appreciation, as such test is applied from time to time. In *Dudgeon*[1] the state's interference with the applicant's freedom to assert his sexual identity was total, covering both consensual and private adult homosexual activity. The court critically analysed the alleged justification advanced upon the grounds of 'protection of ... morals' and 'protection of the rights and freedoms of others' under art 8(2)[2]. It started from the premise that some degree of regulation of male homosexual conduct was inevitable, the overall aim being to preserve public order and decency and to protect the vulnerable. But these social and legislative objectives did not amount to 'a pressing social need' justifying the restriction of private, consensual acts between adults. Given the scale of the interference occasioned, which was tantamount to a complete ban of homosexuality, and the differences of treatment within the UK, the particularly serious reasons needed to justify such an intrusive policy had simply not been demonstrated by the state[3].

1   *Dudgeon v United Kingdom* (1981) 4 EHRR 149, E Ct HR.
2   There was no question in *Dudgeon v United Kingdom* (1981) 4 EHRR 149, E Ct HR that the requirement that restrictions be in accordance with law was satisfied. The UK's action in Application 9702/82 *X v United Kingdom* 30 DR 239 (1982), EComHR, was justified as necessary to protect the rights of others as there was evidence of the use of force on the applicant's part in the sexual relations in question: see paras 134–136.
3   Contrast with *Laskey, Jaggard and Brown v United Kingdom* (1997) 24 EHRR 39, E Ct HR, paras 42–49, where the ostensibly violent nature of the sexual activities in question were felt to widen the state's margin of appreciation very considerably. For the decision of the domestic court, see *R v Brown* [1994] 1 AC 212, HL.

4.8.46   However in *Dudgeon*[1], a prohibition on sexual conduct below the age of 21 was said not to be a breach of art 8 rights[2], nor was it discriminatory pursuant to art 14. That issue was revisited in the *Sutherland* case[3]. The Commission was persuaded, particularly in the light of recent, consistent medical developments that suggested sexual orientation was to all intents and purposes fixed by the age of 16 and that men above that age were not in need of special protection. Even if there were a few individuals above the age of 16 who would be potentially disturbed by a homosexual experience, it would nevertheless be disproportionate to expose both them and the older sexual partner to potential criminal sanctions in all cases[4].

1   *Dudgeon v United Kingdom* (1981) 4 EHRR 149, E Ct HR.
2   Consistent in this respect with the Commission's reasoning in Application No 8383/78 *X v Federal Republic of Germany* 17 DR 227 (1979) at 55–56; and *X v United Kingdom* (1981) 3 EHRR 63 (where the applicant was in part challenging the discriminatory age of consent in the UK fixed at 21 for homosexuals). Both cases also decided that differing treatment of male and female homosexuals in terms of the ages of consent could also be objectively justified on the basis of increased risk in the case that male homosexuals would seek to attract adolescents.
3   Application 25186/94 *Sutherland v United Kingdom* (1 July 1997, unreported).
4   See paras 63–66 of the majority opinion. Applications pending in Strasbourg include a challenge to the UK ban on homosexuals serving in the armed forces as considered in *R v Ministry of Defence, ex p Smith* [1996] QB 517, CA.

3   JUSTIFICATION: FAMILY LIFE

4.8.47   Given the interests at stake in the family life cases, the E Ct HR's approach to justification is a comparatively strict one. First, the need for certainty or interferences 'in accordance with the law' plays an important role in this context, particularly interferences of a severe and stark nature such as the separation of children from their natural parents[1]. In *Johansen v Norway*[2] the E Ct HR considered a case where a child had been in local authority care since the age of two weeks. The court did not criticise the state for taking the care proceedings or for maintaining the care order. However it did find a violation of art 8 in respect of the state's action to terminate parental contact so that the child be adopted, stating:

'In the present case the applicant has been deprived of her parental rights and access in the context of a permanent placement of her daughter in a foster home with a view to adoption by the foster parents. The measures were particularly far-reaching in that they totally deprived the applicant of her family life with the child and were inconsistent with the aim of reuniting them. Such measures should only be applied in exceptional circumstances and could only be justified if they were motivated by an overriding requirement pertaining to the child's best interests.[3']

1   *Olsson v Sweden (No 2)* (1992) 17 EHRR 134, E Ct HR; *Eriksson v Sweden* (1990) 12 EHRR 183, E Ct HR (where there was no legal basis for the conditions imposed to restrict parental access to childern in state care); and *Olsson v Sweden* (1988) 11 EHRR 259, E Ct HR (the E Ct HR's concerns about similar Swedish laws were assuaged by domestic procedural safeguards).
2   *Johansen v Norway* (1996) 23 EHRR 33, E Ct HR; see also *Andersson v Sweden* (1992) 14 EHRR 615, E Ct HR; *Hokkanen v Finland* (1994) 19 EHRR 139, E Ct HR.
3   *Johansen v Norway* (1996) 23 EHRR 33, E Ct HR.

4.8.48   Equally in such family separation cases the E Ct HR applies the proportionality test in a rigorous fashion to ensure that such separation truly is necessary. As the court stated in *W v UK*[1] this is a 'domain in which there is an even greater call than usual for protection against arbitrary interference' and as such substantial procedural safeguards, such as notification of important decisions to natural parents, consultation, the provision of information and an opportunity for meaningful, speedy legal redress, are critical to the assessment of the proportionality of any decision reached. There is a positive obligation to involve parents procedurally in any decisions reached and such decisions must be arrived at upon the basis of 'relevant and sufficient' reasons[2], with the positive (albeit not absolute) duty of reuniting parent and child[3]. The substantive decisions of social and care workers are subject to a wider margin of appreciation, though even here the court will find a violation when, for instance, unnecessary restrictions are imposed in conditions of access and communication with the child in care[4].

1   *W v United Kingdom* (1987) 10 EHRR 29, E Ct HR.
2   *Olsson v Sweden* (1989) 11 EHRR 259, E Ct HR.
3   *Olsson v Sweden (No 2)* (1992) 17 EHRR 134, E Ct HR.
4   See *Andersson (M and R) v Sweden* (1992) 14 EHRR 615, E Ct HR; contrast with *Hokkanen v Finland* (1994) 19 EHRR 139, E Ct HR at para 55; and *Rieme v Sweden* (1993) 16 EHRR 155, E Ct HR.

4.8.49   Closely related is the E Ct HR's approach to justification in cases where the application of national immigration rules will have the effect of splitting up the family unit. *Berrehab*[1] represents the starting point of the court's stricter jurisprudence. The fact that the applicant who, although divorced and therefore no longer entitled to a right to remain in the Netherlands, had close ties with his daughter which would in all probability be all but permanently severed by such deportation, led to a positive obligation upon the state not to deport him. Subsequent cases have turned heavily on their facts, though a substantial inclination to prevention of deportation can be detected in the results. Where deportation is based upon criminal activity, it must go beyond 'repeat petty crime' and involve something more serious[2]. As yet all cases dealing with the refusal of a grant of access to facilitate family life (as opposed to the breaking up of a family actually established in the Convention territory) have fallen at the fair balance stage.

1   *Berrehab v Netherlands* (1989) 11 EHRR 322, E Ct HR.
2   This approach was followed more controversially in the cases of *Moustaquim v Belgium* (1991) 13 EHRR 802, E Ct HR and *Beljoudi v France* (1992) 14 EHRR 801, E Ct HR. In both cases the applicants were accomplished petty criminals but with substantial family ties to parents and siblings in the first case, and to a wife in the second; contrast with *Boughanemi v France* (1996) 22 EHRR 228, E Ct HR, paras 42–45 (where deportation was held not to be disproportionate, in particular because of the serious crimes in question and the substantial links retained with Tunisia); and *Bouchelkia v*

France (1997) 25 EHRR 686 (where the applicant was a convicted rapist who, additionally, could not benefit from a family founded after the deportation order was executed).

4   JUSTIFICATION: HOME AND ENVIRONMENT

4.8.50   The range of legitimate interests that can be pursued so as to justify an interference with the respect for the home are numerous: prevention of crime; protection of the rights of others, environmental and public health goals and so on. In terms of justification much depends on the sense of 'home' being protected.

4.8.51   Thus where the notion of a 'home' overlaps heavily with property rights and the interference stems from the operation of general planning, environmental or health regimes, such as was the case in *Buckley*[1], the difficulties in showing a disproportionate action are substantial[2]. However, in cases such as these the facts of *Gillow*[3] show the important need to distinguish carefully between the legitimacy of the general legislative regime and the manner of its application to particular facts. In that case the E Ct HR held that whilst the Guernsey residence legislation was not objectionable in and of itself, there was on the facts nevertheless a violation. This conclusion was arrived at because, inter alia, the Gillows had been refused licences to occupy their home (whether permanent or temporary to permit a considered sale of the property) and had been convicted and fined for doing so even though they were the only possible occupants of the property in view of its dilapidated state[4].

1   *Buckley v United Kingdom* (1996) 23 EHRR 101, E Ct HR.
2   *Buckley v United Kingdom* (1996) 23 EHRR 101, E Ct HR, at paras 62–63 and 84–85.
3   *Gillow v United Kingdom* (1986) 11 EHRR 335, E Ct HR.
4   The action taken was therefore considered to be disproportionate to the legitimate aims pursued by the Guernsey legislation: see *Gillow v United Kingdom* (1986) 11 EHRR 335, E Ct HR at 352–353.

4.8.52   When the notion of 'home' overlaps heavily with the concepts of 'private life' so as to connote peaceful enjoyment of one's home environment the margin of appreciation accorded can be expected to be narrower, particularly where forced physical entry is obtained[1]. In such cases the E Ct HR will undertake a careful analysis of the proportionality of the action in question and the application of the particular national laws; as *Chappell* shows an even stricter approach may be adopted in the context of civil proceedings[2].

1   *Funke v France* (1993) 16 EHRR 297, E Ct HR (where the failure to obtain judicial authorisation was fundamental); *Niemietz v Germany* (1993) 16 EHRR 97, E Ct HR (where the warrant was drawn in overly wide terms). The approach in these cases naturally overlaps heavily with the strict approach adopted in correspondence cases : see paras **4.8.53–4.8.56**.
2   *Chappell v United Kingdom* (1990) 12 EHRR 1, E Ct HR.

5   JUSTIFICATION: CORRESPONDENCE AND CONFIDENTIALITY

4.8.53   The requirement for certainty plays a particularly prominent part in the justification process in the E Ct HR's case law in the fields of interception of correspondence and communications: for example, in case of *Herczegfalvy*[1] the court held that the provisions upon which the Austrian mental health authorities relied in order to interfere with the correspondence of the hunger-striking applicant (who had a violent criminal background) were too vague to justify the action in question as they did not specify the scope or conditions of exercise of this discretionary power. This concern was particularly acute as correspondence represented a mental patient's only form of contact with the outside world. The national rules thus conflicted with the rule of law or the rule against arbitrariness[2]. Similarly, in *Malone* the UK failed to convince the court that its telephone tapping régime had a sufficiently clear legal basis; a mere administrative practice regulating such tapping which was regularly adhered to was insufficient[3]. The more serious and intrusive the nature of interference, the greater the requirement for certainty; moreover as the case of *Kruslin* shows the test is a demanding one requirement the removal of any potential (if not actual) uncertainty[4].

1   *Herczegfalvy v Austria* (1992) 15 EHRR 437, E Ct HR.
2   *Silver v United Kingdom* (1983) 5 EHRR 347, E Ct HR, paras 88–95; *McCallum v United Kingdom* (1991) 13 EHRR 596, E Ct HR, paras 31 and 43–48 of the Commission Opinion; *Campbell v United Kingdom* (1992) 15 EHRR 137, E Ct HR (where such a claim of uncertainty was rejected at para 37).
3   *Malone v United Kingdom* (1984) 7 EHRR 14, paras 67–68; contrast with Application 21482/93 *Christie v United Kingdom* 78-A DR 119 (1994), EComHR, where the contention that the Interception of Communications Act 1985 introduced to remedy the problems identified in *Malone* itself failed to provide sufficient certainty were declared inadmissible; see also *Hewitt and Harman v United Kingdom* (1992) 14 EHRR 657, EComHR, esp paras 39–42; *N v United Kingdom* 67 DR 123 (1989); *Kruslin v France* (1990) 12 EHRR 528, para 29; *Halford v United Kingdom* (1997) 24 EHRR 523 where there was found to be a complete absence of legal basis for the tapping in question.
4   *Kruslin v France* (1990) 12 EHRR 528, paras 33–35. This consideration prompted the E Ct HR to treat the French court's explanatory case-law with considerable circumspection.

4.8.54   The range of legitimate interests advanced to justify interception of correspondence and communications range from the prevention of crime, to the more exceptional such as protecting national security, and public safety. The importance of the interest at stake and the nature of the countervailing interest asserted will determine the degree and nature of interference authorised. Thus criminal search warrants are routinely required to be judicially authorised and narrowly focused (particularly to exclude legally privileged material) in order to be considered proportionate[1]. By contrast, in a case that involved threats from serious, organised and sophisticated international terrorists and spies 'exceptional conditions' existed which by turn could justify exceptional surveillance measures and the margin of appreciation accorded to contracting states is correspondingly wider[2].

1   *Niemietz v Germany* (1993) 16 EHRR 97, E Ct HR; *Funke v France* (1993) 16 EHRR 297, E Ct HR; and *Miailhe v France* (1993) 16 EHRR 332, E Ct HR.
2   *Klass v Federal Republic of Germany* (1978) 2 EHRR 214, E Ct HR; see also *Leander v Sweden* (1987) 9 EHRR 433, E Ct HR. In such cases the E Ct HR's jurisprudence places greater emphasis on prior procedural controls and is less inclined to question the proportionality of the decision in question.

4.8.55   The identity of the correspondents or recipients is of central importance to the E Ct HR's approach to the balancing test, as is illustrated by the cases on interception of prisoner's mail. The court has had no difficulty in deciding that controls such as the opening and inspection of mail pursue a potentially legitimate interest, namely the prevention of crime[1]. Indeed, in the context of incarceration some measure of control over prisoner's correspondence had been recognised as compatible with the Convention[2]. However, it must still be proportionately pursued. Thus the stopping of a letter to a prisoner on remand that recommended a lawful tactic, namely the assertion of the right to silence was not permitted, being undirected to the attainment of a legitimate aim and having the effect of frustrating art 6 Convention rights[3]. Equally, in *Silver*, the stopping of correspondence with persons other than relatives or friends and restrictions on complaints about prison conditions were held to be unnecessary in a democratic society[4]. Further as the cases of *Golder* and *Campbell* illustrate, interference with communication or correspondence with lawyers will be subject to particularly intense scrutiny[5]. As the E Ct HR stated in *Campbell*:

'The right to respect for correspondence is of special importance in a prison context where it may be more difficult for a legal advisor to visit his client in person because, as in the present case, of the distant location of the prison ... [T]he objective of confidential communication with a lawyer could not be achieved if this means of communication were the subject of automatic control.'

The court therefore went on to find that the opening of correspondence for reasonable cause as opposed to on a routine basis provided a sufficient and less intrusive protection against the possibility of abuse of legal correspondence[6]. Equally, lawyer-client privilege is accorded a high degree of protection in non-prisoner cases, for instance those involving, as in *Niemietz,* the search and seizure of materials at lawyers' premises[7].

1   *Campbell v United Kingdom* (1992) 15 EHRR 137, E Ct HR, paras 41 and 60; *Silver v United Kingdom* (1983) 5 EHRR 347, E Ct HR, paras 99–104.
2   *Golder v United Kingdom* (1975) 1 EHRR 524, E Ct HR, para 45; *Silver v United Kingdom* (1983) 5 EHRR 347, E Ct HR, para 98; *Campbell v United Kingdom* (1992) 15 EHRR 137, E Ct HR, para 45.
3   *Schönenberge and Durmaz v Switzerland* (1988) 11 EHRR 202.
4   *Silver v United Kingdom* (1983) 5 EHRR 347, E Ct HR, para 99; see also *Pfeifer and Plankl v Austria* (1992) 14 EHRR 692, paras 43–48, E Ct HR.
5   *Golder v United Kingdom* (1975) 1 EHRR 524, E Ct HR; *Campbell v United Kingdom* (1992) 15 EHRR 137, E Ct HR, paras 46–55 relying on *S v Switzerland* (1991) 14 EHRR 670, para 48 ff.
6   In *Campbell v United Kingdom* (1992) 15 EHRR 137, paras 47–48, the E Ct HR rejected the distinction that the UK authorities had attempted to introduce in the light of *Golder v United Kingdom* (1975) 1 EHRR 524, E Ct HR and the friendly settlement in Application 10621/83 *McComb v United Kingdom* 50 DR 81 (1986), between correspondence relating to pending litigation and that relating to prospective litigation.
7   *Niemietz v Germany* (1993) 16 EHRR 97, E Ct HR, para 37.

4.8.56   As regards disclosure of confidential information, there may be an unjustified interference with art 8(2) where such material even if legitimately collated is disseminated without cause or for a purpose other than the one for which it was gathered. Whether there has been a violation in any particular case will depend on whether there is a pressing social need for such information to be collected and on the proportionality of the interference with privacy. There is no invariable and absolute right for a person to know that information about him has been collected and retained, though adequate and effective safeguards are necessary for the measure to be deemed proportionate[1]. Merely because information has been properly gathered and used does not mean that future retention or use is also justified or proportionate. Thus, fingerprints taken but eliminated from enquiries or equivalent DNA samples may have to be destroyed after use unless there is some further goal or specific consideration legitimately pursued[2].

1   *Leander v Sweden* (1987) 9 EHRR 433, E Ct HR; Application 19404/92 *Williams v United Kingdom,* (1992), unreported, EComHR; *Hewitt and Harman v United Kingdom* (1992) 14 EHRR 657, EComHR; *N v United Kingdom* 67 DR 123 (1989), EComHR.
2   *Friedl v Austria* (1995) 21 EHRR 83, EComHR, para 66 (though no violation was found on the facts of that case given the slight interference in question); Application 19404/92 *Williams v United Kingdom* (1992), unreported, EComHR (DNA samples).

> ## Article 9 Freedom of thought, conscience and religion
>
> 1. Everyone has the right to freedom of thought, conscience and religion; this right includes freedom to change his religion or belief and freedom, either alone or in community with others and in public or private, to manifest his religion or belief, in worship, teaching, practice and observance.
> 2. Freedom to manifest one's religion or beliefs shall be subject only to such limitations as are prescribed by law and are necessary in a democratic society in the interests of public safety, for the protection of public order, health or morals, or for the protection of the rights and freedoms of others.

A Introduction

4.9.1 Together with the closely related rights to freedom of expression[1], assembly and association[2], the values of art 9[3] are at the foundations of democratic society. The E Ct HR has observed of art 9 that: 'It is, in its religious dimension, one of the most vital elements that go to make up the identity of believers and their conception of life, but it is also a precious asset for atheists, agnostics, sceptics and the unconcerned'[4]. The protection of personal opinion afforded by arts 9 and 10 in the shape of freedom of thought, conscience and religion is one of the purposes of the freedom of association expressly guaranteed by art 11[5].

1 See para **4.10**.
2 See para **4.11**.
3 Cf the Universal Declaration of Human Rights (Paris, 10 December 1948), art 18; and the International Covenant on Civil and Political Rights (1977), art 18.
4 *Kokkinakis v Greece* (1993) 17 EHRR 397, E Ct HR, para 31.
5 *Young, James and Webster v United Kingdom* (1981) 4 EHRR 38, E Ct HR, para 57.

4.9.2 It is to be noted that in the structure of this article, it is *only* the manifestation of religion or beliefs which may be subject to limitations set out in art 9(2), and that the general freedoms of thought, conscience and religion are absolute rights[1] which may not be subject to any limitation or restriction, including the limitations which appear in art 15 of the Convention[2]. This fact makes it attractive for an applicant to frame his case as falling under art 9 in addition to, for example, arts 10 and 11. However, the limited jurisprudence of the E Ct HR and Commission on art 9 bears testament to the fact that the court has resisted the attempts of applicants to raise issues under art 9 when they may be considered as falling under some other article of the Convention. Examples of this include complaints regarding custody of children between parents of different religious beliefs[3], refusal to join trades unions[4], maintenance of an established church[5], and the right to marry at an age which was lower than that permitted under domestic law but permissible under the applicant's religion[6].

1 The E Ct HR noted the fundamental nature of the rights guaranteed by art 9(1) in *Kokkinakis v Greece* (1994) 17 EHRR 397, E Ct HR, para 33.
2 See para **2.14.1** above.
3 *Hoffmann v Austria* (1993) 17 EHRR 293, E Ct HR, which was considered under art 8 (family life).
4 *Young, James and Webster v United Kingdom* (1981) 4 EHRR 38, E Ct HR, where the E Ct HR

decided the applicants' claims (which related to compulsory union membership) under art 11 (freedom of association) rather than art 9 although one of the main grounds of their objection to joining the union was personal conviction.

5   *Darby v Sweden* (1990) 13 EHRR 774, E Ct HR, which was decided under art 1, first protocol (the right to property) and art 14 (arbitrary discrimination).

6   Application 11579/85 *Khan v United Kingdom* 48 DR 253 (1986), EComHR, considered under art 12 (marriage).

B   Scope

4.9.3   The rights protected by art 9 cannot be enjoyed by corporate entities[1], and it has been held that associations are not capable of exercising the right to freedom of conscience[2]. In *Vereniging v Rechtswinkels Utrecht v Netherlands*[3], the Commission dismissed as manifestly ill-founded a complaint by a prisoners' rights association which challenged the refusal of the Dutch authorities to grant it access to prisons. The Commission observed that art 9 primarily protects the sphere of personal beliefs and religious creeds and acts which are intimately linked to such beliefs or creeds including acts of worship or devotion, rather than aims of an idealistic nature.

1   See Application 3798/68 *Church of X v United Kingdom* 12 YB 306 (1969), EComHR, and Application 7865/77 *Company X v Switzerland* 16 DR 85 (1981), EComHR.
2   Application 11308/84 *Vereniging Rechtswinkels Utrecht v Netherlands* 46 DR 200 (1986), EComHR, and Application 11921/86, *Kontakt-Information-Therapie and Hagen v Austria* 57 DR 81 (1988), EComHR.
3   Application 11308/84 *Vereniging Rechtswinkels Utrecht v Netherlands* 46 DR 200 (1986), EComHR.

4.9.4   Article 9 rights may, however, be enjoyed by an organisation such as a church which is in reality no more than a collection of its adherents[1]. The Commission has also held that a church itself is capable of having its own interests to protect[2]. In *Johnston v Ireland*[3], the E Ct HR rejected a complaint that art 9 was infringed by the absence of domestic provisions permitting divorce which the applicant alleged forced him to live, contrary to his conscience, with a person to whom he was not married. The court held that art 9 could not provide a basis for a right to divorce that could not otherwise be found in the Convention.

1   Application 7805/77 *X and Church of Scientology v Sweden* 16 DR 68 (1979), EComHR; Application 12587/86 *Chappell v United Kingdom* 53 DR 241 (1987), EComHR, reversing the earlier position in *Church of X v United Kingdom* (1969) 12 YB 306, EComHR, where the Commission had held that legal as opposed natural persons were incapable of having or exercising the rights referred to in art 9(1). See also Application 8118/77 *Omkaranda and Divine Light Zentrum v Switzerland* 25 DR 105 (1981), EComHR.
2   Application 12587/86 *Chappell v United Kingdom* 53 DR 214 (1987), EComHR.
3   (1986) 9 EHRR 203, E Ct HR.

4.9.5   The conviction of a conscientious objector for failure to perform a substitute service in place of military service is not a violation of art 9(1)[1], and the application of generally applicable laws to persons who have reasons of conscience not to obey such laws does not infringe art 9(1)[2]. Accordingly, the use of a proportion of tax revenue for military purposes does not infringe art 9(1) even if the taxpayer objects, on grounds of religion or conscience, to such expenditure[3].

1   Because of the terms art 4(3)(b) of the Convention (see para **4.4**) (which excludes from the prohibition of forced or compulsory labour, military service or, where conscientious objectors are

recognised, alternative national service) it has been held that the state may, but need not, recognise conscientious objectors, and have a discretion whether to provide an alternative to military service: Application 2299/64 *Grandrath v Federal Republic of Germany* 10 YB 626 (1966), Com Rep, EComHR. If a state provides alternative forms of national service, it does not violate art 9(1) of the Convention if such service is for a longer period than military service, or if it takes measures to enforce such alternative service: Application 17086/90 *Autio v Finland* 72 DR 245 (1991), EComHR; Application 10600/83 *Johansen v Norway* 44 DR 155 (1985), EComHR. There was no violation of art 9 and art 14 where a conscientious objector complained that Swedish law permitted only Jehovah's Witnesses to enjoy exemption from both military and alternative national service: Application 10410/83 *N v Sweden* 40 DR 203 (1984), EComHR. See also paras **4.4.11–4.4.13** above.

2   Application 8811/79 *Seven Individuals v Sweden* 29 DR 104 (1982), EComHR.
3   See Application 10358/83 *C v United Kingdom* 37 DR 142. The State may, however, choose to respect the views of a conscientious objector and grant some form of exemption from domestic legal provisions without falling foul of Article 14 when it is invoked against it by persons who are not so exempted: Application 11595/85 *Suter v Switzerland* 51 DR 160 (1986), EComHR.

C   Religion and belief

4.9.6   The notions of 'religion and belief' have been given a wide interpretation by the Commission and have been held to include matters such as a non-religious belief[1]. The Commission has held, for example that pacifism falls within the ambit of the right to freedom of thought and conscience on the basis that it is a 'philosophy'[2].

1   *Kokkinakis v Greece* (1993) 17 EHRR 397, E Ct HR, para 31.
2   Application 7050/75 *Arrowsmith v United Kingdom* 19 DR 5 (1980), EComHR. Considered further at para **4.9.9**. See also Van Dijk and Van Hoof *Theory and Practice of the European Convention on Human Rights* (1998, 3rd edn) at p 548, where the authors express the view that art 9 is wide enough to cover not only traditional religious and non-religious beliefs but also minority views which attain a certain level of cogency, seriousness and importance to the person.

4.9.7   Article 9 provides a guarantee against indoctrination of religious beliefs by the state[1]. However, the existence of an established state church does not, of itself, violate the Convention if membership is voluntary[2]. The burden is on a complainant to show that he is in fact an adherent of a particular religion and that the practice or belief that he relies upon is an essential aspect of that religion[3]. Only those manifestations which actually express the belief concerned are protected by art 9(1)[4]. The state has a responsibility to ensure that the holders of religious beliefs can effectively enjoy their rights under the Convention[5]. For example, in the *Otto Preminger Institut*[6] case a film portraying God, Jesus and Mary in a manner which could have been deeply offensive to Christians was forfeited by the authorities. The E Ct HR held, by a majority, that the interference was justified and stressed the duty of those who exercise freedom of expression to avoid comment which does not contribute to public debate and is gratuitously offensive to others. Advertisements directed at the commercial sale of devices produced by a particular religious group are not protected manifestations of religion[7]. A law which criminalised the practice of parental chastisement of children was not an interference with art 9(1) even where the applicants maintained that their religion required such measures[8]. A church minister in dispute with his church regarding doctrine cannot invoke art 9(1) since he is free to leave the church and to continue to hold his beliefs[9].

1   Application 10491/83 *Angelini v Sweden* 51 DR 41 (1986), EComHR.
2   *Darby v Sweden* (1990) 13 EHRR 774, E Ct HR.
3   Application 8160/78 *X v United Kingdom* 22 DR 27 (1981), EComHR; Application 10180/82 *D v France* 35 DR 199 (1983), EComHR. The applicant must also adduce evidence that he actually wished to undertake certain acts of religious worship: see *Guzzardi v Italy* (1980) 3 EHRR 333, E Ct HR, para 110.

4　Application 7050/75 *Arrowsmith v United Kingdom* 19 DR 5 (1980), EComHR. See also Application 8118/77 *Omkaranda and Divine Light Zentrum v Switzerland* 25 DR 105 (1981), EComHR.

5　See, in relation to the right to education under art 2 of the first protocol, para**4.20** below and *Kjeldsen, Busk Madsen and Pedersen v Denmark* (1976) 1 EHRR 711, E Ct HR.

6　*Otto-Preminger Institute v Austria* A 295-A (1994), 19 EHRR 34, E Ct HR. See para **4.10.8** below. See, however, the earlier Commission decision, Application 17439/90 *Choudhury v United Kingdom* 12 HRLJ 172 (1991) EComHR, where the Commission held that the absence of criminal sanctions against publications which offended against non-Christian belief was not a violation of art 9.

7　Application 7805/77 *X and Church of Scientology v Sweden* 16 DR 68 (1979), EComHR, which concerned the prohibition of the use of certain words in advertisements for the Hubbard Electrometer sold by the Church of Scientology. The Commission distinguished between words in publicity material which related to the beliefs of the church and words aimed at selling. The former fell within art 9(1), but the latter did not since they were aimed at selling goods at a profit and were not a manifestation of belief.

8　Application 8811/79 *Seven Individuals v Sweden* 29 DR 104 (1982), EComHR. See also Application 8160/78 *X v United Kingdom* 22 DR 27 (1981), EComHR (refusal of school to allow Moslem teacher to attend prayers at mosque during school hours).

9　Application 12356/86 *Karlsson v Sweden* 57 DR 172 (1988), EComHR. See, however, Application 11045/84 *Knudsen v Norway* 42 DR 247 (1985), EComHR.

4.9.8　The most detailed consideration of art 9 to date is to be found in the E Ct HR decision in *Kokkinakis v Greece*[1]. In that case the applicants were Jehovah's Witnesses who had been convicted under Greek domestic law of the offence of proselytism as a result of their actions in seeking to persuade others to join their sect. The court held that the right to manifest one's religion by 'bearing witness in words and deeds'[2] including trying to convince one's neighbours of the merits of one's sect, fell within art 9 as long as such attempts at persuasion could not be characterised as 'improper prosyletism'[3]. The court also observed that freedom to manifest one's religion is not only exercisable in community with others in public or with a circle of those who share the same faith but also alone and in private.

1　(1993) 17 EHRR 397, E Ct HR.

2　(1993) 17 EHRR 397, E Ct HR, para 31.

3　(1993) 17 EHRR 397, E Ct HR, para 48, where the E Ct HR described improper proselytism as 'a corruption or deformation of [bearing Christian witness] which was not compatible with respect for freedom of thought, conscience and religion'. On the facts the court held that the Greek Government had not justified the interference with the applicants' rights under art 9(2) by a pressing social need: see para **4.9.10** below. See also *Larrisis v Greece* (1997) 4 BHRC 370, E Ct HR, where the E Ct HR held that restrictions on Greek air force officers from encouraging personnel under their command to convert to the Pentescostal religion were justified.

4.9.9　The second part of art 9(1) expressly refers to manifesting religion or belief 'in worship, teaching, practice and observance'. However, in *Arrowsmith v United Kingdom*[1] the applicant's complaint regarding her conviction for the distribution of leaflets opposing the policy of the United Kingdom government in Northern Ireland failed because the Commission held that the practice of pacifism did not include acts which do not directly express belief even though motivated by such belief.

1　Application 7050/75 19 DR 5 (1980), EComHR.

C　Article 9(2)

4.9.10　The power to interfere with freedoms under art 9(1) is limited to manifestations of religion and belief; and the right to hold beliefs, or to abandon beliefs, is wholly immune from interference by the state[1]. Accordingly, any form of compulsion to express certain thoughts, to alter one's opinions, or to disclose one's religious beliefs to others may be an infringement of art 9(1). No form of penalty or sanction can be imposed for holding a certain view, belief or conviction if it is not outwardly manifested in some form. The view has been expressed that the exercise of physical or mental pressure on an accused person to obtain a confession, or the use of lie detectors or hypnosis may infringe art 9(1) in addition to being violation of art 3[2].

1 See para **4.9.2** above. In *Buscarini v San Marino*, 18 February 1999, E Ct HR, para 39, the E Ct HR held that a resolution of the General Grand Council of San Marino requiring the applicants to take an oath of the Gospels on pain of forfeiting their seats in the Council was incompatible with art 9.
2 Van Dijk and Van Hoof *Theory and Practice of the European Convention on Human Rights* (2nd edn), at p 397, notes 1032 and 1033. Such practices may also breach other articles of the Convention.

4.9.11 In *Kokkinakis v Greece*[1] the E Ct HR found that the relevant domestic provisions were 'prescribed by law' when considered against a body of settled national case law and that the legislation pursued the legitimate aim of protecting the rights of others not to be subjected to improper influences by way of proselytising. However, despite the margin of appreciation accorded to states to assess the existence and extent of the necessity of an interference, the court held that the contested measure was not proportionate to the legitimate aim pursued[2].

1 (1993) 17 EHRR 397, E Ct HR. See para **4.9.8** above.
2 For examples of justified intereferences, see: Application 7992/77 *X v United Kingdom* 14 DR 234 (1978), EComHR, where a requirement that all motorcyclists, including Sikhs, wear crash helmets was justified, and Application 1068/61 *X v Netherlands* 5 YB 278 (1962), EComHR, where is was held that the conviction of a farmer who, on religious grounds, refused to take part in a compulsory health scheme designed to prevent illness amongst farm animals was necessary for the protection of health.

Article 10 Freedom of expression

1. Everyone has the right to freedom of expression. This right shall include freedom to hold opinions and to receive and impart information and ideas without interference by public authority and regardless of frontiers. This article shall not prevent States from requiring the licensing of broadcasting, television or cinema enterprises.

2. The exercise of these freedoms, since it carries with it duties and responsibilities, may be subject to such formalities, conditions, restrictions or penalties as are prescribed by law and are necessary in a democratic society, in the interests of national security, territorial integrity or public safety, for the prevention of disorder or crime, for the protection of health or morals, for the protection of the reputation or rights of others, for preventing the disclosure of information received in confidence, or for maintaining the authority and impartiality of the judiciary.

A   Introduction

4.10.1   Freedom of expression[1] constitutes one of the essential foundations of a democratic society[2], and is central to the working of the political process[3]. The E Ct HR has emphasised the pre-eminent role of the press in a state governed by the rule of law and has observed that 'freedom of the press affords the public one of the best means of discovering and forming an opinion of the ideas and attitudes of their political leaders'[4]. The freedom to hold opinions, including political beliefs, which is protected by art 10 is closely related to the freedom of thought guaranteed by art 9[5], and the freedoms of assembly and association enshrined in art 11[6]. Article 10 is similar to the International Covenant on Civil and Political Rights, but it is, in several important respects, cast in weaker language. In particular, art 10 of the Convention does not, in its terms, create an independent right to hold opinions without interference (cf art 19(1) of the Covenant), nor does it expressly refer to the right to seek information[7] (cf art 19(2) of the Covenant). The limitations and restrictions of the right permitted by art 10(2) of the Convention also go beyond those permitted by art 19(3) of the Covenant.

1 Cf the Universal Declaration of Human Rights (Paris, 10 December 1948), art 19; and the International Covenant on Civil and Political Rights, art 19.
2 *Handyside v United Kingdom* (1976) 1 EHRR 737, E Ct HR.
3 Emphasised by the E Ct HR in *Bowman v United Kingdom* (1998) 26 EHRR, 1, 18, para 42.
4 *Castells v Spain* (1992) 14 EHRR 445, E Ct HR, para 43.
5 See para **4.9**.
6 See para **4.11**.
7 The right to receive information prohibits a government from restricting a person from receiving information that others may wish or may be willing to impart to him, but it does not impose on governments an obligation to supply him with it: *Leander v Sweden* (1987) 9 EHRR 433, E Ct HR, where the E Ct HR held that the applicant had no right of access to a government register containing information on his personal life. See also *Gaskin v United Kingdom* (1989), 12 EHRR 36, E Ct HR. In *Guerra v Italy* (1998) 26 EHRR 357, para 53, E Ct HR, the E Ct HR held that the freedom to receive information referred to in para 2 of art 10 prohibits a government from restricting a person from receiving information that others wish or may be willing to impart to him but is not to be construed as imposing on a state positive obligations to collect and disseminate information of its own motion.

B   Scope

4.10.2   The nature and the forms of expression protected by art 10 are extensive and include not only information and ideas which are favourably received but also expression which would be regarded as offensive and which would offend, shock or disturb the state or any sector of the population[1]. Article 10 protects not only the substance of ideas or information expressed, but also the form in which they are conveyed. This includes, for example, a polemical or aggressive tone which a journalist adopts in an attack upon a subject of political interest[2]. Freedom of expression is not limited to the written or spoken word, and although political expression is at the centre of the range of protected speech[3], it has been held to include a wide range of forms of expression including artistic works[4], images[5] and dress[6]. Some types of expression have, however, been regarded as deserving of lesser (or no) protection against restrictions by the state: examples include racist literature[7] and expressions of political support for terrorism[8]. Commercial speech and professional communications are protected by art 10[9], and all legal entities, irrespective of their corporate status or the fact that they pursue commercial objectives benefit from the protection of art 10[10]. However, as appears at para **4.10.8**, the E Ct HR has generally deferred to national authorities on the question of the necessity of interferences with commercial and artistic speech by contrast to political speech.

1   *Sunday Times v United Kingdom* (1979) 2 EHRR 245, E Ct HR, and reiterated recently by the E Ct HR in *Oberschlick v Austria (No 2)* (1998) 25 EHRR 357, E Ct HR.

2   *Jersild v Denmark* (1994) 19 EHRR 1, E Ct HR, and *De Haes and Gijsels v Belgium* (1997) 25 EHRR 1, E Ct HR.

3   *Lingens v Austria* (1986) 8 EHRR 407, E Ct HR and *Handyside v United Kingdom* (1976) 1 EHRR 737, E Ct HR. This reflects the policy of English common law: 'It is of the highest public importance that a democratically elected government body, or indeed any governmental body, should be open to uninhibited public criticism'. The threat of a civil action for defamation must inevitably have an inhibiting effect on freedom of speech, see *Derbyshire County Council v Times Newspapers Ltd* [1993] AC 534, HL, per Lord Keith at 547F. See also the seminal decision in the libel case *New York Times v Sullivan* 376 US 254 (1964) (United States Supreme Court) per Brennan J who observed for the majority '...we consider this case against a background of a profound national commitment to the principle that debate on public issues should be uninhibited, robust and wide open, and that it may well include vehement, caustic, and sometimes unpleasantly sharp attacks on government and public officials ...'. A substantial body of Commonwealth jurisprudence has developed in relation to the protection of speech on political subjects from libel actions. The High Court of Australia has held that the Commonwealth Constitution includes an implied freedom to publish material discussing political matters: *Theophanous v Herald & Weekly Times Ltd* (1994) 182 CLR 104 and *Stephens v West Australian Newspapers Ltd* (1994) 182 CLR 211. See also: *R Rajagopal v State of Tamil Nadu* (1994) 6 SCC 632 (Supreme Court of India); *Hill v Church of Scientology of Toronto* [1995] 2 SCR 1130 (Supreme Court of Canada); *Lange v Atkinson and Australian Consolidated Press NZ Ltd* [1997] 2 NZLR 22 (New Zealand High Court); *Holomisa v Argus Newspapers Ltd* 1996 (2) SA 588 (Supreme Court of South Africa, Witswatersrand Local Division); *Sata v Post Newspapers Ltd (No 2)* [1995] 2 LRC 61 (High Court of Zambia); and Sir Brian Neill, 'The Media and the Law' (1995) Yearbook of Media and Entertainment Law, p 3.

4   *Muller v Switzerland* (1988) 13 EHRR 212, E Ct HR which concerned confiscation from an artist of paintings depicting sexual relations between men and animals. The E Ct HR found that this interfered with the artist's right to freedom of expression but was justified under art 10(2) as necessary for the protection of morals.

5   *Chorherr v Austria* (1993) 17 EHRR 358, E Ct HR.

6   Application 11674/85 *Stevens v United Kingdom* 46 DR 245 (1986), EComHR. The Commission has, however, held that inability to engage in sexual relationships due to incarceration is not an interference with expression since physical expression of feelings is not within art 10(1): see Application 7215/75 *Case of X* 19 DR 66 (1977), EComHR.

7   Applications 8384, 8406/78 *Glimmerveen and Hagenbeck v Netherlands* 18 DR 187 (1979) EComHR, and Application 9325/81 *X v Federal Republic of Germany* 29 DR 194 (1982) EComHR. See, however, *Jersild v Denmark* (1989) 19 EHRR 1 where a television journalist was convicted

under criminal legislation prohibiting dissemination of racist insults; even though he had solicited such contributions and had edited them to give prominence to the most offensive, the European Court of Human Rights found that his conviction was not proportionate to the interest of protecting the rights of others, in the context of a factual programme about the holding of racist opinions; see also *Beauharnais v Illinois* 343 US 250 (1952) (United States Supreme Court); *Collin v Smith* 578 F 2d 1087 1978 (US Court of Appeals, Seventh Circuit); and the discussion of racist speech in Barendt *Freedom of Speech* (1990) at pp 161–167.

8   Application 15484/89 *Purcell v Ireland* 70 DR 262 (1991), EComHR. See also Applications 18714, 18759/81 *Brind and McLaughlin v United Kingdom* 77-A DR 42 (1994), EComHR.

9   See *Casado Coca v Spain* (1994) 18 EHRR 1, E Ct HR; *Markt Intern Verlag v Federal Republic of Germany* (1989) 12 EHRR 161, E Ct HR; *Jacubowski v Germany* (1994) 19 EHRR 64, E Ct HR; *Open Door Counselling and Dublin Well Woman v Ireland* (1992) 15 EHRR 244, E Ct HR. In *Colman v United Kingdom* (1993) 18 EHRR 119, E Ct HR, an application by a British doctor challenging the GMC rules banning advertising by doctors did not proceed to a hearing before the E Ct HR when the application became academic through a change in GMC rules, and when the UK government agreed to pay, without admission of liability, compensation. In *Hertel v Switzerland* E Ct HR, 25 August 1998, the E Ct HR held that an injunction prohibiting a scientist from disseminating views that microwave ovens were dangerous was disproportionate to the legitimate aim of protecting the rights of others, in particular the rights of suppliers and manufacturers of microwave ovens to be protected from acts of unfair competition. See also *Virginia State Board of Pharmacy v Virginia Citizens Consumer Council* 425 US 748 1976 (United States Supreme Court) where Blackmun J, delivering the opinion of the court, stated that the economic purposes of the speaker and the recipient in cases of commercial speech did not disqualify such speech from First Amendment protection.

10   *Autronic AG v Switzerland* (1990) 12 EHRR 485, E Ct HR.

C   Interference

4.10.3   Where the impact upon speech or expression is collateral[1] to the exercise by the state of authority for other purposes, both the European Court of Human Rights and the European Commission of Human Rights have been reluctant to consider that the interference falls within art 10 of the Convention for the Protection of Human Rights. Thus, in *Kosiek v Federal Republic of Germany*[2] claims by teachers that conditions attached to their employment by German *lander* interfered with their rights under art 10 of the Convention were held to be, in reality, claims of rights of access to public employment which had been deliberately excluded from the Convention[3]. There will also be no interference by the state where an individual has agreed or contracted to limit his freedom of expression[4].

1   See, for example, Application 7729/76 *Agee v United Kingdom* 7 DR 164 (1976), EComHR, where the Commission held that the relevant interference was a necessary but unintended corollary of the exercise of the state's authority in deporting illegal immigrants).

2   (1986) 9 EHRR 328, E Ct HR. See also *Glasenapp v Federal Republic of Germany* (1986) 9 EHRR 25, E Ct HR.

3   See, however, Application 10293/83 *B v United Kingdom* 45 DR 41 (1985), EComHR; Application 11389/85 *Morissens v Belgium* 56 DR 127 (1988), EComHR; and *Vogt v Germany* (1996) 21 EHRR 205, E Ct HR where the E Ct HR held that an interference with civil servants' right to freedom of expression was not justifiable. See also *Ahmed v United Kingdom* (1998) 5 BHRC 111, E Ct HR (referred to at para **4.10.14** below) and *Defreitas v Ministry of Agriculture* (1998) 3 WLR 675, PC, where the Privy Council held that a blanket restraint upon civil servants from making any expression on matters of political controversy was excessive and disproportionate.

4   See Application 11308/84 *Vereiging Rechtswinkels Utrecht v Netherlands* 46 DR 200 (1986), EComHR.

4.10.4   The protection from interference is not limited to prior censorship[1] of expression and includes the prohibitions by way of post-expression sanctions as in *Lingens v Austria*[2]. Other types of restraints on expression have included forfeiture of property[3], the denial of a licence[4], and libel damages and an injunction[6]. Penalties imposed by the Spanish Bar Council, a public law corporation, upon a lawyer for engaging in advertising was held to be interference by a public authority with the lawyer's freedom of expression: see *Casado Coca v Spain*[6]. In *Lingens v Austria*[7] a journalist published two articles in a magazine which were strongly critical of the Austrian Chancellor, Bruno Kreisky. Following a successful private prosecution for defamation, Lingens was fined. The E Ct HR upheld his complaint of an interference with this art 10 rights, observing that the fine imposed on Lingens was effectively a type of censure which was likely to discourage criticisms of the type made and was not necessary in a democratic society for the protection of the reputation of others[8].

1   The E Ct HR emphasised recently, however, in *Wingrove v United Kingdom* (1997) 24 EHRR 1, E Ct HR, that prior restraints upon expression require special scrutiny. In *Observer and Guardian v United Kingdom* (1991) 14 EHRR 153, E Ct HR, para 60, the E Ct HR stated that prior restraints required the most careful scrutiny.
2   (1986) 8 EHRR 407, E Ct HR.
3   *Müller v Switzerland* A 133 (1988) 13 EHRR 212, E Ct HR.
4   *Autronic AG v Switzerland* A 178 (1990) 12 EHRR 485, E Ct HR, and *Radio ABC v Austria* (1998), 25 EHRR 185, E Ct HR.
5   *Tolstoy v United Kingdom* (1995) 20 EHRR 442, E Ct HR.
6   (1994) 18 EHRR 1, E Ct HR. See also Application 12242/86 *Rommelfanger v Federal Republic of Germany* 62 DR 151 (1989), EComHR.
7   (1986) 8 EHRR 407, E Ct HR.
8   See also *Oberschlick v Austria* (1991) 19 EHRR 389, E Ct HR.

4.10.5   The state is under a positive obligation to take action where a threat to an individual's freedom of expression comes from a private source, as in *Plattform Artze für das Leben v Austria*[1] where the E Ct HR held that authorities were obliged to take steps to prevent disruption of a demonstration by a hostile mob.

1   (1988) 13 EHRR 204, E Ct HR.

D   Broadcasting, radio and film

4.10.6   The means of protected expression extend beyond speech to include print media, radio, television, broadcasting and film. However, as opposed to the press, broadcast media are subject by the express terms of art 10(1) to licensing[1] provisions. Early cases[2] suggested that the maintenance of public service monopolies in broadcasting was compatible with the Convention. When France ratified the Convention in 1974 it was with an interpretative declaration relating to art 10 designed to protect its state radio and television monopolies[3]. More recently, however, the compatibility of a broadcasting monopoly with art 10 has been considered under art 10(2) rather than art 10(1), and requires in each case the justification of being necessary in a democratic society[4]. The E Ct HR has observed that the purpose of the third sentence of art 10(1) is to make clear that states are permitted to regulate, by a licensing system, the way in which broadcasting is organised in their territories, particularly in technical aspects. Private individuals or organisations do not enjoy a general right to be afforded broadcasting time or a licence to advertise on television[5]. Nor do they have a right to the grant of a licence for a commercial radio station[6].

1   The United States Supreme Court has held that, even absent express provisions as appear in the Convention, the regulatory control of broadcasting by the Federal Communications Commissions does not abridge free speech: *National Broadcasting Co Inc v United States* 319 US 190 (1943).

2   Application 3071/67 *X v Sweden* 26 CD 71 (1968), EComHR where it was held that licensing did
    not exclude a public television monopoly; Application 8266/78 *X v United Kingdom* 16 DR 190
    (1978); Application 10799/84 *Radio X, S, W and A v Switzerland* 37 DR 236 (1984), EComHR.
3   YB VII (1964) p 454.
4   *Nydahl v Sweden* (1993) 16 EHRR CD15, EComHR; and *Informationsverein Lentia v Austria*
    (1993) 17 EHRR 93, E Ct HR.
5   Application 4515/70 *X and Association Z v United Kingdom* 38 CD 86 (1971), EComHR. This is
    subject to exceptional circumstances such as the exclusion of one party from making broadcasts
    when others have been given such an opportunity: see Application 250060/94 *Haider v Austria* 85
    DR 66 (1995) 66, EComHR.
6   Application 4750/71 *X v United Kingdom* 40 CD 29 (1972), EComHR. A refusal by the authorities
    to grant subsidies for theatre performances is not a violation of the Convention: Application 2834/
    66 *X v Germany* 13 YB 260 (1970), EComHR. See also Application 2690/65 *NV Televizier v
    Netherlands* 9 YB 521 (1966), 11 YB 782 (1968), Friendly Settlement.

4.10.7   In *Informationsverein Lentia*[1], the applicants had been refused licences for
television and radio broadcasting because the Austrian Broadcasting Corporation held
a monopoly. The Austrian government submitted that the monopoly was necessary
because it enabled it to regulate the technical aspects of broadcasts and also their role
and place in modern society. Considering the case under art 10(2), the E Ct HR
observed that audio-visual media, as a means of imparting information and ideas of
general interest which the public are entitled to receive[2], are just as important in
modern society[3] as the press, and that limiting audio-visual broadcast capability to
state entities required a very pressing need in order to be justifiable; the necessity for
any restriction must be therefore be 'convincingly established'[4]. The court found that
the interference was not justified, particularly since there was a widespread practice
among states of allowing private stations to co-exist alongside state stations. Given the
technical progress in broadcast media, justifications for restrictions such as the limits
on the numbers of frequencies available are no longer acceptable as providing
justification for state broadcasting monopolies[5].

1   *Informationsverein Lentia v Austria* A 276 (1993), 17 EHRR 93, E Ct HR.
2   In *Autronic AG v Switzerland* (1990) 12 EHRR 485, E Ct HR, the E Ct HR observed that the public
    have a right to receive broadcasts.
3   In *Jersild v Denmark* (1994) 19 EHRR 1, ECtHR, the E Ct HR noted the importance of media
    broadcasting by reason of its immediacy of impact.
4   See also *Radio ABC v Austria* (1997), 25 EHRR 185, E Ct HR.
5   *Radio ABC v Austria* (1997), 25 EHRR 185, E Ct HR. See also *Columbia Broadcasting System v
    Democratic National Committee* 412 US 94 (1973) at 102 (United States Supreme Court).

E   Freedom of expression: art 10(2)

4.10.8   In addition to requiring that interferences with freedom of expression be
prescribed by law[1] and are necessary in a democratic society[2] in the interests of a
legitimate aim, art 10(2) emphasises that the justification for restrictions is that the
right to free expression carries with it certain responsibilities. For example, in the *Otto
Preminger Institut*[3] case a film portraying God, Jesus and Mary in a manner which
could have been deeply offensive to Christians was forfeited by the authorities. The
E Ct HR held that the interference was justified and stressed the duty of those who
exercise freedom of expression to avoid expression which does not contribute to
public debate and is gratuitously offensive to others. The nature of the expression
which is restrained or interfered with by the state will determine the strength and
cogency of the justification for the interference required by the court. Accordingly,
where the interference is with political speech rather than commercial or artistic

speech, the court generally requires the strongest reasons to justify impediments to the exercise of such speech[4].

1   See para **3.13** above.
2   See paras **3.15–3.16**. The adjective 'necessary' within the meaning of art 10(2) implies the existence of a 'pressing social need': *Sunday Times v United Kingdom* (1979) 2 EHRR 245, E Ct HR, para 59.
3   *Otto-Preminger Institute v Austria* (1994) 19 EHRR 34, E Ct HR. See also *Engel v Netherlands* (1976) 1 EHRR 647, E Ct HR; Application 10293/83 *B v United Kingdom* 45 DR 41 (1985), EComHR; Application 11389/85 *Morissens v Belgium* 56 DR 127 (1988), EComHR; Application 8010/77 *X v United Kingdom* 16 DR 101 (1979), EComHR; and *Handyside v United Kingdom* (1976) 1 EHRR 737, E Ct HR where the E Ct HR emphasised the responsibilities of publishers of a book.
4   See, for example, *Castells v Spain* (1992) 14 EHRR 445 where the E Ct HR found that the state had not shown it was necessary to resort to the criminal law to punish the applicant who had made serious factual allegations of wrongdoing (which might have been true) with regard to the conduct of the police in the Basque country. In *Oberschlick v Austria* (1991) 19 EHRR 389, E Ct HR, and *Lingens v Austria* (1986) 8 EHRR 407, E Ct HR, the E Ct HR held that a law requiring the proof of truth of opinions held about political figures was not necessary in a democratic society. This is to be compared to the treatment of commercial advertising in cases such as *Casado Coca v Spain* (1994) 18 EHRR 1, E Ct HR, and *Markt Intern Verlag v Federal Republic of Germany* (1989) 12 EHRR 161, ECtHR, where the E Ct HR refused to substitute its own evaluation for that of the national courts as to whether the advertising restrictions were necessary. See also *Jacubowski v Germany* (1994) 19 EHRR 64, E Ct HR. As to the wide margin of appreciation accorded to the state in the regulation of artistic expression, see *Muller v Switzerland* (1988) 13 EHRR 212, E Ct HR, considered at para **4.10.2**, n 4.

4.10.9   Foreseeability is inherent in the phrase 'prescribed by law'[1]. In *Goodwin v United Kingdom*[2], the E Ct HR held that the Contempt of Court Act 1981, s 10 (on disclosure of journalistic sources), was sufficiently precise to satisfy this test; and in both *Groppera Radio AG v Switzerland*[3], and *Autronic AG v Switzerland*[4] the state was allowed to rely upon norms of public international law which were applied in municipal law as satisfying the test of legal certainty. The court has held that honest commercial practice, as required by German unfair competition legislation, was prescribed by law since in areas such as competition, in which the situation was constantly changing, absolute precision could not be achieved, and developed case law contributed to foreseeability: see *Markt Intern Verlag v Federal Republic of Germany*[5]. In *Tolstoy v United Kingdom*[6], the court held that the legal rules concerning libel damages were formulated with sufficient precision, and that art 10(2) of the Convention did not require an individual to be able to anticipate the quantum of a jury award. Libel awards were therefore not too uncertain to be 'prescribed by law'.

1   *Sunday Times v United Kingdom* (1979) 2 EHRR 245, E Ct HR; *Müller v Switzerland* A 133 (1988) 13 EHRR 212, E Ct HR. See also Application 10038/82 *Harman v United Kingdom* 38 DR 53 (1984), EComHR. See generally para **3.13** above on 'prescribed by law'.
2   (1997) 22 EHRR 123, E Ct HR.
3   (1990) 12 EHRR 321, E Ct HR.
4   (1990) 12 EHRR 485, E Ct HR.
5   (1989) 12 EHRR 161, E Ct HR. See also *Barthold v Federal Republic of Germany* (1986) 13 EHRR 431, E Ct HR.
6   (1995) 20 EHRR 442, E Ct HR.

1   NATIONAL SECURITY

4.10.10   In *Observer and Guardian Newspapers v United Kingdom*[1], the E Ct HR held that the interlocutory injunction restraining publication by newspapers of information obtained from the book *Spycatcher* written by a former member of security services, Peter Wright, pursued the two legitimate aims, for the purposes of art 10(2), of maintaining the authority of the judiciary and safeguarding the operation of the security service, but that the continuance of the injunction, in the face of widespread importation of copies of the book published overseas, was disproportionate. *Vereinigung Demokratischer Soldaten Österreichs and Berthold Gubi v Austria*[2] concerned a penalty imposed on a soldier who distributed, contrary to military regulations, a satirical journal within military barracks and upon whom a penalty was, as a consequence, imposed. The E Ct HR concluded that the soldier's art 10 rights had been unjustifiably interfered with and that the discussion and ideas contained in the journal were of a nature that had to be tolerated within the military[3]. State restrictions upon broadcasting news items relating to organisations connected with, or supporting terrorism were held to be justified as being within the margin of appreciation permitted to states within the area of national security[4].

1   (1991) 14 EHRR 153, E Ct HR.
2   (1994) 20 EHRR 56, E Ct HR. See also *Vereniging Weekblad 'Bluf' v Netherlands* (1995) 20 EHRR 189, E Ct HR.
3   In *Hadjianastassiou v Greece* (1992) 16 EHRR 219, E Ct HR, the E Ct HR emphasised that freedom of expression is enjoyed by military personnel as well as ordinary citizens. The applicant soldier's conviction for disclosure of minor military secrets was, however, held not to be in violation of his art 10 rights since any such disclosure was likely to compromise national security. See also *Grigoriades v Greece* (1997) 4 BHRC 41, E Ct HR.
4   Application 15404/89 *Purcell v Ireland* 70 DR 262 (1991), EComHR; and Applications 18714, 18759/81 *Brind and McLaughlin v United Kingdom* 77-A DR 42 (1994), EComHR.

2   TERRITORIAL INTEGRITY

4.10.11   In *Piermont v France*[1] administrative orders expelling a Member of the European Parliament from French territories in the Caribbean were held by the E Ct HR to pursue the legitimate aims of preventing disorder and territorial integrity, but were not necessary in a democratic society since a fair balance had not been struck between these aims and the freedom of expression of the applicant.

1   (1995) 20 EHRR 301, E Ct HR.

3   PUBLIC SAFETY, AND THE PREVENTION OF DISORDER OR CRIME

4.10.12   The E Ct HR has held that restricting expression in order to prevent disorder within the armed forces is a legitimate aim for the purposes of art 10(2) of the Convention: *Engel v Netherlands*[1]. In *Ahmed Sadik v Greece*, the Commission has held that the institution of criminal proceedings for statements made in the context of an electoral campaign may only be justified insofar as there is clear evidence of incitement to violence[2]. A ban on cable retransmissions in Switzerland of programmes broadcast from Italy did not infringe the applicants' right to impart information and ideas regardless of frontiers because it was designed to maintain orderly international telecommunications[3] (which was held to be a legitimate aim).

1   (1976) 1 EHRR 647, E Ct HR, and *Vereniging Democratischer Soldaten Österreichs and Gubi v Austria* (1994) 20 EHRR 56, E Ct HR. As to prevention of disorder or crime in relation to demonstrations and assemblies, see para **4.11.3**. In *Janowski v Poland*, 21 January 1999, E Ct HR, para 34, the E Ct HR held that the conviction of a journalist for using abusive words towards municipal guards was a proportionate response to the legitimate aim of the prevention of disorder. At para 31, the E Ct HR emphasised that the applicant used such language in circumstances where he was acting as a private individual rather than as a journalist.
2   (1995) 24 EHRR 323. The E Ct HR found that domestic remedies had not been exhausted and so declined to consider the merits of the claim. In *Incal v Turkey* (1997) 4 BHRC 476, E Ct HR found

that the conviction of an individual for circulating a leaflet criticising the local authorities and urging Kurds to combine and make certain political demands was disproportionate to achieving the legitimate aim of preventing disorder because the language used in the leaflet could not be taken as inciting violence, hostility or hatred. Compare *Zane v Turkey* (1997) 4 BHRC 241, E Ct HR.
3   *Groppera Radio AG v Switzerland* (1990) 12 EHRR 321, E Ct HR.

4   PROTECTION OF HEALTH OR MORALS

4.10.13   The case-law of the E Ct HR and Commission in this area has recognised that, because of the wide range of domestic standards, States must enjoy a wide margin of appreciation as to appropriate restrictions on freedom of expression. In *Handyside v United Kingdom*[1], the publisher of a book for children containing a substantial chapter on sex and entitled 'The Little Red Schoolbook' was convicted on an obscenity charges, and the book was banned. The E Ct HR observed that art 10 is intended to protect material which is likely to offend, shock, or disturb a sector of the population. However, the court went on to hold that a ban on the book in the United Kingdom was a proportionate and justifiable interference with freedom of expression within the state's margin of appreciation as being necessary for the protection of public morals. This was despite the fact that the book had not been banned in the majority of the contracting states. Similarly, in *Müller v Switzerland*[2] the punishment of an artist for exhibiting obscene paintings was within the state's margin of appreciation. It is primarily for a state to assess the content of morals, but the court will, however, scrutinise a claim that the action taken by the state to protect its own conception of morals is necessary in a democratic society[3].

1   (1976) 1 EHRR 737, E Ct HR
2   (1988) 13 EHRR 212, E Ct HR.
3   *Open Door Counselling and Dublin Well Woman v Ireland* (1992) 15 EHRR 244, E Ct HR, where the applicants succeeded by reason of the perpetual and absolute nature of the injunction which restrained persons, regardless of age, health reasons, or necessity, from seeking counselling on termination of unwanted pregnancies. By reason of this fact the E Ct HR found that although the injunction pursued the legitimate aim of protecting health and morals it was disproportionate in its effect.

5   PROTECTION OF THE REPUTATION OR RIGHTS OF OTHERS

4.10.14   The E Ct HR held in *Otto Preminger Institut v Austria*[1] that the seizure and banning of a film which was potentially offensive to Christians was justified as pursuing the legitimate aim of protecting the religious rights of others guaranteed by the Convention[2]. The protection of reputation or rights of others covers the imposition of civil or criminal sanctions for defamation. The court, however, rejected the argument that the conviction of Peter Lingens for defamation of the Austrian Chancellor, Bruno Kreisky, was justifiable on the grounds that it was necessary to protect Mr Kreisky's reputation[3]. The limits of acceptable criticism of politicians acting in their public capacity are wider than in relation to a private individual and politicians are therefore expected to display a greater degree of tolerance[4]. In *Otto E F A Remer v Germany*[5] a conviction for incitement to race hatred, by publishing materials denying gassing of Jews in Nazi Germany, was held to be an interference with the applicant's rights under art 10 of the Convention, but was necessary in a democratic society for the protection of the rights and reputations of others. In *Bowman v United Kingdom*[6], the E Ct HR held that the Representation of the People Act 1983, s 75 (restricting expenditure in support of or against an election candidate) infringed the applicant's right to freedom of expression, although s 75 served the legitimate aim of 'protecting the rights of others' by securing equality between electoral candidates in terms of campaign expenditure. The court held that the restrictions imposed by the legislation were not proportionate to this legitimate aim given that the restriction on expenditure prevented Mrs Bowman from publishing information to local voters, but there were no restrictions placed upon political parties advertising at a national or regional level without reference to any particular constituency or candidate. In *Ahmed v United Kingdom*[7], the E Ct HR held that restrictions on civil servants' participation in political activity through political parties and applications for candidature in elections pursued the legitimate aim of ensuring proper functions of political democracy and were sufficiently limited so as not to constitute a disproportionate interference with the applicator's rights under art 10(1).

1   (1994), 19 EHRR 34, E Ct HR. See also para **4.9.7** above.
2   See also *Wingrove v United Kingdom* (1996) 24 EHRR 1, E Ct HR, where the E Ct HR found that the refusal of the British Board of Film Classification to grant a licence for the distribution of the video *Visions of Ecstasy* was a justifiable interference with the applicant's freedom of expression with the legitimate aim of protecting the rights of Christians. The court observed that given their more direct contact with the 'vital forces' of their countries, the state authorities were in a better position than the international judge to give an opinion on what is required nationally to prevent offence to persons of particular religious beliefs.
3   *Lingens v Austria* (1986) 8 EHRR 407, E Ct HR. See also *Oberschlick v Austria (No 2)* (1997) 25 EHRR 357, E Ct HR, where the E Ct HR found that applicant journalist's conviction for calling a political figure a *trottel* (idiot) in an article concerning a speech made by that person was an unjustifiable interference with the applicant's freedom of expression.
4   *Castells v Spain* (1992) 14 EHRR 445, E Ct HR.
5   Application 25096/94 82-A DR 117 (1995), EComHR.
6   (1998) 26 EHRR 1, E Ct HR.
7   (1998) 5 BHRC 111, E Ct HR.

6   PREVENTING THE DISCLOSURE OF INFORMATION RECEIVED IN CONFIDENCE

4.10.15   The E Ct HR held in *Goodwin v United Kingdom*[1] that a court order requiring a journalist to disclose his sources was not necessary in a democratic society when the disclosure was sought to enable a company to identify a disloyal employee. This interest did not outweigh the vital public interest in the protection of the applicant's source.

1   (1997) 22 EHRR 123, E Ct HR. See also *Camelot Group plc v Centaur Communications Ltd* [1998] 1 All ER 251, CA and *Fressoz and Roire v France*, 21 January 1999, E Ct HR.

7   MAINTAINING THE AUTHORITY AND IMPARTIALITY OF THE JUDICIARY

4.10.16   In *Barfod v Denmark*[1] the conviction of an amateur journalist for criminal defamation in an article containing unfounded allegations of bias on the part of certain lay judges was within the margin of appreciation allowed to states, and was not considered by the E Ct HR to be an unacceptable limit on his ability to express criticism of the judgments of these judges. In *Sunday Times v United Kingdom*[2] the E Ct HR rejected the submission that the interference by way of an injunction restraining publication was necessary to protect the authority and impartiality of the judiciary in relation to a pending legal action. Because of the requirements of art 6(1) (see para **4.6**), the state may have a duty to interfere with freedom of expression if the right of an individual to a fair trial would be prejudiced by publication of information about the proceedings[3]. Recently, in *Worm v Austria*[4], the E Ct HR found that the conviction of a journalist for writing an article accusing a former politician (who was charged with offences of tax evasion) of guilt was a justifiable interference with the applicant's freedom of expression which served the legitimate aim of upholding the authority and impartiality of the judiciary. The court observed that impartiality denotes a lack of prejudice or bias on the part of the courts which the public are entitled to assume are the proper forum within art 6 for the determination of guilt or innocence on a criminal charge. The courts, as the guarantors of justice, and whose role is fundamental in any state based upon the rule of law, must enjoy public confidence, and should be protected, to a certain degree, from attacks[5]. A conviction for breaching the confidentiality of proceedings in court was not justifiable when the matters disclosed were at the time of disclosure already in the public domain[6].

1　(1989) 13 EHRR 493, E Ct HR, paras 61–64.
2　(1979) 2 EHRR 245, E Ct HR, para 59. On the issue of protecting the authority and impartiality of the judiciary see also *Schopfer v Switzerland*, E Ct HR, 20 May 1998, dismissing a complaint about a disciplinary sanction imposed on a lawyer for public criticisms of judicial decisions in cases in which he represented clients.
3　*Observer and Guardian v United Kingdom* (1991) 14 EHRR 153, E Ct HR, para 61. See also Application 24770/94 *Associated Newspapers Ltd, Stewart Steven and Clive Wolman v United Kingdom*, 30 November 1994, EComHR, dismissing a complaint about a fine imposed for publishing details of the deliberations of a jury in a criminal trial.
4　(1997) 25 EHRR 454, E Ct HR.
5　See also *De Haes and Gijsels v Belgium* (1997) 25 EHRR 1, E Ct HR, where the E Ct HR found that the necessity for the interference with the journalists' freedom of expression in criticising certain judges had not, on the facts, been established.
6　See *Weber v Switzerland* (1990) 12 EHRR 508, E Ct HR.

> ## Article 11 Right to freedom of peaceful assembly and association
>
> 1. Everyone has the right to freedom of peaceful assembly and to freedom of association with others, including the right to form and join trade unions for the protection of his interests.
> 2. No restrictions shall be placed on the exercise of these rights other than such as are prescribed by law and are necessary in a democratic society in the interests of national security or public safety, for the prevention of disorder or crime, for the protection of health or morals or for the protection of rights and freedoms of others. This article shall not prevent the imposition of lawful restrictions on the exercise of these rights by members of the armed forces, of the police or of the administration of the state.

A Introduction

4.11.1 The separate but related rights of freedom of peaceful assembly and freedom of association appear together in a single provision of the Convention[1]. Both freedoms are central to the workings of the political process. Notwithstanding the autonomous and particular spheres of application of art 11, the protection of personal opinions including political beliefs, expressly secured by arts 9 and 10 of the Convention[2], is one of the objectives of the freedoms of assembly and association enshrined in art 11[3].

1 Cf the Universal Declaration of Human Rights (Paris, 10 December 1948), arts 20(1) and 23(4); International Covenant on Civil and Political Rights, arts 5, 6, 11 and 21; ILO Convention No. 87 Concerning Freedom of Association and Protection of the Right to Organise (9 July 1948); the European Social Charter (Turin, 8 October 1961).
2 See paras **4.9** and **4.10**.
3 *Vogt v Germany* (1995) 21 EHRR 205, E Ct HR, para 64. In *Young, James and Webster v United Kingdom* (1981) 4 EHRR 38, E Ct HR, at para 52 the court observed that one of the purposes of art 11, in the context of a refusal to join a trade union on grounds of personal belief, was the protection of the individual's freedom of thought and conscience. Freedom of association consequence of the First and Fourteenth Amendment protections of freedom of speech, the right of the people to peaceful assembly, and freedom to petition: see *Healey v James* 408 US 169 (1972); *Baird v State Bar of Arizona* 401 US 1 (1971); *NAACP v Alabama ex rel Patterson* 357 US 449 (1958). Cf Canadian Charter of Rights and Freedom 1982, s 2(c) and s 2(d). The scope of the latter provision, which guarantees freedom of association, was considered in *Re Public Services Employee Relations Act* [1987] 1 SCR 313 (Can SC), with reference to the Convention and United States case law.

B Freedom of peaceful assembly

1 SCOPE

4.11.2 The right to peaceful assembly is recognised as a right fundamental[1] to a democratic society, and is not to be restrictively interpreted[2]. Where applicants have complained of violations of their right to freedom of expression under art 10 in cases concerning meetings or assemblies, the Commission has analysed the complaint in terms of art 11 as being the operative provision, and by subsuming the rights to freedom of expression within it[3]. The right covers not only static meetings or assemblies, but also public processions and marches, such as the demonstration by an anti-racist church organisation in the case *Christians against Racism and Fascism v United Kingdom*[4], which fell under a general ban on demonstrations made under the Public Order Act 1936. The right includes both the right to hold private meetings and meetings in public[5]. Subjecting peaceful demonstrations to a prior authorisation procedure does not, however, encroach upon the essence of the right[6] which can be regulated in its exercise. The right of peaceful assembly is not engaged when those who organise and participate in a demonstration have violent intentions which result in public disorder[7]. Following the decision of the E Ct HR in *Plattform 'Ärzte für das Leben' v Austria*[8], it is clear that, in addition to the state not taking steps unjustifiably to restrict the freedom of peaceful assembly, it is under a positive duty in the sphere of relations between private individuals to take reasonable and appropriate measures to enable lawful demonstrations to take place, without the participants being subjected to physical violence or other threats. In this case, the applicants complained of a lack of protection from the police against counter-demonstrators. The court considered that in a democracy the right to counter-demonstrate could not extend to inhibiting the exercise of the right to demonstrate, but went on to hold that on the facts of the case, the Austrian authorities had, within the wide discretion accorded to them as to the means to be used, taken reasonable protective steps. Penalties imposed on an individual following his participation in a demonstration amount to an infringement of the right to peaceful assembly[9].

1　*The Greek Case*, Yearbook XII (1969) 170. As to the scope of the common law right of peaceful assembly and its relation to art 11, see *DPP v Jones* (4 March 1999, unreported).
2　Application 13079/87 *G v Federal Republic of Germany* 60 DR 256 (1989), EComHR.
3　See Application 8191/78 *Rassamblement Jurrasien Unité v Switzerland* 17 DR 93 (1979), EComHR, and Application 10126/82 *Plattform 'Ärzte für das Leben' v Austria* 44 DR 65 (1985), EComHR.
4　Application 8440/78 21 DR 148 (1980), EComHR.
5　Application 8191/78 *Rassamblement Jurrasien Unité v Switzerland* 17 DR 93 (1979), EComHR.
6　Application 8191/78 *Rassamblement Jurrasien Unité v Switzerland* 17 DR 93 (1979), EComHR.
7　Application 13079/87 *G v Federal Republic of Germany* 60 DR 256 (1989), EComHR, p 263.
8　A 139 (1988) 13 EHRR 204, E Ct HR.
9　*Ezelin v France* A 202 (1991) 14 EHRR 362, E Ct HR.

2　FREEDOM OF PEACEFUL ASSEMBLY: ARTICLE 11(2)

4.11.3　Where an interference with the right to freedom of assembly has been found, this interference has normally been held to have been justified by the state as necessary for the prevention of disorder or crime within art 11(1). In *Rassamblement Jurrasien Unité v Switzerland*[1], the Commission held that once a foreseeable danger of disorder was identified the state had a wide margin of appreciation as to the nature of the measures it adopted to avert such disorder. In *Christians against Racism and Fascism v United Kingdom*[2], the Commission found that a ban which had been imposed to prevent demonstrations by a certain group, but which effectively prohibited all demonstrations for a certain period of time, was justified particularly since the applicant was free to organise its demonstration a few days after the ban ceased, and because during the ban itself the applicant was able to organise and hold meetings. In *Ezelin v France*[3], the applicant (a lawyer and trade union official) took part in a demonstration against certain judges of the court of Guadaloupe. Following violence at the demonstration, the applicant (who was not involved in the violence), was disciplined by the local Court of Appeal for not disassociating himself from the march, and for not cooperating with the police. By a majority decision the E Ct HR found that although the disciplinary proceedings and sanction were aimed at the prevention of disorder, they were disproportionate to that aim and consequently an unjustified infringement of the applicant's rights under art 11(1).

1　Application 8191/78 17 DR 93 (1979), EComHR.
2　Application 8440/78 21 DR 148 (1980), EComHR. See also *The Greek Case* 12 YB 1 (1969) 170, EComHR.
3　*Ezelin v France* (1991) 14 EHRR 362, E Ct HR.

C　Freedom of association

1　SCOPE

4.11.4　Association within the meaning of the Convention presupposes a voluntary grouping for a common goal[1], and does not include the right merely to share the company of others[2]. Political parties are a form of association essential to the proper functioning of democracy and fall within the scope of this provision[3]. In *Ahmed v United Kingdom*[4] the E Ct HR held that interference with civil servants' rights to engage in political activity was justified as pursuing the legitimate aim of ensuring the proper functioning of political democracy. The right to form and join trade unions is a special aspect of freedom of association which protects, first and foremost, against state action. An individual has no right to join an association, and an association is equally under no obligation to allow the individual to remain a member[5]. Similarly, an individual should not be disadvantaged if he refuses to become a member of an association, and it has now been clearly established through the trade union 'closed shop' cases (considered below at para **4.11.5**) that there exists a negative right of freedom not to associate[6]. The Commission ruled inadmissible a complaint by a student association that art 11 was violated when the university authorities refused to accord it the same status which had been given to the official student body[7]. Requirements of compulsory membership of professional bodies, which have a separate legal status in national law and perform public law regulatory functions, do not violate art 11, since such bodies do not qualify as 'associations' within the meaning of the article. Thus, in *Le Compte, Van Leuven and De Meyere v Belgium*[8] the E Ct HR held that an obligation to join the *Ordre de Medecins* in order to practise medicine in Belgium did not violate art 11 since doctors were free to form their own associations even though they were also compelled to join the *Ordre*. The Commission applied this case law with the same result in *A v Spain*[9], a case which concerned mandatory membership of local Bar associations. More recently, the E Ct HR has held that a legal requirement in law that a taxi licence holder be a member of an association of taxi drivers was a violation of art 11 since the association was not of a truly public law character, and also because membership had not been proved to be ncessary for the administration of the taxi service in the public interest[10].

1　See *Young, James and Webster v United Kingdom* (1982) 4 EHRR 38, E Ct HR. In Application 6094/73 *Association X v Sweden* 9 DR 1 (1978) EComHR, the Commission observed that freedom of association is a 'general capacity for the citizens to join without interference by the state in association in order to attain various ends'. Political parties clearly fall within the term 'association': see Application 250/57 *KPD v Federal Republic of Germany* 1 YB 222 (1957), EComHR.
2　See Application 8317/78 *McFeeley v United Kingdom* 20 DR 44 (1980), EComHR where the Commission held, at p 48, that prisoners had no right to contact with one another under art 11, and observed that art 11 was principally concerned with the right to form or to be affiliated with a group or organisation pursuing a particular aim.

3   *United Communist Party of Turkey v Turkey* (1998) 26 EHRR 121, E Ct HR. See also *Sidropoulos v Greece* (1997) 4 BHRC 550, E Ct HR.
4   (1998) 5 BHRC 111, E Ct HR.
5   See Application 10550/83 *Cheall v United Kingdom* 42 DR 178 (1985), EComHR, p 185, and *Damyanti v Union* [1971] 3 SCR 840 (Supreme Court of India).
6   *Sigurour A Sigurjonnson v Iceland* (1993) 16 EHRR 462, E Ct HR, para 35.
7   *Association X v Sweden* 9 DR 5 (1973), EComHR. Cf *Healey v James* 408 US 169 (1972)(US Supreme Court).
8   A 43 (1981) 4 EHRR 1, E Ct HR.
9   66 DR 1988 (1990), EComHR. See also *Bathold v Germany* (1985) 7 EHRR 383, E Ct HR, and *Revert and Legallis v France* 62 DR 309 (1989), EComHR.
10   *Sigurour A Sigurjonsson v Iceland* (1993) 16 EHRR 462, E Ct HR.

2   TRADE UNIONS

4.11.5   The freedom to form and join a trade union does not guarantee any particular treatment of trade unions, or their members, such as the right to strike or to be consulted[1]. The scope and nature of the rights attaching to trade unions as associations within the Convention was considered in the case of *Swedish Engine Drivers' Union v Sweden*[2], where the E Ct HR held that the words 'for the protection of his interests' appearing in art 11 denoted a 'right to be heard', but that each state had a choice as to the means to be used to achieve this end. It was further held that the state enjoyed a wide 'margin of appreciation' as to the means to be employed[3]. Thus, a state policy of restricting the number of organisations with which collective agreements are to be concluded is not in itself incompatible with art 11[4], nor is a policy of concluding collective agreements with only a restricted number of unions[5]. Neither policy breaches any right inherent in the right to form and join trade unions as guaranteed by the Convention[6]. The right does not include the right to manage or organise associations[7]. In the case of *Young, James and Webster v United Kingdom*[8], the applicants were dismissed from British Rail following their refusal, on grounds of personal conviction, to join unions with which British Rail had concluded closed shop agreements. The E Ct HR held that the threat of dismissal for refusing to join a trade union following the conclusion of closed shop agreements between employers and unions is an interference which strikes at the very substance of the right to freedom of association[9]. This case was distinguished by the E Ct HR in *Sibson v United Kingdom*[10], in circumstances where the applicant refused to re-join a union which he had left, unless he received a personal apology from the union, where his decision was not on grounds of personal convictions relating to union membership. Unions remain free to decide, in accordance with union rules, questions concerning admission to and expulsion from the union, and the protection afforded by art 11 is primarily against interference by the state[11]. However, the state must, as a matter of positive obligation, protect the individual against abuse of a dominant position by a union as in the *Young, James and Webster* case, or where the exclusion or expulsion of the member was not in accordance with the union's rules or was wholly unreasonable and arbitrary[12]. The E Ct HR has held that the state, when acting as employer, is susceptible to regulation under art 11[13], rejecting the argument that in the sphere of work and employment conditions, the Convention cannot impose upon the state obligations that are not incumbent on a private employer.

1   See *National Union of Belgian Police v Belgium* (1975) 1 EHRR 578, E Ct HR. The E Ct HR referred to and relied upon art 6(1) of the Social Charter of 18 October 1961 (Council of Europe) which does not, in terms, provide unions with a right to consultation. In *Smith v Arkansas State Highways Commission* 441 US 463 (1979), the United States Supreme Court held that a state body is under no First Amendment duty to negotiate with a union about individual employees' grievances. See also *Schmidt and Dahlstrom v Sweden* (1976) 1 EHRR 632, where the E Ct HR

held that the right to strike was not expressly enshrined in art 11 and could be subject to regulation. The Canadian Supreme Court has also interpreted s 2(d) of the Canadian Charter of Rights and Freedoms as not including a right to bargain collectively or a right to strike: *Re Public Service Employee Relations Act* [1987] 1 SCR 313 (Can SC). Cf O'Boyle, Harris and Warbrick *The Law of the European Convention on Human Rights* (1995) at p 430, who consider that the right to strike should be considered as an indispensable aspect of art 11 protection. See also *Collymore v A-G of Trinidad and Tobago* [1970] AC 538, PC, and *All India Bank Employees' Association v National Industrial Tribunal* [1962] 3 SCR 269 (Supreme Court of India).

2 (1976) 1 EHRR 617, E Ct HR, para 40.

3 See also *Gustafsson v Sweden* (1996) 22 EHRR 409, E Ct HR, para 45. In this case, the court also observed, at para 62, that art 11 did confer a right on an employer not to enter into a collective agreement.

4 *Swedish Engine Drivers' Union v Sweden* (1976) 1 EHRR 617, E Ct HR, para 42.

5 *National Union of Belgian Police v Belgium* (1975) 1 EHRR 578, E Ct HR.

6 See Application 1038/61 *Schmidt and Dahlstrom v Sweden* (1976) 1 EHRR 632, E Ct HR, para 34.

7 See *X v Belgium* 4 YB 324 (1961), EComHR.

8 (1981) 4 EHRR 38, E Ct HR. See also *Sigurour A Sigurjonnson v Iceland* (1993) 16 EHRR 632, E Ct HR, para 35, where the E Ct HR referred to the various international treaties and instruments (including the Universal Declaration on Human Rights, and the Community Charter of the Fundamental Social Rights of Workers) which expressly protect the right of every employer and worker to join or not to join professional organisations or trade unions without any personal or occupational damage being suffered by them as a consequence. In the United States, the Supreme Court held in *Abood v Detroit Board of Education* 341 US 209 (1977) that compulsory payment by employees of union dues was a violation of the plaintiffs' First Amendment freedoms.

9 See also the following cases, the subject of friendly settlements, which concerned dismissals from employment following refusals to join trade unions, or expulsion from unions in compliance with closed shop agreements: *Reid v United Kingdom* 34 DR 107 (1983), EComHR; *Eaton v United Kingdom* 39 DR 11 (1984), EComHR; and *Conroy v United Kingdom* 46 DR 66 (1986), EComHR.

10 (1993) 17 EHRR 193, E Ct HR, para 29.

11 See Application 10550/83 *Cheall v United Kingdom* 42 DR 178 (1985), EComHR, p 185. In this case, the Commission considered that the expulsion of the applicant from the union was itself an act of a private body exercising its Convention rights under art 11. In its decision, at p 185, the Commission took into account arts 3 and 5 of the International Labour Organisation Convention No 87 which recognise the rights of unions to draw up their own rules, to administer their own affairs, and to join trade union federations.

12 Application 10550/83 *Cheall v United Kingdom* 42 DR 178 (1985), EComHR, p 185.

13 See *Swedish Engine Drivers' Union v Sweden* (1976) 1 EHRR 617, E Ct HR, and *Schmidt and Dahlstrom v Sweden* (1976) 1 EHRR 632, E Ct HR.

3 FREEDOM OF ASSOCIATION: ARTICLE 11(2)

4.11.6 In *Council of Civil Service Unions v United Kingdom*[1], the Commission held that the banning of unions at GCHQ was an interference with the art 11(1) rights of the employees but, given the nature of the activities carried out at GCHQ, it was justified under art 11(2) as being a lawful In *Vogt v Germany*[2], the E Ct HR considered that on the facts of that case, which concerned the dismissal of a state school teacher who refused to dissociate herself from a political party, the notion of 'administration of the state' should be narrowly interpreted in light of the post held by the applicant. The court held that even if teachers were to be regarded as part of the administration of the state for the purposes of art 11(2), the applicant's dismissal was disproportionate to the legitimate aim pursued. The E Ct HR in *United Communist Party of Turkey v Turkey*[3] observed that the exceptions set out in art 11 are, where political parties are concerned, to be construed strictly and that only convincing and compelling reasons could justify any restriction on such parties' freedom of association.

1 Application 11603/85 50 DR 228 (1987), EComHR.

2 (1996) 21 EHRR 205, E Ct HR, paras 66–68.

3 (1998) 25 EHRR 121, E Ct HR, paras 45–46.

> ### Article 12   Right to marry and found a family
>
> Men and women of marriageable age have the right to marry and to found a family according to the national laws governing the exercise of this right.

A   Introduction

4.12.1   The right guaranteed by art 12 to marry and found a family[1] has received a narrow interpretation from the Commission and E Ct HR, by contrast with the broader right to private and family life under art 8[2].

1   The right is similar to that guaranteed by the Universal Declaration of Human Rights, art 16 and the International Covenant on Civil and Political Rights, art 23(2).
2   See para **4.8**.

B   The nature and scope of the right

4.12.2   The use of the singular, 'this right', in the drafting of art 12 suggests that the right to marry and to found a family are related aspects of a single entitlement. The E Ct HR stated in *Rees v United Kingdom*[1] that 'article 12 is mainly concerned to protect marriage as the basis of the family'.

1   (1986) 9 EHRR 56, 68, E Ct HR, para 49. See also *Sheffield and Horsham v United Kingdom* (1998) 27 EHRR 83, 97, E Ct HR, para 66.

4.12.3   However, the Commission has accepted that the right to marry can apply even where there is no ability to found a family, for example in relation to prisoners who have no right to cohabit with their spouse. That is because, in the view of the Commission, '[t]he essence of the right to marry ... is the formation of a legally binding association between a man and a woman. It is for them to decide whether or not they wish to enter such an association in circumstances where they cannot cohabit'[1]. The Commission held that there was no justification for the United Kingdom to refuse to make arrangements to allow prisoners to marry, thereby delaying the date at which they could marry until they were released from detention[2].

1   Application 7114/75 *Hamer v United Kingdom* 24 DR 5 (1979), 16, EComHR, para 71 and Application 8186/78 *Draper v United Kingdom* 24 DR 72 (1980), 81, EComHR, para 60. In each case, the Report of the Commission was approved by the Committee of Ministers: see 24 DR at pp 17 and 83. Prisoners have no right to conjugal relations with their spouse (or anyone else) because (in the view of the Commission) loss of such an opportunity is the natural corollary of the loss of liberty and is necessary to maintain prison security and good order: Application 6564/74 *X v United Kingdom* 2 DR 105 (1975), EComHR and Application 8166/78 *X and Y v Switzerland* 13 DR 241 (1978), EComHR. In *Hamer* and *Draper*, the Commission concluded that, by contrast, personal liberty was not a necessary pre-condition to the exercise of the right to marry, which could easily take place under supervision, and involved no risk to prison security and good order.
2   Application 7114/75 *Hamer v United Kingdom* 24 DR 5 (1979), EComHR. As a result, the Marriage Act 1983 was enacted to enable marriages of detained persons to be solemnized at the place where

they reside. The Commission has rejected complaints that financial detriments consequent on marriage (loss of disability benefits, or adverse income tax implications) establish an interference with the right to marry contrary to art 12: see *Kleine Staarman v Netherlands* 42 DR 162 (1985), EComHR, and Application 11089/84 *Lindsay v United Kingdom* 49 DR 181 (1986), EComHR.

4.12.4   Article 12 confers the right to remarry for those whose previous marriage has ended as a matter of national law[1]. In *F v Switzerland*, a Swiss civil court imposed a three year prohibition on remarriage by the applicant following the break-up of his third marriage, which the Swiss court considered was caused by the applicant's unacceptable attitude. The E Ct HR held that this was a breach of art 12, emphasising that the provision did not distinguish between marriage and remarriage, and that a prohibition on remarriage could well adversely affect the person who the applicant now wished to marry and any children born out of wedlock[2].

1   But art 12 confers no right to divorce where national law makes no such provision: see para **4.12.12**.
2   (1987) 10 EHRR 411, E Ct HR. The judgment was by 9 votes to 8. The dissenting minority concluded that the restriction was based on legitimate reasons (being designed to protect both the institution of marriage and any future spouse of the applicant, who had been found to have grossly violated the obligations of a married person), was not arbitrary, and was temporary. In the view of the minority, the reference to 'national laws' in art 12 conferred a broad discretion on contracting states.

4.12.5   Article 12 rights are confined to married persons, or to persons who wish to marry. In dismissing a complaint that the parents of an illegitimate child did not have the same rights as a married couple, the E Ct HR rejected the suggestion that art 12 requires that 'all the legal effects attaching to marriage should apply equally to situations that are in certain respects comparable to marriage'[1]. An unmarried father cannot rely on art 12 as the basis for a claim to custody of his child[2], and art 12 does not entitle an unmarried person to adopt a child[3].

1   *Marckx v Belgium* (1979) 2 EHRR 330 at 356, E Ct HR, para 67. But note that even though art 12 does not apply, art 8 may well provide protection in relation to family and private rights: see para **4.8**.
2   Application 9639/82 *B, R and J v Federal Republic of Germany* 36 DR 130 (1984), EComHR.
3   Application 6482/14 *X v Belgium and Netherlands* 7 DR 75 (1975), EComHR. Article 12 does apply to adoption by a married couple: see para **4.12.8**.

C   General restrictions on the right

4.12.6   Article 12 states that the exercise of the right to marry and to found a family shall be subject to the national laws of the contracting states. But any limitations adopted by national laws 'must not restrict or reduce the right in such a way or to such an extent that the very essence of the right is impaired'[1]. So although art 12 confers a general right to marry and found a family, contracting states may impose proportionate restrictions on the right in pursuit of legitimate aims[2].

1   *Rees v United Kingdom* (1986) 9 EHRR 56 at 68, E Ct HR, para 50. See also *Sheffield and Horsham v United Kingdom* (1998) 27 EHRR 163, E Ct HR, para 66.
2   In *F v Switzerland* (1987) 10 EHRR 411, 422, E Ct HR, para 40, the E Ct HR held that the ban on remarriage which 'affected the very essence of the right to marry', was 'disproportionate to the legitimate aim pursued'. In Application 7114/75 *Hamer v United Kingdom* 24 DR 5 (1979), 14, EComHR, para 60, the Commission said that art 12 'does not mean that the scope afforded to national law is unlimited. If it were, article 12 would be redundant. The role of national law, as the wording of the article indicates, is to govern the exercise of the right'.

4.12.7   It is therefore generally a matter for national law to decide on such matters as capacity to marry, and the relevant formalities for marriage[1].

1   Application 7114/75 *Hamer v United Kingdom* 24 DR 5, (1979) 14, EComHR, para 62: 'Such laws may thus lay down formal rules governing matters such as notice, publicity and the formalities whereby marriage is solemnised ... They may also lay down rules of substance based on generally recognised considerations of public interest. Examples are rules concerning capacity, consent, prohibited degrees of consanguinity or the prevention of bigamy ... However, in the Commission's opinion national law may not otherwise deprive a person or category of persons of full legal capacity of the right to marry. Nor may it substantially interfere with their exercise of the right.' See Application 6167/73 *X v Federal Republic of Germany* 1 DR 64 (1974), EComHR (the applicant was not entitled to have his marriage recognised by German law simply because the applicant considered himself married after reading from the Bible and having sexual intercourse with a woman); Application 9057/80 *X v Switzerland* 26 DR 207 (1980) (assessment of whether the applicant remained married to another person under an applicable foreign law); and Application 11579/85 *Khan v United Kingdom* 48 DR 253 (1986), EComHR (marriageable age).

D   Adoption and other means of founding a family

4.12.8   National rules regulating the adoption of children by a married couple are, in principle, within the scope of art 12 because adoption is a means by which a married couple may found a family. However, a state has a broad discretion as to the content of the rules it adopts to regulate adoptions[1].

1   Application 7229/75 *X and Y v United Kingdom* 12 DR 32 (1977), EComHR; and *X v Netherlands* 24 DR 176 (1981), EComHR. See paras **4.12.6** and **4.12.7** on the general scope of the discretion enjoyed by contracting states in relation to regulation of the right to marry.

4.12.9   Similarly, other means by which a married couple may found a family, such as artificial insemination, are within the scope of art 12, in principle, but the state has a broad discretion as to the content of the regulatory rules it applies.

E   Homosexual and transsexual marriages

4.12.10   The E Ct HR has concluded that 'the right to marry guaranteed by art 12 refers to the traditional marriage between persons of opposite biological sex'[1]. So states are entitled, consistently with art 12, to refuse to allow two persons of the same sex to marry[2].

1   *Rees v United Kingdom* (1986) 9 EHRR 56 at 68, E Ct HR, para 49. In *Cossey v United Kingdom* (1990) 13 EHRR 622 at 642, E Ct HR, para 46, the E Ct HR said that there was no evidence in contracting states of 'any general abandonment of the traditional concept of marriage'. See also *Sheffield and Horsham v United Kingdom* (1998) 27 EHRR 163, E Ct HR, para 66. It would be surprising if homosexual relationships were within the scope of art 12 when the Commission has concluded that such relationships do not fall within the scope of 'family life' under art 8: see Application 11716/85 *S v United Kingdom* 47 DR 274 (1986), EComHR. See para **4.8**.
2   In English law, the parties to a marriage must be, respectively, male and female: Matrimonial Causes Act 1973, s 11.

4.12.11   The E Ct HR has rejected suggestions that art 12 entitles a post-operative transsexual to marry a person of the sex opposite to that in which the transsexual now lives socially, psychologically and (as a result of medical treatment) physically. The E Ct HR has held that art 12 entitles a state to adopt biological criteria for determining a person's sex for the purposes of marriage and so entitles a state to refuse to recognise (for this purpose) that gender reassignment surgery alters a person's sex for the law of marriage[1].

1   *Cossey v United Kingdom* (1990) 13 EHRR 622, 642-643, E Ct HR, para 46, upholding the validity of the English law rule in *Corbett v Corbett* [1971] P 83 (High Court). See also *Sheffield and Horsham v United Kingdom* (1998) 27 EHRR 163, E Ct HR, para 66.

F   Divorce

4.12.12   Article 12 does not confer a right to divorce. The E Ct HR so held in *Johnston v Ireland*[1], rejecting a complaint about the prohibition of divorce in Ireland.

1   (1986) 9 EHRR 203, E Ct HR. Despite the existence of a right to divorce in other European states, the E Ct HR adopted a narrow approach to the application of art 12. Having regard to the travaux préparatoires, the court said, at p 219, para 53, that it could not 'by means of an evolutive interpretation, derive … a right which was not included therein at the outset. This is particularly so here, where the omission was deliberate'. Article 12 can be contrasted, in this respect, with the Universal Declaration of Human Rights, art 16, which provides equal rights for the parties 'during marriage and its dissolution'. The judgment in *Johnston* is not easy to reconcile with *F v Switzerland* (see para **4.12.4**) on the right to remarry: a refusal to allow a married person to obtain a divorce will prevent that person and their new partner from marrying each other, and will have an adverse effect on any child born of that union, factors which concerned the court in *F v Switzerland*.

> ## Article 13   Right to an effective remedy
>
> Everyone whose rights and freedoms as set forth in this Convention are violated shall have an effective remedy before a national authority notwithstanding that the violation has been committed by persons acting in an official capacity.

A   Introduction

4.13.1   Article 13 is autonomous but subsidiary. It is the link between the Convention and the national legal systems[1]. The United Kingdom's dualist system has (before the entry into force of the Human Rights Act) meant that Convention rights, in common with other international treaties, cannot be directly invoked in domestic proceedings. By virtue of art 13, however, the Convention is itself violated if the national legal system fails to provide an effective domestic remedy[2]. A breach of art 13 cannot amount to a free-standing violation. It does not guarantee a national remedy against all illegality. It must be linked to a claim that another Convention right has been violated, although there can be a breach of art 13 in the absence of any other breach. A determination of the extent of the state's obligations under art 13 can be made only by reference to the nature of the claim that another art has been violated. Moreover, art 13 contains only minimum procedural safeguards. The rest of the Convention sometimes imposes higher standards[3]. States may also provide their own higher level of procedural protection and, where they do, an applicant must exhaust the additional procedures under art 35 (formerly art 26).

1   See, similarly, the United Nations International Covenant on Civil and Political Rights, art 2 (1966). The United Nations Human Rights Committee has criticised the United Kingdom's failure to give the Covenant some statutory force so as to ensure that it can be invoked before domestic courts, tribunals and administrative agencies: see McGoldrick *The Human Rights Committee* (1991), Summary Record 89, at para 83, pp 278–279.
2   Article 35 requires that effective national remedies are used and exhausted before any application to the E Ct HR is made. Together, arts 13 and 35 enshrine a principle of subsidiarity (requiring a complaint to be tested, and a remedy secured, locally wherever reasonably possible). On the application of art 35, see Mr Justice Bratza and Alison Padfield [1998] JR 220.
3   See in particular arts 5 and 6: paras **4.5** and **4.6**.

4.13.2   The Convention rights to which the Human Rights Act 1998 gives effect do not include art 13. However, courts in the United Kingdom are likely to continue to have regard to art 13 in order to ensure the provision of effective domestic remedies[1].

1   See para **2.1.2**.

B   Scope

4.13.3   In its judgment in *Aksoy v Turkey*[1] the E Ct HR declared that:

'Article 13 guarantees the availability at national level of a remedy to enforce the substance of the Convention rights and freedoms in whatever form they might happen to be secured in the domestic legal order. The effect of this article is thus to require the provision of a domestic remedy allowing the competent national authority both to deal with the substance of the relevant Convention complaint and to grant appropriate relief, although contracting states are afforded some discretion as to the manner in which they conform to their obligations under this provision. The scope of the obligation under article 13 varies depending on the nature of the applicant's complaint under the Convention. Nevertheless, the remedy required by article 13 must be "effective" in practice as well as in law, in particular in the sense that its exercise must not be unjustifiably hindered by the acts or omissions of the authorities of the respondent state.'[2].

1   (1997) 23 EHRR 553, E Ct HR, para 95 and (1996) 1 BHRC 625.
2   See, similarly, *Chahal v United Kingdom* (1996) 23 EHRR 413, E Ct HR, paras 145–155 (art 3 read with art 13).

4.13.4   In order to invoke art 13 it is not necessary to establish a violation of another Convention right or to demonstrate that the applicant would have succeeded before the national authority[1]. It is sufficient to twin art 13 with a *claim* for another violation[2]. Thus, in *Klass v Federal Republic of Germany*[3] the E Ct HR stated:

'Article 13 requires that where an individual considers himself to have been prejudiced by a measure allegedly in breach of the Convention, he should have a remedy before a national authority in order both to have his claim decided and, if appropriate, to obtain redress. Thus, article 13 must be interpreted as guaranteeing an "effective remedy before a national authority" to everyone who claims that his rights and freedoms under the Convention have been violated.'

1   *Costello-Roberts v United Kingdom* (1993) 19 EHRR 112, E Ct HR, para 40 (civil action for assault met with the defence of 'reasonable chastisement' of a pupil by a teacher).
2   This is despite the curious opening words of art 13 ('Everyone whose rights and freedoms as set forth in this Convention *are violated* shall have an effective remedy ...' (emphasis added)) which suggest that the article's purpose was to guarantee a national remedy for grievances already upheld in Strasbourg.
3   (1978) 2 EHRR 214, E Ct HR, para 64.

4.13.5   The claim of a Convention violation must be arguable not fanciful[1]. The test of arguability is closely linked to whether a claim is inadmissible (under art 35, formerly art 27) as manifestly ill-founded[2]. The E Ct HR has held that the tests of arguability and manifestly ill-founded are identical[3]. In *Powell and Rayner v United Kingdom*[4] the E Ct HR regarded the coherence of the dual system of the Convention's enforcement through arts 13 and 35 (formerly 27) as:

'at risk of being undermined if article 13 is interpreted as requiring a national law to make available an "effective remedy" for a grievance classified under article 27(2) as so weak as not to warrant examination on its merits at the international level.'

1   *Silver v United Kingdom* (1983) 5 EHRR 347, E Ct HR, para 113 (control of prisoners' correspondence; Application 10746/84 *Verein Alternatives Lokolradio, Bern v Switzerland* 49 DR 126 (1986), EComHR, page 143; and *Leander v Sweden* (1987) 9 EHRR 433, E Ct HR, para 79 (arguable, but ultimately unsuccessful, violation of another article held to be sufficient to establish a breach of ART 13).
2   See Harris, O'Boyle and Warbrick *Law of the European Convention on Human Rights* (Butterworths, 1995), pp 627–628.
3   *Boyle and Rice v United Kingdom* (1988) 10 EHRR 425, E Ct HR, para 54 (alleged discriminatory interferences with prisoners' rights to family life and private correspondence: held, no breach of art 13 although several breaches of other articles were found).
4   (1990) 12 EHRR 355, E Ct HR, para 33. For a criticism of this approach, see Hampson 39 ICLQ 891 (1990).

4.13.6 The national authority capable of providing the remedy need not be judicial[1], although a judicial remedy will normally[2] be good enough. What is important is that, in practice: (i) the remedial authority is sufficiently independent of the national body which is challenged[3]; and (ii) the authority's powers are sufficiently strong to provide effective redress[4]. The characteristics of judicial remedies[5] are used as indicia[6].

1   *Leander v Sweden* (1987) 9 EHRR 433, E Ct HR, para 77 and *Chahal v United Kingdom* (1996) 23 EHRR 413, E Ct HR, para 152. In *Klass v Federal Republic of Germany* (1978) 2 EHRR 214, E Ct HR, para 21 the E Ct HR was satisfied with the effectiveness of a parliamentary commission and in *Silver v United Kingdom* (1983) 5 EHRR 347, E Ct HR, para 116 was satisfied, in general, with a petition to the Home Secretary. Nor need the national authority satisfy the requirements of art 6(1) of the Convention: see *Golder v United Kingdom* (1975) 1 EHRR 524, E Ct HR, para 33.
2   In the *Greek Case* 12 YB 1 (1969), EComHR, at page 174 the Commission accepted that the Greek courts were not independent and impartial after the military coup.
3   *Silver v United Kingdom* (1983) 5 EHRR 347, E Ct HR, para 116 (remedy ineffective because the Home Secretary was not independent in relation to a complaint about the validity of an order or instruction given by him); *M and E F v Switzerland* 51 DR 283 (1987), EComHR; and *Leander v Sweden* (1987) 9 EHRR 433, E Ct HR, para 81 (the Chancellor of Justice held to be independent of the government in practice).
4   *Silver v United Kingdom* (1983) 5 EHRR 347, E Ct HR, para 115 (Prison Board of Visitors lack the necessary element of enforceability).
5   For example, impartiality, access and binding decisions: see paras **4.6.50–4.6.55**.
6   But they are not exhaustive: see *Leander v Sweden* (1987) 9 EHRR 433, E Ct HR (consistent, but unenforceable, national practice was held to be sufficiently effective) and*Soering v United Kingdom* (1989) 11 EHRR 439, E Ct HR (absence of interim relief against the Crown held not to breach art 13).

4.13.7 The most direct way to improve the effectiveness of national remedies would be to interpret art 13 to require the incorporation of the Convention into domestic law but the E Ct HR has declined to go so far[1]. Article 13 is not designed to give direct effect to the Convention by guaranteeing that the content of national laws and the decisions of national decision-makers conform with it but, rather, to provide the opportunity to test, in the national legal system, whether the Convention has been violated[2]. Thus, art 13 cannot be used to test the compatibility of primary legislation with the Convention. In *Leander v Sweden*[3] the E Ct HR stated:

'Article 13 does not guarantee a remedy allowing a contracting state's laws as such to be challenged before a national authority on the ground of being contrary to the Convention or equivalent domestic norms.'

Accordingly, claims challenging the validity of the Representation of the People Act 1949[4] and the Aircraft and Shipbuilding Industries Act 1977[5] have failed. The immunity is, however, confined to primary legislation. In *Abdulaziz, Cabales and Balkandali v United Kingdom*[6] the applicants, all women lawfully settled in the United Kingdom, had applied for their husbands to join them. The applications were refused under the Immigration Rules then in force, even though the requirements for women to join their settled husbands were less strict. The applicants' primary challenge was under arts 8 and 14 but, in relation to art 13, the United Kingdom contended that the Immigration Rules had legislative status (being laid before the House of Commons) and, therefore, did not need to be capable of challenge in domestic law. The Commission concluded that the Rules were neither primary nor purely delegated legislation but a 'hybrid of delegated legislation and administrative guidelines' drawn up by the Home Secretary and binding on the Immigration appellate Authority. The E Ct HR agreed that the Rules did not have the immunity conferred on legislation and, because there was no effective national remedy to measure the Rules against

Convention standards, held that art 13 had been violated. Article 13 must allow the substance of a Convention claim to be put[7]. The Commission has held that art 13 is violated where the domestic court hears a complaint but national law does not permit it to apply the Convention criteria to it[8].

1   *Ireland v United Kingdom* (1978) 2 EHRR 25, E Ct HR, para 239. Article 13 does not, therefore, require national legal systems to provide a remedy against a decision of the final domestic appellate court: see Applications 8603, 8722, 8723 and 8729/79 *Crocianietal v Italy* 22 DR 147 (1981), EComHR, at pages 223-224; Application 10746/84 *Verein Alternatives Lokalradio, Bern v Switzerland* 49 DR 126 (1986), EComHR, at page 142; Application 10153/82 and *Z and E v Austria* 49 DR 67 (1986), EComHR, at 74.
2   *Silver v United Kingdom* (1983) 5 EHRR 347, E Ct HR, para 113. Neither art 13 nor the Convention in general prescribe any particular *manner* for ensuring the effective domestic protection of the rights guaranteed. States are generally free to determine how they will discharge their international obligations.
3   (1987) 9 EHRR 433, E Ct HR, para 77. See also *James v United Kingdom* (1986) 8 EHRR 123, E Ct HR, para 85.
4   *Liberal Party v United Kingdom* (1980) 4 EHRR 106, EComHR (complaint that the United Kingdom's 'first past the post' electoral system disproportionately favoured the two main parties).
5   *Lithgow v United Kingdom* (1986) 8 EHRR 329, E Ct HR (challenge by shareholders in various shipbuilding companies, which had been nationalised, to the formula for compensation).
6   (1985) 7 EHRR 471, E Ct HR, esp paras 92–93. See para **4.14.5**. See also *Murray v United Kingdom* (1994) 19 EHRR 193, E Ct HR.
7   *Soering v United Kingdom* (1989) 11 EHRR 439, E Ct HR, para 122; *Vilvarajah v United Kingdom* (1991) 14 EHRR 248, E Ct HR, paras 117–127; and Application 11603/85 *Council of Civil Service Unions v United Kingdom* 50 DR 228 (1987) at 242–243.
8   Application 9471/81 *Warwick v United Kingdom* 60 DR 5 (1989) at 18 (held that a civil action offered no realistic hope of successfully challenging corporal punishment in school as a breach of art 3 because of the defence of 'reasonable chastisement' in domestic law). The Commission took a similar view in *Costello-Roberts v United Kingdom* (1993) 19 EHRR 112, E Ct HR, Com Rep para 59. The breach of Article 13 is even more stark when primary legislation precludes a remedy and the application of Convention criteria: see *Baggs v United Kingdom* (1985) 9 EHRR 235 EComHR (the Civil Aviation Act 1982 excluded liability in nuisance caused by aircraft noise near airports in certain circumstances) and *Firsoff v United Kingdom* (1993) 15 EHRR CD 111, EComHR (the Post Office Act 1969, s 29 gave the Post Office a statutory immunity from liability in tort for interferences with mail).

4.13.8   The E Ct HR has suggested that the more important the Convention right invoked, the more effective must be the national remedy[1]. On the other hand, the remedial effectiveness which is required by art 13 may be curtailed if justified by the type of state power in question (for example, remedies against intrusions for national security reasons)[2].

1   *Klass v Federal Republic of Germany* (1978) 2 EHRR 214, E Ct HR, para 55. In *Aksoy v Turkey* (1997) 23 EHRR 553, para 98, above para **4.13.3**, the E Ct HR observed that the nature of the right safeguarded has implications for art 13. In the context of art 3, 'given the fundamental importance of the prohibition of torture and the especially vulnerable position of torture victims, Article 13 imposes, without prejudice to any other remedy available under the domestic system, an obligation on States to carry out ... in addition to the payment of compensation where appropriate ... a thorough and effective investigation capable of leading to the identification and punishment of those responsible [for incidents of torture] and including effective access for the complainant to the investigatory procedure'. The court also held that implicit in the notion of an effective remedy is a duty to proceed to a 'prompt and impartial' investigation whenever there is a reasonable ground to believe that an act of torture has been committed.
2   In *Klass v Federal Republic of Germany* (1978) 2 EHRR 214, E Ct HR, paras 69-72, the E Ct HR considered a German law which permitted state surveillance without prior or later notice. It held that art 13 requires only a remedy that is 'as effective as can be' having regard to the restricted scope for legal recourse inherent in any system of secret surveillance. In *Leander v Sweden* (1987) 9 EHRR 433, E Ct HR, paras 80–84, it applied the same approach to a challenge seeking access to secret personal information. In the United Kingdom, this is relevant to the remedial provisions contained in the Interception of Communications Act 1985, s 7, the Security Service Act 1989, s 5 and the Intelligence

Services Act 1994, s 9. Challenges to those parts of the first two of these three statutes have not progressed beyond the Commission: see, respectively, Application 21482/93 *Christie v United Kingdom* 78-A DR 119 (1994) and Application 18601/91 *Esbester v United Kingdom* (1993) 18 EHRR CD 72. But see, in contrast, *Chahal v United Kingdom* (1996) 23 EHRR 413, E Ct HR, paras 148-155 (refusal of asylum and deportation of Sikh separatist leader defended by the Home Secretary on national security grounds: the E Ct HR found that the 'as effective as can be' approach was not appropriate in respect of a complaint that a person's deportation would expose him to a real risk of treatment in breach of art 3 to which national security issues were immaterial and found a violation of art 13).

4.13.9 It is unlikely that the closing words of art 13 ('notwithstanding that the violation has been committed by persons acting in an official capacity') are intended to do more than make clear that there can be no immunity for public or state officers carrying out their official functions. The words do not mean that the state is required to provide effective domestic remedies which can be invoked by individuals *inter se* for breaches of Convention rights. The state has no direct responsibility for breaches of the Convention by private individuals. But in some circumstances the Convention imposes a positive obligation on a state so that there is a duty to ensure that domestic law provides remedies for such breaches[1].

1   For example, *Gaskin v United Kingdom* (1989) 12 EHRR 36. See also para **2.6.3**, esp at n 3.

C   The effectiveness of the remedy

4.13.10 The national authority must be able properly to consider the applicant's substantive arguments based on the Convention[1]. Thus, although the Convention need not be incorporated, its norms and jurisprudence must be given some status in national law. The exact status and weight required is unclear. In a series of cases involving the United Kingdom, the Commission and E Ct HR have examined this question by reference to the scope for reliance upon Convention rights in judicial review proceedings. Despite the repeated emphasis given in domestic jurisprudence to the restrictive nature of judicial review as a means of challenging executive and administrative action, the E Ct HR[2] has in some cases accepted that an application for judicial review generally secures an adequate adjudication of claims based on substantive Convention rights[3].

1   *Soering v United Kingdom* (1989) 11 EHRR 439, E Ct HR, para 121. See, however, *Costello-Roberts v United Kingdom* (1993) 19 EHRR 112, E Ct HR where the E Ct HR made reference only to the technical availability of a remedy and none to whether the applicant would have been able to put forward arguments based on his Convention rights.
2   See paras **4.13.10–4.13.12**. The Commission took a rather more sceptical view.
3   For a similarly liberal approach in relation to Austria, see *VDSO and Gubi v Austria* (1994) 20 EHRR 55, E Ct HR, paras 54–55.

4.13.11 Prior to the coming into force of the Human Rights Act 1998, public authorities, such as ministers of the Crown, exercising discretionary powers, had no duty to act consistently with the Convention, although the courts recognised that in assessing whether the decision was reasonable (and so lawful) the human rights context would be taken into account[1].

1   See para **2.03**, especially at nn 8–9. See also de Smith, Woolf and Jowell *Judicial Review of Administrative Action* (5th edn, 1995), at pp 593–607; and *R v Secretary of State for the Home Department, ex p Ahmed and Patel* (30 July 1998, unreported), CA.

4.13.12   The United Kingdom has argued in Strasbourg that this very limited degree of scrutiny gives sufficient scope for Convention rights to be invoked before the national courts. In *Soering v United Kingdom*[1] the Commission disagreed. Mr Soering complained that his extradition to the United States of America would breach art 3 of the Convention (since he was likely to receive the death penalty in Virginia and suffer a prolonged wait for execution amounting to 'death row syndrome') but that judicial review excluded consideration of such a complaint in the national courts. The Commission accepted the argument (although, by a majority of one, it found no breach of art 3)[2]. But the E Ct HR rejected it[3], holding that the national court could have examined the strength of Mr Soering's claim to a violation of art 3 and could have concluded that it was irrational for the Home Secretary to have sought to extradite Mr Soering to a country where it was established that there was a real risk of such a violation. The United Kingdom was similarly successful in *Vilvarajah v United Kingdom*[4], a case concerning a claim for asylum by Tamil refugees from Sri Lanka. The Tamils arrived in the United kingdom at various times in 1987. Their asylum applications were rejected by the Home Secretary and they were removed to Sri Lanka[5]. Before their removal they lodged applications with the Commission claiming violations of arts 3 and 13. The Commission agreed that the Tamils had no effective means of ventilating their art 3 claim[6] before the national authorities. Judicial review effectively excluded it as a ground and the right of appeal was insufficient because it had to be pursued from Sri Lanka. The E Ct HR disagreed, holding that a national court could have concluded that it was irrational for the Home Secretary to remove the Tamils in breach of art 3. A different approach was adopted by the E Ct HR in *Chahal v United Kingdom*[7]. The applicant was a Sikh separatist leader who was refused asylum in the United Kingdom and faced with deportation to India on national security grounds. He was entitled to seek judicial review and to make representations to an advisory panel. As in the *Vilvarajah* case, he claimed, inter alia, that deportation would expose him to a real risk of torture or inhuman and degrading treatment contrary to art 3. The E Ct HR held unanimously that there had been a violation of art 13 read with art 3. The former demands independent scrutiny of the claim that there exist substantial grounds for fearing a real risk of treatment contrary to the latter. This scrutiny must be carried out without regard to what the person may have done to warrant expulsion or to any perceived threat to the national security of the expelling state. *Vilvarajah* was distinguished[8] because, in the national security context, judicial review of the substance of the decision is effectively acknowledged[9].

1   (1989) 11 EHRR 439.
2   Com Rep paras 114–168, especially 166. Before the Commission the United Kingdom did not argue that Mr Soering had failed to exhaust his local remedies by failing to seek judicial review: 58 DR 219 (1988). See also the Commission's rejection of the effectiveness of judicial review for the purposes of art 26 in Application 17419/90 *Wingrove v United Kingdom* 76-A DR 26 (1994).
3   (1989) 11 EHRR 439, paras 116–124.
4   (1991) 14 EHRR 248, E Ct HR, paras 124–126.
5   Although not until the decision to remove them had been (unsuccessfully) challenged in judicial review proceedings: see *R v Secretary of State for the Home Department, ex p Sivakumaran* [1988] AC 958 and [1988] 1 All ER 193, HL. On their return to Sri Lanka they were arrested, detained and ill-treated. Their out-of-country appeal was then allowed by the immigration adjudicator and they were allowed to return to the United Kingdom.
6   Which it rejected by a majority of one.
7   (1996) 23 EHRR 413m E Ct HR, paras 145–155.
8   Along with *Klass v Federal Republic of Germany* (1978) 2 EHRR 214, E Ct HR and *Leander v Sweden* (1987) 9 EHRR 433, E Ct HR. In *Chahal* the E Ct HR did not need to examine national security issues but only whether there was a real risk of Mr Chahal being exposed to treatment in breach of art 3 if he were to be deported (a more fundamental right).
9   Another case where judicial review has been found to be an effective remedy was *D v United Kingdom* (1997) 24 EHRR 423.

4.13.13 The E Ct HR has also been generous to contracting states in assessing the sufficiency of private law remedies. In *Costello-Roberts v United Kingdom*[1] (corporal punishment in independent schools) the E Ct HR refused to speculate about the outcome that would have been reached by the English courts applying the defence of 'reasonable chastisement' but was satisfied with merely a possibility that a local civil action could have given rise to a favourable result[2].

1   (1995) 19 EHRR 112, E Ct HR, especially para 40. But see also Application 25599/94 *A v United Kingdom* (Com Rep 18 September 1997) (corporal punishment in the home).
2   See also *Murray v United Kingdom* (1994) 19 EHRR 193, E Ct HR, paras 100–101 (taking and retention of photographs of applicant by police was permitted by primary legislation and, as such, no effective national remedy was required) and *Air Canada v United Kingdom* (1995) 20 EHRR 150, E Ct HR, paras 57–62.

4.13.14 Article 13 is intended to guarantee, in general terms, the availability of a suitable national procedure capable of providing a remedy in an appropriate case but not a favourable result on the facts of any particular case[1]. On the other hand, the availability of the remedy should not depend on the discretion of the national authority (to provide or withhold the remedy) or the discretion of the national body under challenge (to give effect to the remedy). Thus, in *Silver v United Kingdom*[2] the remedy of complaint to the Parliamentary Commissioner for Administration (the Ombudsman) was ineffective because it depended on voluntary compliance with a report presented to Parliament. The national authority cannot be advisory; an element of enforceability is needed[3]. Sometimes, however, a consistent national practice and a tradition of respecting pronouncements which are not formally binding will be good enough[4]. For example, the general practice of the Home Office refraining from implementing a decision against which leave to move for judicial review has been granted is sufficiently effective to make up for the difficulties of obtaining interim relief against the Crown[5]. Moreover, the discretionary nature of relief in judicial review proceedings will not breach art 13[6].

1   *Soering v United Kingdom* (1989) 11 EHRR 439 E Ct HR, para 120; Application 11603/85 *Council for Civil Service Unions v United Kingdom* 50 DR 228 (1987), EComHR, at 243; and *Murray v United Kingdom* (1994) 19 EHRR 193, E Ct HR, para 100.
2   (1983) 5 EHRR 347 E Ct HR, especially paras 54 and 115. See also *Campbell and Fell v United Kingdom* (1984) 7 EHRR 165, E Ct HR, especially paras 51 and 126. Similarly, *Silver v United Kingdom* (1983) 5 EHRR 347, E Ct HR; para **4.13.6** at n 3.
3   *Chahal v United Kingdom* (1996) 23 EHRR 413, E Ct HR, para 154.
4   *Leander v Sweden* (1987) 9 EHRR 433, E Ct HR, para 82.
5   *Soering v United Kingdom* (1989) 11 EHRR 439, E Ct HR, para 123 and *Vilvarajah v United Kingdom* (1992) 14 EHRR 248, E Ct HR, para 153. For confirmation that the English courts now have jurisdiction to grant interim relief against the Crown, see *Re M* [1994] 1 AC 377 sub nom *M v Home Office* [1993] 3 All ER 537, HL.
6   *Vilvarajah v United Kingdom* (1992) 14 EHRR 248, E Ct HR, para 126.

4.13.15 The remedial authority must be different from, and sufficiently independent of, the authority alleged to have breached the Convention[1]. This standard can, however, be met by a right of internal review or appeal to a person within the same decision-making body: provided the second decision-maker looks at the matter de novo and does not merely rubber-stamp the decision of the first[2]. 'Independent' under art 6(1) of the Convention means independent of the executive, of the parties and of Parliament[3]. Because this is a higher standard than that imposed by art 13, a body which satisfies this standard will be independent for the purposes of art 13.

1   *Silver v United Kingdom* (1983) 5 EHRR 347, E Ct HR, para 116 and *Leander v Sweden* (1987) 9 EHRR 433 E Ct HR para 81.

2   Application 12573/86 *M and EF v Switzerland* 51 DR 283 (1987), EComHR. For example, because both are bound by the same internal policy.
3   *Campbell and Fell v United Kingdom* (1984) 7 EHRR 165, E Ct HR, para 81. See paras **4.6.51– 4.6.52**.

4.13.16   The remedy must be available in practice, not just in theory[1]. The remedy must, for example, be available before the implementation of the challenged decision robs it of its effectiveness. Thus, in *Vilvarajah v United Kingdom* the Commission decided that a right of appeal against the refusal of asylum exercisable only from outside the United Kingdom was not effective in practice to consider an allegation that the return itself violated art 3 of the Convention[2].

1   See, generally, *Airey v Ireland* (1979) 2 EHRR 305, E Ct HR.
2   (1992) 14 EHRR 248, EComHR, para 153. In practice, the right of appeal would normally have to be exercised from inside the very state where the applicant claimed to fear persecution. The E Ct HR did not consider the point because it was persuaded that judicial review, a remedy capable of having pre-emptive effect, was sufficient. See also *Andersson (M and R) v Sweden* (1992) 14 EHRR 615, E Ct HR, paras 98–103.

4.13.17   Finally, the effectiveness of national redress must be judged in cumulative terms. Although no single national remedy may, taken alone, be sufficiently effective to satisfy art 13 and none is an appeal from the other, the E Ct HR has stated that the aggregate of such remedies may do so[1]. This is a difficult principle to understand. *Silver v United Kingdom* concerned interference with correspondence between a prisoner and his lawyer by the prison authorities under the Prison Rules (made by the Home Secretary under the Prison Act 1964, as amended). The United Kingdom relied upon four possible remedies: application to the prison's Board of Visitors, application to the Parliamentary Commissioner for Administration (the Ombudsman), petition to the Home Secretary and application to the High Court for judicial review. The first two were incapable of being effective because neither the Board of Visitors nor the Commissioner could give decisions binding upon the prison authorities. The third was effective as regards decisions applying the Prison Rules. A petition to the Home Secretary was, in effect, an appeal against the decision of a prison governor. The fourth was effective for challenges to the legality of the Prison Rules themselves (which the third was not because the Home Secretary was incapable of reviewing his *own* rules). The effectiveness of these remedies did not, however, depend upon their *aggregation*. Rather the *Silver* case demonstrates that where a complaint is made against more than one type of decision, an effective national remedy must be available against each type. It has been pointed out, moreover, that it is difficult to understand how the principle of the aggregation of remedies operates[2]. If a single remedy is effective, there is no need to consider others. If none is effective, and none is an appeal from another, why should the accumulation of a series of inadequate remedies be sufficient? The E Ct HR has, however, not yet explained the practical impact of the aggregation of remedies.

1   *Silver v United Kingdom* (1983) 5 EHRR 347, E Ct HR, paras 116–118; *Leander v Sweden* (1987) 9 EHRR 433, E Ct HR, paras 77–84; *Lithgow v United Kingdom* (1986) 8 EHRR 329, E Ct HR, paras 20–207; and *Chahal v United Kingdom* (1996) 23 EHRR 413, E Ct HR, para 145.
2   See Harris, O'Boyle and Warbrick *Law of the European Convention of Human Rights* (1995, Butterworths) pages 457–458 and Drzemczewski and Warbrick (1987) 7 YEL 364–367.

> ## Article 14   Freedom from discrimination in respect of Convention rights
>
> The enjoyment of the rights and freedoms set forth in this Convention shall be secured without discrimination on any ground such as sex, race, colour, language, religion, political or other opinion, national or social origin, association with a national minority, property, birth or other status.

A   Introduction

4.14.1   The Convention, unlike other international human rights instruments[1], contains no free-standing guarantee of equal treatment without discrimination. Instead, art 14 is restricted to a parasitic prohibition of discrimination in relation only to the substantive rights and freedoms set out elsewhere in the Convention. As a result, many important areas of discrimination, notably in the fields of employment[2] and other economic and social rights[3], fall outside the scope of the article.

1   See in particular the International Covenant on Civil and Political Rights (1966), especially art 26 (see para **5.14**); the International Convention on the Elimination of All Forms of Racial Discrimination (1966) (see para **5.28**); and the International Convention on the Elimination of Discrimination against Women (1979) (see para **5.40**).
2   As to which, see the International Labour Organisation's Discrimination (Employment and Occupation) Convention (1958); and the European Social Charter (1961) (see para **5.91**), preamble and first protocol, art 1. Note also that certain employment-related benefits may fall within the ambit of art 8 of the Convention, or of art 1 of the first protocol, and thus give rise to art 14 claims: see respectively *Petrovic v Austria* (1998) 5 BHRC 232, E Ct HR (parental leave allowance) and *Gaygusuz v Austria* (1997) 23 EHRR 364, E Ct HR, paras 36–41 (emergency social assistance payments).
3   In the UK, discrimination on grounds of sex (or marital status), race, disability and (in Northern Ireland) religious belief or political opinion is prohibited by statute in the fields of (inter alia) employment and the provision of goods and services: see respectively the Sex Discrimination Acts 1975 and 1986 (together with the Equal Pay Act 1970); the Race Relations Act 1976; the Disability Discrimination Act 1995; and the Fair Employment (Northern Ireland) Acts 1976 and 1989, and para **5.16**.

4.14.2   The fundamental nature of the principle of equality of treatment[1] is recognised not only in international law[2] but also in European Community law[3] and by the common law[4]. The principle is, moreover, enshrined in the constitutions of common law jurisdictions outside the United Kingdom[5].

1   A principle specifically recognised by the E Ct HR in A 257-E *Salesi v Italy* (1998) 26 EHRR 187, E Ct HR, para 19.
2   See the United Nations Charter, art 1(3); the Universal Declaration of Human Rights (1948), arts 2 and 7; and the instruments referred to at para **4.14.1**, n 1.
3   The general principle of equality has been held by the European Court of Justice (ECJ) to be 'one of the fundamental principles of Community law': Case 152/81: *Ferrario v Commission* [1983] ECR 2357 at 2367. The ECJ draws inspiration and guidance from the constitutional traditions common to its member states and from international treaties such as the Convention: see eg Case 4/73: *Nold v Commission* [1974] ECR 491, ECJ. The EC Treaty contains specific enunciations of the principle of equality in, inter alia, art 6 (prohibiting discrimination on grounds of nationality) and art 119 (which enshrines the principle of equal pay for men and women).
4   Equality of treatment is a principle of lawful administration laid down by the common law: see de Smith, Woolf and Jowell *Judicial Review of Administrative Action* (5th edn, 1995), paras 13-040 to 13-045; *Matadeen v Pointu* [1998] 3 WLR 18, PC, per Lord Hoffmann at 26F–G (treating like cases alike and unlike cases differently is a 'general axiom of rational behaviour'); and para **5.15**.

5   See eg the Canadian Charter of Rights and Freedoms, s 15 (equal protection without discrimination);
     the Indian Constitution, art 14 (equality before the law and equal protection of the law); the New
     Zealand Bill of Rights Act 1990, ss 19 (freedom from discrimination) and 20 (rights of minorities);
     the South African Constitution, s 8 (equal protection and freedom from discrimination) and the
     United States Constitution, Fourteenth Amendment (equal protection of the law).

B   Article 14

1   SCOPE

4.14.3   The guarantee of non-discrimination[1] in art 14 extends only to the substantive
rights and freedoms set out in the Convention[2]. This includes the substantive rights set
out in the Protocols, which are to be regarded as additional articles to the Convention[3].

1   The E Ct HR has yet to make clear whether the article, in addition to placing a negative obligation
     on states to avoid discrimination, involves a positive obligation on states to take action to secure
     equal treatment. (Cf the position under art 8 of the Convention, where the existence of positive
     obligations is well-established.)
2   See para **4.14.1** and, eg, *Pierre-Bloch v France* (1997) 26 EHRR 202, E Ct HR, para 62.
3   First protocol, art 5; fourth protocol, art 6(1); sixth protocol, art 6; seventh protocol, art 7.

4.14.4   The application of the article does not, however, presuppose a breach of any
of the substantive provisions of the Convention: such an interpretation would leave no
practical function for art 14. A measure which in itself conforms with the substantive
article of the Convention may violate art 14 because it is discriminatory in nature[1].

1   *Belgian Linguistics Case (No 2)* (1979-80) 1 EHRR 252, E Ct HR, para 9; *Airey v Ireland* (1979)
     2 EHRR 305, E Ct HR, para 30; *Marckx v Belgium* (1979-80) 2 EHRR 330, E Ct HR, para 32.

4.14.5   In particular, art 14 extends not only to those elements of a substantive right
which a state is required by the Convention to guarantee, but also to aspects of the right
which the state chooses to guarantee, without being obliged under the Convention to
do so[1]. For example[2], art 6 of the Convention does not compel states to institute a
system of appeal courts[3]. However, there would be a violation of art 14 if a state
provided a right of appeal to some individuals, while unjustifiably debarring others in
similar circumstances from appealing. Accordingly, it is not open to a state seeking to
avoid liability under art 14 to argue that it has acted more generously than the
Convention requires. Thus, in *Abdulaziz, Cabales and Balkandali v United Kingdom*[4],
the United Kingdom allowed resident, alien men with the right to remain to be joined
by their wives (who had no independent right to enter and remain in the United
Kingdom). The same treatment was not afforded to resident, alien women, whose
husbands were, accordingly, not allowed to join them in the United Kingdom in similar
circumstances. There was no obligation on the United Kingdom, under the Convention,
to allow the wives to join their husbands. The E Ct HR nevertheless considered that
the question fell within the ambit of the substantive right to respect for family life[5] and
went on to assess whether the differential treatment was discriminatory contrary to
art 14[6].

1   *Belgian Linguistics Case (No 2)* (1979-80) 1 EHRR 252, E Ct HR, para 9.
2   This example was given by the E Ct HR in the *Belgian Linguistics Case (No 2)* (1979-80) 1 EHRR
     252, E Ct HR, para 9.
3   See [cross-ref to Article 6 section on this point]
4   (1985) 7 EHRR 471, E Ct HR, para 82. Contrast, on similar facts Application 11278/84 *Family K
     and W v Netherlands* 43 DR 216 (1985), EComHR (rights of spouses to obtain Dutch nationality:

Commission held that art 14 did not apply because the right to nationality, unlike the right to family life, is not a Convention right)
5 See para **4.8** on art 8.
6 The E Ct HR found a violation of art 14 read with art 8: see paras 70–85 of its judgment.

4.14.6 A claim under art 14 cannot, however, succeed unless the facts of the case fall within the 'ambit' of one or more of the substantive articles[1]. This test will be satisfied if the 'subject-matter of the disadvantage [complained of] ... constitutes one of the modalities of the exercise of a right guaranteed'[2] or the measures complained of are 'linked to the exercise of a right guaranteed'[3]. Thus, in *Petrovic v Austria*, a claim relating to parental leave allowance was held to come within the scope of art 8 of the Convention because by granting such an allowance states were 'able to demonstrate their respect for family life within the meaning of [that article]': art 14 (taken together with art 8) was therefore applicable[4].

1 See eg *Van der Mussele v Belgium* (1984) 6 EHRR 163, E Ct HR (requirement that a student advocate should undertake defence work without remuneration was within the ambit of art 4); *Rasmussen v Denmark* (1985) 7 EHRR 371, E Ct HR (discrimination relating to paternity proceedings was within ambit of arts 6 and 8); *Inze v Austria* (1988) 10 EHRR 394, E Ct HR (discrimination against an illegitimate child heir in relation to inheritance fell, on the facts, within the ambit of art 1 of the first protocol); *Botta v Italy* (1998) 26 EHRR 241, E Ct HR, paras 39–40 (right of disabled person to access to holiday beach did not fall within ambit of art 8, so art 14 inapplicable).
2 *National Union of Belgian Police v Belgium* (1979-80) 1 EHRR 578, E Ct HR, para 45.
3 *Schmidt and Dahlström v Sweden* (1976) 1 EHRR 632, E Ct HR, para 39.
4 Judgment of 27 March 1998, E Ct HR, paras 28–29.

4.14.7 If an applicant alleges a violation of a substantive article both taken alone and in conjunction with art 14, then if the E Ct HR finds that there is no separate violation of the substantive article, it will usually[1] go on to consider the claim under art 14. If, on the other hand, the E Ct HR finds a violation of the substantive article taken alone, then while it is not precluded from going on to consider art 14[2], the court frequently does not do so[3]. The test applied by the court in deciding whether to consider an art 14 claim in these circumstances is whether a clear inequality of treatment in the enjoyment of the substantive right is a 'fundamental aspect' of the case[4].

1 But cf, for example, *X, Y and Z v United Kingdom* (1997) 24 EHRR 143, E Ct HR, para 56 (majority of E Ct HR holding it 'unnecessary' to consider complaint under art 14 of discrimination against transsexuals, because it was 'tantamount to a restatement of' the complaint under art 8, which the court had rejected).
2 *Marckx v Belgium* (1979-80) 2 EHRR 330, E Ct HR.
3 For examples, see *Kroon v Netherlands* (1995) 19 EHRR 263, E Ct HR, para 42; *Tinnelly and McElduff v United Kingdom* (1998) Times, 16 July.
4 *Airey v Ireland* (1979) 2 EHRR 305, E Ct HR, para 30. For cases where the E Ct HR considered it unnecessary to examine the claim under art 14 even though the essence of the complaint was of differential treatment, see *Vereinigung Demokratischer Soldaten Österreichs and Gubi v Austria* (1994) 20 EHRR 56, E Ct HR, para 56 (applicant publishing a periodical for servicemen complained that it was the only such publication denied access to distribution by the army); *Tsirlis and Kouloumpas v Greece* (1997) 25 EHRR 198, E Ct HR, para 70 (E Ct HR found breach of applicants' right to liberty was 'of a discriminatory nature' (para 60), yet found it unnecessary to consider art 14 aspect of case).

2 PROHIBITED GROUNDS OF DISCRIMINATION

4.14.8 Article 14 prohibits discrimination on grounds of sex, race[1], colour, language, religion, political or other opinion, national[2] or social origin, association with a national minority, property, birth or 'other status'. The list of prohibited grounds is, thus, not exhaustive. The term 'other status' includes sexual orientation[3], marital status[4], illegitimacy[5] and professional[6] or military[7] status.

1   Racial discrimination may also amount to 'degrading' treatment contrary to the substantive right in art 3 of the Convention. For allegations of racial bias by juries, contrary to art 6 of the Convention, see paras **4.5.55–4.5.57**.
2   The Convention, however, permits states to place restrictions on the political activities of aliens: see para **4.16** on art 16.
3   See eg Application 10389/83 *Johnson v United Kingdom* 47 DR 72 (1986), EComHR; *Dudgeon v United Kingdom* (1983) 4 EHRR 149, E Ct HR. Cf the present position in European Community and United Kingdom domestic employment law, where discrimination on grounds of sexual orientation is not unlawful: Application 25186/94 *Sutherland v United Kingdom*, report of 1 July 1997, EComHR, para 51 (leaving open the question of whether discrimination based on sexual orientation properly to be considered as on grounds of 'sex' or of 'other status'; Case C-249/96: *Grant v South-West Trains Ltd* [1998] All ER (EC) 193, ECJ, but cf *Smith v Gardner Merchant Ltd* [1998] IRLR 510, CA; but note that the Treaty of Amsterdam will insert into the EC Treaty an art 6a which will allow for legislation prohibiting such discrimination. Discrimination on grounds of gender re-assignment is, by contrast, already prohibited in the employment field by EC law: Case C-13/94: *P v S and Cornwall County Council* [1996] ECR I-2143, ECJ. For failed claims of discrimination against transsexuals under the Convention, see, eg, *X, Y and Z v United Kingdom* (1997) 24 EHRR 143, E Ct HR; *Sheffield and Horsham v United Kingdom* (1998) 27 EHRR 163, E Ct HR. For recent consideration of sexual orientation discrimination outside Europe, see *Romer v Evans* (1996) 1 BHRC 178 (Supreme Court, United States of America: ordinances removing right to claim discrimination on grounds of sexual orientation violated Constitutional guarantee of equal protection of the law); *National Coalition for Gay and Lesbian Equality v Minister of Justice*, unreported, judgment of 9 October 1998 (Constitutional Court of South Africa)(common law offence of sodomy violated constitutional rights to equality, dignity and privacy); *Vriend v Alberta* (1998) 4 BHRC 140 (Supreme Court of Canada)(exclusion of sexual orientation from grounds of discrimination prohibited under provincial law was unjustified violation of principle of equality before the law set out in s 15 of the Canadian Charter of Rights and Freedoms); and *Quilter v A-G of New Zealand* (1998) 3 BHRC 461 (Court of Appeal, New Zealand: New Zealand Bill of Rights did not require reinterpretation of existing legislation so as to allow same-sex marriages).
4   Note that in the fields, inter alia, of employment and the provision of goods and services, discrimination on grounds of marital status is also prohibited in United Kingdom domestic law: Sex Discrimination Act 1975, s 3.
5   Eg *Inze v Austria* (1988) 10 EHRR 394, E Ct HR.
6   *Van der Mussele v Belgium* (1984) 6 EHRR 163, E Ct HR.
7   *Engel v Netherlands* (1979-80) 1 EHRR 647, E Ct HR.

4.14.9   Although art 14 specifically outlaws discrimination on grounds of 'property'[1], the E Ct HR has shown itself reluctant to hold that the article prohibits discrimination on grounds of financial status. In *Airey v Ireland*[2], where the question arose directly, the court preferred to hold that a failure to provide civil legal aid to an indigent litigant was a substantive breach of art 6, taken alone[3], then finding it unnecessary to consider the applicant's claim under that article taken with art 14[4].

1   And between categories of property-owners: *James v United Kingdom* (1986) 8 EHRR 123, E Ct HR.
2   (1979-80) 2 EHRR 305, E Ct HR, para 30.
3   See para **4.6.17** on *Airey v Ireland* (1979) 2 EHRR 305, E Ct HR.
4   See also *Johnston v Ireland* (1987) 9 EHRR 203, E Ct HR (applicants argued that the fact that they could not afford to travel abroad to obtain a divorce, not available in Ireland, amounted to discrimination on grounds of financial status: E Ct HR held that the true ground of discrimination was domicile not financial means).

3   THE CONCEPT OF DISCRIMINATION

(a)   Introduction

4.14.10   A claim of discrimination contrary to art 14 will be made out if the applicant shows that he or she has (within the ambit of a Convention right[1]) been treated differently, on a prohibited ground[2], from people in a similar, or analogous, situation; and if, further, that different treatment has no reasonable and objective justification[3].

1   See paras **4.14.3–4.14.6** above.
2   See para **4.14.8** above.
3   *Belgian Linguistic Case (No 2)* (1979-80) 1 EHRR 252, E Ct HR, para 9 at para 10.

4.14.11   The E Ct HR has yet to rule definitively on whether art 14 prohibits indirect discrimination[1] (as well as direct discrimination). It would be surprising, however, if such discrimination were held to be excluded from the scope of the article given that the concept of indirect discrimination is well established in European Community law[2] and elsewhere[3].

1   That is, discrimination resulting from a rule or practice applied equally to all individuals without differentiation but which has a disproportionate and unjustified adverse impact on members of a particular group or minority.
2   See eg Case 170/84: *Bilka-Kaufhaus GmbH v Weber von Hartz* [1987] ICR 110, [1987] IRLR 317, ECJ; Case C-127/92: *Enderby v Frenchay Health Authority* [1994] ICR 112, [1993] IRLR 591, ECJ.
3   Indirect, as well as direct, discrimination is prohibited in the United Kingdom by the Sex Discrimination Act 1975, s 1(1)(b) and the Race Relations Act 1976, s 1(1)(b). The Disability Discrimination Act 1995 does not contain a precisely similar proscription on indirect discrimination, although a similar result is achieved by its broad prohibition on discrimination for a reason which relates to a person's disability (s 5), together with the duty to make reasonable adjustments (s 6). The origin of the legal concept of indirect discrimination is found in United States law – see *Griggs v Duke Power* Co 401 US 424 (1971)(US Supreme Court). The concept is also established in Canadian law: see eg *Eldridge v A-G of British Columbia and another* (1997) 3 BHRC 137, Can SC.

4.14.12   Positive or reverse discrimination will not violate the article if it has an objective and reasonable justification[1].

1   See the *Belgian Linguistics Case (No 2)* (1979-80) 1 EHRR 252, E Ct HR, para 9, at para 10 ('certain legal inequalities tend only to correct factual inequalities'); and eg Application 11089/84 *DG and DW Lindsay v United Kingdom* 49 DR 181 (1986) at 190-1, EComHR (tax advantage for married women had 'an objective and reasonable justification in the aim of providing positive discrimination' to encourage married women back to work). Positive discrimination (or 'affirmative action') is also permissible, in certain circumstances, under the International Covenant on Civil and Political Rights, art 26: Human Rights Committee General Comment 18, and decision in *Stalla Costa v Uruguay* (1985) No 198. As to the position in European Community sex discrimination law, see Case C-409/95: *Marschall v Land Nordrhein-Westfalen* [1998] IRLR 39, ECJ (German law giving preference to equally qualified women for promotion where they were under-represented at the level of the relevant post, but with provision for exceptions to be made allowing male candidates to be promoted in specific cases, not contrary to the Equal Treatment Directive (76/207/EEC)); but cf Case C-450/93 *Kalanke v Freie Hansestadt Bremen* [1995] IRLR 660, ECJ. Note also the provision in the Treaty of Amsterdam amending art 119 to allow positive discrimination in certain circumstances. The position in UK sex and race discrimination law is that in general, subject to specified exceptions for training in areas where minorities are under-represented (Sex Discrimination Act 1975, ss 47–48; Race Relations Act 1976, ss 35, 37 and 38), positive discrimination is unlawful (see, eg, *Jepson v Labour Party* [1996] IRLR 116, IT) (but cf the duty to make reasonable adjustments set out in the Disability Discrimination Act 1995).

(b)   Differential treatment of persons in comparable situations

4.14.13   The burden lies upon the applicant to establish[1] that he or she has been less favourably treated than others in comparable circumstances, and that the basis for this differential treatment was a prohibited ground[2]. The E Ct HR has shown itself unsympathetic to claims by applicants that the true reason for less favourable treatment is a covert or hidden discriminatory motive other than that put forward by the state[3].

1 An allegation of discrimination contrary to art 14 will fail if, on the facts, there is a lack of evidence of differential treatment on a prohibited ground: for examples, see *Selçuk and Asker v Turkey* (1998) 26 EHRR 477, E Ct HR, para 102; *Mentes v Turkey* (1998) 26 EHRR 595, E Ct HR, para 96.
2 See above, para **4.14.8**.
3 See eg *Abdulaziz, Cabales and Balkandali v United Kingdom* (1985) 7 EHRR 471, E Ct HR, para 82 at paras 85–86; *Handyside v United Kingdom* (1979-80) 1 EHRR 737, E Ct HR, paras 52, 66; *Stjerna v Finland* (1994) 24 EHRR 195, E Ct HR, paras 49–51.

4.14.14 If the E Ct HR does not consider the situation of the applicant and his or her comparator(s) to be analogous (or 'relevantly similar'[1]), there will be no obligation on the state to justify the differential treatment complained of, and no discrimination contrary to art 14[2]. For example, in *Stubbings v United Kingdom*[3], the applicant victims of childhood sexual abuse sought to compare themselves with victims of injuries inflicted negligently, rather than intentionally, in relation to whom more generous limitation periods applied. The court rejected the victims' claim under art 14, describing the comparison sought to be made as 'artificial'[4]. It may, further, be difficult for applicants to establish, as a matter of evidence, that those who have been more favourably treated are in an analogous situation to their own[5].

1 *National & Provincial Building Society v United Kingdom* (1997) 25 EHRR 127, E Ct HR, para 88.
2 For claims which failed on this ground, see eg *Van der Mussele v Belgium* (1983) 6 EHRR 163, E Ct HR; *Lithgow v United Kingdom* (1986) 8 EHRR 329, E Ct HR; *Spadea and Scalabrino v Italy* (1995) 21 EHRR 482, E Ct HR, para 46.
3 (1996) 23 EHRR 213, E Ct HR, paras 68–71.
4 (1996) 23 EHRR 213, E Ct HR, para 71.
5 As in *Fredin v Sweden* (1991) 13 EHRR 784, E Ct HR, para 60 (the applicants were the only business engaged in extracting gravel to have their permit revoked: their argument, that it was for the state to explain the respects in which their business differed from others, was rejected, and their claim failed because they had not established that the applicants were similar to the surviving operators).

C Objective and reasonable justification for differential treatment

1 GENERALLY

4.14.15 A difference in treatment will be held to be discriminatory (contrary to art 14) if it has 'no objective and reasonable justification'[1]. In order to prove such justification, the respondent government must show that the difference in treatment pursues a 'legitimate aim', and that there is a 'reasonable relationship of proportionality between the means employed and the aim sought to be realised'[2].

1 *Belgian Linguistic Case (No2)* (1979-80) 1 EHRR 252, E Ct HR, para 9, at para 32.
2 See eg *Darby v Sweden* (1991) 13 EHRR 774, E Ct HR, para 31; *Petrovic v Austria* (1998) 5 BHRC 232, E Ct HR, at para 30. For the test of objective justification (for sex discrimination) enunciated by the ECJ see Case 170/84: *Bilka-Kaufhaus GmbH v Weber von Hartz* [1986] ECR 1607, ECJ. For justification in other jurisdictions, see *Romer v Evans* (1996) 1 BHRC 178 at 187H–I and *United States v State of Virginia* (1997) 1 BHRC 265 (Supreme Court, United States of America); *Prinsloo v van der Linde* (1997) 2 BHRC 334 (South African Constitutional Court). For the test of justification under the International Covenant on Civil and Political Rights, art 26, see *Adam v Czech Republic* (1997) 1 BHRC 451, UN Human Rights Committee, at para 12.4, 457G–I.

(a) Legitimate aim

4.14.16 The state must put forward a rational aim for any differential treatment proved by the applicant to have occurred: if it does not do so, the applicant's claim under art 14 will succeed[1]. The E Ct HR has accepted as legitimate for the purposes of the article the aims (for example) of supporting and encouraging the traditional family; of protecting the labour market and public order; and of developing linguistic unity[2].

1   As in *Darby v Sweden* (1991) 13 EHRR 774, E Ct HR, para 31, where the state declined to put forward any justification to the E Ct HR.
2   See, respectively, *Marckx v Belgium* (1979-80) 2 EHRR 330, E Ct HR, para 32 and (in relation to the rights of unmarried fathers) *McMichael v United Kingdom* (1995) 20 EHRR 205, E Ct HR, para 98 (but cf *Fraser v Children's Court* (1997) 1 BHRC 607, Constitutional Court, South Africa); *Abdulaziz, Cabales and Balkandali v United Kingdom* (1985) 7 EHRR 471, E Ct HR, para 82; *Belgian Linguistic Case (No 2)* (1979-80) 1 EHRR 252, E Ct HR, para 9.

(b)   Proportionality

4.14.17   If differential treatment is established by the state to pursue a legitimate aim, the E Ct HR will go on to consider whether there is a reasonable relationship of proportionality between the means employed and the aim sought to be achieved[1]. What is required is that the differences in treatment 'strike a fair balance between the protection of the interests of the community and respect for the rights and freedoms safeguarded by the Convention'[2]. A claim of justification by a state may well fail if it is based upon generalisations without objective evidence in support thereof[3].

1   If an applicant can identify a non-discriminatory alternative means of achieving the same end, this may be evidence of a lack of proportionality: see eg *Inze v Austria* (1987) 10 EHRR 394, E Ct HR, at para 44. On the principle of proportionality, see para **3.10**.
2   *Belgian Linguistic Case (No 2)* (1968) 1 EHRR 252, E Ct HR, para 9.
3   See eg the E Ct HR's rejection in *Marckx v Belgium* (1979-80) 2 EHRR 330, E Ct HR, para 32, of a suggestion (unsupported by any evidence) that mothers of illegitimate children were more likely to abandon them. For a similar approach in a United States case, see *United States v State of Virginia* (1997) 1 BHRC 265, Supreme Court, United States of America.

(c)   The margin of appreciation

4.14.18   Contracting states enjoy a margin of appreciation[1] in relation to the question of justification, which depends upon the circumstances, subject matter and background of the case[2].

1   As to which, see generally para **3.20**.
2   *Rasmussen v Denmark* (1985) 7 EHRR 371, E Ct HR, para 40.

4.14.19   The breadth of the margin of appreciation will vary according to the grounds upon which persons are differently treated. The E Ct HR has identified discrimination on certain grounds as particularly serious[1], with the result that very weighty reasons will have to be advanced by a state to justify such discrimination[2]. Discrimination on grounds of sex[3], illegitimacy[4] and nationality[5] have been expressly stated by the court to fall within this category. Discrimination on grounds of race (outside the sphere of nationality) has not been explicitly identified in this way; but it seems certain (given the approach taken in the *East African Asians*[6], *Abdulaziz*[7] and *Gaygusuz*[8] cases) that it would attract the same protection.

1   Compare the notion of 'suspect categories' in United States constitutional law: see McKean*Equality and Discrimination under International Law* (1983) at pp 237–240.
2   *Abdulaziz, Cabales and Balkandali v United Kingdom* (1985) 7 EHRR 471, E Ct HR, para 82, at para 78.
3   *Abdulaziz, Cabales and Balkandali v United Kingdom* (1985) 7 EHRR 471, E Ct HR, para 82; and see eg *Schuler-Zgraggen v Switzerland* (1993) 16 EHRR 405, E Ct HR; *Burghartz v Switzerland* (1994) 18 EHRR 101, E Ct HR; *Petrovic v Austria* (1998) 5 BHRC 232, E Ct HR, at para 37. Note

also the statement in *Van Raalte v Netherlands* (1997) 24 EHRR 503, E Ct HR, para 42 that 'compelling reasons' must be adduced to justify differences in treatment as between men and women in relation to (gender-specific) exemptions from the obligation to pay social security contributions. As to discrimination on grounds of sexual orientation, see Application 25186/94 *Sutherland v United Kingdom*, report of 1 July 1997, EComHR, paras 56–57 (margin of appreciation 'must be relatively narrow' where discrimination between heterosexuals and homosexuals).

4   *Inze v Austria* (1988) 10 EHRR 394, E Ct HR.
5   *Gaygusuz v Austria* (1997) 23 EHRR 365, E Ct HR, para 42.
6   (1981) 3 EHRR 76, EComHR.
7   *Abdulaziz, Cabales and Balkandali v United Kingdom* (1985) 7 EHRR 471, E Ct HR, para 82.
8   *Gaygusuz v Austria* (1997) 23 EHRR 365, E Ct HR, para 42.

4.14.20   The assessment of whether a state has acted within its margin of appreciation may, further, depend on the existence, or otherwise, of a common European standard (in the Convention states) relating to the matter at issue[1].

1   See *Rasmussen v Denmark* (1985) 7 EHRR 371, E Ct HR, para 30 (Danish law distinguishing between husbands and wives in relation to time limits for paternity proceedings did not differ from that in several other European states: held, the distinction fell within Denmark's margin of appreciation). For a recent example, see *Petrovic v Austria* (1998) 5 BHRC 232, E Ct HR, at paras 38 and 42 (Austrian system, subsequently replaced, allowed for payment of parental leave allowances to mothers but not fathers; no common European standard for payment of such allowances to fathers; indeed, a 'very great disparity' existed between the legal systems of the contracting states in the field, with very few granting allowances to fathers; held, despite need for 'very weighty reasons' to justify sex discrimination, no violation of art 14). See also para **3.05** at nn 3 and 4.

4.14.21   The E Ct HR may also have regard to the existence of international agreements prohibiting discrimination on particular grounds when assessing the weight to be given to particular types of discrimination[1].

1   See *Inze v Austria* (1988) 10 EHRR 394, E Ct HR (illegitimacy: E Ct HR referred to 1977 European Convention on the Legal Status of Children Born out of Wedlock).

Article 15   Derogations

1.   In time of war or other public emergency threatening the life of the nation any High Contracting Party may take measures derogating from its obligations under this Convention to the extent strictly required by the exigencies of the situation, provided that such measures are not inconsistent with its other obligations under international law.

2.   No derogation from Article 2, except in respect of deaths resulting from lawful acts of war, or from Articles 3, 4 (paragraph 1) and 7 shall be made under this provision.

3.   Any High Contracting Party availing itself of this right of derogation shall keep the Secretary General of the Council of Europe fully informed of the measures which it has taken and the reasons therefor. It shall also inform the Secretary General of the Council of Europe when such measures have ceased to operate and the provisions of the Convention are again being fully executed.

4.15.1   For commentary see para **2.14**.

> ## Article 16   Restrictions on the political activities of aliens
>
> Nothing in Articles 10[1], 11[2] and 14[3] shall be regarded as preventing the High Contracting Parties from imposing restrictions on the political activity of aliens.

1   The right to freedom of expression: see para **4.10**.
2   The right to freedom of assembly and association (including the freedom to join a trade union): see para **4.11**.
3   The prohibition on discrimination: see para **4.14**.

4.16.1   Article 1 of the Convention provides that everyone within the jurisdiction of a contracting state is to enjoy Convention rights. However, art 16 creates an exception permitting considerable interference with the political activities of aliens[1] and over-rides the guarantees for nationals contained in arts 10, 11 and 14. Although art 14 prohibits discrimination on the grounds of, inter alia, national origin in the enjoyment of the rights and freedoms set forth in the Convention, the state may, therefore, discriminate against aliens in relation to any Convention rights concerned with political activity: for example, the right to vote and to stand for election may be based on nationality criteria[2].

1   Aliens include stateless persons: see explanatory reports on the fourth protocol, H(71)11 (1971), p 50. Explanatory reports provide guidance only and are not binding on the Commission or E Ct HR.
2   See *Mathieu-Mohin and Clerfayt v Belgium* (1988) 10 EHRR 1, E Ct HR, para 54 (French-speaking Belgian citizens and elected representatives prevented from participating in Flemish-speaking elections and assemblies). The E Ct HR held that the right to vote guaranteed by art 3 of the first protocol 'under conditions which will ensure the free expression of the opinion of *the people* in the choice of the legislature' (emphasis added) contained a principle of equality of treatment of all 'citizens'. See, similarly, the International Convention on Civil and Political Rights, art 25 (which guarantees the right to vote only to citizens) and the United Nations Declaration on the Human Rights of Individuals who are not Nationals of the Country in which They Live (GA Res 40/53) (which gives no protection to aliens' political rights).

4.16.2   The apparent width of art 16 has, however, been limited by the adoption of a restrictive interpretation of the term 'alien'[1]. In addition, like all exceptions to the human rights guaranteed by the Convention, art 16 is strictly construed[2]. In *Piermont v France*[3] the E Ct HR considered a complaint brought by a member of the European Parliament, representing a German constituency. She had visited French Polynesia at the invitation of a local politician and, while there, had taken part in a pro-independence and anti-nuclear demonstration. Just before her departure she was served with an order expelling and excluding her and she was later excluded from New Caledonia. She alleged a violation of her right to freedom of expression under art 10 read with art 14. The E Ct HR upheld this allegation[4] and rejected the French government's defence that the restrictions on the applicant's political activity were permitted by art 16[5]. The E Ct HR refused to accept that the application of art 16 was precluded by the applicant's European citizenship since, at the relevant time (1986), the Community treaties did not recognise any such citizenship[6]. Nevertheless, it considered that her possession of the nationality of a member state of the European Union and, in addition, her status as a member of the European Parliament prevented reliance on art 16 against her (especially in view of the participation of the people of French overseas territories in European Parliament elections). The dissenting minority[7] emphasised that the applicant was 'indubitably an alien in the eyes of French law' at the relevant time and felt themselves compelled to give art 16 at least some relevance. However, they accepted that the E Ct HR should take account of the object and purpose of art 16 in assessing, under art 10.2, the proportionality of the interference with the applicant's freedom of expression. Both the majority and the minority appear to have recognised that art 16 is becoming increasingly outdated in an age of transnational organisations and cross-border politics[8]. As long ago as 1977 the Parliamentary Assembly of the Council of Europe advocated the deletion of art 16[9], and it seems likely that it will be construed very restrictively so as not to impair the essence of the rights guaranteed by arts 10, 11 and 14 of the Convention.

1   It remains to be seen how narrow an interpretation of 'political activity' will be adopted.
2   See para **3.12**.
3   *Piermont v France* (1995) 20 EHRR 301, E Ct HR.
4   *Piermont v France* (1995) 20 EHRR 301, E Ct HR, paras 50–59 and 65–86.
5   *Piermont v France* (1995) 20 EHRR 301, E Ct HR, paras 60–64.
6   Had the chronology been different, however, the majority imply that the applicant would have been able to invoke her European citizenship under the Maastricht Treaty (EC Treaty, art 8(1)).
7   *Piermont v France* (1995) 20 EHRR 301, E Ct HR, paras 4–5 of the joint partly dissenting opinion of Judges Ryssdal, Matscher, Sir John Freeland and Jungwiert.
8   The Commission also emphasised the new notion of 'aliens' enshrined by the European Union and the transnational role of the European Parliament: see paras 57–69 of the Commission's opinion.
9   Recommendation 799 (1977) on the Political Rights and Position of Aliens, 28th Ordinary Session of the Parliamentary Assembly (3rd Part).

4.16.3   In addition to art 16 of the Convention, the fourth and seventh protocols confer a variety of rights on aliens and nationals and duties on contracting states as follows:

(1)   freedom of movement within a state and freedom to leave its territory[1];

(2)   the right of a national not to be expelled from, and the right to enter, a state's territory[2];

(3)   freedom of aliens from collective expulsion[3];

(4)   restrictions on the individual expulsion of aliens[4].

Although the United Kingdom has not yet ratified either of these protocols, their provisions are described here since there are reasonable prospects that they will be ratified and, meanwhile, they may have indirect relevance to rights under European Community law[5]. At international level, freedom of movement is expressly protected by the International Covenant on Civil and Political Rights, art 12, which provides that everyone lawfully within the territory of a state shall, within that territory, have the right to liberty of movement and freedom to choose his residence[6]. The International Covenant on Civil and Political Rights, art 13, provides that an alien lawfully in the territory of a state may be expelled only in pursuance of a decision reached in accordance with law and only after he has been allowed certain procedural safeguards (the right to receive reasons, to have a review and to be represented). However, the United Kingdom has made a wide and general reservation covering immigration and nationality for its reports to the United Nations Human Rights Committee[7].

1   Article 2 of the fourth protocol.
2   Article 3 of the fourth protocol.
3   Article 4 of the fourth protocol.
4   Article 1 of the seventh protocol.
5   Like the sixth protocol, the rights contained in the fourth and seventh protocols have been added mainly

to reflect the wider range of rights included in the International Covenant on Civil and Politicial Rights: see arts 12 and 13. The fourth protocol was signed by the United Kingdom in 1963 but has never been ratified because of concerns about the exact extent of the duty to recognise a right of entry: see the White Paper *Rights Brought Home: The Human Rights Bill* (Cm 3782) at para 4.10. The White Paper at para 4.11, also states that the government regards the rights guaranteed in the fourth protocol as important rights which should be given formal recognition in domestic law. But it continues: 'we also believe that existing laws in relation to different categories of British nationals must be maintained. It will be possible to ratify the fourth protocol only if the potential conflicts with our domestic laws can be resolved. This remains under consideration but [the government does] not propose to ratify the fourth protocol at present'. The seventh protocol has not yet been ratified by the United Kingdom because of concerns that a few provisions of domestic law may be incompatible with it: see the White Paper at para 4.15. The White Paper also states, however, that the government believes that it would be particularly helpful to give the principles contained in the seventh protocol the same legal status as other Convention rights by ratifying and incorporating the seventh protocol. A promise is given that this will be done once legislation has removed the incompatibilities. As with so many human rights, however, freedom of movement has a long pedigree. The Magna Carta, chapter 42 provided that '[i]t shall be lawful for any person, for the future, to go out of our Kingdom, and to return, safely and securely, by land or by water, saving his allegiance to us, unless it be in time of war, for some short space, for the common good of the Kingdom ...'. So far as European Community law is concerned, see Case C-168/91: *Konstandinis v Stadt Altensteig* [1993] ECR I-1191, ECJ where, at para 46 of his opinion, Advocate-General Jacobs suggested that an EU national has the right to be treated according to a common code of fundamental values, including the Convention, when in the territory of another member state.

6   Article 12(1). Article 12(2) provides that everyone shall be free to leave any country, including his own. Article 12(3) precludes restrictions on the rights guaranteed by art 12(1) and (2) except such as are provided by law or are necessary to protect national security, public order, public health or morals or the right and freedoms of others. Article 12(4) provides that no one shall be arbitrarily deprived of the right to enter his own country.

7   The reservation was made when the United Kingdom ratified the Convention and reads: 'The Government of the United Kingdom reserve the right to continue to apply such immigration legislation governing entry into, stay in and departure from the United Kingdom as they may deem necessary from time to time; and accordingly their acceptance of Article 12(4) and of the other provisions of the Covenant is subject to the provisions of any such legislation as regards persons not at the time having the right under the law of the United Kingdom to enter and remain in the United Kingdom. The United Kingdom also reserves a similar right in regard to each of its dependent territories.' See CCPR/C/Rev 3, 32 (1992).

Article 2 of the Fourth Protocol   Freedom of movement within a state and freedom to leave its territory

1.   Everyone lawfully within the territory of a state shall, within that territory, have the right to liberty of movement and freedom to choose his residence.

2.   Everyone shall be free to leave any country, including his own.

3.   No restrictions shall be placed on the exercise of these rights other than such as are in accordance with law and are necessary in a democratic society in the interests of national security or public safety, for the maintenance of 'ordre public', for the prevention of crime, for the protection of health or morals, or for the protection of the rights and freedoms of others.

4.   The rights set forth in paragraph 1 may also be subject, in particular areas, to restrictions imposed in accordance with law and justified by the public interest in a democratic society.

4.16.4   Article 2(1) provides for freedom of movement and residence within a state's territory[1] for everyone[2] lawfully[3] there. This right contemplates much less severe limits on a person's movements than the guarantee contained in art 5(1) of the Convention not to be deprived of one's liberty[4]. In *Piermont v France*[5] the E Ct HR held that there had been no violation of art 2 of the fourth protocol: first, the applicant was served with the expulsion order only as she was leaving French Polynesia so no restrictions had been placed on her freedom of movement while she was there; second, she was served with the order expelling her from New Caledonia on her arrival there so was never 'lawfully within' that territory.

1   A state's embassy abroad is not part of its territory: see Application 17392/90 *V v Denmark* (1992) 15 EHRR CD 28.
2   This includes nationals of the state concerned, nationals of other states and stateless persons.
3   The state retains the right to regulate, through its domestic law, the terms and conditions on which an alien may enter and remain within its territory.
4   On art 5.1, see para **4.5**. The relationship between the two provisions was discussed in *Guzzardi v Italy* (1981) 3 EHRR 333, E Ct HR paras 92–93 (residence confined by judicial order to a small village on a remote island: held, that the 'intensity' of the confinement is determinative and that such factors as the duration, social effects and manner of the confinement are as relevant as geographical limits).
5   (1995) 20 EHRR 301, E Ct HR, paras 40–49. See para **4.16.2**.

4.16.5   Article 2(1) must be read subject to the exceptions contained in art 2(3). These mirror the exceptions set out in arts 8(2), 9(2), 10(2) and 11(2) of the Convention and should be interpreted in the same way[1]. Article 2(4) contains a more novel, and potentially wider, exception: namely, *'in particular areas ... restrictions imposed in accordance with law and justified by the public interest in a democratic society'*. However, like the exceptions set out in art 2(3), it must be construed narrowly and in accordance with the principle of proportionality[2]. Its most obvious application is to permit planning controls which zone residential locations away from commercial, industrial or agricultural areas.

1   See paras **3.12–3.16**.
2   See para **3.10**.

4.16.6   Under art 2(3), the following have been regarded by the Commission as falling within the exceptions: moving mobile home residents from one site to another[1]; withdrawing, after a criminal conviction, a liquor licence linked to a place of residence[2]; a requirement that a bankrupt should not leave a defined area without permission[3]; and bail conditions restricting freedom of movement[4]. However, no exception can apply unless the restriction is imposed 'in accordance with law' and is necessary on the facts of the individual case[5].

1   Application 13628/88 *Van de Vin v Netherlands* 3 HRCD 93 (1992) (justified 'for the maintenance of "ordre public"').
2   Application 8901/80 *X v Belgium* 23 DR 237 (1980) (justified 'for the prevention of crime' as well as 'the protection of health or morals').
3   Application 8988/80 *X v Belgium* 24 DR 198 (1981) (justified 'for the maintenance of "ordre public"' and 'for the protection of rights and freedoms of others').
4   Application 10670/83 *Schmid v Austria* 44 DR 195 (1985) ('justified by the public interest in a democratic society').
5   In *Raimondo v Italy* (1994) 18 EHRR 237, E Ct HR, paras 39-40 (1994) a court order that a mafia suspect should be kept under house arrest was held by the E Ct HR to be justified as necessary 'for the maintenance of "ordre public"' and 'for the prevention of crime'. But the E Ct HR went on to find a violation of art 2 of the fourth protocol in relation to a period of 18 days during which, unknown to the applicant, the arrest order had been revoked. This was a breach of Italy's own procedures and, so, not 'in accordance with law'. See also Application 12541/86 *Ciancimino v Italy* 70 DR 103 (1991).

4.16.7   Under art 2(2), everyone must be free to leave[1] any country, including his own. This right is subject to the exceptions contained in art 2(3) but not that set out in art 2(4). Accordingly, a national or alien may be imprisoned or have his passport seized in, respectively, his own or a foreign state in relation to pending criminal proceedings provided this is done genuinely 'for the maintenance of "ordre public"' or 'the prevention of crime'[2].

1   The right of an individual physically to leave does not imply a right also to remove all one's possessions: see Application 10653/83 *S v Sweden* 42 DR 224 (1985) and *Loizidou v Turkey* (1995) 20 EHRR 99, E Ct HR, esp Com Rep para 98.
2   Application 7680/76 *X v Federal Republic of Germany* 9 DR 190 (1977) and Application 3962/69 *X v Federal Republic of German* 13 YB 688 (1984) (imprisonment); Application 10670/83 *Schmid v Austria* 44 DR 195 (1985) and Application 10307/83 *M v Federal Republic of Germany* 37 DR 113 (1984) (withdrawal of passport).

Article 3 of the Fourth Protocol   The right of a national not to be expelled from, and the right to enter, a state's territory

1.   No one shall be expelled, by means either of an individual or of a collective measure, from the territory of the state of which he is a national.
2.   No one shall be deprived of the right to enter the territory of the state of which he is a national.

4.16.8   A person is expelled from a state of which he is a national when he is 'obliged permanently to leave the territory ... without being left the possibility of returning later'[1]. Expulsion does not include extradition[2]. Moreover, the person being expelled must already have been recognised as a national of the expelling state. The existence of a pending application for nationality is insufficient, although if the application is later granted a right to return as a national will arise[3]. It is for each contracting state to define its citizenship requirements and to identify its citizens. Although it is for the Convention authorities to interpret the terms of art 3 of the fourth protocol, it is very unlikely that they would decline to recognise a state's grant or refusal of its own nationality[4].

1   Application 6189/73 *X v Austria and Federal Republic of Germany* 46 CD 214 (1974). An order that a person be deported from the United Kingdom under the Immigration Act 1971, ss 3(5) and (6) and 5, as amended, may not satisfy that description. It continues in force until such time as it is revoked by the Home Secretary. Application for revocation can be made at any time but normally three years must have elapsed from the making of the deportation order. The revocation of the order does not, however, authorise re-admission. It merely qualifies the ex-deportee to apply for admission under the Immigration Rules when he will usually need to identify a material change of circumstances or new information coming to light since deportation: see the Immigration Act 1971, s 5(2), as amended, and the Immigration Rules, paras 390–392 (HC 395). See, generally, Ian Macdonald and Nicholas Blake *Macdonald's Immigration Law and Practice* (4th edn), paras 15.78–15.80.
2   Application 6242/73 *Bruckmann v Federal Republic of Germany* 17 YB 458 (1974). As to extradition and art 3 of the Convention, see paras **4.3.18–4.3.23**.
3   Application 10564/83 *L v Federal Republic of Germany* 40 DR 262 (1984); Application 3916/69 *X v Sweden* 32 CD 51 (1969); and Application 3745/68 *X v Federal Republic of Germany* 31 CD 107 (1969).
4   Indeed, a principle prohibiting a state from withdrawing nationality in order to expel him was deliberately excluded from art 3 of the fourth protocol: see explanatory report on the fourth protocol, H(71)11 (1971), p 48.

4.16.9   The exclusion of a person from the state[1] of his nationality would violate art 3(2) of the fourth protocol but it may, depending on the circumstances, also violate art 3 of the Convention[2]. Apart from certain categories of Commonwealth citizen, only British citizens (and no other classes of British passport holder) enjoy the right of abode in the United Kingdom[3].

1   For the purposes of the fourth protocol, a state's embassy abroad is not part of its territory: see Application 17392/90 *V v Denmark* (1992) 15 EHRR CD 28.
2   See the separate opinion of Mr Fawcett in the *East African Asians Case* (1973) 3 EHRR 76 Com Rep para 242. As to art 3, see paras **4.3.18–4.3.23**.
3   The Immigration Act 1971, ss 1 and 2, as amended by the British Nationality Act 1981, s 39. British citizens are expressly exempt from deportation and an existing deportation order ceases to have effect if the deportee becomes a British citizen: see the Immigration Act 1971, ss 3(5) and (6) and 5(2), as amended. See, generally, Ian Macdonald and Nicholas Blake *Macdonald's Immigration Law and Practice* (4th edn), ch 6, especially paras 6.75–6.81, and Laurie Fransman *Fransman's British Nationality Law* (2nd edn).

Article 4 of the Fourth Protocol   The freedom of aliens from collective expulsion

Collective expulsion of aliens is prohibited.

4.16.10   Although aliens have no right under the Convention to 'enter, reside or remain in a particular country'[1], they are, once there, given some protection against expulsion. Collective expulsion means 'any measure of the competent authority compelling aliens as a group to leave the country, except where such a measure is taken after and on the basis of a reasonable and objective examination of the particular cases of each individual alien of the group'[2]. The expulsion of individual aliens[3] is dealt with by art 1 of the seventh protocol[4]. 'Expulsion' should be given the same meaning as in art 3 of the fourth protocol[5].

1   Application 12068/86 *Paramanathan v Federal Republic of Germany* 51 DR 237 (1986) at 240.
2   Application 7011/75 *Becker v Denmark* 4 DR 215 (1975) at 235; Application 14209/88 *A v Netherlands* 59 DR 274 (1988) (the mere fact that a number of asylum-seekers from the same country are all refused asylum on similar grounds does not amount to collective expulsion where each receives an individualised, reasoned decision); and Application 18560/91 *A, B and C v France* (1993) 15 EHRR CD 39, EComHR.
3   As to the meaning of 'aliens', see para **4.16**, n 2 and para **4.16.2**.
4   See paras **4.16.11–4.16.14**.
5   See paras **4.16.8–4.16.9**.

Article 1 of the Seventh Protocol   Restrictions on the individual expulsion of aliens

1.   An alien lawfully resident in the territory of a state shall not be expelled therefrom except in pursuance of a decision reached in accordance with law and shall be allowed:
(a) to submit reasons against his expulsion,
(b) to have his case reviewed, and
(c) to be represented for these purposes before the competent authority or a person or persons designated by that authority.
2.   An alien may be expelled before the exercise of his rights under paragraph 1, a, b and c of this Article, when such expulsion is necessary in the interests of public order or is grounded on reasons of national security.

4.16.11   Unlike art 4 of the fourth protocol, art 1 of the seventh protocol does not prohibit expulsion. It demands, much more modestly, merely that the expulsion procedure applied to individual aliens[1] should comply with the rule of law. Expulsion has the same meaning as in arts 3 and 4 of the fourth protocol and does not include extradition[2]. In practice, the impact of this article in domestic law is even more limited. It applies only to aliens who are expelled while 'lawfully resident' in the state's territory. Under United Kingdom immigration law, an alien is expelled either by removal or deportation. Broadly, those who have never been granted a valid leave to enter and so are illegal entrants (for example because they entered clandestinely or because they obtained leave to enter by deception) are removed; while those who have been granted leave to enter but who can no longer rely on that leave (for example because it has expired or because they have broken conditions applying to it) are deported. In both cases the person is being expelled precisely because he is not 'lawfully resident' when expulsion action is commenced[3].

1   As to the meaning of 'aliens', see para **4.16.1**, n 1 and para **4.16.2**.
2   See paras **4.16.8–14.16.9**.
3   A person who is granted 'temporary admission' pending consideration of whether to grant leave to enter is not 'lawfully resident'. The explanatory memorandum on the seventh protocol (CE Doc H (83) 3, page 7) explains that those who are still in transit or who have been admitted for non-residential purposes or who are awaiting a decision on residence are not included. The words 'lawfully resident' must mean more than just lawfully present. As a matter of immigration law, a person with temporary admission is deemed by s 11 of the Immigration Act 1971 not to have entered the United Kingdom.

4.16.12   The protection afforded to an alien by the review referred to in art 1(1)(b) falls far short of that conferred on others by art 6[1] of the Convention. First, the 'competent authority' need not be a judicial body. Second, it need not be independent of the body deciding on expulsion. The expelling body may review its own decisions. Third, it may have only the power to recommend rather than decide. Fourth, it need not confer an oral hearing.

1   See para **4.6**.

4.16.13   The expulsion of an alien (whether collectively or individually) may raise issues under art 8 of the Convention if it would prejudice the enjoyment of family life[1]. There seems no reason to suppose that the words 'in accordance with law' in art 1 of the seventh protocol should have a meaning different from that in art 8(2) of the Convention[2].

1   See para **4.8**.
2   See para **3.13**.

4.16.14   The exception set out in art 1(2) of the seventh protocol should be construed narrowly, applying the principle of proportionality. It is designed only to delay, not to deny, the procedural rights contained in art 1(1)[1].

1   The explanatory memorandum on the seventh protocol, above (CE Doc H (83) 3, p 9) suggests that the state should demonstrate the necessary requirements of public order in each individual case or class of case but that the mere assertion of national security is conclusive.

4.17

> ## Article 17   Prohibition of abuse of rights
>
> Nothing in this Convention may be interpreted as implying for any State, group or person any right to engage in any activity or perform any act aimed at the destruction of any of the rights and freedoms set forth herein or at their limitation to a greater extent than is provided for in the Convention.

4.17.1   For commentary see para **3.17**.

4.18

Article 18   Limitations on use of restrictions on rights

The restrictions permitted under this Convention to the said rights and freedoms shall not be applied for any purpose other than those for which they have been prescribed.

4.18.1   For commentary see para **3.14**.

Article 1 of the First Protocol   Right to property

Every natural or legal person is entitled to the peaceful enjoyment of his possessions. No one shall be deprived of his possessions except in the public interest and subject to the conditions provided for by law and by the general principles of international law.

The preceding provisions shall not, however, in any way impair the right of a state to enforce such laws at it deems necessary to control the use of property in accordance with the general interest or to secure the payment of taxes or other contributions or penalties.

A   Introduction

4.19.1   Article 1 of the first protocol to the Convention in substance guarantees the right of property[1]. This right is recognised in the Universal Declaration of Human Rights[2], in the law of the United Kingdom[3], and in the constitutions of other common law jurisdictions[4]. The inclusion of the right to property in the European Convention, however, was controversial. After an initial failure to reach agreement between states[5], the provision was left over until the first protocol. The formulation that was eventually adopted provides a qualified right to property.

1   *Marckx v Belgium* (1979) 2 EHRR 330, E Ct HR, para 63.
2   Article 17 of the Universal Declaration of Human Rights provides: '1. Everyone has the right to own property alone as well as in association with others. 2. No one shall be arbitrarily deprived of his property.'. See Alfredsson, in Eide et al, *The Universal Declaration of Human Rights* (1992) pp 252–262. See ch 1, especially paras **1.10–1.11**, and para **7.04**.
3   See *Entick v Carrington* (1765) 19 State Tr 1029: 'The great end for which men entered society was to secure their property. That right is preserved sacred and incommunicable in all instances where it has not been abridged by some public law for the good of the whole.' (per Camden CJ at 1060); *A-G v De Keyser's Royal Hotel* [1920] AC 508, HL.
4   For the position in Canada, see Hogg, *Constitutional Law of Canada* (1992), pp 703–709, and *Manitoba Fisheries v R* [1979] 1 SCR 101. For Australia, see PH Lane, *The Australian Constitution* (1997), ch 23. For the United States, see Antieau, *Modern Constitutional Law* (1997), ch 20. As to the position in South Africa, see *Harksen v Lane NO* (1998) 3 BHRC 519. For Zimbabwe, see *Davies v Minister of Land, Agriculture and Water Development* [1997] 1 LRC 123. See also the decisions of the Privy Council concerning the Constitution of Mauritius in *Société United Docks v Government of Mauritius* [1985] AC 585 and *La Compagnie Sucrière de Bel Ombre Ltée v Government of Mauritius* [1995] 3 LRC 494.
5   See Robertson, 28 BYIL 359 (1951) and Peukert (1981) 2 HRLJ 37 at 38–42.

B   Article 1 of the first protocol

1   SCOPE

4.19.2   A wide range of economic interests are protected under art 1 of the first protocol. These include movable or immovable property, tangible or intangible interests, such as shares[1], patents[2], a landlord's entitlement to rent[3], an arbitral award[4], the economic interests connected with the running of a business[5], the right to exercise a profession[6], the entitlement to a pension[7], a legitimate expectation that a certain state of affairs will apply[8], and a legal claim (provided it is a concrete, adequately specified claim)[9].

1   See Applications 8588/79, 8589/79 *Bramelid and Malmstrom v Sweden* 29 DR 64 (1982), EComHR.
2   See Application 12633/87 *Smith Kline and French Laboratories v Netherlands* 66 DR 70 (1990), EComHR.
3   See *Mellacher v Austria* (1989) 12 EHRR 391, E Ct HR, paras 43–44; and Application 10741/84 *S v United Kingdom* 41 DR 226 (1984), EComHR, concerning the benefit of a restrictive covenant and entitlement to annual rent. See also Application 11185/84 *Herrick v United Kingdom* (1985) 8 EHRR 66, EComHR, where the entitlement to use property was held to fall within the scope of art 1 of the first protocol.
4   See *Stran Greek Refineries v Greece* (1994) 19 EHRR 293, E Ct HR, paras 61–62.
5   See *Tre Traktörer Aktiebolag v Sweden* (1989) 13 EHRR 309, E Ct HR, para 53. See also Application 10426/83 *Pudas v Sweden* 40 DR 234 (1984), EComHR.
6   See *Van Marle v Netherlands* (1986) 8 EHRR 483, E Ct HR, paras 41–42. The E Ct HR held that the applicants' professional clientele constituted an asset protected by art 1 of the first protocol.
7   Application 5849/72 *Müller v Austria* 3 DR 25 (1975), EComHR.
8   See *Pine Valley Developments Ltd v Ireland* (1991) 14 EHRR 319, E Ct HR, para 51.
9   See *Pressos Compania Naviera SA v Belgium* (1995) 21 EHRR 301, E Ct HR; *National Provincial Building Society v United Kingdom* (1997) 25 EHRR 127, E Ct HR, paras 69–70.

4.19.3   The protection of art 1 of the first protocol does not apply unless and until it is possible to lay a claim to the property concerned[1]. Thus, expectations which a person has as an heir during the testator's lifetime are not protected, as it is only existing property and not the right to acquire property which is protected[2].

1   See Application 8410/78 *X v Federal Republic of Germany* 18 DR 216 (1979), EComHR, where the Commission held that an expectation that notaries' fees would not be reduced by law was not protected under art 1 of the protocol unless and until there was an actual claim for services rendered.
2   See *Marckx v Belgium* (1979) 2 EHRR 330, E Ct HR, para 50; *Inze v Austria* (1987) 10 EHRR 394, E Ct HR, paras 37–38.

4.19.4   In order to rely on art 1 of the first protocol an applicant needs to establish that he has a property right which he is entitled to enjoy as a matter of domestic law[1]. However, the fact that domestic law does not recognise a particular interest as a property right is not conclusive, as the concept of 'possession' is autonomous[2].

1   See Application 11716/85 *S v United Kingdom* 47 DR 274 (1986), EComHR, where the Commission held that the occupation of property without a legal right was not protected under art 1 of the protocol.
2   See *Tre Traktörer Aktiebolag v Sweden* (1989) 13 EHRR 309, E Ct HR, para 53, recognising that the established economic interests in connection with the running of a business attracted the protection of art 1 of the protocol, although they did not constitute property rights as a matter of Swedish law.

4.19.5   Corporate bodies are protected, provided that the applicant is the real victim of a violation[1]. Although a substantial majority shareholder has been held to be a victim in respect of damage suffered by a company[2], the general rule is that shareholders have no claim based on damage to a company. Piercing the corporate veil will be justified only in exceptional circumstances, in particular when it is clearly established that the company cannot apply through the organs set up pursuant to its articles of incorporation, or through its liquidators[3].

1   See Application 9266/81 *Yarrow v United Kingdom* 30 DR 155 (1983), EComHR, at 185.
2   See Application 1706/62 *X v Austria* 21 CD 34 (1966), EComHR, at 44.
3   See Application 9266/81 *Yarrow v United Kingdom* 30 DR 155 (1983); *Agrotexim v Greece* (1995) 21 EHRR 250, E Ct HR.

2 THE THREE RULES

4.19.6 In its landmark judgment in *Sporrong and Lönnroth v Sweden*[1] the E Ct HR observed that art 1 of the first protocol comprises three distinct rules. The first rule, which is of a general nature, states the principle of peaceful enjoyment of property. It is set out in the first sentence of the first paragraph. The second rule covers deprivation of possessions and subjects it to certain conditions. It appears in the second sentence of the same paragraph. The third rule recognises that states are entitled, amongst other things, to control the use of property in accordance with the general interest, by enforcing such laws as they deem necessary for that purpose. This rule is contained in the second paragraph of art 1 of the first protocol. This observation has frequently been reiterated and applied by the E Ct HR in subsequent judgments[2].

1 (1982) 5 EHRR 35, E Ct HR, para 61.
2 See eg. *James v United Kingdom* (1986) 8 EHRR 123, E Ct HR, para 37; *Lithgow v United Kingdom* (1986) 8 EHRR 329, E Ct HR, para 106; *AGOSI v United Kingdom* (1986) 9 EHRR 1, E Ct HR, para 48; *Erkner and Hofauer v Austria* (1987) 9 EHRR 464, E Ct HR, para 73; *Poiss v Austria* (1987) 10 EHRR 231, E Ct HR, para 63; *Mellacher v Austria* (1989) 12 EHRR 391, E Ct HR, para 42; *Tre Traktörer Aktiebolag v Sweden* (1989) 13 EHRR 309, E Ct HR, para 54; *Holy Monasteries v Greece* (1994) 20 EHRR 1, E Ct HR, para 56; *Pressos Compania Naviera SA v Belgium* (1995) 21 EHRR 301, E Ct HR, para 33; *Scollo v Italy* (1996) 22 EHRR 514, E Ct HR, para 26; *National Provincial Building Society v United Kingdom* (1997) 25 EHRR 127, E Ct HR, para 78.

4.19.7 In considering whether there has been a violation of art 1 of the first protocol, it is necessary first to consider which of these three rules apply. However, the three rules are not 'distinct' in the sense of being unconnected: the second and third rules are concerned with particular interferences with the right to peaceful enjoyment of property and should therefore be construed in the light of the general principle enunciated in the first rule[1].

1 See eg *Lithgow v United Kingdom* (1986) 8 EHRR 329, E Ct HR, para 106; *Mellacher v Austria* (1989) 12 EHRR 391, E Ct HR, para 42; *National Provincial Building Society v United Kingdom* (1997) 25 EHRR 127, E Ct HR, para 78.

(a) The first rule

4.19.8 The first rule applies where the relevant interference with property falls short of a taking, and is not intended to control the use of property, but nevertheless has the effect of interfering with the use or enjoyment of property[1]. Thus, in *Erkner and Hofauer v Austria*[2] the provisional transfer of the applicants' land to other landowners was neither a formal nor a de facto expropriation, and was not essentially designed to restrict or control the use of land, with the result that the second and third rules did not apply. Consequently, the first rule applied. Similarly, in *Stran Greek Refineries v Greece*[3] where an arbitral award in the applicants' favour had been made void and unenforceable by legislation, the interference was held to fall within the first rule of art 1 of the first protocol, as it did not involve a de facto or de jure deprivation of property within the second rule, nor a measure to control the use of property.

1 See *Sporrong and Lönnroth v Sweden* (1982) 5 EHRR 35, E Ct HR, para 65. For the application of the first rule, see also Application 7456/76 *Wiggins v United Kingdom* 13 DR 40 (1978), EComHR, at pp 46–47; Application 7889/77 *Arrondelle v United Kingdom* 19 DR 186 (1980), EComHR.
2 (1987) 9 EHRR 464, E Ct HR, para 74.
3 (1994) 19 EHRR 293, E Ct HR, para 68.

(b)   The second rule

4.19.9   In determining whether there has been a deprivation of possessions within the second rule, it is necessary to consider not only whether there has been a formal taking or expropriation of property, but to:

'look behind the appearances and investigate the realities of the situation complained of … Since the Convention is intended to guarantee rights that are "practical and effective"…, it has to be ascertained whether the situation amounted to a de facto expropriation'[1].

1   See *Sporrong and Lönnroth v Sweden* (1982) 5 EHRR 35, E Ct HR, para 63; *Vasilescu v Romania*, judgment of the E Ct HR (22 May 1998, unreported), paras 44–54. This approach to the question of what amounts to a taking of property coincides with the approach adopted by general international law, that: '… measures taken by a state can interfere with property rights to such an extent that these rights are rendered so useless that they must be deemed to have been expropriated, even though the state does not purport to have expropriated them and the legal title to the property formally remains with the original owner': *Case concerning Starrett Housing Corpn and the Government of the Islamic Republic of Iran*; Interlocutory award of December 1983 by Iran-United States Claims Tribunal; 23 ILM (1984) 1090. See also *Société United Docks v Government of Mauritius* [1985] AC 585 and *La Compagnie Sucrière de Bel Ombre Ltée v Government of Mauritius* [1995] 3 LRC 494.

4.19.10   Thus, in *Papamichalopoulos v Greece*[1] the applicants were deprived of the use of (but not the title to) their land by virtue of a Greek law passed in 1967, which transferred the land to the Navy Fund. The applicants applied unsuccessfully to the Greek courts for restoration of their land. The E Ct HR considered that the applicants' loss of all ability to dispose of the land in issue, taken together with the failure of the attempts made to remedy the situation complained of, entailed sufficiently serious consequences for the applicants' land de facto to have been expropriated in a manner incompatible with their right to the peaceful enjoyment of their possessions.

1   (1993) 16 EHRR 440, E Ct HR, para 45. See also *James v United Kingdom* (1986) 8 EHRR 123, E Ct HR, para 38; *Hentrich v France* (1994) 18 EHRR 440, E Ct HR, paras 34–35.

(c)   The third rule

4.19.11   The third rule applies where the interference in question is intended to control the use of property[1]. It was found to apply, for example, in *Mellacher v Austria*[2], where the rent chargeable by the applicant in respect of his properties was subject to legislative control, and in *Pine Valley Developments Ltd v Ireland*[3], where the applicant's property was subjected to planning controls[4].

1   Where the interference has the effect of interfering with the use or enjoyment of property, but is not intended to do so, the first rule of art 1 of the protocol will apply. See *Sporrong and Lönnroth v Sweden* (1982) 5 EHRR 35, E Ct HR, para 65.
2   (1989) 12 EHRR 391, E Ct HR.
3   (1991) 14 EHRR 319, E Ct HR.
4   For the application of the third rule in relation to the control of use of property, see also *AGOSI v United Kingdom* (1986) 9 EHRR 1, E Ct HR; *Inze v Austria* (1987) 10 EHRR 394, E Ct HR; *Fredin v Sweden* (1991) 13 EHRR 784, E Ct HR; *Vendittelli v Italy* (1994) 19 EHRR 464, E Ct HR; *Spadea and Scalabrino v Italy* (1995) 21 EHRR 482, E Ct HR; *Scollo v Italy* (1995) 22 EHRR 514, E Ct HR.

4.19.12   The third rule also applies to measures which secure the payment of taxes or other contributions or penalties[1].

1   See Application 11036/84 *Svenska Management Gruppen v Sweden* 45 DR 211 (1985), EComHR; Application 13013/87 *Wasa Liv Ömsesidigt v Sweden* 58 DR 163 (1988), EComHR, at 185–187;

Gasus Dosier-und Fördertechnik v Netherlands (1995) 20 EHRR 403, E Ct HR, para 59; *Van Raalte v Netherlands* (1997) 24 EHRR 503, E Ct HR, paras 34–35; *National Provincial Building Society v United Kingdom* (1997) 25 EHRR 127, E Ct HR, para 79.

3   WHEN AN INTERFERENCE WILL BE JUSTIFIED

(a)   The public or general interest

4.19.13   As the text of art 1 of the first protocol makes clear, a taking of property within the second, 'deprivation', rule of this provision can only be justified if it is in the public interest. Interferences with property falling within the first and third rules are similarly required to be in the public, or general, interest[1].

1   The requirement that a measure be in the 'general interest' is expressly mentioned in relation to the third rule, but it is inherent in art 1 of the protocol as a whole. See *Sporrong and Lönnroth v Sweden* (1982) 5 EHRR 35, E Ct HR, paras 69, 73, where the first rule applied; *Scollo v Italy* (1995) 22 EHRR 514, E Ct HR, para 32, where the third, 'control of use', rule applied; and *Gasus Dosier-und Fördertechnik v Netherlands* (1995) 20 EHRR 403, E Ct HR, para 62, where the third rule applied in relation to a taxing measure. A discriminatory interference with property would be unlikely to be in the public or general interest, unless there was objection and reasonable justification for the differential treatment. See paras **4.14.1–4.14.21** on art 14.

4.19.14   However, the scope of review of the object or purpose of a legislative measure or other interference with property is limited. It is well-established that the national authorities have a wide margin of appreciation in implementing social and economic policies, and that their judgment as to what is in the public or general interest will be respected unless that judgment is 'manifestly without reasonable foundation'[1].

1   See *James v United Kingdom* (1986) 8 EHRR 123, E Ct HR, para 46. The E Ct HR also observed that although it could not substitute its own assessment for that of the national authorities, it was nevertheless bound to review the contested measures under art 1 of protocol 1 and, in so doing, inquire into the facts with reference to which the national authorities acted (see para 46). On the concept of a margin of appreciation, see para **3.20**.

(b)   Proportionality

4.19.15   Whichever of the three rules of art 1 of the first protocol applies, an interference with property must not only be in the public or general interest, but must also satisfy the requirement of proportionality, that is, that there is a reasonable relationship of proportionality between the means employed and the aim sought to be realised. As the E Ct HR has repeatedly stated, a fair balance must be struck between the demands of the general interest of the community and the requirements of the protection of the individual's fundamental rights, the search for such a fair balance being inherent in the whole of the Convention[1].

1   See *Sporrong and Lönnroth v Sweden* (1982) 5 EHRR 35, E Ct HR, paras 69 and 73; *James v United Kingdom* (1986) 8 EHRR 123, E Ct HR, para 50; *Lithgow v United Kingdom* (1986) 8 EHRR 329, E Ct HR, para 120; *AGOSI v United Kingdom* (1986) 9 EHRR 1, E Ct HR, para 52; *Mellacher v Austria* (1989) 12 EHRR 391, E Ct HR, para 48; *Tre Traktörer Aktiebolag v Sweden* (1989) 13 EHRR 309, E Ct HR, para 59; *Hentrich v France* (1994) 18 EHRR 440, E Ct HR, paras 45–49; *Stran Greek Refineries v Greece* (1994) 19 EHRR 293, E Ct HR, para 74; *Holy Monasteries v Greece* (1994) 20 EHRR 1, E Ct HR, para 70; *Air Canada v United Kingdom* (1995) 20 EHRR 150, E Ct HR, para 29; *Pressos Compania Naviera SA v Belgium* (1995) 21 EHRR 301, E Ct HR, para 38; *Scollo v Italy* (1995) 22 EHRR 514, E Ct HR, para 32; *National Provincial Building Society v United Kingdom* (1997) 25 EHRR 127, E Ct HR, para 80. On the principle of proportionality, see generally para **3.10**.

4.19.16   The powers of the state to secure the payment of taxes or other contributions or penalties (the third rule) are particularly wide, but a taxing measure is nevertheless subject to the requirement of proportionality[1].

1   See *Gasus Dosier-und Fördertechnik v Netherlands* (1995) 20 EHRR 403, E Ct HR, para 62; *National Provincial Building Society v United Kingdom* (1997) 25 EHRR 127, para 80.

4.19.17   Although art 1 of the first protocol does not expressly require the payment of compensation in respect of a taking of, or other interference with, property, the payment of compensation is generally required for the taking of property. In *James v United Kingdom* the E Ct HR observed that:

'... under the legal systems of the contracting states, the taking of property in the public interest without payment of compensation is treated as justifiable only in exceptional circumstances ... As far as article 1 is concerned, the protection of the right of property it affords would be largely illusory and ineffective in the absence of any equivalent principle. Clearly, compensation terms are material to the assessment whether the contested legislation represents a fair balance between the interests at stake and, notably, whether it does not impose a disproportionate burden on the applicants ...'[1].

1   (1986) 8 EHRR 123, E Ct HR, para 54. See also *Lithgow v United Kingdom* (1986) 8 EHRR 329, E Ct HR, para 120; *Holy Monasteries v Greece* (1994) 20 EHRR 1, E Ct HR, paras 70–75; *Hentrich v France* (1994) 18 EHRR 440, E Ct HR, para 48; and *Pressos Compania Naviera SA v Belgium* (1995) 21 EHRR 301, E Ct HR, para 38, where the E Ct HR observed that: 'Compensation terms under the relevant legislation are material to the assessment whether the contested measure respects the requisite fair balance and, notably, whether it imposes a disproportionate burden on the applicants'; *Guillemin v France* (1998) 25 EHRR 435, E Ct HR, paras 52–57; *Aka v Turkey*, judgment of the E Ct HR (23 September 1998, unreported), paras 41–51.

4.19.18   So far as the standard of compensation is concerned, the taking of property without the payment of an amount reasonably related to its value will normally constitute a disproportionate interference. Article 1 does not, however, guarantee a right to full compensation in all circumstances. Legitimate objectives of 'public interest', such as are pursued in measures of economic reform or measures designed to achieve greater social justice, may call for less than reimbursement of the full market value[1].

1   See *James v United Kingdom* (1986) 8 EHRR 123, E Ct HR, para 54; *Lithgow v United Kingdom* (1986) 8 EHRR 329, E Ct HR, para 121; *Holy Monasteries v Greece* (1994) 20 EHRR 1 E Ct HR, para 71.

(c)   Legal certainty

4.19.19   An interference with property must also satisfy the requirement of legal certainty. This requirement is expressly stated in the second sentence of the first paragraph of article 1 of the protocol, where it is provided that a deprivation of property must be 'subject to the conditions provided for by law' ('prevu par la loi'). It is, however, not restricted to the second of the three rules of art 1: the principle of legal certainty, or legality, is inherent in the Convention as a whole[1].

1   See *Winterwerp v Netherlands* (1979) 2 EHRR 387, E Ct HR, para 45. See generally para **3.13**.

4.19.20   Legal certainty requires the existence of and compliance with adequately accessible and sufficiently precise domestic legal provisions, which satisfy the essential requirements of the concept of 'law'. Although the phrase 'subject to the conditions provided for by law' refers in part to domestic law, the matter is not restricted to domestic law alone[1].

1   See *Lithgow v United Kingdom* (1986) 8 EHRR 329, E Ct HR, para 110. See also *Winterwerp v Netherlands* (1979) 2 EHRR 387, E Ct HR, para 45, where the E Ct HR observed (in the context of the right to liberty) that the notion underlying the term 'prescribed by law' is one of fair and proper procedure, namely, that the measure in question should issue from and be executed by an appropriate authority and should not be arbitrary. The E Ct HR stated that: 'In a democratic society subscribing to the rule of law, no determination that is arbitrary can ever be regarded as lawful.' (at para 39).

4.19.21 There must also be procedural safeguards against the misuse of powers of the state. For example, in *Hentrich v France*[1], concerning the pre-emption of the applicant's property by the French revenue authorities, the E Ct HR held that the principle of legality had been breached because the pre-emption 'operated arbitrarily and selectively and was scarcely foreseeable, and it was not attended by the basic procedural safeguards'.

1   (1994) 18 EHRR 440, E Ct HR, para 42.

(d)   General principles of international law

4.19.22 A taking of property must also be subject to the conditions provided for by the general principles of international law. This does not, however, mean that art 1 incorporates the standards of general international law for the benefit of nationals. The reference to general international law applies only to alien property holders[1].

1   See *James v United Kingdom* (1986) 8 EHRR 123, E Ct HR, paras 58-66; *Lithgow v United Kingdom* (1986) 8 EHRR 329, E Ct HR, paras 111-119.

Article 2 of the First Protocol   Right to education

No person shall be denied the right to education. In the exercise of any functions which it assumes in relation to education and to teaching, the state shall respect the right of parents to ensure such education and teaching in conformity with their own religious and philosophical convictions.

A   Introduction

4.20.1   The negative formulation of the opening sentence of art 2 of the first protocol indicates the qualified scope of the right to education[1]. The article has, nevertheless, attracted a high number of reservations including one from the United Kingdom (its only reservation). In view of certain provisions of the Education Acts in force in the United Kingdom at the time when the reservation was made[2], the principle affirmed in the second sentence of art 2 is accepted by the United Kingdom only so far as it is compatible with the provision of efficient instruction and training and the avoidance of unreasonable public expenditure. Moreover, art 2 itself leaves the structure and funding of public education to the state's discretion. It is the manner in which this discretion is exercised which dictates the scope of individual rights. Article 2 also refrains from prescribing the content or purpose of the education and teaching to be provided[3]. It would not, therefore, be violated by the inclusion or exclusion of a particular subject within the National Curriculum, unless the subject's addition or omission were to be so serious as to preclude the provision of proper education. In short, contracting states are given a wide margin of appreciation to administer and finance their own systems of education[4]. Successful challenges are likely to be scarce provided the system is both efficient and sufficiently flexible to permit a reasonable measure of parental choice (through, for example, a diverse independent sector).

1   The original text adopted the positive formulation ('[e]very person has the right to education') more commonly used in the Convention. However, some contracting states were concerned that this could prove to be unduly onerous: see Opsahl, in Robertson, *Privacy and Human Rights* (1973), pp 220–243.
2   That is, when the first protocol was signed on behalf of the United Kingdom (20 March 1952), see *Campbell and Cosans v United Kingdom* (1982) 4 EHRR 293, E Ct HR, para 37 ('under art 64 of the Convention, a reservation in respect of any provision is permitted only to the extent that any law in force in a contracting state's territory at the time when the reservation is made is not in conformity with the provision'). As to the United Kingdom's reservation, see para **2.15.2**.
3   Contrast this omission with the Universal Declaration of Human Rights, art 26(2) which provides: 'Education shall be directed to the full development of the human personality and to the strengthening of respect for human rights and fundamental freedoms. It shall promote understanding, tolerance and friendship among all nations, racial or religious groups, and shall partner the activities of the United Nations for the maintenance of peace'. Article 26(3) provides that '[p]arents have a prior right to choose the kind of education that shall be given to their children'.
4   See *S P v United Kingdom*, Application 28915/95 (17 January 1997) [1997] EHRLR 287, (where the Commission recognised that there must be a wide measure of discretion left to the appropriate authorities as to how to make the best use possible of the resources available to them in the interests of disabled children generally). As to children with special educational needs, see further, para **4.20.15**.

4.20.2   Nevertheless, the right to education is acknowledged in international human rights instruments as both an economic, social and cultural right[1] and a civil and political right[2]. Moreover, the E Ct HR has confirmed that, while art 2 must be read as a whole, it is dominated by its first sentence; the second sentence being an adjunct to the fundamental right to education[3]. The court has also stressed the distinction between 'education' and 'teaching'[4].

1   International Covenant on Economic, Social and Cultural Rights, art 13(1) contains an explicit recognition by the state parties of the right of everyone to education. Article 13(3) provides that the state parties undertake to have respect for the liberty of parents to choose for their children non-state schools which conform to minimum educational standards and to ensure the religious and moral education of their children in conformity with their own convictions. Article 13(4) states that no part of art 13 shall be construed so as to interfere with the liberty of individuals and bodies to establish and direct educational institutions provided they meet minimum standards. The United Kingdom ratified this Covenant in 1976 without any relevant reservation. The United Kingdom is also a party to the Covenant Against Discrimination in Education (UNESCO 1960), art 2 of which permits the establishment and maintenance of private educational institutions provided they supplement rather than replace state education and provided they meet minimum standards. For a survey of constitutional guarantees of the right to education elsewhere in Europe, see 'A Joint Opinion by Anthony Lester QC and David Pannick' (ISIS Document No 11) April 1987. See also, interpreting art 42 of the Irish Constitution, 'In the Matter of Article 26 of the Constitution and in the Matter of the School Attendance Bill 1942' [1943] IR 334. As to the right to education in the United States of America, see the decisions of the Supreme Court in *Meyer v Nebraska* 262 US 390 (1923), *Pierce v Society of Sisters* 268 US 510 (1925) and *Wisconsin v Yoder* 406 US 205 (1972).
2   United Nations International Covenant on Civil and Political Rights, art 18(4) (1966), which the United Kingdom has also ratified, records the state parties' undertaking to have respect for the liberty of parents to ensure the religious and moral education of their children in conformity with their own convictions. See also the Universal Declaration of Human Rights, art 26(2) (see para **4.20.1**, n 3) and the United Nations Convention on the Rights of the Child, art 28(1) (20 November 1989), both of which have been ratified by the United Kingdom.
3   See *Kjeldsen, Busk Madsen and Pedersen v Denmark* (1976) 1 EHRR 711, E Ct HR, para 52, and *Campbell and Cosans v United Kingdom* (1982) 4 EHRR 293, E Ct HR, paras 36 and 40 (the right to education by its very nature calls for regulation by the state but such regulation must not injure the substance of the right or conflict with other rights enshrined in the Convention or its Protocols). Both these cases are discussed in greater detail in para **4.20.13**.
4   See *Campbell and Cosans v United Kingdom* (1982) 4 EHRR 293, E Ct HR, para 33 ('... the education of children is the whole process whereby, in any society, adults endeavour to transmit their beliefs, culture and other values to the young, whereas teaching or instruction refers in particular to the transmission of knowledge and to intellectual development': a school's disciplinary system is an integral, even indispensable, part of the educational process).

4.20.3   In England and Wales the right to education is recognised by statute[1]. The Secretary of State for Education and Employment is required to promote the education of the people of England and Wales[2].

1   The relevant domestic statute law dealing with nursery, primary and secondary education has been consolidated in the Education Act 1996: see especially ss 13–14 (general responsibility for education of local education authorities and their obligation to provide primary and secondary schools in their areas); and s 7 (duty on parents to ensure that their children of compulsory schools age receive suitable full-time education by regular attendance at school or otherwise): *R v Inner London Education Authority, ex p Ali* (1990) 2 Admin LR 822; *Meade v Haringey London Borough Council* [1979] 1 WLR 637, CA; *Birmingham City Council v Equal Opportunities Commission* [1989] AC 1155, HL. Within the public education system and subject to certain provisos, parents may choose the school which their children should attend: see the Education Act 1996, s 411; and see *R v Cleveland County Council, ex p Commission for Racial Equality* [1994] ELR 44, CA; *R v Governors of Bishop Challoner Roman Catholic Comprehensive Girls' School, ex p Choudhury* [1992] 2 AC 182, HL; *Cumings v Birkenhead Corpn* [1972] 1 Ch 12, CA. This right circumscribes the power of local education authorities to place children in schools. In certain circumstances a child can be excluded from school: see eg *R v Headmaster of Fernhill Manor School, ex p Brown* [1994] ELR 67 (private school); *R v Board of Governors of Stoke Newington School, ex p M* [1994] ELR 131; as to publicly-funded schools see the Education Act 1996, ss 156–160. As to further education, see also the Further and Higher Education Act 1992. See, generally, the *Law of Education* (9th edn, Butterworths).
2   See the Education Act 1996, s 10. See also s 11 for the general duties of the Secretary of State in relation to primary, secondary and further education. For domestic judicial review cases in which reference has been made to the right to education under art 2 (especially in the context of parental preferences) see *R v Secretary of State for Education and Science, ex p Talmud Torah Machzikei Haddass School Trust* (1985) Times, 12 April, (Woolf J), *R v Lancashire County Council, ex p Huddleston* (7 May 1985, unreported) (Webster J), *R v Secretary of State for Education and Science,*

ex p G (1989) Times, 7 July), DC, *R v Rochdale Metropolitan Borough Council, ex p Schemet*(1993) 91 LGR 425 at 443 (Roch J) and *R v Lancashire County Council, ex p Foster* [1995] ELR 33, DC.

B   Scope

4.20.4   The general right to education comprises four separate rights (none of which is absolute[1]):

(1)   a right of access to such educational establishments as exist;

(2)   a right to an effective (but not the most effective possible) education;

(3)   a right to official recognition of academic qualifications[2]; and

(4)   a right, when read with the freedom from discrimination guaranteed by art 14 of the Convention[3], not to be disadvantaged in the provision of education[4] on any ground such as sex, race, colour, language, religion, political or other opinion, national or social origin, association with a national minority, property, birth or other status[5] without reasonable and objective justification.

1   The state is entitled to regulate these rights, taking account of individual and community needs and resources, provided it does not 'injure the substance of the right to education nor conflict with other rights enshrined in the Convention': see the *Belgian Linguistic Case (No 2)* (1968) 1 EHRR 252 E Ct HR, para 5. The regulation may vary from time to time and from place to place.

2   As to these first three rights and the general scope of art 2, see the *Belgian Linguistic Case (No 2)* (1968) 1 EHRR 252 E Ct HR, para 5, pp 30–36, and *Campbell and Cosans v United Kingdom* (1982) 4 EHRR 293, E Ct HR, para 37 at paras 40–41.

3   See para **4.14**.

4   This would encompass education in the wide sense and should include, for example, funding of school sports facilities for girls.

5   It is likely that 'other status' would encompass discrimination on grounds of physical or mental disability and so cover the provision of education to those with special educational needs, on which see para **4.20.5**.

4.20.5   As regards the right of access to such educational establishments as exist at a given time, contracting states are under no duty to establish at their own expense, or to subsidise, education of any particular type or at any particular level[1]. Parents have no right to insist on the provision of single-sex or selective schools. Thus, in *W & DM and M & HI v United Kingdom*[2] the applicants' children were refused places at selective grammar schools. Because the admission quota could not be exceeded without prejudicing efficient education and the efficient use and distribution of resources, they were obliged to go to non-selective comprehensive schools (there being no other schools available in the locality). The Commission declared the complaint inadmissible because there was no lack of pluralism or interference with the parents' role in education, in particular in the transmission of their values or philosophical convictions[3]. Nor are contracting states required to recognise or continue to recognise any particular institution as an educational establishment[4]. Nor are they precluded from imposing entry requirements for access to educational establishments, in particular in relation to higher education[5]. But contracting states do have a power to oblige parents to send their children to school or to ensure that parents secure the provision of adequate education at home[6]. The need to ensure pluralism means that private and independent schools (charging fees and providing assisted places), so long as they reach minimum standards, are not only permitted but their right to exist is guaranteed[7]. Contracting states are, however, entitled to refuse to assist private and independent schools with public funds provided this does not lead to unjustifiable discrimination[8]. Article 2 does not restrict the right to education to those under any particular age: it applies to both elementary and secondary education[9]. There is no unfettered right to further or higher education, where contracting states may make it a condition of admission that a student has the capacity to benefit[10]. Article

2 does not extend to vocational training[11], nor necessarily to specialist advanced studies[12] (although European Union law applies to both). Nor does art 2 in principle exclude recourse to disciplinary measures, including those of suspension and expulsion even if the effect is to prevent the applicant from enrolling at any other educational establishment[13].

1   See the *Belgian Linguistic Case (No 2)* (1968) 1 EHRR 252 E Ct HR, para 5, p 31, and Application 7782/77 *X v United Kingdom* 14 DR 179 (1978), EComHR. This would be an answer to a challenge to the alleged under-funding of education or to its structure. See also Application 9411/81 *Rosengren v Sweden* 29 DR 224 (1982) EComHR. Contracting states would be accorded a wide margin of appreciation to fix school starting and leaving ages.

2   Applications 10228/82 and 10229/82, 37 DR 96 (1984) EComHR.

3   On the other hand, a state monopoly in education or discrimination in access to educational opportunities would breach art 2 read alone and together with art 14 of the Convention.

4   See Application 3798/68 *Church of X v United Kingdom* 12 YB 306 (1969), EComHR.

5   See Application 8840/80 *X v United Kingdom* 23 DR 228 (1980), EComHR; Application 6598/74 5 Digest 783. Similarly, foreign students and prospective students have no right to pursue their education in a particular country: see Application 7671/76 *15 Foreign Students v United Kingdom* 9 DR 185 (1977), EComHR (foreign students subjected to immigration control and refused leave to remain in the United Kingdom).

6   See Application 10233/83 *Family H v United Kingdom* 37 DR 105 (1984), EComHR. See the Education Act 1996, s 7.

7   See 'A Joint Opinion by Anthony Lester QC and David Pannick' (ISIS Document No 11) April 1987. The Opinion relies on the international instruments cited in para **4.20.2**, the first protocol's travaux préparatoires and the Strasbourg jurisprudence in concluding that the abolition of fee-paying, independent education would violate art 2 and that the removal of charitable status from, and the imposition of VAT on, independent schools would probably do so too.

8   See Application 10476/83 *W and KL v Sweden* 45 DR 143 (1985), at 148–149 and Application 11533/85 *Ingrid Jordebo Foundation of Christian Schools and Ingrid Jordebo v Sweden* 51 DR 125 (1987) 128. Even if not covered by the first sentence of art 2, the right to attend a private school is probably secured by the second sentence (the duty on a state to 'respect the right of parents to ensure such education and teaching in conformity with their own ... philosophical convictions').

9   See Application 5962/72 *X v United Kingdom* 2 DR 50 (1975), EComHR, and Application 7671/76 *15 Foreign Students v United Kingdom* 9 DR 185 (1977), EComHR (art 2 is concerned 'primarily with elementary education'). Article 2 applies to both voluntary and compulsory public educaton (including nursery education): see Application 6853/74 *40 Mothers v Sweden* 9 DR 27 (1977), EComHR.

10   See Application 5962/72 *X v United Kingdom* 2 DR 50 (1975), EComHR, and Application 11655/85 *Glazewska v Sweden* 45 DR 300 (1985).

11   See Application 5962/72 *X v United Kingdom* 2 DR 50 (1975), EComHR.

12   See Application 24515/94 *Sulak v Turkey* 84-A DR 98 (1996).

13   See Application 24515/94 *Sulak v Turkey* 84-A DR 98 (1996) (expulsion for repeatedly cheating in examinations led to a denial of access to any other university: held manifestly ill-founded).

4.20.6   As regards the right to an effective education, for the right to education to be meaningful the quality of the education must reach a minimum standard[1]. It must also be pluralist. Neither the curriculum nor individual teachers may seek to advance only one view or to indoctrinate pupils[2].

1   As the E Ct HR observed in the *Belgian Linguistic Case (No 2)* (1968) 1 EHRR 252, E Ct HR, para 5, at p 31, 'the right to education would be meaningless if it did not imply in favour of its beneficiaries the right to be educated in the national language or in one of the national languages, as the case may be'. Beyond this, however, the Commission has expressed its reluctance to assess standards of teaching and allegations of educational negligence: see Application 28915/95 *S P v United Kingdom* (17 January 1997) [1997] EHRLR 287, (parental complaint that successive schools had failed to pay proper regard to child's special needs – dyslexia and short-term memory – thereby contributing to behavioural, emotional and social problems: declared inadmissible).

2   This does not prevent contracting states from imparting information or knowledge of a directly or indirectly religious or philosophical kind through education, but the state must take care that such information or knowledge included in the curriculum must be conveyed in an objective, critical and pluralist manner: *Kjeldsen, Busk Madsen and Pedersen v Denmark* (1976) 1 EHRR 711, E Ct HR, para 52 (compulsory sex education in state schools did not violate art 2 since it was intended to impart

knowledge objectively and in the public interest, and heavily state-subsidised private schools, in which sex education was not compulsory, were also available). See also art 9 of the Convention which guarantees freedom of thought, conscience and religion: see, para **4.9**.

4.20.7 The right to official recognition of academic qualifications and, thereby, the possibility of drawing profit from the education received has not produced any notable Strasbourg jurisprudence.

4.20.8 The right to equal educational opportunities prevents segregated schools and educational systems[1] as well as discrimination in access to education. But it does not preclude all differential treatment. The leading case is the *Belgian Linguistic Case*[2]. Belgium has three official languages: Flemish, French and German. Flemish is spoken by the majority, French by about one third, the remainder are bilingual and a very small number speak only German. Brussels is situated in the Flemish-speaking area but has a large bilingual population. The applicants were French speaking parents who wanted their children to be educated in French and who objected to sending their children outside the area where they lived for that purpose when the children of the Flemish speaking majority suffered no such discrimination. The E Ct HR held that the Belgian government's policy of assimilation was objectively and reasonably justified. It pursued a legitimate aim (the creation of unilingual regions in most of the country) by reasonably proportionate means and did not violate art 2 read with art 14 of the Convention[3]. Nor did it breach the second sentence of art 2 of the first protocol read alone[4] because the material characteristic was language not a 'religious or philosophical conviction'. Where, however, a contracting state provides financial support to grant-maintained schools it cannot, without reasonable and objective justification, discriminate between establishments on religious or philosophical grounds[5]. Under domestic law, sex and race discrimination in education is prohibited by statute[6].

1   Unless, without their own schools, the convictions of parents who are members of religious or philosophical minorities could not be accommodated. Segregation is prohibited on any of the grounds, except sex, listed in para **4.20.4** at (4). Single sex schools are permitted. As to the prohibition on racial segregation in the United States of America, see *Brown v Board of Education* 347 US 483 (1954)(US Supreme Court).
2   (1968) 1 EHRR 252, E Ct HR, para 5, especially pp 33–36.
3   Except in respect of those children who, because of the place of residence of their parents, were denied access to French language schools in certain communes on the edge of Brussels. This amounted to a violation of art 2 read with art 14 of the Convention because the equivalent Dutch language schools accepted all children regardless of the place of residence of their parents.
4   See paras **4.20.11–4.20.15**.
5   In this regard, it is notable that Christian and Jewish grant-maintained establishments have recently been joined by the first Muslim grant-maintained school. It is strongly arguable that a comprehensive failure to fund Muslim schools (or the schools of any other ethnic or religious minority) would violate art 2, read with art 14 of the Convention, unless the differential treatment is objectively justifiable. See, however, Application 23419/94 *Verein Gemeinsam Lernen v Austria* 82-A DR 41 (1995), EComHR where the Commission repeated that, although art 2 guarantees the right to start and run a private school, there is no positive obligation on a state to subsidise any particular form of education (Austrian secular school was refused a staff subsidy which was available to church schools: held, that the differential treatment was objectively and reasonably justified because the church schools were so widespread that if the educational services they provided had to be taken over by the state there would be a considerable burden on public funds).
6   Sex Discrimination Act 1975, ss 22–28, and the Race Relations Act 1976, ss 17–19: see also, respectively, *Halsbury's Laws* (1998 Cum Supp) para 771:20A and *Halsbury's Laws*, volume 4(2), paras 169–170.

4.20.9 While parents are given certain rights over the way in which their child is educated (especially when the child is young), the right to education is normally that of the pupil or student. Where the right resides in, or is exercised by, the parents, it continues while the child is in care[1]. But if the child is adopted, the right is assumed by the adoptive parents[2]. If one parent gains custody of the child, the right ceases for the other parent[3].

1   See Application 10554/83*Aminoff v Sweden* 43 DR 120 (1985), EComHR, at 144 and *Olsson v Sweden* A 130 (1988), 11 EHRR 259, E Ct HR.
2   See Application 7626/76*X v United Kingdom* 11 DR 160 (1977), EComHR.
3   See Application 7911/77*X v Sweden* 12 DR 192 (1977), EComHR.

4.20.10   The detention of a minor by lawful order in a reformatory for the purpose of educational supervision is authorised by art 5(1)(d) of the Convention[1]. Detention in a remand prison as a preliminary to a transfer speedily to such an institution would also be permitted[2].

1   See para **4.5**.
2   See *Bouamar v Belgium* A 129 (1988) 11 EHRR 1, E Ct HR (detention of a 16-year-old boy in a remand prison with no educational facilities, pursuant to a court order, for 119 days in one year was held to violate art 5(1)(d)).

C   Respect for the religious and philosophical conviction of parents

4.20.11   The criteria upon which access to education is granted must be consistent with the parents'[1] right to ensure that their child's education conforms with their own religious or philosophical convictions[2]. This applies equally to private and public education as well as to any other functions (academic, disciplinary and administrative) which contracting states exercise in relation to education[3].

1   The second sentence of art 2 focuses on the rights of parents whereas the first sentence concerns the rights of children. See para **4.20.9**.
2   See *Campbell and Cosans v United Kingdom* (1982) 4 EHRR 293, E Ct HR, paras 36–41 (the suspension of a boy from school for almost a full school year would have ended only if his parents had agreed to expose him to the risk of corporal punishment, contrary to their philosophical convictions). But see the Education Act 1996, s 550 (a person shall not be deprived of access to education because s 548 of the 1996 Act on the abolition of inhuman and degrading corporal punishment applies to him). As to the prohibition on inhuman and degrading corporal punishment in the United Kingdom, see below, para **4.20.14** at n 4. As to the prohibition under art 3 of the Convention, see above, para **4.3.24**. Linguistic preferences (for example, a parental enthusiasm to give a child an entirely Welsh language education) do not amount to philosophical convictions: see the *Belgian Linguistic Case (No 2)* (1968) 1 EHRR 252, E Ct HR, para 5 (where the E Ct HR referred to the travaux préparatoires which showed that philosophical convictions were added to religious convictions in order to protect agnostics and atheists). See the Education Act 1996, s 9 (pupils to be educated in accordance with parents' wishes, so far as that is compatible with the provision of efficient instruction and training and the avoidance of unreasonable public expenditure).
3   See *Campbell and Cosans v United Kingdom* (1982) 4 EHRR 293, E Ct HR, at paras 33–36.

4.20.12   A 'conviction' is more than an 'opinion' or an 'idea'. It is akin to a 'belief' which attains 'a certain level of cogency, seriousness, cohesion and importance'[1]. It must also be genuinely held and the parent bears a heavy burden of showing that it is the real reason for the objection[2]. Moreover, the types of convictions which qualify are narrowly interpreted[3]. Philosophical convictions are 'such convictions as are worthy of respect in a "democratic society" ... and are not incompatible with human dignity; in addition, they must not conflict with the fundamental right of the child to education'[4].

1   See *Campbell and Cosans v United Kingdom* (1982) 4 EHRR 293, E Ct HR, at para 36.
2   See Application 9471/81 *Warwick v United Kingdom* 60 DR 5 (1989) at 18. The reason for the objection should be raised initially with the national education authorities: see Application 9303/81

B and D v United Kingdom 49 DR 44 (1986) at 50. Compare the dissenting judgments of Judges Thor Vilhjalmsson and Jambrek in *Valsamis v Greece* (1996) 24 EHRR 294, E Ct HR (advocating a different burden of proof: parental objection must be accepted 'unless it is obviously unfounded and unreasonable').

3 They do not, for example, include a preference (however strongly held) as to the language of teaching: see the *Belgian Linguistic Case (No 2)* (1968) 1 EHRR 252, E Ct HR, para 5, p 32.

4 See *Campbell and Cosans v United Kingdom* (1982) 4 EHRR 293, E Ct HR, at para 36 and *Young, James and Webster v United Kingdom* (1981) 4 EHRR 38, para 63. In *Campbell and Cosans v United Kingdom* (1980) 3 EHRR 531, EComHR, at para 92, the Commission described religious and philosophical convictions as embracing 'ideas based on human knowledge and reasoning concerning the world, life, society, etc, which a person adopts and professes according to the dictates of his or her conscience'. It is suggested that this would cover parental views about the desirability of sex education, co-education and progressive teaching methods as well as religious instruction.

4.20.13 The extent of parents' rights to object has arisen most prominently in relation to school discipline and sex education. In *Campbell and Cosans v United Kingdom*[1] the applicants complained that the use of corporal punishment in Scottish schools infringed their rights under art 2 to ensure the education and teaching of their children in accordance with their philosophical convictions. The E Ct HR accepted that parental objections to the use of threatened use of corporal punishment in schools were 'philosophical' because they related to a weighty and substantial aspect of human life and behaviour (namely, the integrity of the person), the propriety or otherwise of the infliction of corporal punishment and the exclusion of the distress which the risk of such punishment entails[2]. The United Kingdom was found to have breached the second sentence of art 2[3]. It is unlikely, however, that parental objections (other than on religious grounds) to school dress codes and curricular requirements for physical education would be given such a status[4]. In *Kjeldsen, Busk Madsen and Pedersen v Denmark*[5] the E Ct HR refused to accept as valid an objection to the teaching of sex education in state schools to pupils aged 9–11. It stressed that the information was conveyed in a neutral, objective, critical and pluralist way. No attempt was made to encourage any particular moral or religious attitude. Thus, the mere inclusion within a curriculum of a view to which parents object does not entitle the parents to insist on the exclusion of their child, provided that the overall curriculum is balanced and integrated[6].

1 (1982) 4 EHRR 293, E Ct HR.

2 (1982) 4 EHRR 293, E Ct HR, para 36. But see the dissenting judgment of Judge Sir Vincent Evans for the view that parental convictions could not affect school administration but only the content of what was taught. On corporal punishment in schools and art 3, see para **4.3.24**.

3 The E Ct HR found the United Kingdom's reservation, above, para **4.20.1**, inapplicable because it was not persuaded that the parents' wishes could not be respected in some other way. See, similarly, *Costello-Roberts v United Kingdom* (1993) 19 EHRR 112, E Ct HR.

4 See *Valsamis v Greece* (1997) 24 EHRR 294, E Ct HR, paras 22–32, where the E Ct HR held that a requirement imposed on a pupil (on pain of suspension) to participate in a Greek National Day parade, which took place outside school hours, did not offend the pacifist convictions of the pupil's parents as Jehovah's Witnesses to an extent prohibited by art 2. The E Ct HR emphasised that art 2 had to be read in the light of arts 8, 9 and 10 of the Convention.

5 (1976) 1 EHRR 711, E Ct HR, para 53.

6 But contrast *Hartikainen v Finland* (40/1975), Doc. A/36/40, page 147 (a decision of the Human Rights Committee on a complaint that compulsory classes for children on religion and ethics violated art 18(4) of the International Covenant on Civil and Political Rights).

4.20.14 'Respect' in the second sentence of art 2 means more than 'take account of' or 'acknowledge' but less than 'comply with'. It implies some positive obligation on the part of contracting states[1]. But each contracting state has a choice of means by which to respect the parents' rights (unless there is, in practice, only one effective means available)[2]. It may, for example, allow the child to miss certain (parts of) lessons or permit a change of school (while ensuring that another suitable school, public or private, exists). In *Campbell and Cosans v United Kingdom*[3] the E Ct HR endorsed the exemption of certain pupils from corporal punishment rather than their removal to another school[4].

1   *Campbell and Cosans v United Kingdom* (1982) 4 EHRR 293, E Ct HR, para 37 (policy of gradually eliminating corporal punishment in state schools did not amount to respect for the applicants' convictions against use of corporal punishment). During the course of the drafting of art 2 of the protocol the words 'have regard to' were replaced by the word 'respect'.
2   See *Kjeldsen, Busk Madsen and Pedersen v Denmark* (1976) 1 EHRR 711 E Ct HR, para 50.
3   (1982) 4 EHRR 293, E Ct HR, para 37.
4   The E Ct HR accepted that a requirement to create a dual system of separate schools in each educational sector would involve unreasonable public expenditure. See, more recently *Costello-Roberts v United Kingdom* (1993) 19 EHRR 112, E Ct HR, paras 26–28, which concerned the corporal punishment of a seven-year-old pupil at an independent school. The E Ct HR held that the United Kingdom has a positive obligation to secure for children their right to education under art 2 which covers the administration of punishment by schools, whether independent or state. The punishment suffered by the pupil did, therefore, engage the responsibility of the United Kingdom even though it was administered by the headmaster of an independent school. Corporal punishment in all schools (whether state, grant-maintained or independent) is abolished by the Education Act 1996, s 546, as substituted by the School Standards and Framework Act 1998, s 131. As to the power of members of staff to restrain pupils, see the Education Act 1996, s 550A.

4.20.15   The views of parents of children with special educational needs should also be taken into account but such children have no absolute right to parity of access with other pupils[1]. The contracting state is not required to provide special facilities to accommodate particular convictions, although art 2 may affect the use of existing facilities. Despite the Commission's recognition of an increasing body of opinion holding that, whenever possible, children with special educational needs should be brought up with other children of their own age, it also acknowledges that this approach cannot be applied to all children with such needs but that a wide measure of discretion must be left to each contracting state's educational authorities to decide how to make the best possible use of resources by balancing the interests of children with special educational needs and the interests of other children[2].

1   See Application 14135/88 *PD and LD v United Kingdom* 62 DR 292 (1989), EComHR, at 296–297, and Application 14688/89 *Simpson v United Kingdom* 64 DR 188 (1989), EComHR, at 194–195, and Application 13887/88 *Graeme v United Kingdom* 64 DR 158 (1990), EComHR. In England and Wales the provision by local education authorities of education for children with special educational needs is regulated by the Education Act 1996, Pt IV, Schs 26 and 27. Section 316 provides that children with special educational needs should, unless it is inconsistent with parental wishes, be educated in mainstream (non-special) schools provided that this is compatible with the receipt of the special educational provision which his learning difficulty calls for, with the efficient education of the other children with whom he is educated and with the efficient use of resources. Under the Education Act 1996, Sch 27, para 3 (1), parents are entitled to express a preference for the exact school their child is to attend. Paragraph 3(3) requires the local education authority to honour this preference unless it can demonstrate: (1) that the school is unsuitable for the child's age, ability or aptitude or for his special educational needs; or (2) that the attendance of the child at the school would be incompatible with the provision of efficient education for the children with whom he would be educated or the efficient use of resources. See also the Education Act 1996, ss 7(b) and 14(6)(b) and the Disability Discrimination Act 1995, especially ss 29–30.
2   See Application 25212/94 *Klerks v Netherlands* 82-A DR 129 (1995) (deaf pupil required to transfer to a school for the hard of hearing: held, assuming (without deciding) that the complaint was based on philosophical convictions, that art 2 does not require the pupil's admission to an ordinary school, with the expense of additional teaching staff or to the detriment of other pupils, rather than placement in a special school). See also Application 28915/95 *SP v United Kingdom* (17 January 1997) [1997] EHRLR 287, (voluntary removal by a parent of a pupil with dyslexia and short-term memory problems from a number of schools: held, inadmissible because the pupil had not been excluded from state educational facilities), *Belilos v Switzerland* (1988) 10 EHRR 466, E Ct HR and *Fischer v Austria* (1995) 20 EHRR 349, E Ct HR.

> ## Article 3 of the First Protocol   Right to free elections
>
> The High Contracting Parties undertake to hold free elections at
> reasonable intervals by secret ballot, under conditions which will ensure
> the free expression of the opinion of the people in the choice of the
> legislature.

4.21.1 The right of free elections to the legislature enshrines a central principle of
an effective political democracy and is therefore of prime importance under the
Convention system[1]. Article 3 applies only to the election of the 'legislature', or at least
one of its chambers if it has two or more[2]. The word 'legislature' does not mean only
the national parliament since it has to be interpreted within the context of the
constitutional structure of the state in question[3]. The test for whether a national body
is a 'legislature' is whether it exercises an independent power to issue decrees having
the force of law. Regional councils in Belgium, for example, are constituent parts of
the legislature, in addition to both houses of the national Parliament[4]. Because the
Commission has emphasized the width of the margin of appreciation left to contracting
states in giving effect to art 3, the Strasbourg case law gives little guidance as to the
likely impact of art 3 in interpreting legislation and administrative action in this
country. Comparative case law on analogous provisions in national constitutions of
Commonwealth countries is likely to be of strong persuasive value.

1 *Mathieu-Mohin and Clerfayt v Belgium* (1987) 10 EHRR 1, E Ct HR, para 47.
2 *Mathieu-Mohin and Clerfayt v Belgium* (1987) 10 EHRR 1, E Ct HR, para 53.
3 This raises the question of whether the European Parliament, as a supra-national representative organ
   which has partly assumed the powers and functions of a national legislature, can be considered a
   'legislature' within the meaning of art 3. On this point, see the E Ct HR's positive decision in
   Application 24833/94 *Matthews v United Kingdom* 18 February 1999 and its consideration of the
   powers of the European Parliament since the entry into force of the Treaty on European Union. On
   the possible impact of the Treaty of Amsterdam, see Harris, O'Boyle and Warbrick *Law of the
   European Convention on Human Rights* (1995), at pp 553–554.
4 The Commission was not satisfied that English metropolitan county councils were legislatures within
   the meaning of art 3, in spite of their power to issue bye-laws, because the power was delegated by
   the Westminster Parliament which could not only define the power but abolish the councils:
   Application 11391/85 *Booth-Clibborn v United Kingdom* 43 DR 236 (1985) (in the context of the
   abolition of the councils). Similarly, the Court has declined to decide whether art 3 applies to
   elections to local authorities: Application 22954/93 *Ahmed v United Kingdom* judgment of 2
   September 1998, para 76. It is however submitted that the Scottish Parliament and the Northern
   Ireland Assembly should be regarded as exercising sufficient legislative powers to constitute an
   integral part of the 'legislature', even though the Westminster Parliament will retain its sovereign
   power to abolish them or to abridge or override the exercise of their devolved legislative powers. The
   fact that such powers will have been devolved following popular referenda means that they can claim
   a special legitimacy based upon popular sovereignty; that is, the free expression of the people in the
   choice of the legislature. In the case of the Scottish Parliament, there are powerful arguments for
   contending that the Westminster Parliament does not enjoy unfettered powers in relation to the
   Scottish legal system and Scottish interests, since the Union Agreement of 1707 constitutes
   fundamental law limiting the legislative powers of the Parliament created by that Agreement: see 5
   Stair Memorial Encyclopaedia (1987), paras 338–364. Whether the National Assembly for Wales
   or the Greater London Assembly should be regarded as part of the 'legislature' raises difficult
   questions.

4.21.2 As regards the method of appointing the 'legislature', art 3 provides for 'free'
elections 'at reasonable intervals', 'by secret ballot' and 'under conditions which will
ensure the free expression of the opinion of the people'. Subject to that, it does not

create any obligation to introduce a specific electoral system, such as proportional representation or majority voting with one or two ballots[1]. The contracting states have a wide margin of appreciation, given that their legislation on the matter varies from place to place and from time to time.

1   *Mathieu-Mohin and Clerfayt v Belgium* (1987) 10 EHRR 1, E Ct HR, para 54.

4.21.3   Any electoral system must be assessed in the light of the political evolution of the country concerned. Features that would be unacceptable in the context of one system may accordingly be justified in the context of another, at least so long as the chosen system provides for conditions which will ensure the 'free expression of the opinion of the people in the choice of the legislature'. This includes a principle of equality of treatment for all citizens[1]. United Kingdom courts and tribunals are in a better position than the E Ct HR to assess whether impugned features of the electoral system for political participation are justified. However, subject to the need to protect minorities against the abuse of power by the rule of the majority, courts will seek to avoid having to decide what are really political rather than judicial questions.

1   *Mathieu-Mohin and Clerfayt v Belgium* (1987) 10 EHRR 1, E Ct HR, para 54.

4.21.4   In the *Liberal Party case*[1], after referring to the case law of the German Federal Constitutional Court and of the American Supreme Court in controlling electoral laws that deny equality of voting, the Commission left open the question whether specific features in voting behaviour could raise an issue under art 3 of the first protocol read with art 14 of the Convention 'if religious or ethnic groups could never be represented because there was a clear voting pattern along these lines in the majority'[2].

1   Application 8765/79 *Liberal Party v United Kingdom* 21 DR 211 (1980), at 225.
2   In the *Liberal Party* case, the Commission adopted an unnecessarily restrictive approach to the standing of a political party in seeking the right, on behalf of its supporters, to participate and campaign effectively in elections: see Harris, O'Boyle and Warbrick *Law of the European Convention on Human Rights* (1995), p 556.

4.21.5   Article 3 has particular significance when read with the principle of equal treatment without discrimination as guaranteed by art 14 of the Convention[1]. Were there, for example, to be a gerrymander of constituency boundaries to weaken the electoral influence of members of religious or ethnic groups, or the use of an electoral system which had a manifestly disproportionately adverse impact upon members of such groups, this would surely result in breaches of these provisions[2]. Complex questions of law involving the principle of proportionality may arise as the result of measures of positive or reverse discrimination[3] to overcome the under-representation of women (or members of religious or ethnic groups) in the legislature, for example, where a political party imposes an all-female short list of candidates for certain constituencies, depriving electors of a choice of candidates from that party of both sexes[4].

1   See para **4.14**, especially at **4.14.2**.
2   Cf *Gomillion v Lightfoot* 364 US 339 (1960) (where the US Supreme Court declared unconstitutional an Alabama law redrawing city boundaries so as to exclude almost all of the city's black population from the city limits). In the absence of a gerrymander or other evidence of an abuse of the democratic process, the courts are unlikely to intervene in legislative decisions about the drawing of constituency boundaries. An example can be found in Australia where the High Court held that there is no requirement that the number of voters in electoral districts should be equal, or equal so far as is reasonably practical: *McGinty v State of Western Australia* [1996] 1 LRC 599. A preferential system

of voting has also been held not to be inconsistent with the Federal Constitution (see *Langer v Australia* [1996] 3 LRC 113) and the High Court has upheld the constitutionality of a law making it a criminal offence to advocate publicly that a person should mark his ballot paper otherwise than in the manner prescribed by law: *Muldowney v South Australia* [1996] 3 LRC 154.

3   See para **4.14.12**.

4   Cf, *Jepson and Dyas-Elliot v Labour Party and Keighley Constituency Labour Party* [1996] IRLR 116, where an industrial tribunal held that the exclusion of two men from being considered as Labour Party candidates in three constituencies because those constituencies were required to have all-women short-lists (in accordance with the Labour Party's policy to increase the number of women MPs) had constituted unlawful direct sex discrimination, in breach of the Sex Discrimination Act 1975, s 13, read with the EEC Equal Treatment Directive 76/207. See also the decision of the French Conseil Constitutionnel in the *Feminine Quotas* case, decision no 82-146 DC, 18 November 1982, Rec 66; AJDA 1983, 128; summarised in Bell, *French Constitutional Law* (1992) at 349 (concerning a 25% quota for women on candidate lists for local elections).

4.21.6   Article 3 may also be significant in the United Kingdom in the context of judicial review of the powers of the Scottish Parliament, and the Welsh and Northern Ireland Assemblies, especially when read with the rights of political participation contained in art 25 of the International Covenant on Civil and Political Rights[1], and with other rights, such as the right to freedom of political thought and expression, and of freedom of peaceful assembly, guaranteed by the Convention. Other difficult legal questions may also arise under the Convention and art 3, in applying the principle of proportionality in the context of political participation; for example, about whether the funding of political parties[2], the requirements of access to the ballot or of candidature for elected public office[3], election broadcasts[4], or the conditions in which a popular referendum is conducted[5], are compatible with principles of representation, democracy, freedom of political thought and debate, and equality of treatment[6]. Convention rights may also be invoked to ensure that Parliament treats its members fairly when exercising disciplinary powers over them[7]. However, United Kingdom courts have no jurisdiction to entertain complaints of breaches of Convention rights by either House of Parliament or a person exercising functions in connection with proceedings in Parliament[8].

1   See paras **5.24–5.25**.

2   If a state chooses to provide public funding of the electoral process it is not precluded from doing so: Application 6850/74 *Association X, Y and Z v Germany* 5 DR 90 (1976), at 94. Neither the Commission nor the E Ct HR has considered limits on contributions to political parties or campaigns, or on election expenses. But see *Bowman v United Kingdom* (1998) 26 EHRR 1, E Ct HR, on freedom of expression and limits on campaign expenditure. See para **4.10.14**. The comparative law and practice on the funding of political parties were reviewed by the Supreme Court of Zimbabwe in *United Parties v Minister of Justice* (1997) 3 BHRC 16. On US law, see *Buckley v Valeo* 424 US 1 (1976). See also *Australian Capital Television Pty Ltd v Commonwealth of Australia* (1992) 177 CLR 106 (Aust HC).

3   Where voting or candidature is subject to conditions, these conditions must not impair the essence of the right by making its exercise burdensome or practically impossible: Harris, O'Boyle and Warbrick *Law of the European Convention on Human Rights* (1995) at p 556.

4   In *A-G v Kabourou* [1995] 2 LRC 757, the Court of Appeal of Tanzania held that broadcasts by Radio Tanzania had unfairly influenced election results. In Application 15404/89 *Purcell v Ireland* 70 DR 262 (1991), the Commission held that individual voters' rights under art 3 did not include the right for all political parties to be granted equal coverage by the broadcasting media, or even any coverage. It is submitted that this is too restrictive an approach and that art 3 (read alone and with arts 10 and 14) requires the fair allocation of broadcasting time to political parties in relation to the electoral process.

5   The Commission has held that referenda do not fall within the scope of art 3: Application 6742/74 *X v Germany* 3 DR 98 (1975); Application 7096/75 *X v United Kingdom* 3 DR 165 (1975). However, it is submitted that this is too restrictive an approach where a referendum is closely connected with the enactment of legislation.

6   See eg, *Piermont v France* (1995) 20 EHRR 301, E Ct HR, discussed in **4.16.2**. The German Federal Constitutional Court has developed rich jurisprudence in this area as a guardian of democracy and

the rule of law: see generally, Kommers *The Constitutional Jurisprudence of the Federal Republic of Germany* (2nd edn, 1997), Ch 5.

7   In *Demicoli v Malta* (1991) 14 EHRR 47, E Ct HR, the E Ct HR held that the Maltese House of Representatives did not satisfy the need, in art 6(1) of the Convention, for an impartial tribunal to determine criminal charges, since two of the members who participated in the applicant's trial for breach of parliamentary privilege were the Members of Parliament criticised in the article that was the subject of the criminal offence.

8   By virtue of the Human Rights Act 1998, s 6(3): see para **2.6.3**, at nn 7–9. This exclusion of judicial review preserves the law relating to parliamentary privilege and contempt of parliament, and the separation of powers between the United Kingdom Parliament and the courts: see further *Halsbury's Laws* (4th edn reissue), paras 1002–1006. However, the E Ct HR has jurisdiction to entertain such a complaint.

Chapter 5
Scotland

A Introduction

5.01 As one of the constituent parts of the United Kingdom, Scotland has been affected by the European Convention on Human Rights along with the remainder of the United Kingdom, particularly since the acceptance of the right of individual petition in 1966[1]. Scotland is of course a separate jurisdiction from England and Wales and Northern Ireland, with its own distinctive legal history and traditions, its own body of common law and statute law, its own system of courts and its own legal profession. Although much of the law is broadly similar in effect to that elsewhere in the United Kingdom – particularly, as one would expect, in the areas of constitutional and administrative law – there is also much that is different, even in the areas just mentioned. In consequence, the impact of the Convention in Scotland has not been identical to that elsewhere in the United Kingdom. The cases which have gone to the Strasbourg institutions from Scotland have often arisen within a distinctively Scottish context; and the treatment of the Convention by the Scottish courts has also had a distinctive history.

1   As explained at para **1.27**, this was delayed so as to prevent any challenge to the War Damage Act 1965, which deprived the pursuers of the fruits of their victory in *Burmah Oil Co (Burmah Trading) Ltd v Lord Advocate* 1964 SC 117, [1965] AC 75, HL.

5.02 The distinctiveness of the impact of the Convention in Scotland is unlikely to diminish in the new constitutional context established by the Scotland Act 1998 (SA 1998) and the Human Rights Act 1998 (HRA 1998). The SA 1998, in particular, by providing Scotland with a Parliament empowered to legislate in most areas of domestic affairs, seems likely to bring about a greater divergence between the law in Scotland and that elsewhere in the United Kingdom. As the Scottish Parliament and Executive cannot (in general) competently act in contravention of the Convention, however, the SA 1998 is apt to create a body of domestic case-law on the Convention which will complement that created both in Scotland and elsewhere under the HRA 1998.

5.03 This chapter will consider the Convention and Scots law under the following headings:

Scottish cases in Strasbourg.

The Convention in the Scottish courts prior to the 1998 Acts.

The Scotland Act 1998 and the Convention.

The Human Rights Act 1998.

B Scottish cases in Strasbourg

5.04 Cases in Strasbourg which emanate from Scotland do not always have a distinctively Scottish dimension. Where the law and practice in Scotland are effectively identical to that elsewhere in the United Kingdom, the national background of a case is of no particular importance. This is reflected in the fact that the law in Scotland has often been altered in response to Strasbourg decisions in cases from other parts of the United Kingdom, just as the law in England and Wales and Northern Ireland is liable to require alteration in consequence of a Strasbourg decision in a Scottish case. Nevertheless, a survey of Scottish cases is likely to be of value to Scottish practitioners, particularly as the issues raised by Scottish applicants have in practice tended to arise from a distinctively Scottish context.

5.05   Several of the Scottish cases decided by the E Ct HR have concerned aspects of criminal procedure: notably the composition of a jury[1]; the examination of witnesses before the Appeal Court[2]; legal aid for criminal appeals[3]; and legal representation in criminal appeals[4]. These issues have been considered under reference to arts 6(1)[5], (3)(c)[6] and (d)[7] of the European Convention on Human Rights. Just satisfaction has been considered in several of these cases[8].

1   *Pullar v United Kingdom* (1996) 22 EHRR 391, E Ct HR.
2   *Pullar v United Kingdom* (1996) 22 EHRR 391, E Ct HR.
3   *Granger v United Kingdom* A No 174 (1990) 12 EHRR 469.
4   *Boner v United Kingdom* A No 300-B (1994) 19 EHRR 246; *Maxwell v United Kingdom* A No 300-C (1994) 19 EHRR 97.
5   *Pullar v United Kingdom* (1996) 22 EHRR 391, E Ct HR.
6   *Granger v United Kingdom* A No 174 (1990) 12 EHRR 469: *Maxwell v United Kingdom* A No 300-C (1994) 19 EHRR 97.
7   *Pullar v United Kingdom* (1996) 22 EHRR 391, E Ct HR.
8   *Granger v United Kingdom* A No 174 (1990) 12 EHRR 469; *Boner v United Kingdom* A No 300-B (1994) 19 EHRR 246; *Maxwell v United Kingdom* A No 300-C (1994) 19 EHRR 97.

5.06   Several cases have concerned aspects of prisoners' rights, such as correspondence[1], visits[2], leave[3] and prison conditions[4]. These issues have been examined under reference to arts 3[5], 8[6], 10[7], 13[8] and 25[9] of the European Convention on Human Rights. Just satisfaction has been considered in all these cases.

1   *Boyle and Rice v United Kingdom* A No 131 (1988) 10 EHRR 425; *McCallum v United Kingdom* A No 183 (1990) 13 EHRR 596; *Campbell v United Kingdom* A No 233-A (1992) 15 EHRR 137.
2   *Boyle and Rice v United Kingdom* A No 131 (1988) 10 EHRR 425.
3   *Boyle and Rice v United Kingdom* A No 131 (1988) 10 EHRR 425.
4   *McCallum v United Kingdom* A No 183 (1990) 13 EHRR 596.
5   *McCallum v United Kingdom* A No 183 (1990) 13 EHRR 596.
6   *Boyle and Rice v United Kingdom* A No 131 (1988) 10 EHRR 425; *McCallum v United Kingdom* A No 183 (1990) 13 EHRR 596: *Campbell v United Kingdom* A No 233-A (1992) 15 EHRR 137.
7   *McCallum v United Kingdom* A No 183 (1990) 13 EHRR 596.
8   *Boyle and Rice v United Kingdom* A No 131 (1988) 10 EHRR 425: *McCallum v United Kingdom* A No 183 (1990) 13 EHRR 596.
9   *Campbell v United Kingdom* A No 233-A (1992) 15 EHRR 137.

5.07   The law relating to children was examined in one case which concerned procedure at a children's hearing and parental rights in relation to an illegitimate child[1]. These issues were examined in relation to arts 6(1), 8 and 14 of the European Convention on Human Rights. Just satisfaction was also considered. In another case corporal punishment in schools was examined in relation to art 3 of the Convention and art 2 of the first protocol[2]. A subsequent judgment[3] dealt with just satisfaction.

1   *McMichael v United Kingdom* A No 307-B (1995) 20 EHRR 205, E Ct HR.
2   *Campbell and Cosans v United Kingdom* A No 48 (1982) 4 EHHR 293, E Ct HR.
3   *Campbell and Cosans v United Kingdom* A No 60 (1983) 13 EHRR 441, E Ct HR.

5.09   The protection of property has been considered in one case concerning the nationalisation of an industry, the adequacy of compensation and the assessment of compensation by a statutory tribunal[1]. These issues were examined in relation to arts 6(1) and 13 of the Convention and art 1 of the first protocol (taken alone and in conjunction with art 14 of the Convention).

1   *Lithgow v United Kingdom* A No 102 (1986) 8 EHRR 329, E Ct HR.

5.09   Two cases arising from the participation of servicemen in nuclear tests raised a wide variety of issues concerning the duties of the Government to protect both the servicemen themselves and their future children; access to records; the recovery of documents; and (before the Commission) the interception of communications and the effectiveness of domestic remedies[1]. These issues were examined under arts 2, 3, 6(1), 8, 10, 11, 13, 14 and 26 of the European Convention on Human Rights.

1   *McGinley and Egan v United Kingdom* (1998) 27 EHRR 1, E Ct HR; *LCB v United Kingdom* (1998) 27 EHRR 212. The Commission's decision on admissibility in *McGinley and Egan* is reported at (1995) 21 EHRR CD 56. Its decision on admissibility in *LCB* is reported at 83-A DR 31 (1995).

5.10   A larger number of Scottish cases were considered by the European Commission on Human Rights prior to the establishment of the new court in November 1998. Although many are not reported in any published series of reports, they are available on the Internet[1]. Broad categories have been used in the following survey to indicate the principal subject matter of the cases, but it should be appreciated that these are not watertight compartments.

1   At http://www.dhdirhr.coe.fr/

5.11   The largest group of cases concerned aspects of criminal procedure. A large number of these concerned the availability of legal aid for trials[1] or appeals[2], and the related problem of appellants being unrepresented. These issues have been examined under arts 6(1) and (3)(c). Some of these cases have ended in friendly settlements[3]. In relation to pre-trial procedure, cases have concerned: the questioning of a suspect by the police without a solicitor being present[4]; detention without access to a solicitor[5]; detention under prevention of terrorism legislation[6]; the adequacy of time and facilities for the preparation of the defence[7]; absence of access to police statements and Crown precognitions[8]; the late instruction of counsel[9]; the refusal of an adjournment of the trial[10]; the obtaining ex parte of a warrant to take hair samples[11]; the forcible execution of such a warrant[12]; and conviction on a charge of obstructing the execution of a warrant to obtain bodily samples and teeth impressions[13]. These issues have been examined under arts 3[14], 5[15], 6(1)[16], (3)(b)[17], (c)[18] and (d)[19] and 7[20]. In relation to trial procedure, cases have concerned: the composition of the jury[21]; the impartiality of the jury[22]; newspaper reporting of the trial[23]; the adequacy of legal representation at the trial[24]; alleged errors of fact in the judge's charge[25]; and deletions from the indictment[26]. These issues have been considered under art 6. Conviction on a basis of concert rather than as an actor has been examined under art 6[27]. Conviction on an individual basis under an indictment for libelling, mobbing and rioting has been examined under art 7[28]. In relation to appeal procedure, cases have concerned: the handcuffing of an appellant during the hearing of his appeal[29]; access to a transcript of the trial[30]; access to a translation of the trial judge's charge and report to the Appeal Court[31]; the withdrawal of counsel[32]; the increase of sentence by the Appeal Court[33]; its refusal to allow the abandonment of an appeal[34]; its impartiality[35]; its refusal of an adjournment[36]; its alleged refusal to allow an appeal to be presented[37]; its receipt of a witness statement[38]; its substitution of a conviction in amended terms[39]; the absence of a right of appeal to the House of Lords[40]; and the absence of a right to compensation[41]. These issues have been examined under art 6 (and, in respect of a right to compensation, arts 5(5) and 13[42]). The length of proceedings has been examined under art 6(1) in a case in which there was a delay in bringing a case to trial[43]. Just satisfaction was also considered. An increase in statutory sentencing powers has been examined under art 7[44]. The ability of a Secretary of State's reference to cure defects in an earlier appeal hearing has also been considered[45]. The question of whether a person has a right to have criminal proceedings instituted against other persons has been considered in relation to arts 5, 6[46] and 13[47].

1 Application 11711/85 *McDermitt v United Kingdom* 52 DR 244 (1987); Application 12322/86 *Bell v United Kingdom*, 13 October 1987; Application 12370/86 *JS v United Kingdom*, 9 December 1987; Application 12917/87 *Drummond v United Kingdom*, 9 December 1987.
2 Application 16212/90 *R v United Kingdom*, 17 April 1991; Application 14778/99 *Higgins v United Kingdom* 73 DR 95 (1992); Application 18711/91 *B v United Kingdom*, 4 May 1993; Application 25523/94 *Murdoch v United Kingdom* 12 April 1996; Application 23934/94 *Middleton v United Kingdom*, 12 April 1996; Application 22112/93 *Wotherspoon v United Kingdom*, 12 April 1996; Application 24487/94 *Given v United Kingdom*, 12 April 1996; Application 25648/94 *Robson v United Kingdom*, 15 May 1996; Application 28891/95 *McAteer v United Kingdom*, 2 July 1997; Application 31021/96 *Taylor v United Kingdom*, 22 October 1997; Application 28944/95 *Faulkner v United Kingdom*, 4 March 1998.
3 Application 11711/85 *McDermitt v United Kingdom* 52 DR 244 (1987); Application 14778/99 *Higgins v United Kingdom* 73 DR 95 (1992).
4 Application 25648/94 *Robson v United Kingdom*, 15 May 1996.
5 Application 13081/87 *Windsor v United Kingdom*, 14 December 1988; Application 25648/94 *Robson v United Kingdom*, 15 May 1996.
6 Application 11641/85 *BC v United Kingdom*, 12 July 1986; Application 15096/89 *McGlinchey v United Kingdom*, 2 July 1990.
7 Application 11396/85 *JWR v United Kingdom*, 11 December 1986; Application 13081/87 *Windsor v United Kingdom*, 14 December 1988; Application 23934/94 *Middleton v United Kingdom*, 12 April 1996.
8 Application 22112/93 *Wotherspoon v United Kingdom*, 12 April 1996.
9 Application 12834/87 *Boyle v United Kingdom*, 3 March 1988
10 Application 26282/95 *Burns v United Kingdom*, 4 September 1996.
11 Application 34723/97 *Mellors v United Kingdom*, 21 May 1998.
12 Application 34723/97 *Mellors v United Kingdom*, 21 May 1998.
13 Application 34723/97 *Mellors v United Kingdom*, 21 May 1998.
14 Application 34723/97 *Mellors v United Kingdom*, 21 May 1998.
15 Application 11641/85 *BC v United Kingdom*, 12 July 1986; Application 15096/89 *McGlinchey v United Kingdom*, 2 July 1990.
16 Application 13081/87 *Windsor v United Kingdom*, 14 December 1988; Application 25648/94 *Robson v United Kingdom*, 15 May 1996.
17 Application 11396/85 *JWR v United Kingdom*, 11 December 1986; Application 13081/87 *Windsor v United Kingdom*, 14 December 1988; Application 23934/94 *Middleton v United Kingdom*, 12 April 1996; Application 22112/93 *Wotherspoon v United Kingdom*, 12 April 1996.
18 Application 13081/87 *Windsor v United Kingdom*, 14 December 1988; *Mellors v United Kingdom* Application 34723/97, 21 May 1998.
19 Application 22112/93 *Wotherspoon v United Kingdom*, 12 April 1996.
20 Application 34723/97 *Mellors v United Kingdom*, 21 May 1998.
21 Application 24399/94 *Mennie v United Kingdom*, 16 October 1994.
22 Application 23934/94 *Middleton v United Kingdom*, 12 April 1996.
23 Application 23934/94 *Middleton v United Kingdom*, 12 April 1996.
24 Application 25523/94 *Murdoch v United Kingdom*, 12 April 1996; Application 23934/94 *Middleton v United Kingdom*, 12 April 1996; Application 25648/94 *Robson v United Kingdom*, 15 May 1996.

25 Application 32874/96 *Moore v United Kingdom*, 11 September 1997.
26 Application 24399/94 *Mennie v United Kingdom*, 16 October 1994.
27 Application 12323/86 *Campbell v United Kingdom*, 57 DR 148 (1988).
28 Application 21266/93 *K v United Kingdom*, 30 June 1993.
29 Application 12323/86 *Campbell v United Kingdom* 57 DR 148 (1988).
30 Application 18077/41 *Montes and Lopez v United Kingdom*, 2 December 1992.
31 Application 18077/41 *Montes and Lopez v United Kingdom*, 2 December 1992.
32 Application 12834/87 *Boyle v United Kingdom*, 3 March 1988.
33 Application 12002/86 *Grant v United Kingdom* 55 DR 218 (1988).
34 Application 12002/86 *Grant v United Kingdom* 55 DR 218 (1988).
35 Application 12002/86 *Grant v United Kingdom* 55 DR 218 (1988).
36 Application 25523/94 *Murdoch v United Kingdom*, 12 April 1996.
37 Application 24487/94 *Given v United Kingdom*, 12 April 1996; Application 26282/95 *Burns v United Kingdom*, 4 September 1996; Application 28944/95 *Faulkner v United Kingdom*, 4 March 1998.
38 Application 24399/94 *Mennie v United Kingdom*, 16 October 1994, applying *Pullar v United Kingdom* (1996) 22 EHRR 391, E Ct HR.
39 Application 24399/94 *Mennie v United Kingdom*, 16 October 1994.
40 Application 24399/94 *Mennie v United Kingdom*, 16 October 1994.
41 Application 24399/94 *Mennie v United Kingdom*, 16 October 1994.
42 Application 24399/94 *Mennie v United Kingdom*, 16 October 1994.
43 Application 21437/93 *Dougan v United Kingdom* 1997 SCCR 56, EComHR.
44 Application 14099/88 *Gillies v United Kingdom*, 14 April 1989.
45 Application 16732/90 *WK v United Kingdom*, 11 January 1993.
46 Application 13081/87 *Windsor v United Kingdom*, 14 December 1988.
47 Application 18077/41 *Montes and Lopez v United Kingdom*, 2 December 1992.

5.12 Aspects of civil procedure have been considered in a number of cases. These include cases concerned with: a vexatious litigant order (and art 6(1))[1]; summary warrant procedure in connection with taxes[2] and rates[3] (and its compatibility with art 6(1)); child maintenance review procedures[4]; directors' disqualification proceedings (in particular, the disclosure of information, the giving of reasons and the effectiveness of judicial review, under art 6(1))[5]; an unfair dismissal hearing before an industrial tribunal following acquittal in criminal proceedings (compatibility with art 6(1) and (2))[6]; the Warsaw Convention (as applied in *Abnett v British Airways plc*[7]) (examined under arts 1, 2, 3, 5, 6(1), 8, 13 and 14 of the Convention, and art 1 of the first protocol)[8]; the treatment of a party litigant[9]; the adequacy of rights of appeal from the Lands Tribunal for Scotland[10]; procedure at a public inquiry (compatibility with art 6(1) and (2))[11]; and the effect of developments in the common law on prior transactions (compatibility with art 1 of the first protocol)[12].

1 Application 11559/85 *H v United Kingdom* 45 DR 281 (1985).
2 Application 25373/94 *Smith v United Kingdom* (1995) 21 EHRR CD 75.
3 Application 25602/94 *ANM & Co v United Kingdom*, 29 November 1995.
4 Application 24875/94 *Logan v United Kingdom* 86-A DR 74 (1996), 22 EHRR CD 178.
5 Application 28530/95 *X v United Kingdom* (1998) 25 EHRR CD 88.
6 Application 11882/85 *C v United Kingdom* 54 DR 162 (1987).
7 1997 SC 26, HL.
8 Application 37650/97 *Manners v United Kingdom*, 21 May 1998.9
9 Application 13475/87 *Kay v United Kingdom*, 2 May 1989.
10 Application 13135/87 *S v United Kingdom*, 4 July 1988.
11 Application 22301/93 *McKenzie v United Kingdom*, 1 December 1993.
12 Application 37857/97 *Bank of Scotland v United Kingdom*, 21 October 1998, considering *Smith v Bank of Scotland* 1997 SC 10, HL.

5.13 Several cases have concerned prisoners' rights. Particular issues have included: interference with correspondence with a solicitor[1]; or with the court[2]; restrictions on lawyers' visits[3]; restrictions on television interviews[4]; solitary confinement[5];

imprisonment in a remote location[6]; the transfer of prisoners to Scotland[7]; denial of access to a telephone[8]; lockdown conditions[9]; parole, in particular the system of periodical reviews and the withdrawal of a release recommendation following an incident which resulted in the prisoner's being charged and acquitted[10]; and the position of child offenders in relation to remission[11]. These issues have been considered under arts 3[12], 5[13], 6[14], 8[15], 10[16], 13[17] and 25[18].

1　Application 10621/83 *McComb v United Kingdom* 50 DR 81 (1986) (friendly settlement); Application 20075/92 *Leech v United Kingdom*, 31 August 1994 (considering *Leech v Secretary of State for Scotland*, 1993 SLT 365).
2　Application 11392/85 *Hodgson v United Kingdom*, 4 March 1987.
3　Application 12323/86 *Campbell v United Kingdom* 57 DR 148 (1988).
4　Application 12656/87 *K v United Kingdom*, 13 May 1988.
5　Application 12323/86 *Campbell v United Kingdom* 57 DR 148 (1988).
6　Application 14462/88 *Ballantyne v United Kingdom*, 12 April 1991.
7　Application 15817/89 *Wakefield v United Kingdom* 66 DR 251 (1990).
8　Application 18077/89 *Montes and Lopez v United Kingdom*, 2 December 1992.
9　Application 18942/91 *Windsor v United Kingdom*, 6 April 1993; Application 25525/94 *Advic v United Kingdom* (1995) 20 EHRR CD 125.
10　Application 20755/92 *Howden v United Kingdom*, 10 October 1994, applying *Wynne v United Kingdom* (1994) 19 EHRR 333, E Ct HR and considering *Howden v Parole Board for Scotland* 1992 GWD 20-1186.
11　Application 11077/84 *Nelson v United Kingdom* 49 DR 170 (1986).
12　Application 18942/91 *Windsor v United Kingdom*, 6 April 1993; Application 25525/94 *Advic v United Kingdom* (1995) 20 EHRR CD 125.
13　Application 20755/92 *Howden v United Kingdom*, 10 October 1994; Application 11077/84 *Nelson v United Kingdom* 49 DR 170 (1986).
14　Application 12323/86 *Campbell v United Kingdom* 57 DR 148 (1988); Application 10621/83 *McComb v United Kingdom*, 50 DR 81 (1986) (friendly settlement); Application 20946/92 *Veenstra v United Kingdom*, 31 August 1994; Application 20755/92 *Howden v United Kingdom*, 10 October 1994.
15　Application 10621/83 *McComb v United Kingdom*, 50 DR 81 (1986) (friendly settlement); Application 11392/85 *Hodgson v United Kingdom*, 4 March 1987; Application 15817/89 *Wakefield v United Kingdom*, 1 October 1990; Application 14462/88 *Ballantyne v United Kingdom*, 12 April 1991; Application 20946/92 *Veenstra v United Kingdom*, 31 August 1994; Application 20075/92 *Leech v United Kingdom*, 31 August 1994.
16　Application 12656/87 *K v United Kingdom*, 13 May 1988.
17　Application 18942/91 *Windsor v United Kingdom*, 6 April 1993; Application 20075/92 *Leech v United Kingdom*, 31 August 1994.
18　Application 12323/86 *Campbell v United Kingdom* 57 DR 148 (1988).

5.14　Immigration law has been considered in one case under Article 8, concerned with re-admission as a returning resident[1]. No special issue of Scots law arose.

1　Application 25525/94 *Advic v United Kingdom* (1995) 20 EHRR CD 125.

5.15　The law governing mentally disordered offenders was considered in a case under art 5(1)(e) and (4) concerned with the absence of a judicial remedy allowing the periodic review of detention[1].

1　Application 10213/82 *Gordon v United Kingdom* 47 DR 36 (1985) (following *X v United Kingdom*, Judgment of 5 November 1981, Series A No 46 (1981) 4 EHRR 188).

5.16　Other cases have concerned a variety of issues, including: the interception of communications[1]; a closed shop agreement[2]; the effects of a child maintenance order on access to the children and on religious observance[3]; the suspension of invalidity benefits during imprisonment[4]; corporal punishment in schools and 'philosophical convictions'[5]; the failure of the state to provide financial assistance for private education[6]; a prohibition, by an order made under the nobile officium[7], of the broadcasting of a television programme until the completion of a criminal trial[8]; compensation for the compulsory purchase of land[9]; differences between valuations for rating in Scotland and in England[10]; the security vetting of prospective employees[11]; the keeping of dossiers on individuals by the Security Services and others[12]; an employer's right to reprimand an employee who wrote to a newspaper without permission[13]; dismissal for a theft of which the employee had not been convicted[14]; the loss of tied accommodation[15]; privilege under the law of defamation[16]; and the Crown's refusal to disclose a post mortem report to a relative of the deceased[17]. Other cases have illustrated issues which may arise in relation to company law[18] and in relation to the taking of children into care[19].

1 Application 21482/93 *Christie v United Kingdom* 78-A DR 119 (1994): art 8.
2 Application 9520/81 *Reid v United Kingdom* 34 DR 107 (1983): art 11.
3 Application 24875/94 *Logan v United Kingdom* 86-A DR 74 (1996), 22 EHRR CD 178: arts 8 and 9.
4 Application 2753/95 *Carlin v United Kingdom* (1997) 25 EHRR CD 75: art 1 of the first protocol.
5 Application 8566/79 *X, Y and Z v United Kingdom* 31 DR 50 (1982): art 2 of the first protocol.
6 Application 9461/81 *X and Y v United Kingdom* 31 DR 210 (1982): art 2 of the first protocol.
7 Ie the High Court of Justiciary's inherent equitable jurisdiction.
8 Application 34324/96 *BBC Scotland, McDonald, Rodgers and Donald v United Kingdom* (1997) 25 EHRR CD 179.
9 Application 13135/87 *S v United Kingdom*, 4 July 1988.
10 Application 13473/87 *P v United Kingdom*, 11 July 1988: art 1 of the first protocol and art 14 of the Convention.
11 Application 12015/86 *Hilton v United Kingdom*, 6 July 1988: art 8. This decision contains a discussion of the statute of the BBC under the Convention.
12 Application 12015/86 *Hilton v United Kingdom*, 6 July 1988.
13 Application 16936/90 *Todd v United Kingdom*, 7 November 1990: art 10.
14 Application 28530/95 *X v United Kingdom* (1998) 25 EHRR CD 88: art 6(2).
15 Application 28530/95 *X v United Kingdom* (1998) 25 EHRR CD 88: art 8.
16 Application 22301/93 *McKenzie v United Kingdom*, 1 December 1993: art 6.
17 Application 11516/85 *WB v United Kingdom*, 13 May 1986: arts 8 and 10.
18 Application 11413/85 *RA v United Kingdom*, 13 May 1986: art 1 of the first protocol.
19 Application 19579/92 *B Family v United Kingdom*, 2 April 1993: arts 3, 5, 6, 8 and 13 of the Convention, and art 2 of the first protocol.

C   The Convention in the Scottish courts prior to the 1998 Act

5.17 Although Scotland has contributed significantly to the jurisprudence of the E Ct HR and the European Commission on Human Rights, the Scottish courts were relatively slow to make use of the Convention. In *Kaur v Lord Advocate*[1] Lord Ross expressed the view that a Scottish court was not entitled to have regard to the Convention, either as an aid to construction or otherwise, unless and until its provisions were given statutory effect. Although obiter dictum[2] this view was approved by the Inner House (again, obiter) in *Moore v Secretary of State for Scotland*[3]. This unduly restrictive approach[4] discouraged reference to the Convention in Scottish cases for many years, although such references appeared in the speeches in the House of Lords in *Lord Advocate v Scotsman Publications Ltd*[5]. This was in contrast to the approach adopted in England and Wales, not least by Scottish judges sitting in the House of Lords[6].

1 1980 SC 319.
2 There was conceded to be no ambiguity in the legislation in issue in *Kaur v Lord Advocate* 1980 SC 319, and thus no room for the use of the Convention as an aid to interpretation: see at 329.

3   1985 SLT 38.
4   The presumption that Parliament does not intend to legislate in a manner inconsistent with the treaty obligations entered into by the Crown was established in Scots Law prior to *Kaur* and *Moore*: see eg *Mortensen v Peters* (1906) 8 F 93.
5   1989 SC 122, [1990] 1 AC 812, HL.
6   Eg *Waddington v Miah* [1974] 1 WLR 683 at 694 per Lord Reid; *A-G v British Broadcasting Corpn* [1981] AC 303 at 352 per Lord Fraser of Tullybelton.

5.18   The Convention began however to have a direct impact upon the Scottish courts, particularly through a number of decisions of the E Ct HR concerned with Scottish criminal proceedings. The first of these decisions, *Granger v United Kingdom*[1], resulted in the issue of a Practice Note by the Lord Justice-General providing for a procedure whereby the High Court of Justiciary (as a court of appeal) could recommend the review of a decision of the legal aid authorities to refuse legal aid for representation at an appeal hearing. Subsequently, the cases of *Boner v United Kingdom*[2] and *Maxwell v United Kingdom*[3] resulted in a significant alteration of the criminal appeal system in Scotland, so as to end the automatic right of appeal against conviction or sentence and to introduce a requirement that leave to appeal be obtained. The High Court's awareness of the implications of the Convention was reflected in *Anderson v H M Advocate*, where Lord Hope of Craighead referred to art 6 as describing 'principles which ... have, for a long time, been established as part of the law of this country[4].

1   *Granger v United Kingdom* A No 174 (1990) 12 EHRR 469.
2   *Boner v United Kingdom* A No 300-B (1994) 19 EHRR 246.
3   *Maxwell v United Kingdom* A No 300-C (1994) 19 EHRR 97.
4   1996 JC 29 at 34.

5.19   Following his appointment as Lord President and Lord Justice-General, Lord Hope made clear extra-judicially his concerns over the difference in approach to the Convention which was at least believed to exist between the Scottish and English courts, and the consequent reluctance of Scottish counsel to make use of the Convention in argument[1]. Subsequently in *T, Petitioner*[2] he took the opportunity to review the status of the Convention in Scots law. In relation to *Kaur*[3], he stated:

'Lord Ross's opinion, although widely quoted in the textbooks as still representing the law of Scotland on this matter, has been looking increasingly outdated in the light of subsequent developments, and in my opinion, with respect, it is time that it was expressly departed from'[4].

Lord Hope then reviewed the series of English cases in the House of Lords, culminating in *R v Secretary of State for the Home Department, ex p Brind*[5], which had established that in construing any provision in domestic legislation which is ambiguous in the sense that is capable of a meaning which either conforms to or conflicts with the Convention, the courts will presume that Parliament intended to legislate in uniformity with the Convention, not in conflict with it. Lord Hope concluded:

'I consider that the drawing of a distinction between the law of Scotland and that of the rest of the United Kingdom on this matter can no longer be justified. In my opinion the courts in Scotland should apply the same presumption as that described by Lord Bridge [in *ex p Brind*], namely that, when legislation is found to be ambiguous in the sense that it is capable of a meaning which either conforms to or conflicts with the Convention, Parliament is to be presumed to have legislated in conformity with the Convention, not in conflict with it.'[6].

1   [1991] JR 122 at 126–127; 'From Maastricht to the Saltmarket', Society of Solicitors in the Supreme Courts of Scotland, Biennial Lecture 1992, at 16–17. See also 'Devolution and Human Rights' [1998] EHRLR 367.

2   1997 SLT 724.
3   *Kaur v Lord Advocate* 1980 SC 319.
4   1997 SLT at 733.
5   [1991] 1 AC 696.
6   1997 SLT 724 at 734.

5.20 Since *T, Petitioner* the Convention has been cited with increasing frequency in the Scottish courts, particularly in the High Court. A notable example is *McLeod v HM Advocate*[1], concerned with the disclosure of documents to the defence in criminal proceedings, where the court carried out a close examination of the Strasbourg case-law under Article 6(1) and was concerned to decide the case in a way which was consistent with art 6(1). Other criminal cases involving the Convention have concerned: the compatibility with arts 5(2) and 6(3)(a) of procedures for dealing with persons who did not speak English[2]; delay in the hearing of an appeal[3]; contempt of court[4]; and the withdrawal of legal aid[5]. The second-last mentioned case contains a perceptive observation by the Lord Justice-General, Lord Rodger of Earlsferry[6], that although a boundary has always existed between freedom of expression and the requirements of the due course of justice, art 10 may have had the consequence of displacing that boundary from the familiar place where once it ran: the boundary may have been redrawn at a point which would not have been chosen by people looking at the matter primarily from the standpoint of the administration of justice. This is a useful reminder that although the Convention gives expression to values which already infuse the law of Scotland, and may be regarded as commonplaces of all western legal systems, it does not always express or balance those values in the same way as Scots law has traditionally done.

1   1998 SCCR 77.
2   *Ucak v HM Advocate*, 1998 SCCR 517.
3   *Ucak v HM Advocate*, 1998 SCCR 517.
4   *Cox and Griffiths, Petitioners*, 1998 SCCR 561.
5   *Shaw, Petitioner; Milne, Petitioner* 1998 GWD 37-1930.
6   At 568.

5.21 The Convention has also featured in a number of civil cases. In *Booker Aquaculture Ltd v Secretary of State for Scotland*[1]. Article 1 of the first protocol to the Convention was considered in the context of the implementation of European Community legislation. Article 8 of the Convention has also been referred to in the context of sexual harassment[2].

1   1998 GWD 21-1089.
2   *Ward v Scotrail Railways Ltd* 1999 SC 255.

5.22 As is apparent from the foregoing discussion, the Convention has already influenced the law and practice in Scotland in many fields. Even before the commencement of the SA 1998 or the HRA 1998, the Convention has begun to be used more creatively by the courts in Scotland, with the consequence that its influence on the law of Scotland is certain to increase.

D   The Scotland Act 1998 and the Convention

5.23 The government elected in May 1997 had a manifesto commitment to a programme of constitutional reform, including devolution to Scotland and the incorporation of the

Convention into UK law. The White Paper on devolution[1], published in July 1997, left open the precise implications for devolution of incorporating the Convention, although making it clear that the Scottish Executive and Parliament would implement the UK's international obligations[2]. There were two broad approaches by means of which this could be achieved in respect of the Convention: by enabling the UK Government to override acts of the Scottish Executive or Parliament which would contravene the Convention, or by making it legally impossible for the Scottish Executive or Parliament to contravene the Convention. The White Paper on the Human Rights Bill[3], published in October 1997, made it clear that the latter approach was to be adopted:

> 'The Government has decided that the Scottish Parliament will have no power to legislate in a way which is incompatible with the Convention; and similarly that the Scottish Executive will have no power to make subordinate legislation or to take executive action which is incompatible with the Convention. It will accordingly be possible to challenge such legislation and actions on the ground that the Scottish Parliament or Executive has incorrectly applied its powers. If the challenge is successful then the legislation or action would be held to be unlawful.'[4].

These proposals were reflected in the provisions of the Scotland Bill, which were enacted (with substantial modifications) in the SA 1998[5]. It should be made clear at the outset that the SA 1998 is complex and raises many difficult questions, and that the following account attempts only to give an outline of the principal features relevant to the Convention. There are numerous qualifications and exceptions on matters of detail, for which reference should be made to the SA 1998 itself.

1   *Scotland's Parliament* (Cm 3658, 1997).
2   *Scotland's Parliament* (Cm 3658, 1997), paras 4.19–4.20.
3   *Rights Brought Home* (Cm 3782, 1997).
4   *Rights Brought Home* (Cm 3782, 1997), para 2.21.
5   Scotland Act 1998, c 46.

1   ACTS OF THE SCOTTISH PARLIAMENT

5.24   The SA 1998, s 29(1) provides that an Act of the Scottish Parliament is not law so far as any provision of the Act is outside the legislative competence of the Parliament. The SA 1998, s 29(2) provides that a provision is outside that competence as far as any of the following paragraphs apply:

(a)   it would form part of the law of a country or territory other than Scotland, or confer or remove functions exercisable otherwise than in or as regards Scotland;

(b)   it relates to reserved matters;

(c)   it is in breach of the restrictions in Schedule 4;

(d)   it is incompatible with any of the Convention rights or with Community law;

(e)   it would remove the Lord Advocate from his position as head of the system of criminal prosecution and investigation of deaths in Scotland.

5.25   Paragraphs (a) and (e) are not concerned with the Convention. In relation to para (b), the observation and implementation of obligations under the Convention are not reserved matters[1]. In relation to para (c), the SA 1998, Sch 4 provides that an Act of the Scottish Parliament cannot modify, or confer power by subordinate legislation to modify, any of a number of provisions including the HRA 1998[2]. The SA 1998, Sch 4 also protects s 29 itself from modification by the Scottish Parliament[3]. In relation to para (d), the expression 'the Convention rights' is defined[4] as having the same meaning as in the HRA 1998 (where it is further defined)[5].

1   SA 1998, Sch 5, para 7(2).
2   SA 1998, Sch 4, para 1(1) and (2)(f).
3   SA 1998, Sch 4, para 4.
4   SA 1998, s 126(1).
5   HRA 1998, s 1.

5.26   The SA 1998 contains provisions to ensure that Bills are scrutinised before their introduction in the Scottish Parliament, and to allow for their further scrutiny prior to their submission for Royal Assent. Under the SA 1998, s 31 a member of the Scottish Executive in charge of a Bill must, on or before introduction of the Bill in the Parliament, state that in his view the provisions of the Bill would be within the legislative competence of the Parliament[1]. In addition, the Presiding Officer[2] must, on or before the introduction of the Bill, decide whether or not in his view the provisions of the Bill would be within the legislative competence of the Parliament and state his decision[3]. In this way, the compatibility of any Bill with the Convention will be scrutinised both within the Scottish Executive and by an independent officer of the Scottish Parliament at an early stage.

1   SA 1998, s 31(1).
2   SA 1998, s 19.
3   SA 1998, s 31(2).

5.27   Once a Bill has been passed, it is for the Presiding Officer to submit it for Royal Assent[1]. There is however a period of four weeks beginning with the passing of a Bill during which the Advocate General[2], the Lord Advocate or the Attorney General can refer the question of whether a Bill or any provision of a Bill would be within the legislative competence of the Parliament to the Judicial Committee of the Privy Council for decision[3]. For this purpose the Judicial Committee will consist of the Lords of Appeal in Ordinary together with any other member of the Committee who has held high judicial office[4]. A law officer cannot however make a reference if he has notified the Presiding Officer that he does not intend to make a reference in relation to the Bill[5]. The Presiding Officer cannot submit a Bill for Royal Assent at any time when any of the law officers is entitled to make a reference, or when any such reference has been made but has not been decided or otherwise disposed of by the Judicial Committee[6]. If the Judicial Committee decide that the Bill or any provision of it would not be within the legislative competence of the Parliament, then the Presiding Officer cannot submit the Bill for Royal Assent in its unamended form[7]. The Bill can however be reconsidered by the Parliament following an adverse decision by the Judicial Committee; and any Bill amended on reconsideration can then be approved or rejected by the Parliament[8]. Where a Bill is approved following its reconsideration, there is then a further four week period during which it can again be referred by a law officer to the Judicial Committee[9]. In principle, the process of referral, decision, amendment on reconsideration, approval and re-referral can be repeated indefinitely[10]. In the event that a reference to the Judicial Committee results in a reference to the European Court of Justice for a preliminary ruling, special provisions apply[11].

1   SA 1998, s 32(1).
2   SA 1998, s 87.
3   SA 1998, s 33(1) and (2)(a).
4   SA 1998, s 103(2).
5   SA 1998, s 33(3).
6   SA 1998, s 32(2)
7   SA 1998, s 32(3).
8   SA 1998, s 36(4).

9   SA 1998, s 33(2)(b).
10 SA 1998, s 36(6).
11 SA 1998, s 34, read with SA 1998, ss 32(3)(b) and 36(4)(b).

5.28   The SA 1998 does not state expressly whether the above arrangements provide the only means whereby the compatibility of a Bill with the Convention can be tested, or whether legal proceedings could be brought by third parties (eg against the member of the Scottish Executive responsible for making a statement under s 31(1); or against the Presiding Officer in respect of his decision under s 31(2); or against the law officers in respect of their exercise of their discretion under s 33(1); or against the Parliament itself in respect of its decision whether to pass a Bill or to approve a Bill amended on reconsideration). It is clear that legal proceedings can in principle be taken against a law officer or a member of the Scottish Executive; and the SA 1998 provides for proceedings against the Parliament or the Presiding Officer, although only a restricted range of remedies are available[1]. A person seeking to challenge a Bill might however have difficulty in establishing title and interest to sue and in overcoming the related problem of prematurity[2]. There is also a question whether issues concerning the legislative competence of the Parliament can, consistently with the scheme of the SA 1998, be raised (other than by a law officer) except as a 'devolution issue' under the SA 1998, s 98. Any person wishing to challenge a Bill on the basis of the Convention would in addition have to be a 'victim' for the purposes of art 34 of the Convention[3]. That test would also apply to a challenge, based on the Convention, of a failure to introduce a Bill[4].

1   SA 1998, s 40. See 593 HL Official Report (5th series) cols 2019–2020 (28 October 1998).
2   See 592 HL Official Report (5th series) cols 1364–1377 (28 July 1998).
3   SA 1998, s 100(1). See para **2.7.2** on the meaning of 'victim'.
4   Crown Proceedings Act 1947, s 21, would also be relevant to the remedies available: see SA 1998, ss 52(2) and (7), and 126(1).

5.29   Issues arising as to the compatibility of an Act of the Scottish Parliament with the Convention are described below under the heading 'Devolution Issues'.

2   ACTS OF THE SCOTTISH ADMINISTRATION

5.30   In order to understand how the Convention applies under the SA 1998 to the Scottish Administration, it is necessary to begin with a rather complicated taxonomy. The Scottish Administration comprises the Scottish Executive (whose members are referred to collectively as the Scottish Ministers[1]), junior Scottish Ministers[2] and the staff of the Scottish administration[3] (ie civil servants). The members of the Scottish Executive are the First Minister, Ministers appointed by the First Minister under s 47, the Lord Advocate and the Solicitor General for Scotland[4]. Statutory functions (ie functions conferred by any enactment, including an Act of the Scottish Parliament or an Act of the Westminster Parliament[5]) may be conferred on the Scottish Ministers as a whole, or on the First Minister alone, or on the Lord Advocate alone[6]. Statutory functions conferred on the Lord Advocate alone after he ceases to be a Minister of the Crown, together with any functions exercisable by him immediately before he ceases to be a Minister of the Crown, comprise his 'retained functions'[7].

1   SA 1998, s 44(2).
2   SA 1998, s 49.
3   SA 1998, s 51.
4   SA 1998, s 44(1).

5   SA 1998, ss 52(7) and 126(1).
6   SA 1998, s 52(1), (2), (5)(a) and 6(b).
7   SA 1998, s 52(6).

5.31   The SA 1998. s 53 provides for the general transfer of existing Ministerial functions to the Scottish Ministers. It applies to three specified categories of function which appear to cover all the functions exercisable by a Minister of the Crown – subject to the important exception of the retained functions of the Lord Advocate – and provides that those functions 'shall, so far as they are exercisable within devolved competence', be exercisable by the Scottish Ministers. The expression 'within devolved competence' is explained in the SA 1998, s 54. This provides first that the making of any provision by subordinate legislation is outside devolved competence if the provision would be outside the legislative competence of the Parliament if it were included in an Act of the Scottish Parliament. In relation to any function other than a function of making, confirming or approving subordinate legislation, s 54 provides that it is outside devolved competence to exercise the function (or exercise it in any way) so far as a provision of an Act of the Scottish Parliament conferring the function (or, as the case may be, conferring it so as to be exercisable in that way) would be outside the legislative competence of the Parliament. These complex provisions are intended to have the effect (informally referred to as 'washing') that the functions transferred to the Scottish Ministers – other than the retained functions of the Lord Advocate – do not include any function which would be outside the legislative competence of the Scottish Parliament, and do not include any power to exercise a function in a way which would be outside the legislative competence of the Parliament. Accordingly, in broad terms, if the exercise of an existing function of a Minister of the Crown is incompatible with any Convention right, then the function is not transferred to the Scottish Ministers. Equally, if the exercise in a particular way of an existing function of a Minister of the Crown is incompatible with any Convention right, then the power to exercise it in that way is not transferred to the Scottish Ministers. The major exception to the last two propositions comprises any function exercisable by the Lord Advocate immediately before he ceases to be a Minister of the Crown: these functions are retained by him.

5.32   Compatibility with the Convention is further addressed in the SA 1998, s 57(2). It provides that a member of the Scottish Executive has no power to make any subordinate legislation, or to do any other act, so far as the legislation or act is incompatible with any of the Convention rights. This general rule is subject to an important exception: it does not apply to an act of the Lord Advocate in prosecuting any offence[1], or in his capacity as head of the systems of criminal prosecution and investigation of deaths in Scotland, which, because of the HRA 1998, s 6(2), is not unlawful under s 6(1). In other words, if as the result of primary legislation the Lord Advocate could not have acted differently, or if he was acting so as to give effect to or enforce provisions of primary legislation (or provisions made under primary legislation) which cannot be read or given effect in a way which is compatible with the Convention rights, then it is not unlawful for him so to act. It is to be noted that the SA 1998, s 57(2) opens up the possibility of review of the Lord Advocate's exercise of his discretionary powers as public prosecutor, which the courts have in the past refused to review. On one view, his decisions may in future be open to review in the Court of Session as well as the High Court of Justiciary.

1   This has been said to be intended to cover the decision to prosecute rather than the conduct of the prosecution: 593 HL Official Report (5th series) col 2042 (28 October 1998).

5.33   As mentioned above, the SA 1998, s 57(2) refers to acts of 'a member of the Scottish Executive'. It is to be expected that the *Carltona*[1] principle will apply, so that acts done in the name of a Minister and on his behalf will be treated as his acts. It may also be that, in relation to s 57(2) and (3), the act of a member of the Procurator Fiscal Service will in practice be treated as the act of the Lord Advocate.

1   *Carltona Ltd v Works Comrs* [1943] 2 All ER 560.

3   DEVOLUTION ISSUES

5.34   The SA 1998, Sch 6 contains elaborate provisions for dealing with 'devolution issues'. These are defined[1] as meaning:

(a)   a question whether an Act of the Scottish Parliament or any provision of such an Act is within the legislative competence of the Parliament;

(b)   a question whether any function (which a person has purported, or is proposing, to exercise) is a function of the Scottish Ministers, the First Minister or the Lord Advocate;

(c)   a question whether the purported or proposed exercise of a function by a member of the Scottish Executive is, or would be, within devolved competence;

(d)   a question whether a purported or proposed exercise of a function by a member of the Scottish Executive is, or would be, incompatible with any of the Convention rights or with Community law;

(e)   a question whether a failure to act by a member of the Scottish Executive is incompatible with any of the Convention rights or with Community law;

(f)   any other question about whether a function is exercisable within devolved competence or in or as regards Scotland and any other question arising by virtue of the Act about reserved matters.

Putative devolution issues which are frivolous or vexatious can be filtered out[2].

1   SA 1998, Sch 6, para 1.
2   SA 1998, Sch 6, para 2.

5.35   Devolution issues may arise in any proceedings before courts or tribunals anywhere in the United Kingdom[1]. They may, for example, arise in proceedings for judicial review instituted for the purpose of challenging legislation of the Scottish Parliament or acts of Scottish Ministers, or collaterally (eg by way of defence in criminal proceedings). They can thus arise in proceedings at any level in the judicial hierarchy. Although most devolution issues are likely to arise in proceedings in Scotland, it is conceivable that they may also arise in proceedings in England and Wales or in Northern Ireland. The SA 1998, Sch 6 accordingly contains separate provisions in respect of each jurisdiction. They are however broadly similar. The present discussion will focus on the Scottish provisions.

1   See the discussion in 594 HL Official Report (5th series) cols 77–79 at 94, 2 November 1998.

5.36   The provisions cover both proceedings for the determination of a devolution issue[1] and other proceedings in which a devolution issue arises[2]. In each case, provision is made for the involvement in the proceedings of the Advocate General and the Lord Advocate.

1   SA 1998, Sch 6, para 4.
2   SA 1998, Sch 6, para 5.

5.37   When a devolution issue arises in civil proceedings before a court other than the House of Lords or any court consisting of three or more judges of the Court of Session, that court has a discretion (subject to any rules made under the Act) to refer the devolution issue to the Inner House[1]. Alternatively, the court can decide the issue itself, and it can thereafter come before the higher courts by way of appeal. Similarly, tribunals must make a reference if there is no appeal from that decision, but otherwise have a discretion[2]. The position in criminal proceedings is similar: a court other than any court consisting of two or more judges of the High Court of Justiciary has a discretion (subject to any rules made) either to refer the devolution issue to the High Court of Justiciary, or to decide the issue itself[3].

1   SA 1998, Sch 6, para 7. This is subject to rules made under SA 1998, Sch 6, para 37.
2   SA 1998, Sch 6, para 8.
3   SA 1998, Sch 6, para 9.

5.38   The court to which the issue is referred must then decide it: it cannot refer the issue to a yet higher court[1]. When the Inner House decides a devolution issue on a reference by a lower court, an appeal lies to the Judicial Committee of the Privy Council[2]. Similarly, when the High Court of Justiciary decides a devolution issue on a reference by a lower court, an appeal again lies to the Judicial Committee, but in this instance it is necessary to obtain the leave of the High Court or, failing such leave, the special leave of the Judicial Committee[3]. The reason why leave is required in this instance, but not from a decision of the Inner House, may be that an appeal ordinarily lies from any final decision of the Inner House to the House of Lords without leave, whereas there has hitherto been no right of appeal beyond the High Court of Justiciary.

1   This is implicit in SA 1998, Sch 6, paras 10 and 11.
2   SA 1998, Sch 6, para 12.
3   SA 1998, Sch 6, para 13.

5.39   If on the other hand a devolution issue arises in proceedings before a court consisting of three or more judges of the Court of Session, or two or more judges of the High Court of Justiciary (typically, but not necessarily, on appeal from a lower court or tribunal), then they can either refer the issue to the Judicial Committee[1] or decide the issue themselves. If they decide the issue themselves, an appeal will normally lie in civil proceedings to the House of Lords; but where in civil proceedings there is no right of appeal to the House of Lords, and in all criminal proceedings, an appeal will lie to the Judicial Committee with leave of the court concerned or, failing such leave, with special leave of the Judicial Committee[2].

1   SA 1998, Sch 6, paras 10 and 11.
2   SA 1998, Sch 6, para 13.

5.40   Where a devolution issue arises in the House of Lords, it must be referred to the Judicial Committee unless the House considers it more appropriate, having regard to all the circumstances, that it should determine the issue[1].

1   SA 1998, Sch 6, para 32.

5.41　The Lord Advocate, the Advocate General, the Attorney General or the Attorney General for Northern Ireland may require any court or tribunal to refer to the Judicial Committee any devolution issue which has arisen in proceedings before it to which he is a party[1]. A law officer may also refer to the Judicial Committee any devolution issue which is not the subject of proceedings[2].

1　SA 1998, Sch 6, para 33.
2　SA 1998, Sch 6, para 34.

5.42　The SA 1998 provides for subordinate legislation for prescribing such matters as the stage in proceedings at which a devolution issue is to be raised or referred, the sisting of proceedings for the purpose of a reference, and the manner and time within which any intimation is to be given[1]. It is to be expected that subordinate legislation will make particular provision for criminal proceedings and for civil proceedings before juries, so as to avoid references during a trial.

1　SA 1998, Sch 6, para 37.

5.43　One noteworthy aspect of the procedure is that the Judicial Committee will in general (but not always) be the final court of appeal in respect of devolution issues, including questions as to the compatibility of Acts of the Scottish Parliament or acts of Scottish Ministers with the Convention. Decisions of the Judicial Committee are thus likely to become an important source of domestic law on the Convention; and the Act provides that they are to be 'binding in all legal proceedings (other than proceedings before the Committee)'[1]. It remains to be seen whether this will be interpreted as meaning that its decisions are to be binding on the House of Lords.

1　SA 1998, s 103(1).

4　OTHER ASPECTS

5.44　There are a number of miscellaneous matters arising under the SA 1998 which require to be borne in mind.

5.45　The SA 1998 contains a number of provisions which should ensure broad congruence with the HRA 1998. First, in relation to standing, the SA 1998 does not enable a person to bring any proceedings on the ground that an act is incompatible with the Convention rights, or to rely on the Convention rights in proceedings, unless he would be a victim for the purposes of art 34 of the Convention (within the meaning of the HRA 1998) if proceedings in respect of the act were brought in the E Ct HR[1]. This imports the same test as the HRA 1998, s 7(7)[2]. Secondly, in relation to damages, the Act does not enable a court or tribunal to award any damages in respect of an act which is incompatible with the Convention rights which it could not award if the HRA 1998, s 8(3) and (4) applied[3]. There are however several points where a contrast can be drawn. These are described below[4].

1　SA 1998, s 100(1).
2　See para **2.7.2**.
3　SA 1998, s 100(3).
4　See paras **5.49–5.52**.

5.46   In the event that a court or tribunal decides that an Act of the Scottish Parliament is outwith its competence, or that subordinate legislation is ultra vires, the court or tribunal has a wide power to make an order removing or limiting any retrospective effect of the decision, or suspending the effect of the decision for any period and on any conditions to allow the defect to be corrected[1]. This power is intended to be exercised only exceptionally in criminal proceedings[2].

The SA 1998 also provides for subordinate legislation to make 'such provision as the person making the legislation considers necessary or expedient' in consequence of an Act of the Scottish Parliament which is not, or may not be, within its competence, or any purported exercise by a member of the Scottish Executive of his functions which is not, or may not be, an exercise or a proper exercise of those functions[3]. Such subordinate legislation can have retrospective effects[4]. It should be noted that these powers, so far as concerned with the Scottish Executive, are not confined to devolution issues but can apply where, on ordinary grounds of administrative law, a Scottish Minister has acted ultra vires[5]. The exercise of these powers may be liable to give rise to a variety of issues under the Convention.

1   SA 1998, s 102. This provision was discussed in 593 HL Official Report (5th series), cols 595–606 (8 October 1998).
2   594 HL Official Report (5th series), col 107 (2 November 1998).
3   SA 1998, s 107.
4   SA 1998, s 114(3).
5   This is the intended effect: 594 HL Official Report (5th series), col 599 (9 November 1998).

E   The Human Rights Act 1998

5.47   The HRA 1998 has already been considered in detail in Chapter 2. The present discussion will merely highlight features of particular importance in Scotland.

5.48   The HRA 1998, s 3 requires primary legislation and subordinate legislation to be read and given effect in a way which is compatible with the Convention rights, so far as it is possible to do so. It has to be borne in mind that Acts of the Scottish Parliament, and certain instruments made by Scottish Ministers, are 'subordinate legislation' as defined in the Act[1]. This principle of interpretation is different from that which applies in determining whether Acts of the Scottish Parliament are within the legislative competence of the Parliament, or whether subordinate legislation is within the powers conferred on Scottish Ministers by the SA 1998: where any provision in such legislation could be read in such a way as to be outside competence, it is to be read as narrowly as is required for it to be within competence, if such a reading is possible[2]. Depending on the circumstances, one or other of these principles of interpretation may be relevant, or both.

1   HRA 1998, s 21(1).
2   SA 1998, s 101. It should also be borne in mind that the Interpretation Act 1978 applies only in part to Acts of the Scottish Parliament: see the SA 1998, Sch 8, para 16.

5.49   The HRA 1998, s 4 enables certain courts to make a declaration that a provision of primary legislation is incompatible with a Convention right; and such a declaration can also be made in respect of a provision of subordinate legislation where primary legislation prevents removal of the incompatibility. In Scottish proceedings, the courts which have the power to make a declaration of incompatibility are the House of Lords, the Judicial Committee of the Privy Council, the High Court of Justiciary sitting otherwise than as a trial court, and the Court of Session[1]. Although an Act of the Scottish Parliament falls within the definition of 'subordinate legislation', the Parliament has no power to enact legislation which is incompatible with the Convention rights[2]: a declaration of incompatibility is accordingly not the appropriate remedy. The same would appear to apply to subordinate legislation made by a Scottish Minister, notwithstanding that it may fall within the definition of 'subordinate legislation' in the HRA 1998, since a Scottish Minister has no power to make subordinate legislation which is incompatible with the Convention rights[3].

1   HRA 1998, s 4(5). See para **2.4.4**.
2   SA 1998, s 29.
3   SA 1998, s 57(2).

5.50   The HRA 1998, s 6 makes it unlawful in general for a public authority to act in a way which is incompatible with a Convention right. The Scottish Parliament and the Scottish Ministers will be 'public authorities' within the meaning of s 6. The application of s 6 to these bodies is however more complicated than in respect of most other bodies, and depends on the interplay of the SA 1998 and the HRA 1998. The Parliament has no power to enact legislation which is incompatible with a Convention right[1]. Scottish Ministers have no powers to make any subordinate legislation which is incompatible with a Convention right[2]. Subject to one exception, Scottish Ministers have no power to do any other act which is incompatible with a Convention right[3]. That exception is an act of the Lord Advocate in prosecuting an offence or in his capacity as head of the system of criminal prosecution and investigation of deaths in Scotland which, because of the HRA 1998, s 6(2), is not unlawful under s 6(1). In other words, the only circumstances in which a Scottish Minister has the power to act in a way which is incompatible with a Convention right is where the Lord Advocate acts (in prosecuting, or in his deaths function) in a way in which he is constrained to act by primary legislation, or is giving effect to or enforcing primary legislation (or provisions made under such legislation) which is incompatible with Convention rights. It remains to be seen whether the courts will regard section 6 as applicable to acts done by Scottish Ministers (providing an alternative route to a challenge under the SA 1998), or not. It should be noted that s 6 covers omissions: and 'act' includes a failure to act[4]. In this respect, a question may arise whether s 6 is wider in scope than the SA 1998's restrictions on the powers of the Scottish Parliament and Executive[5]. In particular, s 6 may be capable of covering a failure by a Scottish Minister to introduce legislation, or a failure by the Scottish Parliament to enact it[6]. Difficult questions may well arise in relation to acts or omissions of the Lord Advocate[7].

1   SA 1998, s 29.
2   SA 1998, s 57(2).
3   SA 1998, s 57(2).
4   HRA 1998, s 6(6).
5   But cf SA 1998, s 100(4)(b), and Sch 6, para 1(e).
6   By implication from HRA 1998, s 6(6).
7   Some of the issues are discussed in 583 HL Official Report (5th series) cols 804–809 (24 November 1997); 584 HL Official Report (5th series) cols 1362–1368 (19 January 1998); 585 HL Official Report (5th series) cols 813–816 (5 February 1998).

5.51   There are a number of important differences between cases brought under the SA 1998 on the basis of the Convention and cases brought under the HRA 1998. The

House of Lords is the court of last resort for issues raised under the HRA 1998 (except in Scottish criminal cases), whereas the Judicial Committee of the Privy Council is normally the court of last resort for devolution issues. Devolution issues can be dealt with by a preliminary reference, whereas issues raised under the HRA 1998 cannot. A one-year limitation period applies to proceedings brought against a public authority under the HRA 1998[1], whereas no such period applies to proceedings under the SA 1998. The powers given to the court under the HRA 1998 where a public authority acts unlawfully are arguably different from those available under the SA 1998[2]. The legislative power given under the SA 1998 to remedy ultra vires acts is wider than that under the HRA 1998[3].

1   HRA 1998, s 7(5). See para **2.7.5**.
2   Compare HRA 1998, s 8 with the SA 1998, s 102.
3   Compare HRA 1998, s 10 with the SA 1998, s 107.

F   Conclusion

5.52   As a result of the SA 1998, the Convention is to be given what may be regarded as a constitutional status in Scotland: it is legally superior to Acts of the Scottish Parliament, and provides standards by which those Acts must be judged. The Parliament has no power to make law which is incompatible with the Convention. The Convention also provides standards by which the acts of Scottish Ministers will be judged: in general, they have no power to act in a way which is incompatible with the Convention. In this way, the Convention will be pivotal to Scottish constitutional law.

5.53   More generally, as elsewhere in the United Kingdom, the Convention will profoundly influence public law in Scotland, as it becomes binding on public authorities as a result of the HRA 1998. Since the courts themselves are public authorities for the purposes of the Act[1], the Convention will guide the courts in the development of the common law generally as well as the interpretation of statutes. Over time, this will inevitably have a profound effect upon the whole of our law.

1   HRA 1998, s 6(3)(a).

Chapter 6
Northern Ireland

A Introduction[1]

6.01 As with Scotland, it is not sensible to consider the effects of the Human Rights Act 1998 (HRA 1998) in Northern Ireland without at the same time taking into account the consequences of devolution. This requires careful scrutiny of certain provisions of the Northern Ireland Act 1998 (NIA 1998), which received Royal Assent ten days after the HRA 1998[2]. In addition, because Northern Ireland was subject to special 'direct rule' arrangements between the prorogation of its Parliament in 1972 and the empowerment of its Assembly in 1999[3], it is necessary to examine the operation of the HRA 1998 on the numerous Orders in Council made under those arrangements[4]. Orders in Council may still be made in relation to some non-transferred matters listed in the NIA 1998[5] and, like the other Orders in Council provided for in the NIA 1998[6], they too may be affected by the HRA 1998.

1   The author gratefully acknowledges the many valuable points made on an earlier draft by Professor Brigid Hadfield and Ms Christine Bell, both of Queen's University, Belfast. Remaining errors are his alone.
2   C 47. This is the Act which implements the Belfast (Good Friday) Agreement of 10 April 1998 (Cmnd 3883).
3   An earlier Assembly was established in January 1974, but it ceased to function in May of that year.
4   These were first authorised by the Northern Ireland (Temporary Provisions) Act 1972 and then by the Northern Ireland Act 1974 (renewed annually since then). The 1974 Act has been entirely repealed by the NIA 1998.
5   NIA 1998, Sch 3, paras 9–17 (see s 85).
6   Eg by the NIA 1998, ss 4(4), 6(4) or 86(1).

6.02 The European Convention on Human Rights is a comparatively well-known document in Northern Ireland, largely on account of the civil unrest that plagued the province after 1968. Many applications have been sent to Strasbourg by people living in Northern Ireland and a number of important decisions by the E Ct HR have been issued in cases emanating from Northern Ireland. Opinions differ over whether the Convention has been effective in curbing abuses of human rights during the 'troubles', but the prevailing view is that, on the whole, the Convention has *not* been much of a restraint on either emergency laws or emergency practices. There is more consensus over the point that the European Convention has not proved a particularly helpful document whenever solutions to Northern Ireland's intractable politico-legal problems are being sought. Indeed the Belfast Agreement of 10 April 1998 recognises this by foreshadowing a Bill of Rights for Northern Ireland, a piece of Westminster legislation that will go *beyond* the Convention and define rights which are:

'… supplementary to those in the European Convention on Human Rights, to reflect the particular circumstances of Northern Ireland, drawing as appropriate on international instruments and experience. These additional rights to reflect the principles of mutual respect for the identity and ethos of both communities and parity of esteem[1]'.

1   Section headed 'Rights, Safeguards and Equality of Opportunity', para 4.

6.03   The Northern Ireland Human Rights Commission, created by the NIA 1998[1], is to be requested by the Secretary of State to provide advice on what should be contained in the Bill of Rights, and the Belfast Agreement envisages the Commission consulting on this issue and considering, inter alia:

> '... the formulation of a general obligation on government and public bodies fully to respect, on the basis of equality of treatment, the identity and ethos of both communities in Northern Ireland; and a clear formulation of the rights not to be discriminated against and to equality of opportunity in both the public and private sectors[2]'.

The Northern Ireland Human Rights Commission – a successor body to the Standing Advisory Commission on Human Rights, created by the Northern Ireland Constitution Act 1973 but with purely advisory powers – is the only body of its kind in the United Kingdom and, as such, will be carefully scrutinised by advocates for such bodies elsewhere in the country[3]. The Republic of Ireland is to have a Human Rights Commission too, 'with a mandate and remit equivalent to that within Northern Ireland'[4], and the two Irish Commissions are to set up a joint committee 'as a forum for consideration of human rights issues in the island of Ireland'[5]. One of the matters which this joint committee will consider is 'the possibility of establishing a charter, open to signature by all democratic political parties, reflecting and endorsing agreed measures for the protection of the fundamental rights of everyone living in the island of Ireland'[6].

1   NIA 1998, ss 68–72 and Sch 7.
2   Belfast Agreement, section headed 'Rights, Safeguards and Equality of Opportunity', para 4. Para 4 is referred to in the NIA 1998, s 69(7).
3   See generally, Sarah Spencer and Ian Bynoe *A Human Rights Commission: The options for Britain and Northern Ireland* (1998).
4   Belfast Agreement, section headed 'Rights, Safeguards and Equality of Opportunity', para 9. At the time of writing (February 1999) it appears that the Irish Commission may be given greater powers of investigation than the Northern body.
5   Belfast Agreement, section headed 'Rights, Safeguards and Equality of Opportunity', para 10.
6   Belfast Agreement, section headed 'Rights, Safeguards and Equality of Opportunity', para 10.

6.04   Northern Ireland has also been given an Equality Commission, being largely an amalgam of the existing anti-discrimination bodies (the Fair Employment Commission for Northern Ireland, the Equal Opportunities Commission for Northern Ireland, the Commission for Racial Equality for Northern Ireland and the Northern Ireland Disability Council), though with greater powers[1]. In particular it has the vital function of assisting with the enforcement of new equality duties placed on public authorities.

1   NIA 1998, ss 73–78 and Schs 8 and 9.

6.05   In its attempts to take on board all of the preceding dimensions this chapter will consider the HRA 1998 and Northern Ireland under the following headings:

Northern Irish cases in Strasbourg.

The Convention in Northern Irish courts prior to the HRA 1998.

Orders in Council for Northern Ireland.

The Northern Ireland Act 1998 and the Convention.

The Northern Ireland Human Rights Commission

The Equality Commission for Northern Ireland.

Conclusion and prospects.

B Northern Irish cases in Strasbourg

6.06 Comprehensive accounts of the numerous Northern Irish cases dealt with in Strasbourg have already been published[1], so only a cursory overview is appropriate here. What characterises the cases is the ingenuity and persistence of the lawyers who have taken them, the rate of failure (giving the lie to the belief, still pervasive amongst the public, that the European Convention can provide a solution to all grievances!), and an approach to decision-making by the E Ct HR which points up the differences between civil and common law approaches to the adjudication process.

1   B Dickson *Northern Ireland and the European Convention,* ch 5 in B Dickson, *Human Rights and the European Convention* (1997); S Livingstone 'Reviewing Northern Ireland in Strasbourg 1969–1994', in G Quinn *Irish Human Rights Yearbook 1995,* pp 15–30.

6.07 Eight cases directly concerning Northern Irish law have reached the E Ct HR. A ninth, *McCann v United Kingdom*[1], although concerning events in Gibraltar rather than in Northern Ireland itself, will be mentioned first because it deals with the most important human right of all, the right to life[2]. In 1988 two men and a woman were shot dead in Gibraltar by undercover British soldiers, who apparently believed that the targets were IRA terrorists planting a bomb in the colony. The victims were indeed IRA terrorists but they were not then in the process of planting a bomb. The Commission of Human Rights held that there had been no violation of the right to life, but it referred the case to the E Ct HR, which held, albeit by just one vote (10 to 9), that art 2 *had* been violated. The soldiers who fired the fatal shots were not condemned, because they were found to have honestly believed that it was necessary to fire in order to prevent one or other of the suspects detonating a bomb, but the Ministry of Defence was held not to have displayed the appropriate care in the control and organisation of the arrest operation. Some of the applicants' legal costs (£38,700) were ordered to be reimbursed by the British government, but no compensation was awarded. The decision provoked a storm of protest from politicians in the United Kingdom, but because it turned on particular facts it did not lead to any change in the law (we can only assume that it led the Ministry of Defence to plan future such operations more carefully). The case is of more importance in European terms, because of the reassuringly strict interpretation the E Ct HR placed on the right to life.

1   (1996) 21 EHRR 97.
2   Protected by art 2 of the Convention. See para **4.2**.

6.08 Of the eight other E Ct HR cases involving Northern Ireland, six concerned the operation of emergency arrest and detention powers. The first in time was what is still the only inter-state application to have reached the E Ct HR, *Ireland v United Kingdom*[1], where the claims were that persons arrested in Northern Ireland under emergency powers had been mistreated, that these powers were themselves inconsistent with the Convention, and that they had been applied in a discriminatory fashion. Although the Commission held that the United Kingdom had both tortured and inhumanly treated detainees, the E Ct HR held that the interrogation techniques did *not* amount to torture but did amount to inhuman and degrading treatment. The court also held that the United Kingdom's derogation notice concerning the arrest and detention powers was valid and that those powers had not been used in a discriminatory manner. Again the decision did not lead to a change in the law in Northern Ireland, only to a change in interrogation practice (put in place long before the court issued its judgment).

1   (1978) 2 EHRR 25.

6.09   The seven-day detention powers in the Prevention of Terrorism (Temporary Provisions) Act 1984 (PTA 1984) were again at issue in *Brogan v United Kingdom*[1]. The four applicants argued that they had not been arrested on suspicion of having committed an 'offence', as required by art 5(1)(c) of the Convention, and that the purpose of their arrest was not to bring them before a competent legal authority but merely to interrogate them. The E Ct HR rejected both arguments. It held that 'terrorism' was 'well in keeping with the idea of an offence' and that there was no reason to believe that the police had not acted in good faith in detaining these men. But the court did accept (again going beyond the Commission) that detention for four days and 11 hours, or longer, without being brought before a judicial officer, was a breach of the requirement in art 5(3) that detainees be brought 'promptly' before such an officer. There was also held to have been a breach of art 5(5), because it requires victims of an art 5(3) abuse to have the right to compensation, but, strangely, not a breach of arts 5(4) or 13, because their requirement of an effective review was satisfied by the availability (even if they were bound to fail!) of habeas corpus proceedings.

1   (1989) 11 EHRR 117.

6.10   In response to *Brogan*[1] the United Kingdom Government could have reduced the maximum permitted duration of detention under the PTA to four days. Instead, it chose to issue another derogation notice excusing itself from complying with art 5(3)[2]. The validity of this notice was challenged in *Brannigan and McBride v United Kingdom*, but without success[3]. The E Ct HR thought the measures taken in Northern Ireland were 'strictly required by the exigencies of the situation' (as required by art 15 of the Convention). The derogation notice, despite the various cease-fires currently operating in both Republican and Loyalist quarters in Northern Ireland, remains in place[4]. Given the E Ct HR's assertion that a wide margin of appreciation should be left to states when deciding whether an emergency exists and what derogations from the Convention are necessary to avert it, it seems unlikely that a new challenge to the derogation notice would succeed even today.

1   *Brogan v United Kingdom* (1989) 11 EHRR 117.
2   The earlier notices had been withdrawn on 22 August 1984.
3   (1993) 17 EHRR 539.
4   It is reproduced (as amended) in the Human Rights Act 1998, Sch 3, Part I. See also para **2.14.2**.

6.11   In *Fox, Campbell and Hartley v United Kingdom*[1] the E Ct HR held that the police's arrest power used against three men was invalid because it required only 'suspicion' and not 'reasonable suspicion'[2]. But the law had already been amended three years earlier[3]. In *Margaret Murray v United Kingdom*[4] the E Ct HR refused to condemn a similar arrest power conferred on the army, because on the facts of the case it thought that there had been enough suspicion of Mrs Murray's illegal fund-raising activities to make that suspicion reasonable as required by art 5(1)(c) of the Convention. In any event, the army arrest power had also already been amended so as to be expressly consistent with the Convention[5]. In *John Murray v United Kingdom* the issue was whether denial of access to a solicitor and/or the drawing of inferences from silence in the face of police questioning was a violation of the fair trial provisions in arts 6(1), (2) and (3)(c) of the Convention. The E Ct HR held that, taken separately, the procedures were not a violation, but that, taken together, they were[6]. Nearly three years after that decision, the Attorney General announced new guidelines whereby police officers and prosecutors must take account of the European Court's ruling[7].

1 (1991) 13 EHRR 157.
2 Northern Ireland (Emergency Provisions) Act 1978, s 1(1): 'Any constable may arrest without warrant any person whom he suspects of being a terrorist'.
3 Northern Ireland (Emergency Provisions) Act 1987, s 6 (replacing the Northern Ireland (Emergency Provisions) Act 1978, s 11) and Sch 1, para 1 (amending Northern Ireland (Emergency Provisions) Act 1978, s 13, which contained a power similar to that in s 11).
4 (1994) 19 EHRR 193.
5 Northern Ireland (Emergency Provisions) Act 1987, Sch 1, para 2.
6 (1996) 22 EHRR 29.
7 [1998] 10 *Bulletin of Northern Ireland Law* para 41.

6.12 Two further decisions of the E Ct HR concern aspects of discrimination law in Northern Ireland. In *Dudgeon v United Kingdom*[1] the E Ct HR ruled that the law making homosexuality a crime, even between adults in private, was in breach of art 8 of the Convention. As a result the government had to secure the making of the Homosexual Offences (NI) Order 1982[2]. In *Tinnelly and McElduff v United Kingdom*[3] the E Ct HR held that art 6 (1) had been breached when firms of contractors had been denied the chance to challenge in court the validity of a 'national security certificate' which the Secretary of State had issued to prevent any inquiry into alleged discrimination on religious or political grounds. The government has responded to this by providing for a Tribunal to examine the justifiability of such certificates, both in cases involving public authorities carrying out functions relating to Northern Ireland[4] and in other cases[5]. It is possible that even this reform will not go far enough to satisfy the requirements of the Convention. The fact that the Attorney General can appoint a person to represent a party before the tribunal in any proceedings from which that party and his or her legal representative are excluded, and that the person appointed 'shall not be responsible to the party whose interests he represents', may mean that art 6(3)(c) is violated[6].

1 (1981) 4 EHRR 149.
2 It should be noted, however, that the age of consent for sexual intercourse in Northern Ireland, whether for heterosexual or homosexual intercourse, is still 17, not 16 as in Great Britain.
3 (1998) 4 BHRC 393.
4 NIA 1998, ss 90–92 and Sch 11.
5 Fair Employment and Treatment (NI) Order 1998, arts 80, 96 and 98.
6 'Everyone charged with a criminal offence has the [right...] (c) to defend himself in person or through legal assistance of his own choosing or, if he has not sufficient means to pay for legal assistance, to be given it free when the interests of justice so require.' See paras **4.6.66–4.6.69**.

6.13 A review of the Northern Irish cases which have terminated in the European Commission of Human Rights makes interesting (if at times depressing) reading for a human rights lawyer. Among the applications declared inadmissible are those concerning: the firing of plastic bullets by the British army during a riot[1]; the shooting dead by a British soldier of a teenage joyrider[2]; the failure to protect the right to life of the family of an ex-member of the Ulster Defence Regiment[3]; the mistreatment by the police of persons who had been arrested[4]; the conditions under which prisoners were held in the Maze Prison[5]; the detaining, questioning, searching, photographing and fingerprinting of travellers passing through ports[6]; the screening of witnesses in criminal trials[7]; the ban on demonstrations relating to Northern Ireland in London's Trafalgar Square[8]; the lack of integrated schooling in Northern Ireland[9]; the use of a different electoral system in Northern Ireland for European elections[10]; and the ban on a person being a member of a British Parliamentary body as well as of a foreign Parliamentary body (the Irish Senate)[11].

1   *Stewart v United Kingdom* (1984) 7 EHRR 453.
2   *Kelly v United Kingdom* (1993) 16 EHRR CD 20.
3   *X v United Kingdom and Ireland* (1983) 5 EHRR 504.
4   *Donnelly v United Kingdom* 43 CD 122 (1973) and 4 DR 4 (1975).
5   *McFeeley v United Kingdom* (1981) 3 EHRR 161.
6   *McVeigh, O'Neill and Evans v United Kingdom* (1983) 5 EHRR 71; *Lyttle v United Kingdom* (1987) 9 EHRR 350.
7   *X v United Kingdom* (1993) 15 EHRR CD 113.
8   *Rai, Allmond and 'Negotiate Now' v United Kingdom* 81-A DR 46 (1995).
9   *X v United Kingdom* 14 DR 179 (1978).
10 *Lindsay v United Kingdom* 15 DR 247 (1979).
11 *Mallon v United Kingdom* 37 DR 129 (1984).

6.14   In three important cases applications were declared admissible by the Commission but still failed to proceed to the E Ct HR. In the first, *Arrowsmith v United Kingdom*[1], the Commission declared the application admissible but rejected it on the merits; somewhat surprisingly perhaps, the Commission held that the prosecution of Ms Arrowsmith for distributing literature to soldiers stationed in Great Britain, urging them not to serve in Northern Ireland, was 'necessary for the protection of national security and the prevention of disorder in the army'[2]. Then, in *Farrell v United Kingdom*[3], having declared the application admissible the Commission succeeded in securing a friendly settlement of the matter, which involved the shooting dead of the applicant's husband by British soldiers because they thought he was in the process of planting a bomb. Finally, in *Orchin v United Kingdom*[4], although the Commission declared the application admissible and upheld it on the merits, the Committee of Ministers resolved, under the then art 32 of the Convention, not to take any further action in the case. This was because the British government had already announced the steps it had taken to ensure that the abuse which arose in the case – a man had been held on bail for four years in connection with alleged firearm offences – would not occur again.

1   (1981) 3 EHRR 218.
2   (1981) 3 EHRR 218 at 233 (para 97).
3   (1983) 5 EHRR 466.
4   (1984) 6 EHRR 391.

C   The Convention in Northern Irish courts prior to the HRA 1998

6.15   The attitude of the Northern Irish courts to the European Convention prior to the HRA 1998 can be summed up in one or two sentences[1]. They were prepared to bear the Convention's standards in mind when faced with a problem of statutory interpretation[2], but they were not prepared to use the Convention when developing the common law[3]. In refusing to do the latter, the Northern Irish judges, normally deferential towards their English counterparts, ran counter to the wishes of the House of Lords who, in cases such as *Derbyshire County Council v Times Newspapers Ltd*[4], were prepared to ensure that the common law developed in step with the Convention. The Northern Irish judges certainly agreed with the House of Lords that administrative bodies were under no obligation to exercise their discretion within the limits set by the Convention[5].

1   For a full account see B Dickson *Human Rights and the European Convention* (1997), pp 169-182.
2   See, eg, the early case of *R v Deery* [1977] NI 164 (Court of Criminal Appeal), referring to art 7 of the Convention.
3   See, eg, *Re Hardy's and Whelan's Applications* [1989] 2 NIJB 81.

4   [1993] AC 534.
5   *R v Dougan* (June 1995, unreported), where MacDermott LJ cited Lord Bridge in *R v Secretary of State for the Home Department, ex p Brind* [1991] 1 AC 696 at 748.

D   Orders in Council for Northern Ireland

6.16   It would seem that Orders in Council made under the NIA 1974 or NIA 1998 are subordinate legislation and, pursuant to the HRA 1998, s 3(1), 'so far as it is possible to do so' they must therefore 'be read and given effect in a way which is compatible with the Convention rights'. This applies to all Orders, whether made before or after the HRA 1998 was passed[1]. Although the HRA 1998 does not expressly state that subordinate legislation can be declared invalid or rendered unenforceable (unlike primary legislation, which can merely be declared to be *incompatible* with a Convention right), the strong implication from s 3(2) is that this can occur[2]. The one lingering doubt arises from the fact that the definition of 'subordinate legislation' in the HRA 1998, s 21(1) excludes from its scope any Order in Council amending a public general Act, and one of the unusual features of Orders in Council made under the NIA 1974 and NIA 1998 is that they can amend such Acts. One can only assume that the exclusion from the definition would be interpreted by a court as extending only to the very provisions of the subordinate legislation which amend the Acts, leaving the other provisions in the subordinate legislation to be declared invalid or unenforceable if appropriate. The exclusion in the HRA 1998, s 21(1), be it noted, does not extend to provisions which *repeal* provisions in an Act, nor to provisions which amend an Act of the Parliament of Northern Ireland, a Measure of the 1974 Northern Ireland Assembly, or an Act of the (new) Northern Ireland Assembly, all of which are themselves categorised as examples of subordinate legislation[3].

1   HRA 1998, s 3(2)(a). On HRA 1998, s 3, see para **2.3**. At the time of writing only five Orders in Council were made under the NIA 1974 since 9 November 1998, the date on which the HRA 1998 received the Royal Assent.
2   HRA 1998, s 3(1)(c) parenthetically mentions the possibility of subordinate legislation being revoked.
3   HRA 1998, s 21(1), sub verbis 'subordinate legislation' at paras (c), (d) and (e).

6.17   It should be noted that, being subordinate legislation, Orders in Council made under the NIA 1974 have always been subject to the courts' power to strike down a piece of subordinate legislation if it is ultra vires the parent Act. This power has not yet had to be exercised. The innovation introduced by the HRA 1998 is that an extra basis for striking down a piece of subordinate legislation has been created. No doubt this power will be just as cautiously applied to Orders in Council as the pre-existing power. Nevertheless, the intriguing possibility remains that the courts may strike down a provision in an Order in Council applying in Northern Ireland but be unable to do so if precisely the same provision exists in a piece of primary legislation in any part of Great Britain. The Police and Criminal Evidence (NI) Order 1989, for example, is therefore much more vulnerable than the virtually identical Police and Criminal Evidence Act 1984 in England and Wales.

E   The Northern Ireland Act 1998 and the Convention

6.18   The primary objective of the NIA 1998, of course, is to provide for the creation of a Northern Ireland Assembly and an Executive Committee. The arrangements have been described as consociational, with elements of confederalism and federalism thrown in[1], but for present purposes it is enough to note that the Assembly will have limited powers transferred to it. These 'transferred matters' are those which are not listed as either 'excepted' or 'reserved' matters in the NIA 1998, Schs 2 and 3, respectively.

1   B O'Leary *The British-Irish Agreement: Power-Sharing Plus*, The Constitution Unit, University College, London, 1998, at p 1.

6.19   A provision of an Act of the Northern Ireland Assembly is not law if it deals with an excepted matter and is not ancillary to other provisions dealing with reserved or transferred matters[1]. Such a provision is said to be outside the legislative competence of the Assembly[2]. Among the most important matters within this 'excepted' category are: elections[3]; international relations, including presumably extradition (but not the surrender of fugitive offenders between Northern Ireland and the Republic of Ireland, which is a reserved matter)[4]; the armed forces of the Crown (subject to what is in the reserved list, below)[5]; immigration[6]; the appointment and removal of judges[7]; and national security, special provisions for dealing with terrorism and official secrets[8]. The observation and implementation of obligations under the European Convention are expressly excluded from the category of excepted matters[9].

1   NIA 1998, s 6(2)(b).
2   NIA 1998, s 6(1).
3   NIA 1998, Sch 2, paras 2 and 12
4   NIA 1998, Sch 2, para 3.
5   NIA 1998, Sch 2, para 4.
6   NIA 1998, Sch 2, para 8.
7   NIA 1998, Sch 2, para 11.
8   NIA 1998, Sch 2, para 17.
9   NIA 1998, Sch 2, para 3(c).

6.20   Reserved matters include those which might one day be transferred to the Assembly but which in the meantime are to be dealt with by an Act at Westminster or by an Order in Council[1]. The Secretary of State can seek to effect their transfer by laying before Parliament a draft Order in Council, but this must be preceded by an Assembly resolution, passed with cross-community support, praying that the matter concerned should cease to be a reserved matter[2]. 'Cross-community support' means what the Belfast Agreement calls either parallel consent or a weighted majority[3]. 'Parallel consent' refers to the support of a majority of the members voting, a majority of the designated Nationalists voting and a majority of the designated Unionists voting; 'a weighted majority' refers to the support of 60 per cent of the members voting, 40 per cent of the designated Nationalists voting and 40 per cent of the designated Unionists voting[4].

1   NIA 1998, s 85(1) allows Orders in Council to be made in relation to the matters listed in the NIA 1998, Sch 3, paras 9–17. Presumably the matters listed in paras 1–8 and 18 et seq have to be dealt with by a Westminster Act. The Assembly can pass Acts dealing with reserved matters if the Secretary of State consents (see NIA 1998, s 8(b) and para **6.22** below).
2   NIA 1998, s 4(2) and (3).
3   *Stand One*, Democratic Institutions in Northern Ireland, para 5(d).
4   NIA 1998, s 4(5).

6.21   Among the most important matters within the 'reserved' category are: stamps and the regulation of postal services[1]; the criminal law[2]; the creation of offences and penalties[3]; the prevention and detection of crime and powers of arrest and detention[4];

prosecutions[5]; the treatment of offenders[6]; compensation for victims of crime[7]; the maintenance of public order, including the conferring of powers on the police and army and the Parades Commission for Northern Ireland[8]; the organisation and control of the RUC[9]; all matters relating to court procedure[10]; regulation of anti-competitive practices[11]; human genetics[12]; consumer safety in relation to goods[13]; and data protection[14].

1   NIA 1998, Sch 3, para 7.
2   NIA 1998, Sch 3, para 9(a).
3   NIA 1998, Sch 3, para 9(b).
4   NIA 1998, Sch 3, para 9(c).
5   NIA 1998, Sch 3, para 9(d).
6   NIA 1998, Sch 3, para 9(e).
7   NIA 1998, Sch 3, para 9(g).
8   NIA 1998, Sch 3, para 10. The Parades Commission was created by the Public Processions (NI) Act 1997.
9   NIA 1998, Sch 3, para 11.
10 NIA 1998, Sch 3, para 15.
11 NIA 1998, Sch 3, para 26.
12 NIA 1998, Sch 3, para 34.
13 NIA 1998, Sch 3, para 37.
14 NIA 1998, Sch 3, para 40.

6.22   Unlike in the Scotland Act 1998[1], there is no provision in the NIA 1998 which expressly says that a provision is outside the legislative competence of the Assembly in so far as it relates to reserved matters. The NIA 1998, s 8(b) merely states that if a Bill contains a provision dealing with a reserved matter it requires the consent of the Secretary of State, while s 10(2)(b) requires the Assembly's Presiding Officer to refer a Bill to the Secretary of State if he or she considers that it contains a provision dealing with a reserved matter. On the other hand, there is nothing in the SA 1998 to mirror the NIA 1998, s 6(2)(e), which says that a provision is outside the legislative competence of the Assembly if 'it discriminates against any person or class of person on the ground of religious belief or political opinion'[2]. But both Acts make it clear that neither the Scottish Parliament nor the Northern Ireland Assembly has the legislative competence to enact provisions which are incompatible with the European Convention on Human Rights or with European Community law[3]. The White Paper preceding the HRA 1998[4] did not specify how a devolved Assembly in Northern Ireland would be obliged to stay within the constraints of the European Convention (indeed Northern Ireland was hardly mentioned at all in the White Paper), but the Belfast Agreement made it clear that courts would be given the power 'to overrule Assembly legislation on grounds of inconsistency'[5].

1   SA 1998, s 29(2)(b). The reserved matters are listed in SA 1998, Sch 5.
2   But section L2 in SA 1998, Sch 5 makes equal opportunities a reserved matter.
3   SA 1998, s 29(2)(d); NIA 1998, s 6(2)(c) and (d).
4   *Rights Brought Home* (Cm 3782, 1997).
5   Section headed 'Rights, Safeguards and Equality of Opportunity', para 2.

6.23   The NIA 1998 provides, in all, eight different ways in which the compatibility of Assembly legislation with the European Convention can be officially checked. Each of them may lead to court proceedings of one kind or another. When dealing with such proceedings, a court is under a duty, if faced with a provision of an Assembly's Bill or Act which could be read as either within or outside the Assembly's legislative competence, to interpret that provision as within the Assembly's competence[1]. The same interpretative duty applies to provisions in dubiously valid subordinate legislation[2]. As far as compatibility with Convention rights is concerned, this is a comparable duty to that imposed on courts by the HRA 1998 when they are interpreting primary and subordinate legislation[3].

1   NIA 1998, s 83(1)(a).
2   NIA 1998, s 83(1)(b).
3   HRA 1998, s 3(1).

6.24   First, by the NIA 1998, s 9 a Minister in charge of a Bill must, on or before its introduction in the Assembly, publish a written statement to the effect that in his or her view the Bill would be within the legislative competence of the Assembly. In the human rights context, this is reminiscent of the HRA 1998, s 19(1)(a), which requires a Minister of the Crown in charge of a Bill in each House of Parliament to make a statement, before the second reading of the Bill, that in his or her view its provisions are, or are not, compatible with the Convention rights (and, if they are not compatible, that the government nonetheless wishes to proceed with the Bill). This has been in force since 24 November 1998[1] and statements have been printed on the face of Bills introduced since then as well as in the explanatory notes accompanying the Bills.

1   Human Rights Act 1998 (Commencement) Order 1998, SI 1998/2882. On HRA 1998, s 19, see para **2.19**.

6.25   Second, by the NIA 1998, s 10(1), a Bill is not to be introduced in the Assembly if the Presiding Officer decides that any of its provisions would not be within the legislative competence of the Assembly. It should be noted, however, that, unlike its Scottish equivalent[1], this provision does not impose a duty on the Presiding Officer to decide in every case whether a Bill is within that legislative competence. This point is underlined by the fact that s 10(2) does require the Presiding Officer to consider *every* Bill, both on its introduction and before the Assembly enters on its final stage (unless it is endorsed with a statement that the Secretary of State has consented to the Assembly considering the Bill[2]), with a view to deciding whether it contains any provision dealing with a reserved matter or with an excepted matter which is ancillary to other provisions (whether in the same Bill or previously enacted) dealing with reserved or transferred matters. If, in this sort of case, the Presiding Officer decides that the Bill does contain any such provision, he or she must refer the Bill to the Secretary of State and the Assembly cannot proceed with the Bill unless the Secretary of State gives his or her consent or indicates that in his or her opinion, *pace* the Presiding Officer, the Bill does *not* contain any such provision. No such power exists to refer a Bill to the Secretary of State in situations where the flaw identified by the Presiding Officer relates to some other instance of the Assembly overstepping its legislative competence (eg by contravening the European Convention). Again one can imagine attempts being made to seek judicial review of the Presiding Officer's statement about the legitimacy of a proposed bill[3]. A Minister in the Executive would be well placed to satisfy the locus standi requirements, but so again would the Human Rights Commission.

1   SA 1998, s 31(2).
2   NIA 1998, s 10(3)(b).
3   See N Bamforth, 'Parliamentary Sovereignty and the HRA 1998' [1998] Public Law 572.

6.26   Third, the Attorney General for Northern Ireland[1] can, within four weeks beginning with the passing of a Bill, refer the question of whether a provision of the Bill would be within the legislative competence of the Assembly to the Judicial Committee of the Privy Council[2]. To sit as a member of the Judicial Committee in such cases a person must be, or have been, a Lord of Appeal in Ordinary (ie a Law Lord) or the holder of other 'high judicial office' (ie a Lord Chancellor, a judge of the High Court or Court of Appeal in England and Wales, a judge of the Court of Session in Scotland, or a judge of the High Court or Court of Appeal in Northern Ireland[3]). The intention is obviously to exclude from the Judicial Committee in such cases the top judges from other Commonwealth jurisdictions who are otherwise authorised to sit by virtue of the Judicial Committee Amendment Act 1895[4], as amended. Foreign judges of a different description will, however, still be involved if the Judicial Committee decides to make a reference to the European Court of Justice for a preliminary ruling on a point of European Community law[5].

1   The holder of this office is (for the time being at least) the same person as the Attorney General for England and Wales. The Northern Ireland Constitution Act 1973, s 10, which brought about this merger of offices, has not been repealed by the NIA 1998.
2   NIA 1998, s 11(1) and (2). Cf the powers mentioned in para **6.37**.
3   The definition provided by the Appellate Jurisdiction Act 1876, s 25, as amended.
4   Judicial Committee Amendment Act 1895, s 1.
5   NIA 1998, s 12(1)(b).

6.27   If the Attorney General notifies the Presiding Officer that he does not intend to make a reference to the Judicial Committee, he or she must not then make one[1], but otherwise a Bill cannot be submitted for Royal Assent (in Northern Ireland this submission is made by the Secretary of State, not, as in Scotland, by the Presiding Officer) if the Attorney General is still within the time allowed to make a reference to the Judicial Committee or if a reference has been made but has not yet been disposed of by the Judicial Committee[2]. The Secretary of State cannot submit a Bill in its unamended form for Royal Assent if the Judicial Committee has decided that any provision in it would not be within the legislative competence of the Assembly[3]. If the Judicial Committee does so decide, the Assembly will have the opportunity to reconsider the Bill[4]. The Assembly can also preempt any decision by the Judicial Committee by resolving that it wishes to reconsider the Bill, in which case the Attorney General must request that the reference to the Judicial Committee be withdrawn[5]. Once a Bill has been reconsidered, there is a further four week period during which the Attorney General can again refer it to the Judicial Committee[6]. As in Scotland, the process of referral and reconsideration can be repeated time and time again[7].

1   NIA 1998, s 11(3).
2   NIA 1998, s 14(2).
3   NIA 1998, s 14(3).
4   NIA 1998, s 13(5)(a).
5   NIA 1998, s 12(2) and 13(5).
6   NIA 1998, s 11(2)(b).
7   NIA 1998, s 13(7); see also para **5.28**.

6.28   A fourth, albeit indirect, method of controlling a Bill's consistency with the European Convention is provided for by the NIA 1998, s 14(5)(a), which allows the Secretary of State not to submit a Bill for Royal Assent if he or she considers that it contains a provision 'incompatible with any international obligations'[1]. Although 'international obligations' is defined as excluding obligations to observe Convention rights[2], other international obligations (ie under the International Covenant on Civil and Political Rights) are virtually identical to those in the European Convention. Again, in such circumstances the Assembly will have the opportunity to reconsider the Bill[3], and the four week period for referrals to the Judicial Committee applies here too. Relevant also is the NIA 1998, s 26, which permits the Secretary of State to direct a Minister or

Northern Ireland department that action must be taken to give effect to international obligations[4] (or action not taken if it would be incompatible with any international obligations[5]). Under this power the Secretary of State could require a Minister in charge of a Bill which the Secretary of State believes contravenes international obligations to amend the Bill accordingly. It is submitted that courts have the power to review the Secretary of State's decision under the NIA 1998, s 14(5)(a), or his or her directions under s 26, since both sections refer to international obligations rather than to international policies. If the international obligations have been incorporated into domestic law (eg the prohibition on torture in the Criminal Justice Act 1988[6], implementing the UN Convention Against Torture and Other Cruel, Inhuman or Degrading Treatment or Punishment 1984), it seems all the more clear that the Secretary of State can be judicially reviewed when making a determination as to the scope of those obligations.

1   Cf SA 1998, s 35(1)(a).
2   NIA 1998, s 98(1).
3   NIA 1998, s 13(5)(c).
4   NIA 1998, s 26(2). Cf SA 1998, s 58(2).
5   NIA 1998, s 26(1). Cf SA 1998, s 58(1).
6   Ss 134–138.

6.29   A fifth method of control, unique to Northern Ireland, is provided for by the NIA 1998, s 13(4), which requires standing orders to be made imposing a duty on the Presiding Officer to send a copy of each Bill, as soon as reasonably practicable after its introduction, to the Northern Ireland Human Rights Commission, and enabling the Assembly to ask the Human Rights Commission, where the Assembly thinks fit, to advise whether a Bill is compatible with human rights (*including* Convention rights). The Commission must then advise the Assembly as soon as reasonably practicable after receipt of a request for advice.[1] The very next paragraph requires the Commission to provide such advice 'on such other occasions as the Commission thinks appropriate'. The crucial question, as to whether the Human Rights Commission can take legal action to try to ensure that its advice in such situations is heeded, is addressed in Section E of this chapter.

1   NIA 1998, s 69(4)(a).

6.30   Whatever the definitive answer to that question, it would seem from another provision in the NIA 1998 that a sixth method for controlling the Assembly's compliance with the European Convention is through exercise of the Attorney General's power to bring proceedings on the ground that any legislation is incompatible with the European Convention[1]. The word 'legislation' is not defined in the NIA 1998, but it would seem odd to interpret it as referring only to legislation which has already been given the Royal Assent and not to legislation which is in the course of being enacted. In any event the same subsection makes it clear that the Attorney General can also go to court to challenge acts of a Minister or Northern Ireland department (including, therefore, acts whereby draft legislation is brought before the Assembly). The SA 1998 expressly allows for proceedings to be instituted against the Scottish Parliament, the Presiding Officer or a deputy, any member of staff of the Parliament, and any member of the Parliament (even though it gives no indication as to the kind of proceedings envisaged)[2], but the NIA 1998 is silent in this regard. It is submitted, however, that this omission does not at common law preclude the Attorney General from challenging legislation or an executive act by bringing judicial review proceedings, or any other proceedings, against the Assembly itself or against any of its officers or members. If a court decides to uphold the Attorney General's challenge to an Act, the same legislative and judicial remedies apply as in the case of decisions taken by the Judicial Committee on a reference from the Attorney General[3]. A successful challenge to a Bill would presumably lead to the Assembly reconsidering the Bill in a new form.

1   NIA 1998, s 71(2).
2   NIA 1998, s 40.
3   See para **6.37**.

6.31   A final channel for challenging the compatibility of Assembly legislation with international human rights standards is the one which characterises the question as a 'devolution issue'. In the NIA 1998 devolution issues are defined (in slightly different terms from those used in the SA 1998[1]), as meaning[2]:

'(a)   a question whether any provision of an Act of the Assembly is within the legislative competence of the Assembly;

(b)   a question whether a purported or proposed exercise of a function by a Minister or Northern Ireland department is, or would be, invalid by reason of section 24[3];

(c)   a question whether a Minister or Northern Ireland department has failed to comply with any of the Convention rights, any obligation under Community law or any order under section 27[4] so far as relating to such an obligation; or

(d)   any question arising under this Act about excepted or reserved matters.'

The compatibility of proposed or actual legislation with the European Convention can qualify as a devolution issue under paras (a), (b) or (c) and the matter may arise either *during* or *outside* court proceedings. These then constitute the seventh and eighth means by which legislation's compatibility with the Convention can be checked.

1   NIA 1998, Sch 6, para 1.
2   NIA 1998, Sch 10, para 1.
3   NIA 1998, s 24 is the equivalent for Ministers and departments to s 6 for the Assembly itself, ie it lists the limits to the power of Ministers and departments to make, confirm or approve any subordinate legislation or to do any act. The first of the limitations relates to incompatibility with any of the Convention rights.
4   NIA 1998, s 27 allows a Minister of the United Kingdom government to make an order providing for the achievement by a Minister or Northern Ireland department of a quantified part of an international obligation.

6.32   As noted in Chapter 5[1], a devolution issue can arise *during* proceedings before any court or tribunal anywhere in the United Kingdom. The NIA 1998, Sch 10 therefore makes provision for what is to happen in relation to a Northern Ireland devolution issue depending on the particular United Kingdom jurisdiction where it arises.

1   At para **5.36**.

6.33   When a devolution issue arises in any court or tribunal in Northern Ireland, other than the Court of Appeal or House of Lords, it may either be referred to the Court of Appeal in Northern Ireland (and if the tribunal is one from which there is no appeal, it *must* refer the issue) or be decided by the court or tribunal itself with the possibility of the issue being taken to a higher court by way of appeal. When the Court of Appeal is faced with a devolution issue *referred* to it, it must determine it, and an appeal can then lie to the Judicial Committee of the Privy Council, provided either the Court of Appeal or the Judicial Committee grants leave[1]. When the Court of Appeal is faced with a devolution issue in an *appeal* from a lower court or tribunal, whether the issue has been raised in the lower forum or not, it *may*, like the lower forum, determine the issue itself or refer it to a higher court, again the Judicial Committee. Similarly, when a devolution issue arises in judicial proceedings in the House of Lords, it must be referred to the Judicial Committee 'unless the House considers it more appropriate, having regard to all the circumstances, that it should determine the issue'. Given that the judges sitting in the Judicial Committee in such cases will most likely be Law Lords themselves, it is difficult to imagine the House referring the issue rather than determining it itself.

1   In Scotland leave is required only in criminal cases, and in civil cases there is the alternative of taking the appeal to the House of Lords: see para **5.40**.

6.34   Within Northern Ireland itself, proceedings for the determination of a devolution issue may be instituted by the Attorney General[1]. In so far as this sub-paragraph also says that the Attorney General may *defend* such proceedings[2], there is a presupposition that someone other than the Attorney General may institute them, but no other individual is specified in the legislation. Para 4(3) simply states that the paragraph as a whole is 'without prejudice to any power to institute proceedings exercisable apart from this paragraph by any person'. Moreover, the Attorney General, or the First Minister and the deputy First Minister acting jointly, or the Advocate General for Scotland, may *require* any court or tribunal to refer to the Judicial Committee any devolution issue which has arisen in proceedings before it to which he or she is or they are a party.

1   NIA 1998, Sch 10, para 4(1).
2   By the NIA 1998, Sch 10, para 4(2), the First Minister and deputy First Minister, acting jointly as always, may also defend such proceedings.

6.35   Importantly, the Attorney General, or the First Minister and deputy First Minister acting jointly, or the Advocate General for Scotland, may personally refer to the Judicial Committee any devolution issue which arises *outside* court or tribunal proceedings[1]. This raises the prospect of, say, the First and deputy First Ministers referring to the Judicial Committee a question whether a Minister in the Executive Committee, through acting or failing to act in a certain way, has complied with a Convention right. The Human Rights Commission might also want to persuade the Attorney General to exercise the referral power in situations where the Assembly is insisting on passing legislation which the Commission feels is contrary to Convention rights. It is submitted, once again, that a decision to refer, or not to refer, a devolution issue to the Judicial Committee is itself one that could be judicially reviewed.

1   NIA 1998, Sch 10, para 34. The same office-holders may require a court or tribunal to refer any devolution issue arising in proceedings before it to the Judicial Committee of the Privy Council: para 33. Cf the Attorney General's time-limited power to make a reference to the Judicial Committee under NIA 1998, s 11 (see para **6.26**). Under the Northern Ireland Constitution Act 1973, s 18, the Secretary of State had a comparable power of recommending a referral to the Privy council, but this power was never exercised.

6.36   If the Judicial Committee decides that a provision of an Act of the Assembly is not within the legislative competence of the Assembly (or that a Minister or Northern Ireland department has acted unlawfully), the Secretary of State may make an order remedying the defect in whatever way he or she thinks is necessary or expedient[1], and such an order may even have retrospective effect[2]. The Judicial Committee itself, when deciding that a provision of an Act is ultra vires, can remove or limit the retrospective effect of its decision or suspend its effect for any period and on any conditions allow the defect in the legislation to be corrected[3]. If the Judicial Committee is considering the exercise of any of these powers it must notify the Attorney General and, (if the decision relates to a devolution issue) the First and deputy First Ministers[4]. It must also have regard to the extent to which persons who are not parties to the proceedings would be affected if the power was not exercised[5].

1   NIA 1998, s 80(1). Cf SA 1998, s 107.
2   NIA 1998, s 80(2)(a).
3   NIA 1998, s 81(2). Cf SA 1998, s 102(2).
4   NIA 1998, s 81(4), read with s 81(7)(a).
5   NIA 1998, s 81(3).

6.37   The Judicial Committee has thus been made into something of a Constitutional Court for the United Kingdom, albeit in the limited area of determining devolution issues. Its decisions in proceedings under the NIA 1998 are to be 'binding in all legal proceedings (other than proceedings before the Committee itself)'[1]. It is worth noting that the Judicial Committee was given a similar role when devolution was first provided for in Northern Ireland under the Government of Ireland Act 1920 (GIA 1920) and of course the Committee has long performed a similar role when asked to interpret constitutional provisions in cases arising from jurisdictions in the Commonwealth. Under the GIA 1920, s 51(1), a reference could be made to the Judicial Committee, by the Governor of Northern Ireland or the Secretary of State, on whether 'any Act ... or any Bill ... is beyond the powers of [the Parliament of Northern Ireland]', but only if it appeared to the Governor or Secretary of State that it was 'expedient in the public interest that steps shall be taken for the speedy determination of the question'. By the GIA 1920, s 51(2) 'such persons as seem to the Judicial Committee to be interested may be allowed to appear and be heard as parties to the case'. Although several petitions were apparently addressed to the Governor and Home Secretary for references to be made to the Judicial Committee[2], only one was ever entertained[3]. That was a petition presented by Belfast Corporation to the Governor, who forwarded it to the Home Secretary and who in turn made the reference. The case concerned the question of whether an obligation imposed on local authorities by the Finance Act (NI) 1934, to levy a rate to help pay for state education, was ultra vires because it violated the prohibition placed on the Stormont Parliament by the GIA 1920, s 22 against imposing 'any tax substantially the same in character' as duties and taxes reserved for the United Kingdom Parliament. The Privy Council concluded that the levy did *not* fall into this category because it did not share the essential characteristic of income tax[4].

1   NIA 1998, s 82(1).
2   Sir Arthur Quekett *The Constitution of Northern Ireland* (Part III, 1946) at p 52.
3   See H Calvert *Constitutional Law in Northern Ireland* (1968) pp 298–301.
4   *Re a reference under the Government of Ireland Act 1920, Re section 3 of the Finance Act (NI) 1934* [1936] AC 352 (known as *The Education Levy* case). The opinion was given by Lord Thankerton. The most junior counsel in the case was Mr J C MacDermott, later the Lord Chief Justice of Northern Ireland and a Law Lord.

F   The Northern Ireland Human Rights Commission

6.38   The main innovation produced by the NIA 1998 on the human rights front is the creation of the Northern Ireland Human Rights Commission. Comprising a full-time Chief Commissioner and nine[1] part-time Commissioners, the new body has been given fairly extensive duties but less extensive powers. These functions were considerably amplified as the Bill progressed through Parliament[2]. The Commission's duties are as follows:

(1)   to advise the Secretary of State on what should be contained in a Bill of Rights for Northern Ireland[3];

(2)   to advise the Secretary of State and the Assembly's Executive on the measures which ought to be taken to protect human rights in Northern Ireland[4]. If, following receipt of advice from the Commission under the first duty, the Secretary of State insists on taking a narrow view of what a Bill of Rights should contain, the other rights which the Commission would like to see protected could be contained in legislative measures drafted in pursuance of this second duty;

(3)   to advise the Assembly on whether a Bill being introduced for debate is compatible with human rights[5]. The Commission, crucially, is not restricted to advising on a Bill's compatibility with the European Convention; it can also measure a Bill against, for instance, the Council of Europe's Revised Social Charter or the United Nations' International Covenants, Conventions and Codes of Conduct;

(4)   to keep under review the adequacy and effectiveness of law and practice relating to the protection of human rights[6]. This requires the Commission to pay close attention to how current laws are actually operating in Northern Ireland with a view to deciding if they are in need of reform. It often happens that laws do not on their face conflict with human rights standards, only when they are being implemented;

(5)   to promote understanding and awareness of the importance of human rights in Northern Ireland[7]. This requires the Commission to undertake educational and research activities; it will entail convincing people, especially, perhaps, those of a unionist disposition, that human rights are for all, not just for one particular community;

(6)   to do all that it can to ensure the establishment of a Joint Committee with Ireland's Human Rights Commission[8];

(7)   to recommend to the Secretary of State within two years how the adequacy and effectiveness of the Commission could be improved[9]. When the Northern Ireland Bill was going through Parliament, strenuous efforts were made to persuade the Government to confer greater powers on the Commission. These efforts largely failed and the furthest the Government would go towards satisfying the critics was to allow the Commission to review its existing powers after a two-year trial[10]. We now turn to those powers.

1   NIA 1998, s 68(2) does not specify the number, but that is how many have been appointed.
2   This was as a result of a long series of meetings with the political parties and others: 593 HL Official Report (5th series) col 172 (5 October 1998).
3   NIA 1998, s 69(7). See para **6.02**.
4   NIA 1998, s 69(3).
5   NIA 1998, s 69(4). See also para **6.29**.
6   NIA 1998, s 69(1).
7   NIA 1998, s 69(6).
8   NIA 1998, s 69(10). See para **6.03**.
9   NIA 1998, s 69(2).
10   593 HL Official Report (5th series) cols 1529–1530 (21 October 1998).

6.39   The Commission's powers are threefold.

(1)   To give assistance to individuals when they are bringing court proceedings, and to bring court proceedings itself[1]. The criteria for deciding when assistance should be given are identical to those in existing anti-discrimination legislation

both in Great Britain and in Northern Ireland[2], which means that a lot will turn on whether it would be 'unreasonable' for a particular applicant to proceed with a case unassisted. The Commission itself will not be able to take cases in which it wishes to rely upon the European Convention on Human Rights because the Convention has been incorporated into United Kingdom law in such a manner as to limit court access to those who qualify as 'victims' within the strict sense of that term in what is now art 34 of the European Convention. But no doubt the Commission will be able to serve as an amicus to the court when appropriate.

(2)   To conduct such investigations as the Commission considers necessary or expedient for the purpose of exercising its functions[3]. The Commission, unlike its counterpart in the Republic of Ireland[4], is not being given the ancillary powers necessary to make investigations really effective – it cannot oblige people to provide sworn evidence and it cannot compel the disclosure of documents – but it may be that public authorities will realise the wisdom of cooperating with investigations, thus rendering the lack of additional powers irrelevant[5]. One or two trial investigations will soon test the position.

(3)   To publish its advice and the outcome of its research and investigations[6]. No one could quarrel with this necessary corollary to the Commission's other functions. If the Commission cannot itself enforce its recommendations, it must at least be able to publicise them.

1   NIA 1998, s 69(5). The scope of this subsection is expanded upon in paras **6.41–6.44**.
2   Sex Discrimination Act 1975, s 75; Sex Discrimination (NI) Order 1976, art 75; Race Relations Act 1976, s 66; Race Relations (NI) Order 1997, art 64; Fair Employment and Treatment (NI) Order 1998, art 45. As yet there is no legislation allowing disabled people to gain assistance of this nature from a public body, but the government has declared its intention to remedy this by amending the Disability Discrimination Act 1995.
3   NIA 1998, s 69(8).
4   *Irish Independent* 11 February 1999, p 14.
5   During the Parliamentary debates on the Northern Ireland Bill the government said it would fully co-operate with any investigation undertaken by the Commission: 593 HL Official Report (5th series) col 1543 (21 October 1998).
6   NIA 1998, s 69(9).

6.40   The Human Rights Commission will obviously play an important role in ensuring that laws and practices in Northern Ireland comply with internationally recognised human rights standards. It will no doubt seek to ensure that the full panoply of standards is taken into account. The important question, though, is whether, at the end of the day, the Commission is primarily an advisory body, like its predecessor the Standing Advisory Commission on Human Rights (SACHR)[1], or whether it can take legal steps to ensure that its advice is implemented.

1   Established by the Northern Ireland Constitution Act 1973, s 20. SACHR's purpose was to advise the Secretary of State 'on the adequacy and effectiveness of the law for the time being in force in preventing discrimination on the ground of religious belief or political opinion and in providing redress for persons aggrieved by discrimination on either ground [and to keep] the Secretary of State informed as to the extent to which [public authorities] have prevented discrimination on either ground by persons or bodies not prohibited from discriminating by that law'. In practice, however, successive Secretaries of State permitted SACHR to report on the full range of human rights issues. Its annual reports (only one of which was ever debated at Westminster) are a rich source of information on human rights concerns in the province.

6.41   By the NIA 1998, s 69(5) the Commission can involve itself in court proceedings in two types of situation. First, it may give assistance to any individual[1] in Northern Ireland who has commenced, or wishes to commence, proceedings which involve law or practice relating to the protection of human rights or in the course of which the individual wishes to rely on such law or practice[2]. Most such proceedings will involve laws already in force, but it is possible to imagine a situation where a person believes that his or her human rights will be affected by an Assembly Bill if it becomes law. Whether that person would have locus standi to seek judicial review of an Assembly decision in relation to the Bill, or of a statement by a Minister or Presiding Officer that the Bill is compatible with human rights, will depend on the existing common law rules on standing[3] and Parliamentary privilege. A fairly certain prospect of personal adverse impact would probably have to be shown. What is clear is that, if an applicant for judicial review wishes to rely on rights conferred by the European Convention, he or she will have to be a 'victim' within the definition given to that term by the Strasbourg jurisprudence based on what was previously art 25, now art 34, of the Convention[4]. The European jurisprudence rarely if ever acknowledges *potential* victims.

1   NIA 1998, s 69(5) uses the word 'individual', while s 70 uses the word 'person'; the latter, it is submitted, must be read subject to the former, which means that *legal* persons will not be able to ask for assistance from the Commission.
2   NIA 1998, s 69(5)(a) read in conjunction with s 70(1).
3   A useful precedent is the Divisional Court's decision in *R v Lord Chancellor, ex p Witham* [1998] QB 575, [1997] 2 All ER 779, where a man on income support, who wished to bring proceedings in person for defamation, successfully challenged the Supreme Court Fees (Amendment) Order 1996, art 3, made by the Lord Chancellor under powers conferred by the Supreme Court Act 1981, s 130, because it repealed provisions in a previous Order relieving litigants in person in receipt of income support from the obligation to pay court fees and thereby abrogated his right of access to the courts.
4   Protocol 11, which abolished the role of the European Commission of Human Rights and made the E Ct HR a full-time body, renumbered the articles in the Convention. As from 1 November 1998 only the new version of the Convention applies. On who is a 'victim' under art 34, see para **2.7.2**.

6.42   If it appears that an individual may be able to get over the obstacles concerning standing, the Human Rights Commission will be able to consider giving assistance on the ground: (a) that the case raises a question of principle; (b) that it would be unreasonable to expect the person to deal with the case without assistance because of its complexity, or because of the person's position in relation to another person involved, or *for some other reason*[1]; or (c) that there are other special circumstances making it appropriate for the Commission to provide assistance[2]. In a case where an individual is challenging an Assembly Bill, it is possible that the Commission would consider that it raises a question of principle under (a) above, or that it constitutes a special circumstance under (c) or, especially if the applicant stands to lose quite a lot financially if the Bill goes ahead, that there is some other reason why it would be unreasonable to expect the individual to deal with the case unassisted. In such cases, of course, the Commission's assistance could itself be provided to help the individual get over any difficulties relating to locus standi. Or the Commission might refuse assistance on the basis that NIA 1998, s 70 must be read as presupposing that the 'law' being challenged has already received Royal Assent.

1   Emphasis added.
2   NIA 1998, s 70(2).

6.43   The second way in which the Human Rights Commission can involve itself in court proceedings is by itself bringing proceedings involving law or practice relating to the protection of human rights[1]. The NIA 1998 is otherwise silent as to the situations where such proceedings can be brought, so again one can only assume that the common law rules on standing will apply. Given the Commission's statutory status, its specific statutory functions, its inclusion in the Belfast Agreement, the attention given to it in the Parliamentary debates, the principles governing Human Rights Commissions approved by the United Nations' General Assembly in 1993, and cases such as *R v Secretary of State for Employment, ex p Equal Opportunities Commission*[2] and *Re the Equal Opportunities Commission for Northern Ireland*[3], it must surely be accepted that the Commission *will* be considered as having standing to challenge Assembly laws in an application for judicial review. And there seems no good reason for limiting this standing to situations where the laws have already been enacted; it should extend to challenges against *proposed* Assembly laws. However it seems unlikely that in any case the Commission will be able to rely specifically on the ground for judicial review provided for by the HRA 1998 – the incompatibility of the Bill with European Convention rights – because the Commission will not be able to show that it is a 'victim'[4]. NIA 1998, s 71(1) precludes any such proceedings brought by a 'person', and this term must be taken to embrace the Commission, a body corporate[5].

1   NIA 1998, s 69(5)(b).
2   [1995] 1 AC 1, HL.
3   [1988] NI 223, where the Equal Opportunitites Commission for Northern Ireland successfully challenged the rules for determining grammar school places in Northern Ireland.
4   On who is a 'victim' in this context, see para **2.7.2**.
5   NIA 1998, s 68(1).

6.44   A case can be made for arguing that the Commission should be able to rely on the ground that a proposed law is incompatible with *other* human rights standards, such as those contained in United Nations' Covenants or Conventions which the United Kingdom has ratified. The best argument in support of this position is the wording of the NIA 1998 itself: s 69(5)(b) expressly authorises the Commission to 'bring proceedings involving law or practice relating to the protection of human rights' and s 69(11)(b) states that in that section "'human rights" *includes* Convention rights'[1]. An additional argument is that part of the spirit running through the Belfast Agreement, which the Northern Ireland Act is intended to implement, was that human rights in Northern Ireland require to be protected in a way which complies with international standards. Indeed the Human Rights Commission is charged with advising the Secretary of State on the legislation required to protect rights supplementary to those in the European Convention, 'drawing as appropriate on international instruments and experience'.

1   Emphasis added.

G   The Equality Commission for Northern Ireland

6.45   On the more specific topic of equality, the Equality Commission will to some extent be breaking new ground. The cornerstone of the equality framework is contained in the NIA 1998, s 75. This section imposes a duty on most public authorities in Northern Ireland to have regard: (a) to the need to promote equality of opportunity; and (b) to the desirability of promoting good relations. They are to do so by devising 'equality schemes', provided for in the NIA 1998, Sch 9. These schemes must be submitted for approval to the Equality Commission within six months of Sch 9 coming into force (or of the establishment of the public authority in question if this is a later date). If not so approved, the draft schemes will then be referred by the Equality Commission to the Secretary of State, who can either require a revised scheme to be submitted or make a scheme himself or herself.

6.46   An equality scheme must show how the public authority in question proposes to fulfil the duties imposed on it by the NIA 1998, s 75. It must conform to any guidelines issued by the Equality Commission, it must specify a timetable for the measures it proposes and it must include details of how the scheme will be published[1]. It must also be preceded by consultations between the public authority and representatives of persons likely to be affected by the scheme (and such other persons specified in directions given by the Equality Commission)[2]. More particularly, the scheme must state what arrangements the authority is making for:

(a)   assessing its compliance with the duties under the NIA 1998, s 75 and consulting on matters to which a duty under that section is likely to be relevant (including details of the persons to be consulted);

(b)   assessing and consulting on the likely impact of policies adopted or proposed to be adopted by the authority on the promotion of equality of opportunity;

(c)   monitoring any adverse impact of policies adopted by the authority on the promotion of equality of opportunity;

(d)   publishing the results of such assessments and monitoring as are mentioned in paras (b) and (c);

(e)   training staff; and

(f)   ensuring, and assessing, public access to information and to services provided by the authority[3].

1   NIA 1998, Sch 9, para 4(3).
2   NIA 1998, Sch 9, para 5.
3   NIA 1998, Sch 9, para 4(2).

6.47   If a person complains that the provisions of an approved equality scheme are not being complied with, the Equality Commission must investigate this complaint or give reasons why it is not investigating, and if the Commission then makes recommendations based on the investigation, but these are not adhered to by the public authority concerned, the matter can be referred to the Secretary of State for directions to be issued to the authority.

6.48   Two prominent public authorities at present excluded from the scope of the NIA 1998, s 75 are the Royal Ulster Constabulary and the Police Authority for Northern Ireland. This is a great disappointment to those who believe that it is the police more than most who need to be paying attention to equality of opportunity and good community relations and it is to be hoped that one of the recommendations of the Commission on Policing in Northern Ireland, chaired by Chris Patten and due to issue its report no later than the summer of 1999, will be to extend the NIA 1998, s 75 duty to both the police and whatever supervisory body is established in relation to the police. But the strength of s 75 is the range of bases upon which equality must be founded. The standard ones of gender, marital status, race, political belief, religion and disability are listed, but so are age, sexual orientation and whether or not a person has dependants[1]. Although the victims of discriminatory treatment based on these last three grounds will still not be able to take court proceedings in Northern Ireland to vindicate themselves, they will at least be able to make a complaint to the Equality Commission.

1   Class, though referred to in the Belfast Agreement, section headed 'Rights, Safeguards and Equality of Opportunity', para 1 is not included.

6.49   The NIA 1998, s 76 repeats existing law[1] which makes discrimination on religious or political grounds a statutory tort, allowing victims to sue for compensation and/or an injunction. This time the police and the Police Authority *are* included within the law's ambit.

1   Northern Ireland Constitution Act 1973, s 19. See generally B Hadfield 'The Northern Ireland Constitution Act 1973: Lessons for Minority Rights' in P Cumper and S Wheatley, 'Minority Rights in the New Europe' (1999), pp 129–146.

6.50   The Equality Commission will be a larger, busier and more powerful body than the Human Rights Commission. Taking over the functions of the four existing anti-discrimination bodies[1], the new Commission will have between 14 and 20 Commissioners[2], as opposed to the HRC's ten. Its powers of investigation will be greater, as will its resources. However, although the members of both Commissions are to be appointed by the Secretary of State[3], the Equality Commission is to be funded by, and is to report primarily to, the Assembly[4], whereas the Human Rights Commission is to be funded by Westminster and is to report to the Secretary of State. The Equality Commission will be subject to oversight by the Commissioner for Complaints in Northern Ireland (ie the local government Ombudsman)[5], but the Human Rights Commission will not.

1   See para **6.04**.
2   NIA 1998, s 73(2).
3   NIA 1998, ss 68(2) and 73(2).
4   NIA 1998, Sch 8, paras 5–7.
5   NIA 1998, Sch 8, para 11.

H   Conclusion and prospects

6.51   No one can predict what the future holds for Northern Ireland in political terms. But almost everyone would agree that there is little chance of there being enduring peace and stability in the area unless the legal system adheres strictly to internationally accepted human rights standards. Through the HRA 1998 and the NIA 1998, Westminster has gone far in providing the appropriate framework for such adherence. The responsibility has now passed, for the time being at least, to the institutions established by those Acts[1], to the judiciary and to lawyers. However, in view of the marginal effect which the European Convention on Human Rights has had to date on the legal system's response to the troubles in Northern Ireland since 1969, it would be wrong to expect these institutions and personnel to be able to alter the landscape radically just because the Convention has been incorporated into domestic law[2]. Judges in Northern Ireland tend to favour judicial restraint rather than judicial activism, even if on many occasions their approach to disputes over emergency laws and practices has been a touch more liberal than that adopted by the Law Lords[3]. The Convention itself is in need of updating, and may in fact soon be at least equalled in significance, if not superseded, by the Council of Europe's Revised European Social Charter, provided improved mechanisms can be devised for that document's enforcement[4]. But the HRA 1998 will undoubtedly give encouragement to lawyers in Northern Ireland when they are investigating whether sustainable arguments can be raised in favour of a challenge to laws or practices. The establishment of a full-time court in Strasbourg, together with more streamlined procedures for reaching that court, also should help to enhance the Convention's standing in Northern Ireland. There are undoubtedly interesting times ahead for all who have a concern for human rights there.

1　The important role of the Parliamentary Joint Committee on Human Rights – in the absence of a Human Rights Commission for Great Britain – should not be ignored.
2　I have explored this point further in 'The Human Rights Act and Northern Ireland' in M Hunt and R Singh *A Practitioner's Guide to the Impact of the Human Rights Act 1998*, ch 25 (due to publish in 1999). The area of law most likely to be affected is that of criminal law and procedure. Unfortunately no specific mention of Northern Ireland's criminal law and procedure is made in either N Richardson 'Criminal Law and Practice', in C Baker *Human Rights Act 1998: A Practitioner's Guide* (1998), pp 127–173, or in D Cheney, L Dickson, J Fitzpatrick and S Uglow *Criminal Justice and the Human Rights Act 1998* (1999).
3　S Livingstone 'The House of Lords and the Northern Ireland Conflict' (1994) 57 MLR 333.
4　See generally D Gomien, D Harris and L Zwaak *Law and Practice of the European Convention on Human Rights and the European Social Charter* (1996), pp 415–430.

Chapter 7
Wales

A Introduction

7.01 Wales has been affected by the European Convention on Human Rights together with the other constituent parts of the United Kingdom. The Laws in Wales Act 1535[1] provided that England and Wales were united and Welshmen and Englishmen were to be subject to the same laws and have the same privileges[2]. Since that time, there has been one legal system for England and Wales. However, forthcoming constitutional changes will provide for a different route whereby the Convention may be applied in Wales to that in England.

1 This short title was conferred by the Statute Law Revision Act 1948.
2 See the Laws in Wales Act 1535, s 1 (repealed); and the Laws in Wales Act 1542 (repealed, except for s 47) by the Welsh Language Act 1993, s 35, Sch 2.

B The National Assembly for Wales

7.02 In 1973 a minority opinion of the Royal Commission on the Constitution[1] recommended the creation of a Welsh Assembly with limited legislative powers[2]. This proposed Welsh Assembly, however, was rejected by the Welsh electorate in a referendum on 1 March 1979. The government elected in May 1997 included in its manifesto commitment to constitutional reform the establishment of a Welsh Assembly. The White Paper, *A Voice for Wales*[3], published in July 1997, proposed that a directly-elected Assembly should assume responsibility for policies and public services then exercised by the Secretary of State for Wales. Unlike Scotland[4], the Welsh Assembly would be able to make secondary legislation only, within the framework laid down in Acts of the Westminster Parliament. In introducing the White Paper the Secretary of State for Wales emphatically stated that Parliament would continue to make primary legislation for Wales, that the Secretary of State for Wales would remain a member of the Cabinet and that Welsh Members of Parliament would remain in full force in the House of Commons[5].

1 See the *Report of the Royal Commission on the Constitution 1963–73* (Cmnd 5460 and 5460–I) (1973) (the 'Kilbrandon Report'), ch 24.
2 *Report of the Royal Commission on the Constitution 1969–73* (Cmnd 5460 and 5460–I) (1973), ch 24.
3 *A Voice for Wales (Llais dros Cymru)* (Cm 3718, 1997).
4 See paras **5.24–5.44**.
5 See 298 HC Official Report (6th series) col 1120 (25 July 1997). Wales is represented by at least 35 members: see Parliamentary Constituencies Act 1986, s 3, Sch 2, para 1.

7.03 These proposals were embodied in the Government of Wales Act 1998[1] (GWA 1998) which received royal assent on 31 July 1998. It provides for the establishment of the National Assembly for Wales or Cynulliad Cenedlaethol Cymru (referred to in the

GWA 1998 as the Assembly)[2]. The Assembly will have the functions which are transferred to it, or made exercisable by it, by virtue of the GWA 1998 or conferred or imposed on it by or under the GWA 1998 or any other Act[3]. By way of an Order in Council any function so far as exercisable by a Minister of the Crown in relation to Wales may be either transferred to the Assembly, or directed to be exercised by the Assembly concurrently with the Minister, or exercisable by the Minister only with the Agreement of, or after consultation with, the Assembly[4]. The Secretary of State for Wales will be entitled to attend and participate in any proceedings of the Assembly, but will not be entitled to vote or to attend or participate in the proceedings of an Assembly committee or sub-committee[5].

1   Government of Wales Act 1998, c 38.
2   GWA 1998, s 1.
3   GWA 1998, s 21.
4   GWA 1998, s 22.
5   GWA 1998, s 76.

7.04   Where a function to make subordinate legislation has been transferred or made exercisable by the Assembly, any relevant Parliamentary procedural provision shall not have effect save where it is made jointly with a Minister or where it relates to a cross-border matter[1]. The procedure of the Assembly shall be regulated by standing orders[2]. The Assembly must establish a committee with responsibilities relating to the scrutiny of relevant Welsh subordinate legislation[3].

1   GWA 1998, s 44.
2   GWA 1998, s 46.
3   GWA 1998, s 58.

7.05   The White Paper on the Human Rights Bill[1], published in October 1997, comparing the incorporation of the Convention in Wales with that in Scotland, stated:

'Similarly, the Welsh Assembly will not have power to make subordinate legislation or take executive action which is incompatible with the Convention. It will be possible to challenge such legislation and action in the courts, and for them to be quashed, on the ground that the Assembly has exceeded its powers.'[2].

1   *Rights Brought Home* (Cm 3782, 1997).
2   *Rights Brought Home* (Cm 3782, 1997), para 2.22.

7.06   Section 107(1) of the GWA 1998 addresses the compatibility with the Convention acts and secondary legislation of the Assembly[1]. It provides that the Assembly has no power to make, confirm or approve any subordinate legislation, or do any other act so far as the subordinate legislation or act is incompatible with any of the Convention rights[2]. This rule does not enable a person to bring any proceedings in a court or tribunal or to rely upon any of the Convention rights in any such proceedings in respect of an act unless he would be a victim for the purposes of art 34 of the Convention if proceedings were brought in the E Ct HR in respect of that act[3]. However, this proviso does not apply to the Attorney General, the Assembly, the Advocate General for Scotland or the Attorney General for Northern Ireland[4]. In relation to damages the GWA 1998 does not enable a court or tribunal to award any damages in respect of an act which is incompatible with the Convention rights, which it could not award if the HRA 1998, s 8(3) and (4) applied[5]. The 'Convention' and the 'Convention rights' are defined as having the same meaning as in the HRA 1998[6] (where they are further defined[7]).

1　At the time of writing the GWA 1998, s 107 has not yet been brought into force. The Government
　　of Wales Act 1998 (Commencment No 1) Order 1998, SI 1998/2244, the Government of Wales
　　Act 1998 (Commencment No 2) Order 1998, SI 1998/2789 and the Government of Wales Act
　　1998 (Commencement No 3) Order 1999, SI 1999/118 have together brought into effect GWA
　　1998, Pts I–VI (except ss 104, 105, 107, 112, 116–118 and 125).
2　The GWA 1998, s 107(1)(b) differs from the Scotland Act 1998 in that 'act' is not defined
　　in the GWA 1998 to include 'failure to act', as it is in respect of the act or failure of a member
　　of the Scottish Executive (see SA 1998, s 100(4)(b)).
3　GWA 1998, s 107(2). See para **2.7.2** on the meaning of 'victim'.
4　GWA 1998, s 107(3).
5　GWA 1998, s 107(4). On HRA 1998, s 8, see para **2.8**.
6　GWA 1998, s 107(5).
7　HRA 1998, s 1. See para **2.1**.

C　Devolution issues

7.07　The GWA 1998 contains a similar but narrower set of provisions for dealing with
'devolution issues' to those found in the Scotland Act 1998[1] (SA 1998). These are
defined[2] in the GWA 1998 as meaning:

(a)　a question whether a function is exercisable by the Assembly;

(b)　a question whether a purported or proposed exercise of a function by the
Assembly is, or would be, within the powers of the Assembly, including by
virtue of being incompatible either with Community law or an obligation arising
from a Ministerial order to implement or comply with a Community obligation
of the United Kingdom, or any of the Convention rights;

(c)　a question whether the Assembly has failed to comply with a duty imposed on
it, including by virtue of being a Community obligation of the United Kingdom
or arising from a Ministerial order to implement or comply with a Community
obligation;

(d)　a question whether a failure to act by the Assembly is incompatible with any
of the Convention rights.

A devolution issue is not taken to arise in any proceedings merely because of any
contention of a party which appears to the court or tribunal to be frivolous or vexatious[3].

1　See paras **5.35–5.44**.
2　GWA 1998, Sch 8, para 1.
3　GWA 1998, Sch 8, para 2.

7.08　In line with the SA 1998[1] the GWA 1998 anticipates that devolution issues may
arise in any proceedings before courts or tribunals anywhere in the United Kingdom.
The GWA 1998 at Sch 8 accordingly makes separate provision for devolution issues
which arise in either England and Wales, Scotland or Northern Ireland. The discussion
below focuses on the provisions for England and Wales.

1　See para **5.36**.

7.09　The provisions cover both proceedings brought for the purpose of determining
a devolution issue[1], and other proceedings in which a devolution issue arises[2]. The
GWA 1998 provides that the Attorney General may institute proceedings for the
determination of a devolution issue[3], but without limitation to any power to institute

proceedings otherwise exercisable by any person[4]. Where a devolution issue arises in other proceedings the court or tribunal shall order notice of it to be given to the Attorney General and the Assembly, unless a party to the proceedings[5].

1   GWA 1998, Sch 8, para 4.
2   GWA 1998, Sch 8, para 5.
3   GWA 1998, Sch 8, para 4(1).
4   GWA 1998, Sch 8, para 4(2).
5   GWA 1998, Sch 8, para 5(1).

7.10   Where a devolution issue arises in civil proceedings before a magistrates' court it may refer it to the High Court[1]. A court, other than a magistrates' court, the Court of Appeal, the House of Lords, or, if the devolution issue arises in proceedings on reference to it from a magistrates, the High Court, may refer any devolution issue which arises in civil proceedings before it to the Court of Appeal[2]. The tribunal must make a reference to the Court of Appeal where there would be no appeal from its decision, but it otherwise has a discretion[3].

1   GWA 1998, Sch 8, para 6.
2   GWA 1998, Sch 8, para 7.
3   GWA 1998, Sch 8, para 8.

7.11   The position in respect of criminal proceedings is similar: a court, other than the Court of Appeal or the House of Lords, may refer any devolution issue arising in proceedings to the High Court if the proceedings are summary proceedings, or to the Court of Appeal if the proceedings are proceedings on indictment[1]. It is to be presumed that where a tribunal does not refer the devolution issue but determines it itself, and neither the Assembly nor the Attorney General are involved, normal existing legal processes would apply, and an application for judicial review may be brought in respect of the decision.

1   GWA 1998, Sch 8, para 9.

7.12   Where the Court of Appeal has a devolution issue referred to it, it is not able simply to refer the issue up to a higher court, but must deal with it itself. However, when a devolution issue has not been referred to the Court of Appeal, but arises in proceedings before it, the Court of Appeal may decide it itself or refer it to the Judicial Committee[1]. When the High Court or the Court of Appeal determines a devolution issue referred to it an appeal lies to the Judicial Committee only with the leave of the court concerned, or failing such leave, with special leave of the Judicial Committee[2].

1   GWA 1998, Sch 8, para 10.
2   GWA 1998, Sch 8, para 11.

7.13   Where a devolution issue arises in the House of Lords, it must be referred to the Judicial Committee unless the House considers it more appropriate, having regard to all the circumstances, that it should determine the issue[1].

1   GWA 1998, Sch 8, para 29.

7.14   The Attorney General, the Advocate General for Scotland, or the Advocate General for Northern Ireland or the Assembly may require any court or tribunal to refer to the Judicial Committee any devolution issue which has arisen in any proceedings before it to which he or it is a party[1]. The Attorney General or the Assembly may refer to the Judicial Committee any devolution issue which is not the subject of proceedings[2]. Where the Attorney General makes such a reference in relation to a devolution issue which relates to the proposed exercise of a function by the Assembly he must notify the Assembly of that fact, and, between the time of the notification and the reference being decided or otherwise disposed of, the Assembly shall not exercise the function in the manner proposed[3].

1　GWA 1998, Sch 8, para 30.
2　GWA 1998, Sch 8, para 31(1).
3　GWA 1998, Sch 8, para 31(2).

7.15 The GWA provides for subordinate legislation for prescribing such matters as the stage in proceedings at which a devolution issue is to be raised or referred, for the staying or sisting of proceedings, and for determining the manner and time within which any notice and intimation is to be given[1].

1　GWA 1998, Sch 8, para 36.

7.16 In line with the SA 1998 the GWA 1998 provides that decisions of the Judicial Committee are to be binding in all legal proceedings (other than proceedings before the Judicial Committee itself)[1].

1　GWA 1998, Sch 8, para 32.

7.17 In the event that a court or tribunal decides that subordinate legislation of the Assembly is ultra vires the court or tribunal may make an order removing or limiting any retrospective effect of the decision, or suspending its effect for any period and on any conditions to allow the defect to be corrected[1].

1　GWA 1998, s 110. See para **5.47** for the analogous provision in the SA 1998.

7.18 Unlike the SA 1998, the GWA makes no specific provision for the making of subordinate legislation considered necessary or expedient in order to remedy ultra vires acts[1].

1　SA 1998, s 107. See para **5.47**.

D The Government of Wales Act 1998 and the Human Rights Act 1998

7.19 The HRA 1998, s 6 makes it unlawful in general for a public authority to act in a way which is incompatible with a Convention right. The Assembly will be a 'public authority' within the meaning of s 6. In principle, therefore, it would be possible to challenge acts done by the Assembly under the HRA 1998 as an alternative route to a challenge under the GWA 1998. However, whether the courts will accept that s 6 provides an alternative route to the GWA 1998 mechanism to challenge the acts of the Assembly remains to be seen. Unlike s 6 the GWA 1998 mechanism does not cover omissions and a failure to act[1].

1　HRA 1998, s 6(6); GWA 1998, s 107(1). On the HRA 1998, s 6, see para **2.6**.

7.20   There are a number of further distinctions between the cases brought under the GWA 1998 on the basis of the Convention and the HRA 1998. If the case were brought under the HRA 1998 the court of last resort would be the House of Lords, whereas if it were brought as a devolution issue it would be the Judicial Committee of the Privy Council. The GWA 1998 provides procedures whereby devolution issues may be dealt with by way of a preliminary reference, whereas the HRA 1998 does not. Whilst there is no limitation period applicable to proceedings under the GWA 1998, under the HRA 1998 a one year limitation period applies to proceedings brought against a public authority[1].

1   HRA 1998, s 7(5). See para **2.7.5**.

7.21   The HRA 1998, s 3 requires primary legislation and subordinate legislation to be read and given effect in a way which is compatible with the Convention rights, so far as it is possible to do so. Subordinate legislation made by the Assembly will be 'subordinate legislation' within the definition in the HRA 1998[1].

1   HRA 1998, s 21(1). On the HRA 1998, s 3, see para **2.3**.

7.22   Further, all such forms of subordinate legislation, including departmental regulations made in London, and such Welsh local authority by-laws as will continue to be made even after the establishment of the Assembly, will be subject to judicial scrutiny in one form or another through the ordinary courts. Subordinate legislation which is made in Whitehall and which is applicable to Wales in fields in which there has been no transfer of functions to the Assembly, will not raise devolution issues. Hence, such subordinate legislation will not fall to be considered under the new procedures.

Chapter 8

International Human Rights Codes and United Kingdom Law

A Introduction

8.01 The United Kingdom is party to many international human rights instruments. This chapter describes the principal international codes and explains the ways in which the protection afforded by them overlaps with and goes beyond the substantive content of the European Convention on Human Rights (ECHR). It also describes the supra-national monitoring and enforcement procedures, together with the ways in which these treaties are of relevance to United Kingdom courts and tribunals and to legal practitioners.

8.02 International treaties cannot be *directly* relied upon before the domestic courts as part of the law of the land, in the absence of statutory incorporation, unless they embody generally recognised principles of customary international law. However, unincorporated international human rights treaties are relevant to statutory interpretation and the development of the common law in the following ways[1]:

(1) where a UK statute is ambiguous, that is, reasonably capable of two interpretations, only one of which is consistent with the appropriate international treaty, the courts will presume that Parliament intended to legislate in conformity with the international treaty;

(2) where the common law is uncertain, unclear or incomplete, the courts will declare it, wherever possible, in a manner which conforms with the UK's international obligations;

(3) when the courts are called upon to construe a statute enacted to fulfil an international obligation, the courts will assume that the statute was intended to be effective to that end;

(4) where the courts are exercising a discretion, they will seek to exercise it in a way which does not violate our treaty obligations;

(5) when the courts are called upon to decide what, in a particular situation, are the demands of public policy, it is legitimate to have regard to our international obligations.

1 These grounds were identified by Lord Bingham in his maiden speech to the House of Lords as Lord Chief Justice (see 574 HL Official Report (5th series) col 1465 (3 July 1996)). See para **2.03**.

8.03 The persuasive value of international and comparative human rights law to national courts has been widely recognised across the Commonwealth in a series of high-level judicial colloquia on the domestic application of international human rights norms. The participants reached consensus on a series of propositions known as 'the Bangalore Principles'[1], which have been referred to by several senior Commonwealth courts. Subsequent Commonwealth judicial colloquia on human rights have developed and refined the basic propositions. They include the following general statements of principle:

- The international human rights instruments and their developing jurisprudence enshrine values and principles of equality, freedom, rationality and fairness, now recognised by the common law. They should be seen as complementary to domestic law in national courts.

- It is the vital duty of an independent, well-qualified judiciary, assisted by an independent well-trained legal profession, to interpret and apply national constitutions and ordinary legislation, and to develop the common law, in the light of these values and principles.

- Both civil and political rights and economic, social and cultural rights are integral, indivisible and complementary parts of one coherent system of global human rights. The implementation of economic, social and cultural rights which are not justiciable can serve as vital points of reference for judges as they interpret their constitutions and develop the common law, making choices which it is their responsibility to make in a free, equal and democratic society.

1   See 'Developing Human Rights Jurisprudence, Volume 7: Seventh Colloquium on the Domestic Application of International Human Rights Norms', (Commonwealth Secretariat and Interights, 1998).

8.04   The foundation of the international human rights legal system is the Universal Declaration of Human Rights proclaimed by the General Assembly of the United Nations on 10 December 1948[1]. The international human rights treaties described below elaborate on the content of the rights referred to in the Universal Declaration and establish supra-national enforcement machinery for their protection. The ECHR is also designed to enable some of the rights referred to in the Universal Declaration to be collectively enforced[2]. There is, therefore, a considerable overlap between the rights contained in the ECHR and in the other international treaties[3]. There will be occasions when UK courts and legal practitioners will find it useful to take account of the jurisprudence which has built up under the international codes to illuminate the contents of the ECHR, when interpreting legislation or when developing the common law[4].

1   See Ch 1, especially paras **1.10–1.11**.
2   ECHR, art 53 (formerly art 60) of the Convention with the implementation of protocol 11.
3   See the table comparing the protection afforded to civil and political rights under the ECHR and International Covenant on Civil and Political Rights.
4   Information on recent developments in human rights law can be found on the UN website (www.un.org) and in the 'INTERIGHTS Bulletin' (INTERIGHTS is an international human rights law centre which focuses on the protection of human rights through legal remedies. For further information, contact INTERIGHTS, Lancaster House, 33 Islington High Street, London, N1 9LH). See also *Butterworths Human Rights Cases* (BHRC) and *International Human Rights Reports* (IHRR) for the leading international and national judgments in this area.

B   International Covenant on Civil and Political Rights

1   NATURE OF THE UK'S IMPLEMENTING OBLIGATIONS

8.05   The International Covenant on Civil and Political Rights[1] ('ICCPR') was ratified by the UK in May 1976.

1   See generally, D Harris and S Joseph *The International Covenant on Civil and Political Rights and United Kingdom Law* (1995) and M Nowak *UN Covenant on Civil and Political Rights: CCPR Commentary* (1993). Reference should also be made to the UK reservations to the ICCPR, reprinted in Appendix VII in Harris and Joseph.

8.06

Article 2

1.   Each State Party undertakes to respect and to ensure to all individuals within its territory and subject to its jurisdiction the rights recognised in the present Covenant, without distinction of any kind, such as race, colour, sex, language, religion, political or other opinion, national or social origin, property, birth or other status.

2.   Each State Party undertakes to adopt such legislative or other measures as may be necessary to give effect to the rights recognised in the present Covenant.

3.   Each State Party undertakes:

(a)   to provide an effective remedy;

(b)   to ensure that any person claiming such a remedy shall have his right thereto determined by competent judicial, administrative or legislative authorities, and to develop the possibilities of judicial remedy; and

(c)   to ensure that the competent authorities shall enforce such remedies when granted.

---

2   ENFORCEMENT

8.07   The Human Rights Committee[1] ('HRC') is the guardian of the ICCPR and a 'judicial body of high standing'[2].

1   See further, D McGoldrick *The Human Rights Committee: Its Role in the Development of the International Covenant on Civil and Political Rights* (1991) and PR Ghandi *Human Rights Committee and the Right of Individual Communication* (1998).
2   See *Tavista v Minister of Immigration* [1994] 2 NZLR 257, NZCA.

(a)   The Reporting System

8.08   The UK submits reports to the HRC every five years on the measures adopted to give effect to the rights in the ICCPR and on the progress made in the enjoyment of those rights. The HRC makes concluding comments on the performance of each state party[1]. The comments include a number of principal subjects of concern, indicating the areas in which the UK may be failing to meet its ICCPR obligations.

1   See IHRR Vol 3, No 1 [1996] 180 for the HRC's most recent concluding comments on the UK's performance.

8.09   The HRC also adopts general comments which elaborate on the content of the substantive guarantees contained in the ICCPR, providing important guidance to the state parties[1].

1   General Comments Nos 1–22, IHRR Vol 1, No 2 [1994] 1; General Comment 23, IHRR Vol 1, No 3 [1994] 1; General Comment 24, IHRR Vol 2, No 1 [1995] 10 and General Comment 25 IHRR Vol 4, No 1 [1997] 1 and General Comment 26, IHRR Vol 5, No 2 [1998].

8.10   Table of Contents of General Comments on the ICCPR

No of Report	Subject Matter	Year Adopted
1	Reporting obligations	1981
2	Reporting obligations	1981
3	Implementation at national level	1981
4	Art 3: Equality	1981
5	Art 4: Derogations	1981
6	Art 6: Right to life	1982
7[1]	Art 7: Torture	1982
8	Art 9: Liberty and security of the person	1982
9[2]	Art 10: Rights of detained persons	1982
10	Art 19: Freedom of expression	1983
11	Art 20: War propaganda and incitement to national, racial and religious hatred	1983
12	Art 1: Self-determination	1984
13	Art 14: Right to a fair trial	1984
14	Art 6: Right to life	1984
15	Position of aliens under the ICCPR	1986
16	Art 17: Respect for privilege, family, home and correspondence	1988
17	Art 24: Protection of the child	1989
18	Non-Discrimination	1989
19	Art 23: Protection of the family and right to marry	1990
20	Art 7: Torture	1992
21	Art 10: Rights of detained persons	1992
22	Art 18: Freedom of thought, conscience and religion	1993
23	Art 27: Protection of minorities	1994
24	Reservations	1994
25	Art 25: Participation in public life	1996
26	Continuity of obligations and denunciations	1997

1   General Comment 7 was replaced by General Comment 20.
2   General Comment 9 was replaced by General Comment 21.

(b)   Inter-state complaint mechanism

8.11   The UK has recognised the competence of the HRC under art 41 to consider complaints against itself made by another state party concerning a violation of its obligations under the ICCPR. The procedure is essentially conciliatory. It has not yet been used.

(c)   Individual Complaint Mechanism

8.12   The HRC also has competence to consider individual communications from private parties, claiming to be victims of a violation of the Covenant[1]. This jurisdiction is derived from the first optional protocol to the ICCPR. The UK Government has however declined to accede to the ICCPR optional protocol[2]. This is unfortunate since the ICCPR and its jurisprudence could be of more immediate value in this country if national decisions were subject to external review by the HRC.

---

1   Individual complaints are considered in two stages. First, the complaint must be held to be admissible. The HRC will then proceed to consider the merits of the communication. The HRC consists of eminent jurists but is not a typical judicial body. It does not, therefore, have the power to enforce its decisions but must rely on the willingness of the state concerned to remedy the violation. The admissibility decisions and views of the HRC can be found in the *International Human Rights Reports* (IHRR).
2   See the written answer of the Home Secretary in 326 HC Official Report (6th series) col 756 (3 March 1999).

3   EXAMPLES OF LINKS WITH UK LAW AND PRACTICE

(a)   Areas of concern identified by the HRC[1]

8.13

- Not every violation of civil and political rights has an effective remedy in accordance with the ICCPR, art 2(3).
- Police and Criminal Evidence Act 1984 (PACE), ss 34–46 and 58: extended periods of detention without charge or access to legal advisors.
- PACE 1984, ss 17–18: entry into private property without judicial warrant.
- Prevention of Terrorism (Temporary Provisions) Act 1989 (PTA), ss 4–8 and Sch 2: imposition of exclusion orders[2].
- PACE 1984, s 1 (see also Code A) and Criminal Justice and Public Order Act 1994 (CJPOA), s 60: stop and search powers (which are executed on disproportionate numbers of members of some ethnic minorities).
- CJPOA 1994, s 34–37: inferences from the accused's silence.
- Prison conditions.
- The treatment of illegal immigrants, asylum-seekers and those ordered to be deported, in particular:
  - (a)   the length of detention of those incarcerated before deportation (the Immigration Act 1971 does not provide time limits for detention[3]);
  - (b)   the use of excessive force in the execution of deportation orders;
  - (c)   the lack of adequate legal representation for asylum seekers' appeals.
- Failure of the authorities to pursue acts of racial harassment not pursued by the authorities with sufficient rigour and efficiency.
- The remaining instances of corporal punishment in some independent schools.

---

1   See the HRC's most recent comments on the UK, IHRR Vol 3, No 1 [1996] 180.
2   The Government has not renewed its powers of exclusion under the Prevention of Terrorism (Temporary Provisions) Act 1989 (Partial Continuance) Order 1998.
3   See further 'Administrative detention in immigration cases: The *Hardial Singh* principles revisited' [1997] PL 623.

(b)   Examples of the difference in protection under the ICCPR and the ECHR

(i)   Non-discrimination[1]

8.14

> ## Article 26   Non-discrimination
>
> All persons are equal before the law and are entitled without any discrimination to the equal protection of the law. In this respect, the law shall prohibit any discrimination and guarantee to all persons equal and effective protection against discrimination on any ground such as race, colour, sex, language, religion, political or other opinion, national or social origin, property, birth or other status.

1   See D Harris and S Joseph *The International Covenant on Civil and Political Rights and United Kingdom Law*, (1995), Ch 17 and M Nowak *UN Covenant on Civil and Political Rights: CCPR Commentary* at 66–72 and 458–480. See also General Comments 4 and 18, IHRR Vol 1, No 2 [1994] 3 and 22.

8.15   This comprehensive and free-standing guarantee of equality before the law and non-discrimination is of particular significance for the protection of rights in the UK because there is no equivalent provision in the ECHR. The ECHR, art 14[1] is a parasitic provision which provides only for freedom from discrimination in the enjoyment of the rights protected in the Convention itself. The HRC's interpretation of art 26 may, therefore, be valuable as an aid to the development of the common law[2] or when interpreting the following legislation[3].

1   See para **4.14**.
2   The common law recognises that equality of treatment is a principle of lawful administration in English law. See de Smith, Woolf and Jowell *Judicial Review of Administrative Action* (5th edn, 1995), paras 13-036 to 13-045. These paragraphs were recently cited with approval in *Matadeen v Pointu* [1998] 3 WLR 18, PC, 26F–G.
3   For a more detailed examination of sex and racial discrimination, see Sections C and D below.

8.16   The UK's anti- discrimination legislation[1] is listed as follows:

Equal Pay Act 1970;

Equal Pay (Northern Ireland) Act 1970;

Sex Discrimination Acts 1975 and 1986;

Sex Discrimination (Northern Ireland) Orders 1976 and 1988;

Race Relations Act 1976;

Race Relations (Northern Ireland) Order 1997;

Disability Discrimination Act 1995;

Northern Ireland Act 1998;

Fair Employment and Treatment (Northern Ireland) Order 1998.

1   The UK is also bound by the EC anti-discrimination provisions which forbid discrimination on the grounds of nationality and sex, see the Treaty Establishing the European Community, arts 6 and 119 (to become arts 12 and 141 when the Treaty of Amsterdam is ratified).

8.17   In General Comment 18[1] the HRC made the following observations:

(1)   'Discrimination' implies any distinction, exclusion, restriction or preference which is based on any ground such as race, colour, sex, language, religion, political or other opinion, national or social origin, property, birth or other status, and which has the purpose or effect of nullifying or impairing the recognition, enjoyment or exercise by all persons, on an equal footing, of all rights and freedoms.

(2)   Discrimination is prohibited in law or in fact in any field regulated and protected by public authorities.

(3)   Not every differentiation of treatment is discriminatory.

(4)   A distinction will not constitute discrimination if it is based on reasonable and objective criteria and if the aim is to achieve a purpose which is legitimate under the Covenant.

1   See para **8.09**, n 10.

8.18   The guarantee of non-discrimination also extends to economic, social and cultural rights[1]. The kinds of issues which have arisen include: conscientious objection; the provision of severance pay, unemployment and children's benefits; the right to disability, veterans' and survivors' pensions; and the right to public health insurance, education subsidies and employment.

1   *Zwaan-de Vries v Netherlands* (182/84).

(ii)   Rights of detainees to humane treatment[1]

8.19

Article 10   Right of detained persons to humane and dignified treatment

1.   All persons deprived of their liberty shall be treated with humanity and with respect for the inherent dignity of the human person.

2.   (a)   Accused persons shall, save in exceptional circumstances, be segregated from convicted persons and shall be subject to separate treatment appropriate to their status as unconvicted persons;

    (b)   accused juvenile persons shall be separated from adults and brought as speedily as possible for adjudication.

3.   The penitentiary system shall comprise treatment of prisoners the essential aim of which shall be their reformation and social rehabilitation. Juvenile offenders shall be segregated from adults and be accorded treatment appropriate to their age and legal status.

---

1   See D Harris and S Joseph *The International Covenant on Civil and Political Rights and United Kingdom Law* (1995), ch 8 and M Nowak *UN Covenant on Civil and Political Rights: CCPR Commentary* (1993), pp 183–196. See also the UN Standard Minimum Rules for the Treatment of Prisoners.

8.20   The ECHR makes no specific reference to detainees. Both the ECHR, art 3[1] and the ICCPR, art 7 prohibit cruel, inhuman and degrading treatment. The standards provided for in the ICCPR, art 10 are, however, more difficult to satisfy and should result in better conditions for those in detention. UK courts may refer to the standards developed by the HRC when considering actions against the Home Office and Prison Governors for ill-treatment of detainees and when it is alleged that the standard of care provided was inadequate[2].

1   See para **4.03**.
2   See also the comments of the European Committee Against Torture in Section G at paras **8.70** ff.

8.21

Basic needs of detainees and prisoners include the provision of:

- food, clean clothes and medical care;
- ventilated and well-lit cells with sanitary facilities;
- recreational facilities and open-air exercise;
- an opportunity to communicate and for privacy.

8.22   In General Comment 21[1] the HRC made the following observations.

(1)   Article 10(1) applies to anyone deprived of liberty under the laws and authority of the state who is held in prisons, hospitals—particularly psychiatric hospitals—detention camps or correctional institutions or elsewhere. State parties should ensure that the principle stipulated therein is observed in all institutions and establishments within their jurisdiction where persons are being held.

(2)   Article 10(1) complements the ban on torture or other cruel, inhuman or degrading treatment or punishment contained in art 7. Thus, not only may persons deprived of their liberty not be subjected to treatment that is contrary to art 7, including medical or scientific experimentation, but neither may they be subjected to any hardship or constraint other than that resulting from the deprivation of liberty; respect for the dignity of such persons must be guaranteed under the same conditions as for that of free persons. Persons deprived of their liberty enjoy all the rights set forth in the Covenant, subject to the restrictions that are unavoidable in a closed environment.

(3)   Treating all persons deprived of their liberty with humanity and with respect for their dignity is a fundamental and universally applicable rule. Consequently, the application of this rule, as a minimum, cannot be dependent on the material resources available in the state party. This rule must be applied without distinction of any kind, such as race, colour, sex, language, religion, political or other opinion, national or social origin, property, birth or other status.

1   IHRR Vol 1, No 2 [1994] 28.

(iii)   Rights of political participation[1]

8.23

Article 25   Rights of political participation

Every citizen shall have the right and the opportunity, without any of the distinctions mentioned in Article 2[1] and without unreasonable restrictions:

(a) to take part in the conduct of public affairs, directly or through freely chosen representatives;

(b) to vote and to be elected at genuine periodic elections which shall be by universal and equal suffrage and shall be held by secret ballot, guaranteeing the free expression of the will of the electors;

(c) to have access, on general terms of equality, to public service in his country.

1 D Harris and S Joseph *The International Covenant on Civil and Political Rights and United Kingdom Law*, (1995), Ch 16 and M Nowak *UN Covenant on Civil and Political Rights: CCPR Commentary* (1993), pp 435–458. See also General Comment 25, IHRR Vol 4 No 1 [1997] 1.
2 The examples of distinctions referred to in art 2(1) are on the grounds of race, colour, sex, language, religion, political or other opinion, national or social origin, property, birth or other status.

8.24 The ICCPR, art 25 has no direct equivalent in the ECHR. The ECHR, art 3 of the first protocol[1] is a more general provision which merely provides for free elections at reasonable intervals by secret ballot under conditions which ensure the free expression of the opinion of the people in the choice of the legislature. The right of British citizens to political participation may, therefore, be guided by the HRC's interpretation of art 25. This could be particularly relevant as regards sex, race or religious discrimination in the selection of parliamentary candidates.

1 See para **4.21**.

8.25 General Comment 25[1] includes the following observations.

(1) Whatever form of constitution or government is in force, the Covenant requires states to adopt such legislation and other measures as may be necessary to ensure that citizens have an effective opportunity to enjoy the rights it protects. Article 25 lies at the core of democratic government based on the consent of the people and in conformity with the principles of the Covenant.

(2) The rights under art 25 are related to, but distinct from the right of peoples to self-determination. By virtue of the rights covered by art 1(1)(the right to self-determination), peoples have the right freely to determine their political status and to enjoy the right to choose the form of their constitution or government. Article 25 deals with the right of individuals to participate in those processes which constitute the conduct of public affairs. Those rights, as individual rights, can give rise to claims under the first optional protocol.

(3) Any conditions which apply to the exercise of those rights protected by art 25 should be based on objective and reasonable criteria. The exercise of these rights by citizens may not be suspended or excluded except on grounds which are established by law and which are objective and reasonable.

(4) The conduct of public affairs, referred to in para (a), is a broad concept which relates to the exercise of political power, in particular the exercise of legislative, executive and administrative powers. It covers all aspects of public administration, and the formulation and implementation of policy at international, national, regional and local levels. The allocation of powers and the means by which individual citizens exercise the right to participate in the conduct of public affairs protected by art 25 should be established by the constitution and other laws.

(5) Where citizens participate in the conduct of public affairs through freely chosen representatives, it is implicit in art 25 that those representatives do in fact

exercise governmental power and that they are accountable through the electoral process for their exercise of that power. It is also implicit that the representatives exercise only those powers which are allocated to them in accordance with the constitutional provisions.

(6)   Freedom of expression, assembly and association are essential conditions for the effective exercise of the right to vote and must be fully protected.

1   See para **8.09**, n 1.

(iv)   Right to life[1]

8.26

> ### Article 6   Right to life
>
> 1.   Every human being has the inherent right to life. This right shall be protected by law. No one shall be arbitrarily deprived of his life.

1   ECHR, art 2; ICCPR, art 6. See D Harris and S Joseph *The International Covenant on Civil and Political Rights and United Kingdom Law*, (1995), Ch 5 and M Nowak *UN Covenant on Civil and Political Rights: CCPR Commentary* (1993), pp 103–126. See General Comments 6 and 14, IHRR Vol 1, No 2 [1994] 4 and 15.

8.27   The HRC has taken a broader approach to the interpretation of the positive obligation on the states to protect the right to life than the ECt HR[1]. General Comments 6 and 14 include the following observations.

(1)   The right to life is the supreme right from which no derogation is permitted even in time of public emergency which threatens the life of the nation.

(2)   States have the supreme duty to prevent wars, acts of genocide and other mass acts of violence causing arbitrary loss of life.

(3)   States should establish effective facilities and procedures to investigate cases of missing and disappeared persons in circumstances which may involve a violation of the right to life.

(4)   It is desirable for state parties to take all possible measures to reduce infant mortality and to increase life expectancy, especially in adopting measures to eliminate malnutrition and epidemics.

(5)   The production, testing, possession, deployment and uses of nuclear weapons should be prohibited and recognised as crimes against humanity.

1   See para **4.02**.

C   International Convention on the Elimination of Racial Discrimination

1   NATURE OF THE UK'S IMPLEMENTING OBLIGATIONS

8.28   The International Convention on the Elimination of All Forms of Racial Discrimination[1] was ratified by the UK in March 1969. The UK is obliged to ensure non-discrimination in the exercise and enjoyment of a broad range of civil, political, economic, social and cultural rights. Racial discrimination is defined[2] as:

'… any distinction, exclusion, restriction or preference based on race, colour, descent, or national or ethnic origin which has the purpose or effect of nullifying or impairing the recognition, enjoyment or exercise, on an equal footing, of human rights and fundamental freedoms in the political, economic, social, cultural or any other field of public life'.

1   See N Lerner *The United Nations Convention on the Elimination of All Forms of Racial Discrimination* (2nd edn, 1980) and M Banton *International Action Against Racial Discrimination* (1996).
2   Article 1(1).

8.29

Article 2

1.   State Parties condemn racial discrimination and undertake to pursue by all appropriate means and without delay a policy of eliminating racial discrimination in all its forms and promoting understanding among all races, and, to this end:
(a)   Each State Party undertakes to engage in no act or practice of racial discrimination against groups of persons or institutions and to ensure that all public authorities and public institutions, national and local, shall act in conformity with this obligation;
(b)   Each State Party undertakes not to sponsor, defend or support discrimination by any persons or organisations.
(c)   Each State Party shall take effective measures to review governmental, national and local policies, and to amend, rescind or nullify any laws and regulations which have the effect of creating or perpetuating racial discrimination wherever it exists;
(d)   Each State Party shall prohibit and bring to an end, by all appropriate means, including legislation as required by circumstances, racial discrimination by any persons, group or organisation.
(e)   Each State Party undertakes to encourage, where appropriate, integrationist, multi-racial organisations and movements and other means of eliminating barriers between races, and to discourage anything which tends to strengthen racial division.
2.   States parties shall, when the circumstances so warrant, take … special and concrete measures to ensure the adequate development and protection of certain racial groups or individuals belonging to them, for the purpose of guaranteeing to them the full and equal enjoyment of human rights and fundamental freedoms. These measures shall in no case entail as a consequence the maintenance of unequal or separate rights for different racial groups after the objectives for which they were taken have been achieved.

Article 6

State Parties shall assure to everyone within their jurisdiction effective protection and remedies, through the competent national tribunals and other state institutions, against any acts of racial discrimination which violate his human rights and fundamental freedoms contrary to this

> Convention, as well as the right to seek from such tribunals just and adequate reparation or satisfaction for any damage suffered as a result of such discrimination.

2   ENFORCEMENT

8.30   The Committee on the Elimination of Racial Discrimination ('CERD') oversees the enforcement of the Convention.

(a)   The Reporting System

8.31   The UK submits reports to CERD every two years on the legislative, judicial and administrative measures which it has adopted and which give effect to the provisions of the Convention[1]. CERD also makes a number of concluding comments on the UK's performance. CERD issues general recommendations[2] which elaborate further on the nature of the states' obligations.

1   The next UK report is due on 1 April 1999.
2   General Recommendations Nos I–XVII, IHRR Vol 1, No 3 [1994] 4; General Recommendations Nos XVIII–XXIII, IHRR Vol 5, No 1 [1998] 17. See in particular, No XIV (non-discrimination), No XV (art 4), No XIX (art 3), No XX (art 5), No XXI (self-determination) and No XXII (refugees).

(b)   Inter-State Complaint Mechanism

8.32   Article 11 of the Convention provides for an obligatory inter-state complaints procedure, which is conciliatory in nature.

(c)   Individual Complaint Mechanism[1]

8.33   An optional system of complaints from individuals or groups of individuals is established under art 14. Like the HRC, CERD can only forward its recommendations and suggestions to the state and the petitioner concerned. The UK has not accepted the right of individual petition.

1   CERD's opinions can be found in the IHRR.

3   EXAMPLES OF LINKS WITH UK LAW AND PRACTICE

8.34   In addition to the common law principle of equality of treatment[1], there are a number of legislative provisions which seek to combat racial discrimination in the UK.

1   See para **8.15**, n 2.

(a)   Race Relations Act 1976[1]

8.35   The Race Relations Act 1976 makes racial discrimination generally unlawful in the fields of employment, education, housing[2] and the provision of goods and services. The duty not to discriminate does not, however, apply to the provision of many central government services and facilities. In *R v Entry Clearance Officer, Bombay, ex p Amin*[3] the House of Lords stated that Government Departments and civil servants are liable for discriminatory acts only if they are akin to those done by private persons in the market-place. Exclusively public duties such as the control of immigration or the administration of justice do not, therefore, fall within the scope of the Act. It is doubtful whether this is in conformity with the UK's obligations under the ICCPR, or the International Conventions on the Elimination of Race and Sex Discrimination.

1 See also the Race Relations (Remedies) Act 1994 which removes the limit upon compensation imposed by the Race Relations Act 1976, s 56.
2 See also the Housing Act 1996, Pt V, Ch 1 which enables local authorities to apply introductory tenancies to all new tenants throughout their housing stock. A twelve-month probationary period is provided for during which tenants whose behaviour is unacceptable can be served with an eviction notice. Actions which might give rise to eviction include racial harassment. (See further UK's Fourteenth Periodic Report to CERD, CERD/C/299/Add 9, p 18.)
3 [1983] 2 AC 818, HL at 835 concerning the analogous provisions of the Sex Discrimination Act 1975.

(b) Race Relations (Northern Ireland) Order 1997

8.36 The Race Relations (Northern Ireland) Order makes racial discrimination unlawful in the fields of employment, training, education, housing and in the provision of goods and services. CERD expressed concern in its Concluding Comments of 1997 that the Order contains two grounds for exemption, namely public safety and public order[1], in addition to those already enshrined in the Race Relations Act 1976. It also noted that bodies working in the field of health, education, social services, planning and housing do not have the same positive duty to eliminate discrimination as applies to local authorities in Britain[2].

1 Section 41. This section has now been revised by the Fair Employment and Treatment (Northern Ireland) Order 1998, s 98
2 RRA 1976, s 71 imposes a general duty on local authorities to carry out their functions with due regard to the need to eliminate unlawful racial discrimination and promote racial equality.

(c) Public Order Act 1986, s 18 and Criminal Justice and Public Order Act 1994, s 154

8.37 The UK is obliged by art 4 to make the following acts offences punishable by law:

(1) dissemination of ideas based upon racial superiority or hatred;

(2) incitement to racial hatred;

(3) acts of violence against any race or group of persons of another colour or ethnic origin;

(4) incitement to such acts; and

(5) participation in organisations and all other propaganda activities which promote and incite racial discrimination.

8.38 The Public Order Act 1986, s 18[1]; the Criminal Justice and Public Order Act 1994, s 154[2]; and the Crime and Disorder Act 1998, Pt II[3] go some way towards meeting the UK's obligations[4]. CERD has however repeatedly expressed concern in its concluding comments at the UK Government's restrictive interpretation of art 4. In particular, CERD has expressed the view that the UK's failure to make it an offence to participate in organisations which promote and incite racial discrimination is in conflict with its obligations under art 4(b).

1 By virtue of POA 1986, s 18 it is an offence for a person to use threatening, abusive or insulting words or behaviour or to display any material which is threatening, abusive or insulting if he

does so with intent to stir up racial hatred, or if in the circumstances racial hatred is likely to be stirred up. The Act also applies to publicising or distributing such materials (s 19), theatrical performances (s 20), the distribution, showing or playing of a recording of visual images or sounds (s 21), and television and radio broadcasts (s 22). Section 23 makes it an offence to possess material which if displayed or published would amount to an offence under the Act.

2   CJPOA 1994, s 154 amends the Public Order Act to include s 4A, creating the offence of intentional harassment, which is designed to address the problems of racial harassment.

3   Part II provides a definition for 'racially aggravated offences'.

4   See also Football (Offences) Act 1991, s 3 which makes 'racialist' or indecent chanting at football matches an offence.

(d)   Asylum and Immigration Act 1996

8.39   CERD has heavily criticised the alterations made by the Asylum and Immigration Act 1996 to law concerning asylum seekers, see paras **8.89–8.85**.

D   Convention on the Elimination of all Forms of Discrimination Against Women

1   NATURE OF THE UK'S IMPLEMENTING OBLIGATIONS

8.40   The Convention on the Elimination of All Forms of Discrimination Against Women was ratified by the UK on 7 April 1986.

8.41

Article 2

State Parties condemn discrimination against women in all its forms, agree to pursue by all appropriate means and without delay a policy of eliminating discrimination against women and, to this end, undertake:

(a) to embody the principle of equality of men and women in their national constitutions or other appropriate legislation if not yet incorporated therein and to ensure, through law and other appropriate means, the practical realisation of this principle;

(b) to adopt appropriate legislative and other measures, including sanctions where appropriate, prohibiting all discrimination against women;

(c) to establish legal protection of the rights of women on an equal basis with men and to ensure through competent national tribunals and other public institutions the effective protection of women against any act of discrimination;

(d) to refrain from engaging in any act or practice of discrimination against women and to ensure that public authorities and institutions shall act in conformity with this obligation;

(e) to take all appropriate measures to eliminate discrimination against women by any person, organisation or enterprise;

(f) to take all appropriate measures, including legislation, to modify or abolish existing laws, regulations, customs and practices which constitute discrimination against women;

(g) to repeal all national penal provisions which constitute discrimination against women.

2   ENFORCEMENT

8.42   The Committee on the Elimination of Discrimination Against Women (CEDAW) considers the reports which the UK submits in accordance with its obligation under art 18 of the Convention. The reporting procedure is the only monitoring or enforcement procedure established under the Convention. CEDAW issues concluding observations on the performance of the state parties. CEDAW also makes General Recommendations, which provide guidance about the content of the provisions of the Convention[1].

---

1   General Recommendations Nos 1-20, IHRR Vol. 1, No 1 [1994] 15, General Recommendation 21, IHRR Vol 2, No 1 [1995] 1, General Recommendations 22 and 23, IHRR Vol 5, No 1 [1998] 6. See in particular No 9 (nationality), No 15 (equality before the law), No 16 (marriage and children), No 21 (equality in marriage and family relations) and No 23 (political and public life).

3   EXAMPLES OF LINKS WITH UK LAW AND PRACTICE

(a)   Sex Discrimination Act 1975

8.43   The Sex Discrimination Act 1975 makes sex discrimination unlawful in employment, vocational training, education and the management and disposal of property. The Act also makes it unlawful for any person concerned with the provision of goods, facilities and services to the public or a section of the public to discriminate on the grounds of sex[1]. It gives individuals complaining of sex discrimination the right of direct access to industrial tribunals or civil courts.

---

1   See para **8.35**, n 3 on the decision in *R v Entry Clearance Officer, Bombay, ex p Amin* [1983] 2 AC 818, HL.

(b)   Equal Pay Act 1970

8.44   Under the Equal Pay Act employees have the right to bring complaints seeking equal pay for like work, work rated as equivalent and work of equal value.

(c)   Recent changes in the law which promote women's rights

8.45   These include:

- the Sex Discrimination and Equal Pay (Miscellaneous Amendments) Regulations 1996 which ensure that employees working part-time are entitled to qualify for statutory employment protection rights on the same basis as those working full-time;

- the Sex Discrimination Act 1975 (Application to Armed Forces etc) Regulations 1994 which removed the exemption for service personnel from the SDA 1975, s 85;

- the Trade Union Reform and Employment Rights Act 1993, s 32 which provides that an individual who has reason to believe that he or she may be affected by the operation of a term in a collective agreement or a rule made by an employer may complain to an employment tribunal that the term or rule discriminates unlawfully;

- the implementation of the EC Directive on the Protection of Pregnant Women at Work (Council Directive 92/85 EC) which, inter alia, gives all pregnant employees an entitlement to 14 weeks' maternity leave and automatic protection from maternity related dismissal, in Part VIII of the Employment Rights Act 1996.

(d)   Sexual harassment and violence

8.46   Sexual harassment may amount to sex discrimination and thus give rise to an complaint under the SDA 1975. The harassment may also amount to an unlawful assault or give rise to a cause of action under the Protection from Harassment Act 1997. The Criminal Justice and Public Order Act 1994, s 154 (CJPOA) establishes the offence of intentional harassment which includes sexual harassment. The Family Law Act 1996, Pt IV[1] gives the court a wide range of powers to deal with domestic violence.

---

1   FLA 1996, Pt IV (other than s 60) came into force on 1 October 1997.

8.47   The UK courts may be guided in the course of their interpretation of these statutory provisions by CEDAW's General Recommendation No 19 which discusses the obligation of the states under the Convention to eliminate violence against women. CEDAW made the following observations.

(1)   The Convention in art 1 defines discrimination against women. The definition of discrimination includes gender-based violence, that is, violence that is directed against a woman because she is a woman or that affects women disproportionately. It includes acts that inflict physical, mental or sexual harm or suffering, threats of such acts, coercion and other deprivations of liberty.

(2)   Gender-based violence, which impairs or nullifies the enjoyment by women of human rights and fundamental freedoms under general international law or under human rights conventions, is discrimination within the meaning of art 1. These rights and freedoms include:

(a)   the right to life;

(b)   the right not to be subjected to torture or to cruel, inhuman or degrading treatment or punishment;

(c)   the right to equal protection according to humanitarian norms in times of international or internal armed conflict;

(d)   the right to liberty and security of the person;

(e)   the right to equal protection under the law;

(f)   the right to equality in the family;

(g)   the right to the highest standard attainable of physical and mental health;

(h)   the right of just and favourable conditions of work.

(3)   Under general international law and specific human rights covenants, states may also be responsible for private acts if they fail to act with due diligence to prevent violations of rights or to investigate and punish acts of violence, and for providing compensation.

(4)   Prostitutes need the equal protection of laws against rape and other forms of violence.

(5)   Equality in employment can be seriously impaired when women are subjected to gender-specific violence, such as sexual harassment in the workplace.

(6)   Sexual harassment includes such unwelcome sexually determined behaviour as physical contact and advances, sexually coloured remarks, showing pornography and sexual demands, whether by words or actions. Such conduct can be humiliating and may constitute a health and safety problem; it is discriminatory when the woman has reasonable grounds to believe that her objection would

disadvantage her in connection with her employment, including recruitment or promotion, or when it creates a hostile working environment.

(7) State parties should take all appropriate and effective measures to overcome all forms of gender-based violence, whether by public or private act.

(8) State parties should ensure that laws against family violence and abuse, rape, sexual assault and other gender-based violence give adequate protection to all women, and respect their integrity and dignity.

(9) Effective complaints procedures and remedies, including compensation, should be provided.

(10) State parties should take all legal and other measures that are necessary to provide effective protection of women against gender-based violence, including, effective legal measures, such as penal sanctions, civil remedies and compensatory provisions to protect women against all kinds of violence, including, inter alia, violence and abuse in the family, sexual assault and sexual harassment in the workplace.

E   Convention on the Rights of the Child

1   NATURE OF THE UK'S IMPLEMENTING OBLIGATIONS

8.48   The Convention on the Rights of the Child[1] was ratified by the UK on 16 December 1991. The general aims of the Convention have been identified[2] as the four 'P's: the participation of children in decisions affecting their own destiny; the protection of children against discrimination and all forms of neglect and exploitation; the prevention of harm to children; and the provision of assistance for their basic needs. While the Convention has not been incorporated into UK law, it was held by Lord Browne-Wilkinson in *R v Secretary of State for the Home Department, ex p Venables and Thompson*[3] to be legitimate 'to assume that Parliament has not maintained on the statute book a power capable of being exercised in a manner inconsistent with the treaty obligations of this country'.

1   See generally, G Van Bueren *The International Convention on the Rights of the Child* (1995). See also A Cleland and EE Sutherland (eds) *Children's Rights in Scotland: Scots Law Analysed in the Light of the UN Convention on the Rights of the Child* (1996). In 1996 the Council of Europe opened the European Convention on the Exercise of Children's Rights for signature. See IHRR Vol 3, No 2 [1996] 505 for the text and the explanatory report.
2   G Van Bueren *The International Convention on the Rights of the Child* (1995) p 15.
3   [1997] 3 WLR 23 at 49F–H.

8.49

Article 4

State Parties shall undertake all appropriate legislative, administrative, and other measures for the implementation of the rights recognised in the present Convention. With regard to economic, social and cultural rights, state parties shall undertake such measures to the maximum extent of their available resources and, where needed, within the framework of international co-operation.

---

2   ENFORCEMENT

8.50   The Committee on the Rights of the Child considers the UK's reports and makes concluding observations[1] on the government's performance. This is the only type of enforcement machinery provided for in the Convention.

1   For the Committee's concluding observations on the UK's last report, see IHRR Vol 2, No 2 [1995] 498.

3   EXAMPLES OF LINKS WITH UK LAW AND PRACTICE

8.51   The Convention has four general principles which are a guide to its implementation and interpretation:

(a)   non-discrimination (art 2);

(b)   best interests of the child (art 3);

(c)   the right to life, survival and development (art 6); and

(d)   the views of the child (art 12).

8.52   The principles enshrined in arts 3 and 12 are reflected in the Children Act 1989[1]. The CA 1989, s 1 states that when a court determines any question with respect to:

(a)   the upbringing of a child; or

(b)   the administration of a child's property or the application of any income arising from it;

the child's welfare shall be the court's paramount consideration.

This formulation of the welfare principle gives greater significance to the welfare of the child than art 3 of the Convention which states that the best interests of the child shall be *a primary consideration.*

1   See generally, A Bainham and S Cretney *Children: The Modern Law* (1993).

8.53   The CA 1989, s 1(3)(a) also states that under certain circumstances the court should have regard to the ascertainable wishes and feelings of the child concerned.

8.54   The Committee on the Rights of the Child has, however, expressed concern in its most recent concluding observations about the insufficiency of measures taken to ensure the implementation of the general principles of the Convention; that is, arts 2, 3, 6 and 12. In particular, the Committee observed that, the best interests of the child do not appear to be reflected in legislation in such areas as health, education and social security which have a bearing on the respect for the rights of the child. The Committee also noted that in many decisions, including exclusion from school, the child is not systematically invited to express his or her opinion and those opinions may not be given due weight.

8.55   The Committee also raised a number of concerns relating to the administration of the juvenile justice system. These included:

•   the low age of criminal responsibility;

•   the possibility of making a 'secure training order' for children aged between 12 and 14, CJPOA 1994, s 1[1]; and

- the increase of sentences for 15, 16 and 17 year olds under the Criminal Justice Act 1982, s 1B, as amended by the CJPOA 1994, s 17.

1 Now repealed by the Crime and Disorder Act 1998, ss 73(7)(b), 120(2) and Sch 10.

F Convention Against Torture and other Cruel, Inhuman and Degrading Treatment or Punishment

1 NATURE OF THE UK'S IMPLEMENTING OBLIGATIONS

8.56 The UK ratified the Convention Against Torture[1] on 8 December 1988. The Convention expands upon the right not to be subjected to torture or to cruel, inhuman or degrading treatment or punishment contained in the ICCPR, art 7.

1 See generally, Burgers, Herman and Danelius *The United Nations Convention Against Torture: A Handbook on the Convention Against Torture and Other Cruel, Inhuman or Degrading Treatment or Punishment* (1988) and N Rodley *The Treatment of Prisoners under International Law* (1987).
2 See also General Comment 20 of the HRC, IHRR Vol 1, No 2 [1994] 26.

8.57

Article 2

1. Each State Party shall take effective legislative, administrative, judicial or other measures to prevent acts or torture in any territory under its jurisdiction.

---

2 ENFORCEMENT

8.58 The Committee Against Torture (CAT) monitors the implementation of the Convention.

(a) The Reporting System

8.59 The UK submits reports to CAT every four years[1].

1 For CAT's Concluding Observations on the UK's last report, see IHRR Vol 4, No 2 [1997] 493.

(b) Inter-State Complaint Mechanism

8.60 The UK has accepted CAT's jurisdiction to receive inter-state complaints under art 21.

(c) Individual Complaint Mechanism

8.61 The UK has not recognised CAT's competence under art 22 to receive complaints from individuals.

3   LINKS WITH UK LAW AND PRACTICE

8.62   CAT's comments on the UK's performance have focused mainly upon police powers in relation to terrorist offences, the treatment of asylum seekers and immigrants[1] and conditions in prisons[2].

1   See paras **8.89–8.85**.
2   See para **8.84**.

(a)   Emergency Legislation

8.63   The Prevention of Terrorism (Temporary Provisions) Act 1989 (PT(TP)A) and the Northern Ireland (Emergency Provisions) Act 1996 (NI(EP)A)[1] extend the powers of the police beyond those contained in the Police and Criminal Evidence (Northern Ireland) Order 1989. These include the power to stop and question; to arrest without warrant; to stop, search and seize; to enter, search and seize and to detain[2].

1   The NI(EP)A 1996 was recently amended by the Northern Ireland (Emergency Provisions) Act 1998.
2   These powers have been further extended by the Criminal Justice (Terrorism and Conspiracy) Act 1998, s 3.

8.64   In particular, the PT(TP)A 1989, s 14 permits the detention of a person suspected of a terrorist offence without charge or being brought before a magistrate for up to 48 hours. The Secretary of State for Northern Ireland may authorise an extension or a number of extensions up to a total of a further five days. The NI(EP)A 1991, s 45 allows access to a lawyer to be withheld for up to 48 hours.

8.65   Under Part II of the NI(EP)A 1996 the army also have extensive powers to stop and question, to conduct personal searches, to examine and seize documents, and to arrest and detain people.

8.66   NI(EP)A 1996, s 12 provides that in order to challenge the admissibility of a statement evidence must be adduced, which on the face of it shows that the accused was subjected to torture, or to inhuman or degrading treatment, or to any violence or threat of violence in order to induce the making of the statement. The prosecution must then satisfy the court that the statement was not obtained in this manner. The court has a discretion to exclude the evidence if it is appropriate to do so in order to avoid unfairness to the accused or otherwise in the interests of justice.

(b)   Criminal Justice Act 1988, s 134

8.67   By virtue of the Criminal Justice Act 1988, s 134 it is an offence for a public official or person acting in an official capacity to torture a person. The offence is punishable with a maximum of life imprisonment. Torture is defined as the intentional infliction of severe pain or suffering, whether physical or mental and whether caused by act or omission.

(c)   Police and Criminal Evidence Act 1984, s 76

8.68   PACE 1984, s 76 provides that where it is alleged that confession evidence was obtained as the result of 'oppression'[1] the court shall not allow the confession to be given in evidence except insofar as the prosecution proves beyond reasonable doubt that it was not obtained that way.

1 Oppression is defined as including torture, inhuman or degrading treatment, and the use or threat of violence (whether or not amounting to torture). See also *R v Fulling* [1987] QB 426 per Lord Lane CJ at 432.

(d) CAT's recommendations

8.69 CAT's recommendations include the following measures:

* the repeal of the emergency legislation;
* the abolition of detention centres in Northern Ireland;
* the extension of taping of interrogations to all cases and not merely those that do not involve terrorist-related activities;
* permitting lawyers to be present at interrogations in all cases;
* a review of the practices relating to deportation and refoulement where such practices may conflict with the UK's obligations under art 2; and
* a reconsideration of the UK's position on corporal punishment.

G European Convention for the Prevention of Torture and Inhuman or Degrading Treatment or Punishment

1 NATURE OF THE UK'S IMPLEMENTING OBLIGATIONS

8.70 The UK ratified the European Convention for the Prevention of Torture and Inhuman or Degrading Treatment or Punishment[1] in June 1988. This Convention is designed to prevent the human rights violations for which a remedy is provided in the ECHR, art 3[2] through a system of visits to places of detention.

1 The Convention was adopted by the Committee of Ministers of the Council of Europe in June 1987. See generally, Council of Europe, Yearbook of the European Convention for the Prevention of Torture and Inhuman or Degrading Treatment or Punishment, Vol 1, 1989–1992 and vol 2, 1993 (Human Rights Law Centre, University of Nottingham).
2 See para **4.03**.

8.71

Article 2

Each State Party shall permit visits, in accordance with this Convention, to any place within its jurisdiction where persons are deprived of their liberty by a public authority.

---

2 ENFORCEMENT

8.72 The European Committee for the Prevention of Torture and Inhuman or Degrading Treatment or Punishment (CPT)[1] has unlimited access to the territory of the UK to make visits to all places where persons are deprived of their liberty. CPT submits a report on its visits to the UK, which include detailed findings of fact and recommendations for action. The UK then responds in writing to the report[2].

1   In carrying out its functions the CPT has the right to avail itself of legal standards contained in the ECHR and in any other relevant human rights instruments (and the interpretation of them by the human rights organs concerned): Paragraph 5, First General Report on the Activities of the CPT, Yearbook of the European Convention for the Prevention of Torture etc, Vol 1, 56–80.
2   See Yearbook, Vol 1, pp 308–411 and the follow-up report in Yearbook, Vol 2, pp 575–601; para **8.70**, n 1.

3   LINKS WITH UK LAW AND PRACTICE

(a)   Police Custody

8.73   The CPT has commented that:

- the rule that no attempt should be made to dissuade a suspect from obtaining legal advice should be stressed to police officers;

- it is important for both police officers and police surgeons to receive specific training in the identification of mentally disordered or handicapped persons or persons experiencing drug-related symptoms;

- the need for the continued application of the exceptional measures relating to the detention of terrorist suspects by the police should be kept under close review[1].

1   See the CPT's report on the UK in the Yearbook of the European Convention for the Prevention of Torture, Vol 1.

(b)   Imprisonment

8.74   CPT found that there was no evidence of torture in prisons. However, it stated that the combination of overcrowding, lack of integral sanitation (resulting in 'slopping out'), poor hygiene (washing, bathing and food serving facilities) and inadequate regime activities (work, education, sport) amounted to inhuman and degrading treatment[1].

1   See the CPT's report on the UK in the Yearbook of the European Convention for the Prevention of Torture, Vol 1.

H   Convention relating to the Status of Refugees

1   NATURE OF UK'S IMPLEMENTING OBLIGATIONS

8.75   The UK ratified the Convention Relating to the Status of Refugees[1] in March 1954 and the Protocol Relating to the Status of Refugees in September 1968. In domestic law and practice, including the exercise of administrative discretion, the UK must attain the international standard of reasonable efficacy and efficiency in the implementation of the treaty provisions[2].

1   See generally, G Goodwin-Gill *The Refugee in International Law* (2nd edn, 1996).
2   G Goodwin-Gill *The Refugee in International Law* (2nd edn, 1996), pp 240–241.

8.76

Article 33   Prohibition of expulsion or return ('refoulement')

1.   No contracting state shall expel or return a refugee in any manner whatsoever to the frontiers of territories where his life or freedom would be threatened on account of his race, religion, nationality, membership of a particular social group or political opinion.

8.77   A refugee is defined by art 1 as a person who:

'… owing to well-founded fear of being persecuted for reasons of race, religion, nationality, membership of a particular social group or political opinion, is outside the country of his nationality and is unable, or owing to such fear, is unwilling to avail himself of the protection of that country; or who, not having a nationality and being outside the country of his former habitual residence as a result of such events, is unable or, owing to such fear, is unwilling to return to it.'

2   ENFORCEMENT

8.78   There is no formal method of enforcement provided for in the Convention. The UK is required to co-operate with the Office of the United Nations High Commissioner for Refugees and must communicate to the Secretary-General of the United Nations the laws and regulations which it adopts to ensure the application of the Convention.

3   LINKS WITH UK LAW AND PRACTICE

8.79   The principal domestic provisions are the Immigration Acts 1971 and 1988 and the Asylum and Immigration Appeals Act 1993 as amended by the Asylum and Immigration Act 1996. Asylum and Immigration Appeals Act 1993, s 2 gives primacy to the Convention relating to the Status of Refugees and its protocol. It states that nothing in the Immigration Rules shall lay down any practice which would be contrary to the Convention.

8.80   After the determination of a claim by the Home Secretary, the asylum seeker may appeal first to a special adjudicator on the ground that his removal would be contrary to the UK's obligations under the Convention relating to the Status of Refugees[1] and then, with leave, to the Immigration Appeal Tribunal[2].

1   Asylum and Immigration Appeals Act 1993, s 8 (AIAA). The Special Immigration Appeals Commission Act 1997 (SIACA) received Royal Assent on 17 December 1997. SIACA 1997, s 2(1)(g) grants the Commission jurisdiction over any matter in relation to which a person would be entitled to appeal under AIAA 1993, s 8(1), (2) or (3), but for AIAA 1993, Sch 2, para 6 (exclusion, removal or deportation in the interests of national security).
2   AIAA 1993, s 9. The SIACA 1997, s 7, provides for appeals from the Commission.

8.81   The AIAA 1993 established a special appeals procedure for claims without foundation[1]. If on an appeal the special adjudicator agrees with the Secretary of State that the claim is without foundation, the appellant has no right of appeal to the Immigration Appeal Tribunal. He may however seek judicial review of the decision in the High Court.

1   AIAA 1993, Sch 2, para 5.

8.82   The Asylum and Immigration Act 1996 (AIA) further removed the right to appeal to the Immigration Appeal Tribunal from a number of asylum seekers. Section 1 extends the special appeals procedure to appellants from countries in which it appears to the Secretary of the State that there is in general no serious risk of persecution. The designation of a country as a 'safe country' will lead to a presumption that any application made by an individual from a listed state is without foundation[1].

1   See further Colin J Harvey, 'The right to seek asylum in the United Kingdom and "safe countries"' [1996] PL 196. See also the Convention determining the state responsible for examining applications for asylum lodged in one of the member-states of the European Communities, signed in Dublin on 15 June 1990.

8.83   AIA 1996, s 3 provides that where the Home Secretary has certified that the government of the country or territory to which the claimant is to be sent would not send him to another country or territory otherwise than in accordance with the Convention (a 'safe third country'), the claimant will not be permitted to appeal against that decision so long as he is within the UK.

8.84   AIA 1996, s 9 restricts the entitlement of the asylum seeker to housing and s 10 removes entitlement to child benefits. Section 11 validates the social security regulations which deprived asylum seekers of the right to receive various social benefits if they had claimed asylum after entering the country and not at the port of entry[1].

1   Reversing the decision of the Court of Appeal in *R v Secretary of State for Social Security, ex p Joint Council for the Welfare of Immigrants* [1997] 1 WLR 275. Note the decision of the Court of Appeal in *R v Hammersmith and Fulham London Borough Council, ex p M* (1997) 30 HLR 10, which held that persons who had applied for political asylum after their arrival in the UK and were thus excluded from a right to income support or housing benefit were entitled to seek assistance from local authorities under the National Assistance Act 1948 provided they fulfilled the relevant criteria.

8.85   Some of these provisions may put the UK in breach of its international obligations with regard to refugees. CERD[1] has also expressed concern that the implementation of these provisions may be detrimental to the protection of asylum seekers against racial discrimination and their effects may nullify or impair the recognition, enjoyment or exercise, on an equal footing, of human rights and fundamental freedoms of the persons affected by the AIA 1996.

1   See Section C above.

I   International Covenant on Economic, Social and Cultural Rights

1   NATURE OF THE UK'S IMPLEMENTING OBLIGATIONS

8.86   The United Kingdom ratified the International Covenant on Economic, Social and Cultural Rights[1] in May 1976.

1   See M Craven *The International Covenant on Economic, Social and Cultural Rights: A Perspective on its Development* (1995).

8.87

> ## Article 2
>
> 1.   Each state party undertakes to take steps individually and through international assistance and co-operation, especially economic and technical, to the maximum of its available resources, with a view to achieving progressively the full realisation of the rights recognised in the present Covenant by all appropriate means, including particularly, the adoption of legislative measures.

8.88   The nature of the states' obligations was elaborated upon in General Comment 3[1].

(1)   Article 2 describes the nature of the general legal obligations, which include both obligations of conduct and obligations of result.

(2)   While the Covenant provides for progressive realisation of the rights and acknowledges the constraints due to the limits of available resources, it also imposes various obligations which are of immediate effect. One is these is the 'undertaking to guarantee' that relevant rights 'will be exercised without discrimination'.

(3)   The other is the undertaking in art 2(1) 'to take steps', which in itself, is not qualified or limited by other considerations. Thus while the full realisation of the relevant rights may be achieved progressively, steps towards that goal must be taken within a reasonably short time after the Covenant's entry into force for the states concerned. Such steps should be deliberate, concrete and targeted as clearly as possible towards meeting the obligations recognised in the Covenant.

(4)   The Committee recognises that in many instances legislation is highly desirable and in some cases may even be indispensable.

(5)   The adoption of legislative measures is by no means exhaustive of the obligations of the state parties.

(6)   Among the measures which might be considered appropriate, in addition to legislation, is the provision of judicial remedies with respect to rights which may, in accordance with the national legal system, be considered justiciable. The Committee notes, for example, that the enjoyment of the rights recognised, without discrimination, will often be appropriately promoted, in part, through the provision of judicial or other effective remedies. In addition, there are a number of other provisions in the Covenant, which would seem capable of immediate application by judicial and other organs in many national legal systems.

(7)   These provisions include:

article 3: the equal right of men and women to the enjoyment of all economic, social and cultural rights;

article 7(a)(i): fair wages and equal remuneration for work of equal value without distinction of any kind, in particular women being guaranteed conditions of work not inferior to those enjoyed by men, with equal pay for equal work;

article 8: the right to form and join trade unions;

article 10(3): special measures of protection and assistance for all children and young persons;

article 13(2)(a): primary education shall be compulsory and free for all;

article 13(3): respect for the liberty of parents and legal guardians to choose schools for their children (including private schools);

article 13(4): no part of art 13 shall be construed so as to interfere with the liberty of individuals and bodies to establish and direct educational institutions; and

article 15(3): respect the freedom indispensable for scientific research and creative activity.

1   IHRR Vol 1, No 1 [1994] 6.

2   ENFORCEMENT

8.89   The Committee on Economic, Social and Cultural Rights is charged with overseeing the implementation of the Covenant. The only enforcement mechanism provided for is a system of reporting. The Committee submits Concluding Observations on the UK's performance[1]. The Committee also produces General Comments[2] to assist and promote the further implementation of the rights contained in the Covenant.

1   The Committee considered the UK's report on 12 December 1997, E/C.12/1/Add.19.
2   General Comments 1–4, IHRR Vol 1, No 1 [1994] 1; General Comment 5, IHRR Vol 2, No 2 [1995] 261; General Comment 6, IHRR Vol 3, No 2 [1996] 253; General Comment 7, IHRR Vol 5, No 1 [1998] 1. See in particular No 4, the right to adequate housing; No 5, persons with disabilities and No 6, the rights of older persons.

3   EXAMPLES OF LINKS WITH UK LAW AND PRACTICE

8.90   The Committee on Economic, Social and Cultural Rights identified a number of principal subjects of concern:

(1)   the limits imposed by the government on access to free legal aid with respect to a number of economic and social rights;

(2)   the unacceptable levels of poverty among certain segments of the population in the state party, particularly in Northern Ireland;

(3)   the failure to incorporate the right to strike into domestic law, in breach of art 8[1];

(4)   the legally accepted practice of allowing employers to differentiate between union and non-union members by giving pay rises to employees who do not join a union, which is incompatible with art 8;

(5)   the significant degree of de facto discrimination against women, black people and other ethnic minorities, despite the legislation for the protection against discrimination;

(6)   the persistence of a substantially higher rate of unemployment among black people and other ethnic minorities and their disproportionate numbers in lesser paid jobs;

(7)   the condition of many children in the care of the government, directly or indirectly, in spite of extensive legislative provisions on the subject;

(8)   the serious incidence of domestic violence against women;

(9)   the length of waiting times for surgery, which indicate that the UK has not made its best efforts to satisfy art 12;

(10) the continued practice of corporal punishment in schools which are privately financed;

(11) the insufficient protection of vulnerable groups such as travellers and ethnic minorities against evictions;[2] and

(12) the low number of integrated schools in Northern Ireland.

1   The Committee considers that the common law approach recognising only the freedom to strike, and the concept that strike action constitutes a fundamental breach of contract justifying dismissal, are not consistent with the protection of the right to strike.
2   See further General Comment No 7, IHRR Vol 5, No 1 [1998] 1.

J European Social Charter

1 NATURE OF UK'S IMPLEMENTING OBLIGATIONS

8.91   The European Social Charter[1] (ESC) was ratified by the UK in 1962. It is the economic and social counterpart of the ECHR. Part I of the ESC contains a list of objectives which the UK must accept as the aim of its policy. Part II contains a set of obligations, a number of which the UK is legally bound to accept[2].

1   See generally Gomien, Harris and Zwaak *Law and Practice of the European Convention on Human Rights and the European Social Charter* (1996). A Revised European Social Charter is open for ratification. The Revised ESC updates the Charter and extends it to protect a new category of rights. See IHRR Vol 3, No 3 [1996] 726 for the text and explanatory report. For information on the status and ratifications of all Council of Europe treaties, see the Council's website at www.coe.fr.
2   The UK has not accepted arts 2(1); 4(3); 7(1), (4), (7) and (8); 8(2), (3) and (4); and 12(2), (3) and (4). Taken from L Samuels *Fundamental Social Rights: Case Law of the European Social Charter* (1997), App III.

2 ENFORCEMENT

(a) The Reporting System

8.92   The UK submits reports to the Secretary-General of the Council of Europe which are then considered by the Committee of Independent Experts. The report of the UK and the conclusions of the Committee of Independent Experts are subsequently examined by a sub-committee to the Governmental Social Committee of the Council of Europe. The sub-committee reports to the Committee of Ministers, which may make any necessary recommendations to each contracting party[1].

1   See the Recommendations of the Committee of Ministers to the UK, IHRR Vol 5, No 1 [1998] 298.

(b) Collective Complaints Protocol

8.93   This optional protocol allows competent organisations to submit complaints to the Committee of Independent Experts alleging the unsatisfactory application of the ESC by a contracting party. It has not yet entered into force and has not been ratified by the UK.

3   LINKS WITH UK LAW AND PRACTICE

8.94   The Committee of Ministers' negative conclusions included the following observations:

(1)   the Merchant Shipping Act of 1970, s 30c enables criminal sanctions to be imposed on striking seamen even when neither the safety of the boat nor the life or health or those on board was threatened, contrary to art 1, para 2 (prohibition of forced labour); and

(2)   the Trade Union Reform and Employment Rights Act 1993, s 13 and the Trade Union and Labour Relations (Consolidation) Act 1992, ss 64–67 constitute an infringement on the rights to organise and bargain collectively.

Appendix 1

Human Rights Act 1998

Human Rights Act 1998

1998 CHAPTER 42

An Act to give further effect to rights and freedoms guaranteed under the European Convention on Human Rights; to make provision with respect to holders of certain judicial offices who become judges of the European Court of Human Rights; and for connected purposes.

[9th November 1998]

BE IT ENACTED by the Queen's most Excellent Majesty, by and with the advice and consent of the Lords Spiritual and Temporal, and Commons, in this present Parliament assembled, and by the authority of the same, as follows:—

Introduction

1 The Convention Rights

(1)　In this Act 'the Convention rights' means the rights and fundamental freedoms set out in—

　(*a*)　Articles 2 to 12 and 14 of the Convention,

　(*b*)　Articles 1 to 3 of the First Protocol, and

　(*c*)　Articles 1 and 2 of the Sixth Protocol,

as read with Articles 16 to 18 of the Convention.

(2)　Those Articles are to have effect for the purposes of this Act subject to any designated derogation or reservation (as to which see sections 14 and 15).

(3)　The Articles are set out in Schedule 1.

(4)　The Secretary of State may by order make such amendments to this Act as he considers appropriate to reflect the effect, in relation to the United Kingdom, of a protocol.

(5)　In subsection (4) 'protocol' means a protocol to the Convention—

　(*a*)　which the United Kingdom has ratified; or

　(*b*)　which the United Kingdom has signed with a view to ratification.

(6)　No amendment may be made by an order under subsection (4) so as to come into force before the protocol concerned is in force in relation to the United Kingdom.

2 Interpretation of Convention rights

(1)　A court or tribunal determining a question which has arisen in connection with a Convention right must take into account any—

　(*a*)　judgment, decision, declaration or advisory opinion of the European Court of Human Rights,

　(*b*)　opinion of the Commission given in a report adopted under Article 31 of the Convention,

　(*c*)　decision of the Commission in connection with Article 26 or 27(2) of the Convention, or

　(*d*)　decision of the Committee of Ministers taken under Article 46 of the Convention,

343

whenever made or given, so far as, in the opinion of the court or tribunal, it is relevant to the proceedings in which that question has arisen.

(2)   Evidence of any judgment, decision, declaration or opinion of which account may have to be taken under this section is to be given in proceedings before any court or tribunal in such manner as may be provided by rules.

(3)   In this section 'rules' means rules of court or, in the case of proceedings before a tribunal, rules made for the purposes of this section—

> (*a*)   by the Lord Chancellor or the Secretary of State, in relation to any proceedings outside Scotland;
>
> (*b*)   by the Secretary of State, in relation to proceedings in Scotland; or
>
> (*c*)   by a Northern Ireland department, in relation to proceedings before a tribunal in Northern Ireland—
>
> > (i)   which deals with transferred matters; and
> >
> > (ii)   for which no rules made under paragraph (*a*) are in force.

Legislation

3 Interpretation of legislation

(1)   So far as it is possible to do so, primary legislation and subordinate legislation must be read and given effect in a way which is compatible with the Convention rights.

(2)   This section—

> (*a*)   applies to primary legislation and subordinate legislation whenever enacted;
>
> (*b*)   does not affect the validity, continuing operation or enforcement of any incompatible primary legislation; and
>
> (*c*)   does not affect the validity, continuing operation or enforcement of any incompatible subordinate legislation if (disregarding any possibility of revocation) primary legislation prevents removal of the incompatibility.

4 Declaration of incompatibility

(1)   Subsection (2) applies in any proceedings in which a court determines whether a provision of primary legislation is compatible with a Convention right.

(2)   If the court is satisfied that the provision is incompatible with a Convention right, it may make a declaration of that incompatibility.

(3)   Subsection (4) applies in any proceedings in which a court determines whether a provision of subordinate legislation, made in the exercise of a power conferred by primary legislation, is compatible with a Convention right.

(4)   If the court is satisfied—

> (*a*)   that the provision is incompatible with a Convention right, and
>
> (*b*)   that (disregarding any possibility of revocation) the primary legislation concerned prevents removal of the incompatibility,

it may make a declaration of that incompatibility.

(5)   In this section 'court' means—

> (*a*)   the House of Lords;
>
> (*b*)   the Judicial Committee of the Privy Council;
>
> (*c*)   the Courts-Martial Appeal Court;
>
> (*d*)   in Scotland, the High Court of Justiciary sitting otherwise than as a trial court or the Court of Session;

(*e*)   in England and Wales or Northern Ireland, the High Court or the Court of Appeal.

(6)   A declaration under this section ('a declaration of incompatibility')—

(*a*)   does not affect the validity, continuing operation or enforcement of the provision in respect of which it is given; and

(*b*)   is not binding on the parties to the proceedings in which it is made.

5 Right of Crown to intervene

(1)   Where a court is considering whether to make a declaration of incompatibility, the Crown is entitled to notice in accordance with rules of court.

(2)   In any case to which subsection (1) applies—

(*a*)   a Minister of the Crown (or a person nominated by him),

(*b*)   a member of the Scottish Executive,

(*c*)   a Northern Ireland Minister,

(*d*)   a Northern Ireland department,

is entitled, on giving notice in accordance with rules of court, to be joined as a party to the proceedings.

(3)   Notice under subsection (2) may be given at any time during the proceedings.

(4)   A person who has been made a party to criminal proceedings (other than in Scotland) as the result of a notice under subsection (2) may, with leave, appeal to the House of Lords against any declaration of incompatibility made in the proceedings.

(5)   In subsection (4)—

'criminal proceedings' includes all proceedings before the Courts-Martial Appeal Court; and

'leave' means leave granted by the court making the declaration of incompatibility or by the House of Lords.

Public authorities

6 Acts of public authorities

(1)   It is unlawful for a public authority to act in a way which is incompatible with a Convention right.

(2)   Subsection (1) does not apply to an act if—

(*a*)   as the result of one or more provisions of primary legislation, the authority could not have acted differently; or

(*b*)   in the case of one or more provisions of, or made under, primary legislation which cannot be read or given effect in a way which is compatible with the Convention rights, the authority was acting so as to give effect to or enforce those provisions.

(3)   In this section 'public authority' includes—

(*a*)   a court or tribunal, and

(*b*)   any person certain of whose functions are functions of a public nature,

but does not include either House of Parliament or a person exercising functions in connection with proceedings in Parliament.

(4)   In subsection (3) 'Parliament' does not include the House of Lords in its judicial capacity.

(5)   In relation to a particular act, a person is not a public authority by virtue only of subsection (3)(*b*) if the nature of the act is private.

(6) 'An act' includes a failure to act but does not include a failure to—

    (*a*)   introduce in, or lay before, Parliament a proposal for legislation; or

    (*b*)   make any primary legislation or remedial order.

7 Proceedings

(1)   A person who claims that a public authority has acted (or proposes to act) in a way which is made unlawful by section 6(1) may—

    (*a*)   bring proceedings against the authority under this Act in the appropriate court or tribunal, or

    (*b*)   rely on the Convention right or rights concerned in any legal proceedings,

but only if he is (or would be) a victim of the unlawful act.

(2)   In subsection (1)(*a*) 'appropriate court or tribunal' means such court or tribunal as may be determined in accordance with rules; and proceedings against an authority include a counterclaim or similar proceeding.

(3)   If the proceedings are brought on an application for judicial review, the applicant is to be taken to have a sufficient interest in relation to the unlawful act only if he is, or would be, a victim of that act.

(4)   If the proceedings are made by way of a petition for judicial review in Scotland, the applicant shall be taken to have title and interest to sue in relation to the unlawful act only if he is, or would be, a victim of that act.

(5)   Proceedings under subsection (1)(*a*) must be brought before the end of—

    (*a*)   the period of one year beginning with the date on which the act complained of took place; or

    (*b*)   such longer period as the court or tribunal considers equitable having regard to all the circumstances,

but that is subject to any rule imposing a stricter time limit in relation to the procedure in question.

(6)   In subsection (1)(*b*) 'legal proceedings' includes—

    (*a*)   proceedings brought by or at the instigation of a public authority; and

    (*b*)   an appeal against the decision of a court or tribunal.

(7)   For the purposes of this section, a person is a victim of an unlawful act only if he would be a victim for the purposes of Article 34 of the Convention if proceedings were brought in the European Court of Human Rights in respect of that act.

(8)   Nothing in this Act creates a criminal offence.

(9)   In this section 'rules' means—

    (*a*)   in relation to proceedings before a court or tribunal outside Scotland, rules made by the Lord Chancellor or the Secretary of State for the purposes of this section or rules of court,

    (*b*)   in relation to proceedings before a court or tribunal in Scotland, rules made by the Secretary of State for those purposes,

    (*c*)   in relation to proceedings before a tribunal in Northern Ireland—

        (i)   which deals with transferred matters; and

        (ii)   for which no rules made under paragraph (*a*) are in force,

        rules made by a Northern Ireland department for those purposes,

and includes provision made by order under section 1 of the Courts and Legal Services Act 1990.

(10)   In making rules, regard must be had to section 9.

(11)   The Minister who has power to make rules in relation to a particular tribunal may, to the extent he considers it necessary to ensure that the tribunal can provide an appropriate remedy in relation to an act (or proposed act) of a public authority which is (or would be) unlawful as a result of section 6(1), by order add to—

(*a*)   the relief or remedies which the tribunal may grant; or

(*b*)   the grounds on which it may grant any of them.

(12)   An order made under subsection (11) may contain such incidental, supplemental, consequential or transitional provision as the Minister making it considers appropriate.

(13)   'The Minister' includes the Northern Ireland department concerned.

8 Judicial remedies

(1)   In relation to any act (or proposed act) of a public authority which the court finds is (or would be) unlawful, it may grant such relief or remedy, or make such order, within its powers as it considers just and appropriate.

(2)   But damages may be awarded only by a court which has power to award damages, or to order the payment of compensation, in civil proceedings.

(3)   No award of damages is to be made unless, taking account of all the circumstances of the case, including—

(*a*)   any other relief or remedy granted, or order made, in relation to the act in question (by that or any other court), and

(*b*)   the consequences of any decision (of that or any other court) in respect of that act,

the court is satisfied that the award is necessary to afford just satisfaction to the person in whose favour it is made.

(4)   In determining—

(*a*)   whether to award damages, or

(*b*)   the amount of an award,

the court must take into account the principles applied by the European Court of Human Rights in relation to the award of compensation under Article 41 of the Convention.

(5)   A public authority against which damages are awarded is to be treated—

(*a*)   in Scotland, for the purposes of section 3 of the Law Reform (Miscellaneous Provisions) (Scotland) Act 1940 as if the award were made in an action of damages in which the authority has been found liable in respect of loss or damage to the person to whom the award is made;

(*b*)   for the purposes of the Civil Liability (Contribution) Act 1978 as liable in respect of damage suffered by the person to whom the award is made.

(6)   In this section—

'court' includes a tribunal;

'damages' means damages for an unlawful act of a public authority; and

'unlawful' means unlawful under section 6(1).

9 Judicial acts

(1)   Proceedings under section 7(1)(*a*) in respect of a judicial act may be brought only—

(*a*)   by exercising a right of appeal;

(*b*)   on an application (in Scotland a petition) for judicial review; or (*c*)   in such other forum as may be prescribed by rules.

(2)   That does not affect any rule of law which prevents a court from being the subject of judicial review.

(3)   In proceedings under this Act in respect of a judicial act done in good faith, damages may not be awarded otherwise than to compensate a person to the extent required by Article 5(5) of the Convention.

(4)   An award of damages permitted by subsection (3) is to be made against the Crown; but no award may be made unless the appropriate person, if not a party to the proceedings, is joined.

(5)   In this section—

'appropriate person' means the Minister responsible for the court concerned, or a person or government department nominated by him;

'court' includes a tribunal;

'judge' includes a member of a tribunal, a justice of the peace and a clerk or other officer entitled to exercise the jurisdiction of a court;

'judicial act' means a judicial act of a court and includes an act done on the instructions, or on behalf, of a judge; and

'rules' has the same meaning as in section 7(9).

Remedial action

10 Power to take remedial action

(1)   This section applies if—

(*a*)   a provision of legislation has been declared under section 4 to be incompatible with a Convention right and, if an appeal lies—

(i)   all persons who may appeal have stated in writing that they do not intend to do so;

(ii)   the time for bringing an appeal has expired and no appeal has been brought within that time; or

(iii)   an appeal brought within that time has been determined or abandoned; or

(*b*)   it appears to a Minister of the Crown or Her Majesty in Council that, having regard to a finding of the European Court of Human Rights made after the coming into force of this section in proceedings against the United Kingdom, a provision of legislation is incompatible with an obligation of the United Kingdom arising from the Convention.

(2)   If a Minister of the Crown considers that there are compelling reasons for proceeding under this section, he may by order make such amendments to the legislation as he considers necessary to remove the incompatibility.

(3)   If, in the case of subordinate legislation, a Minister of the Crown considers—

(*a*)   that it is necessary to amend the primary legislation under which the subordinate legislation in question was made, in order to enable the incompatibility to be removed, and

(*b*)   that there are compelling reasons for proceeding under this section,

he may by order make such amendments to the primary legislation as he considers necessary.

(4)   This section also applies where the provision in question is in subordinate legislation and has been quashed, or declared invalid, by reason of incompatibility with a Convention right and the Minister proposes to proceed under paragraph 2(*b*) of Schedule 2.

(5)   If the legislation is an Order in Council, the power conferred by subsection (2) or (3) is exercisable by Her Majesty in Council.

(6)   In this section 'legislation' does not include a Measure of the Church Assembly or of the General Synod of the Church of England.

(7)   Schedule 2 makes further provision about remedial orders.

Other rights and proceedings

11 Safeguard for existing human rights

A person's reliance on a Convention right does not restrict—

- (*a*)   any other right or freedom conferred on him by or under any law having effect in any part of the United Kingdom; or

- (*b*)   his right to make any claim or bring any proceedings which he could make or bring apart from sections 7 to 9.

12 Freedom of expression

(1)   This section applies if a court is considering whether to grant any relief which, if granted, might affect the exercise of the Convention right to freedom of expression.

(2)   If the person against whom the application for relief is made ('the respondent') is neither present nor represented, no such relief is to be granted unless the court is satisfied—

- (*a*)   that the applicant has taken all practicable steps to notify the respondent; or

- (*b*)   that there are compelling reasons why the respondent should not be notified.

(3)   No such relief is to be granted so as to restrain publication before trial unless the court is satisfied that the applicant is likely to establish that publication should not be allowed.

(4)   The court must have particular regard to the importance of the Convention right to freedom of expression and, where the proceedings relate to material which the respondent claims, or which appears to the court, to be journalistic, literary or artistic material (or to conduct connected with such material), to—

- (*a*)   the extent to which—

   - (i)   the material has, or is about to, become available to the public; or

   - (ii)   it is, or would be, in the public interest for the material to be published;

- (*b*)   any relevant privacy code.

(5)   In this section—

'court' includes a tribunal; and

'relief' includes any remedy or order (other than in criminal proceedings).

13 Freedom of thought, conscience and religion

(1)   If a court's determination of any question arising under this Act might affect the exercise by a religious organisation (itself or its members collectively) of the Convention right to freedom of thought, conscience and religion, it must have particular regard to the importance of that right.

(2)   In this section 'court' includes a tribunal.

Derogations and reservations

14 Derogations

(1)   In this Act 'designated derogation' means—

- (*a*)   the United Kingdom's derogation from Article 5(3) of the Convention; and (*b*) any derogation by the United Kingdom from an Article of the Convention, or of any protocol to the Convention, which is designated for the purposes of this Act in an order made by the Secretary of State.

(2) The derogation referred to in subsection (1)(*a*) is set out in Part I of Schedule 3.

(3) If a designated derogation is amended or replaced it ceases to be a designated derogation.

(4) But subsection (3) does not prevent the Secretary of State from exercising his power under subsection (1)(*b*) to make a fresh designation order in respect of the Article concerned.

(5) The Secretary of State must by order make such amendments to Schedule 3 as he considers appropriate to reflect—

(*a*) any designation order; or

(*b*) the effect of subsection (3).

(6) A designation order may be made in anticipation of the making by the United Kingdom of a proposed derogation.

15 Reservations

(1) In this Act 'designated reservation' means—

(*a*) the United Kingdom's reservation to Article 2 of the First Protocol to the Convention; and

(*b*) any other reservation by the United Kingdom to an Article of the Convention, or of any protocol to the Convention, which is designated for the purposes of this Act in an order made by the Secretary of State.

(2) The text of the reservation referred to in subsection (1)(*a*) is set out in Part II of Schedule 3.

(3) If a designated reservation is withdrawn wholly or in part it ceases to be a designated reservation.

(4) But subsection (3) does not prevent the Secretary of State from exercising his power under subsection (1)(*b*) to make a fresh designation order in respect of the Article concerned.

(5) The Secretary of State must by order make such amendments to this Act as he considers appropriate to reflect—

(*a*) any designation order; or

(*b*) the effect of subsection (3).

16 Period for which designated derogations have effect

(1) If it has not already been withdrawn by the United Kingdom, a designated derogation ceases to have effect for the purposes of this Act—

(*a*) in the case of the derogation referred to in section 14(1)(*a*), at the end of the period of five years beginning with the date on which section 1(2) came into force;

(*b*) in the case of any other derogation, at the end of the period of five years beginning with the date on which the order designating it was made.

(2) At any time before the period—

(*a*) fixed by subsection (1)(*a*) or (*b*), or

(*b*) extended by an order under this subsection,

comes to an end, the Secretary of State may by order extend it by a further period of five years.

(3) An order under section 14(1)(*b*) ceases to have effect at the end of the period for consideration, unless a resolution has been passed by each House approving the order.

(4) Subsection (3) does not affect—

(*a*) anything done in reliance on the order; or

(*b*) the power to make a fresh order under section 14(1)(*b*).

(5) In subsection (3) 'period for consideration' means the period of forty days beginning with the day on which the order was made.

(6) In calculating the period for consideration, no account is to be taken of any time during which—

(*a*) Parliament is dissolved or prorogued; or

(*b*) both Houses are adjourned for more than four days.

(7) If a designated derogation is withdrawn by the United Kingdom, the Secretary of State must by order make such amendments to this Act as he considers are required to reflect that withdrawal.

17 Periodic review of designated reservations

(1) The appropriate Minister must review the designated reservation referred to in section 15(1)(*a*)—

(*a*) before the end of the period of five years beginning with the date on which section 1(2) came into force; and

(*b*) if that designation is still in force, before the end of the period of five years beginning with the date on which the last report relating to it was laid under subsection (3).

(2) The appropriate Minister must review each of the other designated reservations (if any)—

(*a*) before the end of the period of five years beginning with the date on which the order designating the reservation first came into force; and

(*b*) if the designation is still in force, before the end of the period of five years beginning with the date on which the last report relating to it was laid under subsection (3).

(3) The Minister conducting a review under this section must prepare a report on the result of the review and lay a copy of it before each House of Parliament.

Judges of the European Court of Human Rights

18 Appointment to European Court of Human Rights

(1) In this section 'judicial office' means the office of—

(*a*) Lord Justice of Appeal, Justice of the High Court or Circuit judge, in England and Wales;

(*b*) judge of the Court of Session or sheriff, in Scotland;

(*c*) Lord Justice of Appeal, judge of the High Court or county court judge, in Northern Ireland.

(2) The holder of a judicial office may become a judge of the European Court of Human Rights ('the Court') without being required to relinquish his office.

(3) But he is not required to perform the duties of his judicial office while he is a judge of the Court.

(4) In respect of any period during which he is a judge of the Court—

(*a*) a Lord Justice of Appeal or Justice of the High Court is not to count as a judge of the relevant court for the purposes of section 2(1) or 4(1) of the Supreme Court Act 1981 (maximum number of judges) nor as a judge of the Supreme Court for the purposes of section 12(1) to (6) of that Act (salaries etc);

(*b*)   a judge of the Court of Session is not to count as a judge of that court for the purposes of section 1(1) of the Court of Session Act 1988 (maximum number of judges) or of section 9(1)(*c*) of the Administration of Justice Act 1973 ('the 1973 Act') (salaries etc);

(*c*)   a Lord Justice of Appeal or judge of the High Court in Northern Ireland is not to count as a judge of the relevant court for the purposes of section 2(1) or 3(1) of the Judicature (Northern Ireland) Act 1978 (maximum number of judges) nor as a judge of the Supreme Court of Northern Ireland for the purposes of section 9(1)(*d*) of the 1973 Act (salaries etc);

(*d*)   a Circuit judge is not to count as such for the purposes of section 18 of the Courts Act 1971 (salaries etc);

(*e*)   a sheriff is not to count as such for the purposes of section 14 of the Sheriff Courts (Scotland) Act 1907 (salaries etc);

(*f*)   a county court judge of Northern Ireland is not to count as such for the purposes of section 106 of the County Courts Act (Northern Ireland) 1959 (salaries etc).

(5)   If a sheriff principal is appointed a judge of the Court, section 11(1) of the Sheriff Courts (Scotland) Act 1971 (temporary appointment of sheriff principal) applies, while he holds that appointment, as if his office is vacant.

(6)   Schedule 4 makes provision about judicial pensions in relation to the holder of a judicial office who serves as a judge of the Court.

(7)   The Lord Chancellor or the Secretary of State may by order make such transitional provision (including, in particular, provision for a temporary increase in the maximum number of judges) as he considers appropriate in relation to any holder of a judicial office who has completed his service as a judge of the Court.

Parliamentary procedure

19 Statements of compatibility

(1)   A Minister of the Crown in charge of a Bill in either House of Parliament must, before Second Reading of the Bill—

(*a*)   make a statement to the effect that in his view the provisions of the Bill are compatible with the Convention rights ('a statement of compatibility'); or

(*b*)   make a statement to the effect that although he is unable to make a statement of compatibility the government nevertheless wishes the House to proceed with the Bill.

(2)   The statement must be in writing and be published in such manner as the Minister making it considers appropriate.

Supplemental

20 Orders etc under this Act

(1)   Any power of a Minister of the Crown to make an order under this Act is exercisable by statutory instrument.

(2)   The power of the Lord Chancellor or the Secretary of State to make rules (other than rules of court) under section 2(3) or 7(9) is exercisable by statutory instrument.

(3)   Any statutory instrument made under section 14, 15 or 16(7) must be laid before Parliament.

(4)   No order may be made by the Lord Chancellor or the Secretary of State under section 1(4), 7(11) or 16(2) unless a draft of the order has been laid before, and approved by, each House of Parliament.

(5)   Any statutory instrument made under section 18(7) or Schedule 4, or to which sub-section (2) applies, shall be subject to annulment in pursuance of a resolution of either House of Parliament.

(6)   The power of a Northern Ireland department to make—

   (*a*)   rules under section 2(3)(*c*) or 7(9)(*c*), or

   (*b*)   an order under section 7(11),

is exercisable by statutory rule for the purposes of the Statutory Rules (Northern Ireland) Order 1979.

(7)   Any rules made under section 2(3)(*c*) or 7(9)(*c*) shall be subject to negative resolution; and section 41(6) of the Interpretation Act (Northern Ireland) 1954 (meaning of 'subject to negative resolution') shall apply as if the power to make the rules were conferred by an Act of the Northern Ireland Assembly.

(8)   No order may be made by a Northern Ireland department under section 7(11) unless a draft of the order has been laid before, and approved by, the Northern Ireland Assembly.

21 Interpretation, etc

(1)   In this Act—

   'amend' includes repeal and apply (with or without modifications);

   'the appropriate Minister' means the Minister of the Crown having charge of the appropriate authorised government department (within the meaning of the Crown Proceedings Act 1947);

   'the Commission' means the European Commission of Human Rights;

   'the Convention' means the Convention for the Protection of Human Rights and Fundamental Freedoms, agreed by the Council of Europe at Rome on 4th November 1950 as it has effect for the time being in relation to the United Kingdom;

   'declaration of incompatibility' means a declaration under section 4;

   'Minister of the Crown' has the same meaning as in the Ministers of the Crown Act 1975;

   'Northern Ireland Minister' includes the First Minister and the deputy First Minister in Northern Ireland;

   'primary legislation' means any—

   (*a*)   public general Act;

   (*b*)   local and personal Act;

   (*c*)   private Act;

   (*d*)   Measure of the Church Assembly;

   (*e*)   Measure of the General Synod of the Church of England;

   (*f*)   Order in Council—

      (i)   made in exercise of Her Majesty's Royal Prerogative;

      (ii)   made under section 38(1)(*a*) of the Northern Ireland Constitution Act 1973 or the corresponding provision of the Northern Ireland Act 1998; or

      (iii)   amending an Act of a kind mentioned in paragraph (*a*), (*b*) or (*c*);

      and includes an order or other instrument made under primary legislation (otherwise than by the National Assembly for Wales, a member of the Scottish Executive, a Northern Ireland Minister or a Northern Ireland department) to the extent to which it operates to bring one or more provisions of that legislation into force or amends any primary legislation;

   'the First Protocol' means the protocol to the Convention agreed at Paris on 20th March 1952;

'the Sixth Protocol' means the protocol to the Convention agreed at Strasbourg on 28th April 1983;

'the Eleventh Protocol' means the protocol to the Convention (restructuring the control machinery established by the Convention) agreed at Strasbourg on 11th May 1994;

'remedial order' means an order under section 10;

'subordinate legislation' means any—

(*a*)   Order in Council other than one—

(i)   made in exercise of Her Majesty's Royal Prerogative;

(ii)   made under section 38(1)(*a*) of the Northern Ireland Constitution Act 1973 or the corresponding provision of the Northern Ireland Act 1998; or

(iii)   amending an Act of a kind mentioned in the definition of primary legislation;

(*b*)   Act of the Scottish Parliament;

(*c*)   Act of the Parliament of Northern Ireland;

(*d*)   Measure of the Assembly established under section 1 of the Northern Ireland Assembly Act 1973;

(*e*)   Act of the Northern Ireland Assembly;

(*f*)   order, rules, regulations, scheme, warrant, byelaw or other instrument made under primary legislation (except to the extent to which it operates to bring one or more provisions of that legislation into force or amends any primary legislation);

(*g*)   order, rules, regulations, scheme, warrant, byelaw or other instrument made under legislation mentioned in paragraph (*b*), (*c*), (*d*) or (*e*) or made under an Order in Council applying only to Northern Ireland;

(*h*)   order, rules, regulations, scheme, warrant, byelaw or other instrument made by a member of the Scottish Executive, a Northern Ireland Minister or a Northern Ireland department in exercise of prerogative or other executive functions of Her Majesty which are exercisable by such a person on behalf of Her Majesty;

'transferred matters' has the same meaning as in the Northern Ireland Act 1998; and

'tribunal' means any tribunal in which legal proceedings may be brought.

(2)   The references in paragraphs (*b*) and (*c*) of section 2(1) to Articles are to Articles of the Convention as they had effect immediately before the coming into force of the Eleventh Protocol.

(3)   The reference in paragraph (*d*) of section 2(1) to Article 46 includes a reference to Articles 32 and 54 of the Convention as they had effect immediately before the coming into force of the Eleventh Protocol.

(4)   The references in section 2(1) to a report or decision of the Commission or a decision of the Committee of Ministers include references to a report or decision made as provided by paragraphs 3, 4 and 6 of Article 5 of the Eleventh Protocol (transitional provisions).

(5)   Any liability under the Army Act 1955, the Air Force Act 1955 or the Naval Discipline Act 1957 to suffer death for an offence is replaced by a liability to imprisonment for life or any less punishment authorised by those Acts; and those Acts shall accordingly have effect with the necessary modifications.

22 Short title, commencement, application and extent

(1)   This Act may be cited as the Human Rights Act 1998.

(2)   Sections 18, 20 and 21(5) and this section come into force on the passing of this Act.

(3)   The other provisions of this Act come into force on such day as the Secretary of State may by order appoint; and different days may be appointed for different purposes.

(4)   Paragraph (*b*) of subsection (1) of section 7 applies to proceedings brought by or at the instigation of a public authority whenever the act in question took place; but otherwise that subsection does not apply to an act taking place before the coming into force of that section.

(5)   This Act binds the Crown.

(6)   This Act extends to Northern Ireland.

(7)   Section 21(5), so far as it relates to any provision contained in the Army Act 1955, the Air Force Act 1955 or the Naval Discipline Act 1957, extends to any place to which that provision extends.

SCHEDULE 1
THE ARTICLES

Section 1(3)

PART I
THE CONVENTION

Rights and Freedoms

Article 2
Right to life

1 Everyone's right to life shall be protected by law. No one shall be deprived of his life intentionally save in the execution of a sentence of a court following his conviction of a crime for which this penalty is provided by law.

2 Deprivation of life shall not be regarded as inflicted in contravention of this Article when it results from the use of force which is no more than absolutely necessary:

    (*a*)   in defence of any person from unlawful violence;

    (*b*)   in order to effect a lawful arrest or to prevent the escape of a person lawfully detained;

    (*c*)   in action lawfully taken for the purpose of quelling a riot or insurrection.

Article 3
Prohibition of torture

No one shall be subjected to torture or to inhuman or degrading treatment or punishment.

Article 4
Prohibition of slavery and forced labour

1 No one shall be held in slavery or servitude.

2 No one shall be required to perform forced or compulsory labour.

3 For the purpose of this Article the term 'forced or compulsory labour' shall not include:

    (*a*)   any work required to be done in the ordinary course of detention imposed according to the provisions of Article 5 of this Convention or during conditional release from such detention;

    (*b*)   any service of a military character or, in case of conscientious objectors in countries where they are recognised, service exacted instead of compulsory military service;

(c)   any service exacted in case of an emergency or calamity threatening the life or well-being of the community;

(d)   any work or service which forms part of normal civic obligations.

Article 5
Right to liberty and security

1 Everyone has the right to liberty and security of person. No one shall be deprived of his liberty save in the following cases and in accordance with a procedure prescribed by law:

(a)   the lawful detention of a person after conviction by a competent court;

(b)   the lawful arrest or detention of a person for non-compliance with the lawful order of a court or in order to secure the fulfilment of any obligation prescribed by law;

(c)   the lawful arrest or detention of a person effected for the purpose of bringing him before the competent legal authority on reasonable suspicion of having committed an offence or when it is reasonably considered necessary to prevent his committing an offence or fleeing after having done so;

(d)   the detention of a minor by lawful order for the purpose of educational supervision or his lawful detention for the purpose of bringing him before the competent legal authority;

(e)   the lawful detention of persons for the prevention of the spreading of infectious diseases, of persons of unsound mind, alcoholics or drug addicts or vagrants;

(f)   the lawful arrest or detention of a person to prevent his effecting an unauthorised entry into the country or of a person against whom action is being taken with a view to deportation or extradition.

2 Everyone who is arrested shall be informed promptly, in a language which he understands, of the reasons for his arrest and of any charge against him.

3 Everyone arrested or detained in accordance with the provisions of paragraph 1(c) of this Article shall be brought promptly before a judge or other officer authorised by law to exercise judicial power and shall be entitled to trial within a reasonable time or to release pending trial. Release may be conditioned by guarantees to appear for trial.

4 Everyone who is deprived of his liberty by arrest or detention shall be entitled to take proceedings by which the lawfulness of his detention shall be decided speedily by a court and his release ordered if the detention is not lawful.

5 Everyone who has been the victim of arrest or detention in contravention of the provisions of this Article shall have an enforceable right to compensation.

Article 6
Right to a fair trial

1 In the determination of his civil rights and obligations or of any criminal charge against him, everyone is entitled to a fair and public hearing within a reasonable time by an independent and impartial tribunal established by law. Judgment shall be pronounced publicly but the press and public may be excluded from all or part of the trial in the interest of morals, public order or national security in a democratic society, where the interests of juveniles or the protection of the private life of the parties so require, or to the extent strictly necessary in the opinion of the court in special circumstances where publicity would prejudice the interests of justice.

2 Everyone charged with a criminal offence shall be presumed innocent until proved guilty according to law.

3 Everyone charged with a criminal offence has the following minimum rights:

(a)   to be informed promptly, in a language which he understands and in detail, of the nature and cause of the accusation against him;

(*b*)   to have adequate time and facilities for the preparation of his defence;

(*c*)   to defend himself in person or through legal assistance of his own choosing or, if he has not sufficient means to pay for legal assistance, to be given it free when the interests of justice so require;

(*d*)   to examine or have examined witnesses against him and to obtain the attendance and examination of witnesses on his behalf under the same conditions as witnesses against him;

(*e*)   to have the free assistance of an interpreter if he cannot understand or speak the language used in court.

Article 7
No punishment without law

1 No one shall be held guilty of any criminal offence on account of any act or omission which did not constitute a criminal offence under national or international law at the time when it was committed. Nor shall a heavier penalty be imposed than the one that was applicable at the time the criminal offence was committed.

2 This Article shall not prejudice the trial and punishment of any person for any act or omission which, at the time when it was committed, was criminal according to the general principles of law recognised by civilised nations.

Article 8
Right to respect for private and family life

1 Everyone has the right to respect for his private and family life, his home and his correspondence.

2 There shall be no interference by a public authority with the exercise of this right except such as is in accordance with the law and is necessary in a democratic society in the interests of national security, public safety or the economic well-being of the country, for the prevention of disorder or crime, for the protection of health or morals, or for the protection of the rights and freedoms of others.

Article 9
Freedom of thought, conscience and religion

1 Everyone has the right to freedom of thought, conscience and religion; this right includes freedom to change his religion or belief and freedom, either alone or in community with others and in public or private, to manifest his religion or belief, in worship, teaching, practice and observance.

2 Freedom to manifest one's religion or beliefs shall be subject only to such limitations as are prescribed by law and are necessary in a democratic society in the interests of public safety, for the protection of public order, health or morals, or for the protection of the rights and freedoms of others.

Article 10
Freedom of expression

1 Everyone has the right to freedom of expression. This right shall include freedom to hold opinions and to receive and impart information and ideas without interference by public authority and regardless of frontiers. This Article shall not prevent States from requiring the licensing of broadcasting, television or cinema enterprises.

2 The exercise of these freedoms, since it carries with it duties and responsibilities, may be subject to such formalities, conditions, restrictions or penalties as are prescribed by law and are necessary in a democratic society, in the interests of national security, territorial integrity or public safety, for the prevention of disorder or crime, for the protection of health or morals, for the protection of the reputation or rights of others, for preventing the disclosure of information received in confidence, or for maintaining the authority and impartiality of the judiciary.

Article 11
Freedom of assembly and association

1 Everyone has the right to freedom of peaceful assembly and to freedom of association with others, including the right to form and to join trade unions for the protection of his interests.

2 No restrictions shall be placed on the exercise of these rights other than such as are prescribed by law and are necessary in a democratic society in the interests of national security or public safety, for the prevention of disorder or crime, for the protection of health or morals or for the protection of the rights and freedoms of others. This Article shall not prevent the imposition of lawful restrictions on the exercise of these rights by members of the armed forces, of the police or of the administration of the State.

Article 12
Right to marry

Men and women of marriageable age have the right to marry and to found a family, according to the national laws governing the exercise of this right.

Article 14
Prohibition of discrimination

The enjoyment of the rights and freedoms set forth in this Convention shall be secured without discrimination on any ground such as sex, race, colour, language, religion, political or other opinion, national or social origin, association with a national minority, property, birth or other status.

Article 16
Restrictions on political activity of aliens

Nothing in Articles 10, 11 and 14 shall be regarded as preventing the High Contracting Parties from imposing restrictions on the political activity of aliens.

Article 17
Prohibition of abuse of rights

Nothing in this Convention may be interpreted as implying for any State, group or person any right to engage in any activity or perform any act aimed at the destruction of any of the rights and freedoms set forth herein or at their limitation to a greater extent than is provided for in the Convention.

Article 18
Limitation on use of restrictions on rights

The restrictions permitted under this Convention to the said rights and freedoms shall not be applied for any purpose other than those for which they have been prescribed.

PART II
THE FIRST PROTOCOL

Article 1
Protection of property

Every natural or legal person is entitled to the peaceful enjoyment of his possessions. No one shall be deprived of his possessions except in the public interest and subject to the conditions provided for by law and by the general principles of international law.

The preceding provisions shall not, however, in any way impair the right of a State to enforce such laws as it deems necessary to control the use of property in accordance with the general interest or to secure the payment of taxes or other contributions or penalties.

Article 2
Right to education

No person shall be denied the right to education. In the exercise of any functions which it assumes in relation to education and to teaching, the State shall respect the right of parents to ensure such education and teaching in conformity with their own religious and philosophical convictions.

Article 3
Right to free elections

The High Contracting Parties undertake to hold free elections at reasonable intervals by secret ballot, under conditions which will ensure the free expression of the opinion of the people in the choice of the legislature.

PART III
THE SIXTH PROTOCOL

Article 1
Abolition of the death penalty

The death penalty shall be abolished. No one shall be condemned to such penalty or executed.

Article 2
Death penalty in time of war

A State may make provision in its law for the death penalty in respect of acts committed in time of war or of imminent threat of war; such penalty shall be applied only in the instances laid down in the law and in accordance with its provisions. The State shall communicate to the Secretary General of the Council of Europe the relevant provisions of that law.

SCHEDULE 2
REMEDIAL ORDERS

Section 10

Orders

1 (1)   A remedial order may—

(a)   contain such incidental, supplemental, consequential or transitional provision as the person making it considers appropriate;

(b)   be made so as to have effect from a date earlier than that on which it is made;

(c)   make provision for the delegation of specific functions;

(d)   make different provision for different cases.

(2)   The power conferred by sub-paragraph (1)(a) includes—

(a)   power to amend primary legislation (including primary legislation other than that which contains the incompatible provision); and

(b)   power to amend or revoke subordinate legislation (including subordinate legislation other than that which contains the incompatible provision).

(3)   A remedial order may be made so as to have the same extent as the legislation which it affects.

(4)   No person is to be guilty of an offence solely as a result of the retrospective effect of a remedial order.

Procedure

2 No remedial order may be made unless—

(a)   a draft of the order has been approved by a resolution of each House of Parliament made after the end of the period of 60 days beginning with the day on which the draft was laid; or (*b*)   it is declared in the order that it appears to the person making it that, because of the urgency of the matter, it is necessary to make the order without a draft being so approved.

Orders laid in draft

3 (1)   No draft may be laid under paragraph 2(*a*) unless—

(*a*)   the person proposing to make the order has laid before Parliament a document which contains a draft of the proposed order and the required information; and

(*b*)   the period of 60 days, beginning with the day on which the document required by this sub-paragraph was laid, has ended.

(2)   If representations have been made during that period, the draft laid under paragraph 2(*a*) must be accompanied by a statement containing—

(*a*)   a summary of the representations; and

(*b*)   if, as a result of the representations, the proposed order has been changed, details of the changes.

Urgent cases

4 (1)   If a remedial order ('the original order') is made without being approved in draft, the person making it must lay it before Parliament, accompanied by the required information, after it is made.

(2)   If representations have been made during the period of 60 days beginning with the day on which the original order was made, the person making it must (after the end of that period) lay before Parliament a statement containing—

(*a*)   a summary of the representations; and

(*b*)   if, as a result of the representations, he considers it appropriate to make changes to the original order, details of the changes.

(3)   If sub-paragraph (2)(*b*) applies, the person making the statement must—

(*a*)   make a further remedial order replacing the original order; and

(*b*)   lay the replacement order before Parliament.

(4)   If, at the end of the period of 120 days beginning with the day on which the original order was made, a resolution has not been passed by each House approving the original or replacement order, the order ceases to have effect (but without that affecting anything previously done under either order or the power to make a fresh remedial order).

Definitions

5 In this Schedule—

'representations' means representations about a remedial order (or proposed remedial order) made to the person making (or proposing to make) it and includes any relevant Parliamentary report or resolution; and

'required information' means—

(*a*)   an explanation of the incompatibility which the order (or proposed order) seeks to remove, including particulars of the relevant declaration, finding or order; and

(*b*)   a statement of the reasons for proceeding under section 10 and for making an order in those terms.

Calculating periods

6 In calculating any period for the purposes of this Schedule, no account is to be taken of any time during which—

(*a*) Parliament is dissolved or prorogued; or

(*b*) both Houses are adjourned for more than four days.

SCHEDULE 3
DEROGATION AND RESERVATION

Sections 14 and 15

PART I
DEROGATION

The 1988 notification

The United Kingdom Permanent Representative to the Council of Europe presents his compliments to the Secretary General of the Council, and has the honour to convey the following information in order to ensure compliance with the obligations of Her Majesty's Government in the United Kingdom under Article 15(3) of the Convention for the Protection of Human Rights and Fundamental Freedoms signed at Rome on 4 November 1950.

There have been in the United Kingdom in recent years campaigns of organised terrorism connected with the affairs of Northern Ireland which have manifested themselves in activities which have included repeated murder, attempted murder, maiming, intimidation and violent civil disturbance and in bombing and fire raising which have resulted in death, injury and widespread destruction of property. As a result, a public emergency within the meaning of Article 15(1) of the Convention exists in the United Kingdom.

The Government found it necessary in 1974 to introduce and since then, in cases concerning persons reasonably suspected of involvement in terrorism connected with the affairs of Northern Ireland, or of certain offences under the legislation, who have been detained for 48 hours, to exercise powers enabling further detention without charge, for periods of up to five days, on the authority of the Secretary of State. These powers are at present to be found in Section 12 of the Prevention of Terrorism (Temporary Provisions) Act 1984, Article 9 of the Prevention of Terrorism (Supplemental Temporary Provisions) Order 1984 and Article 10 of the Prevention of Terrorism (Supplemental Temporary Provisions) (Northern Ireland) Order 1984.

Section 12 of the Prevention of Terrorism (Temporary Provisions) Act 1984 provides for a person whom a constable has arrested on reasonable grounds of suspecting him to be guilty of an offence under Section 1, 9 or 10 of the Act, or to be or to have been involved in terrorism connected with the affairs of Northern Ireland, to be detained in right of the arrest for up to 48 hours and thereafter, where the Secretary of State extends the detention period, for up to a further five days. Section 12 substantially re-enacted Section 12 of the Prevention of Terrorism (Temporary Provisions) Act 1976 which, in turn, substantially re-enacted Section 7 of the Prevention of Terrorism (Temporary Provisions) Act 1974.

Article 10 of the Prevention of Terrorism (Supplemental Temporary Provisions) (Northern Ireland) Order 1984 (SI 1984/417) and Article 9 of the Prevention of Terrorism (Supplemental Temporary Provisions) Order 1984 (SI 1984/418) were both made under Sections 13 and 14 of and Schedule 3 to the 1984 Act and substantially re-enacted powers of detention in Orders made under the 1974 and 1976 Acts. A person who is being examined under Article 4 of either Order on his arrival in, or on seeking to leave, Northern Ireland or Great Britain for the purpose of determining whether he is or has been involved in terrorism connected with the affairs of Northern Ireland, or whether there are grounds for suspecting that he has committed an offence under Section 9 of the 1984 Act, may be detained under Article 9 or 10, as appropriate, pending the conclusion of his examination. The period of this examination may exceed 12 hours if an examining officer has reasonable grounds for suspecting him to be or to have been involved in acts of terrorism connected with the affairs of Northern Ireland.

Where such a person is detained under the said Article 9 or 10 he may be detained for up to 48 hours on the authority of an examining officer and thereafter, where the Secretary of State extends the detention period, for up to a further five days.

In its judgment of 29 November 1988 in the Case of *Brogan and Others*, the European Court of Human Rights held that there had been a violation of Article 5(3) in respect of each of the applicants, all of whom had been detained under Section 12 of the 1984 Act. The Court held that even the shortest of the four periods of detention concerned, namely four days and six hours, fell outside the constraints as to time permitted by the first part of Article 5(3). In addition, the Court held that there had been a violation of Article 5(5) in the case of each applicant.

Following this judgment, the Secretary of State for the Home Department informed Parliament on 6 December 1988 that, against the background of the terrorist campaign, and the over-riding need to bring terrorists to justice, the Government did not believe that the maximum period of detention should be reduced. He informed Parliament that the Government were examining the matter with a view to responding to the judgment. On 22 December 1988, the Secretary of State further informed Parliament that it remained the Government's wish, if it could be achieved, to find a judicial process under which extended detention might be reviewed and where appropriate authorised by a judge or other judicial officer. But a further period of reflection and consultation was necessary before the Government could bring forward a firm and final view.

Since the judgment of 29 November 1988 as well as previously, the Government have found it necessary to continue to exercise, in relation to terrorism connected with the affairs of Northern Ireland, the powers described above enabling further detention without charge for periods of up to 5 days, on the authority of the Secretary of State, to the extent strictly required by the exigencies of the situation to enable necessary enquiries and investigations properly to be completed in order to decide whether criminal proceedings should be instituted. To the extent that the exercise of these powers may be inconsistent with the obligations imposed by the Convention the Government has availed itself of the right of derogation conferred by Article 15(1) of the Convention and will continue to do so until further notice.

Dated 23 December 1988.

The 1989 notification

The United Kingdom Permanent Representative to the Council of Europe presents his compliments to the Secretary General of the Council, and has the honour to convey the following information.

In his communication to the Secretary General of 23 December 1988, reference was made to the introduction and exercise of certain powers under section 12 of the Prevention of Terrorism (Temporary Provisions) Act 1984, Article 9 of the Prevention of Terrorism (Supplemental Temporary Provisions) Order 1984 and Article 10 of the Prevention of Terrorism (Supplemental Temporary Provisions) (Northern Ireland) Order 1984.

These provisions have been replaced by section 14 of and paragraph 6 of Schedule 5 to the Prevention of Terrorism (Temporary Provisions) Act 1989, which make comparable provision. They came into force on 22 March 1989. A copy of these provisions is enclosed.

The United Kingdom Permanent Representative avails himself of this opportunity to renew to the Secretary General the assurance of his highest consideration.

23 March 1989.

PART II
RESERVATION

At the time of signing the present (First) Protocol, I declare that, in view of certain provisions of the Education Acts in the United Kingdom, the principle affirmed in the second sentence of

Article 2 is accepted by the United Kingdom only so far as it is compatible with the provision of efficient instruction and training, and the avoidance of unreasonable public expenditure.

Dated 20 March 1952. Made by the United Kingdom Permanent Representative to the Council of Europe.

SCHEDULE 4
JUDICIAL PENSIONS

Section 18(6)

Duty to make orders about pensions

1 (1)   The appropriate Minister must by order make provision with respect to pensions payable to or in respect of any holder of a judicial office who serves as an ECHR judge.

(2)   A pensions order must include such provision as the Minister making it considers is necessary to secure that—

    (*a*)   an ECHR judge who was, immediately before his appointment as an ECHR judge, a member of a judicial pension scheme is entitled to remain as a member of that scheme;

    (*b*)   the terms on which he remains a member of the scheme are those which would have been applicable had he not been appointed as an ECHR judge; and

    (*c*)   entitlement to benefits payable in accordance with the scheme continues to be determined as if, while serving as an ECHR judge, his salary was that which would (but for section 18(4)) have been payable to him in respect of his continuing service as the holder of his judicial office.

Contribution

2 A pensions order may, in particular, make provision—

    (*a*)   for any contributions which are payable by a person who remains a member of a scheme as a result of the order, and which would otherwise be payable by deduction from his salary, to be made otherwise than by deduction from his salary as an ECHR judge; and

    (*b*)   for such contributions to be collected in such manner as may be determined by the administrators of the scheme.

Amendments of other enactments

3 A pensions order may amend any provision of, or made under, a pensions Act in such manner and to such extent as the Minister making the order considers necessary or expedient to ensure the proper administration of any scheme to which it relates.

Definitions

4 In this Schedule—

    'appropriate Minister" means—

        (*a*)   in relation to any judicial office whose jurisdiction is exercisable exclusively in relation to Scotland, the Secretary of State; and

        (*b*)   otherwise, the Lord Chancellor;

    'ECHR judge" means the holder of a judicial office who is serving as a judge of the Court;

    'judicial pension scheme" means a scheme established by and in accordance with a pensions Act;

'pensions Act" means—

(*a*)   the County Courts Act (Northern Ireland) 1959;

(*b*)   the Sheriffs' Pensions (Scotland) Act 1961;

(*c*)   the Judicial Pensions Act 1981; or

(*d*)   the Judicial Pensions and Retirement Act 1993; and

'pensions order" means an order made under paragraph 1.

Appendix 2
Human Rights Instruments

Convention for the Protection of Human Rights and Fundamental Freedoms

Rome, 4.XI.1950

The governments signatory hereto, being members of the Council of Europe;

Considering the Universal Declaration of Human Rights proclaimed by the General Assembly of the United Nations on 10th December 1948;

Considering that this Declaration aims at securing the universal and effective recognition and observance of the Rights therein declared;

Considering that the aim of the Council of Europe is the achievement of greater unity between its members and that one of the methods by which that aim is to be pursued is the maintenance and further realisation of human rights and fundamental freedoms; Reaffirming their profound belief in those fundamental freedoms which are the foundation of justice and peace in the world and are best maintained on the one hand by an effective political democracy and on the other by a common understanding and observance of the human rights upon which they depend;

Being resolved, as the governments of European countries which are like-minded and have a common heritage of political traditions, ideals, freedom and the rule of law, to take the first steps for the collective enforcement of certain of the rights stated in the Universal Declaration,

Have agreed as follows:

Notes
1. Headings added according to the provisions of Protocol No. 11 (ETS No. 155).

Article 1[1]
Obligation to respect human rights

The High Contracting Parties shall secure to everyone within their jurisdiction the rights and freedoms defined in Section 1 of this Convention.

SECTION 1[1] — RIGHTS AND FREEDOMS

Article 2[1]
Right to life

1 Everyone's right to life shall be protected by law. No one shall be deprived of his life intentionally save in the execution of a sentence of a court following his conviction of a crime for which this penalty is provided by law.

2 Deprivation of life shall not be regarded as inflicted in contravention of this article when it results from the use of force which is no more than absolutely necessary:

a   in defence of any person from unlawful violence;

b   in order to effect a lawful arrest or to prevent the escape of a person lawfully detained;

c   in action lawfully taken for the purpose of quelling a riot or insurrection.

Article 3[1]
Prohibition of torture

No one shall be subjected to torture or to inhuman or degrading treatment or punishment.

Article 4[1]
Prohibition of slavery and forced labour

1   No one shall be held in slavery or servitude.

2   No one shall be required to perform forced or compulsory labour.

3   For the purpose of this article the term 'forced or compulsory labour' shall not include:

a   any work required to be done in the ordinary course of detention imposed according to the provisions of Article 5 of this Convention or during conditional release from such detention;

b   any service of a military character or, in case of conscientious objectors in countries where they are recognised, service exacted instead of compulsory military service;

c   any service exacted in case of an emergency or calamity threatening the life or well-being of the community;

d   any work or service which forms part of normal civic obligations.

Article 5[1]
Right to liberty and security

1   Everyone has the right to liberty and security of person. No one shall be deprived of his liberty save in the following cases and in accordance with a procedure prescribed by law:

a   the lawful detention of a person after conviction by a competent court;

b   the lawful arrest or detention of a person for noncompliance with the lawful order of a court or in order to secure the fulfilment of any obligation prescribed by law;

c   the lawful arrest or detention of a person effected for the purpose of bringing him before the competent legal authority on reasonable suspicion of having committed an offence or when it is reasonably considered necessary to prevent his committing an offence or fleeing after having done so;

d   the detention of a minor by lawful order for the purpose of educational supervision or his lawful detention for the purpose of bringing him before the competent legal authority;

e   the lawful detention of persons for the prevention of the spreading of infectious diseases, of persons of unsound mind, alcoholics or drug addicts or vagrants;

f   the lawful arrest or detention of a person to prevent his effecting an unauthorised entry into the country or of a person against whom action is being taken with a view to deportation or extradition.

2   Everyone who is arrested shall be informed promptly, in a language which he understands, of the reasons for his arrest and of any charge against him.

3   Everyone arrested or detained in accordance with the provisions of paragraph 1.c of this article shall be brought promptly before a judge or other officer authorised by law to exercise judicial power and shall be entitled to trial within a reasonable time or to release pending trial. Release may be conditioned by guarantees to appear for trial.

4   Everyone who is deprived of his liberty by arrest or detention shall be entitled to take proceedings by which the lawfulness of his detention shall be decided speedily by a court and his release ordered if the detention is not lawful.

5   Everyone who has been the victim of arrest or detention in contravention of the provisions of this article shall have an enforceable right to compensation.

Article 6[1]
Right to a fair trial

1   In the determination of his civil rights and obligations or of any criminal charge against him, everyone is entitled to a fair and public hearing within a reasonable time by an independent and impartial tribunal established by law. Judgment shall be pronounced publicly but the press and public may be excluded from all or part of the trial in the interests of morals, public order or national security in a democratic society, where the interests of juveniles or the protection of the private life of the parties so require, or to the extent strictly necessary in the opinion of the court in special circumstances where publicity would prejudice the interests of justice.

2   Everyone charged with a criminal offence shall be presumed innocent until proved guilty according to law.

3   Everyone charged with a criminal offence has the following minimum rights:

a   to be informed promptly, in a language which he understands and in detail, of the nature and cause of the accusation against him;

b   to have adequate time and facilities for the preparation of his defence;

c   to defend himself in person or through legal assistance of his own choosing or, if he has not sufficient means to pay for legal assistance, to be given it free when the interests of justice so require;

d   to examine or have examined witnesses against him and to obtain the attendance and examination of witnesses on his behalf under the same conditions as witnesses against him;

e   to have the free assistance of an interpreter if he cannot understand or speak the language used in court.

Article 7[1]
No punishment without law

1   No one shall be held guilty of any criminal offence on account of any act or omission which did not constitute a criminal offence under national or international law at the time when it was committed. Nor shall a heavier penalty be imposed than the one that was applicable at the time the criminal offence was committed.

2   This article shall not prejudice the trial and punishment of any person for any act or omission which, at the time when it was committed, was criminal according to the general principles of law recognised by civilised nations.

Article 8[1]
Right to respect for private and family life

1   Everyone has the right to respect for his private and family life, his home and his correspondence.

2   There shall be no interference by a public authority with the exercise of this right except such as is in accordance with the law and is necessary in a democratic society in the interests of national security, public safety or the economic well-being of the country, for the prevention of disorder or crime, for the protection of health or morals, or for the protection of the rights and freedoms of others.

Article 9[1]
Freedom of thought, conscience and religion

Everyone has the right to freedom of thought, conscience and religion; this right includes freedom to change his religion or belief and freedom, either alone or in community with others and in public or private, to manifest his religion or belief, in worship, teaching, practice and observance.

2   Freedom to manifest one's religion or beliefs shall be subject only to such limitations as are prescribed by law and are necessary in a democratic society in the interests of public safety,

for the protection of public order, health or morals, or for the protection of the rights and freedoms of others.

Article 10[1]
Freedom of expression

1   Everyone has the right to freedom of expression. This right shall include freedom to hold opinions and to receive and impart information and ideas without interference by public authority and regardless of frontiers. This article shall not prevent States from requiring the licensing of broadcasting, television or cinema enterprises.

2   The exercise of these freedoms, since it carries with it duties and responsibilities, may be subject to such formalities, conditions, restrictions or penalties as are prescribed by law and are necessary in a democratic society, in the interests of national security, territorial integrity or public safety, for the prevention of disorder or crime, for the protection of health or morals, for the protection of the reputation or rights of others, for preventing the disclosure of information received in confidence, or for maintaining the authority and impartiality of the judiciary.

Article 11[1]
Freedom of assembly and association

1   Everyone has the right to freedom of peaceful assembly and to freedom of association with others, including the right to form and to join trade unions for the protection of his interests.

2   No restrictions shall be placed on the exercise of these rights other than such as are prescribed by law and are necessary in a democratic society in the interests of national security or public safety, for the prevention of disorder or crime, for the protection of health or morals or for the protection of the rights and freedoms of others. This article shall not prevent the imposition of lawful restrictions on the exercise of these rights by members of the armed forces, of the police or of the administration of the State.

Article 12[1]
Right to marry

Men and women of marriageable age have the right to marry and to found a family, according to the national laws governing the exercise of this right.

Article 13[1]
Right to an effective remedy

Everyone whose rights and freedoms as set forth in this Convention are violated shall have an effective remedy before a national authority notwithstanding that the violation has been committed by persons acting in an official capacity.

Article 14[1]
Prohibition of discrimination

The enjoyment of the rights and freedoms set forth in this Convention shall be secured without discrimination on any ground such as sex, race, colour, language, religion, political or other opinion, national or social origin, association with a national minority, property, birth or other status.

Article 15[1]
Derogation in time of emergency

1   In time of war or other public emergency threatening the life of the nation any High Contracting Party may take measures derogating from its obligations under this Convention to the extent strictly required by the exigencies of the situation, provided that such measures are not inconsistent with its other obligations under international law.

2   No derogation from Article 2, except in respect of deaths resulting from lawful acts of war, or from Articles 3, 4 (paragraph 1) and 7 shall be made under this provision.

3 Any High Contracting Party availing itself of this right of derogation shall keep the Secretary General of the Council of Europe fully informed of the measures which it has taken and the reasons therefor. It shall also inform the Secretary General of the Council of Europe when such measures have ceased to operate and the provisions of the Convention are again being fully executed.

Article 16[1]
Restrictions on political activity of aliens

Nothing in Articles 10, 11 and 14 shall be regarded as preventing the High Contracting Parties from imposing restrictions on the political activity of aliens.

Article 17[1]
Prohibition of abuse of rights

Nothing in this Convention may be interpreted as implying for any State, group or person any right to engage in any activity or perform any act aimed at the destruction of any of the rights and freedoms set forth herein or at their limitation to a greater extent than is provided for in the Convention.

Article 18[1]
Limitation on use of restrictions on rights

The restrictions permitted under this Convention to the said rights and freedoms shall not be applied for any purpose other than those for which they have been prescribed.

SECTION II[1] — EUROPEAN COURT OF HUMAN RIGHTS

Article 19
Establishment of the Court

To ensure the observance of the engagements undertaken by the High Contracting Parties in the Convention and the Protocols thereto, there shall be set up a European Court of Human Rights, hereinafter referred to as 'the Court'. It shall function on a permanent basis.

Article 20
Number of judges

The Court shall consist of a number of judges equal to that of the High Contracting Parties.

Article 21
Criteria for office

1 The judges shall be of high moral character and must either possess the qualifications required for appointment to high judicial office or be jurisconsults of recognised competence.

2 The judges shall sit on the Court in their individual capacity.

3 During their term of office the judges shall not engage in any activity which is incompatible with their independence, impartiality or with the demands of a full-time office; all questions arising from the application of this paragraph shall be decided by the Court.

Article 22
Election of judges

1 The judges shall be elected by the Parliamentary Assembly with respect to each High Contracting Party by a majority of votes cast from a list of three candidates nominated by the High Contracting Party.

2 The same procedure shall be followed to complete the Court in the event of the accession of new High Contracting Parties and in filling casual vacancies.

Article 23
Terms of office

1   The judges shall be elected for a period of six years. They may be re-elected. However, the terms of office of one-half of the judges elected at the first election shall expire at the end of three years.

2   The judges whose terms of office are to expire at the end of the initial period of three years shall be chosen by lot by the Secretary General of the Council of Europe immediately after their election.

3   In order to ensure that, as far as possible, the terms of office of one-half of the judges are renewed every three years, the Parliamentary Assembly may decide, before proceeding to any subsequent election, that the term or terms of office of one or more judges to be elected shall be for a period other than six years but not more than nine and not less than three years.

4   In cases where more than one term of office is involved and where the Parliamentary Assembly applies the preceding paragraph, the allocation of the terms of office shall be effected by a drawing of lots by the Secretary General of the Council of Europe immediately after the election.

5   A judge elected to replace a judge whose term of office has not expired shall hold office for the remainder of his predecessor's term.

6   The terms of office of judges shall expire when they reach the age of 70.

7   The judges shall hold office until replaced. They shall, however, continue to deal with such cases as they already have under consideration.

Article 24
Dismissal

No judge may be dismissed from his office unless the other judges decide unanimously that he has ceased to fulfil the required conditions.

Article 25
Registry and legal secretaries

The Court shall have a registry, the functions and organisation of which shall be laid down in the rules of the Court. The Court shall be assisted by legal secretaries.

Article 26
Plenary Court

The plenary Court shall

a   elect its President and one or two Vice-Presidents for a period of three years; they may be re-elected;

b   set up Chambers, constituted for a fixed period of time;

c   elect the Presidents of the Chambers of the Court; they may be re-elected;

d   adopt the rules of the Court, and

e   elect the Registrar and one or more Deputy Registrars.

Article 27
Committees, Chambers and Grand Chamber

1   To consider cases brought before it, the Court shall sit in committees of three judges, in Chambers of seven judges and in a Grand Chamber of seventeen judges. The Court's Chambers shall set up committees for a fixed period of time.

2   There shall sit as an *ex officio* member of the Chamber and the Grand Chamber the judge elected in respect of the State Party concerned or, if there is none or if he is unable to sit, a person of its choice who shall sit in the capacity of judge.

3   The Grand Chamber shall also include the President of the Court, the Vice-Presidents, the Presidents of the Chambers and other judges chosen in accordance with the rules of the Court. When a case is referred to the Grand Chamber under Article 43, no judge from the Chamber which rendered the judgment shall sit in the Grand Chamber, with the exception of the President of the Chamber and the judge who sat in respect of the State Party concerned.

Article 28
Declarations of inadmissibility by committees

A committee may, by a unanimous vote, declare inadmissible or strike out of its list of cases an application submitted under Article 34 where such a decision can be taken without further examination. The decision shall be final.

Article 29
Decisions by Chambers on admissibility and merits

1   If no decision is taken under Article 28, a Chamber shall decide on the admissibility and merits of individual applications submitted under Article 34.

2   A Chamber shall decide on the admissibility and merits of inter-State applications submitted under Article 33.

3   The decision on admissibility shall be taken separately unless the Court, in exceptional cases, decides otherwise.

Article 30
Relinquishment of jurisdiction to the Grand Chamber

Where a case pending before a Chamber raises a serious question affecting the interpretation of the Convention or the protocols thereto, or where the resolution of a question before the Chamber might have a result inconsistent with a judgment previously delivered by the Court, the Chamber may, at any time before it has rendered its judgment, relinquish jurisdiction in favour of the Grand Chamber, unless one of the parties to the case objects.

Article 31
Powers of the Grand Chamber

The Grand Chamber shall

a   determine applications submitted either under Article 33 or Article 34 when a Chamber has relinquished jurisdiction under Article 30 or when the case has been referred to it under Article 43; and

b   consider requests for advisory opinions submitted under Article 47.

Article 32
Jurisdiction of the Court

1   The jurisdiction of the Court shall extend to all matters concerning the interpretation and application of the Convention and the protocols thereto which are referred to it as provided in Articles 33, 34 and 47.

2   In the event of dispute as to whether the Court has jurisdiction, the Court shall decide.

Article 33
Inter-State cases

Any High Contracting Party may refer to the Court any alleged breach of the provisions of the Convention and the protocols thereto by another High Contracting Party.

Article 34
Individual applications

The Court may receive applications from any person, non-governmental organisation or group of individuals claiming to be the victim of a violation by one of the High Contracting Parties of the rights set forth in the Convention or the protocols thereto. The High Contracting Parties undertake not to hinder in any way the effective exercise of this right.

Article 35

Admissibility criteria

1　The Court may only deal with the matter after all domestic remedies have been exhausted, according to the generally recognised rules of international law, and within a period of six months from the date on which the final decision was taken.

2　The Court shall not deal with any application submitted under Article 34 that

a　is anonymous; or

b　is substantially the same as a matter that has already been examined by the Court or has already been submitted to another procedure of international investigation or settlement and contains no relevant new information.

3　The Court shall declare inadmissible any individual application submitted under Article 34 which it considers incompatible with the provisions of the Convention or the protocols thereto, manifestly ill-founded, or an abuse of the right of application.

4　The Court shall reject any application which it considers inadmissible under this Article. It may do so at any stage of the proceedings.

Article 36
Third party intervention

1　In all cases before a Chamber of the Grand Chamber, a High Contracting Party one of whose nationals is an applicant shall have the right to submit written comments and to take part in hearings.

2　The President of the Court may, in the interest of the proper administration of justice, invite any High Contracting Party which is not a party to the proceedings or any person concerned who is not the applicant to submit written comments or take part in hearings.

Article 37
Striking out applications

1　The Court may at any stage of the proceedings decide to strike an application out of its list of cases where the circumstances lead to the conclusion that

a　the applicant does not intend to pursue his application; or

b　the matter has been resolved; or

c　for any other reason established by the Court, it is no longer justified to continue the examination of the application.

However, the Court shall continue the examination of the application if respect for human rights as defined in the Convention and the protocols thereto so requires.

2　The Court may decide to restore an application to its list of cases if it considers that the circumstances justify such a course.

Article 38
Examination of the case and friendly settlement proceedings

1　If the Court declares the application admissible, it shall

a　pursue the examination of the case, together with the representatives of the parties, and if need be, undertake an investigation, for the effective conduct of which the States concerned shall furnish all necessary facilities;

b　place itself at the disposal of the parties concerned with a view to securing a friendly settlement of the matter on the basis of respect for human rights as defined in the Convention and the protocols thereto.

2   Proceedings conducted under paragraph 1.b shall be confidential.

Article 39
Finding of a friendly settlement

If a friendly settlement is effected, the Court shall strike the case out of its list by means of a decision which shall be confined to a brief statement of the facts and of the solution reached.

Article 40
Public hearings and access to documents

1   Hearings shall be in public unless the Court in exceptional circumstances decides otherwise.

2   Documents deposited with the Registrar shall be accessible to the public unless the President of the Court decides otherwise.

Article 41
Just satisfaction

If the Court finds that there has been a violation of the Convention or the protocols thereto, and if the internal law of the High Contracting Party concerned allows only partial reparation to be made, the Court shall, if necessary, afford just satisfaction to the injured party.

Article 42
Judgments of Chambers

Judgments of Chambers shall become final in accordance with the provisions of Article 44, paragraph 2.

Article 43
Referral to the Grand Chamber

1   Within a period of three months from the date of the judgment of the Chamber, any party to the case may, in exceptional cases, request that the case be referred to the Grand Chamber.

2   A panel of five judges of the Grand Chamber shall accept the request if the case raises a serious question affecting the interpretation or application of the Convention or the protocols thereto, or a serious issue of general importance.

3   If the panel accepts the request, the Grand Chamber shall decide the case by means of a judgment.

Article 44
Final judgments

1   The judgment of the Grand Chamber shall be final.

2   The judgment of a Chamber shall become final

   a   when the parties declare that they will not request that the case be referred to the Grand Chamber; or

   b   three months after the date of the judgment, if reference of the case to the Grand Chamber has not been requested; or

   c   when the panel of the Grand Chamber rejects the request to refer under Article 43.

3   The final judgment shall be published.

Article 45
Reasons for judgments and decisions

1   Reasons shall be given for judgments as well as for decisions declaring applications admissible or inadmissible.

2   If a judgment does not represent, in whole or in part, the unanimous opinion of the judges, any judge shall be entitled to deliver a separate opinion.

Article 46
Binding force and execution of judgments

1   The High Contracting Parties undertake to abide by the final judgment of the Court in any case to which they are parties.

2   The final judgment of the Court shall be transmitted to the Committee of Ministers, which shall supervise its execution.

Article 47
Advisory opinions

1   The Court may, at the request of the Committee of Ministers, give advisory opinions on legal questions concerning the interpretation of the Convention and the protocols thereto.

2   Such opinions shall not deal with any question relating to the content or scope of the rights or freedoms defined in Section 1 of the Convention and the protocols thereto, or with any other question which the Court or the Committee of Ministers might have to consider in consequence of any such proceedings as could be instituted in accordance with the Convention.

3   Decisions of the Committee of Ministers to request an advisory opinion of the Court shall require a majority vote of the representatives entitled to sit on the Committee.

Article 48
Advisory jurisdiction of the Court

The Court shall decide whether a request for an advisory opinion submitted by the Committee of Ministers is within its competence as defined in Article 47.

Article 49
Reasons for advisory opinions

1   Reasons shall be given for advisory opinions of the Court.

2   If the advisory opinion does not represent, in whole or in part, the unanimous opinion of the judges, any judge shall be entitled to deliver a separate opinion.

3   Advisory opinions of the Court shall be communicated to the Committee of Ministers.

Article 50
Expenditure on the Court

The expenditure on the Court shall be borne by the Council of Europe.

Article 51
Privileges and immunities of judges

The judges shall be entitled, during the exercise of their functions, to the privileges and immunities provided for in Article 40 of the Statute of the Council of Europe and in the agreements made thereunder.

SECTION III[1,2] — MISCELLANEOUS PROVISIONS

Notes
1. Headings in this section added according to the provisions of Protocol No. 11 (ETS No. 155).
2. The articles of this section are renumbered according to the provisions of Protocol No. 11. (ETS No. 155).

Article 52[1]
Inquiries by the Secretary General

On receipt of a request from the Secretary General of the Council of Europe any High Contracting Party shall furnish an explanation of the manner in which its internal law ensures the effective implementation of any of the provisions of the Convention.

Article 53[1]
Safeguard for existing human rights

Nothing in this Convention shall be construed as limiting or derogating from any of the human rights and fundamental freedoms which may be ensured under the laws of any High Contracting Party or under any other agreement to which it is a Party.

Article 54[1]
Powers of the Committee of Ministers

Nothing in this Convention shall prejudice the powers conferred on the Committee of Ministers by the Statute of the Council of Europe.

Article 55[1]
Exclusion of other means of dispute settlement

The High Contracting Parties agree that, except by special agreement, they will not avail themselves of treaties, conventions or declarations. in force between them for the purpose of submitting, by way of petition, a dispute arising out of the interpretation or application of this Convention to a means of settlement other than those provided for in this Convention.

Article 56[1]
Territorial application

1[2]   Any State may at the time of its ratification or at any time thereafter declare by notification addressed to the Secretary General of the Council of Europe that the present Convention shall, subject to paragraph 4 of this Article, extend to all or any of the territories for whose international relations it is responsible.

2   The Convention shall extend to the territory or territories named in the notification as from the thirtieth day after the receipt of this notification by the Secretary General of the Council of Europe.

3   The provisions of this Convention shall be applied in such territories with due regard, however, to local requirements.

4[2]   Any State which has made a declaration in accordance with paragraph 1 of this article may at any time thereafter declare on behalf of one or more of the territories to which the declaration relates that it accepts the competence of the Court to receive applications from individuals, non-governmental organisations or groups of individuals as provided by Article 34 of the Convention.

Notes
1. Heading added according to the provisions of Protocol No. 11 (ETS No. 155).
2. Text amended according to the provisions of Protocol No. 11 (ETS No. 155).

Article 57[1]
Reservations

1   Any State may, when signing this Convention or when depositing its instrument of ratification, make a reservation in respect of any particular provision of the Convention to the extent that any law then in force in its territory is not in conformity with the provision. Reservations of a general character shall not be permitted under this article.

2   Any reservation made under this article shall contain a brief statement of the law concerned.

Article 58[1]
Denunciation

1   A High Contracting Party may denounce the present Convention only after the expiry of five years from the date on which it became a party to it and after six months' notice contained in a notification addressed to the Secretary General of the Council of Europe, who shall inform the other High Contracting Parties.

2   Such a denunciation shall not have the effect of releasing the High Contracting Party concerned from its obligations under this Convention in respect of any act which, being capable of constituting a violation of such obligations, may have been performed by it before the date at which the denunciation became effective.

3   Any High Contracting Party which shall cease to be a member of the Council of Europe shall cease to be a Party to this Convention under the same conditions.

4[2]   The Convention may be denounced in accordance with the provisions of the preceding paragraphs in respect of any territory to which it has been declared to extend under the terms of Article 56.

Notes
1. Heading added according to the provisions of Protocol No. 11 (ETS No. 155).
2. Text amended according to the provisions of Protocol No. 11 (ETS No. 155).

Article 59[1]
Signature and ratification

1   This Convention shall be open to the signature of the members of the Council of Europe. It shall be ratified. Ratifications shall be deposited with the Secretary General of the Council of Europe.

2   The present Convention shall come into force after the deposit of ten instruments of ratification.

3   As regards any signatory ratifying subsequently, the Convention shall come into force at the date of the deposit of its instrument of ratification.

4   The Secretary General of the Council of Europe shall notify all the members of the Council of Europe of the entry into force of the Convention, the names of the High Contracting Parties who have ratified it, and the deposit of all instruments of ratification which may be effected subsequently.

Done at Rome this 4th day of November 1950, in English and French, both texts being equally authentic, in a single copy which shall remain deposited in the archives of the Council of Europe. The Secretary General shall transmit certified copies to each of the signatories.

Protocol [No. 1]
to the Convention for the Protection
of Human Rights and Fundamental Freedoms[1]

Paris, 20.III.1952

The governments signatory hereto, being members of the Council of Europe,

Being resolved to take steps to ensure the collective enforcement of certain rights and freedoms other than those already included in Section 1 of the Convention for the Protection of Human Rights and Fundamental Freedoms signed at Rome on 4 November 1950 (hereinafter referred to as 'the Convention'),

Have agreed as follows:

Article 1
Protection of property

Every natural or legal person is entitled to the peaceful enjoyment of his possessions. No one shall be deprived of his possessions except in the public interest and subject to the conditions provided for by law and by the general principles of international law.

The preceding provisions shall not, however, in any way impair the right of a State to enforce such laws as it deems necessary to control the use of property in accordance with the general interest or to secure the payment of taxes or other contributions or penalties.

Notes
1. Headings of articles added and text amended according to the provisions of Protocol No. 11 (ETS No. 155) as from its entry into force.

Article 2
Right to education

No person shall be denied the right to education. In the exercise of any functions which it assumes in relation to education and to teaching, the State shall respect the right of parents to ensure such education and teaching in conformity with their own religious and philosophical convictions.

Article 3
Right to free elections

The High Contracting Parties undertake to hold free elections at reasonable intervals by secret ballot, under conditions which will ensure the free expression of the opinion of the people in the choice of the legislature.

Article 4[1]
Territorial application

Any High Contracting Party may at the time of signature or ratification or at any time thereafter communicate to the Secretary General of the Council of Europe a declaration stating the extent to which it undertakes that the provisions of the present Protocol shall apply to such of the territories for the international relations of which it is responsible as are named therein.

Any High Contracting Party which has communicated a declaration in virtue of the preceding paragraph may from time to time communicate a further declaration modifying the terms of any former declaration or terminating the application of the provisions of this Protocol in respect of any territory.

A declaration made in accordance with this article shall be deemed to have been made in accordance with paragraph 1 of Article 56 of the Convention.

Notes
1. Text amended according to the provisions of Protocol No. 11 (ETS No. 155).

Article 5
Relationship to the Convention

As between the High Contracting Parties the provisions of Articles 1, 2, 3 and 4 of this Protocol shall be regarded as additional articles to the Convention and all the provisions of the Convention shall apply accordingly.

Article 6
Signature and ratification

This Protocol shall be open for signature by the members of the Council of Europe, who are the signatories of the Convention; it shall be ratified at the same time as or after the ratification of the Convention. It shall enter into force after the deposit of ten instruments of ratification. As regards any signatory ratifying subsequently, the Protocol shall enter into force at the date of the deposit of its instrument of ratification.

The instruments of ratification shall be deposited with the Secretary General of the Council of Europe, who will notify all members of the names of those who have ratified.

Done at Paris on the 20th day of March 1952, in English and French, both texts being equally authentic, in a single copy which shall remain deposited in the archives of the Council of Europe. The Secretary General shall transmit certified copies to each of the signatory governments.

Protocol No. 4
to the Convention for the Protection
of Human Rights and Fundamental Freedoms
securing certain rights and freedoms
other than those already included in the Convention
and in the First Protocol thereto[1]

Strasbourg, 16.IX.1963

Notes
1. Headings of articles added and text amended according to the provisions of Protocol No. 11 (ETS No. 155) as from its entry into force.

The governments signatory hereto, being members of the Council of Europe,

Being resolved to take steps to ensure the collective enforcement of certain rights and freedoms other than those already included in Section 1 of the Convention for the Protection of Human Rights and Fundamental Freedoms signed at Rome on 4th November 1950 (hereinafter referred to as the 'Convention') and in Articles 1 to 3 of the First Protocol to the Convention, signed at Paris on 20th March 1952,

Have agreed as follows:

Article 1
Prohibition of imprisonment for debt

No one shall be deprived of his liberty merely on the ground of inability to fulfil a contractual obligation.

Article 2
Freedom of movement

1   Everyone lawfully within the territory of a State shall, within that territory, have the right to liberty of movement and freedom to choose his residence.

2   Everyone shall be free to leave any country, including his own.

3   No restrictions shall be placed on the exercise of these rights other than such as are in accordance with law and are necessary in a democratic society in the interests of national security or public safety, for the maintenance of ordre public, for the prevention of crime, for the protection of health or morals, or for the protection of the rights and freedoms of others.

4   The rights set forth in paragraph 1 may also be subject, in particular areas, to restrictions imposed in accordance with law and justified by the public interest in a democratic society.

Article 3
Prohibition of expulsion of nationals

1   No one shall be expelled, by means either of an individual or of a collective measure, from the territory of the State of which he is a national.

2   No one shall be deprived of the right to enter the territory of the state of which he is a national.

Article 4
Prohibition of collective expulsion of aliens

Collective expulsion of aliens is prohibited.

Article 5
Territorial application

1   Any High Contracting Party may, at the time of signature or ratification of this Protocol, or at any time thereafter, communicate to the Secretary General of the Council of Europe a declaration stating the extent to which it undertakes that the provisions of this Protocol shall apply to such of the territories for the international relations of which it is responsible as are named therein.

2   Any High Contracting Party which has communicated a declaration in virtue of the preceding paragraph may, from time to time, communicate a further declaration modifying the terms of any former declaration or terminating the application of the provisions of this Protocol in respect of any territory.

3[1]   A declaration made in accordance with this article shall be deemed to have been made in accordance with paragraph 1 of Article 56 of the Convention.

4   The territory of any State to which this Protocol applies by virtue of ratification or acceptance by that State, and each territory to which this Protocol is applied by virtue of a declaration by that State under this article, shall be treated as separate territories for the purpose of the references in Articles 2 and 3 to the territory of a State.

5[2]   Any State which has made a declaration in accordance with paragraph 1 or 2 of this Article may at any time thereafter declare on behalf of one or more of the territories to which the declaration relates that it accepts the competence of the Court to receive applications from individuals, non-governmental organisations or groups of individuals as provided in Article 34 of the Convention in respect of all or any of Articles 1 to 4 of this Protocol.

Notes
1. Text amended according to the provisions of Protocol No. 11 (ETS No. 155).
2. Text added according to the provisions of Protocol No. 11 (ETS No. 155).

Article 6[1]
Relationship to the Convention

As between the High Contracting Parties the provisions of Articles 1 to 5 of this Protocol shall be regarded as additional Articles to the Convention, and all the provisions of the Convention shall apply accordingly.

Notes
1. Text amended according to the provisions of Protocol No. 11 (ETS No. 155).

Article 7
Signature and ratification

1   This Protocol shall be open for signature by the members of the Council of Europe who are the signatories of the Convention; it shall be ratified at the same time as or after the ratification of the Convention. It shall enter into force after the deposit of five instruments of ratification. As regards any signatory ratifying subsequently, the Protocol shall enter into force at the date of the deposit of its instrument of ratification.

2   The instruments of ratification shall be deposited with the Secretary General of the Council of Europe, who will notify all members of the names of those who have ratified.

In witness whereof the undersigned, being duly authorised thereto, have signed this Protocol.

Done at Strasbourg, this 16th day of September 1963, in English and in French, both texts being equally authoritative, in a single copy which shall remain deposited in the archives of the Council of Europe. The Secretary General shall transmit certified copies to each of the signatory states.

Protocol No. 6
to the Convention for the Protection
of Human Rights and Fundamental Freedoms
concerning the Abolition of the Death Penalty[1]

Strasbourg, 28.IV.1983

The member States of the Council of Europe, signatory to this Protocol to the Convention for the Protection of Human Rights and Fundamental Freedoms, signed at Rome on 4 November 1950 (hereinafter referred to as 'the Convention'),

Considering that the evolution that has occurred in several member States of the Council of Europe expresses a general tendency in favour of abolition of the death penalty;

Have agreed as follows:

Notes
1. Headings of articles added and text amended according to the provisions of Protocol No. 11 (ETS No. 155) as from its entry into force.

Article 1
Abolition of the death penalty

The death penalty shall be abolished. No-one shall be condemned to such penalty or executed.

Article 2
Death penalty in time of war

A State may make provision in its law for the death penalty in respect of acts committed in time of war or of imminent threat of war; such penalty shall be applied only in the instances laid down in the law and in accordance with its provisions. The State shall communicate to the Secretary General of the Council of Europe the relevant provisions of that law.

Article 3
Prohibition of derogations

No derogation from the provisions of this Protocol shall be made under Article 15 of the Convention.

Article 4[1]

Prohibition of reservations

No reservation may be made under Article 57 of the Convention in respect of the provisions of this Protocol.

Notes
1. Text amended according to the provisions of Protocol No. 11 (ETS No. 155).

Article 5
Territorial application

1   Any State may at the time of signature or when depositing its instrument of ratification, acceptance or approval, specify the territory or territories to which this Protocol shall apply.

2   Any State may at any later date, by a declaration addressed to the Secretary General of the Council of Europe, extend the application of this Protocol to any other territory specified in the declaration. In respect of such territory the Protocol shall enter into force on the first day of the month following the date of receipt of such declaration by the Secretary General.

3   Any declaration made under the two preceding paragraphs may, in respect of any territory specified in such declaration, be withdrawn by a notification addressed to the Secretary General. The withdrawal shall become effective on the first day of the month following the date of receipt of such notification by the Secretary General.

Article 6
Relationship to the Convention

As between the States Parties the provisions of Articles 1 and 5 of this Protocol shall be regarded as additional articles to the Convention and all the provisions of the Convention shall apply accordingly.

Article 7
Signature and ratification

The Protocol shall be open for signature by the member States of the Council of Europe, signatories to the Convention. It shall be subject to ratification, acceptance or approval. A member State of the Council of Europe may not ratify, accept or approve this Protocol unless it has, simultaneously or previously, ratified the Convention. Instruments of ratification, acceptance or approval shall be deposited with the Secretary General of the Council of Europe.

Article 8
Entry into force

1   This Protocol shall enter into force on the first day of the month following the date on which five member States of the Council of Europe have expressed their consent to be bound by the Protocol in accordance with the provisions of Article 7.

2   In respect of any member State which subsequently expresses its consent to be bound by it, the Protocol shall enter into force on the first day of the month following the date of the deposit of the instrument of ratification, acceptance or approval.

Article 9
Depositary functions

The Secretary General of the Council of Europe shall notify the member States of the Council of:

a   any signature;

b   the deposit of any instrument of ratification, acceptance or approval;

c   any date of entry into force of this Protocol in accordance with Articles 5 and 8;

d   any other act, notification or communication relating to this Protocol.

In witness whereof the undersigned, being duly authorised thereto, have signed this Protocol.

Done at Strasbourg, this 28th day of April 1983, in English and in French, both texts being equally authentic, in a single copy which shall be deposited in the archives of the Council of Europe. The Secretary General of the Council of Europe shall transmit certified copies to each member State of the Council of Europe.

Protocol No. 7
to the Convention for the Protection
of Human Rights and Fundamental Freedoms[1]

Strasbourg, 22.XI.1984

Notes

1. Headings of articles added and text amended according to the provisions of Protocol No. 11 (ETS No. 155) as from its entry into force.

The member States of the Council of Europe signatory hereto,

Being resolved to take further steps to ensure the collective enforcement of certain rights and freedoms by means of the Convention for the Protection of Human Rights and Fundamental Freedoms signed at Rome on 4 November 1950 (hereinafter referred to as 'the Convention'),

Have agreed as follows:

Article 1
Procedural safeguards relating to expulsion of aliens

1   An alien lawfully resident in the territory of a State shall not be expelled therefrom except in pursuance of a decision reached in accordance with law and shall be allowed:

a   to submit reasons against his expulsion,

b   to have his case reviewed, and

c   to be represented for these purposes before the competent authority or a person or persons designated by that authority.

2   An alien may be expelled before the exercise of his rights under paragraph 1.a, b and c of this Article, when such expulsion is necessary in the interests of public order or is grounded on reasons of national security.

Article 2
Right of appeal in criminal matters

1   Everyone convicted of a criminal offence by a tribunal shall have the right to have his conviction or sentence reviewed by a higher tribunal. The exercise of this right, including the grounds on which it may be exercised, shall be governed by law.

2   This right may be subject to exceptions in regard to offences of a minor character, as prescribed by law, or in cases in which the person concerned was tried in the first instance by the highest tribunal or was convicted following an appeal against acquittal.

Article 3
Compensation for wrongful conviction

When a person has by a final decision been convicted of a criminal offence and when subsequently his conviction has been reversed, or he has been pardoned, on the ground that a new or newly discovered fact shows conclusively that there has been a miscarriage of justice, the person who has suffered punishment as a result of such conviction shall be compensated according to the law or the practice of the state concerned, unless it is proved that the nondisclosure of the unknown fact in time is wholly or partly attributable to him.

Article 4
Right not to be tried or punished twice

1   No one shall be liable to be tried or punished again in criminal proceedings under the jurisdiction of the same state for an offence for which he has already been finally acquitted or convicted in accordance with the law and penal procedure of that state.

2   The provisions of the preceding paragraph shall not prevent the reopening of the case in accordance with the law and penal procedure of the State concerned, if there is evidence of new or newly discovered facts, or if there has been a fundamental defect in the previous proceedings, which could affect the outcome of the case.

3   No derogation from this Article shall be made under Article 15 of the Convention.

Article 5
Equality between spouses

Spouses shall enjoy equality of rights and responsibilities of a private law character between them, and in their relations with their children, as to marriage, during marriage and in the event of its dissolution. This Article shall not prevent States from taking such measures as are necessary in the interests of the children.

Article 6
Territorial applications

1   Any State may at the time of signature or when depositing its instrument of ratification, acceptance or approval, specify the territory or territories to which this Protocol shall apply and state the extent to which it undertakes that the provisions of this Protocol shall apply to this or these territories.

2   Any state may at any later date, by a declaration addressed to the Secretary-General of the Council of Europe, extend the application of this Protocol to any other territory specified in the declaration. In respect of such territory the protocol shall enter into force on the first day of the month following the expiration of a period of two months after the date of receipt by the Secretary-General of such declaration.

3   Any declaration made under the two preceding paragraphs may, in respect of any territory specified in such declaration, be withdrawn or modified by a notification addressed to the Secretary-General. The withdrawal or modification shall become effective on the first day of the month following the expiration of a period of two months after the date of receipt of such notification by the Secretary-General.

4[1]   A declaration made in accordance with this Article shall be deemed to have been made in accordance with paragraph 1 of Article 56 of the Convention.

5   The territory of any State to which this Protocol applies by virtue of ratification, acceptance or approval by that State, and each territory to which this Protocol is applied by virtue of a declaration by that State under this Article, may be treated as separate territories for the purpose of the reference in Article 1 to the territory of a State.

6[2]   Any State which has made a declaration in accordance with paragraph 1 or 2 of this Article may at any time thereafter declare on behalf of one or more of the territories to which the declaration relates that it accepts the competence of the Court to receive applications from individuals, non-governmental organisations or groups of individuals as provided in Article 34 of the Convention in respect of Articles 1 to 5 of this Protocol.

Notes
1. Text amended according to the provisions of Protocol No. 11 (ETS No. 155).
2. Text added according to the provisions of Protocol No. 11 (ETS No. 155).

Article 7[1]
Relationship to the Convention

As between the States Parties, the provisions of Article 1 to 6 of this Protocol shall be regarded as additional Articles to the Convention, and all the provisions of the Convention shall apply accordingly.

Notes
1. Text amended according to the provisions of Protocol No. 11 (ETS No. 155).

Article 8
Signature and ratification

This Protocol shall be open for signature by member States of the Council of Europe which have signed the Convention. It is subject to ratification, acceptance or approval. A member State of the Council of Europe may not ratify, accept or approve this Protocol without previously or simultaneously ratifying the Convention. Instruments of ratification, acceptance or approval shall be deposited with the Secretary General of the Council of Europe.

Article 9
Entry into force

1   This Protocol shall enter into force on the first day of the month following the expiration of a period of two months after the date on which seven member States of the Council of Europe have expressed their consent to be bound by the Protocol in accordance with the provisions of Article 8.

2   In respect of any member State which subsequently expresses its consent to be bound by it, the Protocol shall enter into force on the first day of the month following the expiration of a period of two months after the date of the deposit of the instrument of ratification, acceptance or approval.

Article 10
Depositary functions

The Secretary General of the Council of Europe shall notify all the member States of the Council of Europe of:

a   any signature;

b   the deposit of any instrument of ratification, acceptance or approval;

c   any date of entry into force of this Protocol in accordance with Articles 6 and 9;

d   any other act, notification or declaration relating to this Protocol.

In witness whereof the undersigned, being duly authorised thereto, have signed this Protocol.

Done at Strasbourg this 22nd day of November 1984, in English and French, both texts being equally authentic, in a single copy which shall be deposited in the archives of the Council of Europe. The Secretary General of the Council of Europe shall transmit certified copies to each member State of the Council of Europe.

European Court of Human Rights
Rules of Court

(4 November 1998)

The European Court of Human Rights,

Having regard to the Convention for the Protection of Human Rights and Fundamental Freedoms and the Protocols thereto,

Makes the present Rules:

Rule 1
(Definitions)

For the purposes of these Rules unless the context otherwise requires:

(*a*) the term 'Convention' means the Convention for the Protection of Human Rights and Fundamental Freedoms and the Protocols thereto;

(*b*) the expression 'plenary Court' means the European Court of Human Rights sitting in plenary session;

(*c*) the term 'Grand Chamber' means the Grand Chamber of seventeen judges constituted in pursuance of Article 27 § 1 of the Convention;

(*d*) the term 'Section' means a Chamber set up by the plenary Court for a fixed period in pursuance of Article 26 (*b*) of the Convention and the expression 'President of the Section' means the judge elected by the plenary Court in pursuance of Article 26 (*c*) of the Convention as President of such a Section;

(*e*) the term 'Chamber' means any Chamber of seven judges constituted in pursuance of Article 27 § 1 of the Convention and the expression 'President of the Chamber' means the judge presiding over such a 'Chamber';

(*f*) the term 'Committee' means a Committee of three judges set up in pursuance of Article 27 § 1 of the Convention;

(*g*) the term 'Court' means either the plenary Court, the Grand Chamber, a Section, a Chamber, a Committee or the panel of five judges referred to in Article 43 § 2 of the Convention;

(*h*) the expression '*ad hoc* judge' means any person, other than an elected judge, chosen by a Contracting Party in pursuance of Article 27 § 2 of the Convention to sit as a member of the Grand Chamber or as a member of a Chamber;

(*i*) the terms 'judge' and 'judges' mean the judges elected by the Parliamentary Assembly of the Council of Europe or *ad hoc* judges;

(*j*) the term 'Judge Rapporteur' means a judge appointed to carry out the tasks provided for in Rules 48 and 49;

(*k*) the term 'Registrar' denotes the Registrar of the Court or the Registrar of a Section according to the context;

(*l*) the terms 'party' and 'parties' mean

— the applicant or respondent Contracting Parties;

— the applicant (the person, non-governmental organisation or group of individuals) that lodged a complaint under Article 34 of the Convention;

(*m*) the expression 'third party' means any Contracting State or any person concerned who, as provided for in Article 36 §§ 1 and 2 of the Convention, has exercised its right or been invited to submit written comments or take part in a hearing;

(*n*)   the expression 'Committee of Ministers' means the Committee of Ministers of the Council of Europe;

(*o*)   the terms 'former Court' and 'Commission' mean respectively the European Court and European Commission of Human Rights set up under former Article 19 of the Convention.

TITLE I
ORGANISATION AND WORKING OF THE COURT

Chapter I
Judges

Rule 2
(Calculation of term of office)

1.   The duration of the term of office of an elected judge shall be calculated as from the date of election. However, when a judge is re-elected on the expiry of the term of office or is elected to replace a judge whose term of office has expired or is about to expire, the duration of the term of office shall, in either case, be calculated as from the date of such expiry.

2.   In accordance with Article 23 § 5 of the Convention, a judge elected to replace a judge whose term of office has not expired shall hold office for the remainder of the predecessor's term.

3.   In accordance with Article 23 § 7 of the Convention, an elected judge shall hold office until a successor has taken the oath or made the declaration provided for in Rule 3.

Rule 3
(Oath or solemn declaration)

1.   Before taking up office, each elected judge shall, at the first sitting of the plenary Court at which the judge is present or, in case of need, before the President of the Court, take the following oath or make the following solemn declaration:

'I swear'—or 'I solemnly declare'—'that I will exercise my functions as a judge honourably, independently and impartially and that I will keep secret all deliberations.'

2.   This act shall be recorded in minutes.

Rule 4
(Incompatible activities)

In accordance with Article 21 § 3 of the Convention, the judges shall not during their term of office engage in any political or administrative activity or any professional activity which is incompatible with their independence or impartiality or with the demands of a full-time office. Each judge shall declare to the President of the Court any additional activity. In the event of a disagreement between the President and the judge concerned, any question arising shall be decided by the plenary Court.

Rule 5
(Precedence)

1.   Elected judges shall take precedence after the President and Vice-Presidents of the Court and the Presidents of the Sections, according to the date of their election; in the event of re-election, even if it is not an immediate re-election, the length of time during which the judge concerned previously held office as a judge shall be taken into account.

2.   Vice-Presidents of the Court elected to office on the same date shall take precedence according to the length of time they have served as judges. If the length of time they have served as judges is the same, they shall take precedence according to age. The same Rule shall apply to Presidents of Sections.

3.   Judges who have served the same length of time as judges shall take precedence according to age.

4.   *Ad hoc* judges shall take precedence after the elected judges according to age.

Rule 6
(Resignation)

Resignation of a judge shall be notified to the President of the Court, who shall transmit it to the Secretary General of the Council of Europe. Subject to the provisions of Rules 24§ 3 *in fine* and 26 § 2, resignation shall constitute vacation of office.

Rule 7
(Dismissal from office)

No judge may be dismissed from his or her office unless the other judges, meeting in plenary session, decide by a majority of two-thirds of the elected judges in office that he or she has ceased to fulfil the required conditions. He or she must first be heard by the plenary Court. Any judge may set in motion the procedure for dismissal from office.

Chapter II
Presidency of the Court

Rule 8
(Election of the President and Vice-Presidents of the Court and the Presidents and Vice-Presidents of the Sections)

1.   The plenary Court shall elect its President, two Vice-Presidents and the Presidents of the Sections for a period of three years, provided that such period shall not exceed the duration of their terms of office as judges. They may be re-elected.

2.   Each Section shall likewise elect for a renewable period of three years a Vice-President, who shall replace the President of the Section if the latter is unable to carry out his or her duties.

3.   The Presidents and Vice-Presidents shall continue to hold office until the election of their successors.

4.   If a President or a Vice-President ceases to be a member of the Court or resigns from office before its normal expiry, the plenary Court or the relevant Section, as the case may be, shall elect a successor for the remainder of the term of that office.

5.   The elections referred to in this Rule shall be by secret ballot; only the elected judges who are present shall take part. if no judge receives an absolute majority of the elected judges present, a ballot shall take place between the two judges who have received most votes. In the event of a tie, preference shall be given to the judge having precedence in accordance with Rule 5.

Rule 9
(Functions of the President of the Court)

1.   The President of the Court shall direct the work and administration of the Court. The President shall represent the Court and, in particular, be responsible for its relations with the authorities of the Council of Europe.

2.   The President shall preside at plenary meetings of the Court, meetings of the Grand Chamber and meetings of the panel of five judges.

3.   The President shall not take part in the consideration of cases being heard by Chambers except where he or she is the judge elected in respect of a Contracting Party concerned.

Rule 10
(Functions of the Vice-Presidents of the Court)

The Vice-Presidents of the Court shall assist the President of the Court. They shall take the place of the President if the latter is unable to carry out his or her duties or the office of President is vacant, or at the request of the President. They shall also act as Presidents of Sections.

Rule 11
(Replacement of the President and the Vice-Presidents)

If the President and the Vice-Presidents of the Court are at the same time unable to carry out their duties or if their offices are at the same time vacant, the office of President of the Court shall be assumed by a President of a Section or, if none is available, by another elected judge, in accordance with the order of precedence provided for in Rule 5.

Rule 12
(Presidency of Sections and Chambers)

The Presidents of the Sections shall preside at the sittings of the Section and Chambers of which they are members. The Vice-Presidents of the Sections shall take their place if they are unable to carry out their duties or if the office of President of the Section concerned is vacant, or at the request of the President of the Section. Failing that, the judges of the Section and the Chambers shall take their place, in the order of precedence provided for in Rule 5.

Rule 13
(Inability to preside)

Judges of the Court may not preside in cases in which the Contracting Party of which they are nationals or in respect of which they were elected is a party.

Rule 14
(Balanced representation of the sexes)

In relation to the making of appointments governed by this and the following chapter of the present Rules, the Court shall pursue a policy aimed at securing a balanced representation of the sexes.

Chapter III
The Registry

Rule 15
(Election of the Registrar)

1.   The plenary Court shall elect its Registrar. The candidates shall be of high moral character and must possess the legal, managerial and linguistic knowledge and experience necessary to carry out the functions attaching to the post.

2.   The Registrar shall be elected for a term of five years and may be re-elected. The Registrar may not be dismissed from office, unless the judges, meeting in plenary session, decide by a majority of two-thirds of the elected judges in office that the person concerned has ceased to fulfil the required conditions. He or she must first be heard by the plenary Court. Any judge may set in motion the procedure for dismissal from office.

3.   The elections referred to in this Rule shall be by secret ballot; only the elected judges who are present shall take part. If no candidate receives an absolute majority of the elected judges present, a ballot shall take place between the two candidates who have received most votes. In the event of a tie, preference shall be given, firstly, to the female candidate, if any, and, secondly, to the older candidate.

4.   Before taking up office, the Registrar shall take the following oath or make the following solemn declaration before the plenary Court or, if need be, before the President of the Court:

'I swear'—or 'I solemnly declare'—'that I will exercise loyally, discreetly and conscientiously the functions conferred upon me as Registrar of the European Court of Human Rights.'

This act shall be recorded in minutes.

Rule 16
(Election of the Deputy Registrars)

1.   The plenary Court shall also elect two Deputy Registrars on the conditions and

in the manner and for the term prescribed in the preceding Rule. The procedure for dismissal from office provided for in respect of the Registrar shall likewise apply. The Court shall first consult the Registrar in both these matters.

2.   Before taking up office, a Deputy Registrar shall take an oath or make a solemn declaration before the plenary Court or, if need be, before the President of the Court, in terms similar to those prescribed in respect of the Registrar. This act shall be recorded in minutes.

Rule 17
(Functions of the Registrar)

1.   The Registrar shall assist the Court in the performance of its functions and shall be responsible for the organisation and activities of the Registry under the authority of the President of the Court.

2.   The Registrar shall have the custody of the archives of the Court and shall be the channel for all communications and notifications made by, or addressed to, the Court in connection with the cases brought or to be brought before it.

3.   The Registrar shall, subject to the duty of discretion attaching to this office, reply to requests for information concerning the work of the Court, in particular to enquiries from the press.

4.   General instructions drawn up by the Registrar, and approved by the President of the Court, shall regulate the working of the Registry.

Rule 18
(Organisation of the Registry)

1.   The Registry shall consist of Section Registries equal to the number of Sections set up by the Court and of the departments necessary to provide the legal and administrative services required by the Court.

2.   The Section Registrar shall assist the Section in the performance of its functions and may be assisted by a Deputy Section Registrar.

3.   The officials of the Registry, including the legal secretaries but not the Registrar and the Deputy Registrars, shall be appointed by the Secretary General of the Council of Europe with the agreement of the President of the Court or of the Registrar acting on the President's instructions.

Chapter IV
The Working of the Court

Rule 19
(Seat of the Court)

1.   The seat of the Court shall be at the seat of the Council of Europe at Strasbourg. The Court may, however, if it considers it expedient, perform its functions elsewhere in the territories of the member States of the Council of Europe.

2.   The Court may decide, at any stage of the examination of an application, that it is necessary that an investigation or any other function be carried out elsewhere by it or one or more of its members.

Rule 20
(Sessions of the plenary Court)

1.   The plenary sessions of the Court shall be convened by the President of the Court whenever the performance of its functions under the Convention and under these Rules so requires. The

President of the Court shall convene a plenary session if at least one-third of the members of the Court so request, and in any event once a year to consider administrative matters.

2. The quorum of the plenary Court shall be two-thirds of the elected judges in office.

3. If there is no quorum, the President shall adjourn the sitting.

Rule 21
(Other sessions of the Court)

1. The Grand Chamber, the Chambers and the Committees shall sit full time. On a proposal by the President, however, the Court shall fix session periods each year.

2. Outside those periods the Grand Chamber and the Chambers shall be convened by their Presidents in cases of urgency.

Rule 22
(Deliberations)

1. The Court shall deliberate in private. Its deliberations shall remain secret.

2. Only the judges shall take part in the deliberations. The Registrar or the designated substitute, as well as such other officials of the Registry and interpreters whose assistance is deemed necessary, shall be present. No other person may be admitted except by special decision of the Court.

3. Before a vote is taken on any matter in the Court, the President may request the judges to state their opinions on it.

Rule 23
(Votes)

1. The decisions of the Court shall be taken by a majority of the judges present. In the event of a tie, a fresh vote shall be taken and, if there is still a tie, the President shall have a casting vote. This paragraph shall apply unless otherwise provided for in these Rules.

2. The decisions and judgments of the Grand Chamber and the Chambers shall be adopted by a majority of the sitting judges. Abstentions shall not be allowed in final votes on the admissibility and merits of cases.

3. As a general rule, votes shall be taken by a show of hands. The President may take a roll-call vote, in reverse order of precedence.

4. Any matter that is to be voted upon shall be formulated in precise terms.

Chapter V
The Chambers

Rule 24
(Composition of the Grand Chamber)

1. The Grand Chamber shall be composed of seventeen judges and three substitute judges.

2. The Grand Chamber shall be constituted for three years with effect from the election of the presidential office-holders referred to in Rule 8.

3. The Grand Chamber shall include the President and Vice-Presidents of the Court and the Presidents of the Sections. In order to complete the Grand Chamber, the plenary Court shall, on a proposal by its President, divide all the other judges into two groups which shall alternate every nine months and whose membership shall be geographically as balanced as possible and reflect the different legal systems among the Contracting Parties. The judges and substitute judges who are to hear each case referred to the Grand Chamber during each nine-month period shall be designated in rotation within each group; they shall remain members of the Grand Chamber until the proceedings have been completed, even after their terms of office as judges have expired.

4.   If he or she does not sit as a member of the Grand Chamber by virtue of paragraph 3 of the present Rule, the judge elected in respect of any Contracting Party concerned shall sit as an *ex officio* member of the Grand Chamber in accordance with Article 27 §§ 2 and 3 of the Convention.

5.   (*a*)   Where any President of a Section is unable to sit as a member of the Grand Chamber, he or she shall be replaced by the Vice-President of the Section.

   (*b*)   If other judges are prevented from sitting, they shall be replaced by the substitute judges in the order in which the latter were selected under paragraph 3 of the present Rule.

   (*c*)   If there are not enough substitute judges in the group concerned to complete the Grand Chamber, the substitute judges lacking shall be designated by a drawing of lots amongst the members of the other group.

6.   (*a*)   The panel of five judges of the Grand Chamber called upon to consider requests submitted under Article 43 of the Convention shall be composed of

   —   the President of the Court,

   —   the Presidents or, if they are prevented from sitting, the Vice-Presidents of the Sections other than the Section from which was constituted the Chamber that dealt with the case whose referral to the Grand Chamber is being sought,

   —   one further judge designated in rotation from among the judges other than those who dealt with the case in the Chamber.

   (*b*)   No judge elected in respect of, or who is a national of, a Contracting Party concerned may be a member of the panel.

   (*c*)   Any member of the panel unable to sit shall be replaced by another judge who did not deal with the case in the Chamber, who shall be designated in rotation.

Rule 25
(Setting up of Sections)

1.   The Chambers provided for in Article 26 (*b*) of the Convention (referred to in

these Rules as 'Sections') shall be set up by the plenary Court, on a proposal by its President, for a period of three years with effect from the election of the presidential office-holders of the Court under Rule 8. There shall be at least four Sections.

2.   Each judge shall be a member of a Section. The composition of the Sections shall be geographically and gender balanced and shall reflect the different legal systems among the Contracting Parties.

3.   Where a judge ceases to be a member of the Court before the expiry of the period for which the Section has been constituted, the judge's place in the Section shall be taken by his or her successor as a member of the Court.

4.   The President of the Court may exceptionally make modifications to the composition of the Sections if circumstances so require.

5.   On a proposal by the President, the plenary Court may constitute an additional Section.

Rule 26
(Constitution of Chambers)

1. The Chambers of seven judges provided for in Article 27 § 1 of the Convention for the consideration of cases brought before the Court shall be constituted from the Sections as follows.

   (*a*)   The Chamber shall in each case include the President of the Section and the judge elected in respect of any Contracting Party concerned. If the latter judge is not a member of the Section to which the application has been assigned under Rule 51 or 52, he or she shall sit as an *ex officio* member of the Chamber in accordance with Article 27 § 2 of the Convention. Rule 29 shall apply if that judge is unable to sit or withdraws.

(*b*) The other members of the Chamber shall be designated by the President of the Section in rotation from among the members of the relevant Section.

(*c*) The members of the Section who are not so designated shall sit in the case as substitute judges.

2. Even after the end of their terms of office judges shall continue to deal with cases in which they have participated in the consideration of the merits.

Rule 27
(Committees)

1. Committees composed of three judges belonging to the same Section shall be set up under Article 27 § 1 of the Convention. After consulting the Presidents of the Sections, the President of the Court shall decide on the number of Committees to be set up.

2. The Committees shall be constituted for a period of twelve months by rotation among the members of each Section, excepting the President of the Section.

3. The judges of the Section who are not members of a Committee may be called upon to take the place of members who are unable to sit.

4. Each Committee shall be chaired by the member having precedence in the Section.

Rule 28
(Inability to sit, withdrawal or exemption)

1. Any judge who is prevented from taking part in sittings shall, as soon as possible,

give notice to the President of the Chamber.

2. A judge may not take part in the consideration of any case in which he or she has a personal interest or has previously acted either as the Agent, advocate or adviser of a party or of a person having an interest in the case, or as a member of a tribunal or commission of inquiry, or in any other capacity.

3. If a judge withdraws for one of the said reasons, or for some special reason, he or she shall inform the President of the Chamber, who shall exempt the judge from sitting.

4. If the President of the Chamber considers that a reason exists for a judge to withdraw, he or she shall consult with the judge concerned; in the event of disagreement, the Chamber shall decide.

Rule 29
(Ad hoc *judges*)

1. If the judge elected in respect of a Contracting Party concerned is unable to sit in the Chamber or withdraws, the President of the Chamber shall invite that Party to indicate within thirty days whether it wishes to appoint to sit as judge either another elected judge or, as an *ad hoc* judge, any other person possessing the qualifications required by Article 21 § 1 of the Convention and, if so, to state at the same time the name of the person appointed. The same rule shall apply if the person so appointed is unable to sit or withdraws.

2. The Contracting Party concerned shall be presumed to have waived its right of appointment if it does not reply within thirty days.

3. An *ad hoc* judge shall, at the opening of the first sitting fixed for the consideration of the case after the judge has been appointed, take the oath or make the solemn declaration provided for in Rule 3. This act shall be recorded in minutes.

Rule 30
(Common interest)

1. If several applicant or respondent Contracting Parties have a common interest, the President of the Court may invite them to agree to appoint a single elected judge or *ad hoc* judge in

accordance with Article 27 § 2 of the Convention. If the Parties are unable to agree, the President shall choose by lot, from among the persons proposed as judges by these Parties, the judge called upon to sit *ex officio.*

2.   In the event of a dispute as to the existence of a common interest, the plenary Court shall decide.

TITLE II
PROCEDURE

Chapter I
General Rules

Rule 31
(Possibility of particular derogations)

The provisions of this Title shall not prevent the Court from derogating from them for the consideration of a particular case after having consulted the parties where appropriate.

Rule 32
(Practice directions)

The President of the Court may issue practice directions, notably in relation to such matters as appearance at hearings and the filing of pleadings and other documents.

Rule 33
(Public character of proceedings)

1.   Hearings shall be public unless, in accordance with paragraph 2 of this Rule, the Chamber in exceptional circumstances decides otherwise, either of its own motion or at the request of a party or any other person concerned.

2.   The press and the public may be excluded from all or part of a hearing in the interest of morals, public order or national security in a democratic society, where the interests of juveniles or the protection of the private life of the parties so require, or to the extent strictly necessary in the opinion of the Chamber in special circumstances where publicity would prejudice the interests of justice.

3.   Following registration of an application, all documents deposited with the Registry, with the exception of those deposited within the framework of friendly-settlement negotiations as provided for in Rule 62, shall be accessible to the public unless the President of the Chamber, for the reasons set out in paragraph 2 of this Rule, decides otherwise, either of his or her own motion or at the request of a party or any other person concerned.

4.   Any request for confidentiality made under paragraphs 1 or 3 above must give reasons and specify whether the hearing or the documents, as the case may be, should be inaccessible to the public in whole or in part.

Rule 34
(Use of languages)

1.   The official languages of the Court shall be English and French.

2.   Before the decision on the admissibility of an application is taken, all communications with and pleadings by applicants under Article 34 of the Convention or their representatives, if not in one of the Court's official languages, shall be in one of the official languages of the Contracting Parties.

3.   (*a*)   All communications with and pleadings by such applicants or their representatives in respect of a hearing, or after a case has been declared admissible, shall be in one of the Court's official languages, unless the President of the Chamber authorises the continued use of the official language of a Contracting Party.

(*b*) If such leave is granted, the Registrar shall make the necessary arrangements for the oral or written translation of the applicant's observations or statements.

4. (*a*) All communications with and pleadings by Contracting Parties or third parties shall be in one of the Court's official languages. The President of the Chamber may authorise the use of a non-official language.

(*b*) If such leave is granted, it shall be the responsibility of the requesting party to provide for and bear the costs of interpreting or translation into English or French of the oral arguments or written statements made.

5. The President of the Chamber may invite the respondent Contracting Party to provide a translation of its written submissions in the or an official language of that Party in order to facilitate the applicant's understanding of those submissions.

6. Any witness, expert or other person appearing before the Court may use his or her own language if he or she does not have sufficient knowledge of either of the two official languages. In that event the Registrar shall make the necessary arrangements for interpreting or translation.

Rule 35
(Representation of Contracting Parties)

The Contracting Parties shall be represented by Agents, who may have the assistance of advocates or advisers.

Rule 36
(Representation of applicants)

1. Persons, non-governmental organisations or groups of individuals may initially present applications under Article 34 of the Convention themselves or through a representative appointed under paragraph 4 of this Rule.

2. Following notification of the application to the respondent Contracting Party under Rule 54 § 3 (*b*), the President of the Chamber may direct that the applicant should be represented in accordance with paragraph 4 of this Rule.

3. The applicant must be so represented at any hearing decided on by the Chamber or for the purposes of the proceedings following a decision to declare the application admissible, unless the President of the Chamber decides otherwise.

4. (*a*) The representative of the applicant shall be an advocate authorised to practise in any of the Contracting Parties and resident in the territory of one of them, or any other person approved by the President of the Chamber.

(*b*) The President of the Chamber may, where representation would otherwise be obligatory, grant leave to the applicant to present his or her own case, subject, if necessary, to being assisted by an advocate or other approved representative.

(*c*) In exceptional circumstances and at any stage of the procedure, the President of the Chamber may, where he or she considers that the circumstances or the conduct of the advocate or other person appointed under the preceding sub-paragraphs so warrant, direct that the latter may no longer represent or assist the applicant and that the applicant should seek alternative representation.

5. The advocate or other approved representative, or the applicant in person if he or she seeks leave to present his or her own case, must have an adequate knowledge of one of the Court's official languages. However, leave to use a non-official language may be given by the President of the Chamber under Rule 34 § 3.

Rule 37
(Communications, notifications and summonses)

1. Communications or notifications addressed to the Agents or advocates of the parties shall be deemed to have been addressed to the parties.

2.   If, for any communication, notification or summons addressed to persons other than the Agents or advocates of the parties, the Court considers it necessary to have the assistance of the Government of the State on whose territory such communication, notification or summons is to have effect, the President of the Court shall apply directly to that Government in order to obtain the necessary facilities.

3.   The same rule shall apply when the Court desires to make or arrange for the making of an investigation on the spot in order to establish the facts or to procure evidence or when it orders the appearance of a person who is resident in, or will have to cross, that territory.

Rule 38
(Written pleadings)

1.   No written observations or other documents may be filed after the time-limit set by the President of the Chamber or the Judge Rapporteur, as the case may be, in accordance with these Rules. No written observations or other documents filed outside that time-limit or contrary to any practice direction issued under Rule 32 shall be included in the case file unless the President of the Chamber decides otherwise.

2.   For the purposes of observing the time-limit referred to in paragraph 1, the material date is the certified date of dispatch of the document or, if there is none, the actual date of receipt at the Registry.

Rule 39
(Interim measures)

1.   The Chamber or, where appropriate, its President may, at the request of a party or of any other person concerned, or of its own motion, indicate to the parties any interim measure which it considers should be adopted in the interests of the parties or of the proper conduct of the proceedings before it.

2.   Notice of these measures shall be given to the Committee of Ministers.

3.   The Chamber may request information from the parties on any matter connected with the implementation of any interim measure it has indicated.

Rule 40
(Urgent notification of an application)

In any case of urgency the Registrar, with the authorisation of the President of the Chamber, may, without prejudice to the taking of any other procedural steps and by any available means, inform a Contracting Party concerned in an application of the introduction of the application and of a summary of its objects.

Rule 41
(Case priority)

The Chamber shall deal with applications in the order in which they become ready for examination. It may, however, decide to give priority to a particular application.

Rule 42
(Measures for taking evidence)

1.   The Chamber may, at the request of a party or a third party, or of its own motion, obtain any evidence which it considers capable of providing clarification of the facts of the case. The Chamber may, *inter alia,* request the parties to produce documentary evidence and decide to hear as a witness or expert or in any other capacity any person whose evidence or statements seem likely to assist it in the carrying out of its tasks.

2.   The Chamber may, at any time during the proceedings, depute one or more of its members or of the other judges of the Court to conduct an inquiry, carry out an investigation on the spot or take evidence in some other manner. It may appoint independent external experts to assist such a delegation.

3.   The Chamber may ask any person or institution of its choice to obtain information, express an opinion or make a report on any specific point.

4.   The parties shall assist the Chamber, or its delegation, in implementing any measures for taking evidence.

5.   Where a report has been drawn up or some other measure taken in accordance with the preceding paragraphs at the request of an applicant or respondent Contracting Party, the costs entailed shall be borne by that Party unless the Chamber decides otherwise. In other cases the Chamber shall decide whether such costs are to be borne by the Council of Europe or awarded against the applicant or third party at whose request the report was drawn up or the other measure was taken. In all cases the costs shall be taxed by the President of the Chamber.

Rule 43
(Joinder and simultaneous examination of applications)

1.   The Chamber may, either at the request of the parties or of its own motion, order the joinder of two or more applications.

2.   The President of the Chamber may, after consulting the parties, order that the proceedings in applications assigned to the same Chamber be conducted simultaneously, without prejudice to the decision of the Chamber on the joinder of the applications.

Rule 44
(Striking out and restoration to the list)

1.   When an applicant Contracting Party notifies the Registrar of its intention not to proceed with the case, the Chamber may strike the application out of the Court's list under Article 37 of the Convention if the other Contracting Party or Parties concerned in the case agree to such discontinuance.

2.   The decision to strike out an application which has been declared admissible shall be given in the form of a judgment. The President of the Chamber shall forward that judgment, once it has become final, to the Committee of Ministers in order to allow the latter to supervise, in accordance with Article 46 § 2 of the Convention, the execution of any undertakings which may have been attached to the discontinuance, friendly settlement or solution of the matter.

3.   When an application has been struck out, the costs shall be at the discretion of the Court. If an award of costs is made in a decision striking out an application which has not been declared admissible, the President of the Chamber shall forward the decision to the Committee of Ministers.

4.   The Court may restore an application to its list if it concludes that exceptional circumstances justify such a course.

Chapter II
Institution of Proceedings

Rule 45
(Signatures)

1.   Any application made under Articles 33 or 34 of the Convention shall be submitted in writing and shall be signed by the applicant or by the applicant's representative.

2.   Where an application is made by a non-governmental organisation or by a group of individuals, it shall be signed by those persons competent to represent that organisation or group. The Chamber or Committee concerned shall determine any question as to whether the persons who have signed an application are competent to do so.

3.   Where applicants are represented in accordance with Rule 36, a power of attorney or written authority to act shall be supplied by their representative or representatives.

Rule 46
(Contents of an inter-State application)

Any Contracting Party or Parties intending to bring a case before the Court under Article 33 of the Convention shall file with the registry an application setting out

(*a*)   the name of the Contracting Party against which the application is made;

(*b*)   a statement of the facts;

(*c*)   a statement of the alleged violation(s) of the Convention and the relevant arguments;

(*d*)   a statement on compliance with the admissibility criteria (exhaustion of domestic remedies and the six-month rule) laid down in Article 35 § 1 of the Convention;

(*e*)   the object of the application and a general indication of any claims for just satisfaction made under Article 41 of the Convention on behalf of the alleged injured party or parties; and

(*f*)   the name and address of the person(s) appointed as Agent;

and accompanied by

(*g*)   copies of any relevant documents and in particular the decisions, whether judicial or not, relating to the object of the application.

Rule 47
(Contents of an individual application)

1.   Any application under Article 34 of the Convention shall be made on the application form provided by the registry, unless the President of the Section concerned decides otherwise. It shall set out

(*a*)   the name, date of birth, nationality, sex, occupation and address of the applicant;

(*b*)   the name, occupation and address of the representative, if any;

(*c*)   the name of the Contracting Party or Parties against which the application is made;

(*d*)   a succinct statement of the facts;

(*e*)   a succinct statement of the alleged violation(s) of the Convention and the relevant arguments;

(*f*)   a succinct statement on the applicant's compliance with the admissibility criteria (exhaustion of domestic remedies and the six-month rule) laid down in Article 35 § 1 of the Convention; and

(*g*)   the object of the application as well as a general indication of any claims for just satisfaction which the applicant may wish to make under Article 41 of the Convention;

and be accompanied by

(*h*)   copies of any relevant documents and in particular the decisions, whether judicial or not, relating to the object of the application.

2.   Applicants shall furthermore

(*a*)   provide information, notably the documents and decisions referred to in paragraph I (h) above, enabling it to be shown that the admissibility criteria (exhaustion of domestic remedies and the six-month rule) laid down in Article 35 § 1 of the Convention have been satisfied; and

(*b*)   indicate whether they have submitted their complaints to any other procedure of international investigation or settlement.

3.   Applicants who do not wish their identity to be disclosed to the public shall so indicate and shall submit a statement of the reasons justifying such a departure from the normal rule of public access to information in proceedings before the Court. The President of the Chamber may authorise anonymity in exceptional and duly justified cases.

4.   Failure to comply with the requirements set out in paragraphs 1 and 2 above may result in the application not being registered and examined by the Court.

5.   The date of introduction of the application shall as a general rule be considered to be the date of the first communication from the applicant setting out, even summarily, the object of the application. The Court may for good cause nevertheless decide that a different date shall be considered to be the date of introduction.

6.   Applicants shall keep the Court informed of any change of address and of all circumstances relevant to the application.

Chapter III
Judge Rapporteurs

Rule 48
(Inter-State applications)

1.   Where an application is made under Article 33 of the Convention, the Chamber constituted to consider the case shall designate one or more of its judges as Judge Rapporteur(s), who shall submit a report on admissibility when the written observations of the Contracting Parties concerned have been received. Rule 49 § 4 shall, in so far as appropriate, be applicable to this report.

2.   After an application made under Article 33 of the Convention has been declared admissible, the Judge Rapporteur(s) shall submit such reports, drafts and other documents as may assist the Chamber in the carrying out of its functions.

Rule 49
(Individual applications)

1.   Where an application is made under Article 34 of the Convention, the President of the Section to which the case has been assigned shall designate a judge as Judge Rapporteur, who shall examine the application.

2.   In their examination of applications Judge Rapporteurs

    (*a*)   may request the parties to submit, within a specified time, any factual information, documents or other material which they consider to be relevant;

    (*b*)   shall, subject to the President of the Section directing that the case be considered by a Chamber, decide whether the application is to be considered by a Committee or by a Chamber.

3.   Where a case is considered by a Committee in accordance with Article 28 of the Convention, the report of the Judge Rapporteur shall contain

    (*a*)   a brief statement of the relevant facts;

    (*b*)   a brief statement of the reasons underlying the proposal to declare the application inadmissible or to strike it out of the list.

4.   Where a case is considered by a Chamber pursuant to Article 29 § 1 of the Convention, the report of the Judge Rapporteur shall contain

    (*a*)   a statement of the relevant facts, including any information obtained under paragraph 2 of this Rule;

    (*b*)   an indication of the issues arising under the Convention in the application;

    (*c*)   a proposal on admissibility and on any other action to be taken, together, if need be, with a provisional opinion on the merits.

5.   After an application made under Article 34 of the Convention has been declared admissible, the Judge Rapporteur shall submit such reports, drafts and other documents as may assist the Chamber in the carrying out of its functions.

Rule 50
(Grand Chamber proceedings)

Where a case has been submitted to the Grand Chamber either under Article 30 or under Article 43 of the Convention, the President of the Grand Chamber shall designate as Judge Rapporteur(s) one or, in the case of an inter-State application, one or more of its members.

Chapter IV
Proceedings on Admissibility

Inter-State applications
Rule 51

1.   When an application is made under Article 33 of the Convention, the President of the Court shall immediately give notice of the application to the respondent Contracting Party and shall assign the application to one of the Sections.

2.   In accordance with Rule 26 § 1 (*a*), the judges elected in respect of the applicant and respondent Contracting Parties shall sit as *ex officio* members of the Chamber constituted to consider the case. Rule 30 shall apply if the application has been brought by several Contracting Parties or if applications with the same object brought by several Contracting Parties are being examined jointly under Rule 43 § 2.

3.   On assignment of the case to a Section, the President of the Section shall constitute the Chamber in accordance with Rule 26 § 1 and shall invite the respondent Contracting Party to submit its observations in writing on the admissibility of the application. The observations so obtained shall be communicated by the Registrar to the applicant Contracting Party, which may submit written observations in reply.

4.   Before ruling on the admissibility of the application, the Chamber may decide to invite the parties to submit further observations in writing.

5.   A hearing on the admissibility shall be held if one or more of the Contracting Parties concerned so requests or if the Chamber so decides of its own motion.

6.   After consulting the Parties, the President of the Chamber shall fix the written and, where appropriate, oral procedure and for that purpose shall lay down the time-limit within which any written observations are to be filed.

7.   In its deliberations the Chamber shall take into consideration the report submitted by the Judge Rapporteur(s) under Rule 48 § 1.

Individual applications

Rule 52
(Assignment of applications to the Sections)

1.   Any application made under Article 34 of the Convention shall be assigned to a Section by the President of the Court, who in so doing shall endeavour to ensure a fair distribution of cases between the Sections.

2.   The Chamber of seven judges provided for in Article 27 § 1 of the Convention shall be constituted by the President of the Section concerned in accordance with Rule 26 § 1 once it has been decided that the application is to be considered by a Chamber.

3.   Pending the constitution of a Chamber in accordance with the preceding paragraph, the President of the Section shall exercise any powers conferred on the President of the Chamber by these Rules.

Rule 53
(Procedure before a Committee)

1.   In its deliberations the Committee shall take into consideration the report submitted by the Judge Rapporteur under Rule 49 § 3.

2. The Judge Rapporteur, if he or she is not a member of the Committee, may be invited to attend the deliberations of the Committee.

3. In accordance with Article 28 of the Convention, the Committee may, by a unanimous vote, declare inadmissible or strike out of the Court's list of cases an application where such a decision can be taken without further examination. This decision shall be final.

4. If no decision pursuant to paragraph 3 of the present Rule is taken, the application shall be forwarded to the Chamber constituted under Rule 52 § 2 to examine the case.

Rule 54
(Procedure before a Chamber)

1. In its deliberations the Chamber shall take into consideration the report submitted by the Judge Rapporteur under Rule 49 § 4.

2. The Chamber may at once declare the application inadmissible or strike it out of the Court's list of cases.

3. Alternatively, the Chamber may decide to

   (*a*) request the parties to submit any factual information, documents or other material which it considers to be relevant;

   (*b*) give notice of the application to the respondent Contracting Party and invite that Party to submit written observations on the application;

   (*c*) invite the parties to submit further observations in writing.

4. Before taking its decision on admissibility, the Chamber may decide, either at the request of the parties or of its own motion, to hold a hearing. In that event, unless the Chamber shall exceptionally decide otherwise, the parties shall be invited also to address the issues arising in relation to the merits of the application.

5. The President of the Chamber shall fix the procedure, including time-limits, in relation to any decisions taken by the Chamber under paragraphs 3 and 4 of this Rule.

Inter-State and individual applications

Rule 55
(Pleas of inadmissibility)

Any plea of inadmissibility must, in so far as its character and the circumstances permit, be raised by the respondent Contracting Party in its written or oral observations on the admissibility of the application submitted as provided in Rule 51 or 54, as the case may be.

Rule 56
(Decision of a Chamber)

1. The decision of the Chamber shall state whether it was taken unanimously or by a majority and shall be accompanied or followed by reasons.

2. The decision of the Chamber shall be communicated by the Registrar to the applicant and to the Contracting Party or Parties concerned.

Rule 57
(Language of the decision)

1. Unless the Court decides that a decision shall be given in both official languages, all decisions shall be given either in English or in French. Decisions given shall be accessible to the public.

2. Publication of such decisions in the official reports of the Court, as provided for in Rule 78, shall be in both official languages of the Court.

Chapter V
Proceedings after the Admission of an Application

Rule 58
(Inter-State applications)

1.   Once the Chamber has decided to admit an application made under Article 33 of the Convention, the President of the Chamber shall, after consulting the Contracting Parties concerned, lay down the time-limits for the filing of written observations on the merits and for the production of any further evidence. The President may however, with the agreement of the Contracting Parties concerned, direct that a written procedure is to be dispensed with.

2.   A hearing on the merits shall be held if one or more of the Contracting Parties concerned so requests or if the Chamber so decides of its own motion. The President of the Chamber shall fix the oral procedure.

3.   In its deliberations the Chamber shall take into consideration any reports, drafts and other documents submitted by the Judge Rapporteur(s) under Rule 48 § 2.

Rule 59
(Individual applications)

1.   Once the Chamber has decided to admit an application made under Article 34 of the Convention, it may invite the parties to submit further evidence and written observations.

2.   A hearing on the merits shall be held if the Chamber so decides of its own motion or, provided that no hearing also addressing the merits has been held at the admissibility stage under Rule 54 § 4, if one of the parties so requests. However, the Chamber may exceptionally decide that the discharging of its functions under Article 38 § 1 (*a*) of the Convention does not require a hearing to be held.

3.   The President of the Chamber shall, where appropriate, fix the written and oral procedure.

4.   In its deliberations the Chamber shall take into consideration any reports, drafts and other documents submitted by the Judge Rapporteur under Rule 49 § 5.

Rule 60
(Claims for just satisfaction)

1.   Any claim which the applicant Contracting Party or the applicant may wish to make for just satisfaction under Article 41 of the Convention shall, unless the President of the Chamber directs otherwise, be set out in the written observations on the merits or, if no such written observations are filed, in a special document filed no later than two months after the decision declaring the application admissible.

2.   Itemised particulars of all claims made, together with the relevant supporting documents or vouchers, shall be submitted, failing which the Chamber may reject the claim in whole or in part.

3.   The Chamber may, at any time during the proceedings, invite any party to submit comments on the claim for just satisfaction.

Rule 61
(Third-party intervention)

1.   The decision declaring an application admissible shall be notified by the Registrar to any Contracting Party one of whose nationals is an applicant in the case, as well as to the respondent Contracting Party under Rule 56 § 2.

2.   Where a Contracting Party seeks to exercise its right to submit written comments or to take part in an oral hearing, pursuant to Article 36 § 1 of the Convention, the President of the Chamber shall fix the procedure to be followed.

3.   In accordance with Article 36 § 2 of the Convention, the President of the Chamber may, in the interests of the proper administration of justice, invite or grant leave to any Contracting State which is not a party to the proceedings, or any person concerned who is not the applicant, to submit written comments or, in exceptional cases, to take part in an oral hearing. Requests for leave for this purpose must be duly reasoned and submitted in one of the official languages, within a reasonable time after the fixing of the written procedure.

4.   Any invitation or grant of leave referred to in paragraph 3 of this Rule shall be subject to any conditions, including time-limits, set by the President of the Chamber. Where such conditions are not complied with, the President may decide not to include the comments in the case file.

5.   Written comments submitted in accordance with this Rule shall be submitted in one of the official languages, save where leave to use another language has been granted under Rule 34 § 4. They shall be transmitted by the Registrar to the parties to the case, who shall be entitled, subject to any conditions, including time-limits, set by the President of the Chamber, to file written observations in reply.

Rule 62
(Friendly settlement)

1.   Since an application has been declared admissible, the Registrar, acting on the instructions of the Chamber or its President, shall enter into contact with the parties with a view to securing a friendly settlement of the matter in accordance with Article 38 § 1 (*b*) of the Convention. The Chamber shall take any steps that appear appropriate to facilitate such a settlement.

2.   In accordance with Article 38 § 2 of the Convention, the friendly settlement negotiations shall be confidential and without prejudice to the parties' arguments in the contentious proceedings. No written or oral communication and no offer or concession made in the framework of the attempt to secure a friendly settlement may be referred to or relied on in the contentious proceedings.

3.   If the Chamber is informed by the Registrar that the parties have agreed to a friendly settlement, it shall, after verifying that the settlement has been reached on the basis of respect for human rights as defined in the Convention and the protocols thereto, strike the case out of the Court's list in accordance with Rule 44 § 2.

Chapter VI
Hearings

Rule 63
(Conduct of hearings)

1.   The President of the Chamber shall direct hearings and shall prescribe the order in which Agents and advocates or advisers of the parties shall be called upon to speak.

2.   Where a fact-finding hearing is being carried out by a delegation of the Chamber under Rule 42, the head of the delegation shall conduct the hearing and the delegation shall exercise any relevant power conferred on the Chamber by the Convention or these Rules.

Rule 64
(Failure to appear at a hearing)

Where, without showing sufficient cause, a party fails to appear, the Chamber may, provided that it is satisfied that such a course is consistent with the proper administration of justice, nonetheless proceed with the hearing.

Rule 65
(Convocation of witnesses, experts and other persons; costs of their appearance)

1.   Witnesses, experts and other persons whom the Chamber or the President of the Chamber decides to hear shall be summoned by the Registrar.

2.   The summons shall indicate

(a)   the case in connection with which it has been issued;

(b)   the object of the inquiry, expert opinion or other measure ordered by the Chamber or the President of the Chamber;

(c)   any provisions for the payment of the sum due to the person summoned.

3.   If the persons concerned appear at the request or on behalf of an applicant or respondent Contracting Party, the costs of their appearance shall be borne by that Party unless the Chamber decides otherwise. In other cases, the Chamber shall decide whether such costs are to be borne by the Council of Europe or awarded against the applicant or third party at whose request the person summoned appeared. In all cases the costs shall be taxed by the President of the Chamber.

Rule 66
(Oath or solemn declaration by witnesses and experts)

1.   After the establishment of the identity of the witness and before testifying, every witness shall take the following oath or make the following solemn declaration:

'I swear'—or 'I solemnly declare upon my honour and conscience'—'that I shall speak the truth, the whole truth and nothing but the truth.'

This act shall be recorded in minutes.

2.   After the establishment of the identity of the expert and before carrying out his or her task, every expert shall take the following oath or make the following solemn declaration:

'I swear'—or 'I solemnly declare'—'that I will discharge my duty as an expert honourably and conscientiously.'

This act shall be recorded in minutes.

3.   This oath may be taken or this declaration made before the President of the Chamber, or before a judge or any public authority nominated by the President.

Rule 67
(Objection to a witness or expert; hearing of a person for information purposes)

The Chamber shall decide in the event of any dispute arising from an objection to a witness or expert. It may hear for information purposes a person who cannot be heard as a witness.

Rule 68
(Questions put during hearings)

1.   Any judge may put questions to the Agents, advocates or advisers of the parties, to the applicant, witnesses and experts, and to any other persons appearing before the Chamber.

2.   The witnesses, experts and other persons referred to in Rule 42 § 1 may, subject to the control of the President of the Chamber, be examined by the Agents and advocates or advisers of the parties. In the event of an objection as to the relevance of a question put, the President of the Chamber shall decide.

Rule 69
(Failure to appear, refusal to give evidence or false evidence)

If, without good reason, a witness or any other person who has been duly summoned fails to appear or refuses to give evidence, the Registrar shall, on being so required by the President of the Chamber, inform the Contracting Party to whose jurisdiction the witness or other person is subject. The same provisions shall apply if a witness or expert has, in the opinion of the Chamber, violated the oath or solemn declaration provided for in Rule 66.

Rule 70
(Verbatim record of hearings)

1. The Registrar shall, if the Chamber so directs, be responsible for the making of a verbatim record of a hearing. The verbatim record shall include

(*a*) the composition of the Chamber at the hearing;

(*b*) a list of those appearing before the Court, that is to say Agents, advocates and advisers of the parties and any third party taking part;

(*c*) the surnames, forenames, description and address of each witness, expert or other person heard;

(*d*) the text of statements made, questions put and replies given;

(*e*) the text of any decision delivered during the hearing by the Chamber or the President of the Chamber.

2. If all or part of the verbatim record is in a non-official language, the Registrar shall, if the Chamber so directs, arrange for its translation into one of the official languages.

3. The representatives of the parties shall receive a copy of the verbatim record in order that they may, subject to the control of the Registrar or the President of the Chamber, make corrections, but in no case may such corrections affect the sense and bearing of what was said. The Registrar shall lay down, in accordance with the instructions of the President of the Chamber, the time-limits granted for this purpose.

4. The verbatim record, once so corrected, shall be signed by the President and the Registrar and shall then constitute certified matters of record.

Chapter VII
Proceedings before the Grand Chamber

Rule 71
(Applicability of procedural provisions)

Any provisions governing proceedings before the Chambers shall apply, *mutatis mutandis,* to proceedings before the Grand Chamber.

Rule 72
(Relinquishment of jurisdiction by a Chamber in favour of the Grand Chamber)

1. In accordance with Article 30 of the Convention, where a case pending before a Chamber raises a serious question affecting the interpretation of the Convention or the protocols thereto or where the resolution of a question before it might have a result inconsistent with a judgment previously delivered by the Court, the Chamber may, at any time before it has rendered its judgment, relinquish jurisdiction in favour of the Grand Chamber, unless one of the parties to the case has objected in accordance with paragraph 2 of this Rule. Reasons need not be given for the decision to relinquish.

2. The Registrar shall notify the parties of the Chamber's intention to relinquish jurisdiction. The parties shall have one month from the date of that notification within which to file at the Registry a duly reasoned objection. An objection which does not fulfil these conditions shall be considered invalid by the Chamber.

Rule 73
(Request by a party for referral of a case to the Grand Chamber)

1. In accordance with Article 43 of the Convention, any party to a case may exceptionally, within a period of three months from the date of delivery of the judgment of a Chamber, file in writing at the Registry a request that the case be referred to the Grand Chamber. The party shall specify in its request the serious question affecting the interpretation or application of the

Convention or the protocols thereto, or the serious issue of general importance, which in its view warrants consideration by the Grand Chamber.

2.   A panel of five judges of the Grand Chamber constituted in accordance with Rule 24 § 6 shall examine the request solely on the basis of the existing case file. It shall accept the request only if it considers that the case does raise such a question or issue. Reasons need not be given for a refusal of the request.

3.   If the panel accepts the request, the Grand Chamber shall decide the case by means of a judgment.

Chapter VIII
Judgments

Rule 74
(Contents of the judgment)

1.   A judgment as referred to in Articles 42 and 44 of the Convention shall contain

   (*a*)   the names of the President and the other judges constituting the Chamber concerned, and the name of the Registrar or the Deputy Registrar;

   (*b*)   the dates on which it was adopted and delivered;

   (*c*)   a description of the parties;

   (*d*)   the names of the Agents, advocates or advisers of the parties;

   (*e*)   an account of the procedure followed;

   (*f*)   the facts of the case;

   (*g*)   a summary of the submissions of the parties;

   (*h*)   the reasons in point of law;

   (*i*)   the operative provisions;

   (*j*)   the decision, if any, in respect of costs;

   (*k*)   the number of judges constituting the majority;

   (*l*)   where appropriate, a statement as to which text is authentic.

2.   Any judge who has taken part in the consideration of the case shall be entitled to annex to the judgment either a separate opinion, concurring with or dissenting from that judgment, or a bare statement of dissent.

Rule 75
(Ruling on just satisfaction)

1.   Where the Chamber finds that there has been a violation of the Convention, it shall give in the same judgment a ruling on the application of Article 41 of the Convention if that question, after being raised in accordance with Rule 60, is ready for decision; if the question is not ready for decision, the Chamber shall reserve it in whole or in part and shall fix the further procedure.

2.   For the purposes of ruling on the application of Article 41 of the Convention, the Chamber shall, as far as possible, be composed of those judges who sat to consider the merits of the case. Where it is not possible to constitute the original Chamber, the President of the Court shall complete or compose the Chamber by drawing lots.

3.   The Chamber may, when affording just satisfaction under Article 41 of the Convention, direct that if settlement is not made within a specified time, interest is to be payable on any sums awarded.

4.   If the Court is informed that an agreement has been reached between the injured party and the Contracting Party liable, it shall verify the equitable nature of the agreement and, where it finds the agreement to be equitable, strike the case out of the list in accordance with Rule 44 § 2.

Rule 76
(Language of the judgment)

1.   Unless the Court decides that a judgment shall be given in both official languages, all judgments shall be given either in English or in French. Judgments given shall be accessible to the public.

2.   Publication of such judgments in the official reports of the Court, as provided for in Rule 78, shall be in both official languages of the Court.

Rule 77
(Signature, delivery and notification of the judgment)

1.   Judgments shall be signed by the President of the Chamber and the Registrar.

2.   The judgment may be read out at a public hearing by the President of the Chamber or by another judge delegated by him or her. The Agents and representatives of the parties shall be informed in due time of the date of the hearing. Otherwise the notification provided for in paragraph 3 of this Rule shall constitute delivery of the judgment.

3.   The judgment shall be transmitted to the Committee of Ministers. The Registrar shall send certified copies to the parties, to the Secretary General of the Council of Europe, to any third party and to any other person directly concerned. The original copy, duly signed and sealed, shall be placed in the archives of the Court.

Rule 78
(Publication of judgments and other documents)

In accordance with Article 44 § 3 of the Convention, final judgments of the Court shall be published, under the responsibility of the Registrar, in an appropriate form. The Registrar shall in addition be responsible for the publication of official reports of selected judgments and decisions and of any document which the President of the Court considers it useful to publish.

Rule 79
(Request for interpretation of a judgment)

1.   A party may request the interpretation of a judgment within a period of one year following the delivery of that judgment.

2.   The request shall be filed with the Registry. It shall state precisely the point or points in the operative provisions of the judgment on which interpretation is required.

3.   The original Chamber may decide of its own motion to refuse the request on the ground that there is no reason to warrant considering it. Where it is not possible to constitute the original Chamber, the President of the Court shall complete or compose the Chamber by drawing lots.

4.   If the Chamber does not refuse the request, the Registrar shall communicate it to the other party or parties and shall invite them to submit any written comments within a time-limit laid down by the President of the Chamber. The President of the Chamber shall also fix the date of the hearing should the Chamber decide to hold one. The Chamber shall decide by means of a judgment.

Rule 80
(Request for revision of a judgment)

1.   A party may, in the event of the discovery of a fact which might by its nature have a decisive influence and which, when a judgment was delivered, was unknown to the Court and could not reasonably have been known to that party, request the Court, within a period of six months after that party acquired knowledge of the fact, to revise that judgment.

2.   The request shall mention the judgment of which revision is requested and shall contain the information necessary to show that the conditions laid down in paragraph 1 have been complied

with. It shall be accompanied by a copy of all supporting documents. The request and supporting documents shall be filed with the Registry.

3.   The original Chamber may decide of its own motion to refuse the request on the ground that there is no reason to warrant considering it. Where it is not possible to constitute the original Chamber, the President of the Court shall complete or compose the Chamber by drawing lots.

4.   If the Chamber does not refuse the request, the Registrar shall communicate it to the other party or parties and shall invite them to submit any written comments within a time-limit laid down by the President of the Chamber. The President of the Chamber shall also fix the date of the hearing should the Chamber decide to hold one. The Chamber shall decide by means of a judgment.

Rule 81
(Rectification of errors in decisions and judgments)

Without prejudice to the provisions on revision of judgments and on restoration to the list of applications, the Court may, of its own motion or at the request of a party made within one month of the delivery of a decision or a judgment, rectify clerical errors, errors in calculation or obvious mistakes.

Chapter IX
Advisory Opinions

Rule 82

In proceedings relating to advisory opinions the Court shall apply, in addition to the provisions of Articles 47, 48 and 49 of the Convention, the provisions which follow. It shall also apply the other provisions of these Rules to the extent to which it considers this to be appropriate.

Rule 83

The request for an advisory opinion shall be filed with the Registry. It shall state fully and precisely the question on which the opinion of the Court is sought, and also

(*a*)   the date on which the Committee of Ministers adopted the decision referred to in Article 47 § 3 of the Convention;

(*b*)   the names and addresses of the person or persons appointed by the Committee of Ministers to give the Court any explanations which it may require.

The request shall be accompanied by all documents likely to elucidate the question.

Rule 84

1.   On receipt of a request, the Registrar shall transmit a copy of it to all members of the Court.

2.   The Registrar shall inform the Contracting Parties that the Court is prepared to receive their written comments.

Rule 85

1.   The President of the Court shall lay down the time-limits for filing written comments or other documents.

2.   Written comments or other documents shall be filed with the Registry. The Registrar shall transmit copies of them to all the members of the Court, to the Committee of Ministers and to each of the Contracting Parties.

Rule 86

After the close of the written procedure, the President of the Court shall decide whether the Contracting Parties which have submitted written comments are to be given an opportunity to develop them at an oral hearing held for the purpose.

Rule 87

If the Court considers that the request for an advisory opinion is not within its consultative competence as defined in Article 47 of the Convention, it shall so declare in a reasoned decision.

Rule 88

1.   Advisory opinions shall be given by a majority vote of the Grand Chamber. They shall mention the number of judges constituting the majority.

2.   Any judge may, if he or she so desires, attach to the opinion of the Court either a separate opinion, concurring with or dissenting from the advisory opinion, or a bare statement of dissent.

Rule 89

The advisory opinion shall be read out in one of the two official languages by the President of the Court, or by another judge delegated by the President, at a public hearing, prior notice having been given to the Committee of Ministers and to each of the Contracting Parties.

Rule 90

The opinion, or any decision given under Rule 87, shall be signed by the President of the Court and by the Registrar. The original copy, duly signed and sealed, shall be placed in the archives of the Court. The Registrar shall send certified copies to the Committee of Ministers, to the Contracting Parties and to the Secretary General of the Council of Europe.

Chapter X
Legal Aid

Rule 91

1.   The President of the Chamber may, either at the request of an applicant lodging an application under Article 34 of the Convention or of his or her own motion, grant free legal aid to the applicant in connection with the presentation of the case from the moment when observations in writing on the admissibility of that application are received from the respondent Contracting Party in accordance with Rule 54 § 3 (*b*), or where the time-limit for their submission has expired.

2.   Subject to Rule 96, where the applicant has been granted legal aid in connection with the presentation of his or her case before the Chamber, that grant shall continue in force for purposes of his or her representation before the Grand Chamber.

Rule 92

Legal aid shall be granted only where the President of the Chamber is satisfied

(*a*)   that it is necessary for the proper conduct of the case before the Chamber;

(*b*)   that the applicant has insufficient means to meet all or part of the costs entailed.

Rule 93

1.   In order to determine whether or not applicants have sufficient means to meet all or part of the costs entailed, they shall be required to complete a form of declaration stating their income, capital assets and any financial commitments in respect of dependants, or any other financial obligations. The declaration shall be certified by the appropriate domestic authority or authorities.

2.   The Contracting Party concerned shall be requested to submit its comments in writing.

3.   After receiving the information mentioned in paragraphs 1 and 2 above, the President of the Chamber shall decide whether or not to grant legal aid. The Registrar shall inform the parties accordingly.

Rule 94

1.   Fees shall be payable to the advocates or other persons appointed in accordance with Rule 36 § 4. Fees may, where appropriate, be paid to more than one such representative.

2.   Legal aid may be granted to cover not only representatives' fees but also travelling and subsistence expenses and other necessary expenses incurred by the applicant or appointed representative.

Rule 95

On a decision to grant legal aid, the Registrar shall

    (*a*)   fix the rate of fees to be paid in accordance with the legal-aid scales in force;

    (*b*)   the level of expenses to be paid.

Rule 96

The President of the Chamber may, if satisfied that the conditions stated in Rule 92 are no longer fulfilled, revoke or vary a grant of legal aid at any time.

TITLE III
TRANSITIONAL RULES

Rule 97
(Judges' terms of office)

The duration of the terms of office of the judges who were members of the Court at the date of the entry into force of Protocol No. 11 to the Convention shall be calculated as from that date.

Rule 98
(Presidency of the Sections)

For a period of three years from the entry into force of Protocol No. 11 to the Convention,

    (*a*)   the two Presidents of Sections who are not simultaneously Vice-Presidents of the Court and the Vice-Presidents of the Sections shall be elected for a term of office of eighteen months;

    (*b*)   the Vice-Presidents of the Sections may not be immediately re-elected.

Rule 99
(Relations between the Court and the Commission)

1.   In cases brought before the Court under Article 5 §§ 4 and 5 of Protocol No. 11 to the Convention the Court may invite the Commission to delegate one or more of its members to take part in the consideration of the case before the Court.

2.   In cases referred to in the preceding paragraph the Court shall take into consideration the report of the Commission adopted pursuant to former Article 31 of the Convention.

3.   Unless the President of the Chamber decides otherwise, the said report shall be made available to the public through the Registrar as soon as possible after the case has been brought before the Court.

4.   The remainder of the case file of the Commission, including all pleadings, in cases brought before the Court under Article 5 §§ 2 to 5 of Protocol No. 11 shall remain confidential unless the President of the Chamber decides otherwise.

5.   In cases where the Commission has taken evidence but has been unable to adopt a report in accordance with former Article 31 of the Convention, the Court shall take into consideration the verbatim records, documentation and opinion of the Commission's delegations arising from such investigations.

Rule 100
(Chamber and Grand Chamber proceedings)

1. In cases referred to the Court under Article 5 § 4 of Protocol No. 11 to the Convention, a panel of the Grand Chamber constituted in accordance with Rule 24 § 6 shall determine, solely on the basis of the existing case file, whether a Chamber or the Grand Chamber is to decide the case.

2. If the case is decided by a Chamber, the judgment of the Chamber shall, in accordance with Article 5 § 4 of Protocol No. 11, be final and Rule 73 shall be inapplicable.

3. Cases transmitted to the Court under Article 5 § 5 of Protocol No. 11 shall be forwarded by the President of the Court to the Grand Chamber.

4. For each case transmitted to the Grand Chamber under Article 5 § 5 of the Protocol No 11, the Grand Chamber shall be completed by judges designated by rotation within one of the groups mentioned in Rule 24 § 3, the cases being allocated to the groups on an alternate basis.

Rule 101
(Grant of legal aid)

Subject to Rule 96, in cases brought before the Court under Article 5 §§ 2 to 5 of Protocol No. 11 to the Convention, a grant of legal aid made to an applicant in the proceedings before the Commission or the former Court shall continue in force for the purposes of his or her representation before the Court.

Rule 102
(Request for interpretation or revision of a judgment)

1. Where a party requests interpretation or revision of a judgment delivered by the former Court, the President of the Court shall assign the request to one of the Sections in accordance with the conditions laid down in Rule 51 or 52, as the case may be.

2. The President of the relevant Section shall, notwithstanding Rules 79 § 3 and 80 § 3, constitute a new Chamber to consider the request.

3. The Chamber to be constituted shall include as *ex officio* members

    (*a*) the President of the Section;

and, whether or not they are members of the relevant Section,

    (*b*) the judge elected in respect of any Contracting Party concerned or, if he or she is unable to sit, any judge appointed under Rule 29;

    (*c*) any judge of the Court who was a member of the original Chamber that delivered the judgment in the former Court.

4. (*a*) The other members of the Chamber shall be designated by the President of the Section by means of a drawing of lots from among the members of the relevant Section.

    (*b*) The members of the Section who are not so designated shall sit in the case as substitute judges.

TITLE IV
FINAL CLAUSES

Rule 103
(Amendment or suspension of a Rule)

1. Any Rule may be amended upon a motion made after notice where such a motion is carried at the next session of the plenary Court by a majority of all the members of the Court. Notice of such a motion shall be delivered in writing to the Registrar at least one month before the session at which it is to be discussed. On receipt of such a notice of motion, the Registrar shall inform all members of the Court at the earliest possible moment.

2.   A Rule relating to the internal working of the Court may be suspended upon a motion made without notice, provided that this decision is taken unanimously by the Chamber concerned. The suspension of a Rule shall in this case be limited in its operation to the particular purpose for which it was sought.

Rule 104
(Entry into force of the Rules)

The present Rules shall enter into force on 1 November 1998.

Universal Declaration of Human Rights, 1948

PREAMBLE

Whereas recognition of the inherent dignity and of the equal and inalienable rights of all members of the human family is the foundation of freedom, justice and peace in the world,

Whereas disregard and contempt for human rights have resulted in barbarous acts which have outraged the conscience of mankind, and the advent of a world in which human beings shall enjoy freedom of speech and belief and freedom from fear and want has been proclaimed as the highest aspiration of the common people,

Whereas it is essential, if man is not to be compelled to have recourse, as a last resort, to rebellion against tyranny and oppression, that human rights should be protected by the rule of law,

Whereas it is essential to promote the development of friendly relations between nations,

Whereas the peoples of the United Nations have in the Charter reaffirmed their faith in fundamental human rights, in the dignity and worth of the human person and in the equal rights of men and women and have determined to promote social progress and better standards of life in larger freedom,

Whereas Member States have pledged themselves to achieve, in co-operation with the United Nations, the promotion of universal respect for and observance of human rights and fundamental freedoms,

Whereas a common understanding of these rights and freedoms is of the greatest importance for the full realization of this pledge.

Now, Therefore,

The General Assembly

proclaims

This universal declaration of human rights as a common standard of achievement for all peoples and all nations, to the end that every individual and every organ of society, keeping this Declaration constantly in mind, shall strive by teaching and education to promote respect for these rights and freedoms and by progressive measures, national and international, to secure their universal and effective recognition and observance, both among the peoples of Member States themselves and among the peoples of territories under their jurisdiction.

Article 1

All human beings are born free and equal in dignity and rights. They are endowed with reason and conscience and should act towards one another in a spirit of brotherhood.

Article 2

Everyone is entitled to all the rights and freedoms set forth in this Declaration, without distinction of any kind, such as race, colour, sex, language, religion, political or other opinion, national or social origin, property, birth or other status.

Furthermore, no distinction shall be made on the basis of the political, jurisdictional or international status of the country or territory to which a person belongs, whether it be independent, trust, non-self-governing or under any other limitation of sovereignty.

Article 3

Everyone has the right to life, liberty and security of person.

Article 4

No one shall be held in slavery or servitude: slavery and the slave trade shall be prohibited in all their forms.

Article 5

No one shall be subjected to torture or cruel, inhuman or degrading treatment or punishment.

Article 6

Everyone has the right to recognition everywhere as a person before the law.

Article 7

All are equal before the law and are entitled without any discrimination to equal protection of the law. All are entitled to equal protection against any discrimination in violation of this Declaration and against any incitement to such discrimination.

Article 8

Everyone has the right to an effective remedy by the competent national tribunals for acts violating the fundamental rights granted him by the constitution or by law.

Article 9

No one shall be subjected to arbitrary arrest, detention or exile.

Article 10

Everyone is entitled in full equality to a fair and public hearing by an independent and impartial tribunal, in the determination of his rights and obligations and of any criminal charge against him.

Article 11

1.   Everyone charged with a penal offence has the right to be presumed innocent until proved guilty according to law in a public trial at which he has had all the guarantees necessary for his defence.

2.   No one shall be held guilty of any penal offence on account of any act or omission which did not constitute a penal offence, under national or international law, at the time when it was committed. Nor shall a heavier penalty be imposed than the one that was applicable at the time the penal offence was committed.

Article 12

No one shall be subjected to arbitrary interference with his privacy, family, home or correspondence, nor to attacks upon his honour and reputation. Everyone has the right to the protection of the law against such interference or attacks.

Article 13

1.   Everyone has the right to freedom of movement and residence within the borders of each state.

2.   Everyone has the right to leave any country, including his own, and to return to his country.

Article 14

1.   Everyone has the right to seek and to enjoy in other countries asylum from persecution.

2.   This right may not be invoked in the case of prosecutions genuinely arising from non-political crimes or from acts contrary to the purposes and principles of the United Nations.

Article 15

1.   Everyone has the right to a nationality.

2.   No one shall be arbitrarily deprived of his nationality nor denied the right to change his nationality.

Article 16

1.   Men and women of full age, without any limitation due to race, nationality or religion, have

the right to marry and to found a family. They are entitled to equal rights as to marriage, during marriage and at its dissolution.

2.   Marriage shall be entered into only with the free and full consent of the intending spouses.

3.   The family is the natural and fundamental group unit of society and is entitled to protection by society and the State.

Article 17

1.   Everyone has the right to own property alone as well as in association with others.

2.   No one shall be arbitrarily deprived of his property.

Article 18

Everyone has the right to freedom of thought, conscience and religion; this right includes freedom to change his religion or belief, and freedom, either alone or in community with others and in public or private, to manifest his religion or belief in teaching, practice, worship and observance.

Article 19

Everyone has the right to freedom of opinion and expression; this right includes freedom to hold opinions without interference and to seek, receive and impart information and ideas through any media and regardless of frontiers.

Article 20

1.   Everyone has the right to freedom of peaceful assembly and association.

2.   No one may be compelled to belong to an association.

Article 21

1.   Everyone has the right to take part in the government of his country, directly or through freely chosen representatives.

2.   Everyone has the right of equal access to public service in his country.

3.   The will of the people shall be the basis of the authority of government; this will shall be expressed in periodic and genuine elections which shall be by universal and equal suffrage and shall be held by secret vote or by equivalent free voting procedures.

Article 22

Everyone, as a member of society, has the right to social security and is entitled to realization, through national effort and international co-operation and in accordance with the organization and resources of each State, of the economic, social and cultural rights indispensable for his dignity and the free development of his personality.

Article 23

1.   Everyone has the right to work, to free choice of employment, to just and favourable conditions of work and to protection against unemployment.

2.   Everyone, without any discrimination, has the right to equal pay for equal work.

3.   Everyone who works has the right to just and favourable remuneration ensuring for himself and his family an existence worthy of human dignity, and supplemented, if necessary, by other means of social protection.

4.   Everyone has the right to form and to join trade unions for the protection of his interests.

Article 24

Everyone has the right to rest and leisure, including reasonable limitation of working hours and periodic holidays with pay.

Article 25

1.   Everyone has the right to a standard of living adequate for the health and well-being of himself and of his family, including food, clothing, housing and medical care and necessary social services, and the right to security in the event of unemployment, sickness, disability, widowhood, old age or other lack of livelihood in circumstances beyond his control.

2.   Motherhood and childhood are entitled to special care and assistance. All children, whether born in or out of wedlock, shall enjoy the same social protection.

Article 26

1.   Everyone has the right to education. Education shall be free, at least in the elementary and fundamental stages. Elementary education shall be compulsory. Technical and professional education shall be made generally available and higher education shall be equally accessible to all on the basis of merit.

2.   Education shall be directed to the full development of the human personality and to the strengthening of respect for human rights and fundamental freedoms. It shall promote understanding, tolerance and friendship among all nations, racial or religious groups, and shall further the activities of the United Nations for the maintenance of peace.

3.   Parents have a prior right to choose the kind of education that shall be given to their children.

Article 27

1.   Everyone has the right freely to participate in the cultural life of the community, to enjoy the arts and to share in scientific advancement and its benefits.

2.   Everyone has the right to the protection of the moral and material interests resulting from any scientific, literary or artistic production of which he is the author.

Article 28

Everyone is entitled to a social and international order in which the rights and freedoms set forth in this Declaration can be fully realized.

Article 29

1.   Everyone has duties to the community in which alone the free and full development of his personality is possible.

2.   In the exercise of his rights and freedoms, everyone shall be subject only to such limitations as are determined by law solely for the purpose of securing due recognition and respect for the rights and freedoms of others and of meeting the just requirements of morality, public order and the general welfare in a democratic society.

3.   These rights and freedoms may in no case be exercised contrary to the purposes and principles of the United Nations.

Article 30

Nothing in this Declaration may be interpreted as implying for any State, group or person any right to engage in any activity or to perform any act aimed at the destruction of any of the rights and freedoms set forth herein.

International Covenant
on Civil and Political Rights, 1966

<small>PREAMBLE</small>

The States Parties to the present Covenant,

Considering that, in accordance with the principles proclaimed in the Charter of the United Nations, recognition of the inherent dignity and of the equal and inalienable rights of all members of the human family is the foundation of freedom, justice and peace in the world,

Recognizing that these rights derive from the inherent dignity of the human person,

Recognizing that, in accordance with the Universal Declaration of Human Rights, the ideal of free human beings enjoying civil and political freedom and freedom from fear and want can only be achieved if conditions are created whereby everyone may enjoy his civil and political rights, as well as his economic, social and cultural rights,

Considering the obligation of States under the Charter of the United Nations to promote universal respect for, and observance of, human rights and freedoms,

Realizing that the individual, having duties to other individuals and to the community to which he belongs, is under a responsibility to strive for the promotion and observance of the rights recognized in the present Covenant,

Agree upon the following articles:

PART I

Article 1

1.   All peoples have the right of self-determination. By virtue of that right they freely determine their political status and freely pursue their economic, social and cultural development.

2.   All peoples may, for their own ends, freely dispose of their natural wealth and resources without prejudice to any obligations arising out of international economic co-operation, based upon the principle of mutual benefit, and international law. In no case may a people be deprived of its own means of subsistence.

3.   The States Parties to the present Covenant, including those having responsibility for the administration of Non-Self-Governing and Trust Territories, shall promote the realization of the right of self-determination, and shall respect that right, in conformity with the provisions of the Charter of the United Nations.

PART II

Article 2

1.   Each State Party to the present Covenant undertakes to respect and to ensure to all individuals within its territory and subject to its jurisdiction the rights recognized in the present Covenant, without distinction of any kind, such as race, colour, sex, language, religion, political or other opinion, national or social origin, property, birth or other status.

2.   Where not already provided for by existing legislative or other measures, each State Party to the present Covenant undertakes to take the necessary steps, in accordance with its constitutional processes and with the provisions of the present Covenant, to adopt such legislative or other measures as may be necessary to give effect to the rights recognized in the present Covenant.

3.   Each State Party to the present Covenant undertakes:

(*a*)   To ensure that any person whose rights or freedoms as herein recognized are violated shall have an effective remedy, notwithstanding that the violation has been committed by persons acting in an official capacity;

(*b*)   To ensure that any person claiming such a remedy shall have his right thereto determined by competent judicial, administrative or legislative authorities, or by any other competent authority provided for by the legal system of the State, and to develop the possibilities of judicial remedy;

(*c*)   To ensure that the competent authorities shall enforce such remedies when granted.

Article 3

The States Parties to the present Covenant undertake to ensure the equal right of men and women to the enjoyment of all civil and political rights set forth in the present Covenant.

Article 4

1.   In time of public emergency which threatens the life of the nation and the existence of which is officially proclaimed, the State Parties to the present Covenant may take measures derogating from their obligations under the present Covenant to the extent strictly required by the exigencies of the situation, provided that such measures are not inconsistent with their other obligations under international law and do not involve discrimination solely on the ground of race, colour, sex, language, religion or social origin.

2.   No derogation from Articles 6, 7, 8 (paragraphs 1 and 2), 11, 15, 16 and 18 may be made under this provision.

3.   Any State Party to the present Covenant availing itself of the right of derogation shall immediately inform the other States Parties to the present Covenant, through the intermediary of the Secretary-General of the United Nations of the provisions from which it has derogated and of the reasons by which it was actuated. A further communication shall be made, through the same intermediary on the date on which it terminates such derogation.

Article 5

1.   Nothing in the present Covenant may be interpreted as implying for any State, group or person any right to engage in any activity or perform any act aimed at the destruction of any of the rights and freedoms recognized herein or at their limitation to a greater extent than is provided for in the present Covenant.

2.   There shall be no restriction upon or derogation from any of the fundamental human rights recognized or existing in any State Party to the present Covenant pursuant to law, conventions, regulations or custom on the pretext that the present Covenant does not recognize such rights or that it recognizes them to a lesser extent.

PART III

Article 6

1. Every human being has the inherent right to life. This right shall be protected by law. No one shall be arbitrarily deprived of his life.

2.   In countries which have not abolished the death penalty, sentence of death may be imposed only for the most serious crimes in accordance with the law in force at the time of the commission of the crime and not contrary to the provisions of the present Covenant and to the Convention on the Prevention and Punishment of the Crime of Genocide. This penalty can only be carried out pursuant to a final judgment rendered by a competent court.

3.   When deprivation of life constitutes the crime of genocide, it is understood that nothing in this Article shall authorize any State Party to the present Covenant to derogate in any way from any obligation assumed under the provisions of the Convention on the Prevention and Punishment of the Crime of Genocide.

4.   Anyone sentenced to death shall have the right to seek pardon or commutation of the sentence. Amnesty, pardon or commutation of the sentence of death may be granted in all cases.

5.   Sentence of death shall not be imposed for crimes committed by persons below eighteen years of age and shall not be carried out on pregnant women.

6.   Nothing in this Article shall be invoked to delay or to prevent the abolition of capital punishment by any State Party to the present Covenant.

Article 7

No one shall be subjected to torture or to cruel, inhuman or degrading treatment or punishment. In particular, no one shall be subjected without his free consent to medical or scientific experimentation.

Article 8

1.   No one shall be held in slavery; slavery and the slave-trade in all their forms shall be prohibited.

2.   No one shall be held in servitude.

3.   (*a*)   No one shall be required to perform forced or compulsory labour;

   (*b*)   Paragraph 3 (*a*) shall not be held to preclude, in countries where imprisonment with hard labour may be imposed as a punishment for a crime, the performance of hard labour in pursuance of a sentence to such punishment by a competent court;

   (*c*)   For the purpose of this paragraph the term 'forced or compulsory labour' shall not include:

   (i)   Any work or service, not referred to in sub-paragraph (b), normally required of a person who is under detention in consequence of a lawful order of a court, or of a person during conditional release from such detention;

   (ii)   Any service of a military character and, in countries where conscientious objection is recognized, any national service required by law of conscientious objectors;

   (iii)   Any service exacted in cases of emergency or calamity threatening the life or well-being of the community;

   (iv)   Any work or service which forms part of normal civil obligations.

Article 9

1.   Everyone has the right to liberty and security of person. No one shall be subjected to arbitrary arrest or detention. No one shall be deprived of his liberty except on such grounds and in accordance with such procedures as are established by law.

2.   Anyone who is arrested shall be informed, at the time of arrest, of the reasons for his arrest and shall be promptly informed of any charges against him.

3.   Anyone arrested or detained on a criminal charge shall be brought promptly before a judge or other officer authorized by law to exercise judicial power and shall be entitled to trial within a reasonable time or to release. It shall not be the general rule that persons awaiting trial shall be detained in custody, but release may be subject to guarantees to appear for trial, at any other stage of the judicial proceedings, and, should occasion arise, for execution of the judgment.

4.   Anyone who is deprived of his liberty by arrest or detention shall be entitled to take proceedings before a court, in order that that court may decide without delay on the lawfulness of his detention and order his release if the detention is not lawful.

5.   Anyone who has been the victim of unlawful arrest or detention shall have an enforceable right to compensation.

Article 10

1.   All persons deprived of their liberty shall be treated with humanity and with respect for the inherent dignity of the human person.

2.   (*a*)   Accused persons shall, save in exceptional circumstances, be segregated from convicted persons and shall be subject to separate treatment appropriate to their status as unconvicted persons;

    (*b*)   Accused juvenile persons shall be separated from adults and brought as speedily as possible for adjudication.

3.   The penitentiary system shall comprise treatment of prisoners the essential aim of which shall be their reformation and social rehabilitation. Juvenile offenders shall be segregated from adults and be accorded treatment appropriate to their age and legal status.

Article 11

No one shall be imprisoned merely on the ground of inability to fulfil a contractual obligation.

Article 12

1.   Everyone lawfully within the territory of a State shall, within that territory, have the right to liberty of movement and freedom to choose his residence.

2.   Everyone shall be free to leave any country, including his own.

3.   The above-mentioned rights shall not be subject to any restrictions except those which are provided by law, are necessary to protect national security, public order *(ordre public),* public health or morals or the rights and freedoms of others, and are consistent with the other rights recognized in the present Covenant.

4.   No one shall be arbitrarily deprived of the right to enter his own country.

Article 13

An alien lawfully in the territory of a State Party to the present Covenant may be expelled therefrom only in pursuance of a decision reached in accordance with law and shall, except where compelling reasons of national security otherwise require, be allowed to submit the reasons against his expulsion and to have his case reviewed by, and be represented for the purpose before, the competent authority or a person or persons especially designated by the competent authority.

Article 14

1.   All persons shall be equal before the courts and tribunals. In the determination of any criminal charge against him, or of his rights and obligations in a suit at law, everyone shall be entitled to a fair and public hearing by a competent, independent and impartial tribunal established by law. The Press and the public may be excluded from all or part of a trial for reasons of morals, public order *(ordre public)* or national security in a democratic society, or when the interest of the private lives of the parties so requires, or to the extent strictly necessary in the opinion of the court in special circumstances where publicity would prejudice the interests of justice; but any judgement rendered in a criminal case or in a suit at law shall be made public except where the interest of juvenile persons otherwise requires or the proceedings concern matrimonial disputes or the guardianship of children.

2.   Everyone charged with a criminal offence shall have the right to be presumed innocent until proved guilty according to law.

3.   In the determination of any criminal charge against him, everyone shall be entitled to the following minimum guarantees, in full equality:

    (*a*)   To be informed promptly and in detail in a language which he understands of the nature and cause of the charge against him;

(*b*)　To have adequate time and facilities for the preparation of his defence and to communicate with counsel of his own choosing;

(*c*)　To be tried without undue delay;

(*d*)　To be tried in his presence, and to defend himself in person or through legal assistance of his own choosing; to be informed, if he does not have legal assistance, of this right; and to have legal assistance assigned to him, in any case where the interests of justice so require, and without payment by him in any such case if he does not have sufficient means to pay for it;

(*e*)　To examine, or have examined, the witnesses against him and to obtain the attendance and examination of witnesses on his behalf under the same conditions as witnesses against him;

(*f*)　To have the free assistance of an interpreter if he cannot understand or speak the language used in court;

(*g*)　Not to be compelled to testify against himself or to confess guilt.

4.　In the case of juvenile persons, the procedure shall be such as will take account of their age and the desirability of promoting their rehabilitation.

5.　Everyone convicted of a crime shall have the right to his conviction and sentence being reviewed by a higher tribunal according to law.

6.　When a person has by a final decision been convicted of a criminal offence and when subsequently his conviction has been reversed or he has been pardoned on the ground that a new or newly discovered fact shows conclusively that there has been a miscarriage of justice, the person who has suffered punishment as a result of such conviction shall be compensated according to law, unless it is proved that the non-disclosure of the unknown fact in time is wholly or partly attributable to him.

7.　No one shall be liable to be tried or punished again for an offence for which he has already been finally convicted or acquitted in accordance with the law and penal procedure of each country.

Article 15

1.　No one shall be held guilty of any criminal offence on account of any act or omission which did not constitute a criminal offence, under national or international law, at the time when it was committed. Nor shall a heavier penalty be imposed than the one that was applicable at the time when the criminal offence was committed. If, subsequent to the commission of the offence, provision is made by law for the imposition of a lighter penalty, the offender shall benefit thereby.

2.　Nothing in this article shall prejudice the trial and punishment of any person for any act or omission which, at the time when it was committed, was criminal according to the general principles of law recognized by the community of nations.

Article 16

Everyone shall have the right to recognition everywhere as a person before the law.

Article 17

1.　No one shall be subjected to arbitrary or unlawful interference with his privacy, family, home or correspondence, nor to unlawful attacks on his honour and reputation.

2.　Everyone has the right to the protection of the law against such interference or attacks.

Article 18

1.　Everyone shall have the right to freedom of thought, conscience and religion. This right shall include freedom to have or to adopt a religion or belief of his choice, and freedom, either individually or in community with others and in public or private, to manifest his religion or belief in worship, observance, practice and teaching.

2.   No one shall be subject to coercion which would impair his freedom to have or to adopt a religion or belief of his choice.

3.   Freedom to manifest one's religion or beliefs may be subject only to such limitations as are prescribed by law and are necessary to protect public safety, order, health, or morals or the fundamental rights and freedoms of others.

4.   The States Parties to the present Covenant undertake to have respect for the liberty of parents and, when applicable, legal guardians to ensure the religious and moral education of their children in conformity with their own convictions.

Article 19

1.   Everyone shall have the right to hold opinions without interference.

2.   Everyone shall have the right to freedom of expression; this right shall include freedom to seek, receive and impart information and ideas of all kinds, regardless of frontiers, either orally, in writing or in print, in the form of art, or through any other media of his choice.

3.   The exercise of the rights provided for in paragraph 2 of this article carries with it special duties and responsibilities. It may therefore be subject to certain restrictions, but these shall only be such as are provided by law and are necessary:

(*a*)   For respect of the rights or reputations of others;

(*b*)   For the protection of national security or of public order *(ordre public),* or of public health or morals.

Article 20

1.   Any propaganda for war shall be prohibited by law.

2.   Any advocacy of national, racial or religious hatred that constitutes incitement to discrimination, hostility or violence shall be prohibited by law.

Article 21

The right of peaceful assembly shall be recognized. No restrictions may be placed on the exercise of this right other than those imposed in conformity with the law and which are necessary in a democratic society in the interests of national security or public safety, public order *(ordre public),* the protection of public health or morals or the protection of the rights and freedoms of others.

Article 22

1.   Everyone shall have the right to freedom of association with others, including the right to form and join trade unions for the protection of his interests.

2.   No restrictions may be placed on the exercise of this right other than those which are prescribed by law and which are necessary in a democratic society in the interests of national security or public safety, public order *(ordre public),* the protection of public health or morals or the protection of the rights and freedoms of others. This Article shall not prevent the imposition of lawful restrictions on members of the armed forces and of the police in their exercise of this right.

3.   Nothing in this article shall authorize States Parties to the International Labour Organization Convention of 1948 concerning Freedom of Association and Protection of the Right to Organize to take legislative measures which would prejudice, or to apply the law in such a manner as to prejudice, the guarantees provided for in that Convention.

Article 23

1.   The family is the natural and fundamental group unit of society and is entitled to protection by society and the State.

2. The right of men and women of marriageable age to marry and to found a family shall be recognized.

3. No marriage shall be entered into without the free and full consent of the intending spouses.

4. States Parties to the present Covenant shall take appropriate steps to ensure equality of rights and responsibilities of spouses as to marriage, during marriage and at its dissolution. In the case of dissolution, provision shall be made for the necessary protection of any children.

Article 24

1. Every child shall have, without any discrimination as to race, colour, sex, language, religion, national or social origin, property or birth, the right to such measures of protection as are required by his status as a minor, on the part of his family, society and the State.

2. Every child shall be registered immediately after birth and shall have a name.

3. Every child has the right to acquire a nationality.

Article 25

Every citizen shall have the right and the opportunity, without any of the distinctions mentioned in Article 2 and without unreasonable restrictions:

(*a*) To take part in the conduct of public affairs, directly or through freely chosen representatives;

(*b*) To vote and to be elected at genuine periodic elections which shall be by universal and equal suffrage and shall be held by secret ballot, guaranteeing the free expression of the will of the electors;

(*c*) To have access, on general terms of equality, to public service in his country.

Article 26

All persons are equal before the law and are entitled without any discrimination to the equal protection of the law. In this respect, the law shall prohibit any discrimination and guarantee to all persons equal and effective protection against discrimination on any ground such as race, colour, sex, language, religion, political or other opinion, national or social origin, property, birth or other status.

Article 27

In those States in which ethnic, religious or linguistic minorities exist, persons belonging to such minorities shall not be denied the right, in community with the other members of their group, to enjoy their own culture, to profess and practise their own religion, or to use their own language.

PART IV

Article 28

1. There shall be established a Human Rights Committee (hereafter referred to in the present Covenant as the Committee). It shall consist of eighteen members and shall carry out the functions hereinafter provided.

2. The Committee shall be composed of nationals of the States Parties to the present Covenant who shall be persons of high moral character and recognized competence in the field of human rights, consideration being given to the usefulness of the participation of some persons having legal experience.

3. The members of the Committee shall be elected and shall serve in their personal capacity.

Article 29

1. The members of the Committee shall be elected by secret ballot from a list of persons possessing the qualifications prescribed in Article 28 and nominated for the purpose by the States Parties to the present Covenant.

2.   Each State Party to the present Covenant may nominate not more than two persons. These persons shall be nationals of the nominating State.

3.   A person shall be eligible for renomination.

Article 30

1.   The initial election shall be held no later than six months after the date of the entry into force of the present Covenant.

2.   At least four months before the date of each election to the Committee, other than an election to fill a vacancy declared in accordance with Article 34, the Secretary-General of the United Nations shall address a written invitation to the States Parties to the present Covenant to submit their nominations for membership of the Committee within three months.

3.   The Secretary-General of the United Nations shall prepare a list in alphabetical order of all the persons thus nominated, with an indication of the States Parties which have nominated them, and shall submit it to the States Parties to the present Covenant no later than one month before the date of each election.

4.   Elections of the members of the Committee shall be held at a meeting of the States Parties to the present Covenant convened by the Secretary-General of the United Nations at the Headquarters of the United Nations. At that meeting, for which two thirds of the States Parties to the present Covenant shall constitute a quorum, the persons elected to the Committee shall be those nominees who obtain the largest number of votes and an absolute majority of the votes of the representatives of States Parties present and voting.

Article 31

1.   The Committee may not include more than one national of the same State.

2.   In the election of the Committee, consideration shall be given to equitable geographical distribution of membership and to the representation of the different forms of civilization and of the principal legal systems.

Article 32

1.   The members of the Committee shall be elected for a term of four years. They shall be eligible for re-election if renominated. However, the terms of nine of the members elected at the first election shall expire at the end of two years; immediately after the first election, the names of these nine members shall be chosen by lot by the Chairman of the meeting referred to in Article 30, paragraph 4.

2.   Elections at the expiry of office shall be held in accordance with the preceding Articles of this part of the present Covenant.

Article 33

1.   If, in the unanimous opinion of the other members, a member of the Committee has ceased to carry out his functions for any cause other than absence of a temporary character, the Chairman of the Committee shall notify the Secretary-General of the United Nations, who shall then declare the seat of that member to be vacant.

2.   In the event of the death or the resignation of a member of the Committee, the Chairman shall immediately notify the Secretary-General of the United Nations, who shall declare the seat vacant from the date of death or the date on which the resignation takes effect.

Article 34

1.   When a vacancy is declared in accordance with Article 33 and if the term of office of the member to be replaced does not expire within six months of the declaration of the vacancy, the Secretary-General of the United Nations shall notify each of the States Parties to the present Covenant, which may within two months submit nominations in accordance with Article 29 for the purpose of fulfilling the vacancy.

2. The Secretary-General of the United Nations shall prepare a list in alphabetical order of the persons thus nominated and shall submit it to the States Parties to the present Covenant. The election to fill the vacancy shall then take place in accordance with the relevant provisions of this part of the present Covenant.

3. A member of the Committee elected to fill a vacancy declared in accordance with Article 33 shall hold office for the remainder of the term of the member who vacated the seat of the Committee under the provisions of that Article.

Article 35

The members of the Committee shall, with the approval of the General Assembly of the United Nations, receive emoluments from United Nations resources on such terms and conditions as the General Assembly may decide, having regard to the importance of the Committee's responsibilities.

Article 36

The Secretary-General of the United Nations shall provide the necessary staff and facilities for the effective performance of the functions of the Committee under the present Covenant.

Article 37

1. The Secretary-General of the United Nations shall convene the initial meeting of the Committee at the Headquarters of the United Nations.

2. After its initial meeting, the Committee shall meet at such times as shall be provided in its rules of procedure.

3. The Committee shall normally meet at the Headquarters of the United Nations or at the United Nations Office at Geneva.

Article 38

Every member of the Committee shall, before taking up his duties, make a solemn declaration in open committee that he will perform his functions impartially and conscientiously.

Article 39

1. The Committee shall elect its officers for a term of two years. They may be re-elected.

2. The Committee shall establish its own rules of procedure, but these rules shall provide, *inter alia,* that:

(a) Twelve members shall constitute a quorum;

(b) Decisions of the Committee shall be made by a majority vote of the members present.

Article 40

1. The States Parties to the present Covenant undertake to submit reports on the measures they have adopted which give effect to the rights recognized herein and on the progress made in the enjoyment of those rights:

(a) Within one year of the entry into force of the present Covenant for the States Parties concerned;

(b) Thereafter whenever the Committee so requests.

2. All reports shall be submitted to the Secretary-General of the United Nations, who shall transmit them to the Committee for consideration. Reports shall indicate the factors and difficulties, if any, affecting the implementation of the present Covenant.

3. The Secretary-General of the United Nations may, after consultation with the Committee, transmit to the specialized agencies concerned copies of such parts of the reports as may fall within their field of competence.

4.   The Committee shall study the reports submitted by the States Parties to the present Covenant. It shall transmit its reports, and such general comments as it may consider appropriate, to the States Parties. The Committee may also transmit to the Economic and Social Council these comments along with the copies of the reports it has received from States Parties to the present Covenant.

5.   The States Parties to the present Covenant may submit to the Committee observations on any comments that may be made in accordance with paragraph 4 of this Article.

Article 41

1.   A State Party to the present Covenant may at any time declare under this article that it recognizes the competence of the Committee to receive and consider communications to the effect that a State Party claims that another State Party is not fulfilling its obligations under the present Covenant. Communications under this article may be received and considered only if submitted by a State Party which has made a declaration recognizing in regard to itself the competence of the Committee. No communication shall be received by the Committee if it concerns a State Party which has not made such a declaration. Communications received under this Article shall be dealt with in accordance with the following procedure:

(*a*)   If a State Party to the present Covenant considers that another State Party is not giving effect to the provisions of the present Covenant, it may, by written communication, bring the matter to the attention of that State Party. Within three months after the receipt of the communication, the receiving State shall afford the State which sent the communication an explanation or any other statement in writing clarifying the matter, which should include, to the extent possible and pertinent, reference to domestic procedures and remedies taken, pending, or available in the matter.

(*b*)   If the matter is not adjusted to the satisfaction of both States Parties concerned within six months after the receipt by the receiving State of the initial communication, either State shall have the right to refer the matter to the Committee, by notice given to the Committee and to the other State.

(*c*)   The Committee shall deal with a matter referred to it only after it has ascertained that all available domestic remedies have been invoked and exhausted in the matter, in conformity with the generally recognized principles of international law. This shall not be the rule where the application of the remedies is unreasonably prolonged.

(*d*)   The Committee shall hold closed meetings when examining communications under this article.

(*e*)   Subject to the provisions of sub-paragraph (c), the Committee shall make available its good offices to the States Parties concerned with a view to a friendly solution of the matter on the basis of respect for human rights and fundamental freedoms as recognized in the present Covenant.

(*f*)   In any matter referred to it, the Committee may call upon the States Parties concerned, referred to in sub-paragraph (b), to supply any relevant information.

(*g*)   The States Parties concerned, referred to in sub-paragraph (b), shall have the right to be represented when the matter is being considered in the Committee and to make submissions orally and/or in writing.

(*h*)   The Committee shall, within twelve months after the date of receipt of notice under sub-paragraph (b), submit a report:

(i)   If a solution within the terms of sub-paragraph (e) is reached, the Committee shall confine its report to a brief statement of the facts and of the solution reached;

(ii)   If a solution within the terms of sub-paragraph (e) is not reached, the Committee shall confine its report to a brief statement of the facts; the written submissions and record of the oral submissions made by the States Parties concerned shall be attached to the report.

In every matter, the report shall be communicated to the States Parties concerned.

2.   The provisions of this Article shall come into force when ten States Parties to the present Covenant have made declarations under paragraph of this Article. Such declarations shall be deposited by the States Parties with the Secretary-General of the United Nations, who shall transmit copies thereof to the other States Parties. A declaration may be withdrawn at any time by notification to the Secretary-General. Such a withdrawal shall not prejudice the consideration of any matter which is the subject of a communication already transmitted under this Article; no further communication by any State Party shall be received after the notification of withdrawal of the declaration has been received by the Secretary-General, unless the State Party concerned has made a new declaration.

Article 42

1.   (a)   If a matter referred to the Committee in accordance with Article 41 is not resolved to the satisfaction of the States Parties concerned, the Committee may, with the prior consent of the States Parties concerned, appoint an *ad hoc* Conciliation Commission (hereinafter referred to as the Commission). The good offices of the Commission shall be made available to the States Parties concerned with a view to an amicable solution of the matter on the basis of respect for the present Covenant;

   (b)   The Commission shall consist of five persons acceptable to the States Parties concerned. If the States Parties concerned fail to reach agreement within three months on all or part of the composition of the Commission the members of the Commission concerning whom no agreement has been reached shall be elected by secret ballot by a two-thirds majority vote of the Committee from among its members.

2.   The members of the Commission shall serve in their personal capacity. They shall not be nationals of the States Parties concerned, or of a State not party to the present Covenant, or of a State Party which has not made a declaration under Article 41.

3.   The Commission shall elect its own Chairman and adopt its own rules of procedure.

4.   The meetings of the Commission shall normally be held at the Headquarters of the United Nations or at the United Nations Office at Geneva. However, they may be held at such other convenient places as the Commission may determine in consultation with the Secretary-General of the United Nations and the States Parties concerned.

5.   The secretariat provided in accordance with Article 36 shall also service the commissions appointed under this article.

6.   The information received and collated by the Committee shall be made available to the Commission and the Commission may call upon the States Parties concerned to supply any other relevant information.

7.   When the Commission has fully considered the matter, but in any event not later than twelve months after having been seized of the matter, it shall submit to the Chairman of the Committee a report for communication to the States Parties concerned.

   (a)   If the Commission is unable to complete its consideration of the matter within twelve months, it shall confine its report to a brief statement of the status of its consideration of the matter.

   (b)   If an amicable solution to the matter on the basis of respect for human rights as recognized in the present Covenant is reached, the Commission shall confine its report to a brief statement of the facts and of the solution reached.

   (c)   If a solution within the terms of sub-paragraph (b) is not reached, the Commission's report shall embody its findings on all questions of fact relevant to the issues between the States Parties concerned, and its views on the possibilities of an amicable solution of the matter. This report shall also contain the written submissions and a record of the oral submissions made by the States Parties concerned.

   (d)   If the Commission's report is submitted under sub-paragraph (c), the States Parties concerned shall, within three months of the receipt of the report, notify the Chairman of the Committee whether or not they accept the contents of the report of the Commission.

8.   The provisions of this Article are without prejudice to the responsibilities of the Committee under Article 41.

9.   The States Parties concerned shall share equally all the expenses of the members of the Commission in accordance with estimates to be provided by the Secretary-General of the United Nations.

10.   The Secretary-General of the United Nations shall be empowered to pay the expenses of the members of the Commission, if necessary, before reimbursement by the States Parties concerned, in accordance with paragraph 9 of this Article.

Article 43

The members of the Committee, and of the *ad hoc* conciliation commissions which may be appointed under Article 42, shall be entitled to the facilities, privileges and immunities of experts on mission for the United Nations as laid down in the relevant sections of the Convention on the Privileges and Immunities of the United Nations.

Article 44

The provisions for the implementation of the present Covenant shall apply without prejudice to the procedures prescribed in the field of human rights by or under the constituent instruments and the conventions of the United Nations and of the specialized agencies and shall not prevent the States Parties to the present Covenant from having recourse to other procedures for settling a dispute in accordance with general or special international agreements in force between them.

Article 45

The Committee shall submit to the General Assembly of the United Nations through the Economic and Social Council, an annual report on its activities.

PART V

Article 46

Nothing in the present Covenant shall be interpreted as impairing the provisions of the Charter of the United Nations and of the constitutions of the specialized agencies which define the respective responsibilities of the various organs of the United Nations and of the specialized agencies in regard to the matters dealt with in the present Covenant.

Article 47

Nothing in the present Covenant shall be interpreted as impairing the inherent right of all peoples to enjoy and utilize fully and freely their natural wealth and resources.

Article 48

1.   The present Covenant is open for signature by any State Member of the United Nations or member of any of its specialized agencies, by any State Party to the Statute of the International Court of Justice, and by any other State which has been invited by the General Assembly of the United Nations to become a party to the present Covenant.

2.   The present Covenant is subject to ratification. Instruments of ratification shall be deposited with the Secretary-General of the United Nations.

3.   The present Covenant shall be open to accession by any State referred to in paragraph 1 of this article.

4.   Accession shall be effected by the deposit of an instrument of accession with the Secretary-General of the United Nations.

5.   The Secretary-General of the United Nations shall inform all States which have signed this Covenant or acceded to it of the deposit of each instrument of ratification or accession.

Article 49

1.   The present Covenant shall enter into force three months after the date of the deposit with the Secretary-General of the United Nations of the thirty-fifth instrument of ratification or instrument of accession.

2.   For each State ratifying the present Covenant or acceding to it after the deposit of the thirty-fifth instrument of ratification or instrument of accession, the present Covenant shall enter into force three months after the date of the deposit of its own instrument of ratification or instrument of accession.

Article 50

The provisions of the present Covenant shall extend to all parts of federal States without any limitations or exceptions.

Article 51

1.   Any State Party to the present Covenant may propose an amendment and file it with the Secretary-General of the United Nations. The Secretary-General of the United Nations shall thereupon communicate any proposed amendments to the States Parties to the present Covenant with a request that they notify him whether they favour a conference of States Parties for the purpose of considering and voting upon the proposals. In the event that at least one third of the States Parties favours such a conference, the Secretary-General shall convene the conference under the auspices of the United Nations. Any amendment adopted by a majority of the States Parties present and voting at the conference shall be submitted to the General Assembly of the United Nations for approval.

2.   Amendments shall come into force when they have been approved by the General Assembly of the United Nations and accepted by a two-thirds majority of the States Parties to the present Covenant in accordance with their respective constitutional processes.

3.   When amendments come into force, they shall be binding on those States Parties which have accepted them, other States Parties still being bound by the provisions of the present Covenant and any earlier amendment which they have accepted.

Article 52

Irrespective of the notifications made under Article 48, paragraph 5, the Secretary-General of the United Nations shall inform all States referred to in paragraph 1 of the same Article of the following particulars:

(*a*)   Signatures, ratifications and accessions under Article 48;

(*b*)   The date of the entry into force of the present Covenant under Article 49 and the (late of the entry into force of any amendments under Article 51.

Article 53

1.   The present Covenant, of which the Chinese, English, French, Russian and Spanish texts are equally authentic, shall be deposited in the archives of the United Nations.

2.   The Secretary-General of the United Nations shall transmit certified copies of the present Covenant to all States referred to in Article 48.

Second Optional Protocol to the International Covenant on Civil and Political Rights, aiming at the abolition of the death penalty

Adopted and proclaimed by General Assembly resolution 44/128 of 15 December 1989

The States Parties to the present Protocol,

Believing that abolition of the death penalty contributes to enhancement of human dignity and progressive development of human rights,

Recalling article 3 of the Universal Declaration on Human Rights, adopted on 10 December 1948, and article 6 of the International Covenant on Civil and Political Rights, adopted on 16 December 1966,

Noting that article 6 of the International Covenant on Civil and Political Rights refers to abolition of the death penalty in terms that strongly suggest that abolition is desirable,

Convinced that all measures of abolition of the death penalty should be considered as progress in the enjoyment of the right to life,

Desirous to undertake hereby an international commitment to abolish the death penalty,

Have agreed as follows:

Article 1

1.   No one within the jurisdiction of a State Party to the present Protocol shall be executed.

2.   Each State party shall take all necessary measures to abolish the death penalty within its jurisdiction.

Article 2

1.   No reservation is admissible to the present Protocol, except for a reservation made at the time of ratification or accession that provides for the application of the death penalty in time of was pursuant to a conviction for a most serious crime of a military nature committed during wartime.

2.   The State party making such a reservation shall at the time of ratification or accession communicate to the Secretary-General of the United Nations the relevant provisions of its national legislation applicable during wartime.

3.   The State Party having made such a reservation shall notify the Secretary-General of the United Nations of any beginning or ending of a state of war applicable to its territory.

Article 3

The States Parties to the present Protocol shall include in the reports they submit to the Human Rights Committee, in accordance with article 40 of the Covenant, information on the measures that they have adopted to give effect to the present Protocol.

Article 4

With respect to the States Parties to the Covenant that have made a declaration under article 41, the competence of the Human Rights Committee to receive and consider communications when a State Party claims that another State Party is not fulfilling its obligations shall extend to the provisions of the present Protocol, unless the State Party concerned has made a statement to the contrary at the moment of ratification or accession.

Article 5

With respect to the States Parties to the first Optional Protocol to the International Covenant on Civil and Political Rights adopted on 16 December 1966, the competence of the Human Rights

Committee to receive and consider communications from individuals subject to its jurisdiction shall extend to the provisions of the present Protocol, unless the State party concerned has made a statement to the contrary at the moment of ratification or accession.

Article 6

1. The provisions of the present Protocol shall apply as additional provisions to the Covenant.

2. Without prejudice tot he possibility of a reservation under article 2 of the present Protocol, the right guaranteed in article 1, paragraph 1, of the present Protocol shall not be subject to any derogation under article 4 of the Covenant.

Article 7

1. The present Protocol is open for signature by any State that has signed the Covenant.

2. The present Protocol is subject to ratification by any State that has ratified the Covenant or acceded to it. Instruments of ratification shall be deposited with the Secretary-General of the United Nations.

3. The present Protocol shall be open to accession by any State that has ratified the Covenant or acceded to it.

4. Accession shall be effected by the deposit of an instrument of accession with the Secretary-General of the United Nations.

5. The Secretary-General of the United Nations shall inform all States that have signed the present Protocol or acceded to it of the deposit of each instrument of ratification or accession.

Article 8

1 The present Protocol shall enter into force three months after the date of the deposit with the Secretary-General of the United Nations of the tenth instrument of ratification or accession.

2 For each State ratifying the present Protocol or acceding to it after the deposit of the tenth instrument of ratification or accession, the present Protocol shall enter into force three months after the date of the deposit of its own instrument of ratification or accession.

Article 9

The provisions of the present Protocol shall extend to all parts of federal States without any limitations or exceptions.

Article 10

The Secretary-General of the United Nations shall inform all States referred to in article 48, paragraph 1, of the Covenant of the following particulars:

(a) Reservation, communications and notifications under article 2 of the present Protocol;

(b) Statements made under articles 4 or 5 of the present Protocol;

(c) Signatures, ratifications and accessions under article 7 of the present Protocol

(d) The date of the entry into force of the present Protocol under article 8 thereof.

Article 11

1. The present Protocol, of which the Arabic, Chinese, English, French, Russian and Spanish texts are equally authentic, shall be deposited in the archives of the United Nations.

2. The Secretary-General of the United Nations shall transmit certified copies of the present Protocol to all States referred to in article 48 of the Covenant.

International Covenant on
Economic, Social, and Cultural Rights, 1966

This appears in the annex to a resolution adopted by the United Nations General Assembly on 16 December 1966. The Covenant entered into force on 3 January 1976; and ninety-nine States have become parties.

TEXT

PREAMBLE

T*he States Parties to the present Covenant,*

Considering that, in accordance with the principles proclaimed in the Charter of the United Nations, recognition of the inherent dignity and of the equal and inalienable rights of all members of the human family is the foundation of freedom, justice and peace in the world,

Recognizing that these rights derive from the inherent dignity of the human person,

Recognizing that, in accordance with the Universal Declaration of Human Rights, the ideal of free human beings enjoying freedom from fear and want can only be achieved if conditions are created whereby everyone may enjoy his economic, social and cultural rights, as well as his civil and political rights,

Considering the obligation of States under the Charter of the United Nations to promote universal respect for, and observance of, human rights and freedoms,

Realizing that the individual, having duties to other individuals and to the community to which he belongs, is under a responsibility to strive for the promotion and observance of the rights recognized in the present Covenant,

Agree upon the following articles:

PART I

Article 1

1.   All peoples have the right of self-determination. By virtue of that right they freely determine their political status and freely pursue their economic, social and cultural development.

2.   All peoples may, for their own ends, freely dispose of their natural wealth and resources without prejudice to any obligations arising out of international economic co-operation, based upon the principle of mutual benefit, and international law. In no case may a people be deprived of its own means of subsistence.

3.   The States Parties to the present Covenant, including those having responsibility for the administration of Non-Self-Governing and Trust Territories, shall promote the realization of the right of self-determination, and shall respect that right, in conformity with the provisions of the Charter of the United Nations.

PART II

Article 2

1.   Each State Party to the present Covenant undertakes to take steps, individually and through international assistance and co-operation, especially economic and technical, to the maximum of its available resources, with a view to achieving progressively the full realization of the rights recognized in the present Covenant by all appropriate means, including particularly the adoption of legislative measures.

2.   The States Parties to the present Covenant undertake to guarantee that the rights enunciated in the present Covenant will be exercised without discrimination of any kind as to race, colour,

sex, language, religion, political or other opinion, national or social origin, property, birth or other status.

3. Developing countries, with due regard to human rights and their national economy, may determine to what extent they would guarantee the economic rights recognized in the present Covenant to non-nationals.

Article 3

The States Parties to the present Covenant undertake to ensure the equal right of men and women to the enjoyment of all economic, social and cultural rights set forth in the present Covenant.

Article 4

The States Parties to the present Covenant recognize that, in the enjoyment of those rights provided by the State in conformity with the present Covenant, the State may subject such rights only to such limitations as are determined by law only in so far as this may be compatible with the nature of these rights and solely for the purpose of promoting the general welfare in a democratic society.

Article 5

1. Nothing in the present Covenant may be interpreted as implying for any State, group or person any right to engage in any activity or to perform any act aimed at the destruction of any of the rights or freedoms recognized herein, or at their limitation to a greater extent than is provided for in the present Covenant.

2. No restriction upon or derogation from any of the fundamental human rights recognized or existing in any country in virtue of law, conventions, regulations or custom shall be admitted on the pretext that the present Covenant does not recognize such rights or that it recognizes them to a lesser extent.

PART III

Article 6

1. The States Parties to the present Covenant recognize the right to work, which includes the right of everyone to the opportunity to gain his living by work which he freely chooses or accepts, and will take appropriate steps to safeguard this right.

2. The steps to be taken by a State Party to the present Covenant to achieve the full realization of this right shall include technical and vocational guidance and training programmes, policies and techniques to achieve steady economic, social and cultural development and full and productive employment under conditions safeguarding fundamental political and economic freedoms to the individual.

Article 7

The States Parties to the present Covenant recognize the right of everyone to the enjoyment of just and favourable conditions of work, which ensure, in particular:

    (*a*)   Remuneration which provides all workers, as a minimum with:

        (i)   Fair wages and equal remuneration for work of equal value without distinction of any kind, in particular women being guaranteed conditions of work not inferior to those enjoyed by men, with equal pay for equal work;

        (ii)   A decent living for themselves and their families in accordance with the provisions of the present Covenant;

    (*b*)   Safe and healthy working conditions;

    (*c*)   Equal opportunity for everyone to be promoted in his employment to an appropriate higher level, subject to no considerations other than those of seniority and competence;

(*d*)   Rest, leisure and reasonable limitation of working hours and periodic holidays with pay, as well as remuneration for public holidays.

Article 8

1.   The States Parties to the present Covenant undertake to ensure:

(*a*)   The right of everyone to form trade unions and join the trade union of his choice, subject only to the rules of the organization concerned, for the promotion and protection of his economic and social interests. No restrictions may be placed on the exercise of this right other than those prescribed by law and which are necessary in a democratic society in the interests of national security or public order or for the protection of the rights and freedoms of others;

(*b*)   The right of trade unions to establish national federations or confederations and the right of the latter to form or join international trade union organizations;

(*c*)   The right of trade unions to function freely subject to no limitations other than those prescribed by law and which are necessary in a democratic society in the interests of national security or public order or for the protection of the rights and freedoms of others;

(*d*)   The right to strike, provided that it is exercised in conformity with the laws of the particular country.

2.   This Article shall not prevent the imposition of lawful restrictions on the exercise of these rights by members of the armed forces or of the police or of the administration of the State.

3.   Nothing in this Article shall authorize States Parties to the International Labour Organization Convention of 1948 concerning Freedom of Association and Protection of the Right to Organize to take legislative measures which would prejudice, or apply the law in such a manner as would prejudice, the guarantees provided for in that Convention.

Article 9

The States Parties to the present Covenant recognize the right of everyone to social security, including social insurance.

Article 10

The States Parties to the present Covenant recognize that:

1.   The widest possible protection and assistance should be accorded to the family, which is the natural and fundamental group unit of society, particularly for its establishment and while it is responsible for the care and education of dependent children. Marriage must be entered into with the free consent of the intending spouses.

2.   Special protection should be accorded to mothers during a reasonable period before and after childbirth. During such period working mothers should be accorded paid leave or leave with adequate social security benefits.

3.   Special measures of protection and assistance should be taken on behalf of all children and young persons without any discrimination for reasons of parentage or other conditions. Children and young persons should be protected from economic and social exploitation. Their employment in work harmful to their morals or health or dangerous to life or likely to hamper their normal development should be punishable by law. States should also set age limits below which the paid employment of child labour should be prohibited and punishable by law.

Article 11

1.   The States Parties to the present Covenant recognize the right of everyone to an adequate standard of living for himself and his family, including adequate food, clothing and housing, and to the continuous improvement of living conditions. The States Parties will take appropriate steps to ensure the realization of this right, recognizing to this effect the essential importance of international co-operation based on free consent.

2.   The States Parties to the present Covenant, recognizing the fundamental right of everyone to be free from hunger, shall take, individually and through international co-operation, the measures, including specific programmes, which are needed:

(*a*)   To improve methods of production, conservation and distribution of food by making full use of technical and scientific knowledge, by disseminating knowledge of the principles of nutrition and by developing or reforming agrarian systems in such a way as to achieve the most efficient development and utilization of natural resources;

(*b*)   Taking into account the problems of both food-importing and food-exporting countries, to ensure an equitable distribution of world food supplies in relation to need.

Article 12

1.   The States Parties to the present Covenant recognize the right of everyone to the enjoyment of the highest attainable standard of physical and mental health.

2.   The steps to be taken by the States Parties to the present Covenant to achieve the full realization of this right shall include those necessary for:

(*a*)   The provision for the reduction of the stillbirth-rate and of infant mortality and for the healthy development of the child;

(*b*)   The improvement of all aspects of environmental and industrial hygiene;

(*c*)   The prevention, treatment and control of epidemic, endemic, occupational and other diseases;

(*d*)   The creation of conditions which would assure to all medical service and medical attention in the event of sickness.

Article 13

1.   The States Parties to the present Covenant recognize the right of everyone to education. They agree that education shall be directed to the full development of the human personality and the sense of its dignity, and shall strengthen the respect for human rights and fundamental freedoms. They further agree that education shall enable all persons to participate effectively in a free society, promote understanding, tolerance and friendship among all nations and all racial, ethnic or religious groups, and further the activities of the United Nations for the maintenance of peace.

2.   The States Parties to the present Covenant recognize that, with a view to achieving the full realization of this right:

(*a*)   Primary education shall be compulsory and available free to all;

(*b*)   Secondary education in its different forms, including technical and vocational secondary education, shall be made generally available and accessible to all by every appropriate means, and in particular by the progressive introduction of free education;

(*c*)   Higher education shall be made equally accessible to all, on the basis of capacity, by every appropriate means, and in particular by the progressive introduction of free education;

(*d*)   Fundamental education shall be encouraged or intensified as far as possible for those persons who have not received or completed the whole period of their primary education;

(*e*)   The development of a system of schools at all levels shall be actively pursued, an adequate fellowship system shall be established, and the material conditions of teaching staff shall be continuously improved.

3.   The States Parties to the present Covenant undertake to have respect for the liberty of parents and, when applicable, legal guardians, to choose for their children schools, other than those established by the public authorities, which conform to such minimum educational standards as may be laid down or approved by the State and to ensure the religious and moral education of their children in conformity with their own convictions.

4.   No part of this Article shall be construed so as to interfere with the liberty of individuals and bodies to establish and direct educational institutions, subject always to the observance of the principles set forth in paragraph 1 of this Article and to the requirement that the education given in such institutions shall conform to such minimum standards as may be laid down by the State.

Article 14

Each State Party to the present Covenant which, at the time of becoming a Party, has not been able to secure in its metropolitan territory or other territories under its jurisdiction compulsory primary education, free of charge, undertakes, within two years, to work out and adopt a detailed plan of action for the progressive implementation, within a reasonable number of years, to be fixed in the plan, of the principle of compulsory education free of charge for all.

Article 15

1.   The States Parties to the present Covenant recognize the right of everyone:

   (*a*)   To take part in cultural life;

   (*b*)   To enjoy the benefits of scientific progress and its applications;

   (*c*)   To benefit from the protection of the moral and material interests resulting from any scientific, literary or artistic production of which he is the author.

2.   The steps to be taken by the States Parties to the present Covenant to achieve the full realization of this right shall include those necessary for the conservation, the development and the diffusion of science and culture.

3.   The States Parties to the present Covenant undertake to respect the freedom indispensable for scientific research and creative activity.

4.   The States Parties to the present Covenant recognize the benefits to be derived from the encouragement and development of international contacts and co-operation in the scientific and cultural fields.

PART IV

Article 16

1.   The States Parties to the present Covenant undertake to submit in conformity with this part of the Covenant reports on the measures which they have adopted and the progress made in achieving the observance of the rights recognized herein.

2.   (*a*)   All reports shall be submitted to the Secretary-General of the United Nations, who shall transmit copies to the Economic and Social Council for consideration in accordance with the provisions of the present Covenant.

   (*b*)   The Secretary-General of the United Nations shall also transmit to the specialized agencies copies of the reports, or any relevant parts therefrom, from States Parties to the present Covenant which are also members of these specialized agencies in so far as these reports, or parts therefrom, relate to any matters which fall within the responsibilities of the said agencies in accordance with their constitutional instruments.

Article 17

1.   The States Parties to the present Covenant shall furnish their reports in stages, in accordance with a programme to be established by the Economic and Social Council within one year of the entry into force of the present Covenant after consultation with the States Parties and the specialized agencies concerned.

2.   Reports may indicate factors and difficulties affecting the degree of fulfilment of obligations under the present Covenant.

3.   Where relevant information has previously been furnished to the United Nations or to any specialized agency by any State Party to the present Covenant, it will not be necessary to reproduce that information, but a precise reference to the information so furnished will suffice.

Article 18

Pursuant to its responsibilities under the Charter of the United Nations in the field of human rights and fundamental freedoms, the Economic and Social Council may make arrangements with the specialized agencies in respect of their reporting to it on the progress made in achieving the observance of the provisions of the present Covenant falling within the scope of their activities. These reports may include particulars of decisions and recommendations on such implementation adopted by their competent organs.

Article 19

The Economic and Social Council may transmit to the Commission on Human Rights for study and general recommendation or as appropriate for information the reports concerning human rights submitted by States in accordance with Articles 16 and 17, and those concerning human rights submitted by the specialized agencies in accordance with Article 18.

Article 20

The States Parties to the present Covenant and the specialized agencies concerned may submit comments to the Economic and Social Council on any general recommendation under Article 19 or reference to such general recommendation in any report of the Commission on Human Rights or any documentation referred to therein.

Article 21

The Economic and Social Council may submit from time to time to the General Assembly reports with recommendations of a general nature and a summary of the information received from the States Parties to the present Covenant and the specialized agencies on the measures taken and the progress made in achieving general observance of the rights recognized in the present Covenant.

Article 22

The Economic and Social Council may bring to the attention of other organs of the United Nations, their subsidiary organs and specialized agencies concerned with furnishing technical assistance any matters arising out of the reports referred to in this part of the present Covenant which may assist such bodies in deciding, each within its field of competence, on the advisability of international measures likely to contribute to the effective progressive implementation of the present Covenant.

Article 23

The States Parties to the present Covenant agree that international action for the achievement of the rights recognized in the present Covenant includes such methods as the conclusion of conventions, the adoption of recommendations, the furnishing of technical assistance and the holding of regional meetings and technical meetings for the purpose of consultation and study organized in conjunction with the Governments concerned.

Article 24

Nothing in the present Covenant shall be interpreted as impairing the provisions of the Charter of the United Nations and of the constitutions of the specialized agencies which define the respective responsibilities of the various organs of the United Nations and of the specialized agencies in regard to the matters dealt with in the present Covenant.

Article 25

Nothing in the present Covenant shall be interpreted as impairing the inherent right of all peoples to enjoy and utilize fully and freely their natural wealth and resources.

PART V

Article 26

1.   The present Covenant is open for signature by any State Member of the United Nations or member of any of its specialized agencies, by any State Party to the Statute of the International Court of Justice, and by any other State which has been invited by the General Assembly of the United Nations to become a party to the present Covenant.

2.   The present Covenant is subject to ratification. Instruments of ratification shall be deposited with the Secretary-General of the United Nations.

3.   The present Covenant shall be open to accession by any State referred to in paragraph 1 of this Article.

4.   Accession shall be effected by the deposit of an instrument of accession with the Secretary-General of the United Nations.

5. The Secretary-General of the United Nations shall inform all States which have signed the present Covenant or acceded to it of the deposit of each instrument of ratification or accession.

Article 27

1.   The present Covenant shall enter into force three months after the date of the deposit with the Secretary-General of the United Nations of the thirty-fifth instrument of ratification or instrument of accession.

2.   For each State ratifying the present Covenant or acceding to it after the deposit of the thirty-fifth instrument of ratification or instrument of accession, the present Covenant shall enter into force three months after the date of the deposit of its own instrument of ratification or instrument of accession.

Article 28

The provisions of the present Covenant shall extend to all parts of federal States without any limitations or exceptions.

Article 29

1.   Any State Party to the present Covenant may propose an amendment and file it with the Secretary-General of the United Nations. The Secretary-General shall thereupon communicate any proposed amendments to the States Parties to the present Covenant with a request that they notify him whether they favour a conference of States Parties for the purpose of considering and voting upon the proposals. In the event that at least one third of the States Parties favours such a conference, the Secretary-General shall convene the conference under the auspices of the United Nations. Any amendment adopted by a majority of the States Parties present and voting at the conference shall be submitted to the General Assembly of the United Nations for approval.

2.   Amendments shall come into force when they have been approved by the General Assembly of the United Nations and accepted by a two-thirds majority of the State Parties to the present Covenant in accordance with their respective constitutional processes.

3.   When amendments come into force they shall be binding on those States Parties which have accepted them, other States Parties still being bound by the provisions of the present Covenant and any earlier amendment which they have accepted.

Article 30

Irrespective of the notifications made under Article 26, paragraph 5, the Secretary-General of the United Nations shall inform all States referred to in paragraph 1 of the same Article of the following particulars:

(*a*)   Signatures, ratifications and accessions under Article 26;

(*b*)   The date of the entry into force of the present Covenant under Article 27 and the date of the entry into force of any amendments under Article 29.

Article 31

1.   The present Covenant, of which the Chinese, English, French, Russian and Spanish texts are equally authentic, shall be deposited in the archives of the United Nations.

2.   The Secretary-General of the United Nations shall transmit certified copies of the present Covenant to all States referred to in Article 26.

International Convention on the Elimination of All Forms of Racial Discrimination, 1966

The States Parties to this Convention,

Considering that the Charter of the United Nations is based on the principles of the dignity and equality inherent in all human beings, and that all Member States have pledged themselves to take joint and separate action, in co-operation with the Organization, for the achievement of one of the purposes of the United Nations which is to promote and encourage universal respect for and observance of human rights and fundamental freedoms for all, without distinction as to race, sex, language or religion,

Considering that the Universal Declaration of Human Rights proclaims that all human beings are born free and equal in dignity and rights and that everyone is entitled to all the rights and freedoms set out therein, without distinction of any kind, in particular as to race, colour or national origin,

Considering that all human beings are equal before the law and are entitled to equal protection of the law against any discrimination and against any incitement to discrimination,

Considering that the United Nations has condemned colonialism and all practices of segregation and discrimination associated therewith, in whatever form and wherever they exist, and that the Declaration on the Granting of Independence to Colonial Countries and Peoples of 14 December 1960 (General Assembly resolution 1514 (XV)) has affirmed and solemnly proclaimed the necessity of bringing them to a speedy and unconditional end,

Considering that the United Nations Declaration on the Elimination of All Forms of Racial Discrimination of 20 November 1963 (General Assembly resolution 1940 (XVIII) solemnly affirms the necessity of speedily eliminating racial discrimination throughout the world in all its forms and manifestations and of securing understanding of and respect for the dignity of the human person,

Convinced that any doctrine of superiority based on racial differentiation is scientifically false, morally condemnable, socially unjust and dangerous, and that there is no justification for racial discrimination, in theory or in practice, anywhere,

Reaffirming that discrimination between human beings on the grounds of race, colour or ethnic origin is an obstacle to friendly and peaceful relations among nations and is capable of disturbing peace and security among peoples and the harmony of persons living side by side even within one and the same State,

Convinced that the existence of racial barriers is repugnant to the ideals of any human society,

Alarmed by manifestations of racial discrimination still in evidence in some areas of the world and by governmental policies based on racial superiority or hatred, such as policies of *apartheid,* segregation or separation,

Resolved to adopt all necessary measures for speedily eliminating racial discrimination in all its forms and manifestations, and to prevent and combat racist doctrines and practices in order to promote understanding between races and to build an international community free from all forms of racial segregation and racial discrimination,

Bearing in mind the Convention concerning Discrimination in respect of Employment and Occupation adopted by the International Labour Organization in 1958, and the Convention against Discrimination in Education adopted by the United Nations Educational, Scientific and Cultural Organization in 1960,

Desiring to implement the principles embodied in the United Nations Declaration on the Elimination of All Forms of Racial Discrimination and to secure the earliest adoption of practical measures to that end,

Have agreed as follows:

PART I

Article 1

1.   In this Convention, the term 'racial discrimination' shall mean any distinction, exclusion, restriction or preference based on race, colour, descent, or national or ethnic origin which has the purpose or effect of nullifying or impairing the recognition, enjoyment or exercise, on an equal footing, of human rights and fundamental freedoms in the political, economic, social, cultural or any other field of public life.

2. This Convention shall not apply to distinctions, exclusions, restrictions or preferences made by a State Party to this Convention between citizens and non-citizens.

3. Nothing in this Convention may be interpreted as affecting in any way the legal provisions of States Parties concerning nationality, citizenship or naturalization, provided that such provisions do not discriminate against any particular nationality.

4. Special measures taken for the sole purpose of securing adequate advancement of certain racial or ethnic groups or individuals requiring such protection as may be necessary in order to ensure such groups or individuals equal enjoyment or exercise of human rights and fundamental freedoms shall not be deemed racial discrimination, provided, however, that such measures do not, as a consequence, lead to the maintenance of separate rights for different racial groups and that they shall not be continued after the objectives for which they were taken have been achieved.

Article 2

1.   States Parties condemn racial discrimination and undertake to pursue by all appropriate means and without delay a policy of eliminating racial discrimination in all its forms and promoting understanding among all races, and, to this end:

(*a*)   Each State Party undertakes to engage in no act or practice of racial discrimination against persons, groups of persons or institutions and to ensure that all public authorities and public institutions, national and local, shall act in conformity with this obligation;

(*b*)   Each State Party undertakes not to sponsor, defend or support racial discrimination by any persons or organizations;

(*c*)   Each State Party shall take effective measures to review governmental, national and local policies, and to amend, rescind or nullify any laws and regulations which have the effect of creating or perpetuating racial discrimination wherever it exists;

(*d*)   Each State Party shall prohibit and bring to an end, by all appropriate means, including legislation as required by circumstances, racial discrimination by any persons, group or organization;

(*e*)   Each State Party undertakes to encourage, where appropriate, integrationist multi-racial organizations and movements and other means of eliminating barriers between races, and to discourage anything which tends to strengthen racial division.

2.   States Parties shall, when the circumstances so warrant, take, in the social, economic, cultural and other fields, special and concrete measures to ensure the adequate development and protection of certain racial groups or individuals belonging to them, for the purpose of guaranteeing them the full and equal enjoyment of human rights and fundamental freedoms. These measures shall in no case entail as a consequence the maintenance of unequal or separate rights for different racial groups after the objectives for which they were taken have been achieved.

Article 3

States Parties particularly condemn racial segregation and *apartheid* and undertake to prevent, prohibit and eradicate all practices of this nature in territories under their jurisdiction.

Article 4

States Parties condemn all propaganda and all organizations which are based on ideas or theories of superiority of one race or group of persons of one colour or ethnic origin, or which attempt to justify or promote racial hatred and discrimination in any form, and undertake to adopt immediate and positive measures designed to eradicate all incitement to, or acts of, such discrimination and, to this end, with due regard to the principles embodied in the Universal Declaration of Human Rights and the rights expressly set forth in Article 5 of this Convention, *inter alia:*

(a) Shall declare an offence punishable by law all dissemination of ideas based on racial superiority or hatred, incitement to racial discrimination, as well as all acts of violence or incitement to such acts against any race or group of persons of another colour or ethnic origin, and also the provision of any assistance to racist activities, including the financing thereof;

(b) Shall declare illegal and prohibit organizations, and also organized and all other propaganda activities, which promote and incite racial discrimination, and shall recognize participation in such organizations or activities as an offence punishable by law;

(c) Shall not permit public authorities or public institutions, national or local, to promote or incite racial discrimination.

Article 5

In compliance with the fundamental obligations laid down in Article 2 of this Convention, States Parties undertake to prohibit and to eliminate racial discrimination in all its forms and to guarantee the right of everyone, without distinction as to race, colour, or national or ethnic origin, to equality before the law, notably in the enjoyment of the following rights:

(a) The right to equal treatment before the tribunals and all other organs administering justice;

(b) The right to security of person and protection by the State against violence or bodily harm, whether inflicted by government officials or by any individual, group or institution;

(c) Political rights, in particular the rights to participate in elections—to vote and to stand for election—on the basis of universal and equal suffrage, to take part in the Government as well as in the conduct of public affairs at any level and to have equal access to public service;

(d) Other civil rights, in particular:

　　(i) The right to freedom of movement and residence within the border of the State;

　　(ii) The right to leave any country, including one's own, and to return to one's country;

　　(iii) The right to nationality;

　　(iv) The right to marriage and choice of spouse;

　　(v) The right to own property alone as well as in association with others;

　　(vi) The right to inherit;

　　(vii) The right to freedom of thought, conscience and religion;

　　(viii) The right to freedom of opinion and expression;

　　(ix) The right to freedom of peaceful assembly and association;

(e) Economic, social and cultural rights, in particular:

(i)　The rights to work, to free choice of employment, to just and favourable conditions of work, to protection against unemployment, to equal pay for equal work, to just and favourable remuneration;

(ii)　The right to form and join trade unions;

(iii)　The right to housing;

(iv)　The right to public health, medical care, social security and social services;

(v)　The right to education and training;

(vi)　The right to equal participation in cultural activities;

(f)　The right to access to any place or service intended for use by the general public, such as transport, hotels, restaurants, cafés, theatres and parks.

Article 6

States Parties shall assure to everyone within their jurisdiction effective protection and remedies, through the competent national tribunals and other State institutions, against any acts of racial discrimination which violate his human rights and fundamental freedoms contrary to this Convention, as well as the right to seek from such tribunals just and adequate reparation or satisfaction for any damage suffered as a result of such discrimination.

Article 7

States Parties undertake to adopt immediate and effective measures, particularly in the fields of teaching, education, culture and information, with a view to combating prejudices which lead to racial discrimination and to promoting understanding, tolerance and friendship among nations and racial or ethnical groups, as well as to propagating the purposes and principles of the Charter of the United Nations, the Universal Declaration of Human Rights, the United Nations Declaration on the Elimination of All Forms of Racial Discrimination, and this Convention.

PART II

Article 8

1.　There shall be established a Committee on the Elimination of Racial Discrimination (hereinafter referred to as the Committee) consisting of eighteen experts of high moral standing and acknowledged impartiality elected by States Parties from among their nationals, who shall serve in their personal capacity, consideration being given to equitable geographical distribution and to the representation of the different forms of civilization as well as of the principal legal systems.

2.　The members of the Committee shall be elected by secret ballot from a list of persons nominated by the States Parties. Each State Party may nominate one person from among its own nationals.

3.　The initial election shall be held six months after the date of the entry into force of this Convention. At least three months before the date of each election the Secretary-General of the United Nations shall address a letter to the States Parties inviting them to submit their nominations within two months. The Secretary-General shall prepare a list in alphabetical order of all persons thus nominated, indicating the States Parties which have nominated them, and shall submit it to the States Parties.

4.　Elections of the members of the Committee shall be held at a meeting of States Parties convened by the Secretary-General at United Nations Headquarters. At that meeting, for which two-thirds of the States Parties shall constitute a quorum, the persons elected to the Committee shall be those nominees who obtain the largest number of votes and an absolute majority of the votes of the representatives of States Parties present and voting.

5.　(a)　The members of the Committee shall be elected for a term of four years. However, the terms of nine of the members elected at the first election shall expire at the end of two years; immediately after the first election the names of these nine members shall be chosen by lot by the Chairman of the Committee.

(*b*) For the filling of casual vacancies, the State Party whose expert has ceased to function as a member of the Committee shall appoint another expert from among its nationals, subject to the approval of the Committee.

6.   States Parties shall be responsible for the expenses of the members of the Committee while they are in performance of Committee duties.

Article 9

1.   States Parties undertake to submit to the Secretary-General of the United Nations, for consideration by the Committee, a report on the legislative, judicial, administrative or other measures which they have adopted and which give effect to the provisions of this Convention: (*a*) within one year after the entry into force of the Convention for the State concerned; and (*b*) thereafter every two years and whenever the Committee so requests. The Committee may request further information from the States Parties.

2.   The Committee shall report annually, through the Secretary-General, to the General Assembly of the United Nations on its activities and may make suggestions and general recommendations based on the examination of the reports and information received from the States Parties. Such suggestions and general recommendations shall be reported to the General Assembly together with comments, if any, from States Parties.

Article 10

1.   The Committee shall adopt its own rules of procedure.

2.   The Committee shall elect its officers for a term of two years.

3.   The secretariat of the Committee shall be provided by the Secretary-General of the United Nations.

4.   The meetings of the Committee shall normally be held at United Nations Headquarters.

Article 11

1.   If a State Party considers that another State Party is not giving effect to the provisions of this Convention, it may bring the matter to the attention of the Committee. The Committee shall then transmit the communication to the State Party concerned. Within three months, the receiving State shall submit to the Committee written explanations or statements clarifying the matter and the remedy, if any, that may have been taken by that State.

2.   If the matter is not adjusted to the satisfaction of both parties, either by bilateral negotiations or by any other procedure open to them, within six months after the receipt by the receiving State of the initial communication, either State shall have the right to refer the matter again to the Committee by notifying the Committee and also the other State.

3.   The Committee shall deal with a matter referred to it in accordance with paragraph 2 of this Article after it has ascertained that all available domestic remedies have been invoked and exhausted in the case, in conformity with the generally recognized principles of international law. This shall not be the rule where the application of the remedies is unreasonably prolonged.

4.   In any matter referred to it, the Committee may call upon the States Parties concerned to supply any other relevant information.

5.   When any matter arising out of this Article is being considered by the Committee, the States Parties concerned shall be entitled to send a representative to take part in the proceedings of the Committee, without voting rights, while the matter is under consideration.

Article 12

1.   (*a*) After the Committee has obtained and collated all the information it deems necessary,

the Chairman shall appoint an *ad hoc* Conciliation Commission (hereinafter referred to as the Commission) comprising five persons who may or may not be members of the Committee. The members of the Commission shall be appointed with the unanimous consent of the parties to the dispute, and its good offices shall be made available to the States concerned with a view to an amicable solution of the matter on the basis of respect for this Convention.

(b) If the States Parties to the dispute fail to reach agreement within three months on all or part of the composition of the Commission, the members of the Commission not agreed upon by the States Parties to the dispute shall be elected by secret ballot by a two-thirds majority vote of the Committee from among its own members.

2. The members of the Commission shall serve in their personal capacity. They shall not be nationals of the States Parties to the dispute or of a State not Party to this Convention.

3. The Commission shall elect its own Chairman and adopt its own rules of procedure.

4. The meetings of the Commission shall normally be held at United Nations Headquarters or at any other convenient place as determined by the Commission.

5. The secretariat provided in accordance with Article 10, paragraph 3, of this Convention shall also service the Commission whenever a dispute among States Parties brings the Commission into being.

6. The States Parties to the dispute shall share equally all the expenses of the members of the Commission in accordance with estimates to be provided by the Secretary-General of the United Nations.

7. The Secretary-General shall be empowered to pay the expenses of the members of the Commission, if necessary, before reimbursement by the States Parties to the dispute in accordance with paragraph 6 of this Article.

8. The information obtained and collated by the Committee shall be made available to the Commission, and the Commission may call upon the States concerned to supply any other relevant information.

Article 13

1. When the Commission has fully considered the matter, it shall prepare and submit to the Chairman of the Committee a report embodying its findings on all questions of fact relevant to the issue between the parties and containing such recommendations as it may think proper for the amicable solution of the dispute.

2. The Chairman of the Committee shall communicate the report of the Commission to each of the States Parties to the dispute. These States shall, within three months, inform the Chairman of the Committee whether or not they accept the recommendations contained in the report of the Commission.

3. After the period provided for in paragraph 2 of this Article, the Chairman of the Committee shall communicate the report of the Commission and the declarations of the States Parties concerned to the other States Parties to this Convention.

Article 14

1. A State Party may at any time declare that it recognizes the competence of the Committee to receive and consider communications from individuals or groups of individuals within its jurisdiction claiming to be victims of a violation by that State Party of any of the rights set forth in this Convention. No communication shall be received by the Committee if it concerns a State Party which has not made such a declaration.

2. Any State Party which makes a declaration as provided for in paragraph 1 of this Article may establish or indicate a body within its national legal order which shall be competent to receive and consider petitions from individuals and groups of individuals within its jurisdiction

who claim to be victims of a violation of any of the rights set forth in this Convention and who have exhausted other available local remedies.

3. A declaration made in accordance with paragraph 1 of this Article and the name of any body established or indicated in accordance with paragraph 2 of this Article shall be deposited by the State Party concerned with the Secretary-General of the United Nations, who shall transmit copies thereof to the other States Parties. A declaration may be withdrawn at any time by notification to the Secretary-General, but such a withdrawal shall not affect communications pending before the Committee.

4.   A register of petitions shall be kept by the body established or indicated in accordance with paragraph 2 of this Article, and certified copies of the register shall be filed annually through appropriate channels with the Secretary-General on the understanding that the contents shall not be publicly disclosed.

5.   In the event of failure to obtain satisfaction from the body established or indicated in accordance with paragraph 2 of this Article, the petitioner shall have the right to communicate the matter to the Committee within six months.

6.   (*a*)   The Committee shall confidentially bring any communication referred to it to the attention of the State Party alleged to be violating any provision of this Convention, but the identity of the individual or groups of individuals concerned shall not be revealed without his or their express consent. The Committee shall not receive anonymous communications.

    (*b*)   Within three months, the receiving State shall submit to the Committee written explanations or statements clarifying the matter and the remedy, if any, that may have been taken by that State.

7.   (*a*)   The Committee shall consider communications in the light of all information made available to it by the State Party concerned and by the petitioner. The Committee shall not consider any communication from a petitioner unless it has ascertained that the petitioner has exhausted all available domestic remedies. However, this shall not be the rule where the application of the remedies is unreasonably prolonged.

    (*b*)   The Committee shall forward its suggestions and recommendations, if any, to the State Party concerned and to the petitioner.

8.   The Committee shall include in its annual report a summary of such communications and, where appropriate, a summary of the explanations and statements of the States Parties concerned and of its own suggestions and recommendations.

9.   The Committee shall be competent to exercise the functions provided for in this Article only when at least ten States Parties to this Convention are bound by declarations in accordance with paragraph 1 of this Article.

Article 15

1.   Pending the achievement of the objectives of the Declaration on the Granting of Independence to Colonial Countries and Peoples, contained in General Assembly resolution 1514 (XV) of 14 December 1960, the provisions of this Convention shall in no way limit the right of petition granted to these peoples by other international instruments or by the United Nations and its specialized agencies.

2.   (*a*)   The Committee established under Article 8, paragraph 1, of this Convention shall receive copies of the petitions from, and submit expressions of opinion and recommendations on these petitions to, the bodies of the United Nations which deal with matters directly related to the principles and objectives of this Convention in their consideration of petitions from the inhabitants of Trust and Non-Self-Governing Territories and all other territories to which General Assembly resolution 1514 (XV) applies, relating to matters covered by this Convention which are before these bodies.

    (*b*)   The Committee shall receive from the competent bodies of the United Nations copies of the reports concerning the legislative, judicial, administrative or other measures directly related to the principles and objectives of this Convention applied by the administering Powers within the Territories mentioned in sub-paragraph (a) of this paragraph, and shall express opinions and make recommendations to these bodies.

3.   The Committee shall include in its report to the General Assembly a summary of the petitions and reports it has received from United Nations bodies, and the expressions of opinion and recommendations of the Committee relating to the said petitions and reports.

4.   The Committee shall request from the Secretary-General of the United Nations all information relevant to the objectives of this Convention and available to him regarding the Territories mentioned in paragraph 2 (a) of this Article.

Article 16

The provisions of this Convention concerning the settlement of disputes or complaints shall be applied without prejudice to other procedures for settling disputes or complaints in the field of discrimination laid down in the constituent instruments of, or in conventions adopted by, the United Nations and its specialized agencies, and shall not prevent the States Parties from having recourse to other procedures for settling a dispute in accordance with general or special international agreements in force between them.

PART III

Article 17

1.   This Convention is open for signature by any State Member of the United Nations or member of any of its specialized agencies, by any State Party to the Statute of the International Court of Justice, and by any other State which has been invited by the General Assembly of the United Nations to become a Party to this Convention.

2.   This Convention is subject to ratification. Instruments of ratification shall be deposited with the Secretary-General of the United Nations.

Article 18

1.   This Convention shall be open to accession by any State referred to in Article 17, paragraph 1, of the Convention.

2.   Accession shall be effected by the deposit of an instrument of accession with the Secretary-General of the United Nations.

Article 19

1.   This Convention shall enter into force on the thirtieth day after the date of the deposit with the Secretary-General of the United Nations of the twenty-seventh instrument of ratification or instrument of accession.

2.   For each State ratifying this Convention or acceding to it after the deposit of the twenty-seventh instrument of ratification or instrument of accession, the Convention shall enter force on the thirtieth day after the date of the deposit of its own instrument of ratification or instrument of accession.

Article 20

1.   The Secretary-General of the United Nations shall receive and circulate to all States which are or may become Parties to this Convention reservations made by States at the time of ratification or accession. Any State which objects to the reservation shall, within a period of ninety days from the date of the said communication, notify the Secretary-General that it does not accept it.

2.   A reservation incompatible with the object and purpose of this Convention shall not be permitted, nor shall a reservation the effect of which would inhibit the operation of any of the bodies established by this Convention be allowed. A reservation shall be considered incompatible or inhibitive if at least two-thirds of the States Parties to this Convention object to it.

3.   Reservations may be withdrawn at any time by notification to this effect addressed to the Secretary-General. Such notification shall take effect on the date on which it is received.

Article 21

A State Party may denounce this Convention by written notification to the Secretary-General of the United Nations. Denunciation shall take effect one year after the date of receipt of the notification by the Secretary-General.

Article 22

Any dispute between two or more States Parties with respect to the interpretation or application of this Convention, which is not settled by negotiation or by the procedures expressly provided for in this Convention, shall, at the request of any of the parties to the dispute, be referred to the International Court of Justice for decision, unless the disputants agree to another mode of settlement.

Article 23

1.   A request for the revision of this Convention may be made at any time by any State Party by means of a notification in writing addressed to the Secretary-General of the United Nations.

2.   The General Assembly of the United Nations shall decide upon the steps, if any, to be taken in respect of such a request.

Article 24

The Secretary-General of the United Nations shall inform all States referred to in Article 17, paragraph 1, of this Convention of the following particulars:

(*a*)   Signatures, ratifications and accessions under Articles 17 and 18;

(*b*)   The date of entry into force of this Convention under Article 19;

(*c*)   Communications and declarations received under Articles 14, 20 and 23;

(*d*)   Denunciations under Article 21.

Article 25

1.   This Convention, of which the Chinese, English, French, Russian and Spanish texts are equally authentic, shall be deposited in the archives of the United Nations.

2.   The Secretary-General of the United Nations shall transmit certified copies of this Convention to all States belonging to any of the categories mentioned in Article 17, paragraph 1, of the Convention.

In faith whereof the undersigned, being duly authorized thereto by their respective Governments, have signed the present Convention, opened for signature at New York, on the seventh day of March, one thousand nine hundred and sixty-six.

ANNEX

The General Assembly,

Recalling the Declaration on the Granting of Independence to Colonial Countries and Peoples contained in its resolution 1514 (XV) of 14 December 1960.

Bearing in mind its resolution 1654 (XVI) of 27 November 1961, which established the Special Committee on the Situation with regard to the Implementation of the Declaration on the Granting of Independence to Colonial Countries and Peoples to examine the application of the Declaration and to carry out its provisions by all means at its disposal,

Bearing in mind also the provisions of Article 15 of the International Convention on the Elimination of All Forms of Racial Discrimination contained in the annex to resolution 2106 A (XX) above,

Recalling that the General Assembly has established other bodies to receive and examine petitions from the peoples of colonial countries,

Convinced that close co-operation between the Committee on the Elimination of Racial Discrimination, established by the International Convention on the Elimination of All Forms of Racial Discrimination, and the bodies of the United Nations charged with receiving and examining petitions from the peoples of colonial countries will facilitate the achievement of the objectives of both the Convention and the Declaration on the Granting of Independence to Colonial Countries and Peoples,

Recognizing that the elimination of racial discrimination in all its forms is vital to the achievement of fundamental human rights and to the assurance of the dignity and worth of the human person, and thus constitutes a pre-emptory obligation under the Charter of the United Nations,

1. *Calls upon* the Secretary-General to make available to the Committee on the Elimination of Racial Discrimination, periodically or at its request, all information in his possession relevant to Article 15 of the International Convention on the Elimination of All Forms of Racial Discrimination;

2. *Requests* the Special Committee on the Situation with regard to the Implementation of the Granting of Independence to Colonial Countries and Peoples, and all other bodies of the United Nations authorized to receive and examine petitions from the peoples of the colonial countries, to transmit to the Committee on the Elimination of Racial Discrimination, periodically or at its request, copies of petitions from those peoples relevant to the Convention, for the comments and recommendations of the said Committee;

3. *Requests* the bodies referred to in paragraph 2 above to include in their annual reports to the General Assembly a summary of the action taken by them under the terms of the present resolution.

1406th plenary meeting

21 December 1965

Convention on the Elimination of all Forms of Discrimination Against Women, 1979

The States Parties to the present Convention,

Noting that the Charter of the United Nations reaffirms faith in fundamental human rights, in the dignity and worth of the human person and in the equal rights of men and women,

Noting that the Universal Declaration of Human Rights affirms the principle of the inadmissibility of discrimination and proclaims that all human beings are born free and equal in dignity and rights and that everyone is entitled to all the rights and freedoms set forth therein, without distinction of any kind, including distinction based on sex,

Noting that the States Parties to the International Covenants on Human Rights have the obligation to ensure the equal right of men and women to enjoy all economic, social, cultural, civil and political rights,

Considering the international conventions concluded under the auspices of the United Nations and the specialized agencies promoting equality of rights of men and women,

Noting also the resolutions, declarations and recommendations adopted by the United Nations and the specialized agencies promoting equality of rights of men and women,

Concerned, however, that despite these various instruments extensive discrimination against women continues to exist,

Recalling that discrimination against women violates the principles of equality of rights and respect for human dignity, is an obstacle to the participation of women, on equal terms with men, in the political, social, economic and cultural life of their countries, hampers the growth of the prosperity of society and the family and makes more difficult the full development of the potentialities of women in the service of their countries and of humanity,

Concerned that in situations of poverty women have the least access to food, health, education, training and opportunities for employment and other needs,

Convinced that the establishment of the new international economic order based on equity and justice will contribute significantly towards the promotion of equality between men and women,

Emphasizing that the eradication of *apartheid,* of all forms of racism, racial discrimination, colonialism, neo-colonialism, aggression, foreign occupation and domination and interference in the internal affairs of States is essential to the full enjoyment of the rights of men and women,

Affirming that the strengthening of international peace and security, relaxation of international tension, mutual co-operation among all States irrespective of their social and economic systems, general and complete disarmament, and in particular nuclear disarmament under strict and effective international control, the affirmation of the principles of justice, equality and mutual benefit in relations among countries and the realization of the right of peoples under alien and colonial domination and foreign occupation to self-determination and independence, as well as respect for national sovereignty and territorial integrity, will promote social progress and development and as a consequence will contribute to the attainment of full equality between men and women,

Convinced that the full and complete development of a country, the welfare of the world and the cause of peace require the maximum participation of women on equal terms with men in all fields,

Bearing in mind the great contribution of women to the welfare of the family and to the development of society, so far not fully recognized, the social significance of maternity and the role of both parents in the family and in the upbringing of children, and aware that the role of women in procreation should not be a basis for discrimination but that the upbringing of children requires a sharing of responsibility between men and women and society as a whole,

Aware that a change in the traditional role of men as well as the role of women in society and in the family is needed to achieve full equality between men and women,

Determined to implement the principles set forth in the Declaration on the Elimination of Discrimination against Women and, for that purpose, to adopt the measures required for the elimination of such discrimination in all its forms and manifestations,

Have agreed on the following:

PART I

Article 1

For the purposes of the present Convention, the term 'discrimination against women' shall mean any distinction, exclusion or restriction made on the basis of sex which has the effect or purpose of impairing or nullifying the recognition, enjoyment or exercise by women, irrespective of their marital status, on a basis of equality of men and women, of human rights and fundamental freedoms in the political, economic, social, cultural, civil or any other field.

Article 2

States parties condemn discrimination against women in all its forms, agree to pursue by all appropriate means and without delay a policy of eliminating discrimination against women and, to this end, undertake;

(a) To embody the principle of the equality of men and women in their national constitutions or other appropriate legislation if not yet incorporated therein and to ensure, through law and other appropriate means, the practical realization of this principle;

(b) To adopt appropriate legislative and other measures, including sanctions where appropriate, prohibiting all discrimination against women;

(c) To establish legal protection of the rights of women on an equal basis with men and to ensure through competent national tribunals and other public institutions the effective protection of women against any act of discrimination;

(d) To refrain from engaging in any act or practice of discrimination against women and to ensure that public authorities and institutions shall act in conformity with this obligation;

(e) To take all appropriate measures to eliminate discrimination against women by any person, organization or enterprise;

(f) To take all appropriate measures, including legislation, to modify or abolish existing laws, regulations, customs and practices which constitute discrimination against women;

(g) To repeal all national penal provisions which constitute discrimination against women.

Article 3

States Parties shall take in all fields, in particular in the political, social, economic and cultural fields, all appropriate measures, including legislation, to ensure the full development and advancement of women, for the purpose of guaranteeing them the exercise and enjoyment of human rights and fundamental freedoms on a basis of equality with men.

Article 4

1.   Adoption by States Parties of temporary special measures aimed at accelerating *de facto* equality between men and women shall not be considered discrimination as defined in the present Convention, but shall in no way entail as a consequence the maintenance of unequal or separate standards; these measures shall be discontinued when the objectives of equality of opportunity and treatment have been achieved.

2.   Adoption by States Parties of special measures, including those measures contained in the present Convention, aimed at protecting maternity shall not be considered discriminatory.

Article 5

States Parties shall take all appropriate measures:

(a)   To modify the social and cultural patterns of conduct of men and women, with a view to achieving the elimination of prejudices and customary and all other practices which are based on the idea of the inferiority or the superiority of either of the sexes or on stereotyped roles for men and women;

(b)   To ensure that family education includes a proper understanding of maternity as a social function and the recognition of the common responsibility of men and women in the upbringing and development of their children, it being understood that the interest of the children is the primordial consideration in all cases.

Article 6

States Parties shall take all appropriate measures, including legislation, to suppress all forms of traffic in women and exploitation of prostitution of women.

PART II

Article 7

States Parties shall take all appropriate measures to eliminate discrimination against women in the political and public life of the country and, in particular, shall ensure to women, on equal terms with men, the right:

(a)   To vote in all elections and public referenda and to be eligible for election to all publicly elected bodies;

(b)   To participate in the formulation of government policy and the implementation thereof and to hold public office and perform all public functions at all levels of government;

(c)   To participate in non-governmental organizations and associations concerned with the public and political life of the country.

Article 8

States Parties shall take all appropriate measures to ensure to women, on equal terms with men and without any discrimination, the opportunity to represent their Governments at the international level and to participate in the work of international organizations.

Article 9

1.   States Parties shall grant women equal rights with men to acquire, change or retain their nationality. They shall ensure in particular that neither marriage to an alien nor change of nationality by the husband during marriage shall automatically change the nationality of the wife, render her stateless or force upon her the nationality of the husband

2.   States Parties shall grant women equal rights with men with respect to the nationality of their children.

PART III

Article 10

States Parties shall take all appropriate measures to eliminate discrimination against women in order to ensure to them equal rights with men in the field of education and in particular to ensure, on a basis of equality of men and women:

(a)   The same conditions for career and vocational guidance, for access to studies and for the achievement of diplomas in educational establishments of all categories in rural as well as in urban areas; this equality shall be ensured in pre-school, general, technical, professional and higher technical education, as well as in all types of vocational training;

(*b*) Access to the same curricula, the same examinations, teaching staff with qualifications of the same standard and school premises and equipment of the same equality;

(*c*) The elimination of any stereotyped concept of the roles of men and women at all levels and in all forms of education by encouraging coeducation and other types of education which will help to achieve this aim and, in particular, by the revision of textbooks and school programmes and the adaptation of teaching methods;

(*d*) The same opportunities to benefit from scholarships and other study grants;

(*e*) The same opportunities for access to programmes of continuing education, including adult and functional literacy programmes, particularly those aimed at reducing, at the earliest possible time, any gap in education existing between men and women;

(*f*) The reduction of female student drop-out rates and the organization of programmes for girls and women who have left school prematurely;

(*g*) The same opportunities to participate actively in sports and physical education;

(*h*) Access to specific educational information to help to ensure the health and well-being of families, including information and advice on family planning.

Article 11

1.   States Parties shall take all appropriate measures to eliminate discrimination against women in the field of employment in order to ensure, on a basis of equality of men and women, the same rights, in particular:

(*a*) The right to work as an inalienable right of all human beings;

(*b*) The right to the same employment opportunities, including the application of the same criteria for selection in matters of employment;

(*c*) The right to free choice of profession and employment, the right to promotion, job security and all benefits and conditions of service and the right to receive vocational training and retraining, including apprenticeships, advanced vocational training and recurrent training;

(*d*) The right to equal remuneration, including benefits, and to equal treatment in respect of work of equal value, as well as equality of treatment in the evaluation of the quality of work;

(*e*) The right to social security, particularly in cases of retirement, unemployment, sickness, invalidity and old age and other incapacity to work, as well as the right to paid leave;

(*f*) The right to protection of health and to safety in working conditions, including the safeguarding of the function of reproduction.

2.   In order to prevent discrimination against women on the grounds of marriage or maternity and to ensure their effective right to work, States Parties shall take appropriate measures:

(*a*) To prohibit, subject to the imposition of sanctions, dismissal on the grounds of pregnancy or of maternity leave and discrimination in dismissals on the basis of marital status;

(*b*) To introduce maternity leave with pay or with comparable social benefits without loss of former employment, seniority or social allowances;

(*c*) To encourage the provision of the necessary supporting social services to enable parents to combine obligations with work responsibilities and participation in public life, in particular through promoting the establishment and development of a network of child-care facilities;

(*d*)   To provide special protection to women during pregnancy in types of work proved to be harmful to them.

3.   Protective legislation relating to matters covered in this article shall be reviewed periodically in the light of scientific and technological knowledge and shall be revised, repealed or extended as necessary.

Article 12

1.   States Parties shall take all appropriate measures to eliminate discrimination against women in the field of health care in order to ensure on a basis of equality of men and women, access to health care services, including those related to family planning.

2.   Notwithstanding the provisions of paragraph i of this Article, States Parties shall ensure to women appropriate services in connexion with pregnancy, confinement and the post-natal period, granting free services where necessary, as well as adequate nutrition during pregnancy and lactation.

Article 13

States Parties shall take all appropriate measures to eliminate discrimination against women in other areas of economic and social life in order to ensure, on a basis of equality of men and women, the same rights, in particular:

(*a*)   The right to family benefits;

(*b*)   The right to bank loans, mortgages and other forms of financial credit;

(*c*)   The right to participate in recreational activities, sports and all aspects of cultural life.

Article 14

1.   States Parties shall take into account the particular problems faced by rural women and the significant roles which rural women play in the economic survival of their families, including their work in the non-monetized sectors of the economy, and shall take all appropriate measures to ensure the application of the provisions of this Convention to women in rural areas.

2.   States Parties shall take all appropriate measures to eliminate discrimination against women in rural areas in order to ensure, on a basis of equality of men and women, that they participate in and benefit from rural development and, in particular, shall ensure to such women the right:

(*a*)   To participate in the elaboration and implementation of development planning at all levels;

(*b*)   To have access to adequate health care facilities, including information, counselling and services in family planning;

(*c*)   To benefit directly from social security programmes;

(*d*)   To obtain all types of training and education, formal and non-formal, including that relating to functional literacy, as well as, *inter alia,* the benefit of all community and extension services, in order to increase their technical proficiency;

(*e*)   To organize self-help groups and co-operatives in order to obtain equal access to economic opportunities through employment or self-employment;

(*f*)   To participate in all community activities;

(*g*)   To have access to agricultural credit and loans, marketing facilities, appropriate technology and equal treatment in land and agrarian reform as well as in land resettlement schemes;

(*h*)   To enjoy adequate living conditions, particularly in relation to housing, sanitation, electricity and water supply, transport and communications.

PART IV

Article 15

1.   States Parties shall accord to women equality with men before the law.

2.   States Parties shall accord to women, in civil matters, a legal capacity identical to that of men and the same opportunities to exercise that capacity. In particular, they shall give women equal rights to conclude contracts and to administer property and shall treat them equally in all stages of procedure in courts and tribunals.

3.   States Parties agree that all contracts and all other private instruments of any kind with a legal effect which is directed at restricting the legal capacity of women shall be deemed null and void.

4.   States Parties shall accord to men and women the same rights with regard to the law relating to the movement of persons and the freedom to choose their residence and domicile.

Article 16

1.   States Parties shall take all appropriate measures to eliminate discrimination against women in all matters relating to marriage and family relations and in particular shall ensure, on a basis of equality of men and women:

(*a*)   The same right to enter into marriage;

(*b*)   The same right freely to choose a spouse and to enter into marriage only with their free and full consent;

(*c*)   The same rights and responsibilities during marriage and at its dissolution;

(*d*)   The same rights and responsibilities as parents, irrespective of their marital status, in matters relating to their children; in all cases the interests of the children shall be paramount;

(*e*)   The same rights to decide freely and responsibly on the number and spacing of their children and to have access to the information, education and means to enable them to exercise these rights;

(*f*)   The same rights and responsibilities with regard to guardianship, wardship, trustee-ship and adoption of children, or similar institutions where these concepts exist in national legislation; in all cases the interests of the children shall be paramount;

(*g*)   The same personal rights as husband and wife, including the right to choose a family name, a profession and an occupation;

(*h*)   The same rights for both spouses in respect of the ownership, acquisition, manage-ment, administration, enjoyment and disposition of property, whether free of charge or for a valuable consideration.

2.   The betrothal and marriage of a child shall have no legal effect, and all necessary action, including legislation, shall be taken to specify a minimum age for marriage and to make the registration of marriages in an official registry compulsory.

PART V

Article 17

1.   For the purpose of considering the progress made in the implementation of the present Convention, there shall be established a Committee on the Elimination of Discrimination against Women (hereinafter referred to as the Committee) consisting, at the time of entry into force of the Convention, of eighteen and, after ratification of or accession to the Convention by the thirty-fifth State Party, of twenty-three experts of high moral standing and competence in the field

covered by the Convention. The experts shall be elected by States Parties from among their nationals and shall serve in their personal capacity, consideration being given to equitable geographical distribution and to the representation of the different forms of civilization as well as the principal legal system.

2.   The members of the Committee shall be elected by secret ballot from a list of persons nominated by States Parties. Each State Party may nominate one person from among its own nationals.

3.   The initial election shall be held six months after the date of the entry into force of the present Convention. At least three months before the date of each election the Secretary-General of the United Nations shall address a letter to the States Parties inviting them to submit their nominations within two months. The Secretary-General shall prepare a list in alphabetical order of all persons thus nominated, indicating the States Parties which have nominated them, and shall submit it to the States Parties.

4.   Elections of the members of the Committee shall be held at a meeting of States Parties convened by the Secretary-General at United Nations Headquarters. At that meeting, for which two thirds of the States Parties shall constitute a quorum, the persons elected to the Committee shall be those nominees who obtain the largest number of votes and an absolute majority of the votes of the representatives of States Parties present and voting.

5.   The members of the Committee shall be elected for a term of four years. However, the terms of nine of the members elected at the first election shall expire at the end of two years; immediately after the first election the names of these nine members shall be chosen by lot by the Chairman of the Committee.

6.   The election of the five additional members of the Committee shall be held in accordance with the provisions of paragraphs 2, 3 and 4 of this Article, following the thirty-fifth ratification or accession. The terms of two of the additional members elected on this occasion shall expire at the end of two years, the names of these two members having been chosen by lot by the Chairman of the Committee.

7.   For the filling of casual vacancies, the State Party whose expert has ceased to function as a member of the Committee shall appoint another expert from among its nationals, subject to the approval of the Committee.

8.   The members of the Committee shall, with the approval of the General Assembly, receive emoluments from United Nations resources on such terms and conditions as the Assembly may decide, having regard to the importance of the Committee's responsibilities.

9.   The Secretary-General of the United Nations shall provide the necessary staff and facilities for the effective performance of the functions of the Committee under the present Convention.

Article 18

1.   States Parties undertake to submit to the Secretary-General of the United Nations, for consideration by the Committee, a report of the legislative, judicial, administrative or other measures which they have adopted to give effect to the provisions of the present Convention and on the progress made in this respect:

(*a*)   Within one year after the entry into force for the State concerned; and

(*b*)   Thereafter at least every four years and further whenever the Committee so requests.

2.   Reports may indicate factors and difficulties affecting the degree of fulfilment of obligations under the present Convention.

Article 19

1.   The Committee shall adopt its own rules of procedure.

2.   The Committee shall elect its officers for a term of two years.

Article 20

1.   The Committee shall normally meet for a period of not more than two weeks annually in order to consider the reports submitted in accordance with Article 18 of the present Convention.

2.   The meetings of the Committee shall normally be held at United Nations Headquarters or at any other convenient place as determined by the Committee.

Article 21

1.   The Committee shall, through the Economic and Social Council, report annually to the General Assembly of the United Nations on its activities and may make suggestions and general recommendations based on the examination of reports and information received from the States Parties. Such suggestions and general recommendations shall be included in the report of the Committee together with comments, if any, from States Parties.

2. The Secretary-General shall transmit the reports of the Committee to the Commission on the Status of Women for its information.

Article 22

The specialized agencies shall be entitled to be represented at the consideration of the implementation of such provisions of the present Convention as fall within the scope of their activities. The Committee may invite the specialized agencies to submit reports on the implementation of the Convention in areas falling within the scope of their activities.

PART VI

Article 23

Nothing in this Convention shall affect any provisions that are more conducive to the achievement of equality between men and women which may be contained:

(*a*)   In the legislation of a State Party; or,

(*b*)   In any other international convention, treaty or agreement in force for that State.

Article 24

States Parties undertake to adopt all necessary measures at the national level aimed at achieving the full realization of the rights recognized in the present Convention.

Article 25

1.   The present Convention shall be open for signature by all States.

2.   The Secretary-General of the United Nations is designated as the depositary of the present Convention.

3.   The present Convention is subject to ratification. Instruments of ratification shall be deposited with the Secretary-General of the United Nations.

4.   The present Convention shall be open to accession by all States. Accession shall be effected by the deposit of an instrument of accession with the Secretary-General of the United Nations.

Article 26

1.   A request for the revision of the present Convention may be made at any time by any State Party by means of a notification in writing addressed to the Secretary-General of the United Nations.

2.   The General Assembly of the United Nations shall decide upon the steps, if any, to be taken in respect of such a request.

Article 27

1.   The present Convention shall enter into force on the thirtieth day after the date of deposit

with the Secretary-General of the United Nations of the twentieth instrument of ratification or accession.

2.   For each State ratifying the present Convention or acceding to it after the deposit of the twentieth instrument of ratification or accession, the Convention shall enter into force on the thirtieth day after the date of the deposit of its own instrument of ratification or accession.

Article 28

1.   The Secretary-General of the United Nations shall receive and circulate to all States the text of reservations made by States at the time of ratification or accession.

2.   A reservation incompatible with the object and purpose of the present Convention shall not be permitted.

3.   Reservations may be withdrawn at any time by notification to this effect addressed to the Secretary-General of the United Nations, who shall then inform all States thereof. Such notification shall take effect on the date on which it is received.

Article 29

1.   Any dispute between two or more States Parties concerning the interpretation or application of the present Convention which is not settled by negotiation shall, at the request of one of them, be submitted to arbitration. If within six months from the date of the request for arbitration the parties are unable to agree on the organization of the arbitration, any one of those parties may refer the dispute to the International Court of Justice by request in conformity with the Statute of the Court.

2.   Each State Party may at the time of signature or ratification of this Convention or accession thereto declare that it does not consider itself bound by paragraph 1 of this article. The other States Parties shall not be bound by that paragraph with respect to any State Party which has made such a reservation.

3.   Any State Party which has made a reservation in accordance with paragraph 2 of this article may at any time withdraw that reservation by notification to the Secretary-General of the United Nations.

Article 30

The present Convention, the Arabic, Chinese, English, French, Russian and Spanish texts of which are equally authentic, shall be deposited with the Secretary-General of the United Nations.

IN WITNESS WHEREOF the undersigned, duly authorized, have signed the present Convention.

Declaration on the Elimination of All Forms of Intolerance and of Discrimination Based on Religion or Belief, 1981

The General Assembly,

Considering that one of the basic principles of the Charter of the United Nations is that of the dignity and equality inherent in all human beings, and that all Member States have pledged themselves to take joint and separate action in co-operation with the Organization to promote and encourage universal respect for and observance of human rights and fundamental freedoms for all, without distinction as to race, sex, language or religion,

Considering that the Universal Declaration of Human Rights and the International Covenants on Human Rights proclaim the principles of non-discrimination and equality before the law and the right to freedom of thought, conscience, religion and belief,

Considering that the disregard and infringement of human rights and fundamental freedoms, in particular of the right to freedom of thought, conscience, religion or whatever belief, have brought, directly or indirectly, wars and great suffering to mankind, especially where they serve as a means of foreign interference in the internal affairs of other States and amount to kindling hatred between peoples and nations,

Considering that religion or belief, for anyone who professes either, is one of the fundamental elements in his conception of life and that freedom of religion or belief should be fully respected and guaranteed,

Considering that it is essential to promote understanding, tolerance and respect in matters relating to freedom of religion and belief and to ensure that the use of religion or belief for ends inconsistent with the Charter of the United Nations, other relevant instruments of the United Nations and the purposes and principles of the present Declaration is inadmissible,

Convinced that freedom of religion and belief should also contribute to the attainment of the goals of world peace, social justice and friendship among peoples and to the elimination of ideologies or practices of colonialism and racial discrimination,

Noting with satisfaction the adoption of several, and the coming into force of some, conventions, under the aegis of the United Nations and of the specialized agencies, for the elimination of various forms of discrimination,

Concerned by manifestations of intolerance and by the existence of discrimination in matters of religion or belief still in evidence in some areas of the world,

Resolved to adopt all necessary measures for the speedy elimination of such intolerance in all its forms, and manifestations and to prevent and combat discrimination on the ground of religion or belief,

Proclaims this Declaration on the Elimination of All Forms of Intolerance and of Discrimination Based on Religion or Belief:

Article 1

1.   Everyone shall have the right to freedom of thought, conscience and religion. This right shall include freedom to have a religion or whatever belief of his choice, and freedom, either individually or in community with others and in public or private, to manifest his religion or belief in worship, observance, practice and teaching.

2.   No one shall be subject to coercion which would impair his freedom to have a religion or belief of his choice.

3.   Freedom to manifest one's religion or beliefs may be subject only to such limitations as are prescribed by law and are necessary to protect public safety, order, health or morals or the fundamental rights and freedoms of others.

Article 2

1.   No one shall be subject to discrimination by any State, institution, group of persons, or person on grounds of religion or other beliefs.

2.   For the purposes of the present Declaration, the expression 'intolerance and discrimination based on religion or belief' means any distinction, exclusion, restriction or preference based on religion or belief and having as its purpose or as its effect nullification or impairment of the recognition, enjoyment or exercise of human rights and fundamental freedoms on an equal basis.

Article 3

Discrimination between human beings on grounds of religion or belief constitutes an affront to human dignity and a disavowal of the principles of the Charter of the United Nations, and shall be condemned as a violation of the human rights and fundamental freedoms proclaimed in the Universal Declaration of Human Rights and enunciated in detail in the International Covenants on Human Rights, and as an obstacle to friendly and peaceful relations between nations.

Article 4

1.   All States shall take effective measures to prevent and eliminate discrimination on the grounds of religion or belief in the recognition, exercise and enjoyment of human rights and fundamental freedoms in all fields of civil, economic, political, social and cultural life.

2.   All States shall make all efforts to enact or rescind legislation where necessary to prohibit any such discrimination, and to take all appropriate measures to combat intolerance on the grounds of religion or other beliefs in this matter.

Article 5

1.   The parents or, as the case may be, the legal guardians of the child have the right to organize the life within the family in accordance with their religion or belief and bearing in mind the moral education in which they believe the child should be brought up.

2.   Every child shall enjoy the right to have access to education in the matter of religion or belief in accordance with the wishes of his parents or, as the case may be, legal guardians, and shall not be compelled to receive teaching on religion or belief against the wishes of his parents or legal guardians, the best interests of the child being the guiding principle.

3.   The child shall be protected from any form of discrimination on the ground of religion or belief. He shall be brought up in a spirit of understanding, tolerance, friendship among peoples, peace and universal brotherhood, respect for freedom of religion or belief of others, and in full consciousness that his energy and talents should be devoted to the service of his fellow men.

4.   In the case of a child who is not under the care either of his parents or of legal guardians, due account shall be taken of their expressed wishes or of any other proof of their wishes in the matter of religion or belief, the best interests of the child being the guiding principle.

5.   Practices of a religion or beliefs in which a child is brought up must not be injurious to his physical or mental health or to his full development, taking into account Article 1, paragraph 3, of the present Declaration.

Article 6

In accordance with Article 1 of the present Declaration, the subject to provisions of Article 1, paragraph 3, the right to freedom of thought, conscience, religion or belief shall include, *inter alia*, the following freedoms:

(*a*)   To worship or assemble in connection with a religion or belief, and to establish and maintain places for these purposes;

(*b*)　To establish and maintain appropriate charitable or humanitarian institutions;

(*c*)　To make, acquire and use to an adequate extent the necessary articles and materials related to the rites or customs of a religion or belief;

(*d*)　To write, issue and disseminate relevant publications in these areas;

(*e*)　To teach a religion or belief in places suitable for these purposes;

(*f*)　To solicit and receive voluntary financial and other contributions from individuals and institutions;

(*g*)　To train, appoint, elect or designate by succession appropriate leaders called for by the requirements and standards of any religion or belief;

(*h*)　To observe days of rest and to celebrate holidays and ceremonies in accordance with the precepts of one's religion or belief;

(*i*)　To establish and maintain communications with individuals and communities in matters of religion and belief at the national and international levels.

Article 7

The rights and freedoms set forth in the present Declaration shall be accorded in national legislation in such a manner that everyone shall be able to avail himself of such rights and freedoms in practice.

Article 8

Nothing in the present Declaration shall be construed as restricting or derogating from any right defined in the Universal Declaration of Human Rights and the International Covenants on Human Rights.

Convention Against Torture and Other Cruel, Inhuman or Degrading Treatment or Punishment, 1984

The States Parties to this Convention,

Considering that, in accordance with the principles proclaimed in the Charter of the United Nations, recognition of the equal and inalienable rights of all members of the human family is the foundation of freedom, justice and peace in the world,

Recognizing that those rights derive from the inherent dignity of the human person,

Considering the obligation of States under the Charter, in particular Article 55, to promote universal respect for, and observance of, human rights and fundamental freedoms,

Having regard to article 5 of the Universal Declaration of Human Rights and article 7 of the International Covenant on Civil and Political Rights, both of which provide that no one shall be subjected to torture or to cruel, inhuman or degrading treatment or punishment,

Having regard also to the Declaration on the Protection of All Persons from Being Subjected to Torture and Other Cruel, Inhuman or Degrading Treatment or Punishment, adopted by the General Assembly on 9 December 1975;

Desiring to make more effective the struggle against torture and other cruel, inhuman or degrading treatment or punishment throughout the world,

Have agreed as follows:

PART I

Article 1

1.   For the purposes of this Convention, the term 'torture' means any act by which severe pain or suffering, whether physical or mental, is intentionally inflicted on a person for such purposes as obtaining from him or a third person information or a confession, punishing him for an act he or a third person has committed or is suspected of having committed, or intimidating or coercing him or a third person, or for any reason based on discrimination of any kind, when such pain or suffering is inflicted by or at the instigation of or with the consent or acquiescence of a public official or other person acting in an official capacity. It does not include pain or suffering arising only from, inherent in or incidental to lawful sanctions.

2.   This article is without prejudice to any international instrument or national legislation which does or may contain provisions of wider application.

Article 2

1.   Each State Party shall take effective legislative, administrative, judicial or other measures to prevent acts of torture in any territory under its jurisdiction.

2.   No exceptional circumstances whatsoever, whether a state of war or a threat of war, internal political instability or any other public emergency, may be invoked as a justification of torture.

3.   An order from a superior officer or a public authority may not be invoked as a justification of torture.

Article 3

1.   No State Party shall expel, return *('refouler')* or extradite a person to another State where there are substantial grounds for believing that he would be in danger of being subjected to torture.

2.   For the purpose of determining whether there are such grounds, the competent authorities shall take into account all relevant considerations including, where applicable, the existence in the State concerned of a consistent pattern of gross, flagrant or mass violations of human rights.

Article 4

1.   Each State Party shall ensure that all acts of torture are offences under its criminal law. The same shall apply to an attempt to commit torture and to commit an act by any person which constitutes complicity or participation in torture.

2.   Each State Party shall make these offences punishable by appropriate penalties which take into account their grave nature.

Article 5

1.   Each State Party shall take such measures as may be necessary to establish its jurisdiction over the offences referred to in article 4 in the following cases:

(*a*)   When the offences are committed in any territory under its jurisdiction or on board a ship or aircraft registered in that State;

(*b*)   When the alleged offender is a national of that State;

(*c*)   When the victim is a national of that State if that State considers it appropriate.

2.   Each State Party shall likewise take such measures as may be necessary to establish its jurisdiction over such offences in cases where the alleged offender is present in any territory under its jurisdiction and it does not extradite him pursuant to article 8 to any of the States mentioned in paragraph I of this article.

3.   This Convention does not exclude any criminal jurisdiction exercised in accordance with internal law.

Article 6

1.   Upon being satisfied, after an examination of information available to it, that the circumstances so warrant, any State Party in whose territory a person alleged to have committed any offence referred to in article 4 is present shall take him into custody or take other legal measures to ensure his presence. The custody and other legal measures shall be as provided in the law of that State but may be continued only for such time as is necessary to enable any criminal or extradition proceedings to be instituted.

2.   Such State shall immediately make a preliminary inquiry into the facts.

3.   Any person in custody pursuant to paragraph 1 of this article shall be assisted in communicating immediately with the nearest appropriate representative of the State of which he is a national, or, if he is a stateless person, with the representative of the State where he usually resides.

4.   When a State, pursuant to this article, has taken a person into custody, it shall immediately notify the States referred to in article 5, paragraph 1, of the fact that such person is in custody and of the circumstances which warrant his detention. The State which makes the preliminary inquiry contemplated in paragraph 2 of this article shall promptly report its findings to the said States and shall indicate whether it intends to exercise jurisdiction.

Article 7

1.   The State Party in the territory under whose jurisdiction a person alleged to have committed any offence referred to in article 4 is found shall in the cases contemplated in article 5, if it does not extradite him, submit the case to its competent authorities for the purpose of prosecution.

2.   These authorities shall take their decision in the same manner as in the case of any ordinary offence of a serious nature under the law of that State. In the cases referred to in article 5, paragraph 2, the standards of evidence required for prosecution and conviction shall in no way be less stringent than those which apply in the cases referred to in article 5, paragraph 1.

3.   Any person regarding whom proceedings are brought in connection with any of the offences referred to in article 4 shall be guaranteed fair treatment at all stages of the proceedings.

Article 8

1.   The offences referred to in article 4 shall be deemed to be included as extraditable offences in any extradition treaty existing between States Parties. States Parties undertake to include such offences as extraditable offences in every extradition treaty to be concluded between them.

2.   If a State Party which makes extradition conditional on the existence of a treaty receives a request for extradition from another State Party with which it has no extradition treaty, it may consider this Convention as the legal basis for extradition in respect of such offences. Extradition shall be subject to the other conditions provided by the law of the requested State.

3.   States Parties which do not make extradition conditional on the existence of a treaty shall recognize such offences as extraditable offences between themselves subject to the conditions provided by the law of the requested State.

4. Such offences shall be treated, for the purpose of extradition between States Parties, as if they had been committed not only in the place in which they occurred but also in the territories of the States required to establish their jurisdiction in accordance with article 5, paragraph 1.

Article 9

1.   States Parties shall afford one another the greatest measure of assistance in connection with criminal proceedings brought in respect of any of the offences referred to in article 4, including the supply of all evidence at their disposal necessary for the proceedings.

2.   States Parties shall carry out their obligations under paragraph 1 of this article in conformity with any treaties on mutual judicial assistance that may exist between them.

Article 10

1.   Each State Party shall ensure that education and information regarding the prohibition against torture are fully included in the training of law enforcement personnel, civil or military, medical personnel, public officials and other persons who may be involved in the custody, interrogation or treatment of any individual subjected to any form of arrest, detention or imprisonment.

2.   Each State Party shall include this prohibition in the rules or instructions issued in regard to the duties and functions of any such persons.

Article 11

Each State Party shall keep under systematic review interrogation rules, instructions, methods and practices as well as arrangements for the custody and treatment of persons subjected to any form of arrest, detention or imprisonment in any territory under its jurisdiction, with a view to preventing any cases of torture.

Article 12

Each State Party shall ensure that its competent authorities proceed to a prompt and impartial investigation, wherever there is reasonable ground to believe that an act of torture has been committed in any territory under its jurisdiction.

Article 13

Each State Party shall ensure that any individual who alleges he has been subjected to torture in any territory under its jurisdiction has the right to complain to, and to have his case promptly and impartially examined by, its competent authorities. Steps shall be taken to ensure that the complainant and witnesses are protected against all ill-treatment or intimidation as a consequence of his complaint or any evidence given.

Article 14

1.   Each State Party shall ensure in its legal system that the victim of an act of torture obtains redress and has an enforceable right to fair and adequate compensation, including the means for

as full rehabilitation as possible. In the event of the death of the victim as a result of an act of torture, his dependants shall be entitled to compensation.

2. Nothing in this article shall affect any right of the victim or other persons to compensation which may exist under national law.

Article 15

Each State Party shall ensure that any statement which is established to have been made as a result of torture shall not be invoked as evidence in any proceedings, except against a person accused of torture as evidence that the statement was made.

Article 16

1. Each State Party shall undertake to prevent in any territory under its jurisdiction other acts of cruel, inhuman or degrading treatment or punishment which do not amount to torture as defined in article 1, when such acts are committed by or at the instigation of or with the consent or acquiescence of a public official or other person acting in an official capacity. In particular, the obligations contained in articles 10, 11, 12 and 13 shall apply with the substitution for references to torture of references to other forms of cruel, inhuman or degrading treatment or punishment.

2. The provisions of this Convention are without prejudice to the provisions of any other international instrument or national law which prohibits cruel, inhuman or degrading treatment or punishment or which relates to extradition or expulsion.

PART II

Article 17

1. There shall be established a Committee against Torture (hereinafter referred to as the Committee) which shall carry out the functions hereinafter provided. The Committee shall consist of ten experts of high moral standing and recognized competence in the field of human rights, who shall serve in their personal capacity. The experts shall be elected by the States Parties, consideration being given to equitable geographical distribution and to the usefulness of the participation of some persons having legal experience.

2. The members of the Committee shall be elected by secret ballot from a list of persons nominated by States Parties. Each State Party may nominate one person from among its own nationals. States Parties shall bear in mind the usefulness of nominating persons who are also members of the Human Rights Committee established under the International Covenant on Civil and Political Rights and who are willing to serve on the Committee against Torture.

3. Elections of the members of the Committee shall be held at biennial meetings of States Parties convened by the Secretary-General of the United Nations. At those meetings, for which two thirds of the States Parties shall constitute a quorum, the persons elected to the Committee shall be those who obtain the largest number of votes and an absolute majority of the votes of the representatives of States Parties present and voting.

4. The initial election shall be held no later than six months after the date of the entry into force of this Convention. At least four months before the date of each election, the Secretary-General of the United Nations shall address a letter to the States Parties inviting them to submit their nominations within three months. The Secretary-General shall prepare a list in alphabetical order of all persons thus nominated, indicating the States Parties which have nominated them, and shall submit it to the States Parties.

5. The members of the Committee shall be elected for a term of four years. They shall be eligible for re-election if renominated. However, the term of five of the members elected at the first election shall expire at the end of two years; immediately after the first election the names of these five members shall be chosen by lot by the chairman of the meeting referred to in paragraph 3 of this article.

6.   If a member of the Committee dies or resigns or for any other cause can no longer perform his Committee duties, the State Party which nominated him shall appoint another expert from among its nationals to serve for the remainder of his term, subject to the approval of the majority of the States Parties. The approval shall be considered given unless half or more of the States Parties respond negatively within six weeks after having been informed by the Secretary-General of the United Nations of the proposed appointment.

7.   States Parties shall be responsible for the expenses of the members of the Committee while they are in performance of Committee duties.

Article 18

1.   The Committee shall elect its officers for a term of two years. They may be re-elected.

2.   The Committee shall establish its own rules of procedure, but these rules shall provide, *inter alia,* that:

    (*a*)   Six members shall constitute a quorum;

    (*b*)   Decisions of the Committee shall be made by a majority vote of the members present.

3.   The Secretary-General of the United Nations shall provide the necessary staff and facilities for the effective performance of the functions of the Committee under this Convention.

4.   The Secretary-General of the United Nations shall convene the initial meeting of the Committee. After its initial meeting, the Committee shall meet at such times as shall be provided in its rules of procedure.

5.   The States Parties shall be responsible for expenses incurred in connection with the holding of meetings of the States Parties and of the Committee, including reimbursement to the United Nations for any expenses, such as the cost of staff and facilities, incurred by the United Nations pursuant to paragraph 3 of this article.

Article 19

1.   The States Parties shall submit to the Committee, through the Secretary-General of the United Nations, reports on the measures they have taken to give effect to their undertakings under this Convention, within one year after the entry into force of the Convention for the State Party concerned. Thereafter the States Parties shall submit supplementary reports every four years on any new measures taken and such other reports as the Committee may request.

2.   The Secretary-General of the United Nations shall transmit the reports to all States Parties.

3.   Each report shall be considered by the Committee which may make such general comments on the report as it may consider appropriate and shall forward these to the State Party concerned. That State Party may respond with any observations it chooses to the Committee.

4.   The Committee may, at its discretion, decide to include any comments made by it in accordance with paragraph 3 of this article, together with the observations thereon received from the State Party concerned, in its annual report made in accordance with article 24. If so requested by the State Party concerned, the Committee may also include a copy of the report submitted under paragraph 1 of this article.

Article 20

1.   If the Committee receives reliable information which appears to it to contain well-founded indications that torture is being systematically practised in the territory of a State Party, the Committee shall invite that State Party to co-operate in the examination of the information and to this end to submit observations with regard to the information concerned.

2.   Taking into account any observations which may have been submitted by the State Party concerned, as well as any other relevant information available to it, the Committee may, if it decides that this is warranted, designate one or more of its members to make a confidential inquiry and to report to the Committee urgently.

3. If an inquiry is made in accordance with paragraph 2 of this article, the Committee shall seek the co-operation of the State Party concerned. In agreement with that State Party, such an inquiry may include a visit to its territory.

4. After examining the findings of its member or members submitted in accordance with paragraph 2 of this article, the Committee shall transmit these findings to the State Party concerned together with any comments or suggestions which seem appropriate in view of the situation.

5. All the proceedings of the Committee referred to in paragraphs 1 to 4 of this article shall be confidential, and at all stages of the proceedings the co-operation of the State Party shall be sought. After such proceedings have been completed with regard to an inquiry made in accordance with paragraph 2, the Committee may, after consultations with the State Party concerned, decide to include a summary account of the results of the proceedings in its annual report made in accordance with article 24.

Article 21

1. A State Party to this Convention may at any time declare under this article that it recognizes the competence of the Committee to receive and consider communications to the effect that a State Party claims that another State Party is not fulfilling its obligations under this Convention. Such communications may be received and considered according to the procedures laid down in this article only if submitted by a State Party which has made a declaration recognizing in regard to itself the competence of the Committee. No communication shall be dealt with by the Committee under this article if it concerns a State Party which has not made such a declaration. Communications received under this article shall be dealt with in accordance with the following, procedure:

   (a) If a State Party considers that another State Party is not giving effect to the provisions of this Convention, it may, by written communication, bring the matter to the attention of that State Party. Within three months after the receipt of the communication the receiving State shall afford the State which sent the communication an explanation or any other statement in writing clarifying the matter, which should include, to the extent possible and pertinent, reference to domestic procedures and remedies taken, pending or available in the matter;

   (b) If the matter is not adjusted to the satisfaction of both States Parties concerned within six months after the receipt by the receiving State of the initial communication, either State shall have the right to refer the matter to the Committee, by notice given to the Committee and to the other State;

   (c) The Committee shall deal with a matter referred to it under this article only after it has ascertained that all domestic remedies have been invoked and exhausted in the matter, in conformity with the generally recognized principles of international law. This shall not be the rule where the application of the remedies is unreasonably prolonged or is unlikely to bring effective relief to the person who is the victim of the violation of this Convention;

   (d) The Committee shall hold closed meetings when examining communications under this article;

   (e) Subject to the provisions of subparagraph (c), the Committee shall make available its good offices to the States Parties concerned with a view to a friendly solution of the matter on the basis of respect for right obligations provided for in this Convention. For this purpose, the Committee may, when appropriate, set up an *ad hoc* conciliation commission;

   (f) If any matter referred to it under this article, the Committee may call upon the States Parties concerned, referred to in subparagraph (b), to supply any relevant information;

   (g) The States Parties concerned, referred to in subparagraph (b), shall have the right to be represented when the matter is being considered by the Committee and to make submissions orally and/or in writing;

(*h*)   The Committee shall, within twelve months after the date of receipt of notice under subparagraph (*b*), submit a report:

(i)   If a solution within the terms of subparagraph (*e*) is reached, the Committee shall confine its report to a brief statement of the facts and of the solution reached;

(ii)   If a solution within the terms of subparagraph (*e*) is not reached, the Committee shall confine its report to a brief statement of the facts; the written submissions and record of the oral submissions made by the States Parties concerned shall be attached to the report.

In every matter, the report shall be communicated to the States Parties concerned.

2.   The provisions of this article shall come into force when five States Parties of this Convention have made declarations under paragraph 1 of this article. Such declarations shall be deposited by the States Parties with the Secretary-General of the United Nations, who shall transmit copies thereof to the other States Parties. A declaration may be withdrawn at any time by notification to the Secretary-General. Such a withdrawal shall not prejudice the consideration of any matter which is the subject of a communication already transmitted under this article; no further communication by any State Party shall be received under this article after the notification of withdrawal of the declaration has been received by the Secretary-General, unless the State Party concerned has made a new declaration.

Article 22

1.   A State Party to this Convention may at any time declare under this article that it recognizes the competence of the Committee to receive and consider communications from or on behalf of individuals subject to its jurisdiction who claim to be victims of a violation by a State Party of the provisions of the Convention. No communication shall be received by the Committee if it concerns a State Party which has not made such a declaration.

2.   The Committee shall consider inadmissible any communication under this article which is anonymous or which it considers to be an abuse of the right of submission of such communications or to be incompatible with the provisions of this Convention.

3.   Subject to the provisions of paragraph 2, the Committee shall bring any communications submitted to it under this article to the attention of the State Party to this Convention which has made a declaration under paragraph 1 and is alleged to be violating any provisions of the Convention.

Within six months, the receiving State shall submit to the Committee written explanations or statements clarifying the matter and the remedy, if any, that may have been taken by that State.

4.   The Committee shall consider communications received under this article in the light of all information made available to it by or on behalf of the individual and by the State Party concerned.

5.   The Committee shall not consider any communications from an individual under this article unless it has ascertained that:

(*a*)   The same matter has not been, and is not being, examined under another procedure of international investigation or settlement;

(*b*)   The individual has exhausted all available domestic remedies; this shall not be the rule where the application of the remedies is unreasonably prolonged or is unlikely to bring effective relief to the person who is the victim of the violation of this Convention.

6.   The Committee shall hold closed meetings when examining communications under this article.

7.   The Committee shall forward its views to the State Party concerned and to the individual.

8.   The provisions of this article shall come into force when five States Parties to this Convention have made declarations under paragraph 1 of this article. Such declarations shall be deposited by the States Parties with the Secretary-General of the United Nations, who shall

transmit copies thereof to the other States Parties. A declaration may be withdrawn at any time by notification to the Secretary-General. Such a withdrawal shall not prejudice the consideration of any matter which is the subject of a communication already transmitted under this article; no further communication by or on behalf of an individual shall be received under this article after the notification of withdrawal of the declaration has been received by the Secretary-General, unless the State Party has made a new declaration.

Article 23

The members of the Committee and of the *ad hoc* conciliation commissions which may be appointed under article 21, paragraph 1(*e*), shall be entitled to the facilities, privileges and immunities of experts on mission for the United Nations as laid down in the relevant sections of the Convention on the Privileges and Immunities of the United Nations.

Article 24

The Committee shall submit an annual report on its activities under this Convention to the States Parties and to the General Assembly of the United Nations.

PART III

Article 25

1. This Convention is open for signature by all States.

2. This Convention is subject to ratification. Instruments of ratification shall be deposited with the Secretary-General of the United Nations.

Article 26

This Convention is open to accession by all States. Accession shall be effected by the deposit of an instrument of accession with the Secretary-General of the United Nations.

Article 27

1. This Convention shall enter into force on the thirtieth day after the date of the deposit with the Secretary-General of the United Nations of the twentieth instrument of ratification or accession.

2. For each State ratifying this Convention or acceding to it after the deposit of the twentieth instrument of ratification or accession, the Convention shall enter into force on the thirtieth day after the date of the deposit of its own instrument of ratification or accession.

Article 28

1. Each State may, at the time of signature or ratification of this Convention or accession thereto, declare that it does not recognize the competence of the Committee provided for in article 20.

2. Any State Party having made a reservation in accordance with paragraph 1 of this article may, at any time, withdraw this reservation by notification to the Secretary-General of the United Nations.

Article 29

1. Any State Party to this Convention may propose an amendment and file it with the Secretary-General of the United Nations. The Secretary-General shall thereupon communicate the proposed amendment to the States Parties with a request that they notify him whether they favour a conference of States Parties for the purpose of considering and voting upon the proposal. In the event that within four months from the date of such communication at least one third of the States Parties favours such a conference, the Secretary-General shall convene the conference under the auspices of the United Nations. Any amendment adopted by a majority of the States Parties present and voting at the conference shall be submitted by the Secretary-General to all the States Parties for acceptance.

2.   An amendment adopted in accordance with paragraph 1 of this article shall enter into force when two thirds of the States Parties to this Convention have notified the Secretary-General of the United Nations that they have accepted it in accordance with their respective constitutional processes.

3.   When amendments enter into force, they shall be binding on those States Parties which have accepted them, other States Parties still being bound by the provisions of this Convention and any earlier amendments which they have accepted.

Article 30

1.   Any dispute between two or more States Parties concerning the interpretation or application of this Convention which cannot be settled through negotiation shall, at the request of one of them, be submitted to arbitration. If within six months from the date of the request for arbitration the Parties are unable to agree on the organization of the arbitration, any one of those Parties may refer the dispute to the International Court of Justice by request in conformity with the Statute of the Court.

2.   Each State may, at the time of signature or ratification of this Convention or accession thereto, declare that it does not consider itself bound by paragraph 1 of this article. The other States Parties shall not be bound by paragraph 1 of this article with respect to any State Party having made such a reservation.

3.   Any State Party having made a reservation in accordance with paragraph 2 of this article may at any time withdraw this reservation by notification to the Secretary-General of the United Nations.

Article 31

1.   A State Party may denounce this Convention by written notification to the Secretary-General of the United Nations. Denunciation becomes effective one year after the date of receipt of the notification by the Secretary-General.

2.   Such a denunciation shall not have the effect of releasing the State Party from its obligations under this Convention in regard to any act or omission which occurs prior to the date at which the denunciation becomes effective, nor shall denunciation prejudice in any way the continued consideration of any matter which is already under consideration by the Committee prior to the date at which the denunciation becomes effective.

3.   Following the date at which the denunciation of a State Party becomes effective, the Committee shall not commence consideration of any new matter regarding that State.

Article 32

The Secretary-General of the United Nations shall inform all States Members of the United Nations and all States which have signed this Convention or acceded to it of the following:

  (*a*)   Signatures, ratifications and accessions under articles 25 and 26;

  (*b*)   The date of entry into force of this Convention under article 27 and the date of the entry into force of any amendments under article 29;

  (*c*)   Denunciations under article 31.

Article 33

1.   This Convention, of which the Arabic, Chinese, English, French, Russian and Spanish texts are equally authentic, shall be deposited with the Secretary-General of the United Nations.

2.   The Secretary-General of the United Nations shall transmit certified copies of this Convention to all States.

Convention on the Rights of the Child, 1989

PREAMBLE

The States Parties to the present Convention,

Considering that, in accordance with the principles proclaimed in the Charter of the United Nations, recognition of the inherent dignity and of the equal and inalienable rights of all members of the human family is the foundation of freedom, justice and peace in the world,

Bearing in mind that the peoples of the United Nations have, in the Charter, reaffirmed their faith in fundamental human rights and in the dignity and worth of the human person, and have determined to promote social progress and better standards of life in larger freedom,

Recognizing that the United Nations has, in the Universal Declaration of Human Rights and in the International Covenants on Human Rights, proclaimed and agreed that everyone is entitled to all the rights and freedoms set forth therein, without distinction of any kind, such as race, colour, sex, language, religion, political or other opinion, national or social origin, property, birth or other status,

Recalling that, in the Universal Declaration of Human Rights, the United Nations has proclaimed that childhood is entitled to special care and assistance,

Convinced that the family, as the fundamental group of society and the natural environment for the growth and well-being of all its members and particularly children, should be afforded the necessary protection and assistance so that it can fully assume its responsibilities within the community,

Recognizing that the child, for the full and harmonious development of his or her personality, should grow up in a family environment, in an atmosphere of happiness, love and understanding,

Considering that the child should be fully prepared to live an individual life in society, and brought up in the spirit of the ideals proclaimed in the Charter of the United Nations, and in particular in the spirit of peace, dignity, tolerance, freedom, equality and solidarity,

Bearing in mind that the need to extend particular care to the child has been stated in the Geneva Declaration of the Rights of the Child of 1924 and in the Declaration of the Rights of the Child adopted by the General Assembly on 20 November 1959 and recognized in the Universal Declaration of Human Rights, in the International Covenant on Civil and Political Rights (in particular in Articles 23 and 24), in the International Covenant on Economic, Social and Cultural Rights (in particular in Article 10) and in the statutes and relevant instruments of specialized agencies and international organizations concerned with the welfare of children,

Bearing in mind that, as indicated in the Declaration of the Rights of the Child, 'the child, by reason of his physical and mental immaturity, needs special safeguards and care, including appropriate legal protection, before as well as after birth',

Recalling the provisions of the Declaration on Social and Legal Principles relating to the Protection and Welfare of Children, with Special Reference to Foster Placement and Adoption Nationally and Internationally; the United Nations Standard Minimum Rules for the Administration of Juvenile Justice (The Beijing Rules); and the Declaration on the Protection of Women and Children in Emergency and Armed Conflict,

Recognizing that, in all countries in the world, there are children living in exceptionally difficult conditions, and that such children need special consideration,

Taking due account of the importance of the traditions and cultural values of each people for the protection and harmonious development of the child,

Recognizing the importance of international co-operation for improving the living conditions of children in every country, in particular in the developing countries,

Have agreed as follows:

PART I

Article 1

For the purposes of the present Convention, a child means every human being below the age of eighteen years unless, under the law applicable to the child, majority is attained earlier.

Article 2

1.   States Parties shall respect and ensure the rights set forth in the present Convention to each child within their jurisdiction without discrimination of any kind, irrespective of the child's or his or her parent's or legal guardian's race, colour, sex, language, religion, political or other opinion, national, ethnic or social origin, property, disability, birth or other status.

2.   States Parties shall take all appropriate measures to ensure that the child is protected against all forms of discrimination or punishment on the basis of the status, activities, expressed opinions, or beliefs of the child's parents, legal guardians, or family members.

Article 3

1.   In all actions concerning children, whether undertaken by public or private social welfare institutions, courts of law, administrative authorities or legislative bodies, the best interests of the child shall be a primary consideration.

2.   States Parties undertake to ensure the child such protection and care as is necessary for his or her well-being, taking into account the rights and duties of his or her parents, legal guardians, or other individuals legally responsible for him or her, and, to this end, shall take all appropriate legislative and administrative measures.

3.   States Parties shall ensure that the institutions, services and facilities responsible for the care or protection of children shall conform with the standards established by competent authorities, particularly in the areas of safety, health, in the number and suitability of their staff, as well as competent supervision.

Article 4

States Parties shall undertake all appropriate legislative, administrative, and other measures for the implementation of the rights recognized in the present Convention. With regard to economic, social and cultural rights, States Parties shall undertake such measures to the maximum extent of their available resources and, where needed, within the framework of international co-operation.

Article 5

States Parties shall respect the responsibilities, rights and duties of parents or, where applicable, the members of the extended family or community as provided for by local custom, legal guardians or other persons legally responsible for the child, to provide, in a manner consistent with the evolving capacities of the child, appropriate direction and guidance in the exercise by the child of the rights recognized in the present Convention.

Article 6

1.   States Parties recognize that every child has the inherent right to life.

2.   States Parties shall ensure to the maximum extent possible the survival and development of the child.

Article 7

1.   The child shall be registered immediately after birth and shall have the right from birth to a name, the right to acquire a nationality and, as far as possible, the right to know and be cared for by his or her parents.

2.   States Parties shall ensure the implementation of these rights in accordance with their national law and their obligations under the relevant international instruments in this field, in

particular where the child would otherwise be stateless.

Article 8

1.   States Parties undertake to respect the right of the child to preserve his or her identity, including nationality, name and family relations as recognized by law without unlawful interference.

2.   Where a child is illegally deprived of some or all of the elements of his or her identity, States Parties shall provide appropriate assistance and protection, with a view to speedily re-establishing his or her identity.

Article 9

1.   States Parties shall ensure that a child shall not be separated from his or her parents against their will, except when competent authorities subject to judicial review determine, in accordance with applicable law and procedures, that such separation is necessary for the best interests of the child. Such determination may be necessary in a particular case such as one involving abuse or neglect of the child by the parents, or one where the parents are living separately and a decision must be made as to the child's place of residence.

2.   In any proceedings pursuant to paragraph 1 of the present Article, all interested parties shall be given an opportunity to participate in the proceedings and make their views known.

3.   States Parties shall respect the right of the child who is separated from one or both parents to maintain personal relations and direct contact with both parents on a regular basis, except if it is contrary to the child's best interests.

4.   Where such separation results from any action initiated by a State Party, such as the detention, imprisonment, exile, deportation or death (including death arising from any cause while the person is in the custody of the State) of one or both parents or of the child, that State Party shall, upon request, provide the parents, the child or, if appropriate, another member of the family with the essential information concerning the whereabouts of the absent member(s) of the family unless the provision of the information would be detrimental to the well-being of the child. States Parties shall further ensure that the submission of such a request shall of itself entail no adverse consequences for the person(s) concerned.

Article 10

1.   In accordance with the obligation of States Parties under Article 9, paragraph 1, applications by a child or his or her parents to enter or leave a State Party for the purpose of family reunification shall be dealt with by States Parties in a positive, humane and expeditious manner. States Parties shall further ensure that the submission of such a request shall entail no adverse consequences for the applicants and for the members of their family.

2.   A child whose parents reside in different States shall have the right to maintain on a regular basis, save in exceptional circumstances personal relations and direct contacts with both parents. Towards that end and in accordance with the obligation of States Parties under Article 9, paragraph 2, States Parties shall respect the right of the child and his or her parents to leave any country, including their own, and to enter their own country. The right to leave any country shall be subject only to such restrictions as are prescribed by law and which are necessary to protect the national security, public order (*ordre public*), public health or morals or the rights and freedoms of others and are consistent with the other rights recognized in the present Convention.

Article 11

1.   States Parties shall take measures to combat the illicit transfer and non return of children abroad.

2.   To this end, States Parties shall promote the conclusion of bilateral or multilateral agreements or accession to existing agreements.

Article 12

1.   States Parties shall assure to the child who is capable of forming his or her own views the

right to express those views freely in all matters affecting the child, the views of the child being given due weight in accordance with the age and maturity of the child.

2.   For this purpose, the child shall in particular be provided the opportunity to be heard in any judicial and administrative proceedings affecting the child, either directly, or through a representative or an appropriate body, in a manner consistent with the procedural rules of national law.

Article 13

1.   The child shall have the right to freedom of expression; this right shall include freedom to seek, receive and impart information and ideas of all kinds, regardless of frontiers, either orally, in writing or in print, in the form of art, or through any other media of the child's choice.

2.   The exercise of this right may be subject to certain restrictions, but these shall only be such as are provided by law and are necessary:

  (*a*)   For respect of the rights or reputations of others; or

  (*b*)   For the protection of national security or of public order (*ordre public*), or of public health or morals.

Article 14

1.   States Parties shall respect the right of the child to freedom of thought, conscience and religion.

2.   States Parties shall respect the rights and duties of the parents and, when applicable, legal guardians, to provide direction to the child in the exercise of his or her right in a manner consistent with the evolving capacities of the child.

3.   Freedom to manifest one's religion or beliefs may be subject only to such limitations as are prescribed by law and are necessary to protect public safety, order, health or morals, or the fundamental rights and freedoms of others.

Article 15

1.   States Parties recognize the rights of the child to freedom of association and to freedom of peaceful assembly.

2.   No restrictions may be placed on the exercise of these rights other than those imposed in conformity with the law and which are necessary in a democratic society in the interests of national security or public safety, public order (*ordre public*), the protection of public health or morals or the protection of the rights and freedoms of others.

Article 16

1.   No child shall be subjected to arbitrary or unlawful interference with his or her privacy, family, home or correspondence, nor to unlawful attacks on his or her honour and reputation.

2.   The child has the right to the protection of the law against such interference or attacks.

Article 17

States Parties recognize the important function performed by the mass media and shall ensure that the child has access to information and material from a diversity of national and international sources, especially those aimed at the promotion of his or her social, spiritual and moral well-being and physical and mental health. To this end, States Parties shall:

  (*a*)   Encourage the mass media to disseminate information and material of social and cultural benefit to the child and in accordance with the spirit of Article 29;

  (*b*)   Encourage international co-operation in the production, exchange and dissemination of such information and material from a diversity of cultural, national and international sources;

(*c*) Encourage the production and dissemination of children's books;

(*d*) Encourage the mass media to have particular regard to the linguistic needs of the child who belongs to a minority group or who is indigenous;

(*e*) Encourage the development of appropriate guidelines for the protection of the child from information and material injurious to his or her well-being, bearing in mind the provisions of Articles 13 and 18.

Article 18

1. States Parties shall use their best efforts to ensure recognition of the principle that both parents have common responsibilities for the upbringing and development of the child. Parents or, as the case may be, legal guardians, have the primary responsibility for the upbringing and development of the child. The best interests of the child will be their basic concern.

2. For the purpose of guaranteeing and promoting the rights set forth in the present Convention, States Parties shall render appropriate assistance to parents and legal guardians in the performance of their child-rearing responsibilities and shall ensure the development of institutions, facilities and services for the care of children.

3. States Parties shall take all appropriate measures to ensure that children of working parents have the right to benefit from child-care services and facilities for which they are eligible.

Article 19

1. States Parties shall take all appropriate legislative, administrative, social and educational measures to protect the child from all forms of physical or mental violence, injury or abuse, neglect or negligent treatment, maltreatment or exploitation, including sexual abuse, while in the care of parent(s), legal guardian(s) or any other person who has the care of the child.

2. Such protective measures should, as appropriate, include effective procedures for the establishment of social programmes to provide necessary support for the child and for those who have the care of the child, as well as for other forms of prevention and for identification, reporting, referral, investigation, treatment and follow-up of instances of child maltreatment described heretofore, and, as appropriate, for judicial involvement.

Article 20

1. A child temporarily or permanently deprived of his or her family environment, or in whose own best interests cannot be allowed to remain in that environment, shall be entitled to special protection and assistance provided by the State.

2. States Parties shall in accordance with their national laws ensure alternative care for such a child.

3. Such care could include, *inter alia,* foster placement, *kafalah* of Islamic law, adoption or if necessary placement in suitable institutions for the care of children. When considering solutions, due regard shall be paid to the desirability of continuity in a child's upbringing and to the child's ethnic, religious, cultural and linguistic background.

Article 21

States Parties that recognize and/or permit the system of adoption shall ensure that the best interests of the child shall be the paramount consideration and they shall:

(*a*) Ensure that the adoption of a child is authorized only by competent authorities who determine, in accordance with applicable law and procedures and on the basis of all pertinent and reliable information, that the adoption is permissible in view of the child's status concerning parents, relatives and legal guardians and that, if required, the persons concerned have given their informed consent to the adoption on the basis of such counselling as may be necessary;

(*b*) Recognize that inter-country adoption may be considered as an alternative means of child's care, if the child cannot be placed in a foster or an adoptive family or cannot in any suitable manner be cared for in the child's country of origin;

(*c*)   Ensure that the child concerned by inter-country adoption enjoys safeguards and standards equivalent to those existing in the case of national adoption;

(*d*)   Take all appropriate measures to ensure that, in inter-country adoption, the placement does not result in improper financial gain for those involved in it;

(*e*)   Promote, where appropriate, the objectives of the present article by concluding bilateral or multilateral arrangements or agreements, and endeavour, within this framework, to ensure that the placement of the child in another country is carried out by competent authorities or organs.

Article 22

1.   States Parties shall take appropriate measures to ensure that a child who is seeking refugee status or who is considered a refugee in accordance with applicable international or domestic law and procedures shall, whether unaccompanied or accompanied by his or her parents or by any other person, receive appropriate protection and humanitarian assistance in the enjoyment of applicable rights set forth in the present Convention and in other international human rights or humanitarian instruments to which the said States are Parties.

2.   For this purpose, States Parties shall provide, as they consider appropriate, co-operation in any efforts by the United Nations and other competent inter-governmental organizations or non-governmental organizations co-operating with the United Nations to protect and assist such a child and to trace the parents or other members of the family of any refugee child in order to obtain information necessary for reunification with his or her family. In cases where no parents or other members of the family can be found the child shall be accorded the same protection as any other child permanently or temporarily deprived of his or her family environment for any reason, as set forth in the present Convention.

Article 23

1.   States Parties recognize that a mentally or physically disabled child should enjoy a full and decent life, in conditions which ensure dignity, promote self-reliance and facilitate the child's active participation in the community.

2.   States Parties recognize the right of the disabled child to special care and shall encourage and ensure the extension, subject to available resources, to the eligible child and those responsible for his or her care, of assistance for which application is made and which is appropriate to the child's condition and to the circumstances of the parents or others caring for the child.

3.   Recognizing the special needs of a disabled child, assistance extended in accordance with paragraph 2 of the present article shall be provided free of charge, whenever possible, taking into account the financial resources of the parents or others caring for the child, and shall be designed to ensure that the disabled child has effective access to and receives education, training, health care services, rehabilitation services, preparation for employment and recreation opportunities in a manner conducive to the child's achieving the fullest possible social integration and individual development, including his or her cultural and spiritual development.

4.   States Parties shall promote, in the spirit of international co-operation, the exchange of appropriate information in the field of preventive health care and of medical, psychological and functional treatment of disabled children, including dissemination of and access to information concerning methods of rehabilitation, education and vocational services, with the aim of enabling States Parties to improve their capabilities and skills and to widen their experience in these areas. In this regard, particular account shall be taken of the needs of developing countries.

Article 24

1.   States Parties recognize the right of the child to the enjoyment of the highest attainable standard of health and to facilities for the treatment of illness and rehabilitation of health. States

Parties shall strive to ensure that no child is deprived of his or her right of access to such health care services.

2.   States Parties shall pursue full implementation of this right and, in particular, shall take appropriate measures:

(a)   To diminish infant and child mortality;

(b)   To ensure the provision of necessary medical assistance and health care to all children with emphasis on the development of primary health care;

(c)   To combat disease and malnutrition, including within the framework of primary health care, through, *inter alia,* the application of readily available technology and through the provision of adequate nutritious foods and clean drinking-water, taking into consideration the dangers and risks of environmental pollution;

(d)   To ensure appropriate pre-natal and post-natal health care for mothers;

(e)   To ensure that all segments of society, in particular parents and children, are informed, have access to education and are supported in the use of basic knowledge of child health and nutrition, the advantages of breast-feeding, hygiene and environmental sanitation and the prevention of accidents;

(f)   To develop preventive health care, guidance for parents and family planning education and services.

3.   States Parties shall take all effective and appropriate measures with a view to abolishing traditional practices prejudicial to the health of children.

4.   States Parties undertake to promote and encourage international co-operation with a view to achieving progressively the full realization of the right recognized in the present article. In this regard, particular account shall be taken of the needs of developing countries.

Article 25

States Parties recognize the right of a child who has been placed by the competent authorities for the purposes of care, protection or treatment of his or her physical or mental health, to a periodic review of the treatment provided to the child and all other circumstances relevant to his or her placement.

Article 26

1.   States Parties shall recognize for every child the right to benefit from social security, including social insurance, and shall take the necessary measures to achieve the full realization of this right in accordance with their national law.

2.   The benefits should, where appropriate, be granted, taking into account the resources and the circumstances of the child and persons having responsibility for the maintenance of the child, as well as any other consideration relevant to an application for benefits made by or on behalf of the child.

Article 27

1.   States Parties recognize the right of every child to a standard of living adequate for the child's physical, mental, spiritual, moral and social development.

2.   The parent(s) or others responsible for the child have the primary responsibility to secure, within their abilities and financial capacities, the conditions of living necessary for the child's development.

3.   States Parties, in accordance with national conditions and within their means, shall take appropriate measures to assist parents and others responsible for the child to implement this right and shall in case of need provide material assistance and support programmes, particularly with regard to nutrition, clothing and housing.

4.   States Parties shall take all appropriate measures to secure the recovery of maintenance for the child from the parents or other persons having financial responsibility for the child, both

within the State Party and from abroad. In particular, where the person having financial responsibility for the child lives in a State different from that of the child, States Parties shall promote the accession to international agreements or the conclusion of such agreements, as well as the making of other appropriate arrangements.

Article 28

1.   States Parties recognize the right of the child to education, and with a view to achieving this right progressively and on the basis of equal opportunity, they shall, in particular:

(*a*)   Make primary education compulsory and available free to all;

(*b*)   Encourage the development of different forms of secondary education, including general and vocational education, make them available and accessible to every child, and take appropriate measures such as the introduction of free education and offering financial assistance in case of need;

(*c*)   Make higher education accessible to all on the basis of capacity by every appropriate means;

(*d*)   Make educational and vocational information and guidance available and accessible to all children;

(*e*)   Take measures to encourage regular attendance at schools and the reduction of drop-out rates.

2.   States Parties shall take all appropriate measures to ensure that school discipline is administered in a manner consistent with the child's human dignity and in conformity with the present Convention.

3.   States Parties shall promote and encourage international co-operation in matters relating to education, in particular with a view to contributing to the elimination of ignorance and illiteracy throughout the world and facilitating access to scientific and technical knowledge and modern teaching methods. In this regard, particular account shall be taken of the needs of developing countries.

Article 29

1.   States Parties agree that the education of the child shall be directed to:

(*a*)   The development of the child's personality, talents and mental and physical abilities to their fullest potential;

(*b*)   The development of respect for human rights and fundamental freedoms, and for the principles enshrined in the Charter of the United Nations;

(*c*)   The development of respect for the child's parents, his or her own cultural identity, language and values, for the national values of the country in which the child is living, the country from which he or she may originate, and for civilizations different from his or her own;

(*d*)   The preparation of the child for responsible life in a free society, in the spirit of understanding, peace, tolerance, equality of sexes, and friendship among all peoples, ethnic, national and religious groups and persons of indigenous origin;

(*e*)   The development of respect for the natural environment.

2.   No part of the present Article or Article 28 shall be construed so as to interfere with the liberty of individuals and bodies to establish and direct educational institutions, subject always to the observance of the principles set forth in paragraph 1 of the present Article and to the requirements that the education given in such institutions shall conform to such minimum standards as may be laid down by the State.

Article 30

In those States in which ethnic, religious or linguistic minorities or persons of indigenous origin exist, a child belonging to such a minority or who is indigenous shall not be denied the right, in community with other members of his or her group, to enjoy his or her own culture, to profess and practise his or her own religion, or to use his or her own language.

Article 31

1. States Parties recognize the right of the child to rest and leisure, to engage in play and recreational activities appropriate to the age of the child and to participate freely in cultural life and the arts.

2. States Parties shall respect and promote the right of the child to participate fully in cultural and artistic life and shall encourage the provision of appropriate and equal opportunities for cultural, artistic, recreational and leisure activity.

Article 32

1. States Parties recognize the right of the child to be protected from economic exploitation and from performing any work that is likely to be hazardous or to interfere with the child's education, or to be harmful to the child's health or physical, mental, spiritual, moral or social development.

2. States Parties shall take legislative, administrative, social and educational measures to ensure the implementation of the present article. To this end, and having regard to the relevant provisions of other international instruments, States Parties shall in particular:

(*a*)   Provide for a minimum age or minimum ages for admission to employment;

(*b*)   Provide for appropriate regulation of the hours and conditions of employment;

(*c*)   Provide for appropriate penalties or other sanctions to ensure the effective enforcement of the present article.

Article 33

States Parties shall take all appropriate measures, including legislative, administrative, social and educational measures, to protect children from the illicit use of narcotic drugs and psychotropic substances as defined in the relevant international treaties, and to prevent the use of children in the illicit production and trafficking of such substances.

Article 34

States Parties undertake to protect the child from all forms of sexual exploitation and sexual abuse. For these purposes, States Parties shall in particular take all appropriate national, bilateral and multilateral measures to prevent:

(*a*)   The inducement or coercion of a child to engage in any unlawful sexual activity;

(*b*)   The exploitative use of children in prostitution or other unlawful sexual practices;

(*c*)   The exploitative use of children in pornographic performances and materials.

Article 35

States Parties shall take all appropriate national, bilateral and multilateral measures to prevent the abduction of, the sale of or traffic in children for any purpose or in any form.

Article 36

States Parties shall protect the child against all other forms of exploitation prejudicial to any aspects of the child's welfare.

Article 37

States Parties shall ensure that:

(*a*)   No child shall be subjected to torture or other cruel, inhuman or degrading treatment or punishment. Neither capital punishment nor life imprisonment without possibility of release shall be imposed for offences committed by persons below eighteen years of age;

(*b*)   No child shall be deprived of his or her liberty unlawfully or arbitrarily. The arrest, detention or imprisonment of a child shall be in conformity with the law and shall be used only as a measure of last resort and for the shortest appropriate period of time;

(*c*)   Every child deprived of liberty shall be treated with humanity and respect for the inherent dignity of the human person, and in a manner which takes into account the needs of persons of his or her age. In particular, every child deprived of liberty shall be separated from adults unless it is considered in the child's best interest not to do so and shall have the right to maintain contact with his or her family through correspondence and visits, save in exceptional circumstances;

(*d*)   Every child deprived of his or her liberty shall have the right to prompt access to legal and other appropriate assistance, as well as the right to challenge the legality of the deprivation of his or her liberty before a court or other competent, independent and impartial authority, and to a prompt decision on any such action.

Article 38

1.   States Parties undertake to respect and to ensure respect for rules of international humanitarian law applicable to them in armed conflicts which are relevant to the child.

2.   States Parties shall take all feasible measures to ensure that persons who have not attained the age of fifteen years do not take a direct part in hostilities.

3.   States Parties shall refrain from recruiting any person who has not attained the age of fifteen years into their armed forces. In recruiting among those persons who have attained the age of fifteen years but who have not attained the age of eighteen years, States Parties shall endeavour to give priority to those who are oldest.

4.   In accordance with their obligations under international humanitarian law to protect the civilian population in armed conflicts, States Parties shall take all feasible measures to ensure protection and care of children who are affected by an armed conflict.

Article 39

States Parties shall take all appropriate measures to promote physical and psychological recovery and social reintegration of a child victim of: any form of neglect, exploitation, or abuse; torture or any other form of cruel, inhuman or degrading treatment or punishment; or armed conflicts. Such recovery and reintegration shall take place in an environment which fosters the health, self-respect and dignity of the child.

Article 40

1.   States Parties recognize the right of every child-alleged as, accused of, or recognized as having infringed the penal law to be treated in a manner consistent with the promotion of the child's sense of dignity and worth, which reinforces the child's respect for the human rights and fundamental freedoms of others and which takes into account the child's age and the desirability of promoting the child's reintegration and the child's assuming a constructive role in society.

2.   To this end, and having regard to the relevant provisions of international instruments, States Parties shall, in particular, ensure that:

(*a*)   No child shall be alleged as, be accused of, or recognized as having infringed the penal law by reason of acts or omissions that were not prohibited by national or international law at the time they were committed;

(*b*)   Every child alleged as or accused of having infringed the penal law has at least the following guarantees:

    (i)   To be presumed innocent until proven guilty according to law;

    (ii)   To be informed promptly and directly of the charges against him or her, and, if appropriate, through his or her parents or legal guardians, and to have legal or other appropriate assistance in the preparation and presentation of his or her defence;

(iii) To have the matter determined without delay by a competent, independent and impartial authority or judicial body in a fair hearing according to law, in the presence of legal or other appropriate assistance and, unless it is considered not to be in the best interest of the child, in particular, taking into account his or her age or situation, his or her parents or legal guardians;

(iv) Not to be compelled to give testimony or to confess guilt; to examine or have examined adverse witnesses and to obtain the participation and examination of witnesses on his or her behalf under conditions of equality;

(v) If considered to have infringed the penal law, to have this decision and any measures imposed in consequence thereof reviewed by a higher competent, independent and impartial authority or judicial body according to law;

(vi) To have the free assistance of an interpreter if the child cannot understand or speak the language used;

(vii) To have his or her privacy fully respected at all stages of the proceedings.

3. States Parties shall seek to promote the establishment of laws, procedures, authorities and institutions specifically applicable to children alleged as, accused of, or recognized as having infringed the penal law, and, in particular:

(*a*) The establishment of a minimum age below which children shall be presumed not to have the capacity to infringe the penal law;

(*b*) Whenever appropriate and desirable, measures for dealing with such children without resorting to judicial proceedings, providing that human rights and legal safeguards are fully respected.

4. A variety of dispositions, such as care, guidance and supervision orders; counselling; probation; foster care; education and vocational training programmes and other alternatives to institutional care shall be available to ensure that children are dealt with in a manner appropriate to their wellbeing and proportionate both to their circumstances and the offence.

Article 41

Nothing in the present Convention shall affect any provisions which are more conducive to the realization of the rights of the child and which may be contained in:

(*a*) The law of a State Party; or

(*b*) International law in force for that State.

PART II

Article 42

States Parties undertake to make the principles and provisions of the Convention widely known, by appropriate and active means, to adults and children alike.

Article 43

1. For the purpose of examining the progress made by States Parties in achieving the realization of the obligations undertaken in the present Convention, there shall be established a Committee on the Rights of the Child, which shall carry out the functions hereinafter provided.

2. The Committee shall consist of ten experts of high moral standing and recognized competence in the field covered by this Convention. The members of the Committee shall be elected by States Parties from among their nationals and shall serve in their personal capacity, consideration being given to equitable geographical distribution, as well as to the principal legal systems.

3. The members of the Committee shall be elected by secret ballot from a list of persons nominated by States Parties. Each State Party may nominate one person from among its own nationals.

4.   The initial election to the Committee shall be held no later than six months after the date of the entry into force of the present Convention and thereafter every second year. At least four months before the date of each election, the Secretary-General of the United Nations shall address a letter to States Parties inviting them to submit their nominations within two months. The Secretary-General shall subsequently prepare a list in alphabetical order of all persons thus nominated, indicating States Parties which have nominated them, and shall submit it to the States Parties to the present Convention.

5.   The elections shall be held at meetings of States Parties convened by the Secretary-General at United Nations Headquarters. At those meetings, for which two thirds of States Parties shall constitute a quorum, the persons elected to the Committee shall be those who obtain the largest number of votes and an absolute majority of the votes of the representatives of States Parties present and voting.

6.   The members of the Committee shall be elected for a term of four years. They shall be eligible for re-election if renominated. The term of five of the members elected at the first election shall expire at the end of two years; immediately after the first election, the names of these five members shall be chosen by lot by the Chairman of the meeting.

7.   If a member of the Committee dies or resigns or declares that for any other cause he or she can no longer perform the duties of the Committee, the State Party which nominated the member shall appoint another expert from among its nationals to serve for the remainder of the term, subject to the approval of the Committee.

8.   The Committee shall establish its own rules of procedure.

9.   The Committee shall elect its officers for a period of two years.

10.   The meetings of the Committee shall normally be held at United Nations Headquarters or at any other convenient place as determined by the Committee. The Committee shall normally meet annually. The duration of the meetings of the Committee shall be determined, and reviewed, if necessary, by a meeting of the States Parties to the present Convention, subject to the approval of the General Assembly.

11.   The Secretary-General of the United Nations shall provide the necessary staff and facilities for the effective performance of the functions of the Committee under the present Convention.

12.   With the approval of the General Assembly, the members of the Committee established under the present Convention shall receive emoluments from United Nations resources on such terms and conditions as the Assembly may decide.

Article 44

1.   States Parties undertake to submit to the Committee, through the Secretary-General of the United Nations, reports on the measures they have adopted which give effect to the rights recognized herein and on the progress made on the enjoyment of those rights:

(*a*)   Within two years of the entry into force of the Convention for the State Party concerned;

(*b*)   Thereafter every five years.

2.   Reports made under the present Article shall indicate factors and difficulties, if any, affecting the degree of fulfilment of the obligations under the present Convention. Reports shall also contain sufficient information to provide the Committee with a comprehensive understanding of the implementation of the Convention in the country concerned.

3.   A State Party which has submitted a comprehensive initial report to the Committee need not, in its subsequent reports submitted in accordance with paragraph 1 (*b*) of the present Article, repeat basic information previously provided.

4.   The Committee may request from States Parties further information relevant to the implementation of the Convention.

5.   The Committee shall submit to the General Assembly, through the Economic and Social Council, every two years, reports on its activities.

6.   States Parties shall make their reports widely available to the public in their own countries.

Article 45

In order to foster the effective implementation of the Convention and to encourage international co-operation in the field covered by the Convention:

(*a*)   The specialized agencies, the United Nations Children's Fund, and other United Nations organs shall be entitled to be represented at the consideration of the implementation of such provisions of the present Convention as fall within the scope of their mandate. The Committee may invite the specialized agencies, the United Nations Children's Fund and other competent bodies as it may consider appropriate to provide expert advice on the implementation of the Convention in areas falling within the scope of their respective mandates. The Committee may invite the specialized agencies, the United Nations Children's Fund, and other United Nations organs to submit reports on the implementation of the Convention in areas falling within the scope of their activities;

(*b*)   The Committee shall transmit, as it may consider appropriate, to the specialized agencies, the United Nations Children's Fund and other competent bodies, any reports from States Parties that contain a request, or indicate a need, for technical advice or assistance, along with the Committee's observations and suggestions, if any, on these requests or indications;

(*c*)   The Committee may recommend to the General Assembly to request the Secretary-General to undertake on its behalf studies on specific issues relating to the rights of the child;

(*d*)   The Committee may make suggestions and general recommendations based on information received pursuant to Articles 44 and 45 of the present Convention. Such suggestions and general recommendations shall be transmitted to any State Party concerned and reported to the General Assembly, together with comments, if any, from States Parties.

PART III

Article 46

The present Convention shall be open for signature by all States.

Article 47

The present Convention is subject to ratification. Instruments of ratification shall be deposited with the Secretary-General of the United Nations.

Article 48

The present Convention shall remain open for accession by any State. The instruments of accession shall be deposited with the Secretary-General of the United Nations.

Article 49

1.   The present Convention shall enter into force on the thirtieth day following the date of deposit with the Secretary-General of the United Nations of the twentieth instrument of ratification or accession.

2.   For each State ratifying or acceding to the Convention after the deposit of the twentieth instrument of ratification or accession, the Convention shall enter into force on the thirtieth day after the deposit by such State of its instrument of ratification or accession.

Article 50

1.   Any State Party may propose an amendment and file it with the Secretary-General of the United Nations. The Secretary-General shall thereupon communicate the proposed amendment to States Parties, with a request that they indicate whether they favour a conference of States Parties for the purpose of considering and voting upon the proposals. In the event that, within four months from the date of such communication, at least one third of the States Parties favour such a conference, the Secretary-General shall convene the conference under the auspices of the United Nations. Any amendment adopted by a majority of States Parties present and voting at the conference shall be submitted to the General Assembly for approval.

2.   An amendment adopted in accordance with paragraph 1 of the present article shall enter into force when it has been approved by the General Assembly of the United Nations and accepted by a two-thirds majority of States Parties.

3.   When an amendment enters into force, it shall be binding on those States Parties which have accepted it, other States Parties still being bound by the provisions of the present Convention and any earlier amendments which they have accepted.

Article 51

1.   The Secretary-General of the United Nations shall receive and circulate to all States the text of reservations made by States at the time of ratification or accession.

2.   A reservation incompatible with the object and purpose of the present Convention shall not be permitted.

3.   Reservations may be withdrawn at any time by notification to that effect addressed to the Secretary-General of the United Nations, who shall then inform all States. Such notification shall take effect on the date on which it is received by the Secretary-General.

Article 52

A State Party may denounce the present Convention by written notification to the Secretary-General of the United Nations. Denunciation becomes effective one year after the date of receipt of the notification by the Secretary-General.

Article 53

The Secretary-General of the United Nations is designated as the depositary of the present Convention.

Article 54

The original of the present Convention, of which the Arabic, Chinese, English, French, Russian and Spanish texts are equally authentic, shall be deposited with the Secretary-General of the United Nations.

In witness thereof the undersigned plenipotentiaries, being duly authorized thereto by their respective Governments, have signed the present Convention.

Convention relating to the Status of Refugees, 1951

The High Contracting Parties,

Considering that the Charter of the United Nations and the Universal Declaration of Human Rights approved on 10 December 1948 by the General Assembly have affirmed the principle that human beings shall enjoy fundamental rights and freedoms without discrimination,

Considering that the United Nations has, on various occasions, manifested its profound concern for refugees and endeavoured to assure refugees the widest possible exercise of these fundamental rights and freedoms.

Considering that it is desirable to revise and consolidate previous international agreements relating to the status of refugees and to extend the scope of and the protection accorded by such instruments by means of a new agreement,

Considering that the grant of asylum may place unduly heavy burdens on certain countries, and that a satisfactory solution of a problem of which the United Nations has recognized the international scope and nature cannot therefore be achieved without international co-operation.

Expressing the wish that all States, recognizing the social and humanitarian nature of the problem of refugees, will do everything within their power to prevent this problem from becoming a cause of tension between States,

Noting that the United Nations High Commissioner for Refugees is charged with the task of supervising international conventions providing for the protection of refugees, and recognizing that the effective co-ordination of measures taken to deal with this problem will depend upon the co-operation of States with the High Commissioner,

Have agreed as follows:

CHAPTER I

General Provisions

Definition of the Term 'Refugee'
Article 1

A.   For the purposes of the present Convention, the term 'refugee' shall apply to any person who:

(1)   Has been considered a refugee under the Arrangements of 12 May 1926 and 30 June 1928 or under the Conventions of 28 October 1933 and 10 February 1938, the Protocol of 14 September 1939 or the Constitution of the International Refugee Organization;

Decisions of non-eligibility taken by the International Refugee Organization during the period of its activities shall not prevent the status of refugee being accorded to persons who fulfil the conditions of paragraph 2 of this section;

(2)   [As a result of events occurring before I January 1951 and] owing to well-founded fear of being persecuted for reasons of race, religion, nationality, membership of a particular social group or political opinion, is outside the country of his nationality and is unable or, owing to such fear, is unwilling to avail himself of the protection of that country; or who, not having a nationality and being outside the country of his former habitual residence [as a result of such events], is unable or, owing to such fear, is unwilling to return to it.

In the case of a person who has more than one nationality, the term 'the country of his nationality' shall mean each of the countries of which he is a national, and a person shall not be deemed to be lacking the protection of the country of his nationality if, without any valid reason based on well-founded fear, he has not availed himself of the protection of one of the countries of which he is a national.

B. (1)   For the purposes of this Convention, the words 'events occurring before I January 1951' in Article 1, Section A, shall be understood to mean either

(*a*)   'events occurring in Europe before 1 January 1951'; or

(*b*)   'events occurring in Europe or elsewhere before 1 January 1951';

and each Contracting State shall make a declaration at the time of signature, ratification or accession, specifying which of these meanings it applies for the purpose of its obligations under this Convention.

(2)   Any Contracting State which has adopted alternative (*a*) may at any time extend its obligations by adopting alternative *(b)* by means of a notification addressed to the Secretary-General of the United Nations.

C.   This Convention shall cease to apply to any person falling under the terms of section A if:

(1)   He has voluntarily re-availed himself of the protection of the country of his nationality; or

(2)   Having lost his nationality, he has voluntarily reacquired it; or

(3)   He has acquired a new nationality, and enjoys the protection of the country of his new nationality; or

(4)   He has voluntarily re-established himself in the country which he left or outside which he remained owing to fear of persecution; or

(5)   He can no longer, because the circumstances in connexion with which he has been recognized as a refugee have ceased to exist, continue to refuse to avail himself of the protection of the country of his nationality;

Provided that this paragraph shall not apply to a refugee falling under section A (1) of this article who is able to invoke compelling reasons arising out of previous persecution for refusing to avail himself of the protection of the country of nationality;

(6)   Being a person who has no nationality he is, because the circumstances in connexion with which he has been recognized as a refugee have ceased to exist, able to return to the country of his former habitual residence;

Provided this paragraph shall not apply to a refugee falling under section A (1) of this article who is able to invoke compelling reasons arising out of previous persecution for refusing to return to the country of his former habitual residence.

D.   This Convention shall not apply to persons who are at present receiving from organs or agencies of the United Nations other than the United Nations High Commissioner for Refugees protection or assistance.

When such protection or assistance has ceased for any reason, without the position of such persons being definitively settled in accordance with the relevant resolutions adopted by the General Assembly of the United Nations, these persons shall *ipso facto* be entitled to the benefits of this Convention.

E.   This Convention shall not apply to a person who is recognized by the competent authorities of the country in which he has taken residence as having the rights and obligations which are attached to the possession of the nationality of that country.

F.   The provisions of this Convention shall not apply to any person with respect to whom there are serious reasons for considering that:

(*a*)   He has committed a crime against peace, a war crime, or a crime against humanity, as defined in the international instruments drawn up to make provision in respect of such crimes;

(*b*)   He has committed a serious non-political crime outside the country of refuge prior to his admission to that country as a refugee;

(*c*)   He has been guilty of acts contrary to the purposes and principles of the United Nations.

General Obligations
Article 2

Every refugee has duties to the country in which he finds himself, which require in particular that he conform to its laws and regulations as well as to measures taken for the maintenance of public order.

Non-discrimination
Article 3

The Contracting States shall apply the provisions of this Convention to refugees without discrimination as to race, religion or country of origin.

Religion
Article 4

The Contracting States shall accord to refugees within their territories treatment at least as favourable as that accorded to their nationals with respect to freedom to practise their religion and freedom as regards the religious education of their children.

Rights Granted Apart from this Convention
Article 5

Nothing in this Convention shall be deemed to impair any rights and benefits granted by a Contracting State to refugees apart from this Convention.

The Term 'In the same circumstances'
Article 6

For the purpose of this Convention, the term in 'the same circumstances' implies that any requirements (including requirements as to length and conditions of sojourn or residence) which the particular individual would have to fulfil for the enjoyment of the right in question, if he were not a refugee, must be fulfilled by him, with the exception of requirements which by their nature a refugee is incapable of fulfilling.

Exemption from Reciprocity
Article 7

1.   Except where this Convention contains more favourable provisions, a Contracting State shall accord to refugees the same treatment as is accorded to aliens generally.

2.   After a period of three years' residence, all refugees shall enjoy exemption from legislative reciprocity in the territory of the Contracting States.

3.   Each Contracting State shall continue to accord to refugees the rights and benefits to which they were already entitled, in the absence of reciprocity, at the date of entry into force of this Convention for that State.

4.   The Contracting States shall consider favourably the possibility of according to refugees, in the absence of reciprocity, rights and benefits beyond those to which they are entitled according to paragraphs 2 and 3, and to extending exemption from reciprocity to refugees who do not fulfil the conditions provided for in paragraphs 2 and 3.

5. The provisions of paragraphs 2 and 3 apply both to the rights and benefits referred to in Articles 13, 18, 19, 21 and 22 of this Convention and to rights and benefits for which this Convention does not provide.

Exemption from Exceptional Measures
Article 8

With regard to exceptional measures which may be taken against the person, property or interests of nationals of a foreign State, the Contracting States shall not apply such measures to a refugee who is formally a national of the said State solely on account of such nationality. Contracting States which, under their legislation, are prevented from applying the general principle expressed in this article, shall, in appropriate cases, grant exemptions in favour of such refugees.

Provisional Measures
Article 9

Nothing in this Convention shall prevent a Contracting State, in time of war or other grave and exceptional circumstances, from taking provisionally measures which it considers to be essential to the national security in the case of a particular person, pending a determination by the Contracting State that that person is in fact a refugee and that the continuance of such measures is necessary in his case in the interests of national security.

Continuity of Residence
Article 10

1.   Where a refugee has been forcibly displaced during the Second World War and removed to the territory of a Contracting State, and is resident there, the period of such enforced sojourn shall be considered to have been lawful residence within that territory.

2.   Where a refugee has been forcibly displaced during the Second World War from the territory of a Contracting State and has, prior to the date of entry into force of this Convention, returned there for the purpose of taking up residence, the period of residence before and after such enforced displacement shall be regarded as one uninterrupted period for any purposes for which uninterrupted residence is required.

Refugee Seamen
Article 11

In the case of refugees regularly serving as crew members on board a ship flying the flag of a Contracting State, that State shall give sympathetic consideration to their establishment on its territory and the issue of travel documents to them or their temporary admission to its territory particularly with a view to facilitating their establishment in another country.

CHAPTER II

Juridical Status

Personal Status
Article 12

1.   The personal status of a refugee shall be governed by the law of the country of his domicile or, if he has no domicile, by the law of the country of his residence.

2.   Rights previously acquired by a refugee and dependent on personal status, more particularly rights attaching to marriage, shall be respected by a Contracting State, subject to compliance, if this be necessary, with the formalities required by the law of that State, provided that the right in question is one which would have been recognized by the law of that State had he not become a refugee.

Movable and Immovable Property
Article 13

The Contracting States shall accord to a refugee treatment as favourable as possible and, in any event, not less favourable than that accorded to aliens generally in the same circumstances, as regards the acquisition of movable and immovable property and other rights pertaining thereto, and to leases and other contracts relating to movable and immovable property.

Artistic Rights and Industrial Property
Article 14

In respect of the protection of industrial property, such as inventions, designs or models, trade marks, trade names, and of rights in literary, artistic and scientific works, a refugee shall be accorded in the country in which he has his habitual residence the same protection as is accorded to nationals of that country. In the territory of any other Contracting State, he shall be accorded the same protection as is accorded in that territory to nationals of the country in which he has his habitual residence.

Right of Association
Article 15

As regards non-political and non-profit-making associations and trade unions the Contracting States shall accord to refugees lawfully staying in their territory the most favourable treatment accorded to nationals of a foreign country, in the same circumstances.

Access to Courts
Article 16

1.   A refugee shall have free access to the courts of law on the territory of all Contracting States.

2.   A refugee shall enjoy in the Contracting State in which he has his habitual residence the same treatment as a national in matters pertaining to access to the courts, including legal assistance and exemption from *cautio judicatum solvi.*

3.   A refugee shall be accorded in the matters referred to in paragraph 2 in countries other than that in which he has his habitual residence the treatment granted to a national of the country of his habitual residence.

CHAPTER III

Gainful Employment

Wage-earning Employment
Article 17

1.   The Contracting States shall accord to refugees lawfully staying in their territory the most favourable treatment accorded to nationals of a foreign country in the same circumstances, as regards the right to engage in wage-earning employment.

2.   In any case, restrictive measures imposed on aliens or the employment of aliens for the protection of the national labour market shall not be applied to a refugee who was already exempt from them at the date of entry into force of this Convention for the Contracting State concerned, or who fulfils one of the following conditions:

(*a*)   He has completed three years' residence in the country.

(*b*)   He has a spouse possessing the nationality of the country of residence. A refugee may not invoke the benefit of this provision if he has abandoned his spouse:

(*c*)   He has one or more children possessing the nationality of the country of residence.

3.   The Contracting States shall give sympathetic consideration to assimilating the rights of all refugees with regard to wage-earning employment to those of nationals, and in particular of those refugees who have entered their territory pursuant to programmes of labour recruitment or under immigration schemes.

Self-employment
Article 18

The Contracting States shall accord to a refugee lawfully in their territory treatment as favourable as possible and, in any event, not less favourable than that accorded to aliens generally in the same circumstances, as regards the right to engage on his own account in agriculture, industry, handicrafts and commerce and to establish commercial and industrial companies.

Liberal Professions
Article 19

1.   Each Contracting State shall accord to refugees lawfully staying in their territory who hold diplomas recognized by the competent authorities of that State, and who are desirous of

practising a liberal profession, treatment as favourable as possible and, in any event, not less favourable than that accorded to aliens generally in the same circumstances.

2.   The Contracting States shall use their best endeavours consistently with their laws and constitutions to secure the settlement of such refugees in the territories, other than the metropolitan territory, for whose international relations they are responsible.

CHAPTER IV

Welfare

Rationing
Article 20

Where a rationing system exists, which applies to the population at large and regulates the general distribution of products in short supply, refugees shall be accorded the same treatment as nationals.

Housing
Article 21

As regards housing, the Contracting States, in so far as the matter is regulated by laws or regulations or is subject to the control of public authorities, shall accord to refugees lawfully staying in their territory treatment as favourable as possible and, in any event, not less favourable than that accorded to aliens generally in the same circumstances.

Public Education
Article 22

1.   The Contracting States shall accord to refugees the same treatment as is accorded to nationals with respect to elementary education.

2.   The Contracting States shall accord to refugees treatment as favourable as possible, and, in any event, not less favourable than that accorded to aliens generally in the same circumstances, with respect to education other than elementary education and, in particular, as regards access to studies, the recognition of foreign school certificates, diplomas and degrees, the remission of fees and charges and the award of scholarships.

Public Relief
Article 23

The Contracting States shall accord to refugees lawfully staying in their territory the same treatment with respect to public relief and assistance as is accorded to their nationals.

Labour Legislation and Social Security
Article 24

1.   The Contracting States shall accord to refugees lawfully staying in their territory the same treatment as is accorded to nationals in respect of the following matters:

(*a*)   In so far as such matters are governed by laws or regulations or are subject to the control of administrative authorities: remuneration, including family allowances where these form part of remuneration, hours of work, overtime arrangements, holidays with pay, restrictions on home work, minimum age of employment, apprenticeship and training, women's work and the work of young persons, and the enjoyment of the benefits of collective bargaining;

(*b*)   Social security (legal provisions in respect of employment injury, occupational diseases, maternity, sickness, disability, old age, death, unemployment, family responsibilities and any other contingency which, according to national laws or regulations, is covered by a social security scheme), subject to the following limitations:

(i)   There may be appropriate arrangements for the maintenance of acquired rights and rights in course of acquisition;

(ii)   National laws or regulations of the country of residence may prescribe special arrangements concerning benefits or portions of benefits which are payable wholly out of public funds, and concerning allowances paid to persons who do not fulfil the contribution conditions prescribed for the award of a normal pension.

2.   The right to compensation for the death of a refugee resulting from employment injury or from occupational disease shall not be affected by the fact that the residence of the beneficiary is outside the territory of the Contracting State.

3.   The Contracting States shall extend to refugees the benefits of agreements concluded between them, or which may be concluded between them in the future, concerning the maintenance of acquired rights in the process of acquisition in regard to social security, subject only to the conditions which apply to nationals of the States signatory to the agreements in question.

4.   The Contracting States will give sympathetic consideration to extending to refugees so far as possible the benefits of similar agreements which may at any time be in force between such Contracting States and non-contracting States.

CHAPTER V

Administrative Measures

Administrative Assistance
Article 25

1.   When the exercise of a right by a refugee would normally require the assistance of authorities of a foreign country to whom he cannot have recourse, the Contracting States in whose territory he is residing shall arrange that such assistance be afforded to him by their own authorities or by an international authority.

2.   The authority or authorities mentioned in paragraph 1 shall deliver or cause to be delivered under their supervision to refugees such documents or certifications as would normally be delivered to aliens by or through their national authorities.

3.   Documents or certifications so delivered shall stand in the stead of the official instruments delivered to aliens by or through their national authorities, and shall be given credence in the absence of proof to the contrary.

4.   Subject to such exceptional treatment as may be granted to indigent persons, fees may be charged for the services mentioned herein, but such fees shall be moderate and commensurate with those charged to nationals for similar services.

5.   The provisions of this article shall be without prejudice to Articles 27 and 28.

Freedom of Movement
Article 26

Each Contracting State shall accord to refugees lawfully in its territory the right to choose their place of residence and to move freely within its territory, subject to any regulations applicable to aliens generally in the same circumstances.

Identity Papers
Article 27

The Contracting States shall issue identity papers to any refugee in their territory who does not possess a valid travel document.

Travel Documents
Article 28

1.   The Contracting States shall issue to refugees lawfully staying in their territory travel documents for the purpose of travel outside their territory, unless compelling reasons of national

security or public order otherwise require, and the provisions of the Schedule to this Convention shall apply with respect to such documents. The Contracting States may issue such a travel document to any other refugee in their territory; they shall in particular give sympathetic consideration to the issue of such a travel document to refugees in their territory who are unable to obtain a travel document from the country of their lawful residence.

2.   Travel documents issued to refugees under previous international agreements by parties thereto shall be recognized and treated by the Contracting States in the same way as if they had been issued pursuant to this Article.

Fiscal Charges
Article 29

1.   The Contracting States shall not impose upon refugees duties, charges or taxes, of any description whatsoever, other or higher than those which are or may be levied on their nationals in similar situations.

2.   Nothing in the above paragraph shall prevent the application to refugees of the laws and regulations concerning charges in respect of the issue to aliens of administrative documents including identity papers.

Transfer of Assets
Article 30

1.   A Contracting State shall, in conformity with its laws and regulations, permit refugees to transfer assets which they have brought into its territory, to another country where they have been admitted for the purposes of resettlement.

2.   A Contracting State shall give sympathetic consideration to the application of refugees for permission to transfer assets wherever they may be and which are necessary for their resettlement in another country to which they have been admitted.

Refugees Unlawfully in the Country of Refuge
Article 31

1.   The Contracting States shall not impose penalties, on account of their illegal entry or presence, on refugees who, coming directly from a territory where their life or freedom was threatened in the sense of Article 1, enter or are present in their territory without authorization, provided they present themselves without delay to the authorities and show good cause for their illegal entry or presence.

2.   The Contracting States shall not apply to the movements of such refugees restrictions other than those which are necessary and such restrictions shall only be applied until their status in the country is regularized or they obtain admission into another country. The Contracting States shall allow such refugees a reasonable period and all the necessary facilities to obtain admission into another country.

Expulsion
Article 32

1.   The Contracting States shall not expel a refugee lawfully in their territory save on grounds of national security or public order.

2.   The expulsion of such a refugee shall be only in pursuance of a decision reached in accordance with due process of law. Except where compelling reasons of national security otherwise require, the refugee shall be allowed to submit evidence to clear himself, and to appeal to and be represented for the purpose before the competent authority or a person or persons specially designated by the competent authority.

3.   The Contracting States shall allow such a refugee a reasonable period within which to seek legal admission into another country. The Contracting States reserve the right to apply during that period such internal measures as they may deem necessary.

Prohibition of Expulsion or Return ('Refoulement')
Article 33

1.   No Contracting State shall expel or return ('refouler') a refugee in any manner whatsoever to the frontiers of territories where his life or freedom would be threatened on account of his race, religion, nationality, membership of a particular social group or political opinion.

2.   The benefit of the present provision may not, however, be claimed by a refugee whom there are reasonable grounds for regarding as a danger to the security of the country in which he is, or who, having been convicted by a final judgment of a particularly serious crime, constitutes a danger to the community of that country.

Naturalization
Article 34

The Contracting States shall as far as possible facilitate the assimilation and naturalization of refugees. They shall in particular make every effort to expedite naturalization proceedings and to reduce as far as possible the charges and costs of such proceedings.

CHAPTER VI

Executory and Transitory Provisions

Co-operation of the National Authorities with the United Nations
Article 35

1.   The Contracting States undertake to co-operate with the Office of the United Nations High Commissioner for Refugees, or any other agency of the United Nations which may succeed it, in the exercise of its functions, and shall in particular facilitate its duty of supervising the application of the provisions of this Convention.

2.   In order to enable the Office of the High Commissioner or any other agency of the United Nations which may succeed it, to make reports to the competent organs of the United Nations, the Contracting States undertake to provide them in the appropriate form with information and statistical data requested concerning:

(*a*)   The condition of refugees,

(*b*)   The implementation of this Convention, and

(*c*)   Laws, regulations and decrees which are, or may hereafter be, in force relating to refugees.

Information on National Legislation

Article 36

The Contracting States shall communicate to the Secretary-General of the United Nations the laws and regulations which they may adopt to ensure the application of this Convention.

Relation to Previous Conventions
Article 37

Without prejudice to Article 28, paragraph 2, of this Convention, this Convention replaces, as between parties to it, the Arrangements of 5 July 1922, 31 May 1924, 12 May 1926, 30 June 1928 and 30 July 1935, the Conventions of 28 October 1933 and 10 February 1938, the Protocol of 14 September 1939 and the Agreement of 15 October 1946.

CHAPTER VII

Final Clauses

Settlement of Disputes
Article 38

Any dispute between parties to this Convention relating to its interpretation or application, which cannot be settled by other means, shall be referred to the International Court of Justice at the request of any one of the parties to the dispute.

Signature, Ratification and Accession
Article 39

1.   This Convention shall be opened for signature at Geneva on 28 July 1951 and shall thereafter be deposited with the Secretary-General of the United Nations. It shall be open for signature at the European Office of the United Nations from 28 July to 31 August 1951 and shall be re-opened for signature at the Headquarters of the United Nations from 17 September 1951 to 31 December 1952.

2.   This Convention shall be open for signature on behalf of all States Members of the United Nations, and also on behalf of any other State invited to attend the Conference of Plenipotentiaries on the Status of Refugees and Stateless Persons or to which an invitation to sign will have been addressed by the General Assembly. It shall be ratified and the instruments of ratification shall be deposited with the Secretary-General of the United Nations.

3.   This Convention shall be open from 28 July 1951 for accession by the States referred to in paragraph 2 of this Article. Accession shall be effected by the deposit of an instrument of accession with the Secretary-General of the United Nations.

Territorial Application Clause
Article 40

1.   Any State may, at the time of signature, ratification or accession, declare that this Convention shall extend to all or any of the territories for the international relations of which it is responsible. Such a declaration shall take effect when the Convention enters into force for the State concerned.

2.   At any time thereafter any such extension shall be made by notification addressed to the Secretary-General of the United Nations and shall take effect as from the ninetieth day after the day of receipt by the Secretary-General of the United Nations of this notification, or as from the date of entry into force of the Convention for the State concerned, whichever is the later.

3.   With respect to those territories to which this Convention is not extended at the time of signature, ratification or accession, each State concerned shall consider the possibility of taking the necessary steps in order to extend the application of this Convention to such territories, subject, where necessary for constitutional reasons, to the consent of the Governments of such territories.

Federal Clause
Article 41

In the case of a Federal or non-unitary State, the following provisions shall apply:

(a)   With respect to those articles of this Convention that come within the legislative jurisdiction of the federal legislative authority, the obligations of the Federal Government shall to this extent be the same as those of Parties which are not Federal States;

(b)   With respect to those Articles of this Convention that come within the legislative jurisdiction of constituent states, provinces or cantons which are not, under the constitutional system of the federation, bound to take legislative action, the Federal Government shall bring such Articles with a favourable recommendation to the notice of the appropriate authorities of states, provinces or cantons at the earliest possible moment.

(c)   A Federal State Party to this Convention shall, at the request of any other Contracting State transmitted through the Secretary-General of the United Nations, supply a statement of the law and practice of the Federation and its constituent units in regard to any particular provision of the Convention showing the extent to which effect has been given to that provision by legislative or other action.

Reservations
Article 42

1.   At the time of signature, ratification or accession, any State may make reservations to Articles of the Convention other than to Articles 1, 3, 4, 16 (1), 33, 36 – 46 inclusive.

2.   Any State making a reservation in accordance with paragraph 1 of this Article may at any time withdraw the reservation by a communication to that effect addressed to the Secretary-General of the United Nations.

Entry into Force
Article 43

1.   This Convention shall come into force on the ninetieth day following the day of deposit of the sixth instrument of ratification or accession.

2.   For each State ratifying or acceding to the Convention after the deposit of the sixth instrument of ratification or accession, the Convention shall enter into force on the ninetieth day following the date of deposit by such State of its instrument of ratification or accession.

Denunciation
Article 44

1.   Any Contracting State may denounce this Convention at any time by a notification addressed to the Secretary-General of the United Nations.

2.   Such denunciation shall take effect for the Contracting State concerned one year from the date upon which it is received by the Secretary-General of the United Nations.

3.   Any State which has made a declaration or notification under Article 40 may, at any time thereafter, by a notification to the Secretary-General of the United Nations, declare that the Convention shall cease to extend to such territory one year after the date of receipt of the notification by the Secretary-General.

Revision
Article 45

1.   Any Contracting State may request revision of this Convention at any time by a notification addressed to the Secretary-General of the United Nations.

2.   The General Assembly of the United Nations shall recommend the steps, if any, to be taken in respect of such request.

Notifications by the Secretary-General of the United Nations
Article 46

The Secretary-General of the United Nations shall inform all Members of the United Nations and non-member States referred to in Article 39:

   (*a*)   Of declarations and notifications in accordance with section B of Article 1;

   (*b*)   Of signatures, ratifications and accessions in accordance with Article 39;

   (*c*)   Of declarations and notifications in accordance with Article 40;

   (*d*)   Of reservations and withdrawals in accordance with Article 42;

   (*e*)   Of the date on which this Convention will come into force in accordance with Article 43;

   (*f*)   Of denunciations and notifications in accordance with Article 44;

   (*g*)   Of requests for revision in accordance with Article 45.

In faith whereof the undersigned, duly authorized, have signed this Convention on behalf of their respective Governments,

Done at Geneva, this twenty-eighth day of July, one thousand nine hundred and fifty-one, in a single copy, of which the English and French texts are equally authentic and which shall remain deposited in the archives of the United Nations, and certified true copies of which shall be delivered to all Members of the United Nations and to the non-member States referred to in Article 39.

Protocol relating to the Status of Refugees of 31 January 1967

United Nations General Assembly, 16 December 1966

4 October 1967

PREAMBLE

The States Parties to the present Protocol,

Considering that the Convention relating to the Status of Refugees done at Geneva on 28 July 1951 (hereinafter referred to as the Convention) covers only those persons who have become refugees as a result of events occurring before 1 January, 1951,

Considering that new refugee situations have arisen since the Convention was adopted and that the refugees concerned may therefore not fall within the scope of the Convention,

Considering that it is desirable that equal status should be enjoyed by all refugees covered by the definition in the Convention irrespective of the dateline 1 January 1951,

Have agreed as follows:

Article 1
General provision

1.   The States Parties to the present Protocol undertake to apply Articles 2 to 34 inclusive of the Convention to refugees as hereinafter defined.

2.   For the purpose of the present Protocol, the term 'refugee' shall, except as regards the application of paragraph 3 of this Article, mean any person within the definition of Article 1 of the Convention as if the words 'As a result of events occurring before 1 January 1951 and ... 'and the words'... a result of such events', in Article 1 A (2) were omitted.

3.   The present Protocol shall be applied by the States Parties hereto without any geographic limitation, save that existing declarations made by States already Parties to the Convention in accordance with Article 1 B (1)(*a*) of the Convention, shall, unless extended under Article 1 B (2) thereof, apply also under the present Protocol.

Article 2
Co-operation of the national authorities with the United Nations

1.   The States Parties to the present Protocol undertake to co-operate with the Office of the United Nations High Commissioner for Refugees, or any other agency of the United Nations which may succeed it, in the exercise of its functions, and shall in particular facilitate its duty of supervising the application of the provisions of the present Protocol.

2.   In order to enable the Office of the High Commissioner, or any other agency of the United Nations which may succeed it, to make reports to the competent organs of the United Nations, the States Parties to the present Protocol undertake to provide them with the information and statistical data requested, in the appropriate form, concerning: (*a*) The condition of refugees; (*b*) The implementation of the present Protocol; (*c*) Laws, regulations and decrees which are, or may hereafter be, in force relating to refugees.

Article 3
Information on national legislation

The States Parties to the present Protocol shall communicate to the Secretary-General of the United Nations the laws and regulations which they may adopt to ensure the application of the present Protocol.

Article 4
Settlement of disputes

Any dispute between States Parties to the present Protocol which relates to its interpretation or application and which cannot be settled by other means shall be referred to the International Court of Justice at the request of any one of the parties to the dispute.

Article 5
Accession

The present Protocol shall be open for accession on behalf of all States Parties to the Convention and of any other State Member of the United Nations or member of any of the specialized agencies or to which an invitation to accede may have been addressed by the General Assembly of the United Nations. Accession shall be effected by the deposit of an instrument of accession with the Secretary-General of the United Nations.

Article 6
Federal clause

In the case of a Federal or non-unitary State, the following provisions shall apply:

(*a*)   With respect to those articles of the Convention to be applied in accordance with Article I, paragraph 1, of the present Protocol that come within the legislative jurisdiction of the federal legislative authority, the obligations of the Federal Government shall to this extent be the same as those of States Parties which are not Federal States;

(*b*)   With respect to those articles of the Convention to be applied in accordance with Article I, paragraph 1, of the present Protocol that come within the legislative jurisdiction of constituent States, provinces or cantons which are not, under the constitutional system of the federation, bound to take legislative action, the Federal Government shall bring such articles with a favourable recommendation to the notice of the appropriate authorities of States, provinces or cantons at the earliest possible moment;

(*c*)   A Federal State Party to the present Protocol shall, at the request of any other State Party hereto transmitted through the Secretary-General of the United Nations, supply a statement of the law and practice of the Federation and its constituent units in regard to any particular provision of the Convention to be applied in accordance with Article I, paragraph 1, of the present Protocol, showing the extent to which effect has been given to that provision by legislative or other action.

Article 7
Reservations and declarations

1.   At the time of accession, any State may make reservations in respect of Article IV of the present Protocol and in respect of the application in accordance with Article I of the present Protocol of any provisions of the Convention other than those contained in Articles 1, 3, 4, 16 (1) and 33 thereof, provided that in the case of a State Party to the Convention reservations made under this Article shall not extend to refugees in respect of whom the Convention applies.

2.   Reservations made by States Parties to the Convention in accordance with Article 42 thereof shall, unless withdrawn, be applicable in relation to their obligations under the present Protocol.

3.   Any State making a reservation in accordance with paragraph 1 of this Article may at any time withdraw such reservation by a communication to that effect addressed to the Secretary-General of the United Nations.

4.   Declarations made under Article 40, paragraphs 1 and 2, of the Convention by a State Party thereto which accedes to the present Protocol shall be deemed to apply in respect of the present Protocol, unless upon accession a notification to the contrary is addressed by the State Party concerned to the Secretary-General of the United Nations. The provisions of Article 40, paragraphs 2 and 3, and of Article 44, paragraph 3, of the Convention shall be deemed to apply mutatis mutandis to the present Protocol.

Article 8
Entry into force

1.   The present Protocol shall come into force on the day of deposit of the sixth instrument of accession.

2.   For each State acceding to the Protocol after the deposit of the sixth instrument of accession, the Protocol shall come into force on the date of deposit by such State of its instrument of accession.

Article 9
Denunciation

1.   Any State Party hereto may denounce this Protocol at any time by a notification addressed to the Secretary-General of the United Nations.

2.   Such denunciation shall take effect for the State Party concerned one year from the date on which it is received by the Secretary-General of the United Nations.

Article 10
Notifications by the Secretary-General of the United Nations

The Secretary-General of the United Nations shall inform the States referred to in Article V above of the date of entry into force, accessions, reservations and withdrawals of reservations to and denunciations of the present Protocol, and of declarations and notifications relating hereto.

Article 11
Deposit in the archives of the Secretariat of the United Nations

A copy of the present Protocol, of which the Chinese, English, French, Russian and Spanish texts are equally authentic, signed by the President of the General Assembly and by the Secretary-General of the United Nations, shall be deposited in the archives of the Secretariat of the United Nations. The Secretary-General will transmit certified copies thereof to all States Members of the United Nations and to the other States referred to in Article V above.

APPENDIX

GENERAL ASSEMBLY RESOLUTION 2198 (XXI)

Protocol relating to the Status of Refugees

The General Assembly, Considering that the Convention relating to the Status of Refugees, signed at Geneva on 28 July 1951, covers only those persons who have become refugees as a result of events occurring before 1 January 1951,

Considering that new refugee situations have arisen since the Convention was adopted and that the refugees concerned may therefore not fall within the scope of the Convention,

Considering that it is desirable that equal status should be enjoyed by all refugees covered by the definition in the Convention, irrespective of the date-line of 1 January 1951,

Taking note of the recommendation of the Executive Committee of the Programme of the United Nations High Commissioner for Refugees that the draft Protocol relating to the Status of Refugees should be submitted to the General Assembly after consideration by the Economic and Social Council, in order that the Secretary-General might be authorized to open the Protocol for accession by Governments within the shortest possible time,

Considering that the Economic and Social Council, in its resolution 1186 (XLI) of 18 November 1966, took note with approval of the draft Protocol contained in the addendum to the report of the United Nations High Commissioner for Refugees and concerning measures to extend the personal scope of the Convention and transmitted the addendum to the General Assembly,

1.   Takes note of the Protocol relating to the Status of Refugees, the text of which is contained in the addendum to the report of the United Nations High Commissioner for Refugees;

2.   Requests the Secretary-General to transmit the text of the Protocol to the States mentioned in article V thereof, with a view to enabling them to accede to the Protocol.

1495th plenary meeting, 16 December 1966.

Angola

Date of accession and entry into force: 23 June 1981

Reservation

In its instrument of accession to the Protocol, the Government of Angola declared, in accordance with Article VII paragraph 1, that it does not consider itself bound by Article IV of the Protocol, concerning settlement of disputes relating to the interpretation of the Protocol.

Botswana

Date of accession and entry into force: 6 January 1969

Reservations

'Subject to the reservation in respect of article IV of the said Protocol and in respect of the application in accordance with article I thereof of the provisions of articles 7, 17, 26, 31, 32 and 34 and paragraph 1 of article 12 of the Convention relating to the Status of Refugees, done at Geneva on 28 July 1951.'

Burundi

Date of accession and entry into force: 15 March 1971

Reservations

The instrument of accession to the Protocol was made subject to the following reservations with respect to the application of the Articles of the Convention to those refugees covered by the Protocol:

'1.   The provisions of Article 22 are accepted, in respect of elementary education, only (a) in so far as they apply to public education, and not to private education; (b) on the understanding that the treatment applicable to refugees shall be the most favourable accorded to nationals of other States.

2.   The provisions of Article 17(1) and (2) are accepted as mere recommendations and, in any event, shall not be interpreted as necessarily involving the régime accorded to nationals of countries with which the Republic of Burundi may have concluded regional, customs, economic or political agreements.

3.   The provisions of Article 26 are accepted only subject to the reservation that refugees: (a) do not choose their place of residence in a region bordering on their country of origin, (b) refrain in any event, when exercising their right to move freely, from any activity or incursion of a subversive nature with respect to the country of which they are nationals.'

Cape Verde

Date of accession: 09 July 1987

Reservations

In all cases where the 1951 Convention relating to the Status of Refugees grants to refugees the most favorable treatment accorded to nationals of a foreign country, this provision shall not be interpreted as involving the régime accorded to nationals of countries with which Cape Verde has concluded regional customs, economic or political agreements.

Chile

Date of accession and entry into force: 27 April 1972

Reservations

1. With the reservation that, with reference to the provisions of article 34, the Government of Chile will be unable to grant to refugees facilities greater than those granted to aliens in general, in view of the liberal nature of Chilean naturalization laws;

2   With reservation that the period specified in article 17, paragraph 2 (a) shall, in the case of Chile, be extended from three to ten years;

3   With the reservation that article 17, paragraph 2 (c) shall apply only if the refugee is the widow or the widower of a Chilean spouse;

4   With the reservation that the Government of Chile cannot grant a longer period for compliance with an expulsion order than that granted to other aliens in general under Chilean law.

China (Peoples' Republic of)

Date of accession and entry into force: 24 September 1982

Reservation

The Government of China declared that it does not consider itself bound by Article IV of the Protocol regarding the settlement of disputes.

Congo

Date of accession and entry into force: 10 July 1970

Reservation

The Government of the Congo does not consider itself bound by Article IV of the Protocol regarding the settlement of disputes.

El Salvador

Date of accession and entry into force: 28 April 1983

Reservations

In its instrument of accession to the above-mentioned Protocol, the Government of El Salvador made a reservation to the effect that article IV would not apply in respect of El Salvador.

Ethiopia

Date of accession and entry into force: 10 November 1969

Reservations

Subject to the following reservation in respect of the application, under article 1 of the Protocol, of the Convention relating to the Status of Refugees, done at Geneva on 28 July 1951:

'The provisions of articles 8, 9, 17 (2), and 22 (1) of the Convention are recognized only as recommendations and not as legally binding obligations.'

Finland

Date of accession and entry into force: 10 October 1968

Reservations

Subject to the reservations made in relation to the Convention relating to the Status of Refugees, in accordance with article I of the Protocol.

Ghana

Date of accession and entry into force: 30 October 1968

Reservation

'The Government of Ghana does not consider itself bound by Article IV of the Protocol regarding the settlement of disputes.'

Guatemala

Date of accession and entry into force: 22 September 1983

Reservations

1.   The Republic of Guatemala accedes to the Convention Relating to the Status of Refugees and its Protocol, with the reservation that it will not apply provisions of those instruments in respect of which the Convention allows reservations if those provisions contravene constitutional precepts in Guatemala or norms of public order under domestic law.

2.   The expression 'treatment as favourable as possible' in all articles of the Convention and of the Protocol in which the expression is used should be interpreted as not including rights which, under law or treaty, the Republic of Guatemala has accorded or is according to nationals of the Central American countries or of other countries with which it has concluded or is entering into agreements of a regional nature.

Honduras

Date of accession: 23 March 1992

Reservation

With respect to Article I(1): The Government of the Republic of Honduras does not consider itself bound by those articles of the Convention to which it has entered reservations.

Israel

Date of accession and entry into force: 14 June 1968

Reservations

The reservations made by Israel to the 1951 Convention (see above) are, in accordance with Article VII(2) of the 1967 Protocol, applicable to its obligations under the latter instrument.

Jamaica

Date of accession and entry into force: 30 October 1980

Reservations

'1.   The Government of Jamaica understands Articles 8 and 9 of the Convention as not preventing it from taking, in time of war or other grave and exceptional circumstances, measures in the interest of national security in the case of a refugee on the ground of his nationality;

2.   The Government of Jamaica can only undertake that the provisions of paragraph 2 of Article 17 of the Convention will be applied so far as the law of Jamaica allows;

3.   The Government of Jamaica can only undertake that the provisions of Article 24 of the Convention will be applied so far as the law of Jamaica allows;

4.   the Government of Jamaica can only undertake that the provisions of paragraphs 1, 2 and 3 of article 25 of the Convention will be applied so far as the law of Jamaica allows;

5.   The Government of Jamaica does not accept the obligation imposed by Article IV of the Protocol Relating to the Status of Refugees with regard to the settlement of disputes.'

Luxembourg

Date of accession and entry into force: 22 April 1971

Reservation

The reservation made by Luxembourg to the 1951 Convention (see above) is, in accordance with Article VII(2) of the 1967 Protocol, applicable to its obligations under the latter instrument.

Malawi

Date of accession and entry into force: 10 December 1987

Declaration

'The Government of the Republic of Malawi reiterates its declaration on recognition as compulsory the jurisdiction of the International Court of Justice made on 12 December, 1966 in conformity with Article 36 paragraph 2 of the Statute of the Court. In this respect, the Government of the Republic of Malawi regards the phrase "settled by other means" in Article 38 of the Convention and Article IV of the Protocol to be those means stipulated in Article 33 of the Charter of the United Nations.'

Malta

Date of accession and entry into force: 15 September 1971

Reservations

The reservations made by Malta to the 1951 Convention (see above) are, in accordance with Article VII(2) of the 1967 Protocol, applicable to its obligations under the latter instrument.

Netherlands

Date of accession and entry into force: 29 November 1968

Reservation

In accordance with article VII of the Protocol, all reservations made by the Kingdom of the Netherlands upon signature and ratification of the Convention relating to the Status of Refugees, which was signed in Geneva on 28 July 1951, are regarded to apply to the obligations resulting from the Protocol.

Territorial Application

The Kingdom of the Netherlands accedes to the said Protocol so far as the territory of the Kingdom situated in Europe is concerned; and, as from 1 January 1986, for Aruba.

Peru

Date of accession: 15 September 1983

Declaration

The Government of Peru hereby expressly declares with reference to the provisions of article I, paragraph 1, and article II of the aforementioned Protocol, that compliance with the obligations undertaken by virtue of the act of accession to that instrument shall be ensured by the Peruvian State using all the means at it disposal, and the Government of Peru shall endeavour in all cases to co-operate as far as possible with the Office ot the United Nations High Commissioner for Refugees.

Portugal

Date of accession and entry into force: 13 July 1976

Declaration

Upon accession, the Government of Portugal stated the following:

'(1)   The Protocol will be applied without any geographical limitation.

(2)   In all cases in which the Protocol confers upon the refugees the most favoured person status granted to nationals of a foreign country, this clause will not be interpreted in such a way as to mean the status granted by Portugal to the nationals of Brazil or to the national of other countries with whom Portugal may establish commonwealth-type relations.'

Republic of Korea

Date of accession: 03 December 1992

Reservation

'The Republic of Korea declares pursuant to article 7 of the Protocol that it is not bound by article 7 of the Convention relating to the Status of Refugees, which provides for the exemption of refugees from legislative reciprocity after fulfilling the condition of three years' residence in the territory of the Contracting States.'

Rwanda

Date of accession and entry into force: 3 January 1980

Reservations

The instrument of accession also contains the following reservation to Article IV: 'For the settlement of any dispute between States Parties, recourse may be had to the International Court of Justice only with the prior agreement of the Rwandese Republic.'

Somalia

Date of accession and entry into force: 10 October 1978

Reservations

'The Government of the Somali Democratic Republic acceded to the Convention and Protocol on the understanding that nothing in the said Convention or Protocol will be construed to prejudice or adversely affect the national status, or political aspiration of displaced persons from Somali territories under alien domination.

It is this spirit, that the Somali Democratic Republic will commit itself to respect the terms and provisions of the said Convention and Protocol.'

Swaziland

Date of accession and entry into force: 28 January 1969

Declaration

The instrument of accession made the following declaration:

'The Government of the Kingdom of Swaziland deems it essential to draw attention to the accession herewith as a Member of the United Nations, and not as a Party to the said Convention by reason of succession or otherwise.'

Reservations

Pursuant to paragraph 1 of Article VII of the Protocol, the accession to the Protocol by Swaziland was made subject to the following reservations in respect of the application, under Article I of the Protocol, of the provisions of the Convention relating to the Status of Refugees:

'(1) The Government of the Kingdom of Swaziland is not in a position to assume obligations as contained in Article 22 of the said Convention, and therefore will not consider itself bound by the provisions therein.

(2) Similarly, the Government of the Kingdom of Swaziland is not in a position to assume the obligations of Article 34 of the said Convention, and must expressly reserve the right not to apply the provisions therein.'

Turkey

Date of accession and entry into force: 31 July 1968

Reservations

The instrument of accession stipulates that the Government of Turkey maintains the provisions of the declaration made under section B of Article 1 of the Convention Relating to the Status of Refugees, according to which it applies the Convention only to persons who have become refugees as a result of events occurring in Europe, and also the reservation clause made upon ratification of the Convention to the effect that no provision of this Convention may be interpreted as granting to refugees greater rights than those accorded to Turkish citizens in Turkey.

Uganda

Date of accession and entry into force: 27 September 1976

Reservations

The reservations made by Uganda to the 1951 Convention (see above) are, in accordance with Article VII(2) of the 1967 Protocol, applicable to its obligations under the latter instrument.

United Kingdom

Date of accession and entry into force: 4 September 1968

Territorial Application

'In accordance with the provisions of the first sentence of Article VII(4) of the Protocol, the United Kingdom hereby excludes from the application of the Protocol the following territories for the international relations of which it is responsible: Jersey, Southern Rhodesia, Swaziland.'

'In accordance with the Provisions of the second sentence of Article VII(4) of the said Protocol, the United Kingdom hereby extends the application of the Protocol to the following territories for the international relations of which it is responsible: St. Lucia, Montserrat.'

United Republic of Tanzania

Date of accession and entry into force: 4 September 1968

Reservation

'The provision of Article IV of the Protocol shall not be applicable to the United Republic of Tanzania except within the explicit consent of the Government of the United Republic of Tanzania.'

United States of America

Date of accession and entry into force: 1 November 1968

Reservations

The instrument of accession contained the following reservations in respect of the application of the Convention, in accordance with Article I of the Protocol:

'The United States of America construes Article 29 of the Convention as applying only to refugees who are resident in the United States and reserves the right to tax refugees who are not residents of the United States in accordance with its general rules relating to non-resident aliens.'

'The United States of America accepts the obligation of paragraph 1(b) of Article 24 of the Convention except in so far as that paragraph may conflict in certain instances with any provisions of title II (old age, survivors' and disability insurance) or title XVIII (hospital and medical insurance for the aged) of the Social Security Act. As to any such provision, the United States will accord to refugees lawfully staying in its territory treatment no less favourable than is accorded to aliens generally in the same circumstances.'

Venezuela

Date of accession and entry into force: 19 September 1986

Declaration

'In implementing the provisions of the Protocol which confer on refugees the most favourable treatment accorded to nationals of a foreign country, it shall be understood that such treatment does not include any rights and benefits which Venezuela has granted or may grant regarding entry into or sojourn in Venezuela has concluded regional or subregional integration, customs, economic or political agreements.'

Reservation

The instrument of accession also contains a reservation in respect of Article IV.

Index